FOREWORD

by John Chamberlain

THIS animated jumbo of a book, which is alive with the savor and color of a long departed time when half-forgotten figures like Oswald Garrison Villard and Raymond Gram Swing were setting our intellectual attitudes, provides fascinating chart readings on the drift of liberal opinion from peace to war between 1931 and 1941. The resulting verdict on liberalism, modern American style, is melancholy any way you take it. Either the liberals were wrong at the beginning of the decade of the 'Thirties, or they were wrong at the end—which says little for the quality of their claim to intellectual leadership of the community. The record is either one of premises falsely checked or axioms mistakenly abandoned.

Starkly put, the somersaults of the liberals can be listed as follows:

1. They began the decade of the 'Thirties as pacifists. When the decade ended they were howling for what Stanley High, writing in *The Nation,* called "The Liberals' War."

2. They began the decade with a full-throttled attack on munitions makers as "merchants of death." They ended the decade with a despairing hunt for armaments to "lend-lease" to Great Britain, and they turned against their own neutrality legislation which had sought to limit arms traffic with belligerent nations.

3. They began the decade as convinced supporters of the "revisionist" treatment of the origins of World War I. They denounced the "Morgan loans," which they said had led to our entanglement in the war on the side of the Allies. They attacked the Treaty of Versailles and the whole "Versailles system" for saddling Germany with impossible reparations and turning Eastern Europe into a satellite preserve for the greater glory of French "imperialism."

When the decade ended they had tacitly abandoned "revisionism." Walter Millis, author of the widely read revisionist *Road To War,* announced to his Yale classmates at a reunion that he had said good-bye to all that. Lewis Mumford, who in the 'Twenties had denounced the role of the British press bureau in snaring the United States back in 1916, spent the last days of the 'Thirties excoriating those who still clung to his former beliefs.

In pointing the finger at flip-flopping liberals I should, perhaps, point a finger at myself. "All of this I saw, and part of this I was." *Touché, messieurs, touché.* I still think that "we liberals"—if I may use a designation that applies to me no longer—were right in our criticism of the Versailles Treaty. The men of Versailles forgot the mellow and forgiving wisdom of such post-Napoleonic figures as Metternich when they met in the Hall of Mirrors to give force to the promises of the secret treaties which so appalled Woodrow Wilson when he learned of them.

But other liberal stereotypes of the early 'Thirties which I once accepted hardly accord with the facts of human nature. The doctrinaire pacifist position may invite destruction at the hands of unprincipled enemies. And the effort to blame bankers and munition makers for causing wars can be cart-before-horse thinking. As William Graham Sumner once said, "If men get mad enough, they will fight. If not, then the ordinary means of diplomacy will do." Recourse to bankers and armament manufacturers is often only an afterthought.

What caused the liberals to make their momentous change-over? What led them to abandon the traditionally wise foreign policy laid down by George Washington that the relations between countries should be based on their attitude towards each other and not on what is going on *within* the borders of neighboring states? When George Washington was our guide we did not feel it necessary, as citizens of a republic, to make war on monarchies if they did not menace or threaten us. From the mid-Thirties onward, however, American liberals introduced and developed the doctrine that we must prepare to be aggressive and militant against any country whose ideology and related policies do not please us.

The odd and intellectually indefensible defect of the liberals was that they ignored the acts of the cruel and brutal dictatorial Soviet regime of Joseph Stalin while they were busy concentrating on what

AMERICAN LIBERALISM AND WORLD POLITICS, 1931-1941

LIBERALISM'S PRESS AND SPOKESMEN
ON THE ROAD BACK TO WAR
BETWEEN MUKDEN AND PEARL HARBOR

JAMES J. MARTIN

FOREWORD BY John Chamberlain

VOLUME I

THE DEVIN-ADAIR COMPANY   NEW YORK   1964

Hitler had learned from Moscow. As a refugee from Bolshevik tyranny put it, "the liberals killed the calf and let the cow go." The liberals' understandable hostility to Nazism went hand in hand with regarding Soviet Russia as a "wave of the future," or as the path to a "brave new world" leading over the corpses of millions of starved or butchered Kulaks and the many and distinguished victims of the orgy of Russian treason trials in the mid-Thirties. The liberals quite neglected to note that Hitler's abhorrent anti-Jewish policies were being carried out on a far greater scale in Poland.

By the summer of 1941 the war fervor of the liberals had so undermined their rational faculties that they failed to recognize that the German attack on Russia in June provided a unique, incredible, and totally unexpected opportunity to eliminate the threat of dictatorship from both the Right and the Left without involving the United States in war, as statesmen like former President Herbert Hoover and Senators Robert A. Taft and Harry S. Truman urged at the time. The rival dictatorships could have been allowed and encouraged to bleed each other to ruin on the vast plains of the East while the democratic nations made use of their perhaps undeserved good fortune to revamp and strengthen their own systems of society and government.

The liberals would have none of this sound and solid statecraft but did everything possible to push us into a war of unconditional surrender and mutual destruction. And the war ended, as Hoover had feared, in a vast extension of Soviet power, the communization or demoralization of most of Asia, the disruption of Africa, and the disastrous aftermath of all this which still faces and threatens the Free World.

The liberal double standard in approaching Germany and Russia made it easy for the Communists to undermine most of the original liberal positions. Thus real pro-American progressives of the Robert La Follette–George Norris western breed, who hoped to isolate the United States from the troubles of Europe and Asia, found themselves deserted by their former allies on the American east coast.

John T. Flynn, who had once remarked that "the *New Republic* is my soap box, *Collier's* is my banker," found himself bereft of both soap box and bank as a penalty of consistency in hewing to the La Follettian line. And Charles A. Lindbergh, loyal son of a Minnesota Congressman who had supported the La Follette-Norris position in World War I times, was dismissed as a Copperhead by President Roosevelt. This, despite the fact that Lindbergh had undertaken two eminently patriotic government missions to Germany, one to discover the actual strength of Hitler's air force, and the other, arranged by the State Department, to bring pressure on Göring in hopes that he could persuade Hitler to let Jews emigrate with at least a portion of their property.

The softness of the liberals for the Communists who became their allies was not reciprocated by Stalin's diplomats. But the liberals nonetheless continued to be blind to the likeness of all totalitarian systems, whether of the black, brown or red variety. Their double-think on this point robbed them of all wariness in approaching the peace. It was liberalism, deluded by the attitudes of the 'Thirties, that called General Patton back from Prague, an act that left the Communists in control of what was to Bismarck the pivotal Bohemia. It was liberalism, again deluded by its equivocal thinking on dictator-ships, that let the Red armies move into Berlin ahead of British and American troops and set the scene for the geographical isolation of West Berlin from the new West German republic and made possible the notorious Berlin Wall as a constant threat to world peace.

Liberalism acquiesced in the terms of Teheran and Yalta, let Tito succeed in Yugoslavia when Mihailovic would have been a far better choice for the West, and failed to make use of the German officers' plot against Hitler. Shrewd and far-sighted United States Army offi-cers such as General Albert C. Wedemeyer, who had counselled a more vigorous movement into central Europe by western armies and had opposed the theory of Unconditional Surrender when it was first elaborated at the Casablanca meeting of Roosevelt and Churchill in 1943, were rudely thrust aside.

The "liberals' war" ended with the liberals' peace at Potsdam. It has been far worse than the Versailles Peace which the liberal intel-lectuals once attacked with so much verve and acumen when they were really in there thinking.

James J. Martin, in his comprehensive documentary study of how the liberal intellectuals came to abandon their brains does not speak as a moral dogmatist. His method is to let the protagonists establish out of their own mouths their own record of wavering and contradic-tion as it appeared in such publications as *The Nation,* the *New Re-public* and *Common Sense.* It provides amazing reading and will pro-duce no little consternation on the part of both participants and readers. Whatever one is to make of Dr. Martin's startling exhuma-tions, the liberal flip-flop is not to be denied.

If the flip-flop had cleansed the world of the totalitarian virus, or at least isolated it, it would have been justified. But that job still remains to be done, and the Liberals' attitude towards the "peace" resulting from their war has only compounded the problems and dangers that they did more than any others to produce.

The heritage of the liberal flip-flop is a universal and vastly expen-sive Cold War, the ever-present threat of nuclear destruction, an enormous expansion of Communist power throughout the Old World and its increasing menace to our own Hemisphere. If one is worried, as any patriotic and humane American should be, about the Berlin

Wall, the suppressed populations of eastern Europe, the fluid and un-certain destiny of the Middle East, the apparently endless troubles in Southeast Asia, the racism-in-reverse of Africa, and the inability of the West to defend itself in the United Nations, Dr. Martin's pages afford us the first complete insight into the manner in which this development got started and gained its ominous momentum, with an outcome that is today as incalculable as it is foreboding.

If it is possible for even the literate public to learn anything from history, here is an unique opportunity to profit by examining the causes and genesis of perhaps the most momentous complex of mis-takes in human experience.

AUTHOR'S PREFACE

Foreign policy is not fashioned in a vacuum and historians of American foreign policy must begin to pay more attention to the dynamics of public opinion if they want their writings to be completely meaningful.

Professor Walter Johnson,
Department of History,
University of Chicago
in *Saturday Review*, April 22, 1950.

WHATEVER the inevitably diversified, conflicting, and emotional reactions of the readers of this book, which grow out of their preconceived opinions as to its theme and content, no informed person can very well deny the importance of the subject itself. It encompasses one of the outstanding transitions in the intellectual and political experience of mankind, and it may well turn out to be the last of these. The evidence to support the latter suggestion is more impressive at the moment than that justifying an optimistic outlook on the human future.

Many American liberals were warm supporters of Woodrow Wilson's foreign policy which led us into war in 1917. Disillusioned with the outcome of this first American crusade in foreign lands, they repudiated their previous position on the First World War, bitterly opposed the Treaty of Versailles, seriously criticized the motives and conduct of our wartime Allies, adopted and supported revisionist historical writing, and became the main bulwark and shocktroops of the peace movement and disarmament for nearly two decades between the two World Wars.

Due to a benign, friendly and optimistic attitude towards the "collective security" foreign policy of Soviet Russia, as "sold" to the

League of Nations by Maxim Litvinov and adopted and propagated by the highly esteemed Popular Front movement in Western Europe during the mid-1930's, and shocked and repelled by what was presented in the public prints and personal reports as the nature of the Fascist systems in Italy and Germany, most American liberals abandoned their erstwhile pacific ideological and crusading complex of 1924 to 1937 and turned to vehement support of President Roosevelt's program of rearmament and war—the fateful transformation which constitutes the main theme of this book. They backed the Second World War with far more enthusiasm and unanimity than the liberals had in the case of the First World War, entered into even closer rapport with the Soviet ideology, activities and program, and approved the harsh policies of the victorious Allies in post-war Europe, including the great gains of Soviet Russia.

After President Truman announced the launching of the Cold War in 1947 the majority of American liberals fell in with the crusade of the Free Nations against what were now designated as the "slave peoples" of Soviet Russia, Communist China, and their allies, only protesting such extremes as "McCarthyism." They stood behind the continuation of the Cold War by Secretary Dulles and his brinkmanship and, with the election of John F. Kennedy, they ardently joined in with a congenial New Frontier ideology and administration which combined domestic liberalism with vast armaments and an unremitting Cold War policy which not even the threat of nuclear extermination could shake or dislodge.

It would be no exaggeration to state that not since the long conservative regime in Europe between 1815 and 1848 dominated by Metternich has there been a period more definitely and continuously controlled by an ideological group than the liberal intellectual hegemony since 1917. It was not seriously upset by the conservative trends in domestic affairs under Harding, Coolidge and Hoover because their foreign policy was pacific and "isolationist," and it completely dominated foreign policy during the Eisenhower administrations. Its tenure and ascendency in controlling our foreign policy appear to be indefinitely prolonged, short of a political revolution or a nuclear Armageddon. It has become one of the most vital and enduring ingredients of the American Establishment.

The author has taken no strong personal stand as to the logic, rectitude or wisdom of the shifting liberal ideologies and policies of the last half-century, but he does hope that he has treated them fairly, honestly and adequately. They seem to bear the stamp of public support today, especially in the matter of global foreign policy, which has become vastly more important in American public life and opinion than the problems and obligations of our domestic political and economic scene. In this momentous transformation the liberals have played the decisive role. This book only tells the story down to American entry into the Second World War. A sequel will deal with the period from the eclipse of the New Deal to the emergence of the New Frontier. The play had been written and the stage set by the revamped liberal ideology before the Japanese planes swooped down on Pearl Harbor at daylight on December 7, 1941.

When the overall subject of the United States and public affairs in the Twentieth Century is under consideration, two broad trends stand out beyond all others. The first is the immense growth of the appointive administrative government on the domestic level, and the consequent subordination of the traditional elective political agencies in the formulation and execution of public policy. The second is the increasingly formidable degree to which the internal domestic policy and administration have been subordinated to foreign policy and foreign relations, both as the center of community and public attention and as the dynamic force supporting and impelling national action. Participation in two stupendous world wars in a single generation has been the chief factor in launching, nourishing and strengthening more centralizing and power-concentrating impulses than all the home-front or internal forces calling for such procedure had succeeded in achieving in our entire national history. The period since the end of the Second World War has, if anything, exceeded the war years in the acceleration and expansion of the American State. This is a natural manifestation of a revolution in foreign policy which finds us committed to endemic conscription and expenditure of billions of dollars annually in support for various foreign political regimes deemed essential to our welfare and safety. It has also led to the maintenance of between four and five thousand military, air and naval bases of all types in this country and in scores of others abroad currently bound to us by one kind of treaty or another. This situation has come to be rather generally and automatically accepted as part of the natural order of things by a large part of our citizenry, along with a concomitant Federal budget now reaching a hundred billion dollars which, year in and year out, devotes approximately eighty cents out of each tax dollar to dealing with the consequences of past wars or preparing for possible future conflicts.

This trend in our public policy has been viewed with dark apprehension by a significant portion of the literate community. From the remarkable book, *As We Go Marching*, of John T. Flynn, in 1944, to Amaury de Riencourt's *The Coming Caesars*, in 1957, and since, we have had a substantial volume of literature rich in comparisons of America's course since 1914 to that of classical empires crushed to death by their own weight, or in predictions of similar dire consequences resulting from extrapolations of current tendencies.

All of these novel and complex developments are part of the harvest of an increasingly homogenized foreign policy during the last quarter of a century in which such controversies as have dominated public attention have been in the main over the details of administering, or paying for, courses of action already adopted with a bare minimum of dissent. To this very day, disputes concerning American traffic with the rest of the world gravitate to an ever-increasing extent around incidental steps and issues, the hard core of our interventionist and global policy position being taken for granted. A whole generation has grown to college age and beyond, ignorant for the most part of the vital fact that our foreign policy was once a hotly-debated item in our public life. At the most, they are only vaguely annoyed today when the correctness of our foreign action is questioned, reacting almost as though such skepticism contained a basic element of impropriety, audacity, or even lack of patriotism.

Notwithstanding this ominous trend, foreign policy is not a product of the scientific laboratory or created by impersonal agents in the stratosphere. The prevalent social grouping of humankind on the largest scale continues to be the national state. The traffic and harmonies or conflicts of interest among these organizations which produce congenial relations or hostilities continue to be of the same order as in times past, and opinions on persons, places and things far from the homeland continue to arise. How these attitudes came about and the responsibility for helping them assume tangible and potent form are public issues of the first magnitude.

A new and portentous ingredient has been added to the situation in relatively recent times which stands out as perhaps the most powerful conditioning factor in helping to make up the minds of those in Nation A as to how they should view Nation B. More and more, Nation A has become concerned with what those in power in Nation B are doing *inside* their own country, rather than with what they are doing to accommodate or alienate the people of Nation A. Anyone who misses or ignores the role that the internal policy of countries plays today in generating bellicosity on the part of those often lodged thousands of miles away, is ignoring what is becoming the major key to understanding the germination and incubation of modern international martial collisions in our time. It is perhaps the most important contribution of the liberals to our current foreign policy and world-wide confusion and conflicts.

The present work consists of an effort to study in detail how contemporary foreign policy has been and still is closely related to highly literate and widely circulated public opinion on foreign affairs. The period selected is that between September 18, 1931 and December 7, 1941, two fateful dates for the entire world. The first, the occasion of the Japanese military action at Mukden, in Manchuria, launched a fifteen-year military campaign in the Far East, and in retrospect has been called by many historians the actual starting date of the Second World War. The second date, of course, is the occasion of the Japanese air attack on the United States naval and air installations at Pearl Harbor in December, 1941, which brought this country into the European War and made it a World War.

Instead of examining the gradual drift of America into involvement during this decade, surely one of the historically most significant ten years since classical antiquity, as reflected in the sophisticated and stylized discourse of formal diplomacy, our procedure consisted in a study of every article written on the subject of United States foreign policy and our relations with the rest of the world by approximately 250 authors, journalists, essayists, professors and related specialists in the realm of the social studies, in a selected group of highly influential periodicals circulated nationally in the United States. Many of these personalities were, and still are, internationally-famous figures in the American and world literary and opinion-making field. Collectively, this body of writers and thinkers represented in the 1930's a saturation with what may be called the liberal outlook and tradition in this country, and they enjoyed a near-monopoly of intellectual-literary activities and production during the time-span involved.

Anyone who undertakes a study of a phase of the history of this century is struck at once by one universal fact: the prodigious quantity of materials, both printed and in handwritten and typescript form. A completely exhaustive examination of all pertinent documents would be a lifetime task in each case. Publication of the findings would have to be delayed until after the lifetime of every writer of such works had ended. The practical resolution of this difficult problem must follow one of two possibilities, with variations. The first is a broad *sampling* of the materials which make up the documentary portion of the study. Selection must be left to the discretion of the writer, and superficiality is the main potential obstacle to surmount. The alternative approach involves a different mode of selection, namely, an intensive examination of a more limited but highly representative range of documentary resources.

In seeking to put on record the foreign-affairs views of a group of persons of a particular world-outlook and inclination, such as the liberals of the United States, it is necessary to face these alternative methods of approach. Excluding agonizing philosophical speculation over definitions, I have designated as "liberals" those persons willing to be identified as such through associations of all sorts and by their proven testimonials of a published nature.

It becomes obvious that to set forth a comprehensive account of their views on United States foreign policy and international affairs during such a hectic decade as that of 1931–1941 would itself turn out to be a task requiring decades of research and writing if it were to be based on a complete reading of everything these people had to say on the subject. The assumption is made here that, since the purpose of the book is to present the content of the liberal thought which went into the actual creation of significant intellectual attitudes in this country, only the published product of their thinking needs to be utilized. The unpublished correspondence, office memoranda, telephone calls, telegrams, and other media not available to the general reader have no place in a study of this kind, no matter what they might reveal. Such material might indicate that the person in question held private views contradictory to his publicly-expressed opinions. In a biography or intimate history this would be of vast importance, but in a study of opinion-making and attitude-influencing it is of far less value; the readers would not be aware of these private attitudes or convictions, due to their confidential nature.

Hence, this study of liberal opinions has been restricted to virtually a line-by-line examination of the contents of a number of selected publications, either those noted for the frequency of their reproduction of liberal views, or those entirely devoted to broadcasting liberal opinion, as such, and designating themselves publicly in this manner. Therefore, two main types of sources have been used: (1) outstanding liberal journals of long-established reputations featuring the work of the best-known liberal commentators and read by a moderate-sized group of vastly greater public influence than their numbers would suggest; and (2) internationally-known monthly and quarterly publications of a more general editorial position, but favorably predisposed toward liberal writers of wide repute, as shown by their tables of contents and lists of authors.

Accordingly, instead of a random sampling of liberal writings in a great number of publications, it was decided to subject a smaller number of more relevant publications to the most intensive research. The inevitable result is a much more valid and detailed exposition of liberal thought on the subject under study, in the most favorable intellectual environments. A better understanding can be obtained from, let us say, thirty successive articles or editorials in a sympathetic organ than from two or three widely-separated pronouncements in a source known to be detached, cool, or even antipathetic. For this reason, continuity of expression and contiguity of those presenting it have been sought for from the beginning, in order to maximize the effectiveness of the summary.

The picture of the permutations and combinations of liberal opinion on foreign policy in the 1930's that unfolds is both rich and complicated, featured by numerous disputes, bitter controversies and frequent defections. It affords a number of significant and revealing insights which contribute to a clearer understanding of the world which the drift to war produced, and the ominous impasse which has enveloped our planet since 1945. It portrays the gradual preparation for, and the ultimate execution of, what was probably the most sensational mass-somersault in opinion ever performed in the intellectual history of this country—one almost equal to a putative transformation of the Abolitionists of 1860 into advocates of a slavery system for Negroes after 1865.

Involved in this process during the decade of the 1930's was the repudiation of many traditional liberal positions on very vital matters, among them their reactions to the First World War, post-war reparations and disarmament, pacifism, the international traffic in implements of war, civil liberties, and international political and economic organization. Along with this gradually came a firm and highly emotional lineup of liberals in a new pattern of antagonistic world powers. This new liberal alignment was based mainly on their reaction to the nature of the *internal* regimes of the detested side. The powerful influence of marked sympathy for the Soviet Union and approval of Soviet foreign policy, as expressed through the Popular Front, guided the liberals in the maintenance of this course until the outbreak of general war late in 1939. Thereafter, came an amazing adoption and sponsorship, once again, of the Franco-British "Allied" cause, although American liberalism had excoriated these powers at length between the two World Wars as the chief agents in bringing about the world chaos after the First World War. The capstone to the great shift of the liberals was the ultimate urging of a war declaration by the United States on behalf of their favored side, well in advance of any action taken by the country's elected representatives, although liberalism had been the main bulwark of the peace movement from around 1924 to 1937.

It has been reported in a variety of sources that Franklin D. Roosevelt and Winston S. Churchill spent some time discussing how they should designate what we have come to know as the Second World War or World War II. It has never been said that they ever considered the name suggested by Stanley High in a celebrated essay he wrote for *The Nation* in June, 1941, which he entitled "The Liberals' War." High intended nothing invidious by this; on the contrary, he was most enthusiastic about such an appellation, and the fact that it was approved by the editorial board of one of America's two most prominent liberal magazines suggests that they did not find such a designation offensive or repellent in the slightest degree.

It is not the intent of this study to establish a thesis of this sort, but rather to document in detail the course of American literary and ideological liberalism in the realm of foreign affairs and foreign policy during the fateful ten years that led to the United States becoming involved in the greatest war the world has yet known.

JAMES J. MARTIN

Deep Springs, California
June, 1964

CONTENTS

ILLUSTRATIONS

AMERICAN LEAGUE F
LET'S FIGHT JAPAN
LET'S FIGHT GERMANY
LET'S DON'T FIGHT
HARRY ELMER BARNES

about preceeding pages

Invited to make the main address at a large and much publicized peace rally in New York City sponsored by the American League for Peace and Democracy on August 6, 1938, Dr. Harry Elmer Barnes, not a member but a leading scholar, journalist and anti-interventionist liberal, was ejected because he proposed to make a speech repudiating involvement in *all* foreign wars. The event dramatized the controversy among American liberals which was reaching its peak at that moment, and was memorialized in this famous cartoon by Jerry Doyle. (For details see Vol. II, pp. 729–730.)

1

THE LIBERAL PRESS, 1931–1941 :

EDITORS, CONTRIBUTORS, NEIGHBORS

AND INFLUENCE

WHO constitute "the liberals" in the context of this study? A vast amount of time, energy, paper and ink can be expended to no good purpose in argument, but for practical reasons, accepting as such those who preferred to be known thusly, in addition to the approval of those who professed to be influenced by their views, provides an acceptable answer. In 1932, Clifton Fadiman, in a symposium published in that year, declared, with reference to the United States, "We have two weeklies of liberal political tendencies, the *Nation* and the *New Republic*. They provide the only really penetrating literary evaluation we have." [1] There can be little doubt that any study of liberal opinion in this time must depend upon these two journals to a very great degree, and upon the contributions of the several editors and the many contributors and correspondents of these two publications in their books and in other magazines. Some of these other influence-making centers will be discussed in due time. The productivity of this large group of greater and lesser literary renown was immense, and assimilation is most difficult, even for a survey which undertakes to examine a particular phase of this activity, the American liberal outlook on American foreign policy and world affairs between Mukden and Pearl Harbor. And their influence was not secondary to their productivity, especially among the nation's leaders, and the articulate and the effective among those who had a large part in the shaping of national opinion in many ways.

When I. F. Stone reviewed Felix Frankfurter's *Law and Politics* for the *Nation* on October 21, 1939, he incidentally presented probably the best single-sentence description of American liberal journalism insofar as its objectives and impact were concerned when he wrote, "If I may be forgiven for speaking of *The Nation*'s weekly comrade-in-arms, the young men who started the *New Republic* were concerned not so much with influencing the masses as with influencing important men." [2] Stone automatically defined the goal of his own journal at the same time, for although both these magazines presumed to speak of and to the common man and presumably were devoted to his welfare above all things, they hardly were concerned with him as a regular reader, in view of their modest circulations, between the 30,000–40,000 figure.

The *Nation* was almost four times as old as the *New Republic* in 1931, and did not hesitate to bill itself on its title page every week "The Leading Liberal Weekly Since 1865." Despite the growth of the junior journal since 1914 and its brilliant assemblage of editors and contributors, the *Nation* unabashedly referred to itself in the decade of the 1930's as "America's most influential weekly" when making subscription appeals. But this did not interfere with the tendency to refer to both of them in the same breath when the liberal press was mentioned. And despite frequent launchings of others, they far outlasted all of them in sustained public acceptance and influence.

Testimonials to their influence were not uncommon, but the occasion of important anniversaries just before the outbreak of World War Two acted as a stupendous underlining of this factor. Senator Gerald P. Nye in the spring of 1937 declared, "I cannot conceive of a forward-looking mind being away from the *Nation* at any time," [3] and the Canadian journalist J. V. McAree pronounced some months later in the *Toronto Globe*, "There is no weekly journal so widely read by newspaper editors on this continent as *The Nation* . . . it is a great institution and over the years has probably indirectly exercised more liberal influence than any other publication, daily or weekly, in the United States." [4] This was indeed impressive praise, but it was matched many times over when the *Nation* published its 75th anniversary issue in February, 1940. A similar sheaf of congratulatory messages greeted the *New Republic*'s 25th anniversary number in November, 1939. The combined editorial and contributor staff of these two publications in this era were a veritable *Who's Who* of American and foreign letters unmatched before or since, and that each claimed to be the more important of the two was irrelevant; together they amounted to a virtual saturation of the American liberal and intellectual scene. They were matched in distinction and prestige only by the figures who applauded them.

The *Nation*'s 75th anniversary issue on February 10, 1940 led off with a stirring banner message from President Franklin D. Roosevelt, in which he stressed the importance of the *Nation* as an influential organ of minority opinion in the most undisguised praise.[5] But spirited tributes from the politically eminent had been arriving and appearing in print for weeks before this. Warm birthday commendations and testimonials had been posted by Harry Hopkins, Attorney General Robert H. Jackson, Henry A. Wallace, Thurman Arnold, Ambassador to Mexico Josephus Daniels, Senator George W. Norris, Governor of New York Herbert H. Lehman and Lieutenant Governor Charles Poletti, David E. Lilienthal, Mordecai Ezekiel, Thomas G. Corcoran, Representative John M. Coffee of Washington, Governor Culbert Olson of California and Carey McWilliams, California Commissioner of Immigration and Housing, and Norman Thomas.

The congratulations from the field of letters competed favorably with the political sphere: Sherwood Anderson, Upton Sinclair, William Allen White, Helen Rogers Reid, Alfred A. Knopf, Raymond Gram Swing, George Fort Milton, Roger A. Baldwin, Bennett Cerf, Clifton Fadiman, Irving Brant, Guy Emery Shipler, editor of the *Churchman,* Oscar Ameringer, Fannie Hurst, H. V. Kaltenborn, Louis Untermeyer, William Rose Benét, Robert S. Allen, William T. Evjue, Wisconsin publisher, along with Arthur Garfield Hays, Bishop Francis J. McConnell, John L. Lewis, and George Gallup, the famous public opinion poll-taker, were some of the more noteworthy, supplemented by European and Asiatic figures such as Jacques Maritain, Juan Negrin, Hu Shih, Jules Romains and Harold J. Laski.

Said Senator Norris: "For a great many years I have been a reader of the *Nation* and one of its humble admirers. . . . I should be happy if I knew that its voice could be heard at every fireside in America." Swing declared, "I can think of no single periodical in the United States whose continuing existence is of more importance to American democracy than *The Nation,*" while Cerf announced, "My congratulations to *The Nation* on its 75th anniversary. I consider it one of the three most important magazines in the United States." Kaltenborn insisted, "*The Nation* should be required reading for every opinion-maker." Sherwood Anderson volunteered, "It has always seemed one of the really important publications of the country to me," while Gallup proposed, "Please accept this reader's salute. I know of no magazine with more consistent vitality and interest." Ambassador Daniels testified, "The independence, fearlessness, and ability of *The Nation* make it an influential agency in an era when leadership without strings is the hope of a drifting world," while William Allen White admitted, "It has been my guide, philosopher and friend. For me it has interpreted the news and often even its opinions are news."

Other declarations of its impact in opinion-making were fully as sweeping. Said Mrs. Reid, "*The Nation* has been a potent force in the formation of public opinion in the United States. It gained this influence because it was read by editors and writers and the articulate opinion-forming people in America, also because the intellectually curious and experimental young people of the country were attracted by its provocative content." Thurman Arnold supported this observation: "There are other magazines of greater circulation but few of greater influence. . . . It is a truly great journal, and it has left its mark on thinking of our time." Representative Coffee proposed, "Its literary tone and quality have all endeared it to the intellectual liberals of America," while Governor Olson observed, "The long and checkered history of American journalism has had at least one bright and steady beacon of truth, integrity and liberalism for the past 75 years in *The Nation*." [6]

This was just a portion of the rich variety of acclaim which came from some of the *Nation*'s nationally-known readers, and it had been similarly matched by a flood of letters to the *New Republic* in the last three months of 1939; Wallace, Thomas, Corcoran, Arnold, Cerf, Hopkins, Senators Alben Barkley and Ernest Lundeen, Ida M. Tarbell, Sherwood Eddy, Charles A. Beard, Herbert Bayard Swope, Bishop McConnell, Arthur Krock, Dorothy Canfield Fisher, Gardner Cowles, Jr., Stuart Chase and Van Wyck Brooks were some of the numerous well-wishers who testified to its vast influence.

"You are a national institution," hailed Eddy. Arnold insisted, "on its 25th Birthday the *New Republic* is entitled to applause and congratulations of every liberal group in the country," while Senator Barkley admitted, "I have been a constant reader of the *New Republic* almost from its beginnings," although the nationally eminent historian Beard exceeded this by confiding to the readers, "I have been a paying subscriber since the first number of the *New Republic* was published." Corcoran, a rising figure in the New Deal, wrote one of the strongest testimonials, offering an interesting extension of remarks, "Every week when I was secretary to Mr. Justice Holmes, he asked me to read the *New Republic* to him." Publisher Cerf stated, "Every issue is read from cover to cover by every member of this firm," and publisher Cowles also admitted reading it for years with profit: "I like it and I need it. I wish more businessmen would get the *New Republic* reading habit."

Harry Hopkins cautiously asserted, "I have always welcomed the liberal views taken in the columns of the *New Republic*. Such an editorial outlook is vital in these days of change and controversy, for it presents a point of view essential to the preservation of our democratic institutions in the progress of our country." But the support of writers and journalists was unqualified. Brooks declared, "Your paper and the *Nation* are indispensable supports of any enlightened view of the world we live in, and far more necessary now than ever before," a view backed by Chase: "I think it deserves more respectful attention than ever before in its career." Krock, the well-known New York *Times* reporter, emphasized the aspect of influencing of views: "The *New Republic,* to my mind, discharges an important function in forming and nourishing public opinion," which novelist Fisher underlined with a measure of personal admission: "I feel that my indebtedness to the *New Republic* is a pretty valid proof of the wide and valuable influence it has exerted on public opinion in the United States." [7]

Had the editors of both weeklies chosen to republish the flattering commendations they had received in the past which had been reproduced in their communications departments, the list would have been about the most impressive collection of nationally-known figures in American public life ever assembled. Examples of the persistence of admissions as to the constant influence of the liberal press might be cited almost at will, and as the celebrated Kansas editor White had pointed out, the liberal weeklies were themselves newsworthy to the daily press of the country. When a major ownership change of the *Nation* occurred in the spring of 1935, some 150 newspapers commented on it editorially, adding very flattering observations on its worth as a liberal organ. The Des Moines *Tribune* declared, "*The Nation* has come to be a recognized leader in the field of liberal journalism," while the Rochester *Times-Union* observed, "*The Nation* has exercised an influence far beyond what might seem indicated by its circulation," a verdict supported even more emphatically by the Richmond *Times-Dispatch:* "We doubt if any other publication in the country with only 35,000 circulation exercises as wide an influence as *The Nation*. Almost every newspaper editor in the country reads it regularly, and so do many teachers, public officials and others in position to sway public opinion." [8] The traffic of journalists from the daily press in and out of the editorial and contributor staffs of the liberal weeklies had a substantial influence in keeping a favorable estimate of them in the columns of the former, although it was almost a trademark of the latter to look with cultivated disdain, if not with blunt disapprobation, upon almost all the country's newspapers. Occasions when the daily press received commendations in their pages were few and far between, and the philosophy and values of the newspaper publishers as a body were under constant attack.

THE EDITORIAL GENERAL STAFFS:
A SCHEMATIC VIEW

Some attention to the personalities occupying the editorial positions on these famed weeklies is in order, in view of the mass of unsigned material published every week that dealt with every imaginable issue, and exceedingly heavily with regards to foreign affairs and American foreign policy, with which this study is concerned. On the eve of the fateful decade ending with Pearl Harbor, the *Nation* especially was to undergo some striking changes in ownership and direction, while both the *Nation* and *New Republic* were to be racked by controversies, resignations and editorial accessions, for the most part growing out of disputes over their respective positions on foreign affairs. An especially busy season of changes was to occur in the last two years before American involvement in the Second World War, a period which will be unfolded in the story of the great policy changes which preceded this event.

In the fall of 1931 the *Nation* was headed up under the editorship of one of the most respected figures in the history of American journalism, Oswald Garrison Villard, who had been connected with its fortunes since 1894, and who was to part company in the furiously contentious days of mid-1940, thus terminating a career of over 46 years with this paper. The associate editors, Dorothy Van Doren and Mauritz Hallgren, had the assistance of Joseph Wood Krutch and Henry Hazlitt in the fields of drama and literature, supported by nine contributing editors of such repute as to make identifying comment utterly superfluous: Heywood Broun, Lewis A. Gannett, John A. Hobson, Freda Kirchwey, Henry L. Mencken, Norman Thomas, Mark and Carl Van Doren, and Arthur Warner.

By January, 1932 the only change had been the addition of Devere Allen to the contributing editor's staff, replaced by Ernest Gruening later in the year. Villard resigned from the chief editorship on January 1, 1933, whereupon some drastic tailoring of the editorial masthead occurred. He was replaced by an editorial board of four: Gruening, Kirchwey, Hazlitt and Krutch. The eminent contributing editors disappeared, replaced by Hallgren and Margaret Marshall, although Villard remained also in this capacity in a separate category, supplying a weekly page of sharp comment titled "Issues and Men," which frequently deviated widely from the general editorial tone of the *Nation.*

Another significant shakeup took place two years later to the week, but a number of important changes happened in between in piecemeal fashion, suggesting the eventual proportions of the editorial policy. Hazlitt left after the issue of October 18, 1933 to become

BRUCE BLIVEN

MALCOLM COWLEY

Photo by Gordon Parks

STUART CHASE

Photo by Halsman

QUINCY HOWE

JOHN T. FLYNN

LOUIS FISCHER

Photo by Wide World

ALFRED BINGHAM

OSWALD GARRISON VILLARD

Photo by Wide World

C. HARTLEY GRATTAN

REXFORD GUY TUGWELL

FREDERICK L. SCHUMAN

Photo by Arni

GEORGE SOULE

editor of the *American Mercury,* on an occasion when both Hazlitt and the *Mercury* were accorded the highest praise.[9] At the same time Dorothy Van Doren was now listed among the contributing editors. Gruening left with the issue of February 21, 1934 to become editor of the New York *Evening Post,* recently acquired by J. David Stern. An editorial paragraph commenting on his new position declared, "In his new capacity Ernest Gruening will have an opportunity to exercise his great gifts as a crusader and as the proponent of a vigorous liberal public policy." [10] Gruening continued to contribute signed material to the *Nation* thereafter, until he was appointed director of the newly created Division of Territories and Island Possessions in the Department of the Interior by FDR in August, 1934, on which occasion the *Nation* swelled with pride.

Hallgren left with the issue of May 16, 1934, replaced for two weeks by Warner, who then also departed. Maxwell S. Stewart joined the associate editors with the issue of August 15, 1934 [11] and Raymond Gram Swing was added to the editorial staff with the issue of September 12, 1934,[12] where he joined Kirchwey and Krutch as a three-person chief editorial staff for some months. Charles Angoff was added to the editorial board in April, 1935, preceded by Heywood Broun's return, this time as a contributor of a signed weekly column, in February of that year.[13] Angoff left in September, four months after a momentous ownership change occurred. The issue of May 8, 1935 announced that henceforth The Nation Fund, an incor porated foundation established by Maurice Wertheim, would be tł owner. Wertheim, a member of the *Nation's* board of directors eleven years, was to be assisted on the board of this fund by Vill Krutch, Kirchwey, Broun and Alvin Johnson, an ex-contribı editor of the *New Republic* and director of the New School for Research. The readers were promised that the existing poli "editorial freedom" would be maintained.[14]

On January 15, 1936 Max Lerner replaced Swing on the editors, contributing signed articles for some time as before devoted to domestic affairs. A major change in format ar ance began with the issue of March 4 of this same year, w Johnson and Broun being designated on the masthead associates." [15] The resignation of Dorothy Van Doren wa with regret in the issue of December 26, ending a ye tranquility, to be promptly followed by a massive exp The immediate cause of the upheaval was a bitter cor the editors and owners over the merits of President for changing the membership of the Supreme Cou attacked Villard and Wertheim in his column, enlarged and prolonged by Villard's own test whole affair precipitating another change of own

when Freda Kirchwey, now associated with the *Nation* for sixteen years, became sole owner.[16]

To Kirchwey this split and change of ownership signalled more than a dispute over a contemporary governmental issue, but grew out of a fundamental disagreement on the part of Wertheim with the new policies of "militant liberalism," which were gaining ground by the week and which to her represented the new direction of the future. Wertheim's unwillingness to stay aboard the new engine of change was at the bottom of it all, so this course had been decided upon because of the conviction that the editorship and "firm control" "should be combined." In an elucidative editorial she explained this almost in the sense of being a duty to the journal's new readers and the altered concept of liberalism now abroad: [17]

Never in our experience has the demand for clearcut, radical analysis been so great. Liberalism itself has achieved a new respect, especially among its former left-wing opponents. The example of fascism in Europe and a half-conscious dread of similar repression in the United States has led even the more dogmatic radicals to seek salvation in democratic method and liberal approach. And liberalism itself has taken warning and toughened its defenses against the day of testing. As a representative of radical democratic thought, of realistic liberalism, *The Nation* has drawn in thousands of new readers who have become friends and advocates.

In this manner did a struggle ostensibly incited by an internal dispute over the wisdom of a domestic policy suggestion lead to the formal announcement of the enlistment of the whole journal in the Popular Front. The issue of August 21, 1937 detailed the next stage of the Big Purge. Krutch, for some time the sole serious critic of Communism on the editorial board, resigned, and became dramatic critic.[18] The editorial associate trio of Villard, Broun and Johnson was dissolved, and in September Broun departed from the staff entirely.[19] Stewart was elevated to an associate editor at about this time as well. And although Villard's weekly column continued, veering steadily away from the tone and direction of the magazine as the months went on, there was now little doubt that the direction of policy was firmly in Miss Kirchwey's hands.

The issue of March 19, 1938 [20] announced the addition of James Wechsler to the staff, although he was not listed as an editor until October 21, 1939. On September 24, 1938 it was made known that Turner had resigned to become a professor of government at Williams College, replaced by a long-time contributor, I. F. Stone.[21] Keith Hutchison, a member of the New York *Herald Tribune*'s London bureau, was also added in editorial capacity, devoting most of his efforts to a column on business and finance in the manner of John Flynn's widely-known *New Republic* column, "Other Peoples'

Money." Wechsler left to become assistant labor editor of the new tabloid New York daily, *PM,* in May, 1940, and Villard left the *Nation* after June 29, 1940, terminating a string of columns which had appeared since January, 1933. Richard Rovere, an ex-editor of the Communist-saturated *New Masses,* was added to the editorial staff the next year, his name appearing on the masthead with the issue of September 20, 1941.[22] At this same time Kirchwey added the names of five more persons to the list of contributing editors: Norman Angell, Jonathan Daniels, Louis Fischer, Reinhold Niebuhr and J. Alvarez del Vayo. This step represented no new blood, however, since all had been frequent contributors previously, Fischer having represented the *Nation* as its Moscow correspondent from the mid-20's until shortly after the outbreak of the Spanish Civil War.[23]

Thus the editorial face of the *Nation* changed during this fateful decade, and some idea of the changing position of the journal may be grasped by observing all the comings and goings of the editorial personnel and personalities. The *New Republic* by comparison had a much more tranquil history, at least until the last two years before the entry of the United States into war.

In 1931 the *New Republic* boasted of as formidable a team of editors, and a stable of just as distinguished regular contributors. It was headed up by a group of five editors: Bruce Bliven, who was also president of the journal in its incorporated status, Malcolm Cowley, Robert Morss Lovett, George Soule and Stark Young. A supporting cast of contributing editors consisted of John Dewey, Waldo Frank, Alvin Johnson, E. C. Lindeman, Lewis Mumford, Gilbert Seldes, Rexford Guy Tugwell and Leo Wolman. Although the contributors to the journal came and passed over the years, this group remained remarkably stable. By 1935 only Johnson had dropped from the staff, joining the *Nation,* while John T. Flynn, who started writing his famous column, "Other People's Money," in 1933,[24] W. P. Mangold and the British liberal socialist H. N. Brailsford had been added.

In mid-February, 1936 the editors remained intact, although Seldes and Wolman had dropped from the contributing editors, replaced by Hamilton Basso and Jonathan Mitchell. In October, 1939, after a series of stirring events which had rocked most of the journals of opinion in the land, the *New Republic's* editorial force still held fast. Dewey, Basso and Mangold had departed from the contributors, replaced by Broun from the *Nation,* and two young men, James Benet and Bruce Bliven, Jr., just out of Stanford and Harvard respectively. Lovett, a well-known member of the University of Chicago faculty, was now the governor-general of Puerto Rico, and Tugwell was the chairman of the New York City Planning Commission, and their activities on the magazine were necessarily much curtailed. But it was an indication that men of quality were related to it, and their names still were carried on the masthead. Great pride had been taken in the career of Tugwell, who had been a member of the famous "Brain Trust" group of advisers to President Roosevelt in 1933 and the holder of other administrative governmental posts since that time.

However, an ugly situation was developing, incubated by the clash between the editorial foreign policy position and that of some of the contributing editors. This, combined with a sudden policy somersault late in 1940, started the same migration which featured the internal history of the *New Republic*'s older sister publication. The war brought a rapid episode of face-changing. Old voices dropped out rapidly, and a British flavor developed with the addition of Julian Huxley, Kingsley Martin and Nigel Dennis from England, aided by a strong current of pro-British sentiment from other sources. Mumford and Frank both resigned in protest over the editorial policy of non-commitment on the war, but reaffirmed their loyalty after editorial policy was tailored in a direction which put the journal squarely behind a position like theirs. Max Lerner returned to liberal journalism as a contributing editor in 1940, and Van Wyck Brooks and Samuel Grafton were also added, followed by Michael Straight, whose addition for the previously nonexistent post of Washington editor was announced in the issue for May 5, 1941.[25]

But these new faces, all urgently in support of the interventionist position newly adopted, were matched by quiet departures of consequence, two of the more important being Edmund Wilson and Flynn, in January and February, 1941. Flynn, the most consistently praised regular contributor, who had been spoken of proudly in the same category with Charles A. Beard by the *New Republic* in 1937, departed in an atmosphere of exceptional rancor and exchange of ungracious observations. Wilson's absence from the literary department was another profound loss attributable largely to his disagreement with the new foreign policy.

In this way both weeklies cleared their decks of the "old liberals" prior to war, and faced the readers with a monolith of agreement on this subject by the time American involvement was a reality. The transformation of liberalism on the issues of war, peace, foreign policy and foreign relations is the subject of this study, which will be examined on the basis of issues, events and opinion in detail. At this point, only a sketch of the traffic of the editorial staffs is under examination.

THE YOUNG MONTHLY COUSIN: COMMON SENSE

The picture of liberal journalism in the decade between Mukden and Pearl Harbor would be seriously incomplete without the inclusion of the liberal monthly flower of the depression, *Common Sense.* Beginning in December, 1932, this modest publication, under the editorship of Alfred M. Bingham and Selden Rodman, mustered a breath-taking assembly of talent from month to month in short time. Strongly oriented toward domestic affairs and deeply involved in plans and discussion of third party politics of a farmer-labor variety, *Common Sense* devoted a minimum of space to foreign affairs until 1937. Unlike the established weeklies, it maintained for the most part a cool and critical front toward the Communists and other Marxist elements, and beginning in 1937 it more and more became the refuge and haven for anti-war and non-interventionist liberals successively estranged or repelled by the frankly more war-willing weeklies. Its readership was built partially by opening its columns to politically prominent liberals of farmer-labor persuasion, particularly of the Midwest, Southwest and Far West. In its first seven years it published more material signed by prominent maverick progressive New Deal congressmen and administration figures than the *Nation* and *New Republic* combined and compounded.

Over the years the names of a famous contingent of contributors adorned the masthead of *Common Sense:* Robert S. Allen, Stuart Chase, Henry Hazlitt, Carleton Beals, John Dos Passos, A. J. Muste, V. F. Calverton, John T. Flynn, James Rorty, John Chamberlain, J. B. S. Hardman, George Soule, John Dewey, C. Hartley Grattan, Philip F. La Follette, Mary Heaton Vorse, Louis Adamic, Horace Gregory, Richard S. Childs, Lewis Mumford, Upton Sinclair, Theodore Dreiser, Roger Baldwin, Congressman Thomas R. Amlie of Wisconsin, Max Eastman, Thomas Benton, Francis J. Gorman, Governor Floyd B. Olson of Minnesota, Harold Loeb, Archibald MacLeish, William Harlan Hale, Herbert Harris, Ernest Sutherland Bates, Frank Hanighen, Peter Drucker, Charles A. Beard and Paul Douglas were some of those who found its pages an outlet for views, and a few books which received vast praise were first previewed in installments as well, including Major General Smedley D. Butler's sensational muck-raking book *War Is A Racket.*

The early specialty of *Common Sense,* powerful attacks on both the New Deal and the Republican opposition, stressed the absence of any decent recovery from the depression, plus the political ideas of nearly two dozen progressive office holders. This material was gradually leavened by more and more contributions on the growing world crisis. Liberals who preferred American involvement gradually separated from *Common Sense,* but until Pearl Harbor it stubbornly supported a non-involvement position, loudly calling for domestic reform and a marked improvement in the quality of American life before investment in junkets to carry political purity and morality overseas. Beyond a few mimeographed newsletters, such as the Writers' Anti-War Bureau's *Uncensored, Common Sense* was the last refuge of those who upheld the American liberal anti-war tradition to the end. The views and positions of its editors and contributors will be dealt with subsequently.

MORE DISTANT RELATIVES ON THE LEFT

Eugene Lyons dubbed the decade of the 1930's *The Red Decade,* as he titled his book dealing with the massive growth in that time of Communist strength and sympathy in the United States. That the following ten-year period was one of such favorable consequences for the burgeoning of Communist influence and penetration as to make the prior one of Lyons' concern seem relatively somnolent by comparison is beside the point here. There can be little doubt nevertheless that a rapid growth of Communist-run or directed organizations was a very significant fact, and the field of publications was not an exception. The major organs of American liberal opinion were especially aware of this activity, and examination reveals not only expressions of welcome and sympathy but a certain amount of parallel participation.

Many left-wing intellectuals were not content with the older organs of expression. Their bolder views saw light in a score or more "little magazines," most of them confined to small audiences and exercising very modest influence. The largest part of these working the fields of politics and foreign affairs had a strong Marxist flavor, and a substantial number were outright Communist transmission belts, their loyalty firmly fixed in promoting the welfare of Soviet Russia first. And it was not uncommon to find liberals contributing to some of them at the height of the Popular Front era, as well as a goodly number of frankly Soviet partisans gaining access to the liberal journals in reciprocation. The heady pro-Communism of American liberal journalism of the pre-Pearl Harbor decade was not a coincidence, nor its flourishing in the wartime period merely an accompaniment to a fortuitous political accident.

Joining older organs of farmer-labor and socialist persuasion such as the *Progressive* and the *New Leader* in the early depression years were journals such as *Our America, Soviet Russia Today,* the *Monthly Review,* the *Partisan Review, Left Front, Left Review, Dynamo, Blast, Anvil, Modern Monthly, New International, Marxist Quarterly, Science and Society,* and others. A certain amount of cross-culturization took place between some of these organs and the established Communist or Communist-dominated periodicals such as the *Daily Worker,* the monthly official organ of the CPUSA, the *Com-*

munist, and the literary monthly (weekly beginning in January, 1934) *New Masses.* Later in the period, beginning in 1937, the effect of Communist penetration into daily and weekly journalism in New York began to be documented by the appearance of house organs parodying the parent publication. Thus, in November, 1937, the first issue of *Better Times* (later retitled *New Times*) appeared, which frankly admitted to being "published by Communist Party Units of the New York *Times.*" [26] In February and April, 1939 came the inside journals *High Time,* put out by Communists on the staff of the weekly *Time* magazine, and the *Hearst Worker.* It is significant that all three of these publications, which added insult to injury by adhering severely to the exact format and style of the parent publication, were all warmly commended by the *New Republic.*[27]

Part of this was a reflection of the hostility toward the New York press in general in this period. Neither liberal weekly was charitable or generous toward any daily paper in the city, frequently criticizing the *Times* and *Herald Tribune* in bitter language and struggling to keep from denouncing them as flatly reactionary most of the time. (Nor were liberals particularly welcome on the pages of either.) The Hearst outlet was excoriated regularly, and the *World-Telegram* dismissed as "pseudo-liberal." Similarly they attacked the *Post* and owner J. David Stern, bitterly resenting his "baiting of the Reds and the Soviet Union," while covering this over with "liberal pretensions" growing out of a general pro-domestic New Deal attitude. Even after its change of ownership in June, 1939 the liberal weeklies withheld full approval. Thus, "inside" publications which purported to tell the news which their employers presumably suppressed enjoyed the sanction of liberals as part of their declared responsibility for respecting freedom of the press. Not until the tabloid daily *PM* appeared in 1940 did a New York newspaper obtain liberal approval.

In some of these journals were to be found the work of persons who were far from unknown in the liberal magazines, especially as contributors of book reviews of very pointed content. *New Republic-Nation* contributors and editors were not intimidated from publishing material in a few of them. Joshua Kunitz, T. A. Bisson and Maxwell S. Stewart occasionally appeared in *Soviet Russia Today,* and contributors Louis M. Hacker, Sidney Hook, Lewis Corey, Bertram D. Wolfe and James Burnham were all members of the board of editors when the first issue of the *Marxist Quarterly* appeared in November, 1936.[28]

There were even journals on the left which the liberal editors disapproved of almost as much as they abominated the commercial daily press. This was especially true of periodicals which championed the cause of Leon Trotsky at a time when the Popular Front mechanism required unswerving adherence to the Stalin faction and Stalinist tendencies everywhere. An example of this was the *New International* of Max Shachtman, one of those most intimately related to Trotsky. Even more aggravating was the revamped *Partisan Review*. Originally, along with *Left Front* and *Left Review,* an organ of the John Reed Club, *Partisan Review* remained in this relationship between February, 1934 and October, 1936. Its reappearance in October, 1937 under the direction of Philip Rahv and F. W. Dupee, whom the Stalinist Communist press railed at as expelled members of the Communist Party, was a signal for liberal scorn as well. Its drifting away from purely literary to political themes and its steadily anti-Soviet tone, especially during the 1938 Moscow trial, which sought to indict Trotsky as the mastermind of an international plot to subvert the Soviet Union, excited angry comments. Its concentration of writers such as Hook, Dwight MacDonald, Burnham, Dupee and Victor Serge did not endear it to liberals, who were exerting themselves to maintain their composure during this serious intramural dispute among the Marxists in America; "Put a green cover on it [*Partisan Review*] and today you could hardly tell it from the *American Mercury,*" Malcolm Cowley protested in the *New Republic* for October 19, 1938.[29] Only Hearst matched the *Mercury* for "reaction" in the estimate of American liberalism by this time, so this was a most unflattering comparison.

Despite temporary flirtations and peripheral relationships, most of the writers with a substantial affiliation with American liberalism in the pre-World War Two decade worked out a pro-Communist position of their own instead of becoming very intimately related with periodicals of deliberate Communist persuasion, even though a sizable traffic persisted across all of them by a number of literary figures. But of all the journals on the left between 1931 and 1941, liberals in some number were to be found mainly in two, the *New Masses* and *The Fight,* the latter a momentarily vigorous monthly which was the organ of the American League Against War and Fascism, the most active and encompassing Communist-dominated front organization of the First Red Decade. Scores of liberals were published in both, especially in the period between 1931 and 1937, after which there was a noticeable replacement by resolute Communists or frank party sympathizers. But there can be little doubt that, in the critical period during which the United States recognized Red Russia, and the League of Nations admitted the Soviets, and during which Hitler Germany got to its feet and started to fashion, among other things, a formidable threat to the Communists, a wide communion of interest and sympathy coursed across both liberal and Communist fields of activity alike. The expression of common views and the exchange of words, ideas, slogans and policies as well as spokesmen are facts which can be established with little difficulty.

The *New Masses* was the lineal descendant of the Marxian socialist *Masses* founded in 1911. Reorganized in 1926 with a change in name suggesting rejuvenation, it championed the newly established Bolshevik state vociferously. On January 2, 1934 it underwent a striking transformation into a weekly, patterned in many ways after the two liberal weeklies, and enjoyed five years of sustained growth and influence, during which it approximated their circulation.[30] Many liberals contributed articles and book reviews, and in turn writers whose reputations rested almost entirely upon steady appearance in *New Masses* found ready reception in liberal publications. A substantial sympathetic understanding undoubtedly existed, and its basis was apparently fully understood by those who consented to having their efforts appear in this medium. Granville Hicks, a professor of English at Rensselaer Polytechnic Institute, important figure in the Young Communist League, and an editor in 1934, explained the journal's stand on book-reviewing: [31]

Certainly the *New Masses* has never given a book to a reviewer who was known to be either anti-Soviet or pro-Fascist. Certainly most *New Masses'* reviewers are Communists or Communist sympathizers. Certainly *New Masses'* critics, though they rigorously analyze the work of revolutionary writers, are in complete sympathy with their principles . . . The *New Masses* has adopted a certain position, and in every issue explains what that position is and why it has been adopted.

It thus hardly can be argued that the numerous liberals who participated in issuing this periodical did not know what they were doing or were innocently taking part in an intellectual adventure which was not devoted to a particular outlook on national and world affairs. In a similar way, the editors of the liberal journals can be assumed to have known what they were doing in publishing the work of *New Masses* editors and steady contributors in their pages. In the ten years prior to United States involvement in the Second World War, articles and book reviews by a dozen *New Masses* editors and members of their editorial board appeared in the liberal press, while over 60 well-known liberal writers had pieces published in the *New Masses* during this same time span. The cordiality between the two cooled off markedly beginning late in 1937, when the controversy over Trotsky and the Moscow purges introduced a serious split in the Marxist camp. The tendency for supporters of Trotsky to gather in the liberal sphere brought sharp cries of angry criticism from the Stalinists, who bluntly accused the liberals of becoming anti-Soviet. Several liberals had sent greetings of praise to the *New Masses* on the occasion of its 25th anniversary issue in the fall of 1936. Two years later only an occasional person allied with liberal journalism was appearing it its pages. But a community of interests and a spiritual bond had long ago been forged which was to be wrenched apart only by the startling non-aggression pact signed between Russia and Germany in August, 1939, an act which produced the most agonizing injury to the sensibilities of American left liberals that they have ever suffered, and from which they have yet to fully recover.

The experiences of liberals during the publication life of *The Fight* [32] were not very much different than they were in the case of the *New Masses*. Its first number appeared in November, 1933, and the ideology behind the organization sponsoring it reflected a number of currents which were flowing strongly at the moment: pacifism, anti-militarism, disarmament and sharp criticism of the manufacture of munitions, and allied sentiments, including condemnation of military or paramilitary organizations and education. The interlocking of its mixed personnel gave it the flavor of a multi-hued group, which has always been the delight of institutional liberalism. The first chairman of the parent organization sponsoring *The Fight,* the American League Against War and Fascism, was J. B. Matthews, at that time also the executive secretary of the pacifist Fellowship of Reconciliation. But its vice chairman was Earl Browder, its secretary was Donald Henderson,[33] two Communist stalwarts, and a contributor in the first issue was Henri Barbusse, one of France's most persuasive pro-Communist apologists. Another first-issue contributor was Roger Baldwin.

However, there was an ominous timing connected with the coming into existence of the American League and its new organ. The emergence of the Hitler regime in Germany and its vociferous anti-Communist attack had more to do with it than anyone at the moment wished to admit. The Mussolini regime had been in existence in Italy since 1922, yet it was not until this late date that such a vigorous response to the challenge of Fascism was deemed imperative. The world-wide Russian Communist apparatus for the creation of anti-Hitler and ultimately anti-German sentiment was swinging into operation, a prominent tool in this campaign being the slowly-fashioned Popular Front with all elements Communists could recruit or could find sympathetic. Within a year of its existence, it was plain that this new organization was a mobilization center for sentiment, not *against* war *and* Fascism, but *for* war *against* Fascism. And in 1937 some anti-war liberals began to shout this loudly. It undoubtedly helped to contribute to the flight of liberals from the League's ranks, but the big break took place in the late summer of 1938, by which time the organization's name had been changed to the American League for Peace and Democracy. Liberals of several shades still adhered to this group, but its persistent championing of the Soviet Union's foreign policy, its clamorous support of the Communist revolutions in Spain and China and its hostility toward anti-collective security sentiments among American liberal pacifists put the ALPD utterly out of harmony with such liberal groups as the Keep America Out of War Congress, and the National Council For the Prevention of War. The culminating blow was the rejection of Harry Elmer Barnes as the scheduled main speaker at a gigantic "Peace Parade" demonstration in New York on August 6, 1938, after learning that his speech was going to stress a forthright call for abstaining from all wars, including those which the Communists happened to favor fighting at the moment.[34] The League never recovered from the anti-war liberal assault on this act in the following weeks, and the last issue of its journal appeared in July, 1939. A few months later, after the Russo-German Pact had obliterated the whole structure of liberal-Communist foreign policy argument of the past decade, the League quietly expired. It was no longer needed in the new dispensation.

But in the crucial opinion-forming years of 1934–1938, liberals contributed to *The Fight* profusely. Its pages were a mirror which also reflected the then amiable state of affairs in the liberal and pro-Communist weeklies, even though editorial policy was obviously becoming a pro-Communist monopoly. In May, 1934 *The Fight* was under a new chairman, Harry F. Ward, and its vice chairmen now consisted of Browder, Lincoln Steffens and the *New Republic* editor, Robert M. Lovett. Its editor Joseph Pass had an advisory editorial committee consisting of Kyle Crichton, who wrote for the *New Masses* under the name of Robert Forsythe, Donald Henderson, David Zablodowsky and Malcolm Cowley, one of the dominant literary voices on the *New Republic*. And among its contributors during its heyday were many who also gained access to the organs of liberalism in the same period, including Babette Deutsch, Bernhard J. Stern, Isador Schneider, Harvey O'Connor, Maxwell S. Stewart, Langston Hughes, C. Hartley Grattan, James T. Farrell, Quincy Howe, John Howard Lawson, Albert Maltz, Murray Godwin, Harold Ward, Egon Erwin Kisch, George R. Leighton, James A. Wechsler, R. Palme Dutt, Pierre van Paassen, Leon Dennen, Welton Brown, Hamilton Basso, H. C. Engelbrecht, Edwin Berry Burgum, George A. Coe, Hy Kravif, John Strachey, Victor Yakhontoff, Carl Dreher, Walter Wilson, George Seldes, Liston M. Oak, Bruce Crawford, George S. Counts, Romain Rolland, Johannes Steel, Jerome Davis, Anna Rochester, William P. Mangold, Carleton Beals, Grace Lumpkin, Joseph P. Lash, Mauritz Hallgren, Keith Sward, Heywood Broun, Dorothy Douglas, Bishop Francis J. McConnell, James Waterman Wise and William Gropper.

Other personalities also figured in *The Fight* in the late 30's, including Harold Laski, Robert Dell, Ralph Bates, Louis Fischer, Ch'ao-ting Chi, editorial board member of *Amerasia,* and even such unlikely personages as Clark M. Eichelberger, director of the League of Nations Association, and Sir Norman Angell. And undoubtedly there were sincere friends of peace and opponents of war during the life-time of this organization among its writers, but the position of the journal and organization was never obscure. It never published a paragraph critical of the Soviet Union in its entire existence, nor commented adversely on Soviet arms and military buildups and strength during its furious attacks on munitions makers and military preparations in other countries, especially those with an anti-Soviet foreign policy. In the case of the Communists involved in China and Spain it employed the familiar double standard of extolling Com-munist war-making efficiency while denigrating their opponents. However, this position should never have been mysterious to a single contributor or reader who read Point 5 of the "Program of the Amer-ican League Against War and Fascism" in the September, 1934 issue of *The Fight:* [35]

To support the peace policies of the Soviet Union, for total and uni-versal disarmament, which today with the support of the masses in all countries constitute the clearest and most effective opposition to war throughout the world. To oppose all attempts to weaken the Soviet Union, whether these take the form of misrepresentation and false propa-ganda, diplomatic maneuvering or intervention by imperialist govern-ments.

This defensive portrait of the Russian Communist state, at a time when Communists were actually making parenthetical comments on Russia's possession of the largest army and air force in the world, and its acceptance as a true representation of the world situation, does not flatter the reputation of those who acted as critics and analysts in those times. The belated withdrawal of many liberals from associa-tion with this formidable front in 1937 and 1938 was recognition at last that they had been mobilized in an agency enlisted to promote the welfare of Communist Russia and the success of its foreign policy.

LIBERAL FOREIGN AFFAIRS WRITING
IN SOME PRESTIGE JOURNALS

The substantial contingent of writers on foreign affairs and United States foreign policy which expressed their views at such length in the liberal press apparently had little rapport with the majority of the limited-circulation monthlies and quarterlies which exercised influence in the same circles they preferred to participate in, as reflected by the tributes on their anniversary issues in 1939 and 1940. Some of these, such as *Foreign Affairs,* the *American Mercury* and *Forum,* rarely were known to carry the writing of a liberal of note, and were under condemnation in the liberal weeklies and by most articulate liberals anyway. *Living Age* served as a major outlet for the views principally of Quincy Howe, whose book reviews and comments were a steady feature of the *New Republic* in the period of warmest controversy over collective security. It was the *Living Age* which sparked the great liberal attack on the munitions business in the 1931–1935 period, and Archibald MacLeish credited Howe as "undoubtedly the man most responsible for the entire American campaign." [36] The *Atlantic Monthly* featured the commentaries of Frank H. Simonds and William Henry Chamberlin throughout the decade before Pearl Harbor, both of whom had long associations with American liberalism between the First World War and the Depression, but gradually became estranged during the ten-year journey on the Moscow Express. But the *Atlantic* occasionally opened its columns to others, primarily Villard, Marcel W. Fodor and single essays by Walter Millis and Frank Hanighen.

Harper's, on the other hand, published liberal foreign affairs comments somewhat more freely, but had a preference for some writers. The most frequent contributors were Nathaniel Peffer and Elmer Davis. Such liberal stalwarts as John T. Flynn and Villard were published just once each in the 1931–1941 era, Charles A. Beard only twice. Several other familiar names in the *Nation, New Republic* and *Common Sense* appeared sporadically during this time, including George Soule, John Gunther, Ludwig Lore, Ben Dorfman, Alfred Vagts, M. E. Ravage, Eliot Janeway, C. Hartley Grattan and Hanighen.

The record in the stiff and aristocratic academic quarterlies of top level influence, such as the *Yale Review* and the *Virginia Quarterly Review,* was much less prominent. Barely a dozen liberal writers dealing with foreign politics were published in these two redoubtable publications, two-thirds of the dozen and a half articles appearing in the 1938–1941 period, when the schism over collective security and intervention in the crisis versus continentalism and neutrality was tearing American liberalism completely asunder. Even the many professors whose work was constantly featured in weekly liberal journalism had scant entry to these more stratospheric heights. The mass penetration of the large New York daily newspapers and the quality literary and opinion press by the academic community was largely a phenomenon of the exploding war liberalism of 1941–1945 and the new era of globalism which set in during the following decade. Its parallel was the almost total eclipse of the segment of American liberal opinion which had once expounded a contradictory view on the proper nature of American attitudes and deportment in the field of foreign affairs and relations.

The scores of contributors to the liberal press who had no acknowledged hand in editorial duties will be mentioned throughout the study, in the appropriate context of their contributions, and related to background and so forth. Since contributors' work was signed, there is no difficulty in locating responsibility, but since it was editorial practice, most of the time, to print all editorials as unsigned material, it poses a serious difficulty for those interested in the possible authors. It is of even greater significance since many startling viewpoints, changes of approach, opinion and policy appear in this same anonymous form. The collective nature of the editorial staffs defied efforts to ascribe one or another noteworthy piece to its likely writer, and no memoir by one or another of these famous liberal journalists over the years has done much to cast real light on this problem of identity to this day.

NOTES

1 *New Republic,* November 23, 1932, p. 47.
2 *Nation,* October 21, 1939, pp. 443–444. The *Nation* announced a readership of 35,000 in their issue of June 7, 1941. (Page 680.)
3 As quoted in subscription promotional material in *Nation,* April 3, 1937, p. 390.
4 *Nation,* January 15, 1938, p. 78.
5 *Nation,* February 10, 1940, p. 145.
6 For the text of the citations by these persons see *Nation,* October 28, 1939, p. 478; January 20, 1940, p. 71; January 27, 1940, p. 112; February 3, 1940, pp. 139–140; February 10, 1940, pp. 191–192, 215; February 17, 1940, pp. 263–264; February 24, 1940, p. 291.
7 Quotations in the foregoing three paragraphs will be found in *New Republic,* October 18, 1939, Special Supplement, p. iv; November 1, 1939, p. 378; December 20, 1939, p. 261; February 26, 1940, p. 288.
8 As cited in *Nation,* May 8, 1935, p. 521.
9 *Nation,* October 18, 1933, p. 423.
10 *Nation,* February 28, 1934, p. 233.
11 *Nation,* August 15, 1934, p. 169.
12 *Nation,* September 12, 1934, p. 281.
13 Broun's column began again in the issue of February 20, 1935. Broun, subsequently president of the American Newspaper Guild, was perhaps the kindest of the liberal journalists in treating the *Daily Worker,* and the Communist press generally, though he never recovered from a *Worker* cartoon by Jacob Burck in 1932 when he was running for Congress on the Socialist ticket. Burck's cartoon depicted Broun as a baby in a perambulator being wheeled up Park Avenue by Norman Thomas, clutching a bottle labeled "gin." "Hey-gin" Broun was a Communist epithet which was repeated for years, but he continued to defend the *Daily Worker* in a spirited manner as "part of the American tradition."
14 *Nation,* May 8, 1935, p. 521, contains the full text of the change.
15 *Nation,* January 15, 1936, p. 57.
16 See Villard, "What Is *The Nation* Coming To?," *Nation,* March 27, 1937, p. 352.

17   Signed editorial, *Nation,* June 19, 1937, p. 695. See also the long statement by Wertheim in *Nation,* June 12, 1937, p. 666, dealing with the matter discussed above.

18   On some of Krutch's views see his urbane *Was Europe A Success?* (Farrar and Rinehart, 1934), which first appeared in the *Nation* as articles. An exceedingly kind and commendatory review by Harry Elmer Barnes appeared in the *Nation* on January 23, 1935, pp. 108–109.

19   *Nation,* September 11, 1937, p. 252. The editorial announced the news "with regret," saying, "Mr. Broun has neither resigned nor been dropped, he has merely moved."

20   *Nation,* March 19, 1938, p. 340.

21   *Nation,* September 24, 1938, p. 283. Stone had been identified in the *Nation* on August 22, 1934, p. 219, as the chief editorial writer of the New York *Post.* His earliest articles in the *Nation* were signed Isador Feinstein.

22   *Nation,* September 20, 1941, p. 257. Rovere was identified as a *New Masses* editor by Wechsler in his *Nation* article on September 30, 1939, pp. 342–345.

23   The *Nation* had no direct dispatches from Russia after the Spanish Civil War broke out. Fischer went to Spain and nobody replaced him in Moscow.

24   Flynn was the most consistently praised columnist on the *New Republic* until after the war broke out in 1939, and the editors proudly bracketed him with Charles A. Beard as a liberal of distinction. *New Republic,* February 10, 1937, p. 22.

25   *New Republic,* May 5, 1941, p. 642.

26   George Seldes discussed this journalistic innovation at length in the *New Republic,* September 7, 1938, pp. 121–125.

27   See comments in *New Republic,* February 15, 1939, p. 31; April 5, 1939, p. 235.

28   See full column advertisement of the first issue, "Devoted to the Exposition, Amplification and Application of Marxism," in *New Republic,* October 21, 1936, p. 331.

29   *New Republic,* October 19, 1938, pp. 311–312.

30   The *New Masses* claimed a circulation of 25,000 in their issue of January 1, 1935, (p. 9) but it was in constant financial trouble from 1937 on, and went through several crises, while admitting running deficits as high as $20,000 a year. See especially the issues of June, 1937, February and October, 1938 and February, 1939.

31   *New Masses,* October 2, 1934, p. 17.

32   The name changed three times. From Volume 1, Number 1 to Volume 5, Number 2, it was titled *The Fight Against War and Fascism* (1933–1937). From Volume 5, Number 3 to Volume 6, Number 7, the name was *The Fight For Peace and Democracy* (1937–1939). The title of the last two issues, Numbers 8 and 9 of Volume 6 (June and July, 1939) was *World For Peace and Democracy.*

33   See Henderson's speech before the Central Committee of the CPUSA, May 25–27, 1935, "The Rural Masses and the Work of Our Party," *The Communist,* September, 1935, pp. 866–880.

34   See the embarrassed editorial comment on this tactical blunder in *The Fight,* September, 1938, p. 31.

35   *The Fight,* September, 1934, p. 14. Consult as well the editorial "Russia Fights For Peace" in the same issue.

36   Cited from MacLeish's review of the Engelbrecht and Hanighen volume *Merchants of Death* and George Seldes's *Iron, Blood and Profits; Nation,* May 23, 1934, p. 596.

2

AMERICAN LIBERALISM REACTS AND ADJUSTS TO THE NEW EUROPEAN COLLECTIVISMS

IN 1941, a short while before the United States became a participant in the Second World War, Professor J. Salwyn Schapiro, of the College of the City of New York, reviewing Benedetto Croce's *History as the Story of Liberty* in the *Journal of the History of Ideas,* rendered an incidental definition of liberalism which has subsequently had wide circulation: [1]

Liberalism is an attitude toward life, not a dogmatic faith; it makes its greatest appeal to the educated and enlightened few, not to the broad masses. It has no fixed goal either in this world or the next; no absolute dogmas the acceptance of which leads to salvation; no "social myths" of a perfect society with which to appeal to the suffering masses. Liberalism is experimental and compromising in its methods, which aim to establish a better world through continuous piecemeal reforms. It espouses "principles" and "ideals" to enlighten and to direct these reforms into the proper channel.

A dozen years later, Joseph S. Clark, Jr., Mayor of Philadelphia, in an article in the *Atlantic Monthly,* delivered another definition of significance, this time of the practitioners of liberalism, also of wide quotable consequences. While discussing the political future of liberals, Clark announced,[2]

A liberal is here defined as one who believes in utilizing the full force of government for the advancement of social, political and economic justice at the municipal, state, national, and international levels.

These two definitions in capsule form tell an extended story of the course of liberalism in America in the past quarter of a century in particular. The obvious change of emphasis and basic assumptions reflected in these two statements represent the result of the capture of liberalism and liberals by the intoxicating attractions of power-holding and close affinity to power-holders and the seat of power-wielding. They imply further a substantial replacement of personnel, in view of the contradictory nature of the content of these statements. This metamorphosis has been achieved with a minimum of conscious awareness of the full impact of the fundamental somersault performed; at the same time the traditional modes of expressing liberalism's content and aspirations have persisted without a similar fundamental alteration.

There is little doubt that America's liberals take for granted that what Professor Schapiro said actually describes their persistent intellectual position. Yet the operational directive plotted by Mayor Clark actually describes the path they have taken, whatever obstacles have appeared to make their course so unpleasant in these more recent years. The conflict has led to a great traffic of persons leaving and entering the liberal fold, but the language of liberalism has remained for the most part serenely unaltered throughout this upheaval. The bland assurances that there has been no basic alteration in liberalism and that its verbal and actual states are identical have been accepted at face value for the most part by a contemporary audience, which is today much more acquainted with then Mayor, now Senator, Clark's estimate than that of Professor Schapiro. In fact, as a steady retreat from the latter stand continues, dedication of the exponents of the new liberalism to the verbal stereotypes has intensified. Out of this has emerged a homogenization which has made specific pinpointing more and more difficult. The shapelessness of liberal verbiage has enabled a tantalizing evasiveness to flourish, although the imprecision has communicated itself to the whole society, and is now an infection running its course at a heightened tempo.

One symptom of the confusion resulting from this blending of verbal reflexes is an increasing number of books which purport to define the broader abstractions, but generally succeed only in making the region of non-definition wider. The increasing circulation in the past decade of the words "liberal" and "liberalism" as positive connotations has also led to their adoption by all manner of folk, which helps to explain why the Clark definition is virtually worthless as an aid in identifying liberals. The entire global political spectrum is encompassed by it. As the tangible stuff of liberalism retreats before attempts to grasp it, discussing its substance and its main tenets and spokesmen becomes increasingly difficult. But this is a problem for an investigator of ideological material of whatever sort; the dividing lines have no clear edges, and progressive blurring along the boundaries of both thought and action guarantees increasing handicaps in the path of those so brash as to attempt analysis.

The late George Orwell displayed in his last decade of life a talent for divining and exposing political charlatanry equalled by few people in the history of criticism. His ability to do this through the medium of a superior literary style made him widely read and famous. His education in the ways of political language began primarily, as he tells us, after his experiences in the Spanish Revolution, described so dramatically in *Homage to Catalonia*. But there is a minor masterpiece of his in the same category, an essay titled "Politics and the English Language" in which he discussed the deterioration of the political vocabulary and the related decay of political writing and discussion. His primary conclusion consisted of the observation that political generalizations had become so sloppy and careless, and that the terminology had become so imprecise, that for all practical purposes this language was useless as a means of defining or explaining political positions and political behavior. Such words as "conservative," "reactionary," "radical," "democratic," "progressive," "liberal," and the like, he maintained, had been used so shamefully that whatever precise meaning they once had was dissipated, and now they had degenerated into simply a vocabulary of epithets, used interchangeably by the ignorant and worthless as a guide to any competent understanding.

It is no wonder that the contemporary political spectrum has no real dimensions and the most shameful kind of distortion has become a veritable industry. "Liberals" and "Conservatives" abound at any given moment, depending largely upon whether the fashionable thinking of the day and that accepted in majority circles is labeled one or the other. The homogenization of opinion since the end of the Second World War has even produced schools of hybrids in the political lexicon, and those students of political expression of the last decade or so are familiar with the "conservative liberal" and "liberal conservative" varieties, among others. Orwell's interpretation has been buttressed by all contemporary trends with a vengeance.

Interpretative studies purporting to explain the "isms" abound, and books dealing with the nature of politico-social philosophy and its varied expressions similarly proliferate. There hardly need to be additional contributions of this kind, nor is a lengthy essay essential as explanatory material to serve the purpose of an introduction to the main task about to be undertaken. Rather than quarrel over-long about definitions, with the risk of becoming trapped in a semantic jungle from which there might not be an escape, it seems suitable to proceed from the original statement, accepting the protagonists on their word and at face value.

THE GREAT COLLECTIVIST TRANSFORMATION

The "general staff of liberalism," as one might designate the editors and the many often world-renowned contributors whose work graced the pages of the liberal press, represented the stage of leadership in liberal circles, admitted or not, a dozen years after the First World War. For the most part it consisted of new faces when the familiar figures of the pre-war and wartime liberal and progressive activities are brought to mind. A number of the latter were still active, but an ideological hurricane was beginning to toss American liberalism about, largely a product of the high winds created by the professedly Marxian socialist experiment in Russia, plus those worked up by the world depression. When the full force had descended upon the scene, the effect upon liberalism was to separate the later from the earlier manifestations into what amounted to camps occupied mainly by strangers to each other. European and Asiatic totalitarian recipes for the solution of the disorders of the world national system produced the most profound effects upon American liberals. One might say that from an ideological point of view this experience was to shatter all schemes for reform in America based on exclusively American diagnosis and primarily for American results.

The liberals were not fully convinced in the early and mid-1930's whether they wished to be known as liberals or not. The main source of the cause for this intellectual disquiet is to be found in the influence of socialism of a variety of sorts upon the standard-bearers of liberalism. The years 1930–1931 are mainly the beginning date for the inundation of American intellectual life by "the approach from the left," gaining in strength since the shattering of the world in the War all through the 1920's and achieving swamping proportions due mainly to the economic debacle beginning in 1929. The original liberal open-minded critical attitude, with its tendency to find satisfaction in piecemeal reforms and partial, short-term gains resulting from extended debate, careful study and empirical methods, encountered at this point a problem of such magnitude that little of the early tradition of progressive reform maintained its appeal. While parliamentary democratic capitalist states were able to keep themselves afloat, the socialist critique consisted mainly of a nuisance or irritant. During this period little comfort could be squeezed from the spectacle of Soviet Russia, engulfed in a complex of problems and not particularly useful as an object lesson of what the preferable way of life was likely to be. Marxian socialism had once been a considerable voice in the affairs of the American labor movement, and in its manifestation as the Industrial Workers of the World it had been the most important revolutionary development in the history of American radicalism.

The First World War had shattered the solidarity of American socialism completely. Its high-water mark of effectiveness had been reached shortly before the out-break of the War, and in the United States it never recovered from the obliterating blows of national patriotism and allied sentiments which the War stimulated, bred, and turned loose in such quantity and volume. After the War the tendency for the unions and the labor movement generally to shy away from socialism had steadily grown. It is indeed curious to observe that as Marxian socialism was dying out among the laboring element in America, it was beginning to capture the literary men.

The attractiveness and appeal of Marxian socialism to an element of American life far removed from canvas gloves and denim work-clothing will remain a puzzling matter for some time to come. It is not pertinent to dwell upon the issue at this point, since a considerable literature on the subject has accumulated in the last decade and a half. But a note might be made of a contemporary interpretation which reverberated for years under one authorship or another. Max Nomad, whose *Rebels and Renegades* appeared in 1932,[3] enlarged on a thesis advanced by the Pole Walter Machajski, which first called attention to a new potential class of powerholders, the "declassé intelligentsia" or "mental workers," vaulting into a privileged position through the utilization of their "capital," higher education. Thus, instead of capitalists or workers, the Nomad-Machajski thesis ran, the new state would be run by and in the interests of a new class of "hereditary, soft-handed intellectuals." Through the decade of the 1930's we find other significant contributions to the "managerial revolution" theory from Lewis Corey, Alfred Bingham and Lucien Laurat, anticipating the famous book of this title by James Burnham in 1940, its first systematic elaboration, and wrought into superb and terrifying literature by George Orwell, first in his *Animal Farm* and reaching its peak in *Nineteen Eighty-four,* the nightmare "distopia" of a society run precisely by the people described by Nomad, Machajski and Burnham.

That overalls had become the uniform of the non-laboring, Inner Party policy-making intelligentsia of Orwell's novel is a bit of symbolism of vast significance.

THE LEFTBOUND LOCAL VERSUS
THE MOSCOW EXPRESS

Setting aside momentarily the subject of liberal pretensions and illusions as to being the advance guard of a proletarianized America according to socialist prescriptions and dimensions, it can be observed that the Marxian scriptures were sufficiently obscure to favor the hatching of a bumper crop of deviates. Ideological splinter groups of such variety as to confuse specialists even after years of study were one of the foremost results of the interminable intellectual rounds based on the main Marxian theme. The most ponderous influence was undoubtedly that of the segment which formed an early and intense attachment to the Soviet experiment. The open and subterranean Communists quickly became a gravitational pole, seeking to attract the hesitant and the bewildered. At a nearby position there was the already established Socialist remnant, seeking to perpetuate and extend its influence and tracing its origins back to the turn of the century and beyond. United in agreement upon the conclusion that capitalism and parliamentary democratic state systems were sure to crash, what was to replace them and how it was to do it was the issue in bitter dispute between them. In between these two major camps fluttered the "deviationists," and this point in the spectrum the liberals also occupied. The choice facing them was obvious, and perplexing. But whatever the choice, it involved partnership with a force which held liberalism and liberals in disrepute. At best, the Socialists and Communists viewed liberalism as a program of timid moderation; at worst, a collection of eviscerated political and economic doctrines inherited from a time when the conditions which had fostered their growth no longer existed. That the literati who had decided that the Soviet Union pointed the way held the liberals and liberalism in contempt was utterly undisguised. The liberal press in these circumstances appeared to be acting as agents for their own discrediting, publishing attacks on liberals from Soviet sympathizers and supporters, although this was partially an act which was probably considered in the direction of helping liberals to resolve the serious decision facing them.

In the *New Republic* for February 10, 1932, there appeared a long article by Edmund Wilson, titled "What Do the Liberals Hope For?" In it, while attacking four prominent liberals, Wilson argued that liberalism was bankrupt, that liberals and their practices, principles and promises had had their day. Their leadership in the pre-war period had resulted in a disappointing achievement, and furthermore, the liberals had made the war and the peace which followed it. Besides all this, they had shown their blindness by resisting the

"Revolution," making it "necessary" for those who seized power to shoot and jail and otherwise dispose of the Russian counterparts of some of the Western liberals, the Mensheviks. The failure of the liberals to applaud the Bolshevik success because of the methods employed was an obvious sign of the emptiness of liberalism, and that in the world crisis they stood beaten and hopeless in a situation crying for direction and advice.

A week later, Lincoln Steffens, the veteran liberal progressive of the earlier era, and one of the four men Wilson had disparaged, answered with a response headed "Bankrupt Liberalism," which consisted mainly of admissions as to the correctness of Wilson's diagnosis. "It is," said Steffens, "heart- and head-breaking to see the job begun and carried on over there by a dictator and a small minority using force when they don't know how otherwise to govern." His "old, stout liberalism" was "shattered by the sight," but still he "rejoiced" that "the deed was done and a path blazed for us":

My (our) victory in Russia did take some of the fight out of me. The growing success over there made all progressive movements and liberal programs seem superficial, long and rather hopeless. And to start out again at the bottom to plan to search deeper toward the roots for a revolution— that looks like a long, hard course to take for an old, habituated Menshevik with only a thick skin of Bolshevism on his hardened arteries. It is pleasanter, easier, to sit on the fence and contemplate our progress in Russia, watch it work over there, and listen to the Wall Street sentries appraising it right—as they do and as the liberals don't—at its true significance for us; while I encourage younger men like Edmund Wilson and his readers to pick up and bear on the burden here in this our backward country.

To find the Russian route affirmed more resolutely by a liberal figure of greater stature than Lincoln Steffens is hard to imagine. But Edmund Wilson was just one of the new school of writers who appeared to have made his choice. A contingent had been embroiled in this controversy since the early 1920's, but the coming of the depression had focussed the problem much more acutely for many others, and by mid-1932 the leftward drift of the writers and the intellectuals had become virtually the major topic of discussion. The point about which the controversy centered was not where, but how far. The furor provoked a major article in the *New Republic* on August 17, 1932, characteristically headed "Leftbound Local." It consisted primarily of a summary of a questionnaire published in the summer issue of the *Modern Quarterly,* a lesser liberal journal, answered by fifteen writers, built around the subject of the relationship between literature and political coloration at that point in the business collapse. All fifteen of the critics, writers and poets were from New York, and the *New Republic* editorial article seemed satisfied that their answers were "a cross section of American literary opinion in the summer of 1932." Twelve of the fifteen answered "yes" when asked, "Do you believe that American capitalism is doomed to inevitable failure and collapse?" Only Henry Hazlitt of the *Nation* replied with an unqualified "No." However, no one felt the collapse would take place in the decade ahead. All fifteen writers, the number including Henry Seidel Canby, C. Hartley Grattan, Granville Hicks, John Dos Passos, Sherwood Anderson, Edwin Seaver, Percy Holmes Boynton and Newton Arvin, were in agreement that the writer should "participate" in the "social crisis" rather than remain aloof. A majority of this group felt that becoming a Communist, "in the sense of accepting a communistic philosophy," would make them more effective participants in the struggle, but balked at actually joining the Communist Party and coming under its discipline. All but two denied that becoming a Socialist would have any possible influence, while insofar as the direction American literature was likely to take in the coming decade, a majority expressed the hope or feeling that it would take the path "of Dos Passos and Michael Gold." In summary the liberal journal concluded: [4]

. . . the "leftward swing" of American writers is a reality. Three years ago, these fifteen critics and novelists were classified either as liberals or else as men wholly uninterested in politics. Today most of them distrust the Socialists for being too conservative, too much involved in the present system. . . . They sympathize with the Communists, but not to the extent of wishing to join the party. . . . But it isn't true that all of them have simultaneously boarded the Red Express; the train in which they are traveling might better be described as a leftbound local.

This liberal estimate contained insights into the choice facing the liberal world. Editorially, this leading liberal journal was satisfied that the vast majority of America's writers had not "boarded an express bound for Moscow and points left," but was on the platform waiting for a slower train bound in the same general direction, and in no haste to get there. This was a comforting estimation of the situation, offering a prospective explanation of the present and suggesting the rectitude of adopting a vague quasi-communist outlook without too deep self-questioning as to what destination such a choice might lead them. As it turned out, both the leftbound local and the Moscow Express left at the same time, and the liberals, trying to decide which to take, in desperation boarded both of them. On domestic affairs, they maintained a tolerably independent leftist approach, but their underlying ideological commitment put them squarely in the Russian Soviet orbit on the subject of foreign and world affairs. The result was a steadily increasing pro-Soviet orientation, which in many cases developed into a close attachment. The liberal journals and editors apologized for this steadily increasing corps of pro-Soviet writers during the ensuing decade as a group of pioneers "in the task of sympathetically interpreting the Soviet Union to the vast American middle class." It need hardly be mentioned that no mercy was shown to those who dared undertake this task on behalf of rival totalitarianisms. Nevertheless, the liberal journals and the people to whom they opened their pages comprised in the early 1930's at least a largely unsettled and disturbed environment, creating a picture of America and the world without consistency, and more often than not, contradictory. The diversity of the contributors partially explains the situation, plus the fact that the liberals were especially interested in criticism and were not at this stage overly fussy as to source, provided that it was of relatively high literary quality. Orthodoxy grew in importance as the decade wore on, as the implications of the liberal choices became apparent, and as the fragments of the exploded post-Versailles world began to settle into a more readily recognizable structure.

SOME LIBERAL TRAILS THROUGH THE IDEOLOGICAL JUNGLE OF THE DEPRESSION

The liberal press spoke with many tongues in the trough years of the depression. Those who read it for information, advice and guidance undoubtedly had constant choices to make among the ideological wares on display there. The editors and the numerous contributors struggled with the situation, but it remained largely unresolved. A sizable segment of them decided to support Norman Thomas and the Socialist Party in the 1932 election, but the Communist supporters remained apart and kept up an unending chorus of raucous criticism. At times their penetration of the liberal journals made it difficult to distinguish their title pages from those of the *Daily Worker* and the *New Masses;* a number of prolific contributors circulated among liberal and Communist publications alike as a common currency. There were in addition a small number of unclassified figures familiar to readers of the liberal press who flirted with a variety of sectarian movements and tendencies not in accord with the recognized channels of the left. An examination of some of the prominent voices in the gloom will provide partial illumination.

The clamor of the guides at the darkened crossroads in 1931–1932 was reaching its peak volume. In the latter year the major publishers turned loose a multi-volumed radical Baedeker, featuring Harry Laidler's *Socialist Planning and a Socialist Program,* Paul H. Douglas's *The Coming of a New Party,* Vernon Calverton's *The Liberation of American Literature,* Waldo Frank's *Dawn in Russia,* Joseph Freeman's *The Soviet Worker,* and G. D. H. Cole's *A Guide Through World Chaos.* But perhaps the most widely-read and persuasive of these manuals was Stuart Chase's *A New Deal,* of which one reviewer declared, "Ten years ago it would have landed author and publisher in jail." [5] Chase summarized the main arguments in this volume in a series in the *New Republic* earlier in the summer of 1932 under the title, "A New Deal for America." Declared Chase: [6]

Both the implications of the current depression and the historical position of the United States today, in respect to her slowing populating curve and the passing of the frontier, call for a drastic change in our economic system . . . Of one thing . . . I think we can be sure. Whatever the change, it is going in the direction of more collectivism, more social control of economic activity, more government "interference," less freedom for private business. . . . There is no other way to go. We cannot stand still; the deflation will not permit it. We cannot go back to the nineteenth century; the engineers have dynamited the bridges. . . . To the left, three main routes branch. One of them we shall travel, but I do not know which.

Chase's "routes" were "the wild and stormy road of violent revolution," Communism; "the stern, steelwalled road of a commercial dictatorship, with political democracy swept down a gulley and constitutional guarantees rolled flat," his own definition of Fascism (there were several others in liberal circles); while the third, which he expressed preference for, was "the road of change within the broad outlines of the law and of the American tradition, with many a zooming curve, but safely banked." Chase belonged to a small number of critics who interpreted Fascism as a form of leftism, in defiance of the Red-oriented majority, whose own definition eventually was to gain dominance. Chase conceded the Communists considered Fascism "the widest of wheels to the right," but insisted that the "acid test" of the matter was the factor of collectivism; "in real fascism, Mussolini is the State: private business must bow to his decree. He has demolished the doctrines of free competition almost as completely as has Stalin." A little further on he changed his definition of Fascism:

. . . a powerful group of businessmen and bankers supersede the government—their corporation attorneys doubtless arranging a legal-sounding charter, create new, gigantic monopolies and attack the problem of distribution primarily with the purpose of furnishing sufficient customers for the products of mass production.

This system, Chase concluded, was "detestable," and the Communists were eminently sound in fighting the coming of such a "dictatorship." But in his chiding of the Soviet protagonists, Chase indicated his own degree of liberal know-nothingism toward the realities of the Russian situation. He stated flatly that the Red experiment in Russia was a success, and admitted his sympathy with the "direct and single minded attack" which it represented; "I believe it to have been necessary and inevitable in Russia. It may some day be inevitable in this country."

There is probably no more concise statement of the predicament facing the depression liberals than this one by Stuart Chase. In summary it included most of the elements of the problem: the conclusion that some form of collectivism was inevitable; the expressed hope that the form likely to emerge in America would be in harmony with non-violent liberal socialist hopes, desires and theories; yet the powerful attraction toward the Communists, while still insisting on physical separation on the action level.

The statements and positions of other prominent liberals of Chase's stature show the same indecision and mixed attitudes. The reaction to major Communist policy statements such as William Z. Foster's *Toward a Soviet America,* also published in 1932, merits attention. Arthur Warner, reviewing it in the *Nation,* of which he was one of the editors, did not even mention that Foster had made it quite plain that the Communists intended to suppress and outlaw all other political parties and interest groups upon winning out in America or any other land. George Soule, in an extended *New Republic* review,[7] expressed the liberal socialist view more sharply. The part of Foster's commentary on the American political scene which injured and repelled Soule was the violent denunciation of all varieties of non-Communist leftists and radicals, and the expressed determination to liquidate all these elements. Said Soule, "To be a capitalist is, in Communist eyes, regrettable, but beware of being a Fascist, and beware most of all of being a Social Fascist." This newly-created category, in which the Soviet enthusiasts had bundled the socialists, syndicalists, anarchists, and all manner of other independent radical and unorthodox spirits, was the one in which the liberals had been consigned, to their distress and sadness. Communists of Foster's stamp would surely have nothing to do with them; as Soule put it, "The more closely one agrees with Mr. Foster without actually being a Communist, the more bitterly he resents it."

John Dewey, reviewing Thomas Woody's *New Minds: New Men?,* still another volume seeking to interpret the Soviet, published in

1932, expressed the liberal socialist's dilemma as to Red Russia. Of Woody's book, Dewey declared,[8]

It will perhaps command the confidence of those of us who have a genuine interest in the Russian undertaking, who would like to see it succeed in its ultimate aims, but retain enough of democratic faith to be skeptical about the ruthlessness of its intellectual as well as its political measures.

Dewey recommended that those whom he described as "all our recent literary converts to Communism" study the book carefully until they had come to terms with all the implications of dictatorship. If they wanted Communism without dictatorship, Dewey admonished, "the most essential thinking" concerning the route necessary to get to that state "still remains to be done."

The heat generated by this clash was more intense than usual, exacerbated by the bickerings of an election year, and being caught in the no-man's-land between the committed Communists and Socialists was a most uncomfortable sensation to quite a few liberals. Both the *Nation* and *New Republic* sought to alleviate the pressure by editorially endorsing Norman Thomas and the Socialist ticket, despite all the unkind things their columns had carried about traditional Socialist politics. But this did not prevent an intermural argument between the *New Republic* and Heywood Broun of the *Nation*, the latter better known through his syndicated column in the Scripps-Howard newspapers. Broun, an intense Thomas partisan, irked his liberal rivals by asserting that Foster and the Communists had made great headway among them, and that their "haul" included "three *New Republic* editors of assorted sizes," one of whom they "threw back." "No *New Republic* editor is a Communist," declared this journal in an editorial denial a month before the election.[9] The angry statement went on to say:

It is this sort of thing which keeps many intelligent persons, whether in the labor movement or out of it, from wanting to affiliate themselves closely with any of the groups which pretend to working class leadership —without really having it.

What of the possibility of another political party, in which the liberals might find more congenial circumstances and presumably more chance of expressing themselves both through policy-making and action? Such yearnings were expressed by Paul Douglas, whose *The Coming of a New Party*, with a foreword by John Dewey, and published in the summer of 1932, was virtually a campaign document of an out-elite whose interest in the pending presidential election was just slightly more than lukewarm in fervor. Given an enthusiastic full-page review in the *New Republic* by Robert Morss Lovett, Douglas's book called for a planned economy under the direction of a newly-constructed party with none of the limitations of the two big parties or the two prominent unorthodox groupings. He expressed the conviction that neither of the two major parties could ever direct a planned system, and hinted dramatically that the continuation of the impasse then existing might easily lead to another American revolution.[10]

A welter of confused calls from other established and budding oracles could be heard. Marxians debated the purity of their various testaments; a bitter exchange occurred in the pages of the *New Republic* in the summer of 1932 between Sidney Hook, Robert Briffault and Ashley-Montagu, with Hook insisting that his views were "in conformity with the Marxist philosophy," but disclaiming membership in the Communist Party.[11] Hook agreed with Briffault that liberalism was "contradictory, hypocritical, antiquated and futile," but frowned on the latter's eagerness for executions; "Mr. Briffault's brand of Communism is uniquely his own." [12] Reviewing Briffault's contribution in the symposium edited by Samuel D. Schmalhausen, *Recovery Through Revolution,* Hook rejected Briffault's call for "a considerable liquidation of irrationalists" as a prelude to the coming of the social and intellectual revolution. Judged Hook, "When intellectuals go gaga they believe that all problems can be solved by the *argumentum ad baculum*—the argument from the big stick." Hook's vulnerability to this argument was revealed years later.

Reinhold Niebuhr, from the fastnesses of Union Theological Seminary, was of slightly different mind, in his *Moral Man and Immoral Society.* John Chamberlain, who reviewed it favorably early in 1933 in the *Nation,* revealed Niebuhr's thesis to be that "violence *per se*" was "not necessarily immoral," provided that it led "to a greater measure of justice in the world." Chamberlain summarized it thusly: [13]

Mr. Niebuhr comes to a final distinction: that violence is not justified in the guise of imperialist war, but may be resorted to by oppressed minorities and by the disinherited of the class struggle if peaceful suasion notoriously fails to work. It comes a little hard for Mr. Niebuhr to admit that the end sometimes justifies the means; this time for violence he leaves to the conscience and intelligence of revolutionary strategists. . . .

Niebuhr's stamp of approval upon violence provided it was made recourse to under the special conditions he mentioned did not take into account the ease by which special pleading might divert such licit violence into the channels of national wars once more, and that there is no end to carefully worded arguments suggesting the practicability of suspending ends-and-means judgments temporarily, in order to prove the value of just one tiny execution. That the liberals could not blend viewpoints such as these and the pacifism and disarmament they espoused so strongly will be demonstrated subsequently.

Among the independent and not easily classified critics to whom the pages of the liberal press were open, the figure of Lawrence Dennis stands out. Dennis, a one-time diplomat and latterly employed by New York brokerage firms, emerged as a serious student of the excesses of American financiers as early as November, 1930, when the *New Republic* ran a series of articles by him revealing the degree to which American investors had been defrauded as a result of being coaxed into buying huge quantities of dubious foreign bonds on which the issuing governments had abruptly defaulted. The liberal journals had followed this affair steadily, and Dennis' prestige increased in the field of financial writing after he appeared as a witness before a Senate Finance Committee investigation of these fraudulent bond scandals in January of 1932.[14] Dennis was featured a number of times in both the *Nation* and *New Republic* in subsequent years both as the author of articles on money and finance, and as a reviewer of books on the subject.[15] Dennis' first book, *Is Capitalism Doomed?*, published in the late spring of 1932, got extended reviews in both journals, that by Maxwell S. Stewart in the *Nation* being especially enthusiastic. George Sinclair Mitchell in the *New Republic* was more restrained.[16] Dennis' theory that the ills of capitalism were largely due to erroneous practices which might be rectified by the adoption of better procedures, even if it meant the steadily increased power of the central government, especially in the administration of banking and credit, did not arouse the liberal elements which were inclined to favor a sweeping, wholesale change in the system. Dennis did not use the Marxian terminology familiar to most liberals, even if Stewart had referred to his central thesis as a "twentieth century version of Karl Marx." But Dennis did not indulge in grandiose apocalyptic condemnation nor recommend execution or any other method of disposing of a select group of personal demons. His favorable references toward the desirability of substituting "some form of state capitalism" for the existing one was a message which eventually brought him into sharp conflict with the Communists, partially brought on by Communist resentment at the implication that the Soviet Union was one form of state capitalism in action. By the spring of 1934 the Communists considered him a sufficiently formidable enough antagonist to bill him as the "Leader of Fascism in America" in a debate with Clarence A. Hathaway, then editor of the *Daily Worker*.[17] It probably was disconcerting to some liberal circles to learn that they had been promoting the ideas of such a presumably ideological opponent, but the level of confusion being what it was, there was room for generous margins of error. Furthermore, when it came to the definition of Fascism and who the Fascists were, the liberals worked an area where most of the definitions were supplied by the Communists. The subject matter apparently had numerous vague lacunae, however, judging from the varying dicta advanced as criteria for concluding that Fascism was present.

THE COMMUNISTS AND LIBERALS SEEK A DEFINITION OF FASCISM

No word appeared in the liberal press during the early depression years more frequently than "fascist" or "fascism." The entrenchment of the German, Italian and Japanese totalitarianisms subsequently immensely stimulated their vogue, until by the end of the decade these words no longer denoted anything specific; they had been reduced to verbal reflexes. Defining Fascism became virtually a major indoor and outdoor sport, with many folk trying their hand at divining its central meaning and basic structure and dynamism. But in the liberal press the pro-Soviet contingent supplied by far the major proportion of the answers.

It is of some significance that the editors of the *New Republic* did not assign the Dugdale abridged translation of Adolf Hitler's *Mein Kampf* to a liberal for review, but to John Strachey, the British aristocrat Marxist whose commitment to the Soviet Union was rather more than nominal. Similarly, the *Nation* assigned Strachey to review Fausto Pitigliano's *The Italian Corporative State,* one of the most exhaustive and persuasive English language studies seeking to explain Mussolini's Italy in a favorable context. Strachey's attack on this book was one of the longest and most bitter to be seen in the liberal press in that time.[18] Another widely self-advertised Marxian disciple, George F. Novack, similarly demolished Pitigliano for the *New Republic.* Other books such as Lothrop Stoddard's *Clashing Tides of Color* became the back-drop for veritable Communist versus Fascist morality plays, as in the case of the Marxian sociologist Bernhard J. Stern's review in the *New Republic.*[19]

Italian Fascism was interpreted variously; it was a "dictatorship," and Novack defined this as "the political form of the rule of monopoly capital." Such a dictatorship existed as a result of crushing the class-conscious proletarians and persevered by "maintaining its power over the working class by force and terror." Another popular gambit was the assumption that fascism consisted simply of the capture of the machinery of the State by the "upper class." Who had controlled it before that was not considered worthy of mention. The most obvious defect in these definitions was the discrepancy between the theory of the capture of the State by the single *condottiere*-adventurer and his conduct of public affairs in the intensely personal manner of the well-known Latin American *caudillo,* the impression one would gather from Chase at one stage, and the alternative interpretation of fascism as a system resulting from the capture of the State by a grim, hard-eyed financial-commercial-industrial combine, running public affairs and the economy for their own benefit and keeping a heavy hand upon the national scene in order to stifle any revolt in its cradle.

Still another interpretation of Fascism gained credence, one which obtained wide broadcast by some Socialists. Instead of the bleak vision of a dictature by Big Business, here was conjured up a spectacle of a ruined, poverty-ridden and desperately angry middle class, victims of the World War and the subsequent dislocations of the following decade. A totalitarian order dominated by this group, with a vague program made up of a hash of populism, nationalism, hostility to unionized labor and other elements not too clearly discerned, resembled a sort of retaliatory *lumpen-bourgeoisie* mishandling public affairs more than a powerful plutocratic clique interested in extending and crystallizing their power. Eventually, both these were blended and day-to-day action explained by appealing to one or the other of these interpretations, whichever one happened to be the most plausible on the occasion at hand.

One of the critical issues involved hinged on the definition of a dictatorship. Communist and near-Communist attackers of Fascism started from the unmentioned and presumably taken-for-granted assumption that Russia did not come under this category. There was never the slightest breath from Communists disparaging Fascism that terrorism and rigid policing were social realities observable in the workings of the Soviet. Fascism was subjected to vast abuse for its suppression of opposition political parties, yet the similarity of Communist practice was not a subject for comment to present before the passive liberal audience accepting Communist opinion on the nature of Fascism. It made it easy to conclude that the rival totalitarianisms were vastly different, that the only threat to liberal democracy was the Fascist variety, and that there could be security in their desire to believe that Communism was a branch of humanitarianism in politics.

An earlier Communist definition of Fascism as a particularly degenerate form of capitalism, inevitably doomed to imminent collapse because of the crushing inner contradictions it harbored, appealed to liberals immensely. It implied that watchful waiting was about all that would be necessary as an attitude prior to the coming of the day when the order of things might be fashioned more after the convictions of its enemies. That the resources of four fifths of the planet eventually had to be mobilized to bring Fascism down to defeat from the outside is a measure of the faulty prediction powers of the Communists and the Socialist liberals.

In all the Communist denunciations of Fascism, a number of which were specifically fabricated for liberal consumption, the fact that these regimes were vigorously anti-Communist received widely-varied treatment. On one occasion it might not even be mentioned, on another it might obtain great stress. There can be little doubt that Soviet well-wishers were gravely repelled by this factor. It may also partially explain Communist impatience and distaste for the wide assortment of folk representing dissatisfied and rebellious sentiments and views but still unable to see the Communist path as the solution to the "social problem." Non-Communist programs were all *potential* Fascist programs. Hence the "Social Fascist" label and the bitter doctrinal disputes. Yet, for all the unhappiness created in liberal ranks by this Communist insistence on unconditional yielding to Communist direction in thought as well as action, there was a general acceptance of the definition of Fascism by way of the Communist press and spokesmen. The Communists were the clear winners on this sector of the ideological front. The liberal, parliamentary democratic, socialistically-inclined centers eventually joined hands with the Communists to destroy Fascism, a factor of serious import in attempting to understand the American liberal world view. A rash of re-affirmations of the established Communist definition of Fascism appeared in print in the first two years of Hitler's regime in Germany, accepted at face value by the liberal editors, and usually assigned to known fellow-travellers for review, as in the case of the British Communist R. Palme Dutt's *Fascism and the Social Revolution,* which Norbert Guterman described without reservation in the *New Republic* of January 16, 1935, as a completely faithful picture of Fascist theory.[20] A more detailed examination will be in order when Russo-German affairs come under analysis.

There can be little doubt that all the dictatorial developments in Europe and Asia represented a marked movement away from liberal ways. An occasional voice in the liberal press noted this with some degree of impartiality, and yearned to have some explanation of these phenomena which rose above the partisan groove. Such a commentary was that of Henry G. Alsberg, reviewing H. Hessell Tiltman's *Terror in Europe* in the *New Republic* in the summer of 1932. Tiltman's cursory and popular survey of all the dictatorships then in business in Europe prompted Alsberg to declare, "The period for the muckraking of dictatorships is over. Today we should like to be told how the drift away from democratic institutions hap-

Photo by George Cserna

JOHN DOS PASSOS

NORMAN ANGELL

Photo by Wide World

EDMUND WILSON

Photo by Lotte Meitner-Graf, London

MICHAEL STRAIGHT

LOUIS M. HACKER

Photo by Chas. Hammer, Jr.

GRANVILLE HICKS

Photo by Edwin Coradi

PETER F. DRUCKER

Photo by Dan Weiner

LEWIS GANNETT

Photo by George Cserna

HAMILTON BASSO

PETER VIERECK

EDUARD C. LINDEMAN

Photo by Brown Bros.

NATHANIEL PEFFER

pened, and why, and by what means the dictatorships came into power. We should like to know what deeper popular currents, if any, encouraged the new drift away from liberalism." Alsberg insisted that all the dictatorships, Russia included, demonstrated marked similarities, and that the time had come for a "political philosopher" "to classify these universal phenomena of tyranny and deduce some general principles for them." "We have wasted enough moral indignation upon dictatorship," Alsberg insisted; "The time has come for a little scientific investigation." [21]

The liberal press as an organ devoted to impartial and substantial critiques of all dictatorships might have provided a service to the nation and the world of inestimable value. But Alsberg's desires were not to be realized. A group was already firmly entrenched in the liberal papers which refused to even mention the word "dictatorship" in the same breath with the Soviet Union. From this camp the moderates took their cue. On the home scene this lopsided preoccupation developed into a virtual neurosis. Like guinea hens panicked by the shadow of a piece of newspaper blowing across the farmyard they reacted vociferously to any domestic situation which even faintly seemed to possess the characteristics of Fascism as outlined in some variety of Communist rhetoric.

One need only examine the skirmish in the *New Republic* in the fall of 1932 stirred up by the professed Socialist Nathaniel Weyl and the amorphous "Khaki Shirts," whose spokesmen, one of whom was Gardner Jackson, denied vehemently Weyl's charge that they represented a group of adventurers preparing to pull a Fascist coup.[22] In December, 1933, with the Hitler regime in full control in Germany, came one of the first comprehensive examinations of American Fascist organizations (by Harold Loeb and Selden Rodman) from the leftist point of view published by a liberal organ, and it ended with the conclusion that a Fascist takeover was just around the corner; "The development of a powerful radical movement is probably the only thing that can save this country from eventually going the way of Western Europe." [23] What might prevent the nation from going the way of Eastern Europe was not prescribed.

The more astute of the liberals who had not capitulated to the Communists but who on occasion pirouetted about the Soviet ideal were far more sophisticated than this. Stuart Chase ranked high here. He ignored the camp which trembled before the antics of spectacular cults of multi-hued shirt-wearers, and strove to explain the nature of the American business community, its probable strategy and tactics, and his reasons for believing it eminently unsuitable to set up a system in which the economic outlines of Fascism might be discerned. In the second of his series of articles in the summer of 1932 titled "A New Deal for America," [24] Chase deprecated the Communist view of a native Fascist regime conducting "an economy of scarcity with gouging land-owners, robber-barons and bloated misers all complete." This was a fantastic caricature of the likely American "black dictatorship," said Chase. The engineers and mass production techniques had destroyed all possibility of such a nightmare world here. What was more likely was a Big Business junta composed of "the more dynamic of our bankers, industrialists and merchants," putting into shape a form of collectivism which would find all economic enterprises shaped into a "series of gigantic trusts," with full control of money and production, and faced primarily with the chore of remodeling the "processes of distribution." Given these circumstances, it was a physical impossibility to set up a social system based on meager incomes and pinched material existence. The technical system was poised to drown the land in goods, and it was the problem of these managers to find a way to circulate these goods so that a tolerable degree of social order might result. Reasoned Chase:

The junta will be greedy as any medieval baron, but reasonable prosperity for the masses furnishes more scope for private wealth and conspicuous consumption than all the methods of gouging practiced for ten thousand years. The principle is simple. You can get more money from a man who has money than from one who has not. . . . The black battalions, if they desire big money, must in their peculiar way solve the problem of distribution, balance mass production against mass consumption, keep the profits small per unit, which means huge profits on ten million units, flowing steadily into their great monopolies and combines.

America's likely Fascist "black battalion," said Chase, wanted to escape the business cycle as much as anyone else, radicals or unemployed; "there is no money to be made out of a jobless man; indeed, the reverse: he has to be provided with a flophouse and soup." To do these things "they must control the currency, new investment, wage rates, speculation. The farther they went along these lines the more they would approach to a functional economy." And "the final objective," Chase advanced, "would be a subservient, inarticulate but reasonably prosperous mass of consumers and workers, catering to a small group of Olympian spenders." Sales resistance would have to be broken down systematically; the schools could be used for the large scale "education of consumers." "We would be deluged with stuff," Chase concluded; "We should be as regimented and standardized as so many slot machines; our books, our art, our recreation would be fed to us on the slot-machine formula."

As to the possibilities of such a system becoming established, Chase felt there was little chance. He based his approach on the conclusion that there was no "class solidarity" nor "sense of state" among the men most likely to bring this about. America had not developed a "class capable of exercising dictatorial powers"; the feudal ancestors had been such a group, but here in America, "the pioneer outlook and the devil-take-the-hindmost habits of a commercial civilization had killed the traditions of the man on horseback." The collisions of interest among the financial, industrial and commercial forces would prevent any such order from becoming entrenched. "The whole class is riven with internal dissensions," Chase explained; "Who is to compose these differences?" He could see no one with the requisite qualifications. The Communists might suggest that the "master owning class" was capable, but Chase questioned the whole theory; "I simply ask whether it has unity and the traditions of organized political power." The owners were not prepared or trained for this exigency; "Caesars need a broader education."

Chase wound up his comprehensive examination of the problem by hazarding what might eventuate in the light of American conditions:

The most we can expect on this road is a temporary compromise dictatorship forced by the present crisis, in which certain bankers and businessmen combine with government officials and a labor leader or two, to set up a steering committee whose watchword will be normalcy at the earliest possible moment—normalcy and disbandment as sudden as that of 1919, when the dollar-a-year men from the Council of National Defense packed their bags.

Throughout this entire dissertation, probably the most comprehensive liberal speculation on the likelihood of a native Fascism up to that time, Chase never once mentioned America's relation to the rest of the world or recourse to war as a source of dynamism for stirring the wheels of the economic system into a healthy whir again.

Numerous other figures in high circles in liberal journalism essayed definitions of Fascism for the enlightenment, and often confusion, of the readers. Louis Fischer, in his remarkable defense of the Soviet Union in the *Nation* of April 4, 1934, titled "Fascism and Bolshevism," insisted that "The first law of Fascist regimes is class collaboration," and that "the Fascists' chief weapon of offense is the stifling of the class war and the spreading of nationalist in place of class doctrine." [25] Raymond Gram Swing, an editor of the *Nation* in these times, provided a most succinct definition, in a form reminiscent of government handbooks for the busy in his widely-sold book *Forerunners of American Fascism*, [26] "A reorganization of society to maintain an unequal distribution of economic power by undemocratic means." This definition fitted in well with the current liberal credo that it was not evil if an unequal distribution of economic power were brought about by the "democratic" means of the "working class majority," since critical intelligence and other lofty qualities were considered to be the prerogative of factory workers and small dirt farmers, and only occasionally found among the "middle classes," the repository of "Fascist" impulses. This was the obvious intent in the reasoning of a *New Republic* editorial on a radio address by General Hugh S. Johnson in 1933 to the American Federation of Labor, in which he outlined the Administration's labor policy under the National Recovery Administration. The editors then suggested that this policy threatened "a rapid drift toward the worst feature of Fascism," which they defined as "a labor movement fettered by the state, forbidden to strike, and subjected, on the plea that the 'public' interest is dominant, to profit-making employers."

But the definition of Fascism continued to evolve in the subsequent years, with the liberal economic analyst Eliot Janeway producing one of the more alarming outlines early in 1939. "The economic institutions of Fascism may be briefly summarized," Janeway declared; [27]

First, the Government becomes the chief customer of industry. Second, because the orders it places are for specialized and ever more efficient equipment and materials, they soon outrun industry's capacity. The Government becomes the financier for this expansion. Then, as in the way of most financiers, it begins to share control and actual ownership of industry with the industrialists.

The main message of this report seemed to be, however, that rather than deviating, the economies of the capitalist, Communist and Fascist states all appeared to be moving in the same direction in varying degrees, and that the Communists had already achieved the ultimate in "Fascist" economic organization, by Janeway's definition. And he had partially achieved what Chase had not considered, namely, an examination of the relation of government policy to the economy which in itself made irrelevant a vast part of all the pro-Russian-Marxist theorizing about Fascism in the previous decade.

Liberal commitments to World War One disillusionment and revision, disarmament and pacifism precluded any sustained intellectual effort in which war figured to any degree of prominence, at this time. If discussed at all, it was in the Marxian context of "imperialist war," an incantation of invidiousness of such breadth as to take the subject into the realm of the emotions completely and inhibit examination on a comprehensive level. Some Marxian-flavored liberal thinking on war was in transition, and was about to discover the munitions-maker as a substitute for the diplomat as the primary agent responsible for opening the sluice gates of war. A separate treatment is in order for this phase of liberal thought and

introspection. But a case study can be made of the result of the inter-
twinings of liberal thinking on Fascism and war, considered in relation to the catalytic function performed by the Communists.

L'AFFAIRE MACLEISH: A CASE STUDY

Early in 1932 the poet-intellectual Archibald MacLeish published a
long poem titled *Conquistador,* largely based on Spanish experiences
in the Western Hemisphere in the sixteenth century, a comfortably-
remote day from the anxious times then perturbing the nation and
the world. In his long review of this work, Allen Tate commented
upon how much the author seemed indebted to Ezra Pound. Tate
was just one of a number of other liberal critics who were impressed
by MacLeish's averred stylistic dependence upon Pound. Eda Lou
Walton repeated it in the *Nation* in January, 1934 when reviewing
his *Poems, 1924–1933,* while in April, 1936 in the same publication
Philip Blair Rice, reviewing MacLeish's *Public Speech,* was impelled
to note of the work that "the falling rhythms which MacLeish took
over from Pound's *Cantos* still predominate." [28]

A number of additional restrained comments came from various
quarters, and there followed a new chapter in the long controversy
already underway in the liberal journals as to the nature and interre-
lation of the arts, poetry and social action and political participation
in the current scene. MacLeish's position in this battle of words was
one of standing fast by his contention that the poet was under no
obligation to take part in politics, or social criticism; his ideal was an
aloof location where the poet might be respected as a "literary mas-
ter-worker," and not required to pay homage to any camp in the
social struggle. At a time when a concerted effort was being made to
mobilize all those who had anything to do with the written or spoken
word and to array them somewhere on the politico-social front line,
MacLeish's sharp cry on behalf of the validity of signing a separate
peace drew loud and angry responses in the superconscious liberal
ranks.

In the issue for October 26, 1932 the *New Republic* precipitated
the quarrel by publishing MacLeish's poem "Invocation to the Social
Muse," an urgent message on behalf of his stand in versified form.
The fourth stanza spoke as follows: "poets Fraulein are persons of
known vocation following troops; they must sleep with stragglers
from either prince and of both views: the rules permit them to further the business of neither." The concluding line asked querulously,
"Is it just to demand of us also to bear arms?" [29]

For the next four months brickbats continued to fall upon the author in the letters to the editor department. One reader dismissed it as "double talk"; a particularly distracted correspondent lashed at it as "sickly, sentimental, self-pitying, self-dramatizing nonsense." [30] The Communistically-inclined were especially outraged by it, and the ensuing result was a heated debate between MacLeish and the Marxians of all hues. To keep the situation ablaze the *New Republic* late in December published MacLeish's article "The Social Cant," a massive attack on Marxism and all its fundamental assumptions. Again MacLeish entered his assertion on behalf of the unattached poet living apart from the controversies of his own day. The Communists were wrong, said the poet-under-fire, in insisting that all poetry be entered in the lists on behalf of the Revolution: [31]

So long as the critics write and read and think in the vocabulary of Marxian dialectic they will fumble the meaning of poetry written in the vocabulary of poetry. And the fact that a poem purports to deal with the events of another century will be to them convincing proof that it has nothing to say to the events of this. The only point worth making in that connection is that contemporary poets have for the most part honorably continued to write poetry and refused to be herded with the sheep.

From this point on, and into the next two years, MacLeish had antagonists to spare. The Communists hammered him constantly with the accusation of favoritism toward Fascist sentiments, a charge ultimately taken up by liberals and the liberal press. Two acrimonious exchanges in particular are worth documenting. The first occurred in the summer of 1933, after John Day had published MacLeish's verses titled *Frescoes for Mr. Rockefeller's City*. The *New Republic* stirred up a storm by engaging the Communist literary beacon light Michael Gold to review it, preceding Gold's review with a brief statement to the effect that Gold was a Communist and "convinced of the political significance of poetry and of the arts in general," while MacLeish was known "as a holder of diametrically opposed views." Neither of the men needed introduction to habitual readers of the journal, but it provided Gold with a fine platform from which to launch a blistering attack on MacLeish, titled "Out of the Fascist Unconscious." [32] His opening salvo had the finesse of a flame thrower:

It has been piously said, there can be no fascism in America. But signs appear in the political sky, and Hitler's program, somewhat veiled in caulks and mysteries of the poetic womb, may also be discerned in these latest verses of Archibald MacLeish.

"Mystic nationalism," charged Gold, was "the first stage of the true fascist mind," and *Frescoes* contained it in abundance. In America, with its numerous racial groups, the substitute for race as a rallying point was nationalistic geography, which Gold maintained MacLeish exploited to the full. Still another indication of the poet's "fascist mission" was his "contempt for Marxists, Jews and those disturbed intellectuals who recently have taken the road to the political left."

One need not be confused by MacLeish's ferocious attack on America's legendary financiers; it was a typical Fascist response, "the revolt of the lower middle class, a cruel and futile rage of little traders who have been wiped out." Remarked Gold, "He hates the Harrimans, Vanderbilts and Morgans who 'screwed America gaunt and scrawny with their seven year panics,' but no more than Hitler attacked finance in Germany. The role he wished them to play was that of heroes, like the pioneers and founding fathers, and found nothing but disappointment in their conduct thus far." MacLeish might only be an "unconscious fascist," Gold observed, "but it is curious that he has lyricized the major attitudes of German and Italian fascists." Especially distasteful was his handling of labor, again typically Fascist: loud praise of work and workers in what they had contributed toward building the nation, but hostility toward those who had become "class-conscious."

The conclusion of Gold's assault reached an impressive level of scorn:

The device of contrasting images is much favored by Mr. MacLeish. This technique in poetry was originated by Ezra Pound; T. S. Eliot made it popular; now it is the property of every college literary snobling. It is also the favorite device of political reactionaries.

The *Nation*'s reviewer of *Frescoes*, who took it up two weeks after Gold had conducted his aggravated assault on it, struggled not to call MacLeish a Fascist, and ended up by labeling him a "traditionalist" and a "patrician," while professing great shock at his "violent contempt for Communism." [33]

Carl Sandburg felt so outraged by Gold's imputation of an anti-Jewish bias to MacLeish that he wrote a sharp letter in rejoinder which the *New Republic* printed late in August. After defending the *Frescoes* as "great poetry," he cited Jewish friends who had read the work with pleasure and without offense, terminating his tribute to the author by imputing paranoid tendencies to the critic.[34]

Gold had the apparent last word with a letter in self-defense early in January of 1934, repeating his charge that "Archibald MacLeish in his political pamphlet-poem displayed all the stigmata of one who was blindly drifting toward fascism," and insisted that no one had bothered to meet that challenge. In response to MacLeish's reaction after the review that Gold was "badly frightened," the latter replied now, "Yes, I am, but not for the reasons he enumerates. I, like many others, fear the specter of American fascism. We see it looming in the persons of NIRA, and in the minds of groping intellectuals like Mr. MacLeish." In challenging MacLeish to respond once more to this original assertion, Gold demanded MacLeish state his position.[35]

The *New Republic* was not through with it at this point. John Strachey renewed Gold's charge that *Frescoes* contained "strong traces of the fascist unconscious" in his book *Literature and Dialectical Materialism*,[36] and Cowley, reviewing it in January, 1935, emphatically supported this view with the observation that Strachey "proved it beyond a doubt." Philip Blair Rice, in the *Nation* in the same month, in a long article discussing what was going on in poetical circles "since our poets began their rather vertiginous scramble down from the ivory tower into the depths of the mine pit," a gratuitous reference to the proletarian fad then gaining favor among former withdrawn academics, was not so harsh. He absolved MacLeish of the Marxian charge that *Frescoes* was "an American version of the hymn to Horst Wessel," the hero of National Socialist Germany; "it is no more fascist than a Fourth of July oration by an Iowa Congressman with a slight leaning toward the Ku Klux Klan." However, Rice was not particularly impressed by MacLeish in his work on contemporary themes; "When he approaches his own time he becomes abusive and incoherent." [37] But Rice had no inkling as to what was to come in the next six years, the extended Marxian courtship of 1935–1938, and the alarmed season as intellectual mobilizer of war attitudes in 1939–1941.

In reality, MacLeish was already abandoning his indifference to the politics of his day, regardless of his expressed choice for that attitude. Months before the famous *Frescoes* trial-by-battle, he had published in the *New Republic* a major unfavorable criticism of technocracy,[38] and in the issue of September 20, 1933, while the furor caused by the clash with Gold was still simmering, came into a head-on collision with one of the most active of the same journal's editors, Malcolm Cowley. The issue here was still another poem by MacLeish, "Lines for an Interment," and his critical review of Lawrence Stallings' *The First World War,* which stung Cowley into an immediate response, and a heated exchange followed two weeks later.

Cowley was more concerned with MacLeish's attitude toward the World War as expressed in his review of the Stallings book than he was over the well-worn controversies, where he tended to sympathize with MacLeish's viewpoint. But on the matter of the War, there was a wide gap. MacLeish insisted that it was a distortion of the truth for Stallings to omit any attention to the dead of the war except to include pictures of their corpses. In this way the book became a more powerful piece of propaganda against war, but the failure to present the dead in terms of what they thought at the time they were fighting MacLeish thought was "morally dangerous." Involved here was the widespread conviction among the largest part of both liberals and non-liberals alike that the first World War was an almost total failure insofar as the achievement of the goals for which it was professedly fought. MacLeish sought at this juncture to deal with the matter subjectively, and confine such judgments to the case of each of the individual dead. Cowley, at the time the review was published, had added a comment of his own upbraiding MacLeish for seeing anything good coming out of the struggle, and remarking at one point, with respect to the slain, "They died bravely, they died in vain." In a second round on the subject, MacLeish once more reverted to the original contention, chiding Cowley for his harsh criticism: [39]

Obviously you and I, alive in the year 1933 and looking back—obviously we can say in your fine phrase: "they died bravely, they died in vain." Every economic consideration proves they died in vain. But what, I demand of you as poet, not as editor, what *is* vanity in death? . . . Is it perhaps conceivable that the measure of vanity in a man's death is to be found not afterwards in a history which to him has no existence, but presently in the circumstances in which his death is met? Is it perhaps conceivable that to die generously and in loyalty to a believed-in cause is not, regardless of the success of that cause, regardless even of its validity, to die in vain?

Cowley was unimpressed with this evaluation and although insisting that their mutual differences were largely a matter of emphasis, he implied that MacLeish was not interested in really examining what the fighting men had actually thought while under combat conditions. Cowley maintained that the "believed-in cause" was largely a state of mind induced by heavy doses of propaganda before even leaving the country for the battle zones, and that it was mainly the officer strata that felt that way, the element he and MacLeish were actually acquainted with, he reminded the latter: [40]

Our friends (in the officers' training camps) soon became patriots; they believed in four minute speeches; they marched to the front convinced they were fighting for Democracy, that they were risking death to remove the menace of the German Beast, to protect their own land from the rape of the invader. You and I know they felt pretty good about it.

That Cowley had nothing but contempt for this now was impossible to conceal; the capitalizations alone expressed his ironic attitude to the sloganeering of the war days. But he lost no time reviewing for MacLeish's benefit the fact that the dead in battle were principally common soldiers, most of whom served long enough to "lose whatever exhilaration they may have felt in the beginning," and the residue in most of the cases was "a dead nausea and the hope that it would be soon over," and they would be able to get home at worst only partially mutilated. He called to mind the mutinies, and described his own experiences with a battalion of French Chasseurs that had done exactly that, only to have their leaders shot and themselves driven back to the front, where, Cowley said, they fought "with the spirit of steers driven into the abattoir." Regardless of their individual attitudes, they and the others were killed; "Patriotism, love of danger, fear, boredom, disgust—all the things that went on in their heads didn't matter. . . . presently they became the things Stallings shows in his photographs."

So, Cowley went on, "We can say that they died generously and in loyalty to a believed-in cause . . . or we can say, measuring their aspirations against the world which their efforts helped to produce, that they died for an illusion, died in vain." The former observation might be "true," but the latter was "terribly true."

Cowley concluded his dissection of MacLeish's argument by asking him what he was doing to help prevent the coming of another war; "The real issue between us is, how shall we regard the dead of the next war?" If phrased that way, there was a "gulf of opposed meanings" involved in their respective cases: [41]

For, if we emphasize the useless deaths of the last war, we can be certain of our attitude toward the next. But if, on the other hand, we emphasize the happy illusions of these men who died defending their country—from whom?—and saving democracy—from what?—then we can look forward more or less calmly to the battles in which other generous and loyal men . . . will die in the same courageous fashion. We may even come to share the illusions of the dead, and we shall in any case defend the system which makes the next war as inevitable as tomorrow.

MacLeish did not respond to Cowley's call, but in March of 1934, when the magazine *Fortune* published its sensational article on the armament makers and argued so vigorously between the lines for peace, the *New Republic* opined that in view of the fact that Mac-Leish was an editor of this publication, "Arms and the Men" represented the first dividend resulting from Cowley's sobering proposition of five months earlier.[42]

The *Nation* assumed he had written it, and included him on their "Honor Roll for 1934" as its author, but in a letter to the editors published in January, 1935 he absolved himself from responsibility, while admitting that he "should very much like to claim the credit which the newspapers have given me." MacLeish credited associate editor Eric Hodgkins with being responsible for organizing the work, adding, "That the publication of the article had my fullest and most enthusiastic approval goes, I hope, without saying." He was especially pleased that the *Nation* thought so highly of this attack on the munitions business; "We are proud indeed to have your approval so publicly expressed." [43]

The personal answer to Cowley was begun two months later, with the benefit performance of MacLeish's play *Panic* before an audience consisting mainly of the supporters and readers of the Marxian New Theatre and *New Masses.* Cowley in review expressed the satisfaction that the much-attacked poet "is coming down from his tower," and lauded the leap to the proletarian theme.[44] V. J. Jerome in the *New Masses* in April went far beyond this modest praise, hailed MacLeish as "America's most splendid singer" who clearly saw "the decline of capitalism and its inevitable fall." Jerome's ecstatic review predicted, "I think the play we have seen this evening justifies us in expecting to see him advance from his present point of transition. . . . to sing the epic of the proletariat advancing through day-to-day struggle to power," [45] and MacLeish's frequent articles in *New Masses* the next two years were evidence that he had joined the Marxist literary picket line.[46]

The full seal of Communist approval came in March, 1936 when Isador Schneider, a *New Masses* editor, reviewed *Public Speech.* MacLeish had now performed a full turn in the estimate of Marxist America since the hostile abuse by Gold in 1932.[47] Cowley noted with high approval MacLeish's politicalization in his review of *Public Speech* in the *New Republic* for April 1, 1936. "Everywhere the poet suggests his hatred of Fascism," Cowley reported with satisfaction. Of course, MacLeish's enlistment in the class war did not answer Cowley's question as to where he stood in the matter of the "next" war, and Cowley was hardly interested during the Popular Front era. This did not come until 1940, by which time MacLeish's flirtation with the Communists had cooled, and his enrollment in the opinion-making brigades of the war-bound New Deal had ensued. His *The Irresponsibles,* chiding a new generation for its lack of enthusiasm for another great global fray, once more brought to mind the mental state he reflected in 1932.

The opinions, views and beliefs of Archibald MacLeish will be followed further, as he represents one of the most important examples of the transformation which turned liberalism inside out on the subject of war and peace in America. His is one of the most striking case studies of a quondam critic emerging in less than ten years as one of the most vociferous advocates of participation in war once more.

The private struggle of Archibald MacLeish with the liberal press and its varied ideological figures is one facet of the flavor of the times. As a separate capsule it involves virtually all the contentious and controversial matters perturbing the liberal intellectual scene, as the jerry-built world of Versailles was beginning to totter and as the world and national catastrophes exerted their respective influences to gain the upper position in the consideration of the liberal intellectuals. A closer look at the domestic political scene is in order, as an additional signpost leading to an understanding of the liberal world view.

NOTES

1 *Journal of the History of Ideas,* Vol. 2, No. 4, p. 507.
2 Joseph S. Clark, Jr., "Can The Liberals Rally?," *Atlantic Monthly,* July, 1953, pp. 27–31 (p. 27).
3 See the review of this book in *New Republic,* August 3, 1932, pp. 321–322, by the future *New Masses* literary editor Isador Schneider, and Nomad's reply in *New Republic,* September 7, 1932, p. 103.
4 Editorial "Leftbound Local," *New Republic,* August 17, 1932, pp. 6–7.
5 Quoted by the publisher (Macmillan) in promotional material from Richmond (Va.) *News-Leader; New Republic,* October 26, 1932. In this book Chase predicted the country would reach a permanent population plateau in 1960.
6 *New Republic,* July 6, 1932, pp. 199–201, for this and succeeding quotations. See also Chase's "The Road of the Fascists," *New Republic,* July 13, 1932, pp. 225–226, for his observations on the approaching managerialism as the form of American Fascism.
7 *New Republic,* September 28, 1932, p. 186. Warner's review was published in *Nation,* July 6, 1932, p. 17.
8 *New Republic,* June 8, 1932, p. 104.
9 "Potting and Kettling," *New Republic,* October 5, 1932, p. 194.
10 Lovett's review appeared in the issue for August 31, 1932.
11 *New Republic,* August 24, 1932, p. 171. Hook declared, "None the less, I believe my views to be in conformity with the Marxist philosophy. What is more important, I believe them to be true."
12 *Nation,* June 28, 1933, p. 733, for this and subsequent citation.
13 *Nation,* February 15, 1933, pp. 185–186.
14 The *New Republic* felt its faith in Dennis corroborated when he was called as witness before this committee in its issue of January 20. See also *Nation,* March 15, 1933, p. 274, for further commendation of Dennis as an advisor on Latin American bonds.
15 Dennis, "Can The Banks Be Made Safe?," *Nation,* March 15, 1933, pp. 280–282; "Money: Master or Means?," *Nation,* March 22, 1933, pp. 310–313. See also his long reviews of Henry Pratt Fairchild, *Profits or Prosperity* (Harper, 1932), and Max Loewenthal's *The Investor Pays,* in the *New Republic* for January 11 and June 21, 1933, respectively.
16 *Nation,* July 27, 1932, p. 89; *New Republic,* June 1, 1932, pp. 78–79.
17 This debate was advertised in the *New Masses* in full page form on February 20 and 27, March 6 and 13, 1934; in the *Nation,* February 28; and *New Republic,* March 7. Strangely enough, Hathaway in his article "A Fascist on Parade," *New Masses,* March 13, 1934, pp. 9–10, declared, "Between a Fascist and a Communist nothing can be settled by debate. This issue will be decided on the barricades."
18 *Nation,* October 18, 1933, pp. 448–449.
19 *New Republic,* May 29, 1935, p. 82.

20   *New Republic*, January 16, 1935, pp. 283–284. Guterman was identified as a "French citizen" and contributor to *Avant Poste,* "A French critical review."

21   *New Republic*, August 17, 1932, pp. 24–25.

22   Nathaniel Weyl, "The Khaki Shirts—American Fascists," *New Republic*, September 21, 1932, pp. 145–146. See also communications from E. F. Everett, National Treasurer of the Khaki Shirts, Jackson and Weyl in *New Republic*, October 19, 1932, p. 263.

23   Harold Loeb and Selden Rodman, "American Fascism in Embryo," *New Republic*, December 27, 1933, pp. 185–187.

24   This was the third part of this essay, subtitled "The Road of the Fascists," published in *New Republic*, July 13, 1932, pp. 225–226. All subsequent references and citations are from this article.

25   *Nation*, April 4, 1934, pp. 381–382.

26   New York: Julian Messner, 1935.

27   Eliot Janeway, "England Moves Toward Fascism," *Harper's*, January, 1939, pp. 111–125 (p. 119).

28   Tate review of MacLeish in *New Republic*, June 1, 1932, pp. 77–78. Walton and Rice in *Nation*, January 10, 1934, pp. 48–49 and April 22, 1936, p. 522.

29   *New Republic*, October 26, 1932, p. 296.

30   Comments by readers David Platt and Marie de L. Welch, *New Republic*, December 14, 1932, pp. 125–126. See also issue of February 8, 1933.

31   *New Republic*, December 21, 1932, pp. 156–158.

32   *New Republic*, July 26, 1933, pp. 295–296. Subsequent references and quotations from this article.

33   *Nation*, August 9, 1933, p. 168.

34   *New Republic*, August 23, 1933, p. 50.

35   *New Republic*, January 3, 1934, p. 228.

36   New York: Covici Friede, 1934; Cowley's review in *New Republic*, January 2, 1935, p. 224.

37   Rice, "Poets and the Wars," *Nation*, January 13, 1935, pp. 189–192.

38   MacLeish, "Machines and the Future," *Nation*, February 8, 1933, pp. 141–142. Of technocracy, MacLeish said, "Its philosophy is merely an infantile doctrine of technological determinism to take the place of the equally infantile Marxian dogma of economic determinism."

39   MacLeish to Cowley, *New Republic*, October 4, 1933, pp. 214–215.

40   Cowley to MacLeish, *New Republic*, October 4, 1933, pp. 215–216; all citations from both in these and other passages from this exchange.

41   Cowley to MacLeish, above.

42   Editorial "Hucksters of Death," *New Republic*, March 7, 1934, pp. 88–89.

43   *Nation*, January 23, 1935, p. 103.

44   *New Republic*, March 27, 1935, pp. 190–191.

45   *New Masses*, April 2, 1935, pp. 43–44.

46   Among MacLeish's contributions were the poems, "The German Girls! The German Girls!," in the *New Masses'* "Anti-Fascist Number," December 15, 1935, p. 23, and "Speech To Those Who Say Comrade," *New Masses*, February 11, 1936, p. 13. See also MacLeish, "Gorky the Artisan," *New Masses*, August 4, 1936, pp. 12–13.

47   *New Masses*, March 24, 1936, pp. 21–22.

3

THE LIBERALS WEIGH THE NATIONAL
POLITICAL SCENE, 1931–1935

THE PRE-CAMPAIGN MEASUREMENT
OF FRANKLIN D. ROOSEVELT

DESPITE the fact that this is specifically a study of American liberalism and its expressions of thought and opinion on the subject of war, peace, international politics and American foreign policy in the ten years prior to United States involvement in the Second World War, a brief examination of liberal attitudes toward the country's leaders in the context of domestic politics is exceedingly pertinent. The fact that the dominant figures in shaping domestic policy between 1933 and 1937 also directed the course of foreign policy in the same period, and increasingly concentrated on external affairs in the period after that, calls for a glance at the reputation of these men in liberal eyes at the beginning of their national leadership careers. The full turn effected by liberal opinion on the subject of war was matched, as will be seen, by a similarly impressive wheeling on the character and abilities of those who were ultimately responsible for the grand maneuver of 1939–1941. The growing impossibility of separating United States domestic and foreign policy, especially from late 1938 onward, suggests that a sharp cleavage between the two for the purpose of study and criticism will always be extremely difficult. For that reason, a look at the country's administrators, from the vantage-point of liberalism, at a time when the two phases of public policy were reasonably distinct, serves as a major aid in recognizing the remarkable shift of affection which took place when domestic and foreign affairs began to blend and fuse.

Liberal disgust with both the Republican and Democratic parties increased in volume as the stock market crash of 1929 deepened into the serious economic collapse of the next three years. Impatience and hostility were reflected constantly, as the administration of Herbert Hoover failed to respond to the emergency in the manner considered essential and effective in liberal and "democratic socialist" estimations. The liberal journals were convinced that when it came to the domestic situation, Hoover simply did not know what to do, and could not make up his mind to do anything even when in the mood to do so, in addition to making things worse by doing some of the things he did. His failure to call the Congress into a special session in the summer of 1931 was considered one of the worst presidential failures of all, since action of a special emergency sort at that time was considered by the liberal press to have been of great importance in lessening the pressure of the economic bad times

As the nation ground into the last few months of Mr. Hoover's third year, with the politicians of all hues growing more and more restive and speculations growing on the following year's nominations and presidential election, the liberal reaction to the possibility of more of Mr. Hoover grew blacker by the day. As for their conventional opposition, no profession of hope in that appeared in print, either. An editorial article in the *Nation* for December 9, 1931, titled "No Plans in the Democratic Party," [1] discussed the paralysis prevailing there, and its failure to suggest anything of superior quality to that already proposed by Republicans. Here also a comment was made about Franklin D. Roosevelt, Governor of New York, referred to already as "the leading Democratic candidate for the Presidential nomination." Not a scrap of faith in him was registered at this time. The editorial was especially irked by his evasiveness when questioned as to his positions on the issues before the country; "He refuses to say where he stands today on prohibition, on the tariff, on unemployment, on (foreign) debts and reparations." The contemporary Congress drew even less applause and approval. On the whole it was written off as a collection of ineffectuals, and as far as the future was concerned, the survey pronounced, "Today the only hope of leadership in Congress comes from a handful of Progressives." Two issues later there was a statement involving great praise for Senators La Follette, Borah, Norris, Gerald Nye and Hiram Johnson.

Later in the winter the *New Republic* landed on Roosevelt, and, incidentally, Newton D. Baker, with both feet. Baker had issued a statement to the effect that the League of Nations would not be an issue in the coming campaign. Observed the journal, "Thereupon Governor Franklin Roosevelt, presumably alarmed by the impetus thus accorded Mr. Baker's cause, has given the League an even more vigorous repudiation." As the article went on to say, the League in existence was not "the League Mr. Wilson envisioned." That one the journal asserted it would still be supporting. The one now in operation was "dominated by selfish European Powers, and America must keep clear of it." The case against Baker and Roosevelt was not entirely their "isolationism," meaning their hesitancy to enter into collective security agreements on the governmental level; these sentiments were integral parts of liberal policy thinking at this time too. It was the inconsistency of these public figures, playing both sides of the street, since they had previously been identified with exactly the opposite of the newly advanced positions; "The statements of Messrs. Roosevelt and Baker give good examples of the old trick of politicians—trying to be all things to all men, to seem isolationist to those who want isolation, and internationalist and cooperative for the other school." [2]

On February 17, 1932 the *Nation* continued the attack with an editorial condemnation of a speech Roosevelt delivered before the New York State Grange in which he deprecated the League and insisted on the necessity of collecting the war debts. "Governor Roosevelt has not the courage to stand out bravely for the internationalism he once sponsored," the editorial grieved, and added, "His attitude on the war debts is equally unrealistic." [3]

The mutual recriminations of potential Democratic candidates in early spring pre-national convention speeches provoked a major *New Republic* article in the April 27 issue. Largely devoted to an analysis of the faction of the party assumed to be behind Alfred E. Smith and his charge that Roosevelt was a demagogue, it came to another unflattering estimate of FDR. Mr. Roosevelt had spoken a few weak words on his own behalf, it was conceded, and made a few vague statements about "social-economic planning" and the need for "a more fundamental policy" than that favored by the wealthy wing of the Democrats, but the readers were warned not to expect much of anything: [4]

Mr. Roosevelt has veered in the right direction, but even if he proceeded less feebly in his words, it is improbable that as a Democratic President he could go far in his deeds. Perhaps even a greater danger to the common man would have developed if, as a result of Mr. Smith's attack, Mr. Roosevelt had been made to appear what he is not—a great and forceful champion of popular justice.

In the *Nation* of the same date appeared the eighth and last of a series of profiles of Democrat presidential hopefuls, that of Roosevelt written by the well-regarded biographer of Theodore Roosevelt, Henry F. Pringle. It was as caustic a piece of political muckraking as this magazine was to publish until its scathing pieces on Wendell Willkie in 1940, exceeded only by Hallgren's long essay, "Franklin D. Roosevelt," on June 1, which was largely devoted to demonstrating that FDR was by long standing "an imperialist and a militarist," and undependable as a potential standard-bearer in the cause liberals professed at this time. Pringle's concluding paragraph also dwelled harshly on Roosevelt's thin layer of qualifications as a likely world leader: [5]

If it is true that a new deal is needed in the world, there is small hope for better things in his [FDR's] candidacy. If it is true that foreign debts must be adjusted downward and reparations forgotten, there is nothing in Roosevelt's philosophy, as far as we know, which gives promise of a better day. He calls for palliatives in world affairs, not cures. His domestic program is hardly more stimulating.

In the same issue the *Nation*'s editors declared: "The *Nation* will support Mr. [Norman] Thomas in the coming election."

As the convention neared, Bruce Bliven vied with Villard of the *Nation* on the editorial level as to which of the two could make the most derogatory observations as to the undesirability of Roosevelt. A major editorial article by Bliven on June 1, "Franklin D. Roosevelt, The Patron of Politics," represented about the most forthright repudiation to that moment. Although Bliven excused one major liberal objection, namely, that Roosevelt was an ardent militarist and an enthusiastic promoter of Caribbean imperialism, there were sufficient blows to be delivered on other levels. Bliven could not forgive him for his tie with Tammany Hall: "If Roosevelt betrayed Tammany, Tammany would cheerfully knife him in the convention or the election. And nobody knows this better than Franklin D.; his alliance with Tammany is his gravest liability." He saved a special blast for FDR's castigation of John Haynes Holmes and Rabbi Stephen S. Wise for recommending to him a state investigation of especially offensive machine politics in New York City. This act, averred Bliven, was "a direct charge against his character." Summarizing his makeup, with especial emphasis on appearances and realities, Bliven declared:

He is a patron of politics: despite the effectiveness with which he plays the game at its realistic worst, he, like Woodrow Wilson, condescends toward the people he would help and the problems he seeks to solve. It is true, he

makes excellent speeches about "the forgotten man"; but he is no spokesman for that man by blood brotherhood; he has just read about him in
books. In this world of desperate problems crying for desperate remedies,
I question the effectiveness of the scholar-gentleman even when he means
as well as anyone can.

Bliven's concluding statement was a cruel back-hand compliment: [6]

Franklin D. Roosevelt is intelligent, personally honest, notably progressive for one of his background; and if you don't want four years of disappointment as the result of your vote, I suggest that you might well vote
for the Socialist candidate, whatever individual (named Norman Thomas)
he happens to be.

By this time, Roosevelt was under attack from several liberal-
socialist sniping posts. No later conservative derogations exceeded in
vehemence those of the *Nation* and of its editorial compatriot Heywood Broun, the latter working from the vantage-point of the
Scripps-Howard press. His column of June 29 was especially disparaging. Like Bliven, Villard had already arrayed the *Nation* behind
Thomas as well. A *Nation* editorial of June 13 looked bleakly upon
the Democratic platform, especially the foreign policy planks,[7] but the
journal and its editor-in-chief rose to remarkable heights of vituperation at the time of the convention. The lead story in its July 6 issue,
commenting on the event, could hardly have been written in stronger
terms: [8]

In the confusion that besets the Democratic convention as we go to press
one thing stands clear and unchallengeable. That is the unashamed renunciation by Franklin D. Roosevelt of his last pretension to progressiv-
ism. . . . We had hoped for something better from Franklin Roosevelt.
We had never deceived ourselves as to his weak and vacillating statesmanship, but we believed him honest and sincere. Instead he stands revealed
as ready to lend his support to any trick or device that will advance his
personal political fortune.

The convention back-stage scuffle for delegates and the state delegation horse-trading prior to Mr. Roosevelt's victory carried a high
price in terms of loss of approval and support from liberals in the
Nation camp.

Villard's post-mortem on the convention a week later was titled
"The Democratic Trough at Chicago." No adherent of Mr. Roosevelt could have found any comfort anywhere in it. Declared the
much-experienced author categorically, "Never have I seen a Presidential ticket named at a national convention with so little enthusi-

asm." The platform on which he was nominated was subjected to much more abuse. Villard maintained it represented "total detachment from the realities of life," and was particularly deficient in the area of foreign relations. He dwelt at some length on its utterly introverted substance: "Nowhere is there a single realization of the vital part Europe has played and is playing in our economic life and in producing our economic distress." He went on to note that there was not the slightest mention of what attitude was to be adopted toward the reparations and disarmament conferences at Lausanne and Geneva, and, in bitter irony, "not a word about that sacred obligation of ours to enter the League of Nations, the child of that immortal Democratic President, the last Democratic President, Woodrow Wilson." In short, the Democrats had fashioned a myopic program which included "nothing to give genuine hope to Europe of immediate, vital, and enlightened cooperation." [9] With this terminal salute the liberal press put away the convention and its results and prepared for the hyperthyroid campaigning days ahead. The positions from which to sally forth were by now well understood and established.

COLLAPSE OF THE LIBERAL OPPOSITION

During the summer campaign months, the liberal press continued to hammer away at what it considered major deficiencies in both the Democratic candidate and platform. In August a *Nation* article ridiculed Roosevelt's position that tariff reduction would eliminate the war debts question as a further item of controversy in this country's overseas ties. The journal maintained he had also supported tariffs as a factor contributing to the maintenance of the American standard of living. Furthermore, he was accused of "serious misrepresentation" in his campaign oratory in attacking the Republican record of insufficient reduction of war debts before 1929; "he attacked them at perhaps their one point of strength for the war debt was consistently reduced at the unparalleled rate of about one billion dollars a year." [10] In the *New Republic,* the oracular "T.R.B." insisted that New York circles assumed Roosevelt was "under Hearst's wing in international matters," a conclusion which was inferred from FDR's prompt declaration against the League of Nations so soon after a Hearst newspaper editorial had demanded a stand by him.[11]

In September, Villard, still tenaciously clinging to the touchy foreign affairs agenda, again pointed out that Roosevelt had still not taken a stand on the war debt, reparations and disarmament problems, a sign to him that the whole area was a veritable vacuum in the outlook of the Democratic Party. In addition, Villard considered it most ominous that the Democratic candidate had been highly praised by Bernard Baruch; to be considered "safe and sound and entirely to be trusted by Wall Street men like himself is certainly hard luck for the Democratic candidate." Villard was sure that "If a few more magnates like Mr. Baruch certify to his soundness, the Middle West will begin to see that Mr. Roosevelt is not the great reformer or radical that he is sedulously cracked up to be." [12]

Late in October, Villard published a long editorial headed "Roosevelt and Hoover Militarists Both." It consisted in essence of a plea for a vote for Norman Thomas on the grounds that the mentioned candidates were unreliable on the question of war and that whichever won, there would surely be a strong push for armaments. There was a long and most unfavorable summary of FDR's career as a naval enthusiast, a remark as to his happiness upon becoming Assistant Secretary of the Navy in the Wilson era, his ease in naval company, his pre-World War pressure for a fleet second only to Great Britain, his favoring of intervention in Mexico, his testimony before House and Senate Committees on Naval Affairs strongly advocating a great naval building program, as well as the part he had played in Haiti, where, Villard charged, he had "connived and welcomed pulling down the Haitian Republic," and had expressed gratification with Marine General Smedley D. Butler's dismissal of the Haitian legislature. Predicted Villard, "If he gets in, and the opportunity arises, he will not only be for a bigger navy than we have had, but he will be thoroughly imperialistic if there is any trouble in the Caribbean." [13]

Liberal voices enough were being raised in support of Thomas during this season. Reinhold Niebuhr, Paul Blanshard, Heywood Broun, Elmer Davis and Paul H. Douglas had all entered the lists on his behalf in the liberal press and in the Socialist organ *New Leader*. Niebuhr, in an open letter to the *New Republic* in August, and speaking as chairman of the New York City Organization Committee for Thomas for President, admonished the readers not to be "neutral" in the coming election, but to support Thomas, a "man of outstanding ability," as well as making their votes count "against the two old parties, which have shown themselves completely unable and unwilling to meet the challenge of misery with any intelligence." [14] Davis called the election preliminaries "preposterous" and urged his readers to vote for Thomas. Douglas, chairman of the Thomas and Maurer Committee in Chicago, published open letters in the liberal organs pleading for Midwest support. Douglas loudly proclaimed that he was one of those who believed that the only liberal votes in the 1932 election which would not be "thrown away" would be those for Thomas.[15] Liberal accord was quite general with all these sentiments, although the *New Republic* did publish an article by Matthew Josephson which disparaged Thomas, only to receive a prompt and urgent rebuttal from Blanshard. Blanshard heaped scorn on the journal for having the gall to sponsor an attack on Thomas from the left, after having supported Al Smith in the previous election. Blanshard indignantly advised them to change their ways: [16]

Judging by the journal's record in the past, Norman Thomas is a hard-boiled revolutionist compared to the editors of the *New Republic*. We who are working with him to build a social revolutionary movement in this country have a right to ask from the *New Republic* constructive cooperation as well as negative criticism.

Blanshard was not correct in accusing the *New Republic* of being hostile to Thomas; it just had not repudiated Foster. Editorial support for Thomas was warm, and it increased as election day approached. A long comment two weeks before the election hoped that there would be a vote of over two million for Thomas, which would give the enthusiasts for a frank labor party a nucleus with which to work, and encouragement in knowing there was this much vigorous good will extant. "A vote for Norman Thomas is a vote for the birth of that party in the next four years." [17] Great confidence was expressed in the wisdom of the "average voter" and his ability to see through both Hoover and Roosevelt, realizing that nothing could be expected of either. Since both parties depended on the same sources of support, to expect to see Roosevelt emerge as a figure of much difference from what had already appeared was illusionary: "Franklin D. Roosevelt, if he were the greatest statesman in the world, could not make this party, with its old habits, its old personnel, and its need for campaign chests, a very different animal once it accedes to power." So to prepare for the new party was by far the wisest action at present, and to wait for four more years. At the end of this period it was considered "a very large possibility" that prosperity would not have returned and that the grievances of the farmers and laborers would be more pronounced, thus providing a fertile field for political tillage.

Despite all this advice, in the very same issue of the journal appeared a long letter by Nathaniel Peffer suggesting that nobody vote at all. Peffer felt so estranged and alienated that he was sure the only answer to the dilemma was to stay home and organize deliberate voters' strikes, to distinguish their behavior from the customary indolence of the approximately one half of the electorate which did not vote anyway. He had high hopes for the invigorating and purgative results of such behavior. A cut in the electorate by another fifty percent would surely produce panic among the professional politicians and ultimately bring ruin to the organized parties. The devoted anti-voters could then build on the wreckage of this old body politic a new one in which it might again be possible to participate "with dignity, self-respect and prospect of accomplishment," coming out of a new "political division on realities, parties with principles and policies, and meaning in the exercise of the suffrage." [18]

Last-minute observations, written shortly before the election but appearing in the issues which were published the day after, too soon for comment, continued in the hopeful vein characteristic of the peak period of hope for Thomas's chances. Roosevelt drew more unfavorable commentaries than Hoover, partially due to the fact that he was being recognized as by far the more formidable vote gatherer of the two. A *New Republic* editorial article, "The Obscene Spectacle," agreed that FDR would get a protest vote of millions, but that it would go to him without enthusiasm, being aimed merely at keeping Hoover from another term. The low level of the campaign tactics of the Democrats must surely have disillusioned almost everyone who expected better things, while the behavior of their candidate had demonstrated without a doubt that there was no material difference between the two: [19]

In issue-dodging, Mr. Roosevelt is quite as adept as Mr. Hoover—witness his long silence and final equivocation on the bonus, his refusal to say whether he favors recognition of Russia, his pretense that the war debts can and will be paid and his impossible promises on the score of economy in the operation of the federal government.

On the domestic level the *New Republic* was confident that not too many would be taken in by the mild expressions on behalf of the wisdom of some degree of change; "No doubt many of Mr. Roosevelt's progressive supporters think his program really embodies a 'new deal,' but it embodies nothing that reaches to the heart of the existing system, and almost nothing that has not long ago been adopted by other capitalist nations," and in reality at least fifteen years overdue even here. No one should be deceived by this social landscape gardening; these brave declarations simply constituted "a belated application of liberalistic meliorism to a civilization which we ought to be engaged in remodeling." [20]

THE REACTION TO DEFEAT
AND THE EARLY NEW DEAL

The liberal press, its editors and principal spokesmen took Roosevelt's victory and their defeat with remarkable equanimity. The comment was unusually sober and restrained for some time after the election. There was for a short time a number of loud and angry reverberations from the bitterly disappointed Thomas supporters. One *New Republic* correspondent reproached the journal's editors for the "calm and phlegmatic" manner in which they had accepted the outcome; "it means the triumph in American life of everything that decent people despise and fight against," this unidentified critic remonstrated; "I don't know which fact has more significance, the landslide of a tenth-rate politician like Roosevelt or the tragic defeat and disappointment of Norman Thomas." [21] Gabriel Heatter, stubborn and unyielding in defeat, wrote an open letter to Thomas published in the December 14 issue of the *Nation,* which exuded confidence of a high order in the future of the Socialist Party if it only reorganized and presented its program to the public in new terminology, and junked the old socialist verbiage. The two old parties were undoubtedly "two wings of the same bird of prey," and could be beaten by a socialist party which approached the people "in language they understand and approve." The problem seemed entirely a verbal one to Heatter.[22] Paul Y. Anderson, of the St. Louis *Post-Dispatch,* and a regular correspondent to the *Nation,* a week before spoke in morose and apocalyptic terms which had a bitter after-taste: "Of course it is not outside the realm of possibility that before another Presidential year arrives our economic system will have crashed, and that we shall have been compelled to junk politicians and turn for leadership to those who really know what it is all about." [23] It sounded strange for a publication which devoted much abuse to the emergency strong men of Italy and Germany apparently to approve of such a heartfelt wish for a crisis order here. But there obviously was a qualitative difference in strong men, in view of the fact that it was part of liberal mores to maintain a respectful distance from Stalin.

Yet on the whole, these persons represented only one segment of the liberal front. Roosevelt's Democratic machine had taught most of the others an impressive lesson in practical politics, and some serious reconsideration was quietly going on among many. There was the alluring choice of abandoning resistance and climbing into the wagons of the winners, thereupon to proceed into the councils of the mighty. As it turned out, this consolation prize became the substitute for being the vanguard of a pure Socialist triumph for the majority. There was no immediate rush, nevertheless. A substantial period of criticizing and heckling Roosevelt, his appointments and the New Deal programs in general ensued. There was no expression of unqualified satisfaction with anything in the first few years. The liberals were very cautious while engaged in their gleanings from the bitter fruit of defeat. To embrace too eagerly a cause which had been so roundly denounced just a short time before smacked of indecency. Conversions to the new dispensation were slow and hesitant.

Late in November, "T.R.B." predicted great future popularity for Roosevelt on the grounds that he had taken a strong stand for the repeal of prohibition, in which case he was definitely "swimming with the popular tide." His cultivation of the Washington newsmen and general affability to the Capitol City press, most of it personally hostile to Hoover, and "wet" besides, was considered another astute undertaking. And, after all, said the *New Republic*'s incognito columnist, "No one really hates Mr. Roosevelt. He goes in with no violent enemies and no popular soreness either because of his campaign, which was without much flavor, or because of his program, which, except for prohibition, was on the whole vague." [24] There was plenty of both time and room to repair the psychological fences.

A preliminary olive branch offering was a nearly full-page unsigned editorial in the *New Republic* for February 8, 1933, "Mr. Roosevelt Must Lead," incorporating a plea in favor of an American variant of the "leadership principle" as unabashed as the liberal papers ever printed. It is ironical that at the foot of the same page was the first paragraph of the story announcing the arrival of Adolf Hitler into power in Germany.[25] A virtual moratorium on verbal bombing of FDR ensued the next three or four months, while the celebrated "100 Days" transpired and the astonishing flood of legislation poured out of Congress which was subsequently wrapped up in the parcel labeled the New Deal. Liberal opinion had been united in the firm conviction that the Democrats were bankrupt in the policy field. It took months before any comprehensive attitude could be developed toward all this activity, due to its volume and spread. It represented the first big break-through in the once solidly hostile liberal front, and Roosevelt's bag of liberal camp followers was not insignificant. The liberal ice-floe began to thaw first in the precincts of the *New Republic,* one of whose contributing editors, Rexford G. Tugwell, had been admitted to high rank in New Deal policy-thinking levels, a prestige achievement of no mean proportions.

The principal product of this early "era of good feeling" was a major policy statement by Bliven in the form of a long article in the July 12 issue of the *New Republic,* "Roosevelt and the Radicals." [26] It was the first real indication that Bliven was getting over his 1931 trip to the Soviet Union, though there was many a twisting thicket to wander through in the years ahead in the shape of policy zig-zags toward the Workers' Fatherland. By "radicals," Bliven meant "Communists." As it was revealed, the principal intent of the story was to defend Roosevelt and his program from Communist charges of Fascism and "going the way of Italy." But a substantial part was devoted to a critique of Marxian theory on the basis of its shortcomings as an explanation of what was now taking place in the industrial nations. Some straightforward talk about serious weaknesses in Russia helped to turn the Communist frontal attack on the New Deal as well.

Bliven demonstrated that he was as confused as the Communists when it came to defining Fascism to the satisfaction of any substantial number. The only elements he could think of worth mentioning as integral aspects of Fascism were "enforced minority rule" and "the suppression of labor unions," two excellent examples of what was transpiring in the Soviet Union. In the former case, dictatorship, it was easy to prove Roosevelt was a product of a majority vote in a regular election—as was Hitler, but not Stalin, which was not considered pertinent to mention. Roosevelt's sympathy with "old fashioned trade unionism" was well-known enough to absolve him from guilt on this charge as well. Insofar as the ideological word-game was involved, Bliven lamely expatiated to an inconclusive suspended position:

Whether Roosevelt is a Fascist depends of course upon what you mean by such a term. Certainly, he is no such thing in any sense which is understood by the great mass of the American people, and propaganda to this effect is therefore (like so much propaganda) intelligible and acceptable only to those who already agree with the propagandists.

In substance Bliven was saying at this point that no precise definition of Fascism existed, and that everyone was free to use it in limited and special senses, primarily to identify opponents prior to the campaign of vituperative abuse necessary to harden the fixed notions of some particular camp of true believers. To let the issue lie in this utterly unscientific state was a disservice to every reader.

On the policy level, Bliven invented a new word to explain the economic nationalist and state capitalist elements which he denoted as important aspects of both the Roosevelt and Stalin governments, not of the Roosevelt and the Hitler and/or Mussolini regimes. Bliven believed he was a pioneer in discovering and explaining this phenomenon, which it was "high time the world understood":

The American government has now adopted a policy of "intranationalism," of trying to make America prosperous first and only thereafter attempting to improve international conditions. There is a striking analogy between this decision and Stalin's acceptance of the idea of letting the world revolution go hang, for the present, while trying to make Communism a success within the borders of the U.S.S.R.

Bliven's persuasive attempt to cancel out Communist criticism of Roosevelt and the New Deal by comparing its economic isolationism with that of Russia was written at the height of the London Economic

Conference, where it was apparent that the President had tied the hands of his representatives on all matters dealing with any genuine international approach to the world economic blind staggers. The apologetic attitude inhibited any effort to examine those elements in the structures of the emergency programs common to all the states mentioned, regardless of the capitalist, Communist or Fascist labels. In view of the persistence of cordial predispositions toward the Russian experiment, an expectation of such a survey was utterly premature. But one could not escape obtaining from this statement the reflection of a changed attitude at least on the part of the *New Republic*'s senior editor toward the New Deal. In retrospect the failure of an attractive term like "intranationalism" to replace the uglier-sounding "isolationism" might be considered the unfortunate part of this episode. Bliven's estimate at this point was one of the most temperate to appear in the liberal press during the first term of Franklin Roosevelt. The majority of the liberal observers and critics were not inclined to be so charitable, and Bliven himself had an unkindly view of the New Deal some ten months later.

SOME EARLY ROOSEVELT APPOINTEES UNDER LIBERAL SCRUTINY

Before the first month of Roosevelt's first term had elapsed, liberal unhappiness with his appointments began to be registered. The *New Republic* castigated his sending of Richard Washburn Child abroad as his "unofficial ambassador," calling to mind Child's deep interest in the welfare of the American oil companies and his behavior at the 1922 Genoa Conference, which was summed up as suspiciously anti-Soviet.[27] The major assault on FDR's diplomatic appointments also occurred in March, 1933 with Villard swinging the ax in a full-page signed *Nation* editorial. He summarily reckoned the assignments as "a series of very poor diplomatic appointments." Villard was incensed at the sending of major campaign contributors and a whole boatload of newspapermen and newspaper proprietors abroad to represent America; "As a journalist I have long been constitutionally opposed to the rewarding of journalistic support of a candidate by any office whatsoever." Villard insisted that there was no more dangerous method of "influencing the press" than distributing political loaves and fishes to the loyal typewriter platoons. In this procedure Villard saw Roosevelt repeating the mistakes of Wilson. He could see no reason to send Robert W. Bingham of the Louisville *Courier-Journal* to the London ambassadorship simply because he was a "pleasant-mannered rich man" and a newspaper owner, nor Josephus Daniels, owner and editor of the Raleigh, North Carolina, *Observer* ("a tired, old man") to Mexico, nor Claude Bowers, chief editorial writer of the New York *Evening Journal* ("merely an employee of Hearst") to Spain. Jesse Straus's appointment to Paris was laid to his campaign contribution, since his expert management of the R. H. Macy department store was not any conceivable preparation for the important ambassadorship to France. Villard sardonically remarked, "It is a pity James M. Cox has declined the Berlin post." As the owner of four papers, by the new standards this would make him "a diplomat four times over." "Report has it that Clark Howell of the Atlanta *Constitution* is to be ambassador to Italy. Step up, journalists, and get yours!", was the *Nation* chief's parting shot.[28]

In the summer the *Nation* lashed Roosevelt for replacing Sumner Welles in Cuba with Jefferson Caffrey, "a tool of oil and banking interests in Colombia." [29] But on the home front too, the antipathy of the liberal press to domestic appointments was expressed in the most unequivocal language. Both major journals denounced the naming of Dean Acheson to the post of Under Secretary of the Treasury and John Dickinson as Assistant Secretary of Commerce, largely on the basis of their employment by Wall Street law firms which had been condemned for defending Charles E. Mitchell in the banking scandals and the Sugar Institute from a Sherman Anti-Trust prosecution.[30] The *New Republic* had a caustic comment to make when in the fall of 1933 Dickinson headed up a committee to study the stock market and suggest procedural changes; it was noted that among the first persons named to this body were Acheson and Arthur Dean, another partner in the Sullivan and Cromwell law firm, the latter no less sinister than the others. To suppose that "three Wall Street lawyers" could "supply the nation with cures for Wall Street's wickedness" was "a piece of inexcusable impudence," was the assessment of the scheme.[31]

Acheson's appointment had been greeted with the abrupt judgment that it "did not inspire much confidence," but neither did a number of others. In the summer of 1933, when speculation had developed as to the possibility of Lewis A. Douglas replacing William H. Woodin in the principal post in the Treasury Department, the *Nation* reflected darkly on its likely impact. The buildup of Adolph A. Berle, Jr., as a multi-expert aroused no enthusiastic gestures; "Mr. Berle is popularly supposed to know about everything," jibed the *New Republic,* but in an aside assured the readers that there were surely "some large round holes in his knowledge," in that particular instance, about the stock market.[32] Additional uncomplimentary preliminary assessments were not rare; they abounded. When Roosevelt first named George N. Peek and General Hugh S. Johnson to important posts, they were promptly dismissed as notorious lackeys of Bernard Baruch, himself a frequent target for liberal poisoned arrows. Bliven, reviewing Harold L. Ickes' book *The New Democracy,* in the fall of 1934, shrugged off the author as "a middle-aged Chicago gentleman with a likeable personality and a preference for inaction." [33] A week later the *Nation* responded to the naming of Francis Biddle to the chairmanship of the National Labor Relations Board with words of warning that here was another corporation lawyer, "among whose clients one can find many anti-union big business enterprises," and that his reputed "liberalism" had to be estimated in this light.[34] Additional attention to this tendency will be devoted subsequently.

SOME LIBERAL JUDGMENTS
ON THE NEW DEAL, 1933–1935

When Paul Douglas reviewed Tugwell's *The Industrial Discipline* for the *Nation* in June, 1933 he was still a captive of his "new party" speculations. He held Tugwell in high esteem, but did not feel the same way about the Administration's program, which the book was written to defend. The industrial program headed up under the National Recovery Administration aroused the least enthusiasm from Douglas. This bureau probably drew more disapprobation from liberals than the rest of the New Deal put together, a number of parts of which, in fact, they heartily supported. Douglas reflected a popular view of the NRA when he defined it as a "program of legalized cartels." The Communists perhaps were the most vociferous critics, and were responsible for first describing the NRA as America's counterpart of the Italian corporations as envisioned in Mussolini's Integral State. Douglas worked from another vantage-point; granting that FDR was "progressive" and his university-recruited aides "able," he doubted that any significant control agency "outside of capitalism" could ever control this program. He was convinced that Tugwell was too optimistic, and had not calculated on the obstreperous behavior of the "owners of industry" should prosperity return. Impatience with control would soon sweep "Rooseveltian liberalism" aside and return business to its old familiar ways: [35]

Along with the Rooseveltian program must go, therefore, the organization of those who are at present weak and who need to acquire that which the world respects, namely, power. Trade unions need to be built up and farmers' cooperatives as well. Finally, the urban and rural workers of hand and brain need a strong party of their own.

Undoubtedly a mighty number of urban "workers of brain" endorsed Douglas' call for a place at the table of influence in the land. His case against gaining it through capillary action in the system of the political party then dominant was that the Democrats in the East "and in some of the Midwest States" depended too heavily upon "machines" which were "in league with the worst forces of the under and upper world." This was considered an insuperable handicap to the arrival to power of the forces in the national community which Douglas considered the main repository of social virtue.

There were all sorts of views of the NRA the first summer. "T.R.B." was interested in the ultimate meaning of the immense volume of printed and spoken words devoted to popularizing the NRA all over the country. He was convinced he had the answer: [36]

From a politician's point of view, the far-flung N.R.A. publicity machine . . . is primarily a vast propaganda agency for building up voting strength for Franklin D. Roosevelt and the New Deal. And, in the circumstances, this is a very necessary thing. It has long been evident that Mr. Roosevelt would not take any step directly challenging the vested interests of American industry until he felt sure of solid popular support behind him. Frank (sic) has none of the love of battle of old Theodore; he is emphatically not a leader of lost, or even doubtful, causes.

Paul Anderson in the *Nation* did not think the NRA was in any danger from the opposition it was getting from the liberals, but felt compelled to warn its director, General Johnson, to beware of the forces represented by the Washington *Post,* the New York *Herald Tribune,* and "other disgruntled Hooverites" who were lying in ambush to "sabotage" the program at the first opportunity: [37]

The Reids and the Meyers are determined people. They have not forgiven Roosevelt for last November's landslide nor are they likely to forgive him. Moreover, they speak for great vested interests which are rapidly arriving at the correct conclusion that the recovery program is a spear aimed at the heart of the existing profit system. If anyone believes that this outfit will surrender without a battle he is unacquainted with the native tenacity of the American hog.

Lewis Mumford, absorbed in the work of the Regional Planning Association of America and writing his *Technics and Civilization,* found a few moments to hit the Administration's public works, public housing and industrial recovery programs, all of which he considered virtually failures. In a letter to the *New Republic* in October, 1933,[38] praising John T. Flynn for a critique of the public works action, Mumford claimed that thus far the Roosevelt Administration had "presented an appalling spectacle of inertia, marking time and stalling," that FDR himself had "a masterful habit of making two diametrically opposite moves in almost the same breath," resulting in "an impotence that is just as paralyzing as Mr. Hoover's distaste for making any decision at all." The President had once likened himself to the quarterback of a football team, Mumford recalled, but thus far he had succeeded only in perfecting "the gallant habit of throwing some of his most beautiful passes into the arms of the opposing end," in addition to concealing from everyone "which goal post his team is headed for." The NRA he wrote off as a self-defeating mechanism.

A year later, Mumford was just as much if not more disenchanted with the New Deal. In a harsh review of Horace M. Kallen's *A Free Society,* he delivered a withering attack on the philosophy of pragmatism and its modern application in meeting the problems of the country. Applying it specifically to the Roosevelt Administration, he ended by indicating very bluntly what he preferred to eventuate: [39]

The present administration, indeed, is pragmatism in action: aimless experiment, sporadic patchwork, a total indifference to guiding principles or definitive goals, and hence an uncritical drift along the lines of least resistance, namely the restoration of capitalism. When its confused and contradictory nostrums patently fail, it will be prepared to kill our democracy with a final dose of fascism—unless the workers exert a strong counter-pressure—rather than save the patient by the institution of communism.

The economic historian Louis Hacker's response to the New Deal's action in the area of farm relief and recovery was a short brochure titled *The Farmer Is Doomed,* reviewed anonymously and with enthusiasm in the *New Republic* in September, 1933. Hacker's thesis was that American agriculture had collapsed permanently, and that no legislative magic whatsoever could resuscitate it. The reviewer believed Hacker had proved with a mass of "solid economic facts and figures" that the farmer was "defeated" and on his way to reduction to "peasantry." [40]

Villard's main signed editorial in the *Nation* for September 13, "Six Months of Franklin D. Roosevelt," was especially condemnatory of his foreign relations record, which he described as "bad, almost disastrous." A *New Republic* editorial on March 14, 1934, "Mr. Roosevelt's First Year," had virtually nothing good to say except for the Tennessee Valley Authority, identified as "an interesting experiment in state capitalism" from which America might expect to learn "several valuable lessons"; the NRA, on the other hand, had "sold the country to big business for a mess of pottage." [41]

In April came another major statement from Bruce Bliven, which lacked what faint hope in the program his long account of the previous year contained: [42]

When we look at Mr. Roosevelt's first thirteen months in office, what do we see? He denounced the money-changers, but they are still in control of America's financial organization. He promised the good life to the masses of our people, but there are still more than ten million unemployed and wages have risen little—for many, not all. . . . Money has been poured out to the farmers, but those among them who needed it most have received the least, and the disparity between agriculture and industry continues.

And on the side of international policy, Bliven continued, the President talked "peace, peace," but still found it possible to approve bills authorizing "a fantastic increase in naval and air defense." When George Soule reviewed Roosevelt's book *On Our Way* a month later, he summarized the situation thusly:

The President's simple faith in the public spirit of private industry and its capacity to plan for the social good has obviously been misplaced. The results up to date are most discouraging to any such attempt. No amount of geniality and noble generality can conceal the failure.

The *Nation* reviewer even doubted that the President had written any of the book beyond the foreword and the brief final chapter.[43]

Ernest Sutherland Bates opened his *New Republic* review of Norman Thomas's *The Choice Before Us* that same month with this observation: "Those who, after reading the President's *On Our Way,* are still tempted to repeat the question which he neglected to answer —'On our way to what?'—may turn with profit to this volume by one of his defeated opponents." Bates recommended reading Thomas's book before Roosevelt's on the grounds that Thomas knew where we were going and the President did not. Bates heartily agreed with the Thomas thesis, proposed by a goodly number of observers now, that the New Deal was a form of state capitalism, which was in reality "a mild substitute for Fascism," and primarily "bolstering up monopoly capitalism." [44]

At the fifteen-month mark of the New Deal, the *Nation* declared that for the vast majority, "materially, life is not much more satisfactory than it was in March, 1933," that the unemployed were "as unemployed as ever," and that the cost of living increases in this period were so high that they effectively wiped out all increases in wage levels which had taken place.[45]

The word "Fascism" was beginning to appear more insistently in the summaries of the New Deal in liberal and liberal-socialist circles by the end of the eighteen month and two year marks of the accession to office of the Roosevelt entourage, but some observers were notably restrained. Harry Elmer Barnes, to whom both the *Nation* and *New Republic* assigned several books by and about New Dealers and the New Deal during this time, both attacks and apologia, maintained a diplomatic and moderate course in often extended reviews, drawing attention to strengths and weaknesses alike. But full rein was given in the unsigned editorial material, where many of the attitudinal trial-balloon essays first appeared.

When, in the fall of 1934, Roosevelt in one of his "fireside chats" appealed to the corporations and labor unions to put off their impending showdown struggle, a *New Republic* editorial estimated its meaning in this manner: [46]

Quite apart from its immediate effects, President Roosevelt's truce is rather ominous for the fascist implications it contains. So many actions of the Roosevelt administration have been labeled fascist that one hesitates to use the term. Yet it is noteworthy that the essence of the President's labor policy—that disputes between capital and labor can and should be adjusted by a third party, preferably the government—is also the essence of Fascist labor policy.

Estimates of the Administration's success began to appear regularly in deeper shades of gray. Late in October the same journal concluded that the recovery program was not working, and that the country was "as far away from recovery" as it had been in the fall of 1933. It went on to recommend to FDR, referred to as "a supple-minded aristocrat," that he try to "bring his wealthy friends to see the wisdom of yielding to popular clamor for standard reforms." [47]

On November 14, 1934 Maxwell S. Stewart had similar views to express in the *Nation:*

Two years have passed since F.D.R. was elected President of the United States . . . but despite unprecedented governmental activity, economic conditions throughout the country are practically on a level with those existing when Herbert Hoover was so emphatically turned out of office.

Editorially, the *Nation* shrugged off the New Deal the following week as a "hodge podge." [48]

But the majority view represented in the liberal papers probably was stated as succinctly as possible by an advertisement by the publisher Covici-Friede in the *New Republic* in mid-October, 1934, reading, "Capitalism *Can't* Be Cured!" [49] The subject was the promotion of Lewis Corey's *The Decline of American Capitalism.*

Corey, dubbed "the American John Strachey" by an enthusiastic Lewis Gannett, was being acclaimed for making "the first real attempt to apply Marx to the American scene." His conclusion, accepted with some gusto, was that permanent mass unemployment, reduced living standards and "possible fascism" were in store in the immediate future and for some time to come.

Liberal editorial commentaries on New Deal congressional victories in the 1934 elections were not very comforting. Nothing outstanding was expected from them as lawmakers, and in one case in particular the *Nation* was in dark doubt as to the quality and character of a new senator from Missouri:

The circumstances which led the sovereign State of Missouri to send Harry S. Truman to the United States Senate are scarcely such as to inspire confidence in our democratic institutions. Last summer the obscure Mr. Truman yearned to quit his office as County Judge of Jackson County and become County Collector of Taxes. The post he held was a humdrum affair, that which he had in his mind's eye paid on a fee basis and paid handsomely.

The account went on to describe the story of "Big Boss Tom" Pendergast, "absolute monarch of Kansas City and leader of the Democratic Party in Missouri," whose other plans for the candidate for the collectorship resulted in his "casting about for something else for his ambitious lieutenant," and hitting on the senatorial nomination. "Disappointed, no doubt, Truman accepted," the editorial concluded, "And so Harry S. Truman will not collect taxes for his county but will vote yes and no on treaties with foreign countries, appointments to the Supreme Court, and things like that." [50] The irony in the final remarks was almost strong enough to taste.

Throughout 1935 a steady drum-fire on FDR, the New Deal, the cabinet and some other appointees appeared in the liberal press. The *Nation* spoke of Harold L. Ickes, Secretary of the Interior and key figure in the relief program, as "that personification of slow motion," while the *New Republic* saved special vitriol for Postmaster General James A. Farley: "The Post Office Department has always been bad, but it has rarely been so outrageous as it is under 'Big Jim,' the man who would Tammanyize the whole United States if he could." It also aimed an editorial arrow at Jefferson Caffrey when he was named ambassador to Cuba, and charged him with acting like a "colonial administrator" and as "a member of the Cuban government." [51]

By far the deepest cuts taken at the New Deal official family were those by Paul W. Ward, Washington correspondent of the Baltimore *Sun*, in a lengthy series of profiles in the *Nation* in the spring of 1935. One of the earliest was a ferocious dismemberment of Secretary of

Labor Frances Perkins, "another secretary *for* Mr. Roosevelt." Ward insisted that she had nothing to do with labor policy but simply put into effect the decrees of the President; "He concocts his own labor-relations policies out of his vast experiences with the teeming toilers of Krum Elbow, the militant laborites of banks and law offices, and the Navy Department's class-conscious admirals," Ward explained contemptuously.

Of Harry Hopkins, administrator of three of the four work and direct relief agencies, Ward had the following diagnosis: "He is a man after Roosevelt's own heart—gay, erratic, and full of those amiable prejudices that are the New Deal substitute for profound social and political convictions." Tugwell he brushed away as "a third-rate Voltaire trying to be a second-rate Rousseau," and Henry Morgenthau, Secretary of the Treasury, as "the Dutchess County apple boy." For Wallace he saved especially sulphuric treatment; "Wallace, one of the most admirable and ridiculous figures of the New Deal, should have been born in the Middle Ages," and concluded that the Secretary of Agriculture was "a queer duck" and "a cultural clodhopper." Ward's title for this piece was "Wallace the Great Hesitater." And of Senate Floor Leader Joseph T. Robinson of Arkansas, Ward said "A hog-caller who had missed his calling." [52]

The *New Republic* editorially attacked what they described as Roosevelt's "purge of the liberals from the Agricultural Adjustment Administration," an act which they insisted was "as revealing as anything that has happened since Roosevelt came to power." Their Washington commentator "T.R.B." repeatedly expressed dark comments on the President and his program, and was of the opinion that his big gamble was the expectation that prosperity would return before the fall of 1936. He was convinced that the real strength of the Administration's position was not the vitality of its own program but "the complete failure of the Republicans to develop an attractive alternative." [53] The editorial line on Roosevelt pounded away on the point that he had not possessed, nor had he subsequently acquired, "any deep philosophical convictions of any kind." [54] The portrait of the President in Hallgren's *The Gay Reformer* was considered a good one, and not too extreme.[55]

By January, 1935, the *New Republic* considered that a major showdown was imminent, and in a piece titled "Roosevelt Confronts Capitalism" [56] suggested that the President was going to have to grapple with this opponent if he "wanted to achieve his declared aims." The significance of this call to battle was a lengthy policy statement accompanying it which to some degree indicated the influence of the *New Masses, Soviet Russia Today,* the *Monthly Review,* and the *New Leader,* especially the first three of these rival publications. The immediately arresting statement was the attempt to disclaim responsibility for being an organ of liberal opinion, and to seek a berth in some kind of independent but undefined socialism. Particularly resented was the Communist charge that the *New Republic*, being liberal, and necessarily deluded, had taken up a position in defense of the New Deal:

The Communists have from the beginning persistently misrepresented the *New Republic*'s attitude toward the New Deal. They tagged us as liberal; their doctrine decreed that liberals must be fooled; therefore they insisted that we were supporters of the New Deal and have been fooled.

This was not true, the statement declared. It pointed out that in the presidential campaign, "we did not support Roosevelt," and while none of the party programs were "wholly satisfactory," "we advised our readers to vote either Socialist or Communist." Furthermore, as the Roosevelt program had developed, it had maintained an aloof attitude, praising or attacking when it saw fit, without "emphasis on individual responsibility of the executive," but merely "an identification of him with his program." The conclusion at this point was that the program was up against a stone wall; they felt vindicated that "social-economic planning for the benefit of the masses could not be successful under capitalism," and that specifically, it was being proven by the failure of the President to achieve his "ambitious announced aims" by "the means he was using."

For its liberal readers who thought the *New Republic* had been too strong in its condemnation of the New Deal "failures," it advised a closer look at the publication itself, with a hint that they might adjust their assumptions about it. "The *New Republic* has not for years described itself as liberal; liberalism in the political sense is certainly not the name of the views of those who see no hope of permanency for economic individualism or capitalism."

There was a persistent strain of literary support for this unrest and yearning for something fundamental in the way of changes. The Marxist analysis of Jerome Davis's *Capitalism and Its Culture* received a very favorable review by Lewis Mumford in the *New Republic* for July 10, 1935, and the revolutionary rumbles in Paul Douglas's *Controlling Depressions,* reviewed a week earlier by Abram L. Harris, were quite unmistakable as well. Douglas reflected more the hoped-for third-party, farmer-labor coalition which was under tireless discussion in *Common Sense,* rather than a purely Communist or Socialist order in imitation of European or other beginnings. But the strong statist nature of most of his proposals for change as outlined in his book promised as much comprehensive departure from what had been part of the American socio-economic system.

The strain provoked by being astride the left-bound local and the

Moscow Express simultaneously was beginning to show openly now. The close ideological course to Marxism, complicated by an uncritical presentation of the Soviet Union as the only viable state in a world of irrational and semi-lunatic orders, when placed in juxtaposition to a persistent refusal to accept Communist comradeship and, no doubt, leadership, in the domestic sphere, placed great pressure on individual choice-making. The Communists no doubt received liberal tributes to the Soviet Union with pleasure and satisfaction, and were more logical than the liberals in seeking their adherence elsewhere. Liberal hesitance could hardly be interpreted in another way but blindness or sheer obstructionism, in the Communist view.

Edging up as close to Communism as possible without risking being too badly splashed was a game that was bound to lead to a serious impasse. The liberal vision of Red Russia which appeared often in parallel columns with their disparagements of the New Deal must be considered as an integral part of the whole liberal outlook, and will be treated separately. Liberal riding of the New Deal question was comfortable, but there was no preparation for following where it eventually led. The problem of the New Deal was eventually dissolved in a much bigger one, the problem of the world. By extending the boundaries of the crisis to the edges of the planet, a large part of the public was prevented from learning that the original problem was never solved. By the time "Doctor New Deal" had been replaced by "Doctor Win-the-War," the patient was already recuperating with vigor from the economic bends of 1929–1941 and in a few years, thanks partially to a very short memory, he no longer believed he had ever been sick. The remedy, consisting of massive doses of war, hot, cold, lukewarm, and in combinations of these, has never been abandoned. The later phases of the New Deal as seen through liberal eyes and its relation to the sharpening economic tensions come under observation in good time. But first the background of liberal thinking on war in general, the First World War in particular, and the by-products of that war in the shape of chronic problems need to be examined.

Historians with a flair for the dramatic have occasionally stated that the Second World War began on September 18, 1931. This date, the occasion of the Mukden Incident and the preliminary Japanese invasion of Manchuria, is surely of vast import. It signified to the world that the grandiose Briand-Kellogg Pact of a little more than three years before had not outlawed war as an instrument for the advancement of national policy, but only declarations of war. In one sense the proper advance action announcing this was the short Russo-Chinese war in 1929, but the eventual size and scope of this new struggle completely overshadowed the earlier. The world political order tailored at Versailles had always strained at the seams, but

Mukden was a major split, widening enough in three years to guarantee that the entire garment would be in tatters very shortly. That Versailles had not provided for a satisfactory Far Eastern situation was made obvious. But for that matter it had made even poorer provisions for the immediate European environs. This was in the simultaneous process of shaking apart as well.

Liberal chagrin at learning the flimsiness of the Kellogg Pact had been preceded on the other hand by nearly a decade of the most realistic dissection of the League of Nations, in which a vote of no confidence had been long outstanding. Parallel to that had been unresisting enthusiastic acceptance of revisionism with respect to the origins of the First War, the steady development of revulsion to the idea of supporting national wars again, and a firm conviction that most of the post-war tension and bad blood derived from the attempt to make the impossible financial, military and territorial settlements of 1919–1921 work. A careful look at these matters is in order.

NOTES

1 *Nation,* December 9, 1931, p. 628.
2 Editorial "Democratic Light Horses," *New Republic,* February 17, 1932, pp. 5–6.
3 *Nation,* February 17, 1932, p. 182.
4 Editorial "Demagogues and Plutogogues," *New Republic,* April 27, 1932, pp. 285–287 (p. 287).
5 Pringle, "Franklin D. Roosevelt—Perched on the Bandwagon," *Nation,* April 27, 1932, pp. 487–489; Hallgren, "Franklin D. Roosevelt," *Nation,* June 1, 1932, pp.616–618. The editors' announcement of support to Thomas was made in an editorial in the same issue on page 618.
6 All citations here and above from Bliven, "Franklin D. Roosevelt, The Patron of Politics," *New Republic,* June 1, 1932, pp. 62–64.
7 *Nation,* June 13, 1932, p. 23.
8 *Nation,* July 6, 1932, p. 1.
9 Villard, "The Democratic Trough At Chicago," *Nation,* July 13, 1932, pp. 26–27.
10 *Nation,* August 8, 1932, p. 113.
11 *New Republic,* August 10, 1932, p. 343.
12 *Nation,* September 21, 1932, p. 247.
13 Villard, "Roosevelt and Hoover Militarists Both," *Nation,* October 26, 1932, p. 390.
14 *New Republic,* August 17, 1932, p. 22.
15 *New Republic,* November 2, 1932, p. 332; *Nation,* November 2, 1932, p. 430. Douglas' new book, *The Coming Of A New Party,* was advertised on page 435 of this issue of the *Nation.*
16 *New Republic,* August 10, 1932, p. 335.
17 Editorial "Voting For A Party," *New Republic,* October 26, 1932, pp. 272–274, and for subsequent quotations in paragraph.
18 This long communication was headed "For a Voters' Strike," and ended with the exhortation, "I propose then: Strike! Don't Vote! Teach your children not to vote! Organize your friends! Be good citizens—blacklist politics!" *New Republic,* October 26, 1932, pp. 291–292.
19 *New Republic,* November 9, 1932, p. 341.
20 Editorial "Roosevelt's Revolution," *New Republic,* November 9, 1932, pp. 340–341.
21 *New Republic,* November 30, 1932, p. 74.
22 Heatter's letter was published in the *Nation* for December 14, 1932.

23 Anderson, "Debts, Beer And Other Troubles," *Nation,* December 7, 1932, pp. 557–558.

24 *New Republic,* November 23, 1932, pp. 43–44.

25 *New Republic,* February 8, 1933, p. 137.

26 *New Republic,* July 12, 1933, pp. 228–230. All subsequent citations in following paragraphs referring to Bliven's statement from this source.

27 *New Republic,* March 21, 1934, p. 143.

28 Villard, "The New Diplomatic Appointments," *Nation,* March 29, 1933, p. 336.

29 *Nation,* August 30, 1933, p. 230.

30 *Nation,* July 5, 1933, p. 335.

31 *New Republic,* October 25, 1933, pp. 290–291.

32 See above citation.

33 *New Republic,* November 21, 1934, p. 52.

34 *Nation,* November 28, 1934, p. 603.

35 Douglas, "Rooseveltian Liberalism," *Nation,* June 21, 1933, pp. 702–703. Douglas was entirely absorbed in problems of domestic import in these times, and had already been appointed to the Consumers Advisory Board of the NRA. *New Republic,* November 29, 1933, p. 57. See also his long letter "A National Program For Unemployment Insurance," *New Republic,* October 3, 1934, pp. 215–216.

36 *New Republic,* August 9, 1933, p. 339.

37 Anderson, "The NRA: Pin Pricks and Brickbats," *Nation,* September 13, 1933, pp. 290–291.

38 *New Republic,* October 11, 1933, pp. 243–244. The issue for May 17, 1933, had contained a passionate plea from Mumford for a wholesale government housing program employing communal units.

39 *New Republic,* October 3, 1934, pp. 222–223. In a reply to a complaint by Kallen, in the issue of December 5, 1934, p. 105, Mumford stated that he objected to Kallen's proposals "because his means are inconsistent with his ends; for his means derive from capitalism, the extension of the NRA, while his ends derive from Communism. My own relation to Marxian Communism is as heretical as Dr. Kallen's, and in several respects I am closer to him than I am to the Seventh Day Adventists and Complete Immersionists among the Marxians. But I do not hold that one can pluck the fruits of Communism off the capitalist tree, with the help of a few moral heroes in Washington."

40 *New Republic,* September 6, 1933, p. 110.

41 *New Republic,* March 14, 1934, pp. 116–117.

42 Bliven, "Not Kerensky: Lloyd George," *New Republic,* April 11, 1934, pp. 231–232.

43 *New Republic,* May 2, 1934, pp. 340–341; *Nation,* May 23, 1934, p. 600. Soule's *New Republic* review was a joint essay on this book and also *Social Change and the New Deal,* edited by W. F. Ogburn.

44 *New Republic,* May 23, 1934, p. 53.

45 *Nation,* July 11, 1934, p. 33.

46 Editorial "The Roosevelt Truce," *New Republic,* October 10, 1934, p. 229.

47 *New Republic,* October 24, 1934, pp. 296–297.

48 Stewart, "Stabilize the Dollar Now!," *Nation,* November 14, 1934, pp. 560–562; editorial "The Death Of the G.O.P.," *Nation,* November 21, 1934, p. 578.

49 *New Republic,* October 17, 1934, p. 289.

50 All citations in above paragraph from *Nation,* November, 21, 1934, p. 577.

51 *Nation,* January 16, 1935, p. 57; *New Republic,* February 20, 1935, p. 30; *New Republic,* July 10, 1935, p. 254.

52 See Ward, "Please Excuse Miss Perkins," *Nation,* March 27, 1935, pp. 353–355; "Dirge For Mr. Hopkins," *Nation,* May 22, 1935, pp. 594–596; "Wallace the Great Hesitater," *Nation,* May 8, 1935, p. 535. Ward's comments on Tugwell and Morgenthau are in the essay on Wallace, his reference to Robinson in *Nation,* April 8, 1936, p. 441.

53 *New Republic,* May 1, 1935, p. 339.

54 *New Republic,* December 11, 1935, p. 115.

55 In contrast to the estimate of John T. Flynn, the editors absolved FDR of Flynn's charge that he had sold out the liberals to big business as unintentional, not deliberate.

56 *New Republic,* January 16, 1935, pp. 279–280; citations in subsequent three paragraphs from this source.

4

THE LIBERALS RECONSIDER THE

FIRST WORLD WAR DURING

THE DEPRESSION

SOME REFLECTIONS ON THE
MEANING OF WOODROW WILSON

Less than a month after war had flamed up in East Asia with the outbreak of Sino-Japanese hostilities at Mukden, a *Nation* editorial declared in part, "Woodrow Wilson slew every liberal movement in America and paved the way for the utter corruption of the Harding Administration and the dull and injurious conservatism of Coolidge." [1] The reference was to the entry of the United States into the World War, considered an unqualified tragedy for America and the world in liberal circles, now that enough time had elapsed to permit sufficient rumination on the entire situation. In one sense this short judgment summarized a vast amount of similar comment from a score or more of liberal literary and academic personalities during this time. It seemed to be one of the verdicts least likely to be subject to reversal in any foreseeable time, in view of the numbers and repute of those who joined in this denunciation of Wilson in the first post-war decade. Even the detached giant of psychoanalysis, Sigmund Freud, had strong views on the subject, according to Max Eastman, who in the *New Republic* quoted Freud as asserting in a conversation with him in Vienna in 1926, "You should not have gone into the war at all. Your Woodrow Wilson was the silliest fool of the century. And he was also probably one of the biggest criminals—

unconsciously, I am quite sure." [2] A battalion of academic and political personages echoed Freud's sentiments to the letter.

The liberals of 1931 were not of the mind that political virtue was an exclusive possession of the Democratic Party, despite their persistent upbraiding of the GOP during its now unbroken decade of tenure in possession of the White House and the Treasury Department. For that and other reasons there was not the slightest compulsion to defend the dead giants of the major political parties. In this sense they were performing in the independent critical liberal tradition, and suffered from no inhibitions which might be traced to debts to the powerful and well-placed, whoever or wherever they might be.

Their harsh estimate of Wilson might be considered a proper fruit of a ten-year exposure to the flood of critical literature on the causes of the War, much of which redressed the wartime sagas in a manner far from laudatory of the conduct of the winning Allies. A weighty library in half a dozen tongues existed by this time, comprising the historical section already referred to as "Revisionism." What had been revised were the one-dimensional and pearly-white accounts issued by the Anglo-Russo-Franco-American Allies while the War was in progress, which purported to tell the whole story as to why the war had come about and where the responsibility for its outbreak should be laid. Since the main purpose of it had been to strengthen the support of the home-front people and gain their undivided energies behind the various national "war efforts," it passed without comment that nothing critical of one side was printed, nor the slightest material in extenuation of the enemy. It served its purpose admirably, but it was the most transparent tale-telling when made to serve the double purpose of passing as the history of the enormous and complex event. The works of several academic historians and the revelations of dozens of prominent wartime political and military figures soon made hash of these simple inspirational accounts, with the result that the literary and intellectual levels which read such material habitually had adopted a completely different approach to the War. It might be mentioned that this reconsideration did not extend very far down the intelligence and educational strata, of very considerable importance when the mobilization of opinion prefatory to the second great blood bath of the century commenced. The gradual conversion of the liberal press, its editors, readers and correspondents to the view that "war guilt" was a well-distributed substance and no monopoly of the losing side need not be chronicled here. It may suffice to say that at no time was Revisionism more thoroughly entrenched in the esteem of liberals than the early 1930's.

No more drastic "revision" had taken place than that of America's wartime President. The indictment of Wilson as the grave-digger of pre-1917 liberalism was utterly unequivocal. There was none of the expert evasion of a later crop of emperor-makers who sought to enthrone Wilson on the basis of the noble things he had said in his life and who attempted to shield him from a comprehensive assay by keeping his domestic and foreign policies and actions in separate water-tight compartments. In the eyes of these critics, Wilson the warrior cancelled out Wilson the progressive domestic reformer. They made a deliberate issue of pointing to the war as the virtual sole generator of the sordid domestic consequences so loudly lamented by presidential admirers. The wartime "war of nerves" waged against the home front in the interests of solidifying their fury against the enemy, and their sanction and support of the Government, could not have resulted otherwise than in a "Red Scare" of some sort or other. The primitive nature of wartime propaganda and its effects deserved more attention than the apologists were inclined to devote in that direction. Human emotions could hardly be regulated like piped water or heat; people could not be turned off and on. Thus it was perfectly natural that the ferocity of the campaign against the wartime enemy, when deprived of its object, could be so easily diverted to local hate objects, in the absence of more accessible demons. The lame and halting excuse that the Attorney-General, A. Mitchell Palmer, was to blame for what transpired got sparse acceptance.

The liberals insisted that the history of civil rights violations and the generous use of domestic violence against the resistant and the non-cooperative, as well as some of the uglier outbreaks of racism and anti-radicalism, be treated from the beginning of the war and not from some more convenient time such as when the President had been invalided. The liberals simply would not purchase the legend of Presidential helplessness. That the most powerful political figure in the world could make the whole planet listen respectfully to his requests yet stand with tied hands during the mass violation of the Constitution at home was incomprehensible. The liberals now insisted that Mr. Wilson could just as easily have stepped in and modified the zeal of the war-time and post-war reaction if so inclined. His failure to do so had unleashed the sentiments which had throttled reform and everything allied to it, thus paving the way for a decade during which the forces of liberalism in America scraped a low point untouched since post-Civil War Reconstruction days.

Wilson had been under attack for years in the liberal journals at the hands of journalists and professional historians alike before the outbreak of the depression war in Asia. They did not stop on that account. In January, 1932 the *New Republic* published John Dos Passos' "Meester Veelson," about as fierce a piece on Wilson and the wartime "liberalism" as ever appeared in any paper in America.[3] The same month, Morris R. Cohen, reviewing James Truslow Adams's

The Epic of America, reverberated the by now well-known charges against the wartime President, concluding, "The collapse of Wilsonian idealism began when in order 'to win the war,' he allowed liberal opinion to be repressed, so that he was without support when the reactionaries got the chance to turn against him." [4]

One of the most effective of the journalist-historians in the liberal revisionist cause for some years was C. Hartley Grattan, whose *Why We Fought,* published in 1929, was to be depended on for years as a source. Late in 1934 Professor Hacker was pointing out to *New Republic* readers that John Chamberlain was relying upon it heavily as a starting point in reviewing new books appearing on the war and its causes for the New York *Times.*[5] Grattan's writings on the subject continued to come out in both major liberal weeklies during this time, including a long story late in 1932 based on Colonel Edward M. House's revelations, indicating that Wilson had considered entering the war early in 1916. His reply to House's self-defense ran into another lengthy article, during which he took time to point out that the Allies' wartime propaganda, that they were fighting to destroy the Prussian ruling class, was utterly fraudulent. He called House's attention to the fact that twelve years after Versailles it was already back in the form of the von Schleicher-von Papen forces directing the German government. His castigation of Wilson, House and Page reached impressive heights of abuse.[6] In the summer of 1933, Grattan had another opportunity to devote extended attention to Wilson, this time in a review of John K. Winkler's book *Woodrow Wilson.* Grattan insisted Wilson had been beaten at Paris by the very forces he had assiduously cultivated in order to get there. Once there, he tried to overcome economic realities by rhetoric, still believing "in the power of moral eloquence to govern the world." His "economic befuddlement" [7]

led to his defeat in two ways: in directing our war policy during the period of neutrality it led him to permit the building up of economic entanglements with the Allies, and during the conflict it led him to turn the conduct of the war over to the strong and merciless.

Probably even less magnanimous was Max Lerner, who took the occasion of his review of a new issue of Wilson's *The New Freedom* to make a number of caustic references to the liberal-reformist reputation of Mr. Wilson. Wilson's "radicalism," Lerner scoffed, consisted "of the sort that took itself out mainly in after-dinner eloquence," and his oratory was mainly composed of "brilliant and yet somehow platitudinous phrases" which were "the product of an era which could still personify the evil forces to be overcome," and when under pressure, "his ideals of freedom were sadly squeezed out in the war." [8] Lerner, sympathetic to the New Deal, sternly warned against assuming it to be a carryover: "The New Deal as a program must be clearly dissociated from Wilson's New Freedom."

The first, and no doubt inadvertent, step in rebuilding the legend of Wilson in liberal ranks took place when the *New Republic* in the summer of 1934 printed a most sympathetic review of Professor Charles Seymour's *American Diplomacy During the World War* by Professor Sidney B. Fay. Fay, along with William L. Langer and Harry Elmer Barnes, had been a top-rank academic revisionist writer, but was now about to reverse the path which he had followed in writing the monumental *Origins of the World War* and begin his trip to a historian's Canossa. Fay's enthusiastic approval of Seymour's reassertion that America's entry in the war had been the exclusive product of Presidential idealism apparently caused consternation among the editorial staff, because an editorial rebuttal was published along with the review, a most unusual procedure, it being customary to accept book reviews at face value and let them stand before the readers on their own merits. Straight-forward language was a regular feature in this publication, but its rebuke to Seymour and Fay belonged almost in a class of its own.

"Mr. Seymour suggests that President Wilson may yet be recognized as an example of success through failure," it began, and "Mr. Fay adds that the world today needs more of the Wilsonian vision." These statements did not impair the scholarship of these "distinguished historians," but it did place their "political judgment" in considerable doubt. There was a "specific lesson" to be gained from contemplating the War President and his consequences; his failure demonstrated [9]

the futility, the downright danger of noble ideas when pursued with inappropriate instruments and when not related to the objective situation. He drew the United States into the War with a web of lofty words concealing the very material pressure to put us in—which existed despite the fact that no member of the Morgan firm may have asked him to declare war. Wilson tried to create a healing peace without reckoning with the imperialistic tendencies of the nations that would have to draft and administer it. He loftily overlooked the secret treaties. He assented to the carving up of Europe according to sentiments of political nationality without recognizing the underlying economic realities, or the strategic interest of France and Italy in weakening their enemies.

All this could not be airily dismissed as inconsequential and parenthetical material, insisted the editorial; the result of all these errors was being seen in the political upheaval going on in Germany and Austria at that very moment, and had to be considered as the predominant reason for the cause of "the new war that will probably come." This sharp rebuke ended with the admonition to restrain undue exhilaration; "It is quite beside the point to counsel the world to return to Wilson's ideals. An abject failure is not ennobled by the fact that its intentions were good."

Professor Hacker followed this with a rousing commendation of the editorial and added a few penetrating comments in extenuation: [10]

Dr. Fay makes it plain that he, in common with Dr. Seymour, holds to an indefensible system of acausal idealism and rejects all efforts to place Woodrow Wilson and the other American war leaders in relation to the economic and social forces of their time. In addition he does not scruple to attribute to those who have engaged in this difficult and delicate kind of study a vulgar materialism of which they are not guilty.

Hacker added, in sharp tones, "I take it as immensely significant that the Harvard professor applauds the Yale professor and expresses the pious wish that this book may become the official version of our entrance into the War." But Professor Fay showed himself quite unruffled by Hacker or the other revisionists in his *Nation* review of the third volume of Lloyd George's *War Memoirs,* in which he professed deep interest in Lloyd George's revelations on the Balfour, Northcliffe and Reading missions to Washington, "which did so much to promote harmony between the two great Anglo-Saxon peoples." No liberal critics chose at the moment to ask by what criteria Fay had reduced America, with its immense German, Irish, Italian, Scandinavian and Slavic sub-groups, to an "Anglo-Saxon people." [11] Such sustenance of the "official mythology" was an indication that there would be a hard road ahead for students of the question who desired to penetrate deeper than the level of official statements.

The Seymour-Fay incident in another sense served as a reminder that a cleavage had probably always existed between the liberals on one side and the historians of such influential universities as Yale, Harvard, Columbia and Chicago on the other, whose views regarding the War could be found closer in harmony with the tenor of a publication such as *Foreign Affairs.* A literary scuffle of this kind had occurred before, when Professor Bernadotte Schmitt's *The Coming of the War, 1914* was awarded the 1931 Pulitzer Prize for history as well as the George Louis Beer Prize by the American Historical Association. Harry Elmer Barnes's critical review in the *New Republic* [12] touched off a long argument, which did not come to a halt until the publication late in 1932 of Professor M. H. Cochran's *Germany Not Guilty in 1914.* This book was reviewed most favorably by Barnes [13] and Grattan in the *New Republic* and *Nation* respectively;

and in view of Cochran's observations on the limitations of Schmitt as a researcher and master of German, cast reflections on the historians who had awarded Schmitt such an important prize. Grattan especially attacked Schmitt, claiming his book was one of the most biased studies ever published on the origins of the war, and showed the devotion of the bamboozled writers of war propaganda to their persistent image. He further commended Cochran's damaging examination of Schmitt, exposing his "distortion, mistranslation, ignoring of chronological sequence, use of secondary sources at crucial points where only primary material should be admitted, use of sources long since exposed as worthless and tipping the balance in favor of the Allied side whenever possible." [14]

In this same month of October, 1932 the *Nation* editorially scorched *Foreign Affairs* on its tenth anniversary of publication: "We wish that its editors and backers could face more realistically the facts of the lost World War and free themselves more completely from the war-time ideology," the statement read. In sizing up this expensively-printed quarterly, the *Nation* concluded that a "very strong percentage of contributions" were submitted by "dyed-in-the-wool upholders of the status quo, and from men in high office or distinguished by the conservative point of view." [15]

REVISIONIST PREDISPOSITIONS:

1. CURRENT EVENTS

The *New Republic* took pride in supporting revisionism and what it had done for it since the war had ended. In a two-column editorial reply to a critical letter by Paul Blanshard early in October, 1931, concerning its support of the war while in progress, among other things, it replied: "Whatever may be said of its War record, it [the *New Republic*] certainly has never ceased pointing out the evil results of mistaken war policies and of the peace." [16] Late that year it greeted the awarding of the Nobel Peace Prize to President Nicholas Murray Butler of Columbia University with a raucous reminder of 1917. "Since the war President Butler has been a conspicuous orator for peace," it noted, but added the following dampener: [17]

As president of the Carnegie Endowment for International Peace, President Butler was a sincere advocate of "the war to end war." He accepted the policy of ruthlessness so far as it could be practiced by a noncombatant. His denunciation of Senator La Follette for fulfilling his responsibilities as a statesman, his dismissal of Professor Cattell for exercising his right as a citizen in protesting against the conscription law, remain high water marks of what it was charitable to call wartime hysteria.

The journal was much more enthusiastic over Jane Addams, who had opposed entry into the war, in the same way that it editorially heaped praise on Jeannette Rankin three years later for her resistance to the coming of the war and her tenacious clinging to subsequent discussion of the causes and costs of the war.[18] And it wound up its memorandum by suggesting that it was now apparent, it hoped, even to President Butler, "that the burden of the war under which the world is staggering was vastly increased by throwing the weight of America into the scales of belligerency." In contrast, a few months later, on the announcement of the coming retirement of President Abbot Lawrence Lowell of Harvard, the *Nation* editorially commended him most warmly for defending Professor Hugo Münsterberg "during the insanity of the World War." [19]

Still another change of direction in the academic community was noted when Lewis Corey reviewed Thorstein Veblen's *Essays in Our Changing Order* in the *Nation* in December, 1934. Corey was loud in praise of this book but chose to note that although "Veblen's intelligence broke down in an acceptance of 'the war to make the world safe for democracy,'" there was some virtue attached to the fact that "he indulged in none of the obscene hysteria of the academic war-mongers and he recovered quickly after the peace." [20] In a few short years both Corey and his detested academic personalities were to demonstrate how defenseless and vulnerable they were in the face of a new tidal wave of war hysteria, which was not to be followed by a quick Veblenian "recovery."

One of the most eloquent readers of revisionist history lessons in the *New Republic* was the British socialist H. N. Brailsford, the most frequently published foreign contributor in the liberal papers in the depression years. Brailsford claimed he had both opposed England's going to war and regretted the entry into the war of the United States, this latter event terminating "the hope of a stalemate and a peace without victory." Like the Americans, he considered the wartime idealism a very faint force; "the idealistic motive, however sincerely the masses entertained it, did not influence the belligerent governments, most of which were brought in and kept in by the booty promised in the secret treaties." [21]

In an extended *New Republic* piece on the economic desperation of Central Europe in the spring of 1932 titled "The Battle of the Danube," he placed the responsibility right on the doorsteps of the Great Powers. It was the "mischief" they did at Paris in Balkanizing Central Europe in response to military considerations instead of economics that was the main cause for the distress. In retrospect he saw the old Dual Monarchy as a far superior solution to that dreamed up in 1919. It at least had been a workable economic area of internal trade. But by the time it had been cut up into half a dozen districts with rival currencies and tariffs, and placed in the hands of inexperienced legal and administrative persons, chaos was about the only thing expectable. There was little reason for the exasperation and wonderment now; furthermore, the forces which had tried to form this area into a vast "Mittel Europa" were becoming restive again, a development of "irresistible economic logic." French hegemony here had been an unhealthy experiment, and he warned that the attempt to increase the scope of the disease as a cure would be a serious mistake.[22]

On the *Nation,* the persistence of editor-in-chief Villard in hammering away on the revisionist theme was unsurpassed. The success of Adolf Hitler in German politics sharpened his reminders as to the relation between the war and what was now taking place. Added to his wry remark that we had gone to war to make the world safe for Communism and Mussolini, was the new theme of the German reaction to a dozen years of botchery of Central Europe. But every bit of day-to-day news which could be used to drive home the disillusionment with the war was employed. A few weeks after the 1931 Manchurian incident, President Hoover's Under-Secretary of State William R. Castle delivered in the course of a disarmament speech an attack on World War idealism which matched the revisionist liberals in vigor, and further averred that it was during the war that "the seeds of the depression were sown." The *Nation* editorially in high enthusiasm called Castle's outspoken conduct "true statesmanship," "the kind of courage and truth telling we have a right to expect from men in high office." [23] On the occasion of the death of the well-known British revisionist G. Lowes Dickinson in the summer of 1932, the *Nation* referred to him as "one of England's most unselfish, wisest and high-minded citizens": [24]

An ardent advocate of peace, he had the courage to remain so when war came, not being accustomed to sloughing off his principles and ideals to suit the happenings of the moment.

In reporting Dickinson's death, the *Nation* felt that his course was fully vindicated by events since the Armistice, "especially his opposition to harsh reparations or retaliatory measures against Germany," now that a belligerent regime had acceded to state power.

The *Nation* hurled an especially bitter editorial on the 15th anniversary of the entry of the United States into the World War. Commenting on the big military parade in Washington, it declared in words dripping with scorn:

For ourselves we rather liked the parade—it gave the lie so clearly to the Great Hypocrisy that we won the war to end war; it emphasized so plainly how thoroughly we have become militarized since we went to war to punish Germany for being so militarized.

The editorial concluded by suggesting that the country also ought to remember the vast debt, the 50,000 dead, the legion of wounded still in the hospitals, and the "stranglehold" of the armed services on Congress, as well as the political consequences; "We have earned the hostility of Europe. The only people who speak well of us in Europe are the Germans we fought. Oh, how wise and farsighted we were to go into that war." [25]

In the fall of 1932 Villard promised to support the National Economy League in its drive toward reducing the number of drawers of war pensions, which were described as "only one of the evil results of our entrance into the World War"; "One might almost ask if any war was ever entered into with more superb disregard of inevitable consequences than the United States showed in 1917." [26]

When Associate Justice Owen J. Roberts of the Supreme Court ruled in favor of Germany in the long-drawn-out 1916 "Black Tom" explosion claims case in December and disallowed any collection of damages, the *Nation* went over the substance of the charges carefully and rejoiced in the decision of the umpire. "This decision shows again how foolish the American people were to swallow the tales spread by Allied propagandists and misguided American patriots who wanted only to drag us into war with Germany." [27]

A three-column editorial, "A Farewell to Republicans," was featured in the *Nation* the week Franklin D. Roosevelt was inaugurated, in which the readers were reminded that "the consequences of the World War and the major responsibility of the Democrats for putting the United States into it must not be forgotten," but a qualification was appended which also called to mind that "the Republicans were as eager to make war," and that both parties remained proud of their positions in 1917.[28]

Probably the most astounding thing written by Villard on the subject of war disillusionment and unhappiness with Woodrow Wilson was a full two-page "Open Letter to Colonel House" published on April 5, 1933. It was an epitome of all that had appeared in like vein in the journal for a dozen years, roasting House and Wilson in an almost unbelievable outburst of invective. It was written in the strongest language yet used in denunciation of America's wartime leaders and declared war aims.[29]

REVISIONIST PREDISPOSITIONS:
2 . SOME LITERARY MEN REMINISCE

War veterans whose writing appeared in the liberal journals in the downswing depression years tended to substantiate all the disillusioned attitudes of the liberal revisionist pacifists toward the war. The spirit of *All Quiet on the Western Front* and Walter Owen's almost indescribably depressing *The Cross of Carl* permeated their contributions. Some writers attained impressive heights of expression in putting their reactions to the war in print. The emphasis, in line with the times, was on the "doughboy." Murray Godwin, a contributor to the liberal press quite frequently, wrote a blistering review of *Squads Write,* a volume of selections from the official service newspaper *Stars and Stripes,* which enjoyed freedom from competition. Godwin abused the book as "tripe" and "rubbish," and contributed a bit of confidential material from his own experience. "When I hung my mess kit, early in 1919, beside a double deck bunk in the Caserne Carnot, I found there was one paper not permitted to be sold in camp. That was the Paris edition of the *Chicago Tribune*." Godwin asserted that the reason for this was that the *Tribune* "opened its columns to the beefing of the bucks," and that the authoritative statements about the universal readership of the service paper to the contrary, practically all the men in his barracks "read nothing but the '*Trib.*'" [30]

When James Rorty reviewed *Stepchild of the Rhine* by the Alsatian Oscar Ludmann, he was refreshed by the author's reference to disillusioned German veterans fraternizing with the French at the eastern extremities of the French-German front, both were determined to keep the sector quiet. Rorty was impelled to recall having seen the same thing, remembered the French soldiers "cultivating lettuce and carrots just back of the trenches," and "cursing the recently arrived Americans who insisted upon carrying on the war." [31] This reflected on the blood-lust of America's ally, but William March's *Company K,* although fictional, struck home in the same way to many of those Americans who remembered the war with loathing. Granville Hicks reviewed it with enthusiasm for the *New Republic* and spoke of it as one of the two or three first-rate American novels of the War. But the pessimism and defeatism in the book even depressed Hicks, who felt that it should have closed on a brighter and more rebellious note.[32]

Malcolm Cowley's articles "The Homeless Generations" in the *New Republic* in the fall of 1932 stand as one of the most effective summarizations of the impact of the war on the youths who fought and lived to reject completely all that the war was presumably fought for. Describing the sensation, Cowley remembered nothing particularly noble about it, and had nothing to say about the sentiments expressed by the leaders who remained in America: [33]

School and college had uprooted us in spirit; now we were physically uprooted, hundreds of us, millions, plucked from our own soil as if by a clam-shell bucket and dumped, scattered among strange people. All our roots were dead now, even the Anglo-Saxon tradition of our literary ancestors, even the habits of slow thrift that characterized our social order. We were fed, lodged, clothed by strangers, commanded by strangers, infected with the poison of irresponsibility and unconcern for the future—the poison of travel, too, for we learned that problems could be left behind us merely by moving elsewhere—and the poison of danger, excitement, that made our old life seem intolerable. Then, as suddenly as it began for us, the War ended.

When the war ended, Cowley said, the "sense of relief was too deep to express, so we all got drunk." But the intoxication and the "tears of joy" did not last long, and soon "the composite fatherland" for which they had fought and "in which some of us still believed" dissolved before they realized what was taking place. Then home, "appropriately," thought Cowley, to New York, "the homeland of the uprooted." And presumably, that was the condition in which they still remained.

At this stage no element in America was so convinced that militarism could not be overcome by militarism and war cured by more war. That there was a high degree of unanimity in the evaluation of the steady flow of books referring to some aspect or other of the war when it came from these men is not surprising. The explosion of more war in Asia and South America was not fully appreciated by many liberals, to a great extent due to the fact that they had not yet recuperated from the numbness produced by that of 1914–1918. Every new memoir and special study rang the same alarm bell, and the reviewers tended to rehearse a large part of a story already told many times, and presumably etched so deeply that nothing seemed capable of erasing its outlines.

REVISIONIST PREDISPOSITIONS:

3. DEPRESSION WAR BOOKS IN REVIEW

Lewis Mumford in the course of a review of the third volume of Egon Friedell's *A Cultural History of the Modern Age* in the *New Republic* for January 11, 1933, made a reference to "the dreary insanity of the World War." In many ways the remark was a fair characterization of the overall picture of the event obtainable from a cross-section of American liberals now fifteen years removed. In presenting to the readers of the liberal journals the gist of the histories and memoirs pertinent to the war, the editors rarely neglected the opportunity to get this message across to the public. In the case of Villard of the

Nation and Robert Morss Lovett of the *New Republic* it approached the dimensions of an obsession, but its existence generally, even in the anonymous contributions, is not open to dispute. Even books which sought to defend wartime courses of action or apologistic memoirs were turned into revisionist lessons by the simple act of mentioning the part of the known story omitted, and letting the matter rest in the hands of the third party, the reader.

The treatment of Harold Nicolson's *Peacemaking* is a pertinent case in point. Villard's review was a revisionist masterpiece, as well as an insight into the division in his mind on past and then current Germany. It was the occasion for another savage dissection of Wilson, Lloyd George and the entire Versailles episode. Griffin Barry's examination derived similar conclusions, ending with the conviction the Germans had been the victims of a breach of contract and showing indignation at the treatment of the German delegates penned in a prisoner's stockade until the time had come to sign the treaty.[34]

Lovett examined Mark Sullivan's *Over Here, 1914–1918* largely as a study in sins of omission. Speaking of the war, Lovett seemed quite convinced that "Mr. Sullivan enjoyed it," and that "In his happy retrospect nothing unpleasant" was "'allowed to recur." Lovett thereupon proceeded to recite a substantial number of incidents involving the Debs and Mooney cases, conscientious objectors, the I.W.W., the handling of the Mennonite and Molokan resistants, the internment of German civilians and sundry military and other government departmental scandals sufficiently voluminous to disturb anyone likely to conclude that Sullivan had made a comprehensive examination of the whole home scene during the war years.[35]

The memoirs of William Graves Sharp, Jusserand and Michel Corday, the last mainly a panorama of civilian Paris in the war, which came out during this time, all received prompt attention. The first two were roundly castigated, but Corday's *The Paris Front* impressed Lovett to the degree that he believed it deserved to rank with Barbusse's *Under Fire* and *All Quiet on the Western Front* insofar as it dealt with the subject of "life and death in the trenches." Corday's account of the joy of the civilian population at the outbreak of the fighting and the transition of the hate of the enemy into the virtual hate of peace itself appalled Lovett. The obstinacy of the leaders to a negotiated peace led Corday to remark, "Blood is the milk of old men," which Lovett approved of. Lovett was sure that Corday's picture of the ferocious side of France was a good curative for the romantic portraits of the country which our propaganda had circulated while preparing our own spiritual mobilization for the struggle against the German Beast. In line with this critical tendency was the *Nation*'s comment in mid-December, 1934, on Lord Riddell's *Intimate Diary of the Peace Conference and After* that it completely confuted "the myth that the Allied crusade against Germany was a high minded adventure to save the world from destruction." [36]

Other famous principals in the war received a no less uncomfortable reception. When the Right Honorable Winston Churchill's *The Unknown War: The Eastern Front* appeared, the *Nation,* which already had shown vast disrespect for Churchill and thought up some of the most uncomplimentary language ever bestowed on a wartime figure to describe him on various occasions, reviewed it most unkindly. The reviewer was repelled by Churchill's attempt to justify the fabulous British disaster at Gallipoli on the Turkish front, and after paying tribute to the author's "stirring" prose, declared that the book contained an over-all "repellent obtuseness to human values," and bitterly reproached him for "his venom for revolutionary Russia —the one nation that had the courage to stop fighting." In conclusion it suggested,[37]

Mr. Churchill, if he has occasion to revise his books, should blot out his crocodile tears over the inhumanity of modern war and the collapse of civilization. All his recent statements show continued loyalty to the system that requires inhuman war and is ready to precipitate the ruin of civilization.

A little over a year later, Villard had much kinder words for Frederick Palmer, the chief censor of the American Expeditionary Forces in France, and his volume of memoirs, *With My Own Eyes.* He rejoiced at Palmer's criticism of Wilson, agreed with him that the Allied leaders were "drunk with power whose source they did not understand," complimented him on his part in trying to undo the wartime atrocity stories and trying to keep them out of the American dispatches. Villard also was gratified to see Palmer denounce the League of Nations mandate system as a hypocritical method of restoring Anglo-French colonialism in Africa and the Near East, and he especially noted Palmer's dictum that "To read the Covenant of the League was to break the heart of a practical pacifist." [38]

Lovett had mixed reactions to Professor Joseph Ward Swain's book, *Beginning the Twentieth Century.* Swain's stress on the influence of nationalism and the popular psychology deriving from it, giving to those Lovett called the "warmakers" a potent field for the mobilization of mass support, got extended attention. Swain built a spiral out of armament and "preparedness" or "defense," which incited hysteria, for which the only answer was more "preparedness," in turn precipitating more nervousness, suspicion and fear. All this rested on a foundation of exaggerated national consciousness and the infection of national prestige, cultivated quietly by the elements of the national community in direct line to gain advantage. Lovett recalled the

Mexican campaign preceding United States entry in the War; "a pleasing, harmless rehearsal, with parades, drums, flags, communiqués, war marriages, noble ideals and casualty lists, which thrilled the people with pride and made them eager for more of the same." Lovett considered Swain's account of our entry and participation in the War in accord with the account already familiar, and Swain's judgment that "Wilson and his friends had created a Frankenstein which turned on them and destroyed them" quite correct. But he was slightly subdued by Swain's kindness to the diplomats, his tendency to soften criticism of their actions and his substitution of the whipping up of the primeval instincts of the masses as a stronger force eventually pushing the nations into the world hostilities.[39]

Villard considered Laurence Stallings' *The First World War: A Photographic History* a superior work, and unique in that it made no attempt to separate victors and vanquished, but, instead, made clear incontrovertibly that [40]

the experience of both sides was identical, that the slaughter was as horrible, as inexcusable, and as useless on one side as on the other. If anyone can look through these pages and not feel that the plain people of both sides were crucified needlessly and with fiendish torture, there must be something wrong with him.

Villard did not consider this book as "gruesome" as the pacifist-sponsored *The Horror of It,* a previously-issued and truly sobering photographic memoir of the effects of an industrial war on human bodies. But he urged with some agitation that a copy should be placed "in every household in the United States, certainly in every one in which there is oncoming cannon-fodder for the next wholesale slaughter of humanity." Writing in the summer of 1933, he was already quite sure another war was on its way; "our so-called statesmen have not the brains or the courage to keep us out of war," he raged. Furthermore, there was already under way "a conspiracy to blot out the horrors of the trenches," made possible because men were forgetting them, and discovering at the same time that these same war experiences were a type of asset, on which they could capitalize in many ways. These same men were the ones now "voting for larger armies and navies, and urging complete military preparations for the next struggle." For this reason Villard pleaded that Stallings' book should be put in the schools and that the youth be exposed thoroughly to it, on the assumption that it would increase their propensity to protest their own militarization.

Villard considered the most effective part of this photographic history of the War that which displayed all the belligerents invoking divine aid in their cause. The picture of the rival generals, "war lords", statesmen and soldiers simultaneously praying to the same God for protection and victory, with the assistance of the clergy everywhere, he looked upon with great distaste; "utterly devastating," he commented. There was no reason for wondering why the "Christian church had steadily lost ground" after seeing these pictures; it was irrevocable evidence of "the criminality of the church."

It seemed most appropriate that Professor Ray H. Abrams' *Preachers Present Arms* should be published shortly thereafter. No more damaging volume dealing with the part of the American clergy in supporting and pushing the goals of the War had yet been printed anywhere. The *New Republic* gave it an unqualified favorable review, while pointing out that the peace movements and societies were filled with clergymen once more, but doubted seriously that the churches had "become immune to hatred" and speculated that another "holy war" would find them performing the same function once more. Villard in the *Nation* said of Abrams' book, "This book belongs on the shelf of indispensable volumes for the use of future historians who wish to paint an unbiased picture of what Christian America looked like when it was teaching the Hun Christian virtues and making the world safe for democracy," and in Villard's estimate, *Preachers Present Arms* revealed "the complete moral bankruptcy of the Christian Church, its utter treason to the Prince of Peace, and its intellectual stupidity as well." [41]

When Harper published the religious dissenter Harold Studley Gray's letters under the title *Character "Bad": The Story of a Conscientious Objector* just before the summer of 1934, a *New Republic* review reported, "Young men who want to know what the next war may be like will be interested in this book." [42] There was a timely aspect to this volume as well, in view of the fact that a few months earlier President Roosevelt had granted an amnesty to the 1500 persons convicted of conspiracy to defeat or evade the draft under the wartime selective service and espionage acts. It was one of the few Presidential actions of 1934 which received uninhibited liberal acclaim, and the long struggle for this goal by the American Civil Liberties Union was particularly commended. [43]

As an indication that liberal veteran memories were still an active index to the degree of hostility and resentment to the War still felt in liberal circles, Thomas Boyd's summary of *Soldiers What Next?* by Katharine Mayo in an April, 1934 issue of the *New Republic* was admirable. "Miss Mayo has brought back to an amazing degree all the fine hysterical flavor of propaganda that inundated us during the World War," declared Boyd. The unhappiness of the common soldier and the poor returns from the war for the servicemen compared to the profits presumably made by those who did not fight were thoroughly rehearsed, with Boyd's approval, qualified by quiet words to the effect that he thought he detected the author pleading for Fascism and "the approaching imperialist war." [44]

WHO / WHAT CAUSES WAR?

The liberal interest in revisionism and their implacable pursuit of it regardless of the consequences was not simply concern for historical accuracy or other admirable aims allied to it. The interests of the most persuasive supporters were somewhat mixed. War was truly "the sum of all villainies" to Oswald Garrison Villard, and to many others in varying degrees. Allen Tate, reviewing MacKinlay Kantor's Civil War novel *Long Remember* in the *Nation* summarized the post-war liberal attitude in the fewest words when he stated, "Mr. Kantor tells us that war is meaningless. It is a respectable thesis, and, given the structure of modern society, one that the present reviewer holds." [45] But a cleavage existed in liberal circles as soon as the cause of war entered the discussion. A fairly wide band of agreement could be found on a resolution that war was the worst social evil of the race, yet a controversy would rage when causes and reasons rose to the top of the agenda. Liberal Socialists who were inclined to accept the Soviet Union as the first beachhead of planetary Socialism also reasoned that the Communists had expunged national patriotism and everything connected with it, and would therefore be immune to the pressures which nudged the capitalist democratic nations into war. From this assumption came another: that the Soviet Union alone among the states was genuinely interested in peace as a permanent state of affairs. In all other states there were scheming groups whose anxiety to get another war commenced could be concealed only with great difficulty. The blending of pro-Socialism at home, pro-Sovietism abroad and hostility toward Russia's enemies plus devotion to pacifism were not considered contradictory; rather, were considered different facets of the same world outlook.

As these ingredients began to jell into the shape of the Popular Front in mid-1934 there probably was no more succinct treatment of the entire situation than that by Lewis S. Gannett in his lead-off article, "They All Lied—And Europe Went to War," in the August 8, 1934 *Nation* twentieth anniversary symposium on the outbreak of the World War, "August, 1914." Gannett adhered closely to the revisionist position on the coming of the war, handled the Kaiser very kindly, and treated Poincaré, the Czar and Sir Edward Grey very abusively. Yet in reference to the contemporary scene, he lapsed into harsh attacks on the Hitler and Mussolini regimes, and found only one redeeming feature of the Europe of twenty years later to promise to inhibit the coming of another war: [46]

But there is one important and really encouraging difference between the Europe of 1914 and the Europe of 1934. There is one Great Power today which is bound by no alliances, secret or open, which is genuinely determined not to become involved in a world war which would spell defeat or setback of a domestic program to which it is passionately devoted, a Power which all the other Great Powers in varying degrees hate and fear, Soviet Russia, of course. Soviet Russia is the chief check-rein on Western Europe today.

Thus, while in the act of denouncing the first World War and claiming a title to a position of detachment, the liberal views were slowly turning toward Russia and their holders were quietly enlisting in the Communist cause in preparation for future trouble, should it come their way. By this time all the factors were present which would be needed to establish the "this-time-it's-different" appeal which performed so mightily in selling another world war to those still disillusioned with the first.

Practically no one at this time except possibly Robert Briffault was inclined to discuss the function war might serve in smashing the system which presumably had set war loose and profited so heavily from it. War as an agent of destruction prior to the arrival of the anti-nationalist, anti-capitalist, classless society, sweeping the old structure away and saving the Communists the messy job of "liquidating the irrationalists" was not a subject for proper discussion. No searching inquiry as to the process that had given birth to Russian communism was conducted. It might possibly be said that if the Socialist liberals were willing to condemn the World War as an unmitigated tragedy, a positive qualifying clause might be in order parenthetically due to the part war played in attending the birth pains of Russia in borning Communism, if the question had been phrased in that way. Liberal revisionism had nothing to do with the Russian Communists. They enjoyed immunity in not having carried the war into execution any longer upon seizing the Russian state, besides being responsible for a major revisionist foothold in having exposed to the curious all over the world the contents of the Czar's diplomatic archives. In many ways this was the most important act in turning loose the information which made the first stages of revisionism possible. And it remained the only important diplomatic break-through, as the other Allied powers sat upon their diplomatic files as if made of glue. Thus the motivation of the various revisionist figures differed, as did their goals. Some were satisfied to get the historical record correct, and stressed the diplomatic breakdown prior to hostilities, with a minimum of attention to the whipping up of popular support for war in each nation, in addition to demolishing the "war guilt" thesis and distributing responsibility around among all the participants in varying degrees.

Now that a supposedly anti-nationalist and anti-militarist classless order was in existence, where the inner mechanisms of the other systems necessarily were absent, its defenders could attack the War as the inevitable product of such mechanisms, as special pleading for their erasure and replacement in the respective states with more versions of the presumably more beatific Russian model. Thus the causes of the war to this camp were a mixture of evil individuals and fully as evil practices, all of which it was hoped would be discredited by the sustained and concentrated application of publicity in the form of endless exposure.

Whatever the brand of revisionism, it was inextricably bound with policy matters somewhere or at some point. Correct action was desired by all, meaning action which would lessen but preferably eliminate the possibility of recourse to war again. At this stage, revisionism, pacifism, and socialism began to merge into the outlines of disarmament, and the assault on the debt and reparations burden inherited from the War settlement, in addition to the diplomatic peace machinery, specifically the League of Nations and the Briand-Kellogg Pact. The ensuing mélange created such confusion that one might hazard that few if any were able to thread their way through and maintain a consistent and logical course. The potential obstacles to such clearheadedness were formidable.

From 1932 on, the revisionists of all inclinations had to face the fact that the world was already back to war, if indeed it had ever terminated the holocaust of 1914-1918. Villard, in his momentous open letter to Colonel House in early April, 1933, was of the mind that it had not. In his indictment of House and Wilson he had loudly called, "as a matter of fact, you and Mr. Wilson did not bring about peace at all. . . . the war has steadily gone on ever since." Enough bloody incidents had occurred since 1919 to give Villard's angry call rather substantial supporting testimony. Some of the liberal critics of the World War continued to act and write as if little had transpired since then, that the world had stopped and assumed the appearance of a still-life study after the Paris suburb treaties. But Mukden, the Chaco jungle war between Bolivia and Paraguay, the Leticia incident in northern South America and the desperate nature of German internal affairs all reminded those trying to fashion a comprehensive outlook that the task was an exhausting one. An attitude toward *another* war *now* was needed as well as one toward the last one, which was a somewhat simpler problem in terms of individual choices. Malcolm Cowley's entreaty of Archibald MacLeish as to what he was doing and what attitude he was taking toward the next war was not merely rhetorical. For most of the liberals, the attitude toward the present chaos was tied umbilically to the attitude they had cultivated about the Great War. They possibly subscribed closely to the words of Raymond Leslie Buell in early December, 1931, upon reviewing Hermann Hagedorn's biography of General Leonard Wood: [47]

This generation has learned something of the nature of war. It believes that "to die for one's country" is to die for the benefit of the yellow journalists, the war profiteers and those who seek military glory.

Essentially this summed up one of the prominent attitudes toward all war among the liberals now. Study and reflection of revisionism had resulted in taking this avenue. Jonathan Mitchell expressed the same attitude when reviewing Norman Angell's *The Unseen Assassins* in the *New Republic* June 15, 1932, extending the list of the guilty to include "cabinet officers, diplomats, admirals and generals, egged on by capitalist market hunters and munition makers." Mitchell's controversy with Angell brought this particular approach to war in a head-on collision with a determined and influential group, personified by Angell, who believed this view of war causation to be wrong. But they did not subscribe to the Wilson-Seymour-Fay theory of unmotivated, acausal, impulsive idealism as the deciding factor in precipitation of war.

In the thinking of the Angell element, it was not capitalism or any of the individuals in high rank in capitalist states who were interested in bringing war on, and who consciously schemed to pitch the planet into war continually, because of the rich profits sure to ensue. The business system had nothing to do with it, in their eyes. It was largely to be laid at the door of nationalism and the defective understanding of the populations of these rival national states, so easily galvanized into fury by the stimulation of their latent and ill-concealed ill will toward each other. The quickly aroused feuds and grievances, encouraged by exposure to generations of "lying school history books," as Angell put it, perpetuated defective views of each other, resulting in a "failure of general wisdom," and the global effect was "international anarchy." The cause of war, in other words, applying the Angell diagnosis, was to be located among the people themselves; they were fundamentally at fault for war, not "a little clique of evil 'interests.' "

Angell read Mitchell a long lecture, printed in the *New Republic* three months after the latter's derogatory review, incorporating these and a few other observations.[48] He disparaged the "war is caused by capitalism" theory, and asserted that he saw no reason for its validity since he had spent thirty years discussing this point with "radical and socialist political colleagues," and never heard convincing verification. He still insisted that the true source of war would be found in the political ideas associated with nationalism and "the erroneous thinking of the people as a whole." In regard to the charge of capitalistic profit from war, he admonished Mitchell to look around the world, where capitalism was in ruins, a large part of which disaster was "directly traceable to the War." It might be proven that some capitalists mistakenly encouraged the coming of the war, but that did not prove that the capitalist system profited from it. It simply demonstrated that some capitalists were misguided, and the evidence was lying all about them in the world depression. That "the people don't want war" and that "some interests profit by war" proved absolutely nothing, charged Angell. The people in the Far East did not want cholera, and some interests there profited from cholera; still, few of the people saw the relation "between medieval sanitary conditions and the disease which kills them." In the same way the populaces which insisted on jealous independence and national selfishness, which preferred to do what they wished even if at the expense of neighbors, got the expectable consequences sooner or later in war.

Angell admitted that the Mitchell thesis as to war origins was directly traceable to the postwar peace treaties and the attitudes they hatched. For ten years after, "all realist discussion of the causes of war was rendered impossible by 'the guilty nation' theory," which he frankly considered a fraud and a deception:

The cause of war was Germans. It was easy, simple, provided a scapegoat; kept agreeable passions awake and sent the public mind completely to sleep. There was no problem—nothing for the virtuous non-Germans to do about war except suppress Teutonic wickedness. We are now in danger of substituting for the guilty nation, the guilty class—the Virtuous People vs. the Wicked Capitalist.

The "political left" was making a serious mistake in Angell's estimation in idealizing the "People" and refusing to consider the problem of nationalism and the factors growing out of it. The new line was one of flatly denying that the average run of folk had any responsibility for "revising old ideas or disciplining old passions," the result being that war, which preceded capitalism by an immense span of years, remained untouched as a subject for investigation. The left might better consider the "defective institutions and follies, fallacies and misconceptions common to the great mass of men" as the hiding place of war, instead of pillorying the war profiteers, which gained them nothing.

But Mitchell, in a rejoinder, insisted that there was an entrenched minority which was interested in maintaining this system of "anarchic, sovereign states," and that the main hope was the application of pressure on this minority from the pacifist movement, which "in the United States and Europe is well organized and has millions of men and women among its adherents." In view of the fact that he declared that "With the exception of Russia, there is not a government in the world today which really cares anything about preventing war, if the test be the abandonment of policies which lead towards war," Mitchell was undoubtedly including in his pacifist millions the Soviet population and the world's Communists and their sympathizers. This stood in rather awkward relation to one of Mitchell's subsequent articles on the munitions manufacturers, some months later, in which he blandly mentioned that the largest military air force in the world was the Soviet Union's.

Angell's argument got indirect support from Elmer Davis in a February, 1933 *New Republic* story on the Chaco War,[49] which played heavily on the idea of irrational national sentiments as the dynamism behind this seemingly pointless struggle, described once as "a fight between two bald-headed men over a comb." As Davis commented satirically, "All right-thinking persons know that wars are made by governments composed of Wicked Old Men, against the will of peacefully disposed peoples," and then proceeded to detail the nationalistic excesses of the rival Latin American belligerents. He ridiculed the rival propaganda stories, accusing the enemy of bombing only hospitals and churches, using prisoners to shield attacking troops, maddening soldiers with rum before sending them "over the top," as reflections of the same fables broadcast from Europe fifteen years earlier. The reported suicide of a despairing Paraguayan commander reminded Davis of the similar World War story when "the German Crown Prince used to commit suicide every month or so."

Davis admitted being up against an insoluble problem; "Boundary disputes in which each side appeals to history are at least as old as the war between Jephthah and the Ammonites, and determination of the aggressor is no easier today than when Herodotus and Thucydides tried twenty-five hundred years ago." The Angell thesis stood out prominently when Davis discussed popular reaction:

Only a few things you can be sure of—when the flag has been fired on, crowds will parade the streets singing the national anthem; and that atrocity stories will be sincerely believed on both sides; and that the readiness of governments to talk peace will depend on the news from the front.

What of the League of Nations and the Briand-Kellogg Pact? Davis declared, "the ponderous and intricate international peace machinery" had accomplished "exactly nothing." As long as "a powerful neutral" sympathized with one side, the application of moral pressure was futile. The "Marxian remedy" of "abolition of economic rivalries" he estimated to be mainly tampering with symptoms instead of a bona fide cure, ending on an Angellian note as far as his rumination on the general situation was concerned:

. . . so long as human nature is so constituted that most of us dislike and distrust the people who live on the other side of the mountains, the principal cause of war is still with us. . . . There can be no peace without a will to peace, a readiness to overlook trivial affronts to "national honor," a willingness to settle disputes by arbitration or adjudication, even at the risk of not getting all you want.

It is appropriate to pass on to an examination of the influence of a number of other World War consequences on liberal thinking in the depression 1930's, as areas of both actual and potential policy that evoked additional attitudes which entered the receptacle holding the other ingredients that went to make up the "liberal mind," so to speak. The denunciation of the post-war "reparations" assessments, the drive to curtail armaments and the attitude toward the League of Nations are of next concern.

NOTES

1 *Nation*, October 14, 1931, p. 380. On September 16, 1931, p. 268, the *Nation* had editorially referred to Wilson and Viscount Cecil as "arrogant self-righteous holy men" for having refused to consider the admission of Mexico to the League of Nations at the time of the Versailles peace-making.
2 Max Eastman, "A Significant Memory of Freud," *New Republic*, May 19, 1941, p. 694.
3 Dos Passos, "Meester Veelson," *New Republic*, January 13, 1932, pp. 240–241. This ultimately appeared as part of Dos Passos' book *1919*.
4 *New Republic*, January 20, 1932, pp. 274–275.
5 Letter to *New Republic*, September 12, 1934, p. 133.
6 Grattan, "Colonel House's Self-Defense," *Nation*, December 14, 1932, pp. 588–589.
7 *New Republic*, August 2, 1933, pp. 322–323.
8 *New Republic*, October 11, 1933, pp. 251–252.
9 *New Republic*, August 15, 1934, p. 2, for all quotations on this issue.
10 *New Republic*, September 12, 1934, p. 133, for Hacker's statement and Fay's reply. Hacker's review of Hermann Hagedorn's biography of General Leonard Wood in *Nation* for October 28, 1931 had a strong revisionist viewpoint.
11 *Nation*, November 14, 1934, p. 571.
12 Barnes reviewed this in the *New Republic* for October 22, 1930. On his controversy with Schmitt see also his letter in *New Republic*, March 16, 1932, p. 131.
13 *New Republic*, April 13, 1932, p. 251. Barnes, reviewing Frederick L. Schuman's *War and Diplomacy in the French Empire* in the *Nation* on January 20, 1932, p. 78, described the book as an "advanced revisionist" work, but was puzzled that Schuman should have praised Schmitt's *Coming of the War* in the *Nation* in 1931 when Schuman's own book undermined Schmitt in the most damaging way.
14 *Nation*, October 5, 1932, p. 316.
15 *Nation*, October 19, 1932, p. 341.
16 *New Republic*, October 7, 1931, pp. 209–210.
17 *New Republic*, December 23, 1931, p. 145.

18 *New Republic,* December 26, 1934, p. 177.

19 *Nation,* December 7, 1932, p. 545.

20 *Nation,* December 26, 1934, p. 745. Corey expressed considerable unhappiness over Veblen's persistent anti-Marxism, however.

21 *New Republic,* April 13, 1932, pp. 207–208.

22 Brailsford, "The Battle of the Danube," *New Republic,* May 11, 1932, pp. 343–344.

23 *Nation,* October 14, 1931, p. 378. "We hope every reader of the *Nation* will send his individual thanks to Mr. Castle," the editors concluded.

24 *Nation,* August 17, 1932, p. 135.

25 *Nation,* April 20, 1932, p. 453.

26 *Nation,* October 5, 1932, p. 298.

27 *Nation,* December 28, 1932, p. 629.

28 *Nation,* March 8, 1933, pp. 249–250.

29 Villard, "An Open Letter To Colonel House," *Nation,* April 5, 1933, pp. 364–365.

30 Godwin, "Tardy Souvenir," *New Republic,* December 2, 1931, p. 76.

31 *New Republic,* October 28, 1931, p. 306.

32 *New Republic,* March 1, 1933, p. 81.

33 Cowley, "The Homeless Generations: II—Ambulance Service," *New Republic,* November 2, 1932, p. 328, and for subsequent quotations.

34 Villard in *Nation,* October 18, 1933, pp. 451–452; Barry in *New Republic,* October 11, 1933, pp. 247–248.

35 In Lovett, "Five New Books About Our America," *New Republic,* December 13, 1933, pp. 140–143.

36 Sharp review unsigned, *Nation,* March 8, 1933, p. 267; *What Me Befell* (Houghton, Mifflin, 1932) by J. J. Jusserand reviewed by Villard, *Nation,* January 3, 1934, p. 23; Corday reviewed by Lovett, *New Republic,* March 14, 1934, p. 137, titled "The Happy Non-Combatants." Note on Riddell in *Nation,* December 12, 1934, p. 679.

37 *Nation,* June 29, 1932, pp. 733–734.

38 *Nation,* February 7, 1934, p. 163.

39 Lovett, "The Historian's Last Chance," *New Republic,* October 4, 1933, pp. 217–218.

40 Villard, "War-Mad World," *Nation,* August 9, 1933, pp. 162–163, for this and subsequent quotations from review of this book, in paragraphs below.

41 *New Republic* review on Abrams, unsigned, February 14, 1934, p. 27; Villard's in *Nation* on July 25, 1934, pp. 108–109.

42 *New Republic,* June 20, 1934, p. 164.

43 *Nation,* January 10, 1934, p. 30.

44 *New Republic,* April 4, 1934, pp. 221–222.

45 *Nation,* April 11, 1934, pp. 420–421.

46 Entire symposium on pp. 149–155 of *Nation,* August 8, 1934.

47 Buell, "The Last Proconsul," *New Republic,* December 9, 1931, pp. 111–112.

48 Citations from the Angell-Mitchell argument below from *New Republic,* September 21, 1932, pp. 153–155.

49 Davis, "Paradigm in Paraguay," *New Republic,* February 22, 1933, pp. 38–41, for all citations in subsequent paragraphs.

5

LIBERAL POLICY POSITIONS AND

WORLD AFFAIRS, 1931–1935

Years before the world dispensation of 1919 began to crack up, most liberals had decided to turn their backs on it and its ideals. The full consequences of war revisionism and general disillusionment with the war in all its aspects made this apparent by the time the world depression was well under way. Even the outbreak of war in Asia and the signal of Europe's new look in the person of Adolf Hitler produced only minor changes in these attitudes, even though a conflict did present itself for solution that eventually required another major reversal.

Liberal sentiment was overwhelmingly in favor of eradicating all the evidences of the War as they still continued in policy form. They were for cancellation of all the war debts owed on the inter-Allied level, on the grounds that payment could never take place. In addition to this, they favored ending the reparations payments being extracted from the losing Central Powers, Germany primarily. As part of this same approach of magnanimity, they favored a revision of the Versailles treaty agreements in a sweeping manner. As accessory to this, the firm conviction that the League of Nations had turned out to be mainly an instrument for the enforcement of Franco-British policy had persuaded the liberals to oppose American participation, and furthermore to enter into no collective security or alliance agreements which called for the application of any pressure greater than moral condemnation and boycott of the offender. Additional elements of liberal desires involved a full commitment to the idea of world pacifism and a loud call for world disarmament, which in America took an additional spiral resulting in a strident demand for the ending of the manufacture of arms by private companies and the absolute prohibition of the sales of munitions of war by the United States to any other country. As an adjunct to international agreement on disarmament, debt cancellation and reparations, it was considered highly advisable that the world economic problems be met through world conferences, with no recourse to the use of any kind of coercion.

DEPRESSION REACTIONS TO WAR DEBTS AND REPARATIONS

One of the few actions taken by President Herbert Hoover which got the unstinted acclaim of the *Nation* was the famous moratorium, the one year suspension on the collection of debts owed the United States incurred by the Allies in the World War. An article in the July 1, 1931 issue was headlined, "President Hoover's Great Action," and proceeded to praise it as the act which constituted "the most far-reaching and the most praiseworthy step taken by an American President since the treaty of peace." That a statement could be phrased this enthusiastically about a President subjected to almost continual abuse on the subject of domestic issues testifies to the strong feeling against the whole matter of financial and material settlements which had been inherited since the treaties of the Paris suburbs. The *Nation* considered this the sign that America had gone back into European affairs, "This time not as in 1917 to make the European situation worse and to postpone for a year and a half the arrival of peace," but now for "pacific and constructive" purposes which were hoped would point to "the direct road toward the restoration of normal conditions abroad." Hoover's action was taken to mean that the United States again was taking "the moral leadership of the world." [1]

In the *Nation*'s opinion, the country was "for once" approaching the nations of Europe "in a spirit of friendship and brotherliness, in that spirit of helpfulness and readiness to aid even at a personal sacrifice," which the editorial believed was "characteristic of the American people in foreign affairs." This credo sharply contradicted other judgments about America abroad, especially in Latin America, which were never this generous, but it was important as an index to the liberal dislike of the whole debt affair, and one could read in between the lines the fervent hope that the payment system would never be resumed.

Liberal centers understood that the moratorium was Hoover's admission that the stand taken by his Democrat opponents was correct, namely, that the war debts and reparations being extracted from the vanquished were part of the same entity. Although the liberal press noted a quick cooling-off among the Democrats as soon as Hoover began an earnest investigation of the whole debt-reparation matter, in view of the impasse rapidly materializing in Europe, mainly in Germany, they did not leave any doubt that they thought the same. The liberal villain in this episode was France. The French were the recipients of many sharp words during these days, mostly for their stubborn refusal to consider either disarmament or the cancellation of the reparations being exacted from Germany. Liberal views on such behavior were quite dark, and the columns of the liberal journals were far from complimentary to the French as a result.

In view of the fact that 1932 was the year scheduled for both reparations and disarmament conferences in Switzerland, Hoover's act on the debts rounded out the picture as it hung over from 1919, although the Japanese added another element with their Manchurian action a few months later, scrambling the scene up completely and adding complexities to already top-heavy complexity.

The *New Republic* and *Nation* openly sided with Senator William Borah when he charged that France was the main barrier to European rehabilitation by its demand of full reparations payment from Germany, maintenance of the strict sanctity of the Versailles settlements, and retention of their present armaments to the last cartridge.[2] On the eve of the reparations gathering, the *New Republic* declared, "The first essential in any possible German recovery is a permanent cessation of reparations payments," and freely granted that no German government of any conceivable sort could be expected to take any other position.[3] With the economy of mid-Europe in shambles, largely due to German collapse, the recovery of Europe without Germany was considered most unlikely. Various liberal figures strongly pressed for cancellation of the whole structure. In January, 1932 John Maynard Keynes wrote for the *New Republic* an article, "Britain For Cancellation," which announced a strong plea for the cancellation of all debts and reparations as a step toward ensuring the continuation of peace, and a reassurance to the Brüning government in Germany.[4] That a political upheaval in Germany was imminent was no secret, and as the months of 1932 slipped by, the attack on reparations at times got stronger than that on the debts.

The French case was interpreted variously. At one time the French were considered adamant against the ending of reparations because of the legal title they had acquired at Versailles, and to yield on this issue was considered too dangerous to the maintenance of the treaty settlements in other respects, especially the boundaries and the new small states carved up at Versailles, all comfortably in a French orbit. As the Lausanne reparations meeting approached, a *New Republic* editorial guessed that the French might be willing to trade cancellation of the reparations and accept disarmament in exchange for a cast-iron pledge of a free hand in Central Europe; plus a guarantee that all the ambitions to revise the Versailles Treaty would be abandoned, then there was the possibility of a bit of horse-trading. The French were trying to "establish permanently French supremacy on the Continent at whatever temporary cost," which was interpreted to mean "a dominating position in German industry and Central European trade." For these, the others might be traded.[5]

The temperature attending the *Nation*'s handling of the issue was somewhat warmer on occasion. The February 3, 1932 editorial, "Nearing the Abyss," was a powerful attack on the delay in coming to an agreement for the abatement of both debts and reparations. It was especially hostile to Laval, Herriot and other French nationalists for their adamant stand rejecting both without a security guarantee from the United States, as well as to Stimson for his warning to the "debtor nations" to abstain from forming a "united front" on the question. In the *Nation*'s opinion, this question was at the core of the world depression now. Again, early in May, it launched an editorial call for United States cancellation of the war debts if accompanied by an Allied *quid pro quo* in the form of a cancellation of German reparations.[6]

As the Lausanne reparations conference was about to start its sessions, the liberal press had concluded that the European powers would be acting alone on the problem. They had given up hope that Hoover would follow up on his moratorium with a frank precipitation of the entire war debt matter as accompaniment to the reparations discussions. A few "barking dogs" in Congress had frightened him, the *New Republic* concluded in a long editorial the last week of June, 1932. It commented favorably on a still more recent suggestion by Keynes on the question, this time quoting from the London press, which suggested that the Lausanne conferees reduce reparations to a mere token, and then move to Washington, inform America what they had done, and ask that the same thing be done on their behalf with respect to the inter-Allied debts. The editorial considered it a disgrace that Europeans should be taking the initiative in this affair, when it was obviously a job for Hoover and the United States government, regardless of the fact that we were the creditor, not the debtor. Our own economic recovery was in the balance as well as theirs, and the welfare of all depended on an across-the-board wiping-out of both reparations from Germany and Franco-British debts to the United States.[7]

Though the Mussolini regime was one of the most detested political administrations in the world in liberal eyes, an odd note was struck in stories on Lausanne, in which Italy won high praise for having the only delegation there which "dared to demand that the financial slate be wiped clean"; "The Italians courageously enough . . . have urged that cancellation be applied equally to all European Powers, creditors and debtors, of reparations and war debts." [8] In an April 20, 1932 editorial the *Nation* claimed that [9]

The soundest, most outspoken, and most realistic statement of international policy by any leading nation in the present crisis has come, of all places, from the Grand Council of Fascism. The Council has put Italy on record with five demands; (1) complete renunciation of reparations and cancellation of war debts; (2) the modification or abolition of oppressive customs barriers; (3) the remedying of conditions in the Danubian and Balkan states; (4) the revision of the peace treaties that are creating the present unrest and may provoke future wars; (5) an end to too frequent international conferences.

For these clear statements of position it was thought that Fascist Italy deserved "at least to be congratulated upon the clarity and courage of its statement of aims." Regardless of the hedging which was going on among the other powers, the *Nation* felt that the whole reparations system, "the barren principles as well as the unmet payments," would have to go. The French were the most reluctant, for sure, what with Versailles and "the status quo in Europe" sure to be badly shaken up by any concessions, but the liberal editorial was confident that "Even the French may have to recognize in the end that the economic security of Germany is just as essential to the peace of Europe as is the political security of France." [10]

Both the *Nation* and *New Republic* hailed the final scaling down of reparations to a small fraction of the original assessment with great joy. The former felt shame that the settlement had been made without the slightest contribution from America, and it urgently called upon the administration to scale down the debts; failure to act accordingly would merit us "the world's ill will and hatred for years." [11] In the *New Republic* the event prompted a long editorial, "The End of Reparations." Great satisfaction was expressed that the "preposterous" reparations figures had been scaled down to such an insignificant sum, and a loud call was made that our action follow promptly, consisting of a similar reduction of the debts. It now was noted that most of the American politicians had stopped talking in terms of the Siamese twin relationship of these two circumstances, and grim jaws were being thrust forward in assertion that the debts would have to be paid, come what may. In conclusion it delivered a few barbs at the critics who had suggested the Allies turn over to us a few West Indian islands in exchange for washing out the debt; just an opportunity to "gain a few more subject islands to govern badly, and at great expense to our pocketbooks and prestige." The wry closing sentence pondered: "What a bitter joke it would be if, having fought to make the world safe for democracy, we should finally come out with the sole booty of one or two of the lesser Antilles." [12]

TRACING THE WAR DEBT SERPENTINE
TO REPUDIATION

With the Hoover moratorium elapsed and the time for war debt payment resumption drawing near, the subject returned to the press of the nation, with liberal figures not a mite reluctant in continuing their persistent challenge. The *New Republic* declared in the fall of 1932 that it could see "opinion in the United States is slowly coming about to the position long held by the *New Republic*—that while these payments are legally and morally due, they must either be cancelled in their entirety or substantially reduced, because of their economic absurdity." The election was now over (November 23), and a note was made to the effect that Hoover had invited the President-elect to a consultation on the debt question, but little was expected from it.[13] Two weeks later the *Nation* headed an attack on both Hoover and Roosevelt "Know-Nothingism Wins." It smartly cracked both for their war debt stands, and singled out FDR for an acid comment on his repudiation of the Democrat stand of years back to the effect that debts and reparations were inseparable. His flat statement that there was no relation "whatsoever" was greeted by the rejoinder: "Few statements could be farther from the truth," and warned that "the attitude of both President Hoover and of Governor Roosevelt reveals an evasion of responsibility and of leadership that must arouse the deepest concern." [14]

A pre-Christmas Congressional proposal, headed by Kenneth McKellar of Tennessee, that a system of reprisals be adopted for application to debt defaulters, was scored in a blunt *Nation* editorial in the issue for December 28, 1932 as an incitation to more European hatred. The "ruins of our prestige and our international friendships" was indeed a "melancholy sight," instructive enough to almost tempt the *Nation*, "since we opposed American entry into the World War and were certain that it could only mean disaster, to stress the hollowness of friendships cemented by blood and founded on a mutual enterprise of mass murder." [15]

When the French Chamber of Deputies voted to default on their December 15 debt installment, the *New Republic* ran a long unsigned editorial, pointing out that the French had just as good an excuse for not paying as Congress had for demanding it. The American moratorium of 1931 had stopped reparations receipts from Germany. When French Premier Laval had visited Hoover shortly after, the understanding they gathered was that if the reparations mess were straightened out by the European nations, they could expect United States cooperation on the debts. The Lausanne meeting had taken care of reparations, but there had been no reciprocal action from America on debts; thus, no reparation, no debt payments. Said the journal, "How do they justify their determination not to pay? It is a perfectly simple train of logic, going back fifteen years. Germany caused the War, and Germany should pay for it. . . . No American . . . ought to blame the French public for not understanding why they could not collect from Germany. Nor can many Congressmen claim exemption from the delusion of German responsibility for the War." [16]

Robert Morss Lovett followed this with a long study in the first issue printed in 1933, "Forgive Us Our Debts," [17] with still another persuasive apologia for the debtors, this one arguing that we were partially responsible for reparations in the first place. Lovett rehearsed the culminating months of the war, when Germany capitulated on the basis of a pre-Armistice agreement with this country that the peace would be based on the Fourteen Points and subsequent Wilsonian utterances, among which was an express condemnation of "punitive damages." This had been sabotaged at Paris, "in spite of the eloquent and cogent arguments of Mr. John Foster Dulles" on behalf of honoring the understanding.

Lovett further asserted that there was a close association between debts and reparations from the beginning; that the Allies had deliberately assessed high reparations because they did not have time to study Germany's actual ability to pay, and were afraid of underestimating it, thus leaving a gap between what they would have to pay to the United States and what they might get from Germany.

In addition to these factors, Lovett charged that the Versailles "war guilt clause" was of partial American manufacture, a "dogma evolved by a commission which included in its membership Secretary (of State) Lansing and Mr. James Brown Scott, secretary of the Carnegie Endowment for International Peace," and that Scott had quoted Lansing as asserting that "the evidence of this moral crime against mankind is convincing and conclusive." Lovett derided them for their part in this; "That the representative of the United States originally took a leading part in affirming this stupid falsehood, one so utterly at variance with the spirit of the terms submitted to the world by Mr. Wilson in January, 1918, so subversive of future peace for the world, is a burden which falls heavily upon the American people. . . ."

Thus it was time that this specious line, that there was no connection between war debts and reparations, should be abandoned by American politicians, even if it had been clung to from Wilson to Roosevelt. The failure to keep their Allies in line at Paris and keep their pre-November 11 word to the Germans, added to the part contributed to the war guilt fantasy, "transferred the whole matter of financial settlement to a realm of unreality and mysticism in which intelligence fails to operate." Lovett agreed with Hoover that the War was directly responsible for the state of the world, but that the full bill had not yet been paid by this country:

In the War, the United States paid cheerfully for the blunders of its commanders with the lives of its men. It will pay with its dollars for the blunders of its statesmen, if not cheerfully, at least, it may be hoped, with a stoical acceptance of its obligations to purchase one element of the peace which our representatives failed so signally to make at Paris.

Other voices occasionally heard in the liberal press were not so kind as Lovett. In the *Nation* Paul Anderson professed to be in opposition to remitting a penny of the French debt. He maintained the French had loaned much of the money borrowed from us to their Polish, Rumanian and Yugoslav satellites, to be used for the purchase of armaments from French manufacturers. There were no French suggesting they cancel any debts to these three powers; "The Poles and Rumanians and Yugoslavs will be eating shoe buttons for huckleberries before France forgives them a dime." [18] Anderson pointed out in great indignation that a few days after the French had defaulted on their debt installment to the United States, they began work on a new battle cruiser, costing nearly one-fourth more than the debt installment, and approved of a loan to Austria almost as large.

Anderson agreed with Hiram Johnson that if debt relief was to be given the French and others, the heavily mortgaged and indebted American farmers and workers were entitled to similar advantages.[19] Irving Brant, then an editorial writer for the St. Louis *Star* and *Times,* published in the *New Republic* a satirical attack on the whole subject titled "A War Debt Catechism," with particular antagonism aimed at the French. An idea, largely a product of French imagination, he said, had been formed which maintained that its debt payments to the United States should consist only of German reparations, and that France suffered from the delusion that what had been loaned her during the war was "a gift to make the world safe for democracy." [20]

The handling of the debt problem by President Roosevelt was no more satisfactory in liberal eyes than by Mr. Hoover. The *Nation*, commenting on FDR's refusal to commit himself on the debt, prior to inauguration, showed "almost pathological fear" of saying anything that meant anything, and had "hardly covered himself with glory." [21] Following the twists and turns of the debt discussions between England and the United States in the first six months of the first term was an agonizing experience for the liberal editors, and they on occasion demonstrated great pique at the fuzziness and vagueness with which the situation was met. To them, the only possible position the British could take was that of requesting debt reduction on a pro rata basis to the already shrunken reparations. This would amount to a slash of over ninety percent, which they were sure the Congress would reject, whatever the President did about it.[22] But they approved of such a cut, and were sure that the British would follow the French into default if this was not done. For a short time, prior to the inaugural, liberal hopes were high that FDR would support such a solution, but this wishful thinking soon vanished. No change took place, and Roosevelt's course became harder to follow by the week.[23] As the London Conference met in session, and in knowledge that the war debt question would not be on the agenda, criticism began to pour out. Roosevelt's attitude toward the war debts and reparations was subject to a strong attack in the *New Republic* of June 21, in which an editorial called it the "least admirable part of his administrative policy."

In September came Villard's block-buster, "Six Months of Franklin D. Roosevelt," in which he charged that the problem had gotten worse under FDR's hesitant direction than it ever had been before.[24] It was slowly starting to dawn upon the world-view-minded liberals that the President was almost wholly immersed in the domestic situation and considered the debt-reparations item a pesky side issue. With the tariff wall there as a barrier to European goods, payment of such a debt was becoming evidently impossible, since the only manner practicable would be the shipping to America of a larger volume of goods than the debtors received in return. But with upwards of twelve million without work in America, and unsold inventories of domestic products an unceasing nightmare, acceptance of more goods was the most unlikely course of action. By the late spring of 1934, the liberals began to conclude that whatever the Administration might say was bound to be evasive.[25]

The passage of the Johnson Debt Default Act at the same time gave the liberals much more than a hint of policy. This was greeted with great indignation and expressions of expectation that the entire war debt claims of some eleven billions of dollars would all be lost now, instead of a token payment of a fraction in one final installment. The breakdown of the debt conversations with the British in June was noted with regret, and the President's war-debt message commented upon, with considerable bleakness, in the *New Republic* for June 13. The conclusion reached in the *Nation* at the same time, was that "Mr. Roosevelt thinks exclusively in political terms," and "Since his domestic program is far more important in his eyes than any temporary disturbance of our relations in Europe, more important even than the possible stimulation of our foreign trade, the question of debts must be subordinated to the more pressing realities at home." [26]

By late June the liberal papers, having followed Roosevelt around every bend and curve since months before his inauguration, were sure he had no understanding of the war debt-reparations question, and simply changed from day to day "in a rather happy-go-lucky manner." They noted that his casual suggestion that the British might make their payments in goods and services had been abruptly dropped. The injury to American producers of goods and furnishers of services, *e.g.* shipping, was surely in line; serious damage loomed should this policy be adopted. The suggestion that Bermuda or Jamaica be ceded to us as settlement was brushed off as "fantastic." In summary, the *New Republic* laid a wreath on the whole debt question tomb by noting that "neither Great Britain or any other debtor now cares in the least whether anything more is paid on the debt. Our suggestions for compromise are just about ten years too late." [27] The finality of the whole matter can be gathered from noting the contribution of a new *Nation* editor, Raymond Gram Swing, in the November 21, 1934 issue of the periodical, titled "Issues Before the New Congress." The term "foreign affairs," and anything else even remotely related to the rest of the world were conspicuously missing.[28]

THE DISARMAMENT TRAIL TO REARMAMENT

It is one of the ironies of our century that Asia should explode at the very moment when the call for disarmament in the Western world reached perhaps its most insistent peak. That the rumblings from the Orient should be so effectively dampened and that the disarmament gatherings should be conducted so doggedly is a testament to the determination to come to some positive and heartening understanding about the issue of arms and their relation to war as an instrument of national policy. Disarmament was one facet of a multi-sided question, which in addition consisted of a drive for significant revision of the Versailles treaty, the cancellation of all debts and reparations inherited from that treaty, and territorial adjustments in the frontier areas which the treaty-makers had created while Balkanizing Europe, presumably on behalf of the principle of "national self-determination." It was almost physically impossible to separate these matters into distinct pigeon-holes, and characteristic of the situation was the tendency for all these matters to come up whenever one of them presumably was mainly the topic at hand. Over all these hovered the League of Nations, the peace machinery ostensibly put in business to supervise the harmonious conduct of the very states which were now beginning to raise their voices in shrill criticism, as the economic collapse added its mighty weight to help the friction between the states become intolerable.

In the 1932 election in the United States, the Socialist Party had adopted a pre-election platform which included among other things a plank supporting the idea of complete abolition of all war debts and reparations, provided that in so doing none of the money saved by any state was released for spending on armaments. This position was largely that of the liberal press and its most prominent contributors as well. It partially explains the vigorous pushing of cancellation and disarmament simultaneously. But disarmament talk had reached substantial heights before any decisions had been made seriously to consider cancellation.

At its inception the League of Nations had committed its members to disarm as a corollary to the disarmament imposed upon the defeated powers. Despite the Washington and London Naval Conferences, the Four and Nine Power Pacts and the ultimate in pacts, the Briand-Kellogg moral commitment against recourse to war in the future except for the purpose of self-defense, the planet still bristled with bayonets at the time of the business collapse in the fall of 1929. Organized pacifism had persisted in working for an arms-free world, with little success. Arms competition had been a major industry and continued to be, but the depression brought the matter up for sharp moral condemnation. Justifying vast arms spending at a time when unemployment and deprivation were so widespread was harder than usual, and concerted pressure everywhere, in varying degrees, brought about the decision to hold a major disarmament conference in Geneva, under League auspices, in February, 1932.

In 1931, disarmament speeches had begun to proliferate, with calls from all quarters. Just a few weeks after the Manchurian incident, former American Ambassador to England and Germany Alanson B. Houghton delivered a notable pacifist speech in Mecca Temple, New York City, at a meeting presided over by Nicholas Murray Butler. Houghton lauded the ill-armed small states of Europe, denounced competitive armament races, and strongly suggested that the United States disarm regardless of what might transpire at Geneva among the League members. Houghton's villain was France, which he claimed was the main obstacle to any comprehensive disarmament in

Europe.[29] A voice in favor of disarmament was heard from another corner, Benito Mussolini. Italy's Il Duce was responsible for a strong statement in approval of the Geneva meeting, and through his foreign secretary, Dino Grandi, issued a plea that an "armament truce" prevail in 1932 while the convention was in progress. The liberal press greeted these two supporters of cutting back arms stock-piling with equal approval, although Mussolini's regime represented the lowest point of esteem possible to achieve in liberal eyes in 1931.

But the demon in the disarmament tangle was not Mussolini. Although liberals had made an indoor sport out of deriding the strutting and bellicose talk in Italy, Italy fared very well at their hands in the assaying of credit for supporting disarmament. The almost sole target was France. Months before the Conference opened, the liberal press discussed the French obstinacy and reacted to it most indignantly. The theme of French sabotage of disarmament continued in the liberal press from before the inception of the talks until the whole conference gradually sagged to its knees of its own unresolved weight in 1934. Even after two German governments had successively fallen and had been replaced by the violently hated Hitler regime, bitterness toward the French persisted.

On February 3, 1932 the *Nation* published a lengthy and dispassionate discussion of the conflict of interests likely to break loose at the Conference by David M. Wainhouse, former assistant director of research for the Council on Foreign Relations. He investigated two main theories, the "wars-cause-arms," and the "arms-cause-wars" interpretations, the logic of the former calling for "security" and that of the latter for "disarmament." The latter, which was the theory entertained by the author and most of the liberal writers as of 1932, advanced the idea that arms were the disease and war the symptom. Therefore getting rid of the arms was the basic step. Three years later there was a powerful drive toward adopting the opposite view, underlined by the strident call for "collective security."

In accord with the "arms-cause-wars" theory, however, the *Nation* interpreted the behavior of Japan; "A disarmed Japan would never have made the onslaught upon Manchuria and Shanghai; it would have sought redress for wrongs in a humane and decent way through the League of Nations, the World Court, or a friendly and sympathetic diplomacy." [30] Forgotten for the moment was the fate of the Austro-German customs union proposal at the hands of the Allied-dominated World Court and other attempts to adjust the post-1918 world. But a vague suspicion of the French had not entirely melted in the face of this moment of elevated generalization.

Even before the first gathering of the Conference, a *New Republic* editorial at Thanksgiving time of 1931 suspected the French would try to use it in an attempt to further "arrange Europe to her own plans," [31] and predicted even before the first meeting was held that the French had no intention of disarming or permitting any revision of the Treaties. Overall, the liberals rarely considered the Conference except with some misgivings, even when at their optimistic peak. The oppressive weight of their interpretation of French policy and assumption of French strategy never let up enough to permit them the luxury of a forthright cheerful stand throughout the sessions. With the exception of a temporary flash of brightness in the summer of 1932, after President Hoover's proffer of an independent plan, darkness tended to characterize their outlook, and in a singular way their suspicion that nothing much would come from it was vindicated with interest. Like their observations on the war debts, the sincere suggestions for disarmament came long after they could possibly have had any effect.

The Conference had hardly gotten under way when a *New Republic* editorial comment [32] on the French proposal to the League for an international military force indicated the degree of distrust of the French. The comment scalded the French as being mainly responsible for the absence of such a small "world police force," internationally controlled and created for use against "bandits and pirates." If any such body had ever been attempted prior to this time, the French surely would have used it "to supplement her own strength in maintaining the injustices fastened upon Europe by the treaties of 1919." In retrospect the editorial considered it a good thing that there had never been any such force, or it would have been used against any states "dissatisfied with the present French dominance." The liberals at this point exhibited a stark hardheadedness and frowned on the use of collective pressure for the benefit of one partner. Europe run to the advantage of the French had no more virtue than an America run for the best interests of Mexico, and all the emotional and moral ejaculations aside, the likelihood of such a body being run in the interests of some to the disservice of others was well understood. The conviction that the French were aware of this was not left implied; "She has never seen the League as anything else than a useful device to pull her chestnuts out of the fire for her," was the blunt tally of this episode. The *Nation*'s reception of this French proposal was even frostier; "The French proposal for an international police force composed of the heavier armaments members of the League of Nations is the *reductio ad absurdum* of the attitude that armed force keeps the peace." The editorial rejoiced that it was getting no serious attention.[33]

A *Nation* editorial on February 24, "Who Wants to Disarm?" [34] had much the same approach. It denounced the French proposals as "hypocritical," and flared: "France has been denounced ever since the War as a militaristic country. The French now wish to get out from under this censure, not by reducing armaments, but by sharing with the rest of the world the responsibility for maintaining a huge war machine." It went on to certify that "international morality" was on Germany's side in reproaching the Allies for failing to honor their word since 1918, promising to disarm, and it expressed grave doubt that the other major powers except Russia, and possibly Italy, were really in favor of any disarmament. Of the Reds the *Nation* alleged, "They can disarm because they have better things to do than fight." [35]

Another *New Republic* pre-Conference summary concluded that the entire Versailles settlement of Europe would collapse at once if any disarmament took place. The states of Central Europe which had been shored up by French military might, once they lost the assurance of this, would have to come to terms with their large and proximate neighbors, who had been left out of the first shuffling. The prediction was made that if any real cutting down of France's army or the navies of the United States and England took place, a fundamental re-structuring of Central Europe and the Far East would follow, with Germany and Japan emerging as the strong nations in these two spheres. For this reason the cold confidence in the failure of the Conference remained. Parallel arms reductions would simply result in relief for the rival governments' budgets anyway, and no alleviation of the "imperialistic, greedy policies and plottings" which required the armies and navies to support them. But a frosty warning was forthcoming: "Diplomaticos might remember that if the present Geneva Conference fails, it will almost certainly be a long time before another disarmament conference is called—perhaps not unitl after the next war." [36]

Four months later in the same journal, H. N. Brailsford reiterated the theme of futility in a long and caustic article, "The End of the Versailles System." Brailsford maintained that not disarmament but the future status of Germany should have been the discussion topic. German demands for a scaling down of armaments to her level on the part of the other nations, if ignored, would surely be followed by wholesale repudiation of the Versailles limitations. It was Brailsford's interpretation that "In 1919 the victors were, in vengeful retrospect, disarming the Germany of the Hohenzollerns: what in fact they disarmed and humiliated was the Republic. Its very life is now at stake." For the French, it was the end of the road. Without German reparations payments the level at which they were armed could never be maintained, since this was where reparations money had been going for years. And if they accepted arms equality with Germany, which was backed by a larger population and superior industrial potential, their advantage would be gone also. Of course, there might be the possibility that "the two neighbors could embark on a wholehearted policy of economic collaboration, throw down tariff walls and work together for the consolidation of all Europe." But this was set aside, due to conditions prevailing in French politics. As far as he could see, Brailsford concluded on the melancholy note that "There is no will to disarm. To that fact one can adjust oneself: it is not precisely novel. But the German problem remains, and it spells the end of an epoch and the liquidation of the Versailles system." [37]

The *Nation*'s equivalent of Brailsford was M. Farmer Murphy, foreign correspondent of the Baltimore *Sun,* and he exceeded the former in fulmination against the French, whose suggestions at the Conference he jeered at as "medieval" and as evidence of serious national deterioration: [38]

In view of the everlasting boast about "French logic," it is strange that French policy is so shortsighted. France is always exalting the League, invoking its various powers, and urging it as the proper instrument in international settlements. Yet most of the failures of the League, most of its disappointments, have been the result of secret French intrigue. If France sincerely believes in the League, the only way to strengthen it is to have it deserve public confidence. It will never have that so long as French machinations continually seek to twist its operations (and too often succeed in it) into the promotion of particular national interests, into the services of greedy enterprises, and into the vindictive perpetuation of injustices. French politicians are forever shouting about "security," but if they were as intelligent as they profess to be they would know that fairness, magnanimity, and neighborliness are a better protection than the greatest army that could be raised.

Murphy followed with another sharp attack three weeks later. In his "Courage Wanted at Geneva" he again blasted the French actions, as well as the emerging British delegation, in the absence of the Italian Grandi and the German Brüning. "The lead has been taken by Sir John Simon of England, who oozes unctuous phrases of indirection, and by Tardieu and his Slav and Balkan stoolpigeons," he reported resentfully.[39]

Editorial policy followed Murphy's reportage from the scene. A March 16 editorial hammered the French for trying to revive once more their Danubian Confederation of 1925, "in the hope of consolidating its political grip on the Balkans and Central Europe," and openly charged them with having provoked the Austrian Creditanstalt collapse deliberately, to push Germany into bankruptcy and Europe into crisis. "Now France is again at work, seeking as in former years to add an economic *cordon sanitaire* to its political wall around Germany." But the editorial predicted that this was a flimsy hope, that German economic ties were too big and important in the Balkans and Central Europe, that France was unable to take the products of this area, and could only use political and economic pressure to keep these regions in line.[40]

Reaction to official American steps or suspected steps varied. The *Nation* feared that Secretary of State Stimson might use the Conference to advance his Asiatic policy. In a May 11, 1932 editorial, "Stimson at Geneva," it announced with a shiver, "Let us hope he did not enter into any secret arrangement that may some day drag us into an unpleasant diplomatic situation in the Far East." [41] But Hoover's proposal late in June of about a one third reduction in the levels of armament was met with considerable approval by the *New Republic,* and the observation was made that virtually only the French, British and Japanese representatives were in opposition. Many kind words were printed about his Quaker and war-relief background, and his earnest interest in disarmament, but it was noted that his suggestions were "pale beside Mussolini's bravura pledge to reduce the Italian army to one division of 10,000 men, or beside Maxim Litvinov's frequent offers to do away with the Red Army altogether." With the Soviet Union taking part in the gatherings there was some opportunity to watch the performance of Litvinov, who seemed to be exercising a wry wit in making these total disarmament suggestions mainly for the discomfiture of the representatives of the "capitalist" powers.

The role of pleader for total disarmament was an easy one in view of the hesitation on the part of the nations to commit themselves to the scrapping of anything. But the size of the Red Army was not known, its operations in Asia received scant notice, and the feeling of Russian remoteness from the problems of Western Europe kept comment about the Soviet to a minimum. But the fact that Litvinov accepted Hoover's proposals was given substantial publicity, and a considerable part of the *New Republic* editorial article "Mr. Hoover Proposes" was devoted to interpreting it. There was little doubt, however, that a one third reduction of armed might would end France's "unquestioned military hegemony on the continent." Thereafter, the article surmised, "A combination of Germany, and Italy, with the benevolent neutrality of Soviet Russia, for instance, would be strong enough to check France's European policies at every turn." But a mighty change was to take place before just this situation was to materialize, and the "benevolent neutrality" by then had assumed other proportions.[42]

The *Nation* took a more detached attitude toward Hoover and his disarmament efforts; his reduction ideas were "dragging us back to 1922," what with the possibility the Japanese might demand the opening up of the whole matter as a result of what this might do to the 5:5:3 naval ratio established at the Washington Naval Conference. The *Nation* was in support of a drive to scrap all battleships, and was convinced they would get no help from Hoover because it was alleged "our big-navy advocates" had diverted him from such a goal, "because of an illegitimate and inept desire to dominate the seas." On the adjournment of the meeting in the summer, the same source exclaimed, "How little progress! What a faint response to the desires of the great masses of the nations of the earth!" [43] A note of commendation was reserved for Mr. Litvinov's rebuke to the Germans upon their threat to take no further part in the proceedings, in line with the theory that the real force behind sincere disbandment of military and naval power was the Soviet Union.

A long on-the-spot report by Robert Dell, the Geneva correspondent of the *Manchester Guardian* and a regular contributor to the *Nation,* was more in line with the other prominent liberal publication. He sympathized with the German and Italian disgust over the endless hedging, and warned, "Unless there is a radical change in British and French policy in this matter," the conference was about through. He placed full responsibility upon the governments, and issued a plea that the French and British people "bring necessary pressure" on the key persons involved. Dell was not enchanted by the French attitude: [44]

The French general staff and the French nationalist politicians are not in the least afraid of Germany. They intend to make sure that German armaments shall never catch up with the French, and what they long for is an excuse for walking into Germany and finishing the war which, in their opinion, as M. Poincaré said not long ago, is not finished yet.

After all of Dell's stern castigation of the British and French, and his favorable attitude toward the Germans and Italians, a few weeks later the *Nation* chided the Germans again for their restlessness and made a plea for continuation of the conference, even if it resulted in sustained inaction. So sure was it that the Allies could and would quickly mop up Germany in resumed fighting if the Versailles agreements were breached that it entreated the Germans under any conditions to "possess their souls in patience a few years longer," rather than risk invasion upon rearming. They would thus "deliberately invite forcible reprisals," and "risk a fresh war which can only have one outcome." The prediction was unusual but the circumstances and procedure much different than expected.[45]

Dell was then of the opinion that the British were more to blame for the sagging of the disarmament talks than anyone else, but they got little attention from the editors of the liberal press, still obsessed with the French obstinacy. However, one acid note entered insofar as the British were concerned. The *Nation* had taken a strong position calling for the outlawing of all forms of chemical, bacteriological and

incendiary warfare, and also backed an agreement to abolish all bombardment from the air. A resolution condemning all but the last had
been taken, but the British balked at the last. When Eduard Benes
of Czechoslovakia apologized late in the session for having made the
public declaration that "bombardment from the air is barbarous and
inhuman," the *Nation* surmised that British pressure had been
responsible, seeing that the Air Ministry had denied that any British
fliers had ever been guilty of barbarous actions. The *Nation*'s comment was no contemporary evasive platitude: [46]

In their development of nice and considerate bombs, which have none of
the horrible messiness of the aerial equipment of other countries, the
British have stolen a march on us. The late Lord Thompson once declared, in answer to a disturbed questioner at a meeting of the Foreign
Policy Association in New York that when dealing with recalcitrant
native populations, the Air Ministry was careful to blow up only revolutionaries. The only thing to do is to turn over all future jobs of bombing
to the British, whose selective bombs in Iraq, the Northwest Frontier of
India and elsewhere have supremely qualified them to perform the rite
of pacification.

In the recess the liberal press continued to commend Hoover for
his restrained and polite contributions to the Conference, but stressing over and over again the impropriety of making secret agreements
with the French, granting them the equivalent of a "Franco-Amer-
ican entente against Germany." Attacks continued to be made against
the French leaders for trying to sabotage conciliatory sentiments
among the French people by making allegations of enormous private
armies and vast caches of arms in Germany; all these yarns were
"utterly fantastic," the *Nation* scoffed.[47]

When the German delegation angrily stormed out of the sessions
on July 20, it was thought by many of the liberals that the meetings
would never resume, but on December 11 an announcement was
made to the effect that some shadowy kind of equality of arms in principle had been accorded Germany, and the sessions were resumed.
Speculation on the behind-the-scenes deals proliferated. The *New
Republic* printed another of Brailsford's tart commentaries, "The
Art of Conferring," [48] in which the theme of the unmet German
problem recurred, "Nowhere did the French propose to remove the
grievances of the Germans before we rearm them," Brailsford pointed
out. If the French had "suggested a means of revising the territorial
clauses of the Versailles Treaty," he continued, the next step would
have been disarmament by all without any special effort. Now the
conferees had proposed permitting Germany to rearm, with all its
real problems not faced. The implication was rather obvious that no
one should be surprised if the Germans, now under an openly nation-

alistic government headed by von Schleicher, should attempt to rectify the situation with these arms.

The item which caused the most concern to the liberal editors was the possibility that Hoover's emissary, Norman H. Davis, might have agreed to a commitment of American aid to the French at some future time; "nothing is more certain than that America will repudiate a new agreement which seriously commits us to support of France— and rightly. What France is protecting is the fruits of Versailles, and those poisonous fruits are responsible for half of the sickness of the world today. . . . nobody is going to guarantee the security of France on French terms." This was the *New Republic* verdict, in a long editorial titled "Another Scrap of Paper." [49] The *Nation* was even more vociferous in its condemnation of a back door collective security pledge. Commending Hoover for having refrained from such understandings up to that time, it stood for the repudiation of any new one resulting from Davis's zeal: [50]

The Hoover government has thus far stood up very straight in refusing to enter into any treaty or obligation which would compel us to come to France's rescue whenever and however that country might decide to engage in war. No agreement signed by Norman Davis should in any way oblige us to be ready to guarantee France's safety.

By the early spring of 1933, the Disarmament Conference had become so overshadowed by the Japanese and German developments that liberal hopes were even lower. The League of Nations was subjected to increasing criticism, even though it was admitted that "the diplomats of Europe have never altered their course because of the League." They were still playing the "old game according to the old rules," and in view of the fact that this had produced a war in 1914, another one was likely if it continued as before. In the March 22 issue, the *New Republic* commented editorially that the Conference had been "dragging along for weary months without getting anywhere," and there now seemed to be less hope for the reduction of arms than at any time since the War ended.[51] And the watch still continued, this time over President Roosevelt's shoulder, to see if he would give the French the security blank check Hoover had refused to remit. With Henry L. Stimson, Norman Davis and even Colonel House still on the scene and contributing advice to the new President, several possibilities existed. But by the fall, the discussion of the doings of the Disarmament Conference usually blended into speculations as to how long it would be before another general European war would break out, and whether the United States could this time forego entering it.

A last-gasp meeting of the Disarmament Conference between May 29 and June 11, 1934 brought one of the final notices of this gathering, a substantial *Nation* editorial which appropriately appeared two days after the sessions lapsed. Already the evidence was in on what was to be pressed vigorously as a substitute. With the Soviet on the verge of joining the League, with Litvinov's diplomacy running up one striking success after another, and with his definitions of aggression and collective security enjoying wide vogue, the tortured trail toward peace seemed to wind its way through the Russian Foreign Office. The foreboding that the Conference was about through hastened the gesture of following the new dispensation of collective security along the Communist formula, and the signal for the assault on "isolation" went out along with it. At least in the *Nation,* henceforth, the contempt for traditional American wariness toward collective security agreements, already bitterly under attack in the Communist and pro-Communist press, became a part of its policy as well. The effect of the changes in Europe which called for this revolution was aptly summarized in a closing paragraph in "War Clouds Over Geneva": [52]

But does not the failure of the Disarmament Conference imply a return to the war system and all that is involved? Perhaps not of necessity, but our first task is clearly to save the Conference if it is humanly possible. If these efforts fail, as now seems inevitable, a general security pact such as Litvinov suggests, involving sanctions against an aggressor, is probably the next best resort. To make such an agreement, . . . it is necessary to enlist active support of all the nations of the world honestly desiring peace. It will also involve implementing the League, the Pact of Paris, and all of the existing machinery of peace by every possible means. All this may be bad news to Mr. Hearst and other isolationists. But if any lesson is to be learned from the ill-fated Disarmament Conference, it is that peace only can be attained at a price. And while the price is infinitely less than that of war, it must be paid in advance.

An uncomfortable season was coming upon the liberals. After having sympathized with the defeated and truncated nations of the War, and repeatedly admitted that the Versailles settlements were virtually the reason for Europe's economic and political frictions, they were being exposed to efforts on the part of the unhappy to adjust these grievances. The spectacle was not very comforting to the liberals for ideological reasons.

The re-apportionment of the world could not have been conducted by political forces more loathed than by those at work by the end of 1933. The European twilight zone of muddled inaction was being entered by actionists with little regard for the niceties which the liberals were known to subject to abuse, even though their commitment to them psychologically was much deeper than suspected. Suggestions for rectification of the Versailles settlements were beginning to emerge in the form of hostile acts, and we find the "aggressor" concept returning to circulation after years of identification as a political counterfeit. The ingredients in the world stew were becoming so numerous that even the experts could not separate them by this stage. Thus, being pulled and pushed in a number of directions simultaneously, the wonder is that a consistent liberal viewpoint, steadfastly fixed on the approaches adopted between the end of the War and the Depression, lasted as long as it did. The antecedents of this policy shift were the defiance of the League of Nations by the Japanese and the beginnings of the German escape under Hitler from the crippling Versailles limitations. These affairs began to influence liberal thinking in a short time, and some reflection began to find them slowly gravitating toward the very forces they had categorically cited for botching Europe since 1919, and before. The full flavor comes out in extended examinations of the liberal responses to Japan and Germany.

But the changes in the political face of the world which the developments of 1933–1934 presaged, bearing a full load of distress for liberals at the same time, were not the only complicating factors. While prominent liberal voices adopted a more and more bristling tone upon contemplation of the events of Europe and Asia, there was the residue of anti-militarism at home which was the bank of sentiment from which was drawn the support for the campaign against the manufacture of the tools of war by private enterprise. This was also one facet of a bigger offensive aimed at all related military activities, which was steadily infiltrated by those who did not mind war and war preparations in America as long as they were directed in a particular channel. But for those liberals who took this crusade against war seriously, the simultaneous development of hostility toward the regimes of several foreign states and a demand to demilitarize the United States presented a grave conflict. Several years were found necessary in order to rationalize concurrent pro- and anti-war stands. Both liberal pacifist action and the denunciation of the munitions trade will draw separate attention subsequently, in the latter case taking shape in an extended examination of the liberal attitude toward the famous Nye Committee investigations, which became a symbol of this particular phase of the struggle.

NOTES

1 *Nation*, July 1, 1931, p. 4.
2 *New Republic*, November 4, 1931, p. 310; *Nation*, November 4, 1931, p. 473.
3 *New Republic*, January 20, 1932, p. 252.

4   *New Republic*, January 27, 1932, pp. 284–285.
5   Editorial "Reparations Deadlock," *New Republic*, February 3, 1932, pp. 308–309.
6   "Nearing the Abyss," *Nation*, February 3, 1932, p. 130; "Why We Must Cancel," *Nation*, May 4, 1932, p. 503.
7   Editorial "A Leaderless World," *New Republic*, June 29, 1932, p. 168.
8   *Nation*, July 13, 1932, p. 19.
9   *Nation*, April 20, 1932, p. 451.
10   *Nation*, July 1, 1932, p. 2.
11   "The Settlement At Lausanne," *Nation*, July 20, 1932, p. 48.
12   "The End of Reparations," *New Republic*, July 20, 1932, pp. 247–248.
13   Editorial "The War Debt Incubus," *New Republic*, November 23, 1932, p. 32.
14   Editorial "Know-Nothingism Wins," *Nation*, December 7, 1932, p. 546.
15   Editorial "Ourselves and Our Debtors," *Nation*, December 28, 1932, p. 630.
16   Editorial "Notes On the French Default," *New Republic*, December 28, 1932, p. 174.
17   *New Republic*, January 4, 1933, pp. 209–211; citations in subsequent four paragraphs from this source.
18   Anderson, "Shoebuttons for Huckleberries," *Nation*, January 4, 1933, p. 9.
19   Anderson, "Congress Studies Relief," *Nation*, January 18, 1933, p. 59.
20   *New Republic*, August 2, 1933, pp. 304–307.
21   *Nation*, January 4, 1933, p. 6.
22   *New Republic*, February 8, 1933, pp. 334–335.
23   See the puzzled editorial comments in the *Nation*, February 8, 1933, p. 133, and February 15, 1933, p. 161, on negotiations with Great Britain.
24   *Nation*, September 13, 1933, pp. 287–288.
25   Particularly critical along these lines was the editorial "Nonsense About War Debts," *New Republic*, May 16, 1934, pp. 3–4.
26   *Nation*, June 13, 1934, p. 659. See also *Nation*, May 23, 1934, p. 576.
27   *New Republic*, June 27, 1934, p. 166.
28   *Nation*, November 21, 1934, pp. 582–583.
29   See report in *Nation*, November 25, 1931, p. 557.
30   Wainhouse, "The Disarmament Conference Meets," *Nation*, February 2, 1932, pp. 137–139; editorial, *Nation*, February 10, 1932, p. 133. See also the bitterly critical (of the French) essay by Lindsay Rogers, "French Logic vs. Customs Unions," *Nation*, February 17, 1931, pp. 177–178.
31   And the editorial charged that "Mr. Hoover has already blessed the attempt"; *New Republic*, November 25, 1931, p. 1.
32   *New Republic*, February 17, 1932, p. 2, for all citations in paragraph below.
33   *Nation*, February 17, 1932, p. 181. This editorial also praised the Russian and Italian delegates as "the only champions of complete disarmament."
34   *Nation*, February 24, 1932, pp. 217–218.
35   *Nation*, February 24, 1932, p. 213.
36   For this citation and preceding material in above paragraph, see editorial "Behind the Scenes At Geneva," *New Republic*, February 3, 1932, pp. 309–310.
37   *New Republic*, June 15, 1932, pp. 115–117.
38   Murphy, "Is There Hope For Disarmament," *Nation*, March 2, 1932, pp. 257–258.
39   Murphy, "Courage Wanted At Geneva," *Nation*, March 23, 1932, pp. 340–341.
40   *Nation*, March 16, 1932, p. 300.
41   *Nation*, May 11, 1932, p. 531.
42   *New Republic*, July 6, 1932, pp. 193–194.
43   *Nation*, July 6, 1932, p. 5; July 13, 1932, p. 20; August 3, 1932, p. 94.
44   Dell, "Sabotage At Geneva," *Nation*, September 7, 1932, pp. 209–210.
45   *Nation*, September 28, 1932, p. 268.
46   *Nation*, August 10, 1932, p. 114.
47   Editorial "The Answer To Germany," *Nation*, October 5, 1932, p. 296.
48   *New Republic*, December 14, 1932, pp. 115–117.
49   *New Republic*, December 21, 1932, p. 148.
50   *Nation*, December 21, 1932, p. 599.
51   Editorial "Storm Clouds Over Europe," *New Republic*, March 22, 1933, p. 146.
52   *Nation*, June 13, 1934, p. 662.

6

THE LIBERAL VISION IN THE

SOVIET UNION

ONE of the most remarkable literary morality plays in history was displayed on the pages of the liberal weeklies, and by their contributors in a variety of other journals and books in the era between the stock market crash and the fall of 1939. By mid-1933 all the villainous characters had made their appearance, and the tableau of virtuous Soviet Russia versus the detestable Japanese, Italian and German societies was more or less complete. An understanding of this dichotomy is absolutely necessary in order to grasp the significance of liberal interpretation of the world during this time, and where this interpretation eventually led them. There can be little doubt that the issue was overbalanced in favor of the Russian Communists from the very time they established themselves in power. The liberal press congratulated itself in the mid-1930's, when the Soviet was beginning to emerge as a formidable state, that it had been among the earliest to plead for "justice for Russia" in the last days of the War and the Treaty period. This favorable predisposition led the liberal press to deal with Russia in the kindest manner, apologizing for it at every step, excusing or denying its excesses, and defending it by attacking its rival totalitarians with great ferocity and never picturing any part of these antagonistic programs in the slightest favorable light.

The watchful attitude for the welfare of Russia, and the eagerness to see in the Soviet state a set of conditions and forces existing nowhere else in the world, is one of the most persistent and recognizable themes to be discovered in a close page-by-page study of both the *Nation* and the *New Republic*. The mythology of the "proletarian state" permeated virtually all the news coming from Russia through travellers and correspondents in residence. One will find virtually no criticism at all of the Communists in the reviews of books. And in the worst depression years in America, no more sacred cow than the Soviet "experiment" can be found in the entire liberal press. Praise and admiration of the Soviet system was commonly expressed without the faintest reservation, and all Soviet claims and statistical releases tended to be taken at face value; doubt was something not to be found when dealing with anything announced by Red authorities as facts.

Slogans resounded everywhere, one of the most wearyingly-repeated being the definition of Russia as "the Socialist sixth of the globe," first given wide circulation at the time of the Eleventh Plenum of the E.C.C.I., the Comintern, in 1931, from whence it flashed across American liberal lips and typewriters undiminished to the outbreak of World War Two. "Defend the Soviet Union" became an unofficial rallying cry of the liberals who supported Russian national policy and nationalistic aims, assiduously sold under the guise of advancing the cause of international socialism. Regardless of the evidence that the Red leaders had abandoned the substance of any international revolutionary socialist movement, if there ever had been any, while continuing the appearance and form, the liberals continued to be flagrant offenders and grievous victims at the same time. These liberals were fully aware during this time that any devotion of their energies to the bolstering of French and British imperialism had nothing to do with reform. Their hostility to the non-Communist totalitarian powers rendered it impossible to mobilize them behind their goals, but the commitment of their energies to the support of the USSR put them on the road assisting in the triumph of Communism in Eastern Europe and a large part of Asia.

A most mischievous paradox eventually trapped the liberal befrienders of Russia and its strategical and tactical program. While struggling to act as the voice of pacifism, they enlisted in the revolutionary class struggle, and gave their sanction to violence on an ostensibly different level. The result was an unconscious schizoid appearance, an olive branch in one hand and an automatic weapon in the other, depending on which direction they might be facing. Parallel columns, one pleading for disarmament and the abolition of national wars, the other for vigorous shaking of clenched fists and jut-jawed encouragement to civil wars, sometimes achieved the level of the ludicrous. The pacifist theme deserves separate treatment, especially after its infiltration by the pro-Soviet elements interested in turning the entire affair into an anti-Fascist, pro-Communist front. The printing of continual exhortations to bristling aggressiveness on the part of the "workers" and the loud applause of all violent labor demonstrations led to a contagion which easily cancelled out the pacifism, and proved to be capable of efficient transfer to the arena of first internal and then international conflicts.

CORRESPONDENTS AND TRAVELERS ON THE SCENE

Throughout the early and middle 1930's, the *Nation* and *New Republic* devoted more space to sympathetic stories about Communist Russia than to all the other nations on the globe combined. A remarkable number of them were demonstrably on-the-spot observations. This fact makes the reports that much more astounding. An excuse could probably be made for adulatory writing on the part of an enthusiast comfortably removed from the scene resorting to excessive and unqualified praise. In this case the reporters were on the scene, and demonstrated a remarkable ability to see what they wanted or came there to see. We might sample the most persuasive voices in this case; Louis Fischer, regular Moscow correspondent for the *Nation,* and a variety of visitors, Michael Farbman, Waldo Frank, Joshua Kunitz, and the editor and president of the *New Republic,* Bruce Bliven. Many lesser lights found expression in frequent letters-to-the-editor columns, all attesting to the same verdict, the success of the Soviet as an economic venture, an island of well-being in a world of bleak misery and want. Assiduous Intourist activity in the tourist field at the height of the depression in the West, featured by fifty percent reductions in Russian railroad fares, brought new groups to see and come home to report.

Bliven, on a European trip which took him across Germany into Russia, reported in the December 2, 1931 *New Republic,* "To go from Germany to Russia in the autumn of 1931 is an extraordinary physical experience. Russia . . . is a land of hope." A subsequent long story, titled "A Postcard from Moscow," displayed his enthusiasm over the Soviet brand of totalitarianism. Both his lengthy reports praised Soviet achievements volubly. There was a curious excuse for the heavy military budgets of the regime, admittedly "spending vast sums on the Red army," as a result of the doctrine that the Western capitalistic powers were planning to smash the "socialist experiment" because it was succeeding too well. The Japanese armed expansion into Manchuria had taken place a few weeks before, and Bliven predicted very early Soviet involvement.[1]

In the *Nation* the readers had a laudatory series of articles by Fischer throughout the year and for some time thereafter, in which some astonishingly heartening news was made available. "No special class removes the cream from the earnings of industry in Russia," assured Fischer; "The Russian worker receives wages, and by that token he is subjected to exploitation, but it is one thing to be exploited by a coal baron in Pennsylvania and another to be exploited by 160,000,000 workers like yourself." In liberal circles nothing quite achieved the soothing power of the fiction of collective ownership. As a footnote to Fischer's report, the *Nation* published "Forced Labor in Russia" by the *Nation*'s former managing editor Henry Raymond Mussey in its November 4 issue, actually a complimentary story ridiculing the very idea, without a word of admission that anything faintly like it existed.

Yet in May, 1932, Mussey wrote one of the most chilling reports on Soviet brutality ever published anywhere, "Russia's New Religion," placing the stamp of approval upon the very things he had not long before denied to be true with a bland obtuseness rarely seen before or after. The report dealt only in part with religion, Mussey reporting as an eyewitness from Moscow that "They are tearing down the churches as fast as they can in Moscow and Leningrad and dozens of other places where the Bolsheviks are driving the revolution ahead at full speed." But it was his use of the religious analogy to explain the savagery toward potential opponents or resistants that made one gasp: [2]

Just as good Christians, in the days when they took their religion seriously, tortured and at need drowned or burned witches and other poor folk unlucky enough to be possessed of devils, so do the Communists, and with equally good conscience, starve off and exile and if necessary execute their fellow-countrymen possessed of the seven devils of bourgeois psychology, the incurable devotion to private property and all its works. I do not instance the slaughter of bad landlords and other property-owners in the first fierce years of revolution and counter-revolution. I prefer to call attention to the systematic suppression of the intellectuals down to this present year of grace, and most strikingly of all, to the liquidation of the kulaks in this high tide of revolutionary success and confidence—the calculated, ruthless stamping out of the whole class of rich peasants, numbering millions of households. The Communists deliberately tax them to death, confiscate their property, exile them by the hundreds of thousands, literally let them starve if necessary—and all with that cheerful Russian cruelty that seems to reck almost nothing of human suffering. And why? Because the mind of the kulak is hopelessly filled with the wrong ideas, so that he hinders the coming of Communism in its fulness; because he is possessed of the devil of capitalism, only they prefer to call it a more high-sounding and modern name. Cruel? Fanatical? Without a doubt; but perhaps it does not become the descendants of Cotton Mather and other New England worthies to be too forward in casting the first stone.

In Mussey's arithmetic, the circumstances attending the unjust treatment of a few 17th century Massachusetts colonials and those sealing the fate of millions of 20th century Russians made these two occurrences a quite well-balanced equation. Yet, a year and a half later, Louis Fischer imperturbably dealt with this question in an identical manner in his piece, "The Soviet Revolution Goes On" (*Nation*, November 22, 1933). Even though the editors and most contributors were fairly frothing over the employment of violence by Hitler in settling Germany's internal problems, no difficulty in the least was encountered in facing the similar situation in the Soviet Union. "The Bolsheviks, of course, have never apologized for compulsion," Fischer blandly explained. " 'Great problems in the lives of nations,' Lenin wrote, 'are solved only by force.' " So although the readers could read a Communist text in explanation of Russian practice, not the slightest breath of apology was permitted the contemporary Germans who had adopted the identical means but on a much more modest scale.

Farbman, in a series in the *New Republic* begun in November, 1932, titled "Russia Revisited," spoke as a seasoned visitor to Eastern Europe. He described in glowing terms the exuberance of the workers in the Soviet, outlining their activities as if part of an exciting game. Russia under the Communists was "a symphony of planning," and assured presumably querulous readers that the recent Party deviations from their program in the internal economy were not to be interpreted as the failure of Communism. However, he did challenge the *New Republic* editorial position that Josef Stalin was not a dictator, but qualified this admission by asserting that there was no opposition to him despite outside incitations.

Waldo Frank was in the neophyte class. His long series appeared in the same journal in the summer of 1932, headed "Russian Pilgrimage." The earnest quality of all these reports did have the flavor of pilgrims coming to some legendary shrine to see for themselves, and Frank reflected this spirit very vividly. In his "The Writer in a New Society," he announced, "Soviet literature on its habitual levels is closer to that of the great religious eras than the literature of any capitalist country." [3] He blamed the dullness of the Soviet newspapers *Pravda* and *Izvestia* upon the fact that Russia had no tradition of free speech, and was not accustomed to numerous opinions on the events of the day. He thought it very significant that a young Russian, on learning that the American press in a single day might print all manner of viewpoints, retorted: "I don't see the use of it. Every problem has a right answer. What is the sense in printing a lot of different points of view, when only one can be right?" Frank claimed that "intellectual absolutism, and the acceptance of it," was "engrained in the average Russian," and did not find it repulsive; "perhaps the want of that flabby relativism which goes by the name of liberalism in the West and which is so often nothing but a want of conviction, is not an unmixed evil." [4] Frank's fourth and final report, "Retreat from Moscow," contained a rhapsodic speculation on the future significance of the Russian peasant and the "uncultured workers of all races." His description of the physical appearance of the Volga *muzhiks* he encountered did not tally with the accounts of Russian prosperity by any possible stretch of the imagination, but he was still able to glean a morsel of comfort by imagining his future promise, phrased in the following manner: [5]

The peasant, the unsophisticated toiler, have a self-knowledge humble but authentic. This, our Western Culture has merely covered and destroyed with a patina of lies. And that is why there is more hope in the uncultured workers of all races, more hope, not because we idealize or romanticize their sodden state, but because the finished product of modern rationalist-capitalist culture is hopeless.

Fischer's reports were more numerous than any others, and they remained on a fairly mundane level, concerned to a large extent with reportage of life in Russia on the basis of his observations. However, he was not averse to accepting official Soviet figures and writing stories in which these statistics were never questioned. The ponderous totalizing of Soviet production sometimes had the quality of the sums emanating from the telescreens of Orwell's *Nineteen-Eighty-four*. A close reading of the lengthy accounts sent home by Fischer often uncovered bland admissions so casually made that one might easily brush by them. His Russian world was almost always presented with the accent on the positive; there were rarely any unpleasant consequences of Soviet policy, no victims or executions, expellees or concentration camps and forced labor, all of which the liberal press reported on at length, during this time and subsequently, taking place in virtually every other nation on the Continent. In 1931–1933 Fischer was especially absorbed in reporting on the Five Year Plan and the agricultural policy. In the dead of winter of 1932 he wrote, in "Soviet Progress and Poverty," "I think there is no starvation anywhere in the Ukraine now." But a month later, in "Stalin Faces the Peasant," admissions of malfeasance and malpractice on the part of the Soviet administrative elite abounded, curiously buttered with strong convictions to the effect that the Five Year Plan would be a success and the additional suggestion that the Bolshevik economy might be somewhat improved if the outside nations sold her one hundred million dollars worth of goods on an 18-month credit.[6] Even the *Nation* was called upon to make an editorial statement to the effect that concessions had been made to angry peasants over the continued forced collectivization, winding up optimistically with the assurance that "a solid foundation for industrial and rural socialism had already been laid." [7] Fischer's estimate of Red foreign policy and its windfall in the shape of diplomatic accord with the "bourgeois" states, upon the jarring of the world by the Japanese and German developments, will be taken up subsequently.

Like Fischer, Kunitz, a sometime editor and featured contributor to the *New Masses,* wrote unqualified praise of Stalin for the *New Republic* readers. In his "Food in Russia," in the issue for May 24, 1933, nothing was said about famine, and lyrical description of ruthless programs continued with no break in stride. Undertaken by Stalin's Italian and German rivals, such developments would have been denounced in the strongest language. Kunitz explained the travail thusly: "A new world, a new classless society, a new collectivist psychology, are being born in the Soviet Union. The pains are the pains of birth." There was less evasion in his description of Soviet culture than most of the other correspondents'.[8] In January, 1934, describing the beginning of the Second Five Year Plan, he frankly admitted the first one had been a vast confusion of botchery, though most of his culprits were "saboteurs" and "wreckers." But now the situation was vastly different; "a solid foundation for a classless society" had been built, and "the Soviet population" stood "solidly behind the government; there is scarcely a Communist, scarcely a person in the Soviet Union today who would seriously doubt the desirability of a planned economy or question the wisdom of the Five Year Plan." [9]

Kunitz freely admitted that at least a million people had been driven out of Russia by the Communists, but said nothing about what number remained there incarcerated under one set of conditions or another.[10] These admissions, being made in the first two years of the Hitler regime in Germany, dwarfed the latter's efforts in producing a different variety of police state, but the liberals conveyed the belief that all these police-state policies had been invented by Stalin's German rival.

Fischer's report on Soviet recovery in 1933, "Russia's Last Hard Year," and supplementary stories, in the summer, eventually were followed by Maxwell S. Stewart's "Good News from Russia," in the *New Republic* in October, a loud and joyful shout upon the receipt of the news, via official Soviet statistical releases, that a bumper agricultural harvest had materialized. Stewart testified to the vigor of the

Red economic come-back and the presumable leap upward in the standard of living in this manner: "One of the most striking changes to be observed in Russia this summer is the vast increase in consumers' goods which are on display in the stores. While it is true that the prices of these articles are for the most part exorbitant, the fact that they can be bought at any price is a distinct gain." [11] Simultaneously, Ludwig Lore was denouncing price increases in Germany, a consequence of the Hitler party's bungling bureaucrats.

But tributes to other facets of Communist life were forthcoming from many quarters in addition to the visitors, the latter increasing in number as the '30's wore on. In the spring of 1933 and 1934, the liberal papers advertised guided tours under the direction of H. V. Kaltenborn, sponsored by the American-Russian Chamber of Commerce, Professor Frederick L. Schuman, best known at the time for his denunciatory articles on Hitler Germany, and Anna Louise Strong, identified by the *New Republic* on June 13, 1934 as a thirteen-year resident of Russia and associate editor of the *Moscow Daily News*.

But the competition among the enthusiasts to exceed each other in extravagant praise led to some truly astounding revelations. William Seagle, in a satirical article in the fall of 1932 titled "All Radicals Are Jews," gave full sanction to the declaration that the Soviet had made "the most determined effort in all history to eradicate all manifestations of anti-Semitism," [12] one of the most prodigious misapprehensions of all time, in view of the fact that two decades later, Jewish organizations were alleging that the Reds had wiped out Jewish culture. Ella Winter, in an article "What the Soviet Child Reads," insisted that fairy tales and similar imaginative material had been replaced in children's books by the Five Year Plan, cherubic stories of Lenin, the Dnieprostroy and the Turksib railroad. "They seem to have quite a special and personal love for their "little Lenin," not at all the dry and perfunctory homage paid by most children to their national heroes." [13] The playing habits of Communist children had changed slightly by two years later, according to Fischer's incredible piece "Young Russia at Play" in the *Nation*. His description of the Soviet Pioneers, the equivalent of the "bourgeois" Boy Scouts, marching to the tune of small drums and bugles in the streets on the way to camp, was remarkably similar to the behavior of the much-criticized Hitler Jugend in Germany, over whom much liberal horror had been expressed.[14] But no one was moved to notice or comment on the similarity then or later. An eight-column article in the *New Republic* by one of its editors, E. C. Lindeman, "Is Human Nature Changing in Russia?" concluded unconditionally in the affirmative.[15] In a loud tribute to Soviet medicine and health practices, John A. Kingsbury, in "Russian Medicine: A Social Challenge," suggested strongly that this country had much to learn from observing what had been done there down to the spring of 1933.[16] And Harry F. Ward, in "Soviet Russia—Land of Youth," was immensely pleased by the military terminology bristling throughout the propaganda of the Soviet domestic program, another curious paradoxical situation in view of the universally-accepted notion in liberal circles that the stronghold of pacifism and likely world disarmament leadership was Red Russia.[17]

LIBERAL JOURNALS REVIEW
THE LITERATURE ON RUSSIA

A regular formula was followed in surveying the new books concerned with Russian affairs during these days of maximum charity toward the Soviet experiment. Books dealing favorably with Communism were treated kindly, invariably reviewed by sympathizers. Critical volumes were usually handled in the reverse, and no adverse comment was permitted to escape being rebuked, even though occasional disparaging material was printed in the liberal press. For inspirational contributions which threw light on foreign affairs in the desired manner, the editors were not above occasional reliance on the stable of contributors to the American Communist journals such as John Strachey, and Anna Louise Strong, Leon Dennen's colleague on the *Moscow Daily News,* among others. It goes without saying that no correspondent to *Der Angriff* was given books on Hitler Germany to review for the liberal weeklies. An amazing number of contributions to both the major liberal journals of a non-editorial nature did not bear the names of the authors. The use of never-identified pseudonyms, the very height of irresponsibility to the readers, was especially heavy for the articles which denounced overseas political regimes held in great loathing. The excuse that these people needed "protection" from "reprisals" was the customary evasion, permitting them to comfortably indulge in the most fiery diatribes without having to face the skeptics or the critics. There was a marked degree of restraint in comments on the same subjects which bore the names of the authors. But in the case of most of the material dealing with the Soviet, the authors were almost never hesitant to identify themselves. An example of this kind might be given. In the *New Republic* for April 6, 1932, a book titled *Stalin: The Career of a Fanatic,* written under a pseudonym, "Essod-Bey," was dismissed as outrageous trash, after a laborious attempt was made to unmask the writer. Yet, on the previous page of the same issue, a furious attack on his German rival, *Hitlerism: The Iron Fist in Germany,* also by an anonymous author, "Nordicus," was received with a warm and unquestioning review by Mary Heaton Vorse, even though Hitler still was nearly a year away from political power in Germany.

For the *Nation* in late 1932, Sidney Hook wrote especially favorable reviews of the books *The Soviet Worker* by Joseph Freeman and *Dawn in Russia* by Waldo Frank, two volumes which described the glories of the Soviet achievements with enthusiasm.[18] H. M. Douty, reviewing the Freeman book in the *New Republic,* rhapsodized: "The Soviet Union is a going concern. In a world of unemployment and want, it is rapidly eliminating the insecurities and oppressions which crush the workers in other countries." [19] No short statement can be found which does a better job of synthesizing what the liberals all were convinced was taking place in Russia.

Fischer reviewed Harry F. Ward's *In Place of Profit* in the spring of 1933, and literally accepted Ward's assertion that the Soviets had introduced a superior kind of motivation, enabling Russian workers to outproduce those of capitalist lands, to eliminate insecurity over the future, and to reduce mental disease in the Soviet Union to "a negligible minimum." He contributed just as amazing a summary of Ella Winter's *Red Virtue: Human Relationships in the New Russia.* Although he had some slight misgivings as to her competence to do such a book, he concluded with confidence that "now perhaps there will be fewer foolish questions at lectures on Russia." [20] Books written by Soviet writers and close compatriots usually were examined less critically than some by friends of the Soviet Union. Lewis Gannett protested in his review of Ilya Ehrenberg's *Out of Chaos,* "This man is no propagandist," while Abram L. Harris, in his review of Walter Wilson's *Forced Labor in the United States,* issued by the Communist house of International Publishers, let slide without any comment Wilson's testament that forced labor did not exist in the Soviet Union.[21] The silence on the Red work camps managed to remain virtually airtight, although the concentration camps of the Hitler regime got more publicity in the liberal papers than anywhere else.

Ella Winter reviewed the New York *Times* Russian correspondent Walter Duranty's *Duranty Reports Russia* for the *New Republic* in the spring of 1934 with virtual ecstatic overtones. The *Nation* reviewed it in the summer, and considered this to be the peak of Russian reporting; of it the review claimed, "Keeping in check his own prejudices, antipathies and sympathies [he] evolved a rationalistic dispassionate method of reporting probably without parallel." [22] The *Nation* at no time held its reporters on Germany to a set of standards of this kind. Herman Simpson, one of the *New Republic*'s most talented Marxian controversialists, found heavy evidence of pro-Bolshevik sympathies expressed by Frazier Hunt, another much-travelled newspaperman, in his book *This Bewildered World.*

Hunt was identified as "an old-fashioned American Democrat who had great hopes for the New Deal in America," but who believed, in 1934, that "the Bolshevik idea is destined to revolutionize Asia." [23]

Extracting morsels of comfort from books written by persons who were not Communists or well-wishers took place as well. J. B. S. Hardman did this in reviewing the symposium *Red Economics,* in which Duranty, William H. Chamberlin, H. R. Knickerbocker and others contributed, and Theodor Siebert's *Red Russia,* another book written by a critic which made admissions of Red material progress.[24] But it was customary to deflate writing of uncomplimentary character about the Soviets by Germans, such as Hans Zörner's essays on Soviet agriculture and Paul Scheffer's *Seven Years in Soviet Russia,* as the output of "German patriots." [25] No one was ever described as a "Russian patriot" in these days.

When International Publishers issued the *Collected Works of V. I. Lenin,* as edited by Alexander Trachtenberg, Professor Schuman reviewed them at length for the *New Republic* in the summer of 1933, when the liberal world was still attempting to recover from the deep state of shock which followed the spectacle of Germany's Communists and Social Democrats tamely rolling over before Hitler, instead of putting on a finish fight at the barricades in line with the exhortatory ideological manuals. Schuman dredged the Lenin writings for advice on fighting the Fascists, to whom he conceded the immediate future. He saw all the "bourgeois democracies" becoming fascist in turn, led by a clan of "dictator-demogogues," and that the "proletarian revolution" would have to change its tactics of taking for granted that the liberal democracies were their target. It was for this reason that Communist strategy was not working out and why they were "helpless" before the new enemy: they were fighting a different one than the one the manuals called for. What Schuman professed to find in Lenin was the advice to change the strategy to one of "secret conspiracy, of underground organization, of smuggled propaganda," until the time when the Fascist state, "half-destroyed by economic strangulation and war, is submerged in a mass revolutionary upheaval." Schuman figured that the period just ahead was going to be one of "world inflation and imperialist war," from which the Communists could make vast gains if they followed Lenin's advice consistently. With the prodigious help of the once-despised "bourgeois democracies" these gains were achieved, not quite in accord with the recommended formula. Professor Schuman's review would have graced the pages of the *New Masses* with substantial merit, even though the Communists did not consider him a dependable Muscovite, but a "modern Machiavelli" instead.[26]

The reduction and demolition of formidable critics of the Soviet was another matter. The degree of unfriendliness to writers who persisted in turning out volumes which questioned or rejected the Red Dream increased steadily from 1932, although occasional kind words for anti-Stalin splinter groups and their leaders managed to appear before the liberal reading audience. Destroying Isaac Don Levine's *Red Smoke* was a chore assigned to Joseph Freeman in the fall of 1932. Freeman's own book *An American Testament,* four years later, is one of the most persuasive books ever written describing how an American became a convert to the Soviet camp. Marquis Childs, then with the St. Louis *Post-Dispatch,* reviewing H. G. Wells's *The Shape of Things to Come,* rebuked Wells sharply for his criticism of Red Russia and ridiculed his expectations, which were referred to collectively as Wells's "middle class millennium." [27]

In the late winter of 1934, Joshua Kunitz had written an article titled "A Million Expatriates" for the *New Republic,* trying to explain the attitude of this immense number of people driven out of Russia by the Bolshevik Revolution. He found it hard to think that any of this number were not imbeciles or reactionaries for rejecting the new order. The first memorable book by one of these people, Tatiana Tchernavin, titled *Escape From the Soviets,* was published not many weeks later, and the same journal published a most derogatory review of it by Ella Winter. The book was written, the latter said, "to explain why nice people had to be arrested so often in Russia," but was written by a person so socially blind that she was unable to describe "any of the myriad economic, social and intellectual boons brought to one hundred and sixty million people." Miss Winter derogated her stories of Soviet prison camps, and brushed her off as "a puppy yapping at the heels of history." But, strangely enough, Edna Kenton's review in the *Nation* was favorable, and contained very little adverse comment.[28]

Among American quality literary talent thrown into a perfect ferment by the endless abstract discussions about Marxism and bagged by the Marxists as a formidable protagonist was Edmund Wilson. His *New Republic* articles of 1932 still stand out as remarkable attempts to make his peace with the philosophy as well as appeals to his contemporaries to be consistent and adopt it frankly if they were going to continue careers as critics, writers, artists or historians in the liberal vein. His October 12 essay, "Marxist History," was notable. In the course of this piece, he had condemned Charles A. Beard for his repeated repudiations of Marxism, a sign of the same kind of liberal weakness he had denoted when he aroused the celebrated response by Lincoln Steffens.[29] Steffens in two years managed to adjust to a considerable degree, being rehabilitated to the extent that he was making occasional literary contributions in the field of defending the Soviet adventure.

To Steffens was given the assignment of tomahawking Max East-

man's *Artists in Uniform* and Will Durant's *The Tragedy of Russia.*
The job was done in a masterly fashion, with particular scorn
reserved for deviationist Eastman, editor of the original *Masses* during World War days and a figure in the revolutionary propaganda
field who needed no introductory profile at that time. Eastman,
referred to by Steffens as "our old pre-Revolutionary Revolutionary,"
and "the Great Liberal," was castigated for his attitude toward
Russia, and exhorted to mend his ways and make the effort to see the
light as had Steffens, a reformer of his generation. In an effort to delve
into Eastman's feet-dragging ways, Steffens thought he discerned the
reason: [30]

But now, Russia revolutionized remains what the Great Liberal called
it and fell for: it's the acid test of liberals. And it begins to look as if the
present author of the book before us were one of that large party of
revolutionary pilgrims to the great Revolution who were waiting at the
station for a local when that express went by, and not only did not stop
for them, but threw dust and smoke all over them and their baggage.
Their Baggage! Maybe that's the matter with Max. Fine old liberals like
Max Eastman might better go to Russia to learn what the Russians can
teach us. . . .

Again, inexplicably, the *Nation* assigned Eastman's book, not to a
critic for demolition because of its anti-Stalin theme, but to Carl
Becker, who wrote a lengthy and approving review. Incidents such
as these lay behind Granville Hick's explosion of wrath in the *New
Masses* against the *Nation's* book-reviewing policies.[31]

A *New Republic* correspondent, observing Steffens' new role of old
liberal as Marxist missionary, probably put it best, remembering the
"left-bound local" and Wilson exhortations of two years earlier, when
he remarked that it occurred to him that Steffens, "having rejected
Pilot Edmund Wilson's parlor-car reservation in the *New Republic's*
'Left-Bound Local,' now seemed to be trying to catch up with the
caboose." [32]

Occasional reviewing stints tended to lend not easily divined
touches to the liberal journals' stand on books pertinent to recent
Russian history and politics. In the *Nation,* another offbeat figure,
Benjamin Stolberg, published a long and favorable review of Leon
Trotsky's *The History of the Russian Revolution,* hardly the acceptable and official version as of the late winter of 1933, while later in
the year in the same weekly William Henry Chamberlin reviewed
three books at a single sitting, the previously mentioned critical volume by Durant; *Russia Day by Day,* by Corliss and Margaret Lamont,
and *This Russian Business,* by one E. T. Brown, the last two favorable in different degrees. Chamberlin kept his remarks so reserved

that no clear picture could be obtained of his own ideas, although sufficient evidence was given to discourage anyone from assuming that his attitude toward the Soviet was unmixed admiration.[33]

Chamberlin's position was made unquestionably clear late in 1934, however, when his own book *Russia's Iron Age* was reviewed in the *Nation* by Maxwell S. Stewart. Chamberlin had "deliberately misrepresented Soviet life," Stewart charged; "he is merely unable to see the forest for the trees." A few weeks before, Stewart, reviewing James P. Warburg's *It's Up to Us,* was similarly repelled by the author and one of his sources, Colonel Frank Knox, publisher of the Chicago *Daily News,* for asserting that the United States "had little to learn from the experiments in planning in Italy, Germany, or the Soviet Union." Stewart called these observations "almost pathetic in their naïvete," although he was more saddened by their grouping the three lands together, since he thought there was much more to learn from the last.[34]

In the case of the old anarchist Emma Goldman, the pro-Soviet liberals had a somewhat different kind of antagonist. Waldo Frank found room for a few kind words about this celebrated rebel in the *New Republic* when her autobiographical *Living My Life* (1931) was published, and momentarily her fierce anti-Red books and pamphlets of the 1920's were forgotten. But the struggle broke out in force in 1934 when she received permission to return to the United States for a few weeks, her first appearance since she had been deported in 1920. The *Nation* was unimpressed by the vociferous welcome she received in New York from the "middle class, middle-aged liberals," and sought to justify the Communists for considering her a "wrong-headed old woman" because of her persistent talk of "freedom" and "repression," with reference to Russia. The absence of the former and the presence of the latter in the Soviet was not felt to be grounds for hostility, the editorial comment went on; these things were "merely aspects of revolutionary techniques, incidental to breaking down a capitalist, and building up a socialist state." [35]

But Emma eventually read the *Nation* a furious lesson on its selectivity in condemning dictatorship when that weekly published her article "The Tragedy of the Political Exiles" in October, 1934: [36]

The barbarity of Fascism and Nazism is being condemned and fought by the persons who have remained perfectly indifferent to the Golgotha of the Russian politicals. And not only indifferent; they actually justify the barbarities of the Russian dictatorship as inevitable. All these good people are under the spell of the Soviet myth. They lack awareness of the inconsistency and absurdity of their protesting against brutalities in capitalist countries when they are condoning the same brutalities in the Soviet Republic.

The voices of protest against this prevalent tide were few and far between insofar as publication was concerned. Editorial discretion has in all cases made it impossible to weigh the opinion of any ideological segment of a publication, whatever its preoccupation or activity. The sample that did make the pages of the liberal weeklies evidenced the fact that not all readers were enchanted by the one-sidedness of the picture, but sometimes they were printed so that someone else might demolish them. Even an editor had been known to express protest, as in the case of Henry Hazlitt of the *Nation* in the fall of 1932, when he lodged a complaint against the quality of the literary output of the new school of Marxist proletarian novelists, among others. He was promptly reproached for this tendency by Granville Hicks. A similar blow was struck in the *New Republic* several months later by a correspondent, Edd Winfield Parks, whose long letter was headed, "Notes on Some Left-Wing Critics." Singled out for particular reprimand was Clifton Fadiman, identified then as editor-in-chief of the publisher Simon and Schuster, and referred to as "Lord High Executioner of the Classics," mainly on account of a corrosive article downgrading Goethe, published not long before in the *Nation*. Fadiman's use of the dialectical materialist verbiage prompted the writer to suggest, "I feel that our better Marxian critics should enlarge their vocabularies." [37]

M. R. Werner was outraged by Wilson's treatment of Beard, and wrote in to equalize the case. Werner brought Wilson up smartly: [38]

He objects to Mr. Charles A. Beard's objection to Russia that "it rules by tyranny and terror, with secret police, espionage and arbitrary executions"—on the ground that the capitalist government of the United States rules by the same means. Mr. Edmund Wilson believes that his personal liberty "is not today worth a cent as soon as you step out of your owning-class orbit, and that you are lucky if you do not land in jail or get run out of town or shot, like the reporters, Brookwood organizers and American Civil Liberties representatives who tried to lend a hand at Harlan or Lawrence." Aside from the obvious fact that fifty million American capitalist wrongs do not make a Russian communist right, I should like to point out that Mr. Wilson has been able in capitalist America to step out of his orbit, or into his new orbit, if he prefers, and to report in the pages of the *New Republic,* sometimes with admirable achievement, what he has found. It is true that since he wrote his article, Mr. Wilson has been run out of capitalist Kentucky, but had Mr. Wilson changed his name to Steel and attempted to report some of the miserable facts of Russian existence for a pamphlet—there are no *New Republics* in Russia —he would today find himself confined to communist jails, if he did not have the horrible misfortune to be shot by some of his comrades, who loosely considered that act a necessity for the good of his soul.

Another isolated case of an aggravated reader of some repute involved an angry response to Steffens' blast-in-review at Will Durant when summarizing *The Tragedy of Russia*. Dr. Gustav F. Beck, director of the Labor Temple School and close associate of John Haynes Holmes, characterized Steffens' review as the maximum of "scurrility and venom," taking off from that point to object strenuously to the *New Republic*'s denunciation of Hitler alone while at the same time finding it possible to "sing the praises of a ring of bullies, bosses and sadists who conceive it to be for the good of Russia to treat her by methods that differ by a hair from those employed by the handsome Adolf." The liberals turned Marxist were acting as if it were "lèse majesté" if one suggested that "Russia had blundered," and Beck asked, "Is it better writing (or for that matter clearer thinking) to cough up some stale Marxist dogma every time the question of Russia is aired in the open?" [39]

In like manner Ludwig Lewisohn was repelled by the unashamed side-taking of the *Nation* and wrote in a loud protest, triggered by Fischer's "Life Grows Easier in Russia" article and the simultaneous publication of a full-page advertisement encouraging *Nation* readers to invest in Soviet bonds. Lewisohn, a man of towering repute in Jewish liberal letters, reproached the *Nation* for editorially attacking Fascism and then "subtly sabotaging" this resistance by assenting to the "barbarism" described so favorably by Fischer. He was especially horrified by Fischer's bland declaration that "non-proletarians" got only half the food ration of those not so classified. Lewisohn expressed the exasperation of a segment of the older liberal persuasion when he heatedly inquired of the editors,[40]

The Fascists offer us their Koran or the sword. The Marxians offer us *their* Koran or the sword. Are there no free minds left who will choose the sword in either case? Well, I do. And you, unless you are faithless to all for which you have stood—you *should*.

However, evidences of such non-conformity among the readers made very infrequent appearances during this time. The greater portion of energy expended went toward the construction of a picture of the millennium arrived in the Soviet Union.

SOVIET INTERNAL AND EXTERNAL POLICIES IN THE LIBERAL SCALES

In the December 21, 1932 issue of the *New Republic* Malcolm Cowley, one of its editors, printed an article, "Red Day in Washington," which described a demonstration in the capital not long before which involved some three thousand "hunger marchers" in a sharp scuffle with city police. Cowley disapproved the blunt police behavior in very strong terms, and sympathized with the marchers, even though nothing was ever said as to what was expected from such bravado other than to add another incident to the depression saga discrediting the Hoover Administration. The following month a correspondent queried, "would the *New Republic* grant me space for just one question: What would happen if three thousand Russian hunger marchers tried to march on the Kremlin to present a petition to Stalin?"

With the daily and liberal press alike printing stories of the Russian famine conditions, it seemed an unlikely time to present the Soviet in a superior light, no matter how bad things were in America, but the letter apparently served the purpose of affording Cowley an opportunity to essay such a task. Cowley objected to the way the question was phrased, since it implied that the two governments were similar in nature, when they obviously were not:

The Soviets are a dictatorship of the proletariat. What would happen if three thousand Russian bourgeois marched on the Kremlin? They would be efficiently suppressed (not executed; the day of mass executions has passed in Russia). What would happen if three thousand proletarians marched on the Kremlin? They wouldn't do so, because the Soviets are their own government. But if they ever did march, the government would yield to them, or cease to be communist.

Cowley concluded his rebuttal, perhaps the most astonishing short lesson in political science ever printed in the liberal press, by sympathizing with the Communist view that although the American government was in theory one of all classes, this was proved fictional by the fact that the police, the agents of one class, attacked another.

In many ways this incident characterizes the majority viewpoint in liberal circles toward Russia. No instance was too awkward to inhibit taking positions like this. No matter what ensued from day to day, the dogged presentation of Red Russia as a classless egalitarian socialist land, with a leadership easily replaceable at any time the proletariat so willed, went on year after year. Editorially the liberal weeklies supported their correspondents to the hilt. Russia was one subject on which there was no clash between the editors and the featured contributors, as there was on several other subjects. Not until early in 1935, shortly after the Kirov assassination and the subsequent imprisonment of the Revolutionary Fathers such as Zinoviev and Kamenev, did any serious doubts begin to seep into the editorial columns as to the state of things in the Workers' Fatherland.[41]

The liberal editorial columns patiently tried to explain that Stalin was not a dictator on the style of the others, in the early depression years, like Mussolini of Italy, Horthy of Hungary or Primo de Rivera of Spain; in the middle thirties, like Hitler. According to this line, there was no more abominable game than comparing the Soviet and German leaders, and it was usually as resented in liberal circles as in the Communist press. The fifteenth and seventeenth anniversaries of the Communist takeover in 1932 and 1934 were commemorated with editorial expressions of congratulation in the *New Republic* and the *Nation*. Admissions of difficulties there were absolved by apologies to the effect that they were growing pains, while those of America were those of a painful and decaying capitalist old age. Russian scarcities "were distributed with some degree of equitableness; our relative plenty . . . so highly concentrated that millions had nothing at all." But one need not worry about Russia; "She knows where she is going and is obstructed only by the steepness of the grade," while in America we were adrift uncharted.[42] In the winter of 1932–1933, it was impossible to suppress the fact that serious dislocations were occurring in Russia, made evident by the expulsion of some two dozen famous old Red figures and the placing of serious "counter-revolutionary" charges against these men. But nothing stood in the way of the bright and optimistic portrait busily being drawn in liberal editorial offices. The reckless haste at building up heavy industry and an enormous army were all explained as part of a comprehensive Stalinite plan to prepare the country for trouble with his neighbors everywhere, one of the difficulties of living "in a socialist state surrounded by potential capitalist enemies."[43]

In the summer of 1933, with a stream of optimistic reports flowing in concerning the Soviet harvest, the editors professed some confusion, trying to reconcile these tales with the counter-stories of famine, hold-overs for two years and more. The previous winter's famine stories were now admitted to be true, but the grain harvests now coming in were larger than any in the memory of any living peasant or what they remembered their forefathers describing, all the way back to 1834, which seemed to be the best year of all. It seemed strange that such a remarkable success should reach a level attained a century before, but no liberal commented on this casual item. An editorial in the *New Republic* on August 30, 1933 asserted that Russia's capitalist neighbors were trying to make political capital out of its food problems, real and imagined, yet showed concern that American correspondents were being denied permission to travel through the grain-producing areas. This was regrettable for sure, since their situation could obviously be better described by sympathetic observers on the scene rather "than to have them magnified 10,000 diameters by the telescopes of those modern astrologers who run the lie factories in Bucharest and Riga."[44] Devotion to a friend in need can rarely be found exceeding the defensiveness of the liberal press for the case of "the revolutionary socialist state."

The *New Republic,* early in January, 1934, greeted the delayed announcement of the Second Five Year Plan with relief, and declared that it was "just as ambitious" as the First. Its projected goals were accepted as if already achieved, even though nothing was said about the unachieved goals of the First. It was blithely assumed, for instance, that the expectation that real wages in Russia would double in the ensuing five years, would be achieved with little trouble. Again, a note was made of the heavy concentration of new heavy industry in new sites east of the Ural Mountains, with the intention of "making the Soviet Union virtually impregnable against outside attacks—whether from the West or from the East." [45] By now it was assumed in liberal foreign policy theory that the principal goals of expansionist and remilitarized Germany and Japan consisted mainly of covetous intentions toward Communist real estate.

Through 1934 the glowing reports of the growing opulence and well-being of Communist life kept issuing from Russia into the liberal papers. Political trouble was soft-pedalled in favor of accounts proving the success of the Soviet brand of socialism. Fischer's *Nation* on-the-scene reports, especially his "Luxury in the U.S.S.R." and "Putilov's Revisited," had to be seen to be believed.[46] Stories of this sort emanating from Germany, Italy or Japan would have been printed in comic book form had they landed in liberal hands. The *Nation's* welcome on the seventeenth anniversary of the Revolution involved the sober ingestion of many new Soviet statistics as to their rapid approach to United States and German steel production, as well as several other categories. But the most incredible part of this birthday greeting was the statement, not even accompanied by a wink, that the Communist state had "abolished" their secret police, the O.G.P.U., as a demonstration of their confidence in their tenure, and widespread public support.[47]

A month later, the *Nation* gave additional evidence of their unimpeachable determination to see the Soviet in a beatific light by making known to its readers, in a tone of great pride, that the Red leaders had promised to abandon the rationing of bread on January 1, 1935.[48] No capitalist or even Fascist state had ever been in such straits as this, but whatever significance this might have had was overlooked completely. An apologetic conclusion pointed out that although bread prices were going up, in consolation the government was also raising wages, thus placing its stamp of approval on the Communist wage-price spiral. As the year ended, a final insight as to the direction of the prevailing wind may be gathered by observing that in their year-end literary sections, the five books which received highest liberal recommendations on Russian, Far East and German affairs were all written or edited by outspoken Soviet sympathizers.

RUSSIA AND AMERICA: THE LIBERAL CASE
FOR MUTUAL GOODWILL

An oft-repeated charge in the liberal press in the depression years which rose sharply in velocity beginning shortly after the Japanese incursion in Manchuria was that the United States had a serious blind spot toward Russia; "we are trying to isolate one-sixth of the world," was a remark that issued forth on a variety of occasions. In one sense the Japanese action was a windfall for the friends of Russia and their hopes of eventual United States recognition of the Communist state. Where once only the loss of the advantages of trade might be presented—not an especially dramatic issue—the presence of an expanding Japan in Asia was a perfectly designed, if utterly unpremeditated, situation to excite American interest in a reconsideration of a political reshuffling of the deck, with an aim to gaining from a new combination.

Heavy pressure for American recognition started not long after Mukden, although the first stage was the presentation of a case for the relaxing of the barrier against Soviet products. The sticky part of this action was the repeatedly-made accusation that a goodly portion of the goods the Russians wished to market here were made in vast prison camps filled with political defectionists. The traffic of prison manufactures had been subject to substantial internal scrutiny for many years here, and putting the problem on an international basis did not make it easier to solve. Furthermore, with vast warehouse inventories of unsold goods here, there had been doubt that any stimulation of trade with the Reds would appreciably alter this matter.

The *Nation* was especially sensitive to this, and in a strong editorial on March 30, 1932, "Cutting Off Our Nose," [49] condemned the Hoover Administration's preliminary move to embargo imports from Russia on the grounds of this "forced labor" charge. It wrote off this accusation as "political propaganda" which had "not stood the test of our official investigations." It cited in support of the case for trading with Russia a statement by James D. Mooney, vice president of General Motors Corporation, who was approvingly quoted as having said the following: "As traders, the complexion of Russia's political system, or system of government, should interest us no more than such complexion in any other of the many countries in which we do business." In a short time the *Nation* was to appreciate the limitations of this suggestion, when it vehemently encouraged United States interference with business with Japan and Germany on the basis of the "complexion" of their political systems. This position was made to look even more strange when the liberal press hailed the Communist building of the White Sea Canal with convict labor a short time later. But to suspect that such prisoners might make products for export was a sinister supposition in liberal eyes during this period.

The convict labor charge may have partially subdued liberal protagonists of Russian policy, but the Manchurian adventure by Japan made it possible to subordinate this part of the question to the much more appealing one of relying on Russia as a barrier to Nipponese penetration of Asia. The implication was that by building Russia up in Asia against Japan we would be gaining an ally for the traditional open door policy and an indirect shield for our Asiatic interests in general. The Japanese threat to the Asiatic ambitions of the Soviet Union was not a fit subject for discussion. The pleas for supporting Russian policy as a resistant to the Japanese never mentioned Soviet expansion into Mongolia during this time, nor was there any speculation about the Russians remaining in Manchuria and China after their hypothetical repulse of the Japanese.

There were, as a result of this, two main arguments in support of recognition of Russia; one, the economic gain likely to result as we added the Soviet to our list of customers; the second, the valuable service the Russians could perform on our behalf as the roadblock to Japanese penetration of East Asia. The success of the recognition program, preceded by Maxim Litvinov's various diplomatic maneuvers at the London Economic Conference, and followed by Russia's entry into the League of Nations, concluded a victorious round of objectives achieved by the mid-thirties, all hailed by the liberals as of vast significance to the welfare of mankind in general. One perplexing consequence of the clash between liberal anxieties for a pacific course for American foreign policy and its simultaneous approval of Communist muscle-flexing in Asia was precipitated, another of the conflicts which helped to keep the pages of the liberal journals out of harmony with each other. All United States naval and other gestures in Asiatic waters were subject to frowning disapproval as incitations to a war with Japan, while at the same time Russian military buildup in Siberia was received with beaming sanction.

A full-page editorial in the *New Republic* in March, 1932, "Why Do We Boycott Russia?" dwelt on the buildup of the Soviet against Japan: [50]

. . . it is known that the Japanese military forces have long cherished an ambition to consolidate a great empire on the Asiatic mainland, including not only Manchuria, but territory now under Russian rule. . . . The chief deterrent to a mad adventure of the kind on the part of Japan would be the fear of successful Russian opposition. . . . We could take no more effective action to prevent the spread of war in Asia than by giving Russia every legitimate aid in strengthening her powers of resistance.

As an example of the other principal appeal, it was put into precise form by Charles H. Preston in his article "America and Russia": [51]

If we believe that we can isolate one-sixth of the world, if we believe that we can overthrow the Soviets by refusing to admit that they exist, if we think we can overthrow the Russian government by force now that it is strong, though we could not complete this task when it was weak, and if we have so little faith in our institutions that we are afraid a handful of Communist agitators can overthrow them, then . . . the logical policy is to continue to refuse recognition to the Soviet Union. If, however, . . . we wish to have our full share of business with one of the greatest potential purchasers of American goods in the world, and if we are earnest in our desire for world peace and the brotherhood of nations, then we will follow the example of every other great nation in the world and give our recognition to Soviet Russia.

The *Nation* pulled out all the stops on the recognition organ in its issue of May 18, 1932, devoting almost the entire issue, six successive articles, to the subject, collecting all of the arguments for it in a most persuasive bundle. Jerome Davis's "What Businessmen Think of Recognition" [52] consisted of a poll of fifty of the nation's "largest and best firms" already doing business with the Soviet, of which only four opposed recognition, according to Davis. Hallgren also played the business theme, "Russia Could Help Us," [53] a plea for reviving the domestic economy via steeply raised trade with the Communists. Joseph Barnes worked another facet, "Cultural Recognition of Russia," [54] in which he argued that American tourists, especially teachers and students, had already accorded full recognition by virtue of their visits and studies of Soviet society. Frederick L. Schuman used the corrosive tactic, "Benighted Diplomacy," [55] a searing attack on the Hoover Administration and the State Department for their Russian policy: "Our non-recognition policy has ever been since [1923] defended in terms which, to anyone familiar with the facts in the case, constitute the most fantastic nonsense ever uttered by one government regarding its relations with another," he raged. Schuman pleaded that the United States had a wide "community of interests" with the Soviet which called "for a type of diplomatic collaboration that the Soviet Government is only too willing to give." He referred here to disarmament and the blocking of Japanese ambitions in Asia. "There is only one other Power which has a genuine interest in these purposes and that is the Soviet Union," Schuman argued for the defendant.

Villard's lead full page editorial combined all these arguments in his "Recognize Russia," [56] an energetic plea to promote both our internal economic as well as our foreign policy by so doing, while citing Senators William Borah, Joseph T. Robinson and Hiram Johnson as jointly urging such a course at once as his main support. Of the two Villard thought the foreign implications more important, and he commented at length on Johnson's statement:

> Far more important is his [Johnson's] second contention that the United States ought to recognize Russia as a move to head off another world war. Speaking of the tension existing on the Manchurian border between Russia and Japan because of the latter's aggression, he says that "a spark may set off the powder barrel at any time. Japan seems to think that Russia's downfall would be acclaimed the world over. Some gesture on the part of the United States therefore, could well be made to rid her of any such idea." We surely have progressed some distance when a United States Senator from the Pacific Coast is willing to have it known that in the event of a conflict between Japan and Russia the moral weight of the United States will be on the side of the wicked Bolsheviks.

Despite Villard's irony, the California Senator's statement did not represent any progress at all but was merely a reflection of the deep-rooted anti-Japanese hostility of Western America and not positive feelings toward Russian Communism, though it carried a mischievous portent as far as the country's future was concerned.

In the winter of 1932, there were frequent articles and editorials recommending both courses. Russian "non-aggression pacts" with Poland and France were cited as examples of her pacific intentions, and a *Nation* editorial spoke brightly, "One naturally hopes that Franklin D. Roosevelt's attitude toward Soviet Russia will be more liberal than that of Herbert Hoover," even though his campaign had been featured by evasion of the question. Hints were made that leaks had already revealed his approach would consist of "positive measures" in the matter, however.[57] Louis Fischer, in a major article in the last issue of the journal for 1932, was much more urgent: "Recognize Russia Now" was his call. Fischer played hard on both the Japanese and the economic issues, with the emphasis on foreign affairs. Poetic, inflammatory descriptions of Japanese action, such as the "rape of Manchuria," helped to provide the proper mood. The characterization of territorial changes brought about by force as "rape" probably deserves a study all by itself, in view of the antiquity of the act and the absence of the term for such long periods of time prior to our own time. Fischer blamed Hoover personally for the failure to recognize the Soviet Union, and wrote at great length of the economic values sure to accrue to America forthwith. He was especially angry at stories of Red propaganda in America and revolutionary world goals; "There is no circumstantial evidence of any organizational connection between the Third International and the Soviet

Government," he confided. But Fischer's main concern was with what the Russians could contribute to the United States as a partner in preventing further Japanese expansion. "Moscow has been a tower of strength to all the nations which have sincerely sought its help," said Fischer in conclusion; "Now America needs Russia's aid in the Pacific. The longer it takes Mr. Roosevelt to see this fact and act upon it, the more Japan will bite off from what Moscow can give the United States." [58] No policy recommendation could have been worded more alluringly. But Fischer apparently had little regard for the *Nation's* deep commitment to pacifism.

In March, 1933, Margaret I. Lamont wrote to inform the *New Republic* that an Independent Committee for the Recognition of Soviet Russia had been formed, with an impressive membership, from the names cited as associates, and solicited help to defeat the "strong and articulate forces opposed to recognition," by contributing to a petition urging the new Washington administration to conclude recognition.[59]

By the end of both the summer and the London Economic Conference, the liberal press began to sense that the Soviet Union had made considerable headway by attending, even though nothing of any importance had been discussed or settled. Behind the facade of the Conference, Litvinov had concluded an impressive series of additional non-aggression pacts and brought about "a complete realignment of the forces of world diplomacy," the *New Republic* pointed out in a long editorial, "Litvinov's London Triumph." Besides marking the beginnings of Franco-Russian "cooperation" against Hitler Germany, the groundwork for recognition by the United States had been laid, which would be extended as soon as "Mr. Roosevelt musters sufficient courage." [60] In the *Nation*, Fischer came to virtually the identical conclusions, in "Russia's Last Hard Year." [61] Fischer's *realpolitik* with respect to Russo-Japanese Far Eastern relations and the United States will be examined further in the chapter on the liberal reaction to Japanese expansion. But one important by-product of this pre-recognition proselytization tended to escape recognition: the stress was upon Russia as a national state instead of a vague, sprawling anti-nationalistic preserve where classless international Socialism had made its first beachhead. From this point on another conflict raged in the liberal ranks, mainly unjoined, as the new defenders of the Soviet nation and their secondary patriotism clashed ideologically with the pacifistic anti-nationalist Socialists. The crisis was mostly unrecognized by the latter, unaware to a large degree of the emergence of another formidable Russian state with crushing military and air power, talking with the "bourgeois capitalist" countries on even terms. It took some time before any significant group recognized that their plumping for the ideals represented by Russia of the 1922–1932 period substantially contributed to the comfort and welfare of a foreign state.

As the recognition day approached in November of 1933, repeated stories and editorials in the *Nation* testified to their pleasure at this coming event. With evidence of all kinds all around them in favor, even from substantial portions of the country which could not have been considered liberal by any possible stretch of the imagination, it was now possible to stop fighting for once and to ride in with the tide. On November 22, 1933 the *Nation* in triumph reprinted its famous editorial of January 4, 1919, "Justice to Russia," to commemorate the occasion.[62] Maxwell Stewart, with premonitory finesse, had suggested in October that he was in agreement with the Russians who were suggesting "that 1933 will go down in Soviet history as having even more lasting significance than 1917." [63] The *New Republic* expressed considerable editorial pleasure over the development as well early in December, but had mixed emotions on its impact on the Far Eastern situation. Recognition of Russia was interpreted to mean a definite abandonment of our hitherto "positively unneutral position which favored Japan" at the expense of the Soviet Union, although doubt was expressed that it meant American participation in another Russo-Japanese war. But it was recognized that Russia's position in the event of such a war had been immeasurably improved by United States recognition. The suggestion that this act "counterbalanced" the withdrawal of Germany and Japan from the League of Nations suggested the next hurdle immediately ahead. But the same editorial, titled "The Bear and the Eagle," [64] lacked the enthusiasm shown by other liberal circles over what an economic stimulus recognition would be. It stated the reverse, and pointed out that with "both Russia and the United States embarked upon policies looking toward greater national self-sufficiency," it was most unlikely that anything spectacular would transpire. Russian desires to "cut both imports and exports to an irreducible minimum," plus the "howling" of American producers of competing goods coming from Russia, would see to that. Thus one of the two great reasons advanced for recognition now was being revealed as having little substance.

In retrospect, liberal comment largely concerned itself with the impact of recognition in heightening Russian prestige, and the new spirit of national consciousness being reflected in Soviet action. What benefit recognition might accrue to America soon was omitted altogether. In many ways the deepest insight into the change that had taken place was contributed by Trotsky, writing to the *New Republic* from Turkey. In a long article, "Russia and World Revolution," the world-famous Bolshevik expellee placed the major share of Russia's new-found respectability upon its behavior at the Geneva Disarmament Conference, which had been slighted in favor of the simultaneous London gathering. It was in accord with the fairly familiar Trotsky position that Stalin and the present Kremlin group were sacrificing the "international revolution" and global socialism in favor of its entrenchment in just the Russian state. Said Trotsky: [65]

The supreme achievement of Soviet diplomacy is the Geneva formula which provides the definition of aggression and of the aggressor nation, a formula which applies not only to the interrelations between the Soviet Union and its neighbors, but also to the interrelations between the capitalist states themselves. In this manner, the Soviet government has assumed officially the duty of safeguarding the political map of Europe, as it has emerged from the Versailles laboratory.

This hurt a number of liberals who still considered the Soviet as the backbone of the sentiment in hostility to the War settlements. Trotsky went on:

The present Soviet diplomacy springs completely from the conservative principle of maintaining the status quo. Its attitude toward war and the warring sides is determined . . . by the legalistic criterion: which one crosses the foreign boundaries first. Thus the Soviet formula sanctions the defense of national territory against aggression for capitalist states as well.

It was the invention and broadcasting of this doctrine that was responsible for the sudden achievement of respectability and recognition, declared Trotsky; the other nations were now admitting it to the club.

The *New Republic* put its editorial stamp of credence in the Trotsky diagnosis, and noted a sharp decline of hostility to Communist propaganda in America of Russian inspiration; "nobody" seemed "much interested in the question any more." It was true that the Russians had "lost much of their old zeal for the world revolution." [66] This interpretation more and more piled the Communists and their associates into the corner behind the Russian state protagonist, even if much of the language of the post-Revolution decade remained the main media of communication. But rooting for "socialism" to succeed somewhere was apparently a valid substitute for favoring its success everywhere concurrently.

Not long before American recognition of Russia, Louis Fischer cabled to the *Nation* a lengthy report, "Russia: Fear and Foreign Policy," which supported all the Soviet moves, regardless of their nature, and found ways of explaining them all. He professed to be mystified by the Red non-aggression pact with Mussolini Italy, but those with Poland and France, and Litvinov's "aggression-defining conventions," he interpreted as the Russian method of retaliation against Hitler Germany's anti-Communist bristling; "careful, well-planned Soviet preparation for paying Germany back in her own coin." For the comfort of distressed liberals who observed that the Stalin regime was treading with a soft step insofar as Hitler was concerned and even maintaining economic relations with the National Socialists, he upheld the pre-Popular Front Russian position of soft-pedalling the revolutionary approach (so dear to the Trotsky wing) in favor of the "socialism-in-one-country" line: [67]

> Russia's economic relations with Germany help the Nazis. But those relations are maintained because they help the Bolsheviks. . . . The Kremlin's first concern is the progress of the revolution. . . . The triumph of agrarian collectivization in the U.S.S.R. is far more important for the world revolution than making faces at Hitler, or calling him names. There ought to be a division of labor: those condemned to sterile anger in bourgeois countries can stick to the faces and names, while the Bolsheviks continue on their difficult climb toward a socialist state.

The final stage of Litvinov's diplomatic advances, now that his aggression doctrine at Geneva had gained respectability and understanding from the Western nations, and his London maneuverings had opened the door to recognition by America, was Russian entry into the League of Nations, to be subsequently converted, as the veteran diplomatic correspondent Sisley Huddleston later remarked, into a "dynamic Communist front." But in the editorial language of the *Nation* in September, 1934, the Soviet Union upon admission was expected to turn the League "into an effective instrument for peace." [68] In the same month, in an editorial, "The New Pattern in Europe," the *New Republic* expressed its satisfaction that entry of the Soviets into the League was assured, formally setting "the seal of recognition upon the realignment of European politics" now in progress for well over a year. Great confidence was expressed that the Russo-French "understanding" would lead to effective isolation of Hitler Germany, which had now replaced France as the center of evil in Europe. [69] The sudden somersault on France was inadvertent and more of a product of the horror at the new order in Germany. The crumbling of liberal pacifism and general sentiments in opposition to violence and war on an international scale before this new adversary will be seen subsequently.

Of course, there were troubled spirits in liberal regions upon seeing the Soviet go the way of the capitalist bourgeois states, the forces of corruption against which the Communists had been on their guard for so long, anticipating invasion and the wrecking of their socialist dream. One of the most unhappy spectators of the new developments was Fischer. "I dislike the idea of the Soviet Union in the League of Nations," he wrote to the *Nation* from Moscow in late June, 1934. [70]

He saw Litvinov's pacts of mutual assistance, especially that with France to offset British softness toward Germany and to give the Communists protection against a joint German-Polish move against the Soviet, as the reason leading to this next move. A month and a half later he offered an extension of his interpretation of the new Soviet look in diplomacy and its compromises with Bolshevist declarations: [71]

If you must trade with the capitalists, and the Bolsheviks must, and if you want some guaranty of peace, then you must have friendly diplomatic relations with the bourgeois Powers—and they exact their price. This is very sad—but it is so. It would be much better if there were Soviets in the United States, England and France. But there aren't.

Nor did Fischer miss the consequences on Red Russia of the other by-products of the German revival and the likelihood of clashes of interest. Besides speeding the Communists into a farcical rush into the arms of one of Russia's 1914 allies against Germany, it was having internal consequences: [72]

The class war is tapering off to a skirmish. The gradual disappearance of such a disrupting element makes room for a unifying substitute. This is a development of vast sociological and political significance. It will be called nationalism. And indeed the latest Soviet slogan is "For the Father-land." Only the future will tell whether Soviet nationalism can be of a different quality than bourgeois nationalism.

With this admission that Russian nationalism had not been expunged after all, undermining the years of patient salesmanship of the Soviet Union as utterly devoid of this sentiment, the decks were about clear for a return to war fought on familiar lines. The threat of Germany seemed to be clearing the air of much high-altitude ideological verbiage of little content.

The plunge into international politics forced liberal well-wishers to reconsider the previous apologetics for Red devotion of so much of their resources to military preparation. It also called for a re-structure of strategical thinking. The presumed determination of the Communists to push for a global proletarian internationalism apparently had been dropped like a hot stone in preference for ties with the satisfied states of Versailles. The presumption was that by such action the Soviets had given a sign that they too were now satisfied with the division of the world as of 1919. The Litvinov declaration that, in so many words, an aggressive nation was one that disturbed the status quo and a defensive one was one that tried to protect it, made uncomfortable reading for liberals nurtured on nearly fifteen years of criticism of Versailles plus the reassurance during that time that the Russians disliked it as well. The whole basis of the liberal outlook was being stretched to the cracking point by this policy turn-about.

The most comforting explanation came in the *New Republic* from H. N. Brailsford, in his "Russia Enters the League." [73] According to Brailsford, Russia still entertained its old contempt for the League, and now that its membership was "corroded by fascism and given up to the pursuit of national or imperial self-sufficiency," there was even less reason to hope it would get at the "root causes of war." He interpreted Russia's joining as a gesture on behalf of obtaining allies in the event of a war with Japan and Germany simultaneously, which otherwise they might have to fight single-handed. He insisted that the understanding with the French was not to be accepted as the equivalent of an alliance, that the French were far more enthusiastic than Russia over it, after having seen the Red Air Force and the Soviet airplane-building potential. As far back as June, however, the editorial policy had begun to swing in this direction as a means of making this sensational change-about without loss of balance. An editorial on June 13, 1934, "Russia Shifts the Scenes," took a similar tack, except that it charged that Europe was now going to depend on Russia to keep the Germans divided as of yore, again to prevent them from achieving their "dreams of world conquest." [74] On September 12, 1934, less than a week before formal admission, the *Nation* added its voice to the stream of favorable visions. "The prospect that the Soviet Union will be officially admitted into the League of Nations with a seat on the Council," its editorial declared, "is one of the most heartening international developments in years," and it reassured readers that henceforth, "with Litvinov at Geneva, League sessions would no longer be dull and lethargic." And indeed they were not.

After having ridiculed for years the Allied World War propaganda about the Kaiser's intention of conquering the planet, the liberal press found it exceedingly easy to begin promulgating the same kind of story about a new and much more dreaded German political order. It is instructive to note that all talk about the professed international revolutionary policy of the Comintern vanished during these times. The buildup of the new German ogre had begun, and the principal beneficiary this time was to be Russia.

One especially sour note continued to be heard as an overtone to the deep comforting chords of American recognition of Russia. This grew out of a conflict over Russian debt hangovers from the era of the Czar and Kerensky, in the few years preceding the Red assumption of power. This was the consequence of the Johnson Act upon future Russo-American trade and economic relations. Liberals were in opposition to the Act anyway because of its relation to the deplored war debt question in general. But its application to Russia brought out a whole series of separate denunciations of the Act. For this purpose the pleasing theory of vast American profits from Russian trade was once more hung in view, even though the immediate post-recognition attitude was one of dampening the hopes from this.

A new round of editorial warnings issued, dealing with the loss of "our valuable export trade to Russia" because of the irritating debt affair, accompanied by suggestions that the debts of the pre-Communist regimes be erased. Failure to make good on these obligations should be overlooked, advised both the liberal weeklies; the *New Republic* even intimated that the Soviet had even larger claims against the United States because of American participation in the Archangel and Siberian expeditions in the wartime and immediate postwar years. The *Nation* did not believe that our Siberian adventure was motivated by anti-Bolshevik considerations, however. They were satisfied that Wilson had committed America here largely to forestall a Japanese penetration of this region while Russia was torn by internal troubles. The Soviet case was out of the ordinary, since virtually all purchases were made by government agencies there, while in other nations, the Johnson Act did not impair the ability of American firms dealing with other private companies in such lands. So hostility to the Johnson Act because it struck a direct blow at the material welfare of the Soviet Union gained a new measure of liberal unfriendliness.[75]

This incident pointed up another area of liberal ambivalence. When the German financier Hjalmar Schacht had suggested to Hitler that the Third Reich might repudiate the unpaid debts of the Hohenzollern and Weimar governments, then strive to rebuild Germany's credit all over again on the merits of the new regime, as had been the custom for generations of Latin-American governments, liberal expressions of revulsion were most profuse.[76] Yet they were not the least discomfited that a quite similar course of action might be undertaken by their totalitarian favorites. The hate of Germany completely obscured the issue of the welfare of the United States. The Johnson Act interfered with our trade with Russia, which was thought injurious. Yet the liberal press was solidly behind a commercial boycott of Germany, as a supplementary aid to liberal political policy, even if such a course of action did this country no good either. And at the very same time, the *Nation* was able to enter still another ingredient to the much mixed-up subject of desirable American commercial policy by condemning American silver inflationist advocates in this country, who argued in part that raising silver prices would have the result in the Orient of forcing up Japanese production costs and thus hurt them as export competitors. The *Nation*, for all its distaste for the Japanese and their threat to the Soviet Union, editorially defined such action as "provoking antagonism of a powerful nation by a deliberate blow at its world trade." [77] By the standards already advanced, therefore, it would seem that in mid-1934 Germany was not yet considered a "powerful nation," since injuring its foreign trade was looked upon as a most desirable course of action. A *Nation* editorial, "Czarist Debts and Soviet Trade," in the August 29, 1934 issue, wrapped up in a neat parcel the elements of the case for erasing old Russian debts from the point of view of easing Russo-American relations to the former's benefit.[78] Late in September, 1934 the *New Republic* still expressed great aggravation that no solution to this impasse was being reached, and was extremely vexed with President Roosevelt for not permitting the facilities of the Import-Export Bank to be utilized to help get over this debt wall, and straighten the trade routes between America and Moscow. It was the editorial conclusion that powerful forces were "sabotaging" the negotiations out of hostility to the Soviet Union. But it was all to our loss; with the Second Five Year Plan import blueprints under consideration, it would serve America right if the Soviet took their business to other lands "in a position to make credit advances suitable to Russian needs." [79]

LIBERAL REACTIONS TO DEPRESSION JUSTICE IN RUSSIA

Self-conditioning had induced in the depth of the depression the firm conviction that the Soviet Union represented a political order far removed from the forms extant in other parts of the world. The uniqueness of Stalin and the differences between his regime and that of other national strong men was a subject on which the literature was prolific. The will to believe was so strong and Russia so far away that the notions in circulation had few limits as far as credibility of hearers were concerned in predominant liberal thought. But some details of life in the new socialist state were vague, and remained that way for some time. The reluctance to discuss in lengthy manner the nature of the administration of the laws, Russian courts and legal personnel, penitentiaries, criminal and civil law and related matters excited curiosity. The belief that there were no lawyers in Russia; that the population was a remarkably docile and law-abiding one; that police functions were mainly gentle and kindly guidance performed in a gruff, good-natured style; that the tiny portion of the community that was unfortunate to run afoul in a nation with the most enlightened concepts of equity and justice was kept in prisons of the most amazing modernity; the sureness of the absence of any noticeable defection from the dominant line, all these could be found in the liberal stereotype of life m Russia. The rest of the world was a cold, grim police state characterized by the desire to place as much of the populace in unemployment and misery as possible, if one were to believe the numerous affidavits presented by liberal weekly editors, their correspondents and travelers, and the reviewers of the books they presented to their readers as significant and worthy.

In the liberal press, the picture presented was a composite of several dozen contributors, with very few incongruities leaking through the cracks. The majority of the uncomfortable matters which did manage to reach the agenda were explained away as necessities in the pushing forward of the frontiers of socialism, in accord with the argument that omelets could not be made without breaking eggs. Therefore, there was almost always a silver lining to display whatever the unpleasantness at hand: expellees, drastic steps in the administration of economic policy decisions, secret police activity, massive military expenditures—all these had easy explanations. The challenge of completely contradictory interpretations by the unfriendly or critical had to be met by the imputing of doubts as to the veracity or character of the person involved; the *argumentum ad hominem* usually was the most effective way to discredit a pesky interrupter bearing thistles instead of roses.

The ease with which the official explanation tended to become the accepted one among a group of people doing their best to explain the new order to a scoffing and unbelieving public is understandable. The notion that Stalin could be removed at any time the Communist Party was displeased with his conduct of public office, persisted long after the expulsion of Trotsky in the liberal press. Espionage and subversion were activities only of the forces hostile to the Soviet, and had nothing to do with the actions of the world revolutionary-minded Comintern. A charge that the Communists made recourse to assassination in advancing their cause elsewhere in the spring of 1932 was met with an incredulous smile in a *New Republic* editorial: "Anybody but a chief of police should be aware that the Communists are rigidly opposed to assassination, placing all their hopes in mass tactics," chided the unidentified rebutter.[80]

In these and similar defensive tracts, liberal loyalty to the accepted viewpoint was in some ways predictable. No manuals were available from Soviet sources which explained the inner workings of their system in practice. Those who were interested in the experiment in socialism had only the chance to know how the order worked in theory, and had to take their information, which was by definition prepared according to an advertised ideal, not furnished with interlineal notes calling attention to discrepancies large and small. In the capitalist democracies, with their multi-viewed newspapers and other publications, a great deal of dirty wash was constantly being hung before the public eye. The malfunctionings of the other powers oozed into the open constantly, and whatever mysteries remained were speculated upon at great length. But few liberals read Russian, and just as few visited Russia. Whatever domestic criticism which prevailed in publications intended exclusively for internal circulation was denied them, and only rarely hinted at by the main sources upon which they depended for enlightenment. It is for this reason that the few occasions on which the Soviet leaders opened up homeland happenings to world judgment are of unusual importance in calculating liberal verdicts and the further effect upon their views of Communist Russia.

The genial image of Stalin got its first jolt in the fall of 1932 with the publication of the news that twenty-four of the most prominent members of the Communist Party had been expelled, after charges had been levelled against them to the effect that they were members of a "counter-revolutionary plot" aiming to overthrow the Soviets and bring about the return of capitalism. This news was featured in the first paragraph of the *New Republic* on October 26, accompanied by general rumblings of discomfiture. Since their expulsion had followed an open letter by eighteen of them accusing Stalin of having botched the Five Year Plan and stifled "democracy" in the Party, and demanding that he resign, it put to a sharp test the fervent liberal belief that Stalin as a Party creature was easily removable. The reaction in the form of the prompt expulsion of the critics dearly tried their powers and will to believe.

The editorial expressed vague doubts as to the truth of the charges, and felt it an inopportune time to air such a scandalous affair before the world. While regretting that the Communist Control Commission "should deem it necessary to discipline eminent Communists at a time when the workers' republic needs the intelligent direction and support of every revolutionist," it went on to admit that this clearly illustrated "to what extent dissatisfaction has permeated party membership and wide circles of the general public."

This subject virtually vanished from the liberal papers thereafter, and undoubtedly a way was discovered to resolve the painful situation this event revealed. A little over two years later, it re-emerged in different and more easily explained circumstances.

Some slight twinges passed through liberal ranks with the breaking of the famous "Case of the English Engineers" in the summer of 1933. This was the first great public trial in this decade which rested on the evidence supplied by confessions on the part of the accused, supplemented by self-incrimination and accusation while on the stand. The proceedings were considered so important for the world to know about that they were translated into English and published under the title *Wrecking Activities at Power Stations in the Soviet Union.* Three hefty volumes totalling 805 pages, the report was reviewed by Vera Micheles Dean in the *Nation* and lengthily in the *New Republic* by a lawyer, Samuel D. Smoleff. Smoleff fabricated a curious sort of apologetic explanation, but the Dean review was especially interesting.

She professed to be puzzled by the verbatim trial reports, because the case was based on pre-trial confessions, and revealed that Soviet and British concepts of justice were quite different. The defending lawyers were chosen from the Soviet "college of advocates," and did little for their clients, in view of their own conclusion that the accused were guilty. The British engineers, charged with working with Russians as accomplices, were accused of sabotaging various electric power stations, and the confessions of the whole group were included in this long report.

Miss Dean was alarmed that the Russians, "with Dostoevskian gusto, literally wallowed in their admissions of guilt, and swore that if their lives were spared by the court, they would expiate their crimes by life-long devotion to the Soviet state." On the other hand, one of the British defendants repudiated his confessions at the trial, she pointed out, "on the ground that they were extracted under 'moral pressure.'" Andrei Vishinsky, the prosecutor, questioned the man involved, and got from him an admission that no "third degree" methods had been used, "but that he had been frightened, tired, and 'brow-beaten,' and had been told that if he made a clean breast of it, 'all would be well.'" In reporting this portion of the trial, Miss Dean gave her liberal readers what was probably their first exposure to what has now become famous as a brainwashing, in addition to their first big show trial where the object was to determine the degree of guilt, rather than guilt or innocence. She concluded, on the basis of the "unexpectedly mild verdict," that there did not appear to be any "denial of justice according to accepted international law," and that the Soviet state felt substantially stronger than it had previously and could afford to deal magnanimously with what were portrayed as serious offenses.[81]

Liberal sensibilities were able to weather another bout of indecision and doubt on the basis of the persuasive Soviet explanation of this episode, and rooting out subversion in Russia was an approved activity even among the liberals, what with rumors that the British engineers accused of sabotage were part of British Intelligence.

The first great test of liberal loyalty to the Russian Communist mirage occurred over a year later, following the electrifying news that a prominent Soviet official, Sergei Kirov, had been assassinated. The roundup of 71 suspects, 66 of whom were quietly tried in closed courts without counsel or appeal and promptly shot, stretched liberal feelings of sympathy for the regime to a thread. Both the liberal weeklies expressed their horror at this act. In their pre-Christmas issues, both publications editorialized very strongly and condemned this "ruthless and bloody reprisal" as an act for which there was no excuse. To many people there was a remarkable similarity between this and the similar brutal behavior of the Hitler National Socialist party almost six months before. The latter's intra-party blood-letting had been condemned with great vigor, and the Communist version of the "blood purge" was too close in affinity merely to pass over.

The reverberations of this event continued to roll over the liberal papers for months. Doubts that there was any sizable gulf between the German and Russian regimes as to methods of disposing of dissident and potentially revolutionary elements existed widely, but the unqualified and final verdict as applied to the Hitlerians did not carry over to the Stalinites. At first, there was much skepticism expressed about the official reasons advanced for this bout of summary executions. The first reactions were very blunt; the *Nation* commented sharply: [82]

. . . these circumstances provide no excuse for the ruthless and bloody reprisal of the Soviet government. . . . Instead of asserting the strength and stability of the Soviet government it creates doubts which had been almost banished by the growing liberalism of Bolshevik rule. A strong government does not ordinarily meet assassination by mass terror . . . The development of legal safeguards in Soviet Russia was a frail growth; at the first breath of opposition terror sprang up, full blown. . . . The Soviet government could not have chosen a worse moment to revive the method of terror. The world have come to look to Germany for exhibitions of frightfulness and to Russia for an example of orderly progress toward responsible statesmanship. The recent mass execution makes it plain that the day of true "revolutionary justice" has not arrived.

The *New Republic* was more inclined to go along with the idea that the Soviet might shoot whom they felt they had to in order to preserve "peace," but wanted proof that those shot were guilty: [83]

The doubts that remain in the minds of even the friendliest critics will not make for confidence in Soviet justice. One assumes, but without official confirmation, that those who were shot were implicated in a plot against the Soviets. All those doubts might have been dispelled by a public trial. One may agree with Karl Radek's statement in *Izvestia* that ". . . we prefer to shoot several hundred if necessary of the White Guard which attempts to defeat peace," and still ask proof that such a plot existed and that the men and women who were put to death were involved beyond reasonable doubt. One can only hope that the trial of

. . . Kirov's assassin will reveal the truth behind a situation that, even to the well wishers of the Soviets, forcibly recalls the thirtieth of June in Germany.

Even the most carping Communist could hardly have asked for a kinder estimate than this. Compared to the flaming attack on the German killings, this was virtual exoneration, and a license to shoot additional hundreds as long as proof could be presented that they were enemies of "peace."

In the back-tracking on the Kirov case, Villard in the *Nation* was a virtually lone exception. His entire December 26, 1934 page was turned over to a mighty blast at the Russians, and a month later, in his rather indicative "The Russian Murders Again," he discussed the situation at length once more. He now insisted that there had been 125 summary executions, and denounced the entire proceedings in strong language; "I must again affirm," he announced, "that any government which stoops to wholesale murder to defend itself betrays its own weakness and enormously damages its cause." He went on to condemn both Hitler and Stalin as "despots," and denied that the press in either country could tell the truth about their respective purges "even if they wanted to do so." Perhaps in the case of the Russians such killing was a minor affair, he commented, since "The Communists admit that no fewer than one million kulaks were torn from their homes and sent to Siberia, many of them to experiences worse than death," and he was horrified to quote a Communist orator referring to this episode as "a mere flea bite of cruelty." But Villard was not to be dissuaded by the atmosphere of apology creeping in; "If American liberals had remained silent about these Russian outrages, they would have been debarred from ever speaking out against what is happening in Germany and heaven knows how many other countries, or any miscarriage of justice in the United States." [84]

Villard persisted in his hostile attitude, debating the question "Are Soviet Methods of Political Justice Defensible?" on March 5, 1935 with John Howard Lawson, the latter defending the Kirov shootings and Villard bitterly objecting. In truth, however, Villard as an individual of prominence in liberal opinion-making, was virtually alone at this time. There were no other liberal notables criticizing Russian actions now. An amazing number of persons who condemned terrorism when used by the Germans now just as vigorously defended such action when undertaken by the Communists.

Slowly, in early 1935, the Communists began to explain, and the critical tone of the liberal attitude mellowed. Hints that this whole affair, which was now followed by the arrest and jailing of Zinoviev, Kamenev and the rest of the 1932 rebels, was the work of German and Russian Fascists sounded plausible and in accord with the new liberal rationale. World demonry had been fashioned into a single form called Fascism, and nothing was more reasonable than to blame all uncomfortable facts on this.

As the Communist publications and spokesmen began to feed in stories of German-subsidized revolutionary attempts and Russian fascist plots based even as far away as Connecticut, the sky was the limit for imaginary riot.[85] Through January, 1935 the liberals wrestled with the factors involved, and once more they began to turn bit by bit toward Moscow. Though the Russians failed to present any but the most tissue-thin arguments in support of a German inspired revolution, the understanding that the Hitlerians were "opposed to Communism on principle" was sufficient to suspect them of all Red charges. Still another explanation, in the *New Republic,* was that the Russians had conclusive evidence of German complicity, but did not want to publish it at that moment, "for fear of provoking a war." [86] This was the most diaphanous argument of all, for the liberals had reassured themselves repeatedly by now that the Red army and airforce were the largest in the world, and with their recent understanding with France, plus the fact that conscription had not yet been adopted in Germany, there was no more opportune time for war to break out, if a crushing defeat of Hitler was the desired result.

How far this liberal journal had come around to rationalize the Communist severity was revealed by an editorial paragraph in the issue for January 30, in answer to several readers who had objected to what they thought was an excusing attitude in the expressed policy: [87]

It is possible to oppose the action [the executions] of the Soviet government in the cases of those executed on the ground that one disapproves of capital punishment under all circumstances, or that accused persons are always entitled to public, civil trials with all the customary safeguards against injustice. One must acknowledge however, that it is not customary for revolutionary governments threatened by violence to act with such circumspection, and in this respect the Soviet government is no more culpable than most others. The main charge of the objectors is . . . that the severity and secrecy were employed to get rid of mere political opponents by a reign of terror. We attempted to show that there is no evidence to support this charge and that judgment on it should be suspended until there is.

So another serious crisis had been weathered, and the editorial board at least had decided that the time was not ripe to despair of Socialism triumphant in Russia in a world saturated with divers political sins. Hated German Fascists were to be properly pilloried before the world for trying to build their state upon blood, but like action in the Soviet was a sober step in the interests of world peace and internal security. From its original stand of demanding proof of guilt of the executed, the *New Republic* now wanted proof of innocence.

And from Louis Fischer direct from Moscow in May, 1935 came still another explanation, which tied in with the Popular Front, the growing vigor of Rusisan diplomacy, and the devotion to making Russia a strong state, whatever happened to the vague planetary socialism most liberal idealists thought the Soviet was championing and encouraging. Fischer's "Behind the Kirov Executions" [88] in the *Nation* insisted that it was simply an episode in Red efforts to promote Soviet nationalism among Russians, regardless of whether they were Communists or not, to unite in the "Soviet Fatherland." He concluded an exhaustive study of this latest political new look with the calm assurance that nothing was fundamentally wrong in Russia and that as of that moment "an important change toward real socialism" was sweeping the land from the local community level on up. The peasants' vote had now been made equal to the workers, he pointed out; prior to February, 1935 one worker's vote had been equal to that of five peasants. And there was no voice of opposition in the country, even the non-Communist writers had now "accepted socialism;" "They were actually Communists, except that they had no party cards." So dissidence was at an end, and those among Russian well-wishers who were still anxious and troubled in America might once more resume the untroubled tenor of their political affinities.

NOTES

1 Bliven, "Russia In Hope," *New Republic*, December 2, 1931, pp. 60–61, and "A Postcard from Moscow," *New Republic*, December 9, 1931, pp. 86–88.
2 *Nation*, May 4, 1932, pp. 511–513.
3 Frank, "The Writer In A New Society," *New Republic*, July 27, 1932, p. 288.
4 Frank, "Conversations In Moscow," *New Republic*, July 20, 1932, pp. 255–256, for all citations after Note 3.
5 Frank, "Retreat From Moscow," *New Republic*, August, 3, 1932, pp. 308–310.
6 *Nation*, December 7, 1932, pp. 552–554; January 11, 1933, pp. 39–41.
7 *Nation*, January 25, 1933, p. 79.
8 *New Republic*, May 24, 1933, pp. 43–44.
9 Kunitz, "The Second Five Year Plan," *New Republic*, January 17, 1934, pp. 275–277.
10 See in particular the critical comment by John Gould Fletcher on Kunitz's rationalizations in his article "A Million Expatriates," in a letter to the editors; *New Republic*, March 14, 1934, p. 132.
11 Fischer in *Nation*, August 9, 1933, pp. 154–156; Stewart in *New Republic*, October 11, 1933, pp. 230–232. The critique of Germany by Lore is on page 232.
12 *Nation*, October 5, 1932, p. 308.

13 *New Republic*, December 14, 1932, pp. 122–124.

14 *Nation*, August 1, 1934, pp. 128–130.

15 *New Republic*, March 8, 1933, pp. 95–99.

16 *New Republic*, April 5, 1933, pp. 204–206.

17 *Nation*, August 3, 1932, pp. 103–104.

18 *Nation*, September 14, 1932, pp. 237–238.

19 *New Republic*, December 7, 1932, pp. 165–167.

20 Fischer's review of Ward in *Nation*, May 10, 1933, pp. 534–535; of Winter in *Nation*, June 14, 1933, p. 676.

21 *Nation*, August 9, 1933, pp. 165–166.

22 *New Republic*, April 18, 1934, pp. 277–278; *Nation*, July 11, 1934, p. 54.

23 *New Republic*, July 25, 1934, p. 300.

24 *Nation*, November 23 1932, pp. 507–508.

25 Zörner's articles on Soviet agriculture were published by the *New Republic*, which took the trouble to point out that he was afflicted by a "bias against Communism" in a full-column editorial. See *New Republic*, July 26, 1933, pp. 274–275. On Scheffer see *Nation*, August 24, 1932.

26 Schuman's review in *New Republic*, August 23, 1933, pp. 51–52. The Marxist Herman Simpson referred to Schuman as "the Machiavelli of our age" in a review of the latter's *International Politics* in *New Republic*, July 12, 1933, p. 241.

27 *New Republic*, October 11, 1933, pp. 248.

28 Winter review in *New Republic*, July 25, 1934, pp. 298–299; Kenton review in *Nation*, July 18, 1934, pp. 79–80.

29 Wilson, "Marxist History," *New Republic*, October 12, 1932, pp. 226–228. His concluding paragraph declared, "I do not mean in the least that all the good writers are coming into the Marxist camp. The Marxists are far from all being geniuses, and some of our best writers are far from Marxism and, from all appearances, likely to remain so. Marxism is not a touch-stone for artistic or intellectual or moral excellence. But if we compared those men of genius outside it with those whom it has inspired, we should recognize it—if we had no other means—as the great political-intellectual movement of the time. That other world is dying at the end of its blind alley; but this other, just coming to maturity, has its immense creative work to do." See also review of Wilson's book *The American Jitters*, by Arthur Warner in *Nation*, July 6, 1932, p. 17.

30 *New Republic*, June 30, 1934, pp. 161–162. Steffens' review of Durant appeared in *New Republic*, August 30, 1933, p. 79.

31 *Nation*, May 30, 1934, pp. 624–625. As early as November 23, 1932, Hicks can be seen reproaching Henry Hazlitt in the *Nation* on the grounds of too critical reception of the new Marxist proletarian literary figures.

32 Paul Heffernan, in *New Republic*, July 11, 1934, pp. 240–241.

33 Stolberg's review in *Nation*, February 15, 1933, pp. 169–171; Chamberlin's in *Nation*, August 30, 1933, pp. 245–246.

34 *Nation*, November 14, 1934, pp. 567–568; October 10, 1934, pp. 415–416.

35 Editorial "Emma Goldman," *Nation*, March 21, 1934, p. 370.

36 *Nation*, October 10, 1934, pp. 401–402.

37 *New Republic*, August 9, 1933, pp. 343–344. Fadiman was identified in the *New Republic* (December 9, 1931, p. 100) as collaborating with the Workers' International Relief helping the National Hunger March, and as one of the five-man Committee For Books For Political Prisoners (with George Novack, Florence Bowen, Samuel Middlebrook and Isador Schneider) in *New Republic*, June 8, 1932, p. 103. See also Fadiman, "How I Came To Communism," *New Masses*, September, 1932, pp. 6–9.

38 *New Republic*, March 9, 1932, p. 103.

39 *New Republic*, September 27, 1933, p. 188.

40 *Nation*, July 4, 1934, p. 21.

41 Exchange between Cowley and Dr. William J. Robinson, *New Republic*, January 18, 1933, p. 272. Lionel Abel in his "History, Snobbery, Criticism," in *New Republic*, April 25, 1934, pp. 474–476, maintained that it was a "fact" that Cowley was a Communist and "fronted" "the contemporary scene from the Marxist point of view."

42 *New Republic*, November 16, 1932, p. 3.

43 *New Republic*, January 18, 1933, p. 253.

44   *New Republic,* August 30, 1933, p. 57.
45   *New Republic,* January 10, 1934, p. 236.
46   *Nation,* January 31, 1934, pp. 120–122; September 26, 1934, pp. 348–350.
47   *Nation,* November 14, 1934, pp. 547–548.
48   *Nation,* December 12, 1934, p. 660.
49   *Nation,* March 30, 1932, p. 357.
50   *New Republic,* March 16, 1932, pp. 112–113.
51   *New Republic,* September 21, 1932, pp. 151–153 (153).
52   *Nation,* May 18, 1932, pp. 567–568.
53   *Nation,* May 18, 1932, pp. 561–562.
54   *Nation,* May 18, 1932, p. 565.
55   *Nation,* May 18, 1932, pp. 563–564.
56   *Nation,* May 18, 1932, p 558.
57   *Nation,* December 14, 1932, p. 580. Soviet negotiations with France and Poland discussed in editorial in *New Republic,* December 7, 1932, p. 82.
58   *Nation,* December 28, 1932, p. 633.
59   *New Republic,* March 22, 1933, p. 162.
60   *New Republic,* August 2, 1933, pp. 303–304.
61   *Nation,* August 9, 1933, pp. 154–156. Fischer was sure that no one should "criticize the Kremlin for maintaining a tremendous military establishment in the Soviet East," yet considered that Litvinov's diplomatic efforts on behalf of the Communists "should make the foreign commissar a powerful contender for the Nobel Peace Prize," adding, "I should not be surprised if he got it and accepted it."
62   *Nation,* November 22, 1933, pp. 582–583. See also *Nation* editorials of November 1 and November 8, 1933, p. 495 and p. 524.
63   Stewart, "Good News From Russia," *New Republic,* October 11, 1933, pp. 230–232.
64   *New Republic,* November 1, 1933, pp. 323–324.
65   *New Republic,* November 1, 1933, pp. 327–329.
66   "The Bear and the Eagle," *New Republic,* November 1, 1933, p. 324.
67   *Nation,* October 11, 1933, pp. 403–405.
68   *Nation,* September 12, 1934, p. 282.
69   *New Republic,* September 26, 1934, p. 173.
70   *Nation,* June 27, 1934, pp. 728–729.
71   *Nation,* August 15, 1934, p. 186.
72   Fischer, "Young Russia At Play," *Nation,* August 1, 1934, p. 130.
73   In *New Republic* for September 12, 1934.
74   *New Republic,* June 13, 1934, pp. 115–116.
75   Editorial "The Rift In Russian Relations," *New Republic,* September 19, 1934; *Nation,* May 16, 1934, p. 547.
76   Editorial "Exit Versailles," *New Republic,* May 2, 1934, p. 324.
77   *Nation,* May 16, 1934, p. 548.
78   *Nation,* August 29, 1934, p. 230.
79   Editorial "Strangling Our Russian Trade," *New Republic,* May 9, 1934, p. 352.
80   *New Republic,* May 18, 1932, p. 2.
81   Dean, "Soviet Justice," *Nation,* August 23, 1933, pp. 220–221. The Smoleff review appeared in the *New Republic* for June 21, 1933.
82   *Nation,* December 19, 1934, p. 696.
83   *New Republic,* December 19, 1934, p. 151.
84   Villard, "The Russian 'Purging,'" *Nation,* December 26, 1934, p. 729; "The Russian Murders Again," *Nation,* January 23, 1935, p. 91.
85   *New Republic,* January 2, 1935, p. 204.
86   *New Republic,* January 16, 1935, p. 259.
87   *New Republic,* January 30, 1935, p. 316.
88   *Nation,* May 8, 1935, pp. 529–531; May 15, 1935, pp. 566–568. Citations from first essay, p. 531. Fischer in his *Nation* essay, "The Soviet Revolution Goes On," November 22, 1933, p. 594, had written, "The Bolsheviks, of course, have never apologized for compulsion." "Great problems in the lives of nations," Lenin wrote, "are solved only by force."

7

THE EXPLOSION OF THE FAR EAST

AND LIBERAL RECONSIDERATIONS

THE JAPANESE INVASION OF MANCHURIA
PRODUCES TOTAL CONFUSION

AMERICAN liberals and their articulate literary organs were no better prepared for outbreak of large-scale military action in the world in 1931 than any other segment of national opinion. The event which was later to be referred to as the first act of the Second World War, the Japanese investment of Manchuria in September of that year, apparently had little immediate significance. Nothing about the Mukden incident appeared in the *Nation,* for instance, for almost three weeks after.[1] And for some time thereafter the absence of consistency made it obvious that no integrated attitude existed on the subject. Editorial policy and contributors of signed material conflicted sharply with little acknowledgment, and less awareness. Virtually every liberal opinion was hurriedly mustered and passed in review insofar as attitudes were concerned. All the existing elements of peace machinery, the League of Nations, the Briand-Kellogg Paris Pact, plus unofficial material boycotts on an informal basis, were invoked in a ritualistic way. An undertone of cool estimation existed, weighing the Far East in terms of *realpolitik,* which even found comforting things to say for the Japanese case. Interwoven in the tangled fabric were the national interests of the Powers, which tended to become obscured by the fervent rhetorical appeals of the

protagonists of peace machinery invocation, those unconscious supporters of the interested parties who were quite contented with things
as they were before the Japanese rudeness. And over all of this tow-
ered the dim figure of United States Secretary of State Henry L.
Stimson.

From an editorial position, at least, the liberal papers did not take
the same outlook on the Manchuria situation at the beginning. The
special stories on the subject also varied considerably, leaning very
heavily on the imperialist approach, and chiding the indignant powers for their attitude although it was obvious that, when it came to
China, none were "without sin," so to speak. The fact that virtually
no editorial comment, large or small, was ever signed renders it
most difficult to determine how the several editors of both journals
lined up. In the *Nation,* the first response was to express surprise and
confusion that the Kellogg Pact was not mentioned in the first diplomatic exchanges following the seizure of Mukden. Successive years
found great importance attached to the Paris agreement, and there
was a tendency for memories to go back no further than 1927. This
gave the case an unreal atmosphere and helped to generate vast
amounts of moral indignation, simply on the basis that Japan was
refusing to abide by the latest change in the rules. In its first substantial comment, the editors queried as to whether the big powers,
including the United States, were going to let the Kellogg Pact
become "simply another scrap of paper." Great discouragement was
expressed over "the lack of enthusiasm shown by the United States
for the anti-war treaty when put to the test in the Manchurian crisis."
If this was the attitude of Stimson and the State Department, then it
did not "augur well for future efforts to ban war by international
agreement." [2]

The 1929 Russo-Chinese, post-Kellogg war was already forgotten
by the *Nation,* but not by the *New Republic.* Its first comment lacked
any urgency, by comparison; "Two years ago Russia taught China a
lesson by a military expedition in the orthodox manner of empires.
Now Japan is doing so in the same manner." No moral position was
advanced at this early stage. It was admitted that the Chinese were
guilty of "provocative acts," and that it was "impossible to determine
the right or wrong of the incidents" which had been going on for
months. But no special disapprobation was entered against Japan at
this time. In the past, it was pointed out, "every power which has
been strong enough has taken from China what it could," and thus
Japan's conduct was unexceptionable. No other state had ever given
up anything there unless forced, and the opinion was put forth that
the other nations "would resume acquisitions if they could." In the
New Republic editorial eye, the problem was "insoluble." The Japanese had fought the Russians to get Manchuria, and were fighting

the Chinese to keep it. The latter had been "whittling away" at Japanese investments there for years, and the tenseness might be eased, it recommended, by the withdrawal of Japanese troops, along with a Chinese abandonment of their boycotts and a "relaxation" of their "aggression against Japanese properties in Manchuria." A dim view was taken of outside pressure; "The League of Nations may send commissions and Mr. Stimson may send notes," it conceded, but as long as they were "merely admonitory," the Japanese would accept them with "punctilious courtesy," and do nothing, unless an attempt might be made to "translate them into action," and in that case the prediction was made that "Japan will resist with force." [3]

Peace policies dominated the *New Republic* coverage of the Manchurian situation through the rest of 1931. Avoidance of war was the main theme, and a petulant moralism did not creep into the tone of its commentaries until after the Japanese had expanded their operations southward against Shanghai in January, 1932. When the Hoover-Stimson decision was made temporarily to join the Council of the League as one of the originators of the Paris Pact, the opinion was expressed that it would be very difficult not to do the same whenever any other international crisis arose. This was a landmark in American policy, and indicated "the official ending of our pretended isolation." [4] An inference was made here indicating that they did not follow the great Democratic Party legend of later years to the effect of Republican "isolation" in the 1921–1933 era. In fact, one of the surprising things about both of the social-democrat-inclined liberal weeklies was their unquestioned support of all the Republican documentary foreign policy instruments of the time: the Washington Naval Conference, the Four and Nine Power pacts, the Briand-Kellogg Pact, the efforts to bring about United States membership in the World Court (a side issue), as well as the Stimson Doctrine, disarmament and war debt reduction.

The accent however was on peace at all costs, and this theme did not waver, except momentarily, for a considerable time. Any suggestions for the application of force through the League were deprecated, except of the moral variety. And a strain of mutual criticism pervaded the views of the first autumn. League warnings about the futility of solving its headaches with the Chinese might have had greater effect on Japan, it was suggested, "if the other members of the League, and the United States, which is cooperating with it, would use their morals on themselves, and in the Occident." [5] The tendency to compare Japan's actions in Asia with those of the United States in Nicaragua and Haiti prevailed for some time. This also was in harmony with the anti-imperialistic pacifism of the day, the Russian influence hovering just over the horizon. A few words on the Soviet were beginning to see print. It was cast in the role of the unqualified seeker of peace at all costs in the autumn of 1931, on the grounds of its alleged complete unpreparedness as well as its "obvious desire" of peace for its own sake.

Much hesitancy in condemning Japan still existed late into the fall, partially due to the fact that even the League had to withhold designations of "aggressor" for three months after the invocation of Article XV. For this reason the *New Republic* considered all talk of economic boycott premature, and but for a momentary weakness, continued to be consistent in its expression of blank opposition to economic boycotts, as we shall see. Early in December it frankly expressed this as policy: "The *New Republic* has, ever since the last war, opposed the project of attempting to maintain peace by the applications of sanctions, whether military or economic."

In December, a long editorial "The Manchurian Crisis and the League" came to the conclusion that there was no sense in concealing any longer the fact that the League had "failed, and failed disastrously." Such pressure of "world opinion" as had been applied so far had done nothing more than to stimulate the Japanese in going about their course more resolutely. The League should have begun years before to get at the roots of the Sino-Japanese dispute, not waited until it had already broken out in flames. Instead of laboriously examining the Manchurian railway treaties, which were declared to be the basic cause of the trouble now, the League had done just what it had done ever since it was founded, "devoting its energy" to the "multiplication of rubegoldbergian [sic] peace machinery," which was usually proved in cases of difficulty "to be so wildly fantastic" no one with any sense dared apply it.[6]

Threatening to use sanctions was likely to mean that the war would spread, the editorial went on, and in subsequent observations the same month, the journal stated, "Short of a new world war, there is no sure way to stop the Japanese armies."[7] But no one "occidental nation" was going to interrupt them now, for sure. As to what to do, it suggested doing nothing. "China, America and England have everything to gain by a pacifist, waiting policy;" "we might as well register our disapproval, cease attempts to negotiate a settlement and sit tight until the military policy brings its inevitable economic reaction to the Japanese people."[8] According to politico-economic theory prevalent then, war and militarism simply aggravated the last stages of a dying capitalism, and waiting until the edifice crashed also made the possibility of a new order more inviting, even if the nature of this order was not clear.

The quality of moral indignation in the *Nation* ranks was much sharper than in its companion publication, although there were also spokesmen here who played loudly on the imperialist organ and although not defending Japan, found little in the conduct of the loudest protestors in the West to attract their support. As in the other journal as well, American cooperation was viewed originally as a mighty constructive step, and Mr. Stimson was hailed as a patron of peace. But any action taken must be in harmony with the League Covenant and the Kellogg Pact, it warned; "China is doubtless not altogether without blame." [9] These expressions of doubt as to the blue-white purity of the Chinese are curious documents, and quite unique. They disappeared almost entirely in a few weeks and a unilateral Japanese devil replaced that balanced criticism. The *Nation*'s tone became increasingly querulous as the autumn wore on into early winter. Great hopes were entertained that the League would succeed in persuading the Japanese to withdraw their armies, and all kinds of moral exhortation were expended in the hopes that that body would not become timid and back down after having "asserted its authority." [10]

But when a committee of businessmen, bankers and lawyers was called together by redoubtable Nicholas Murray Butler to find a way if possible to apply economic sanctions, a little foot-dragging began. Editorially the *Nation* made one of its very rare admissions to the effect that it was "one thing to speak of bringing economic pressures against an aggressor nation in time of war, but the trick lies in determining just what constitutes aggression." [11] But these wrestling matches with the greatest semantic booby trap invented in the twentieth century were exceedingly scarce. Usually the word "aggression" was used as loosely and confidently as the word "snake." As a sign that this had been only temporary sobriety, three weeks after this hesitant reservation, an unconditional condemnation was issued: "We are entirely convinced that no matter what the Chinese provocation there is no defense for the Japanese aggression." [12]

On the other hand, two weeks before this, one of the *Nation*'s editors, Mauritz A. Hallgren, had published a long signed article, "Japan Defies the Imperialists," which sought to deal in history which went back a little further than Mr. Kellogg's all-transcendent pact. Japan's defense of its interests in foreign lands was in close accord with the dictum of Calvin Coolidge, Hallgren claimed, by which standards the property and persons of a country's citizens were "part of the national domain even when abroad." Hallgren cited the United States action in the Caribbean since 1900, the British at Singapore, the multi-slicing of China in 1898, Russian action in Manchuria in 1900, American accession of the Philippines and Puerto Rico, and the division of the World War spoils, especially the splitting up of the German colonies by the victors, as the raw material which made up Japan's education on the subject. According to Hallgren, the United States put up precisely the same argument in sending the Marines to Nicaragua, Haiti and Cuba as Japan had in its Manchurian troop concentration. Hallgren tried to absolve himself of defending the Japanese action, and insisted that the nations now trying to interfere in the Far East in the name of "world peace" had come "into court with unclean hands," and that the Japanese people were fully aware of it.

At Washington in 1921, Hallgren further reminded the *Nation* readers, these same "imperialist powers" gave their blessing to the 1915 treaties by which Japan had made her major claims on China, and now they were "condemning the logical consequences." He further explained one reason why: when the Chinese had complained at Washington that they had been forced to accept the treaties, and wished relief, the Japanese had pointed out to the gathering that the adoption of the principle that treaties signed under duress were not binding would have serious effect all over the world. And the assembled powers, in full knowledge of the circumstances under which the Paris suburbs treaties had been signed, "quietly agreed that the Japanese were right." And now? These same powers, "having thus confirmed the validity of the treaties . . . are now in effect denying Japan the right to defend them against what it insists are violations of those treaties by the Chinese." [13] So the argument was back to Spinoza's observation that wars were contests between, not right and wrong, but right and right.

While reviewing six books on Japan in the *Nation*'s January 13, 1932, issue, Hallgren returned to this unsettling theme with another reference to historical positions: [14]

In speaking before the Council on Foreign Relations last winter, Secretary Stimson sought to excuse American activity in Central America and the Caribbean countries partly on the ground that the present position of the United States in that region must be maintained in the interest of national security. The same excuse can be advanced with regard to Japan's position on the Asiatic mainland.

Nor was Hallgren the only student of the Manchuria incident who disagreed with the editorial position. A. E. Hindmarsh, an assistant dean at Harvard University, argued at length two weeks later that there was no definition for the action which the Japanese had taken at Mukden, that it was equivalent to the use of force by the big powers in the nineteenth century against weaker ones. He further reminded readers that the Japanese were not "pioneering" here, since there was the 1923 Italian bombardment of the Greek island of Corfu on the record, and since the Kellogg Pact and the League of Nations Covenant were entirely *moral* agreements. Hindmarsh argued that the trouble was with these documents in failing to prohibit wars of self-defense against "aggression"; "Until aggression is defined (and it has not been), every war is apt to be regarded as a self-defensive war." He also declared that it was possible for Japan to argue that her actions were within the terms of the Nine Power Treaty of 1921–1922, again a matter of charges and counter-charges over terms "wholly defying definition." And he concluded, "It seems apparent that modern peace-preserving efforts are glaringly defective so long as they fail to include prohibition of all force methods." [15] This sober and hardheaded analysis could not have been more at variance with the fulminating editorial of January 6 which yelled that "Japan is running amuck in the family of nations," urging the withdrawal of ambassadors from Tokyo and a strong protest by the Hoover government.[16]

A much similar approach was that of Louis Fischer, in his *Nation* dispatch in December, 1931, "Russia and Japan in Manchuria": [17]

Neither the United States, which rams its will down the throats of Nicaragua and Haiti, nor England, which holds Egypt, India and Cyprus by main force, nor yet France, which half-destroyed the beautiful city of Damascus in order to "pacify" Syria, has any moral right to protest when Japan proceeds to make Manchuria a second Korea. Nor has the League of Nations, for the League completes and confirms the Versailles Treaty with all its vivisection of Germany and its colony-snatching.

So the counsels issuing forth were clamorous, and conflicting. The lack of cohesion between the editorial and feature departments continued for some time, and a clash of some sort probably accounted for it. While Fischer was declaring the League to be hypocritical in its stand on the Manchuria case, an editorial blared, "Nobody has any right whatever to criticize the League and the United States for acting." The editors of the *Nation* now backed both a boycott and League sanctions, and insisted the Japanese be made to adhere to the Nine Power Treaty and the Kellogg Pact.[18] (Hallgren maintained that the Japanese lease to the Kwantung area until 1997 and rights to the South Manchuria Railway to 2002 were untouched by any of the treaties of the early 1920's.)

But bit by bit the fervor of the fall wore off as the dark days of December revealed that the powerful did not share the resoluteness of the *Nation*'s editorial stand. There were hints that the State Department was "supporting" the Japanese,[19] and morose ruminations to the effect that it now appeared that any strong member of the League could defy it when it pleased to do so.[20] Even more disconcerting, it commented on Stimson's note to Japan and China concerning Manchuria and noted with some agitation that apparently the State Department did not intend "to interfere in any arrangement whereby the sovereignty of Manchuria might be transferred to Japan if that transfer is made peacefully," and if the Manchurian "Open Door" were not closed. It shuddered at the possibility of a new Japanese base adjoining Siberia.[21] As a final redoubt, it fell back on the consolation that eventually the economic problem of conducting this enterprise would force Japan to the wall, and a combination of the boycott and desperate finance would eventually cause the whole endeavor to collapse.

In the spring of 1932 came a very serious flirtation with sanctions. Sanctions were considered at the beginning as a non-violent type of action, and a comfortable substitute for guns. Only after the sanctions craze had dissipated itself did the liberals who had been so light-heartedly casting it back and forth realize that they had lent their support to a device as capable of producing widespread warfare as any weapons known. In all this campaign, the *New Republic* alone in its editorial stand patiently stuck to the issue that economic war via sanctions was simply the preliminary step to organized violence. But no permanent cure was effected, since liberal opinion drifted back again and again to this magnetically attractive device in the subsequent decade.

The re-opening of the war in January, 1932 by Japan and its extension southward galvanized several groups in America into actionism of one type or another, besides stimulating the naval expansionists, casting a dark pall over the not-yet-met Geneva Disarmament Conference, and paving the way for another disturbance later on. This was based on the Stimson Doctrine and the Lytton Report on behalf of the League of Nations. Slowly making its way through the jungle of opinion was the case for the Soviet Union, patiently being put together as the paralysis of inaction among the League powers and the United States provided a backdrop for a steadily brightening Russian position in the chaos of the Far East.

In its issue of February 10 the *Nation* reported the operations of the Japanese at Shanghai in indignant prose, then braked to a smoking conclusion, "We wish no one to believe that we are inciting people to take up arms in order to 'revenge' these acts and kill a lot of Japanese who committed these bloody wrongs under the orders of a medieval government." As for the United States it issued a blunt one-way course; "the only policy for us is to get our nationals out of Shanghai and then withdraw ships and soldiers as rapidly as possible." [22]

As far as supporting the French scheme of a League-sponsored international army, to the liberals it was unconditionally out of the question. A serious attack was already on against France as Europe's "chief military nation" of the day, and the French suggestion got a frigid reception. The *New Republic* editorially labeled France a "military peace-maker," little more than a twin of the Japanese, except that what it wished to keep conquered was the area it gained dominance over in 1919; "France's Manchuria is Central Europe," and considered both Japanese and French solutions equally "fantastic." "Any nation which accepts a partnership with the French in this endeavor is sure to be involved in war, sooner or later," was the blunt warning; ". . . we cannot think of anything more unrealistic in the long run than to accept any share in guaranteeing the kind of peace which may be established by force." [23]

Robert Dell's irritated *Nation* dispatch of January 24 sounded this same note, "Is France Backing Japan?", and expressed anger that only one non-Socialist or non-Communist paper in Paris attacked Japan, which revealed an interest in the welfare of another power in addition to China.[24]

It may have been that the French intentions of using such force in Asia were rather feeble, but such a possibility was read into the project as brought up for consideration by the French. What disturbed the *New Republic* was the observation that neither the French nor British had joined with Stimson when he protested Japanese action on the grounds of violation of the Kellogg Pact and Nine Power Treaty. It concluded that the foreign offices of both nations were "notoriously pro-Japanese" and that the League was absorbing defeat after defeat in the Manchurian matter, while in the process it was "only partially successful in its usual device of laying the blame on the United States." [25] The original legend of the failure of the League for lack of American entry had been compounded through the years by now, and at this particular stage there was growing impatience with it, in view of virtual complete agreement in depression-time America that remaining out of the League was an act of exceptional perspicacity. Having already attacked the League as an instrument manipulated since Versailles by British and French politicians, the liberal press found itself in another uncomfortable corner. Cheering on the League to hobble the Japanese and at the same time to keelhaul it for its shortcomings was not a mark of consistency.

An agony of indecision was evident in the liberal fold by the end of the winter of 1931–1932 concerning how now to interpret the Far Eastern situation. At one time the liberals had been of the opinion that the reluctance of the Powers to get away from diplomatic piety and rhetorical balloon-chasing on Manchuria was that they did not want to open up the entire question of all *their* investments in the region, which would surely result if any dredging operations were conducted on the rock-bottom reasons for the Sino-Japanese blood-letting. But a deviation occurred as the months wore on, and more and more liberals began to emerge with the same degree of treaty veneration as the elements they had originally disparaged. On the strength of faith in the temporary substitution of the fine-sounding words of diplomatic exchange for the pork chops of Asiatic reality, a number enlisted fervently in the great sanctions discussion of the spring and summer of 1932.

Thus the diplomatic fad of the moment, sanctions, managed to become rationalized as a most helpful supplement to pacifistic watchful waiting. The exponents of a non-governmentally organized boycott were still on the premises, adding their quasi-belligerence to the other ingredients and goading the pacifists to abandon their "grosser forms of sentimentalism" and join in a general boycott of all Japanese goods sold in America.[26] The boycotters had great faith that this gesture alone would force the Japanese economy into such straits that the leaders would withdraw their armies from the Asiatic mainland with alacrity. Perhaps they were no more ill-informed as to the situation than the supporters of a multi-nation sanctions proceeding along the League of Nations prescription.

Shortly before loud shouting for sanctions and rebuilding the fleet began, the *New Republic,* in February, 1932, re-stated its position in a long editorial, "Can Japan Be Stopped?" [27] Its condemnation of that land was much stronger now, and the belief was expressed that by now, with her greatly expanded military action, she was "guilty of aggression, of violating solemn treaties and promises, in a sense far more clear and less likely to be revised by the subsequent judgment of historians than was Germany when she invaded Belgium in 1914." This statement displayed conclusively that the same kind of prejudgment which led to all the later repudiated impulsive verdicts in 1914–1918 had not been dislodged by all the revisionism since that date, and final decisions were still in fashion on the basis of a small part of the facts, as before.

After again citing the fact that the other powers had done much the same in the past and that there had been Chinese provocation, and warning Americans not to adopt an air of "superior national morality" about it, in view of our past acts, the point was stubbornly clung to that none of this excused the Japanese. Those who had always vigorously objected to this kind of act, "no matter what government has indulged in it," were sound in adhering to a condemnatory stand. Furthermore, "if peace is ever to be safeguarded, this sort of action must stop sometime," and provocation could not be made "an excuse for military action" in violation of treaties.

Beyond supporting Stimson's position that this country would not recognize any settlement reached through war, the recommendations for action sounded much like they had some five months before. As far as the United States was concerned,

The first duty is that which our government has apparently begun vigorously to pursue—to get our citizens in China out of harm's way as soon as possible. . . . We have no interest in the Far East which justifies the sacrifice of a single American, Chinese or Japanese life. It would be intolerable to do anything which might lead to hostilities in the protection of national interests there. We hope not only that we get out of China but that we stay out until we are ready to go back at the invitation of a Chinese government to live under Chinese laws and to submit to Chinese courts.

This obviously did not touch at all on the main issue: what attitude was to be adopted toward Japan now? The advice was still to wait and do nothing, to try to isolate Japan in world opinion and stand by for the expected economic collapse, a dialectical materialist derivation. But all the active schemes were repudiated:

Admitted that she has outlawed herself, that she is a guilty nation, the world's experience in attempting to serve the future of peace by punishing a "guilty nation" in 1914 and thereafter does not lend us to advocate a repetition of the enterprise. The *New Republic* has consistently opposed the principle of military sanctions; you cannot have peace by substituting a world war for a two party conflict.

Stimson's mixed positions baffled the *Nation* as well. On March 9 it editorially praised him for charging that Japan had violated the Nine Power and Briand-Kellogg Pacts, which was the *Nation*'s position as well. It also noted that he had carefully refrained from tagging either China or Japan as the "aggressor," but it did not care for his inference that the United States would act to "keep the Open Door inviolate at all costs," which it repudiated as "foolhardy business of rattling the American saber" as well as one of a number of "dangerous threats to use force." [28]

In March, with boycott petitions signed by the "best people" becoming the latest maneuver, the *New Republic* came out in a vigorous attack [29] on the whole idea in another long unsigned editorial, "Boycott Leads to War." Boycotts were not substitutes for war, as it was becoming the fashion to believe; on the other hand, they *were* war in another form, and a particularly vicious form, which bore "most heavily on the weakest and poorest elements" of the boycotted nation. Instead of causing unemployment, starvation and disease this way, it was more humane to send over the incendiary and gas bomb squadrons. Furthermore, the caution went on, a nation backed to the wall by boycotts would not tamely submit but would fight with all the resources at its command. It was a fond but empty dream of all time that the nation faced by a big enough force of opposition would surrender instead of fight.

Calling attention to the practical side of this, the magazine held that this country would bear by far the biggest burden. We did three times as much business with Japan as the next largest country, China, and no European nation had a Japanese stake anywhere near the size of ours. Thus the nations urging a boycott would be relatively immune, while the brunt would fall directly on the United States. Besides, Japanese reprisals would fall on us first; we were the nearest enemy within reach. "This is not a time to deceive ourselves," the editorial admonished, "We are drifting toward a war with Japan, and those pacifists whose plan to safeguard peace is based on the League conception of sanctions constitute the principal force in that drift." The real issue here was whether "we ought to fight Japan, even as allies of the rest of the world, in order to punish her for the guilt already passed on her?" Editorial rejection of this course was unconditional;

The *New Republic* believes with all the force of its conviction that we should not. The world has had one unhappy experience in the use of war to end war. It has tried to outlaw treaty-breaking by the punishment of a "guilty nation." In 1917 the *New Republic* was naïve enough to urge American participation in this endeavor. By 1919 the tragic consequences were already so clearly apparent that this journal was unwilling to approve the result as expressed in the Treaty of Versailles, or to conspire in creating another world war of the same sort by advocating participation by the United States in the League of Nations.

The worst thing in the whole League Covenant was undoubtedly Article 16, which included the machinery for keeping the peace through employing sanctions, and sanctions, the editorial pointed out, was just "a polite word for war." To suggest violence to stop the Japanese was simply to rehearse the same arguments used for employing it against Germany, and that simply was not satisfactory.

The *Nation*'s position was identical; its March 2 editorial "No War With Japan" [30] was a testy reaction to the sudden burst of tough talk from "college professors, amateur diplomats, and munitions makers who are advocating an economic boycott," while claiming that the temper of the majority was unquestionably inimical to war gestures of this or any other kind.

This was undoubtedly a very courageous position at this superheated moment, with letters to the editors urging support for a Japanese boycott coming from all sides. One of the most compulsive was printed by the *New Republic* a week later, written by Raymond Leslie Buell, one of the principal voices in the liberal boycott ranks.[31] But there was much milling around on the part of other figures. Jonathan Mitchell and John Dewey were other puzzled liberals advancing one or another approach in the hopes that out of the confusion some clear avenue might loom up. Mitchell in February was convinced that Japan was led by "a band of utterly irresponsible half-mad generals and admirals," and that "between them and the forces of civilization, no useful communication" seemed possible. The "forces of civilization" were not identified. Two months later, however, he stung the people protesting the Japanese invasion by pointing out that not another country was willing to withdraw from its real estate land grabs in China except the United States, and that no settlement of the current situation was possible until the abolition of extraterritoriality. No anti-Japanese feeling was evident in this dispatch at all.[32]

The *Nation's* response to the boycott argument was across-the-board rejection; "The economic boycott is not a peace weapon, but one of the deadliest of war weapons, and there is not the slightest doubt that the Japanese would consider it as such." Its counterbalance to Buell was Professor Edwin Borchard of Yale, along with Charles A. Beard the most impressive academic arguers for neutrality in the country. On March 16 the *Nation* accorded loud praise to Borchard's attack on boycotts in the New York *Times,* agreed that his best point was that the boycott was in fact a war measure, "And in the United States, where anti-Japanese sentiment has existed for many years, it is tampering with dynamite to augment and agitate that sentiment by proposals to outlaw trade with Japan." A week later the *Nation* turned over space to Borchard to amplify on his case against boycotts for their readers, resulting in the granitic and bleakly negative "No Economic Boycott." It was the most emphatic contribution of the season which emphasized the *Nation's* editorial position, "We must make peace with the methods of peace, and not with the weapons of war."

Various editors also felt called upon mildly to reproach their esteemed British contributor Mr. Brailsford for coming out in favor of an anti-Japanese boycott in April. They especially disagreed with his picture of British-American opinion on the Japanese situation, in which he placed most of the forces against Japan in this country among the naval enthusiasts, and other "self-seeking and reactionary forces." The *New Republic* further pointed out to Brailsford that even though there were those in America who fitted his description, "the agitation for the boycott in this country" was almost entirely a product of "ardent and idealistic supporters of the League of Nations," who presumably had no material interest in the affair. The journal also hinted that he was not up to his usual incisive self in standing by the assertion that the Powers now trying to obstruct Japan had "nothing to gain" by such behavior and were acting in a purely selfless and disinterested manner.[33]

The coolness of the Hoover Administration toward supporting boycott or sanction plans as expressed on occasion by such as William R. Castle in May was considered a heartening development, and the liberals hostile to such plans continued to drum away at the relation between steps of this kind and shooting war. It did no good to emphasize "measures of restraint" to be used against nations which did not uphold pledges; "If nations persist in aggression, there is no possibility of avoiding war in any case; the problem then becomes to delimit its area." Thus the *New Republic* put forth the case for neutrality and abstention from all collective security pressures.[34]

The *Nation* agreed with the no-boycott position of the Administration even more emphatically in its May 18, 1932 editorial: [35]

That the United States will not join with other powers or with the League of Nations in coercive action to "enforce peace" has now been made clear beyond dispute by the Undersecretary of State, William R. Castle, Jr. . . . We wholly agree with Mr. Castle, as we have repeatedly stated in recent issues of *The Nation,* that peace is not to be secured by resort to economic sanctions, boycotts, embargoes, or blockades.

The magniloquence of Secretary Stimson was another situation completely. Considerable veering persisted on his numerous utterances and his famous "doctrine," ostensibly shared by President Hoover. But there was a tendency to detect in his overall attitude gestures of a threatening nature to Japan; by the end of 1932 the conviction of some of the more articulate liberals was that Stimson's course, logically followed, led straight to war with Japan. The *New Republic* was of this sentiment as early as the time of his widely-broadcast letter of February 24 to Senator Borah. Shortly thereafter, it published an editorial comment of considerable length, in which it spoke in a commendatory manner of the Secretary of State's dictum that territorial gains made by Japan in violation of existing treaties would not be recognized. But on study of all the letter, the view was expressed that Stimson intended to follow up Japan's "modification" of the Nine Power Treaty by similar "modifications" of other treaties, and that spelled a naval armaments race and furious naval base construction. The object apparently was the protection of United States trade with China, if protection of said trade could not be achieved through treaty, and in view of current Japanese action, it could not. The *New Republic* flatly called this "a challenge which looks straight in the direction of imperialistic war," and expressed the fervent hope that the American people would have nothing to do with it. This was "power politics of the most naked and discreditable sort," and if this was all that could modify Japanese behavior in Asia, then "it would be far better to leave any interference in Oriental affairs completely out of our calculations;" [36]

American trade in China is not worth one drop of American blood. And arming to fight, at the other side of the Pacific Ocean in behalf of a self-government of the Chinese people which is still far from being achieved, would be as recklessly quixotic as any national policy ever adopted in the history of the world.

John Dewey detected the same conflicting elements in Stimson's Borah letter, and in the course of a long dispatch titled "Peace—By Pact Or Covenant?" [37] thought that mixing "an appeal to force with an appeal to observe the pledge to employ only pacific means" weakened the effect considerably. Dewey's approach was one of setting aside all the League of Nations force potential represented in Articles 15 and 16 and staking the whole issue on the Briand-Kellogg Pact; in fact, he recommended the abrogation of these "force clauses" in the League Covenant in order to bring it into harmony with the Paris Pact, which he said was "to be put to the front and kept there." Denying themselves coercive force was to Dewey the only possible action for "lovers of peace."

The *Nation* cast Stimson more strongly in the role of world peacemaker than other liberal centers. When he extended his "Doctrine" of January as to Manchuria in the summer to the explosive Bolivia-Paraguay dispute in South America, great hopes were expressed that it would prevent war there. But despite the *Nation*'s hope, "there is every reason to believe it will," the Gran Chaco promptly flamed into a brutal three-year war.[38] In like manner it sought to see grand achievements from Stimson's diplomacy elsewhere and gave great praise to his address before the Council on Foreign Relations on August 7, 1932. "It is . . . a momentous happening when an American Secretary of State solemnly reiterates his belief that war is not only outmoded, but impossible at the present state of the world's history as a means of settling international disputes." [39] Other liberals were not inclined to get so enthusiastic, remembering his Borah letter six months earlier.

Singled out for special attention was Stimson's declaration that the old conception of war was that it was a private fight with no neutrals invited, but now, since the Kellogg Pact, "instead of a war being nobody's business, it is everybody's business," and that now, "a neutral nation not only had the *right* to speak out if it chooses but even had a *duty* to do so in order to preserve peace." Again a testament of great faith was made in the belief in talk as an inhibitor of war, and no consideration of the incitation and exacerbation of neutrals by thus engaging in the affairs of others, laying the groundwork for the time when sufficient anger had been built up to make attractive the exchange of words for guns. One of the regrets of the *Nation* during this period of approbation of the Stimson Doctrine was the "ominous

silence" of both the French and British diplomatic and public spokesmen. The fact that neither nation had given it their approval and
backing was held to be the main reason the Japanese had taken such
a determined stand against it. Yet, no matter what happened, the
hope was expressed that whatever the Japanese did in the line of
expressing contempt for the Stimson approach, "it cannot be met by
resort to war." [40]

The *New Republic*'s response to Stimson's Council speech began
where the *Nation* left off; "The Threat in the Stimson Doctrine" was
the title of a very lengthy cautionary editorial. There was nothing
abstract about this formula; "Stripped of generalities, placed in its
diplomatic setting and given the connotation with which it will be
read by foreign governments, it unequivocally commits the United
States in the Far East." Now that Japan had created a "puppet state"
out of Manchuria and named it Manchukuo, the issue was whether
Japan would heed the Stimson position and get out of Asia proper, or
whether the United States would back down eventually and acknowledge the Japanese action. The alternative to giving in by either party
was obviously war, and no European nation in its opinion was the
least bit interested in fighting Japan "for the sake of the Kellogg-
Briand Pact." If it meant that the United States was going to have to
fight, the strong doubt was expressed that the American people were
being represented by our Far Eastern policy, and whether "the masses
of Americans employed or unemployed" were "sufficiently concerned
in the status of Manchuria to be willing to stake their lives and fortunes on changing the flag which flies over it." The editorial doubted
if there were many Americans who even knew where Manchuria was.
Short of a real opening up of the causes of trouble in Asia, which had
been brushed under the rug at Washington in 1921, it might help
clear the air, it was thought, if each of the Powers now expressing
eloquent remarks about the necessity of keeping the peace be polled
as to what it was willing to *do* to preserve that state, "and it might
enlighten the people of each nation as to what they would in time be
called upon to die for." It was all very fine for the "vocal statesmen"
to feel sincere in their present words, but if they really meant "the
opinion of the world" when they spoke so feelingly, then it had to
mean, in addition to foreign ministers, the opinion "of the masses
who pay the price," and there was no evidence they were being consulted by anybody. [41]

Thus the *New Republic* stuck to its position of no American
involvement in Asia beyond a protest over the Japanese violation of
the Kellogg Pact; no sanctions, no boycott, no international army,
and, above all, no unilateral military interventon on the part of the
United States.

One last gasp on behalf of the League was registered in the fall on the occasion of the report of the commission headed by Lord Lytton of England, fixing responsibility upon Japan in the case of the Manchurian trouble. Both liberal journals considered it an able and eminent summarization of the situation, but expected it to have slight effect, which proved to be good diagnosis. With Japanese rejection, and cautious side-stepping by both the French and British governments, the report, which in the words of the *New Republic,* embodied "so many of the virtues of realistic, well-intentioned liberalism," was a "tragic futility." The "unplanned, capitalistic civilization," of which it was a product, was to blame mainly for this condition, and reservations were expressed as to the possibility that any "solution of the Far Eastern problem" could "arrive by the liberal route." The remedy was approaching through "the growth of a revolutionary movement in the East" which was going "to engulf liberal and imperialist alike and change the whole basis of economic organization," thus rescuing "a civilization struggling in the net of contradictions" of self-created origin.[42] The *New Republic* was hinting that after a year of traditional talk and fence-sitting, it would be the Communists who would bring about a totally unconsidered answer to the Asiatic dispute. A well-formed case for the Communists and Russia was already in circulation, as will be seen.

The *Nation,* in a series of editorial comments of some length in the fall,[43] also accepted the Lytton report without reservations, and called for "a common front" among the Western Powers against Japan in support of the report. For a short season it went back to the familiar verbal magic, calling for the expulsion of Japan from the League, the withdrawal of the United States Ambassador from Tokyo, and an international embargo on arms and loans to Japan and Manchukuo, in the latter case echoing the recommendation of the previously much-maligned Nicholas Murray Butler and his committee. None of these actions would result in war, and would surely hasten the rapid crumbling of the puppet and master alike. The deep conviction of imminent Japanese collapse died a slow death.

By winter all the eager hopefulness in the success of one or another of the suggestions of the past fifteen months had vanished. The League was being denounced as "cowardly" for doing nothing about the Lytton Report, France and Britain castigated for their open sympathy with the Japanese and their unwillingness to support Stimson, and the awareness of the perilous position of the United States in being the only big power to refuse to recognize the Japanese Asiatic penetration was slowly sinking home. Instead of recommending Japanese expulsion from the League, there was dread now that she would leave on her own initiative, an act which was thought sure to be the League's finish. In fact, the *Nation* was convinced the League had done nothing because it feared it would be destroyed by the internal dissension following Japanese secession. Like its companion publication, it boiled the French and British in oil for their "responsibility" for all this, having by their inaction "sabotaged the Covenant and the Kellogg Pact at almost every turn." [44]

Summarizing the Manchurian incident, the *New Republic* concluded that it had one salutary effect, "puncturing the pretension that the League powers want peace," or had the slightest intention of making any sacrifices of a personal kind in order to bring it about. It finished where it began, despondent of any possible good coming out of a capitalistic imperialistic world order and all its diplomatic show: [45]

Peace and international capitalistic imperialism are incompatible. As long as Britain, France and Italy are struggling among themselves and with other powers for control of foreign markets, for monopolies of foreign raw materials, for colonies and dominions, they cannot come into court with clean hands as judges of Japanese imperialism—and they not only can't, but don't intend to.

This was approximately where the liberal journals had come into the affair in the first place. After fifteen months of precarious and often perilous riding on the global diplomatic roller coaster, expressing one hopeful sigh after another that some way might be found to set matters in Asia to the heart's choice of the Occident, the comfortable retreat into lofty impartial comprehensive condemnation had presented itself as the best possible reduction of the entire unpleasant interlude. For those liberal partisans who had been watching the whole drama through the spectacles of the Russian and Asiatic Communists, there was mostly satisfaction and little regret. Occupation and the exercise of influence and power were much more satisfying than abstract diplomatic word-play.

THE SOVIET UNION ENTERS THE MANCHURIAN PICTURE

A catalog of the motives involved in liberal side-taking in the instance of Japan in Manchuria would include unconsciously a reflection of traditional American hostility toward a Japanese entrenchment on the mainland of Asia. When inextricably tangled with liberal pacifistic leanings and the undeniably genuine desires for an international community devoted to the general welfare, the dimensions of all were somewhat transformed. A new ingredient began to move into this blend as the months wore on and no satisfactory resolution appeared. The emergence of Soviet Russia as an interested and deeply involved participant, in addition to the quiet expansion of Communism into central Asia while hardly anyone seemed to be looking, soon presented a situation that in retrospect makes one wonder at the wisdom of the world diplomats with their obsessive concern with peace machinery. While completely engrossed in preventing the absorption of Northern and Central Asia by Japanese from the East, the area in default was occupied by Communists from the West and their converts. One is also inclined to wonder where the persons who rubbed their eyes in dismay in 1948 were during the previous twenty years. During this period the question became phrased: Russia is the only force standing in the way of Japanese hegemony over Northeast Asia. When the dust had cleared, after the Second World War, faces were too red to state it on the contrary, although the fumblings of policy-makers since 1945 make it evident that a vigorous Japan in this area of the world would be eagerly and jubilantly received now.

In the same way, whatever its shortcomings, the liberal press and some of its spokesmen faithfully and sympathetically chronicled the advance of Communism in China and Mongolia throughout the same period. And in like manner, the bewildered blinking and astonished outcries in the late 1940's upon seeing a Communist regime engulf all of China seem superfluous. No more logical result could have succeeded the policies followed by the white Western powers in the nearly two decades before the take-over. For the West, the situation was, in the long run, a most distressing one. Whichever protagonist was victorious, there was no part in its plans for the Occident. For the West, it has become a permanent project of trying to dislodge an enemy from a grip on Northeast Asia, although in recent years the scope of the removal contemplated has immensely widened, thanks to the contagion of Communism spreading over additional vast areas.

That the liberal attitude in general was far more favorable to the Soviet Union and its philosophy as the desirable dominant force in Asia rather than the Japanese, or even the Western powers, after a while, is not surprising. The expansion of a favorable pre-disposition is a logical process. And in view of the hate which the West showed toward Japan in the period of most active conflict over the Manchurian episode, no better environment could have aided the Soviet dream of becoming the determining force in Far Eastern affairs. In fact, the continuous buildup of Russia as an eventual checkmate must be considered as one of the factors which ended the Soviet's pariah status as a nation, and helped to facilitate a shoddy respectability via the Disarmament Conference, the London Economic Conference, recognition by the United States, and entry into the League of Nations.

Those on the outlook for the welfare of Russia went to work quite soon after Mukden. For several months a variety of speculations appeared upon Soviet reaction and possible Soviet moves, all in accord with the fixation of Russia as a weak state so absorbed with internal affairs that it desired nothing so desperately as peace with its neighbors everywhere. Some ingenious theories were set afloat from time to time. Louis Fischer, in a late fall Moscow dispatch to the *Nation* not quite three months after Mukden, revealed that the eagerness of the Western Powers to disturb Japan was motivated by a policy which strove to prevent a Chinese-Russian understanding as of the 1924–1927 Borodin era of good relations with Chiang Kai-shek. Knowing both China and Russia were anti-Versailles, the project at hand consisted of a great show of Sinophile tendencies, and at the same time adopting an approach which would exclude Russia in the campaign of dislodging Japan. They would thereupon snatch the trade with China which Japan would lose at the conclusion of its expulsion from the mainland.

As a supplement to this story that another Sino-Soviet agreement was being torpedoed, Fischer predicted that no war with Japan would result, despite Japanese provocation. He was especially repelled by Japanese charges of the "Red Menace," and Russian subsidization of the Chinese resistance. He also did not fancy Japanese comparisons of their action with the 1929 Russian sally against the Chinese. Nothing was said about the bustling Soviet state being fabricated in Outer Mongolia.[46]

Stories of a buildup of Soviet troop concentrations on the Siberian border of Manchuria were slightly out of harmony with the picture of a toiling and utterly domestically-oriented Soviet Union. In the *New Republic,* in February of 1932, this was explained as part of precautions against a likely invasion by White Russian counter-revolutionaries under Japanese incitation, or even an extension by the Japanese themselves.[47]

This latter rumor ballooned up into generous proportions the following spring, and it eventually went in with the remaining materials from which a principal policy in liberal circles was fashioned, namely, the desirability of recognizing and supporting the Soviet Union as a sure and reliable check against the Japanese hopes of major territorial aggrandizement in Asia. A wave of "White Guards" stories accompanied this, which sought to tie together the Japanese and the anti-Bolshevik Russians known to be in Manchuria and China since revolutionary days. In April the *New Republic* ran a lengthy account of Soviet efforts at keeping the peace, which now included the stationing of 100,000 troops on the Siberian border, referred to as "a very practical means" of maintaining peace. This of course contradicted flatly its main philosophy that peace could not be maintained by arms, and that disarmament was the only way out. Still another story of Japanese war-plotting against the Soviet consisted of a theory that Japan was trying to stimulate a concerted two-front attack, with the Poles and Rumanians undertaking a joint invasion from the West, presumably with the tacit support of their French backers. "A general crusade against communism, participated in by all the border states and financed by French capital would be . . . a very serious matter for the future of the world," this speculation on the possibility of a wholesale anti-Soviet onslaught closed.[48]

Throughout the spring of 1932 the theme of an impending Japanese attack on Russia recurred in the liberal dispatches, accompanied by insistent calls for stepping up trade relations with the Soviet as a means of providing a "powerful measure of peace insurance in the Far East." The Soviet "powers of resistance" would be "immensely strengthened" if she were enabled to buy all she needed here. If we insisted on not boycotting Japan, there was no reason why we did Russia, the reasoning followed. Reference was made to the fact that the Scripps-Howard newspaper chain and Congressmen had started talking about the advisability of recognition and enlarged trade relations, an encouraging sign.

Jonathan Mitchell and Fischer kept the pot boiling in the summer with ominous stories of an impending Japanese attack on Siberia. Mitchell was convinced the Japanese had the backing of "important reactionary elements in Europe," and was furious with Marshal Pétain of France for his repeated philippics about "the coming menace of the Red Army." It was Mitchell's belief that there was one thing America should do at once, and that was to recognize Russia. This would surely stop "European incitement of Japan," and should the long expected war break out, this recognition would "help make possible an early negotiated peace."[49] How this wonderful result might come about because of Russian recognition by the United States was not too persuasively illustrated.

The *New Republic* supported Mitchell with a long accompanying editorial, "In Time of Peace, Prevent War," which accepted the veracity of its correspondent and added a few elements of its own. The principal theme, however, was the possibility of a "world crusade against Communism," in which the unknown factor at this time, June, 1932, was Germany. The chances of Hitler's taking over control of Germany with French support and then joining in a major concerted Western anti-Soviet invasion timed with a similar one in Siberia by Japan, was discussed with great and serious foreboding. The recommended course for America consisted of support for the anti-Hitler forces in Germany and the ending of the humiliating hangovers of the War out of which Hitler's movement made such capital, and, of course, recognition and stepped-up trade with the Soviet Union. The latter would aid in speeding Russian industrialization "on which their powers of military resistance depend," at the same time serving notice on Japan that it could not "count on the Bolshevik bogey" in order to build up alliances.[50] The odd part of this blueprint was the *New Republic*'s mark of approval on an industrial military buildup in Russia at the very time it was praising Litvinov's disarmament speeches and taking seriously his puzzling suggestions at Geneva that all the nations of the world scrap all their armaments. That it was out of step with a simultaneous contemporary call for unconditional pacifism goes without saying. But the super-market of ideas which the liberal papers were becoming made it most difficult for thorough readers to make out any consistent philosophy. War and peace on the same page was about to become commonplace.

Fischer in the *Nation* had already taken the Russians and Japanese to war. His July dispatch, "The Soviet-Japanese War," was even more urgent in its call for American support of the Communists: [51]

A friendly American gesture toward Russia could strengthen Russia's hand . . . and guarantee a greater measure of peace in the Pacific. The only consideration which will finally sober the Japanese militarists is the knowledge that in the event of war against the Soviet Union, America might help the Soviets. To be sure, the United States government does not like Bolsheviks and will not recognize a regime now approaching its fifteenth anniversary celebration. But if America wishes to prevent another war in which it is likely to be involved, the best thing to do is to improve Washington's relations with the Kremlin.

Fischer reviewed the embarrassment already being suffered by America, plus the expense of keeping a fleet in the Pacific and the contemplation that Japan would surely get the Philippines if we set them free. In addition to this was the closing of Manchuria to United States investments and exports. The situation would be threatening for some time, he promised, but "final security" lay in the mounting industrial power of the Soviet Union and in the economic decline of Japan.

Two weeks after this report, Owen Lattimore's *Manchuria: Cradle of Conflict* was reviewed in the *Nation* by a Korean named Younghill Kang, at that time a member of the English Department of New York University, and the person to whom most books about Japan, especially favorable ones, were for a time turned over for criticism. Kang told the readers that Lattimore predicted in his book that Russia and not Japan or China would win Manchuria. He also expressed pleasure at Lattimore's on-the-spot revelation that Russia was "rapidly developing a specifically Russian non-Western technique of warfare," which he thought was "the cause of intense interest

and no little alarm to Western nations." Also considered of particular interest to the readers of America's outstanding pacifist literary
weekly was the statement, "The Russian Army is an engine of
unknown power and very great importance." [52] It was now possible to
turn and read of Litvinov's scolding of the Germans for seeking arms
equality while the Soviet built in secrecy and in numbers nobody
felt competent enough to guess.

Again in September, in its editorial "Meeting Japan's Challenge,"
the *Nation* plugged strongly for Russian recognition, this time in
order to forestall a hinted Russian recognition of Manchukuo in
return for Japanese trade privileges, and also "to make Soviet Russia
a part of the common front against Japan." [53] In 1932, the liberals
were anticipating, not a Hitler-Stalin pact, but a Stalin-Japanese pact.
Fischer's November dispatch, "A Soviet-Japanese Deal Against America?" stressed the same possibility, excused because of Russian fears
of Japan as a close neighbor. To inhibit the two from coming to an
understanding there was no better prescription than American recognition; Fischer hopefully suggested: "If there were any real statesmen
in Washington, they would know how to take advantage of this
situation." [54]

The surprise announcement of the resumption of diplomatic relations between the Chinese Nationalists and the Soviet late in December was added to the fuel burning under the recognition pot, as soon
as an interpretation could be made which did no grievous damage to
the explanation of Asiatic events up to that time. It was also the occasion for one of the amazingly casual accounts of the astonishing
spread of Communism in China, carefully separated from all possible
connection with Russia, and viewed with warm approval. The *New
Republic* [55] ascribed China's willingness to forget the unpleasantries
of five years before with the Soviet and resume full diplomatic relations to the fact that the Communists had made even bigger inroads
in the western part of the country than the Japanese had in the east,
and therefore Chiang was in grave need of a "friend," Russia being
recognized as "the logical partner." The incredible aspect of this stupendous interpretation was the easy assumption that the Soviet would
be an accessory to the Chiang Kai-shek Nanking government's long-
range plan for crushing Communism in China as well as Japanese
ambitions.

In the case of the USSR, after all the second-guessing about the
imminence of a Russo-Japanese pact, it was now conceded that "a
workers' government could hardly make an alliance, explicit or
implicit, with such a band of Fascist adventurers" as ruled Japan at
that time, and that their only logical course was also to forget past
grievances toward Nanking and embrace Chiang once more. In a
casual closing sentence in the paragraph in which this appealing

divination appeared, the editorial remarked blandly, "We do not know what price the USSR was able to obtain by way of concessions by the Chinese, but it is certainly fair to assume that it was a high one." So it was admitted that the benevolent friend of peace in Asia was not above the sharpest kind of diplomatic horse-trading, although its confidence in the purity of the "workers' government" was exceedingly premature. Such unmodified innocence helped make the 1939 Stalin-Hitler pact the psychological and moral catastrophe it was.

The *Nation* was not derailed by this new step. Everything that happened in Asia at this point all suggested the same thing: the United States was under compulsion to recognize Russia. This might be the first stage in a Russo-Sino-Japanese Asiatic bloc directed against the United States in particular, and the easy way to throw it out of joint was for this country to woo the Soviet away through diplomatic recognition. Warned a strong editorial, "Checkmating Japan," [56] "If the United States continues to ignore Moscow, the Russians may decide that it is to their best interests to come to terms with the Japanese." And of course there were the imperatives of preventing a Red recognition of Manchukuo, a dread probability, and the need for keeping open "the Chinese door which we have struggled for thirty years to keep open." This, after publishing the news that America was doing from three to four times as much business with Japan as China. "We should have little to lose by dealing honestly with Soviet Russia, and much to gain by keeping the Japanese in check and so helping to maintain the peace of the Far East," was the closing exhortation of this well-worded statement, the last in a long line of special pleas for the improvement of Russian Asiatic fortunes in 1932. But this Soviet step with Nationalist China was a foreshadowing of things to come. The Communist search for friends in 1933 was to be most fruitful, especially under the astute coaching of Maxim Litvinov. And for the ultimately discomfited liberals, "the workers' government" demonstrated its ability to "come to terms" with the Japanese even *after* American recognition.

THE COMMUNISTS DRAW A NOD
OF APPROVAL IN CHINA

The liberal press and its most articulate figures have been dealt with at considerable length thus far as champions of peace, disarmament, the renunciation of war as an instrument of national policy, and as leading exponents of pacifism as a desirable global philosophy. It might have been a trifle puzzling to a careful and reflective reader to see its lapses into belligerency and vociferous approval of the arming of the Soviet Union, for example, but this still was explained as a measure of support for a preventive kind of military medicine. Massive armies and war supplies accumulated by the Communists in Russia all went to help make the outbreak of a war against them less likely. But there was a war in progress which got no censure from the liberals: the extensive struggle going on in China between Communists and the Nationalists. The liberal division of war into "imperialist" and "class" categories mainly accounts for this. The liberal book of pacifist rules contained no clause applying to domestic bloodshed. Strikes, riots and demonstrations ending in bloodshed conducted in the name of the "workers" were not covered by the blanket of ostracism which applied to all violence under the auspices of uniformed personnel in the interests of national states. This was "imperialist war." Similarly, "revolutionary class" carnage which helped push ahead the world socialist mirage was licit, and only interference with this reprehensible; the smashing of such developments was "reaction." The intellectual trail led to the Communist door, and the opinion-makers of the liberal press did not shake off its influence, whatever they may have found objectionable about the discipline of the Party itself. Liberals of the post-World War Two era developed a facile explanation for the demise of pacifism of this earlier time by blaming it all on Adolf Hitler. But the socialist pacifists did their share in killing pacifism by their repeated reservations with respect to the utilization of violence by political compatriots. The uncamouflaged sympathy with the Communists in China did much to prepare the liberals for the day when the values seen in good old fashioned war could once more be polished and displayed without embarrassment, or feelings of guilt.

The general subject of Russian Soviet penetration of Asia was rarely touched in the liberal press or by the great majority of liberal writers. The vast area between the Urals and central China, north of India and south of Siberia, was for all practical purposes missing from the globe for a decade and a half after the Russian Revolution. The seepage of Red influence here and the creation of ill-defined new Soviet "republics" went on under a near-perfect cover of silence until Communization was a reality over almost the whole region. There were all manner of storm signals in the shape of books written about various parts of this domain, read mainly by persons in tune with the authors' enthusiasm for what was happening. The far greater part of the political fold which later on considered the Communist grasp on Asia an unmitigated calamity might have profited by coming in at the beginning of the performance, because the opportunity was always available. The Communist press was never to blame for this. A fair amount of space there was devoted to exulting over the spread of the Soviet influence. But the liberals found little room for the topic, except occasionally to admit it existed, and to issue congratulations.

To omit this conditioning on behalf of spreading Communism and the anxiety for its success especially in China is to lose sight of a very significant facet of liberal reporting and opinionizing on Japan and its industrious crunching across Manchuria and into Eastern Inner Mongolia and northern China. When the Communists took up a position of resolute resistance to the Japanese, it became fashionable to accord the former unlimited praise without any great fear of repercussions. The buildup of an anti-Japanese world propaganda by the peace-machinery-conscious Western states gave friends of China's Communists all the protective coloration they needed. Collaboration with and aid from Russia did not even have to be alluded to, and after the performance of the Red Chinese at Shanghai in the last months of the winter of 1931–32, it was the fashion for years after to simply refer to this force as "the Nineteenth Route Army." A healthy contingent of pro-Communist journalists, both in and out of the commercial press, did the greater part of the task of popularizing the label and reputation of this Communist-infiltrated armed force. In the *Nation* the first to perform this function was Agnes Smedley. Her article "The Horrors at Shanghai," [57] the first substantial atrocity story from the Sino-Japanese conflict, which was an incitatory and repetitive account of alleged Japanese butcheries, glowed with approbation of the performance of this "autonomous Cantonese" legion. However, the issue at hand was the spectacle of the liberal pacifists cheering on an enormous army of Asiatics whose goals were as remote from liberalism as if they were at large on another planet.

It is of more than ordinary import at this point to conduct a brief examination of the subject of Communism in China and the spread of Communist influence as documented by American Communist and Communist-dominated publications of substantial impact, during the years between Mukden and the beginning of the Popular Front. The relation between their account and that of the liberal press will become significant upon comparison.

There was no official Communist comment on the Japanese action in Manchuria in September until the December, 1931 issue of the *Communist* appeared, in which Harry Gannes commented briefly in restrained, quiet prose, in his "Wall Street and the Organization of the Anti-Soviet Front," that this Japanese action was simply the first stage in the preparation of Manchuria as an "anti-Soviet base." [58] But after the much more extensive Shanghai operations in January, 1932, the agitation and alarm among the Communists moved up sharply. The April issue of the *Communist,* in the article "The World Is Drifting Into An Imperialist War," urgently implored the Communist Party all over the world wherever it was engaged in transportation and communication "to organize their action against the transport of war material to Japan, against the use of the railways, and especially of the harbors and mercantile fleets, for supplying the Japanese imperialists with munitions, weapons and poison gases." The emergency view was not left in doubt in the slightest; "that is the command not only of the day but of the hour," it ordered.[59] The same month's issue of the *New Masses* sounded the same note; "Japan's campaign in Manchuria is not aimed against the Chinese people alone. It is part of the world-wide preparation for an imperialist war against the Soviet Union." [60] It was plain that the motives behind the particular type of reportage of the struggle in China were not going to be simple, and that loyalties were going to be strained in several directions, as the mixed ambitions of Russia, Japan, Britain, the United States, and two major factions in China came into collision. The Communists were undoubtedly easiest to follow, however.

The *New Masses* and *Communist* reported not only the clash with Japan; they detailed the war between the Chinese Communists and Chiang Kai-shek's Nationalists as well, in a series of communiques which read like the general ones of the daily press in 1918, or subsequently, of 1943. But most of all they stressed the amazing progress of Communism in China. In April, 1932 it was claimed that the Reds already controlled a sixth of China, containing a population of 70 millions, while fighting with great success against all comers; "The Soviets maintain a large and well-disciplined army," the *New Masses* said, "which, with the enthusiastic support of the workers and peasants, has won victory after victory against the Nanking (Chiang) forces. The army consists of about 150,000 men. It is supported by about 200,000 organized peasant troops and Communist Young Guards." The Communist guerrilla "resistance" warfare which was to cause such astounding damage in Europe in the Second World War was having its trial run in East Asia. In June, 1932, came an amazing tribute to the fighting qualities of the Nineteenth Route Army, already adopted by world Communism, made rather ridiculous in the *New Masses* by a juxtaposed appeal for the creation of pacifist organizations in America through the ministry of the John Reed Clubs.[61]

The theme of Red Chinese growth appeared time after time in ensuing years. In March, 1934 the *New Masses* announced, "One fourth of China is Red. Soviet China is bigger than any capitalist country in Western Europe—an area totalling 1,348,180 kilometers, with a population of nearly seventy-five millions." Its army was now asserted to be 950,000 including "irregulars." [62] The *Communist* the following month claimed a "stable Soviet China" state as large as Great Britain.[63] In July further information on the efficiency of the Red Chinese army was obtained direct by the *New Masses,* when they published General Chou En-lai's revealing article, "How the Chinese

Red Army Fights." [64] And in December, 1934, a roundup article summarizing the gains until that time was accompanied by a detailed map of China showing the eight enormous areas of the country already under direct Communist control and the even larger adjacent regions described as "Red Partisan Areas." [65] But even this vast beachhead and buffer did not seem to develop much of a sense of security among those whose loyalty was to the Russian instead of the Japanese or British Empire; "The danger of war against the Soviet Union is graver now than at any time in recent months," the *New Masses* solemnly announced. [66]

Beginning in the spring and summer of 1932 one can also observe a growing column of lineage devoted to the activities of the Chinese Communists among American liberals. The subject of Russo-Chinese relations of a Communist nature was prudently omitted, and left to authors of books on Asia. In the journals the weight was placed on Communist gains at both the expense of Japan and the official Chinese government Nationalist forces. This little war within a war stands as one of the fascinating topics of this era. That it received scant attention from the respectable seekers for world morality, who were still trudging toward the horizon of the millennium represented by the Kellogg Pact and the treaty paraphernalia of the 1920's, is evident in the size of the present-day military and naval budgets earmarked for the Far East, a most promising zone for perpetual war in our time.

In the spring and summer of 1932, stories of Communism's growth and spread in China were an important supplement to the liberal portrayal of Japanese evil on the mainland, the necessity of preserving the substance of anti-war treaties and agreements, and need for recognition of Communist Russia. For much of the time it was not quite clear whom they were fighting, in view of the hostility toward Chiang's Kuomintang. Even shortly after the Mukden incident, the *Nation* had attacked him openly as a "militarist" who maintained his party in office largely through conducting systematic beheadings of dissidents and driving out the "radicals" from his ranks. His demise was eagerly looked forward to, because this might "mark the end of militarist government in China." [67] What kind of a government was likely to persevere in a country torn by war from end to end was not elaborated upon. But after the remarkable publicity gained by the Chinese Reds in the Shanghai fighting, it was no longer a secret just what element was most apt to replace Chiang. The *New Republic,* relying on the "most trustworthy estimates" it could find, summed up the situation as of May 1 by putting the area of China already in Soviet hands as that occupied by 50,000,000 people, "defended" by an army of 150,000 but very poorly armed. The separation of these Communist zones by portions of territory "still controlled by government forces" was considered to be the most unhappy aspect of this, but in some areas, the readers were told that there were schools, newspapers, armories and banks, the last issuing "Soviet money." [68] When used in this way, the intention was always that of conveying that the Chinese Soviets were an utterly distinct branch from the Russian, and allusions to Russian missionary work in getting Communism started never were considered worth making. The last subject one was likely to see at this time was that of the traffic of Russians and Chinese between Moscow and the war-ridden areas of China. As in Russia, war was serving as the very efficient mid-wife in bringing another vigorous Red offspring into existence. The ability to talk continually of the ineffable virtues of peace and at the same time to reinvest the dividends of war-smashed areas for compound political profit remains the peak contribution of the Communists to the field of political dynamics in this century. The predominant part of their opponents have not yet learned that, and still yearn to dissolve the communist infection resulting from the poisons of war by administering massive doses of the poison, which helps to illustrate why more of the world moves in the direction of collectivism while giving the impression its aim is the prevention of the establishment of collectivism.

Item after item appeared in the liberal weeklies as the talkfest over possible sanctions against Japan was going on, detailing Chinese Soviet gains at the expense of the Nationalists, and intimating that important leaders and troop detachments were deserting to them. In May, Communist uprisings were reported in points of north and south China some sixteen hundred miles apart, in addition to the remorseless advance of the Reds in the west and interior. The predicament of the "Canton warlords" was cause for gratification, and the prospects for a Soviet Asia considered bright.[69] The Russian hand nowhere was in sight, although a *New Republic* feature story in the summer from west-central Asia by Joshua Kunitz of the *New Masses*, "At the Gates of Hindustan," gave enthusiastic tribute to Russian penetration of the region, and expressed considerable delight at the superimposition of the Communist way of life over that of the traditional Muslim ways.[70]

And in June, 1932 the *Nation* expertly if unconsciously described the intimate relation between war devastation and the ripening of Communism in China, while trying to divert attention from the Soviet Union as a material agent in its fashioning: [71]

Military rule in China, as elsewhere through the East, is rapidly driving the masses toward revolutionary action. Whole provinces in the interior of China are under the control of the Communists. But these radicals are natives, not agents of Moscow. . . . It is these people who make up the bulk of the Red Armies which have been organized to combat the military forces employed by Chiang Kai-shek and the Kuomintang to suppress the Communists.

American liberal apologists, on the verge of the "agrarian reformers" label for Chinese Communism, really meant that the area was going Communist as a consequence of the military chaos, not military rule. Systematic destruction of life and vast amounts of property and capital were producing the same fertile seedbed for Chinese Communism as that of the First World War provided for the Russian variety. The Leninist prescription for turning "imperialist" war into a civil one was being followed out with a vengeance.

Late in the summer the liberal journals began to editorialize at length on the "Great Communist Suppression" campaign in South China, where Chiang was reported to be marching into the Kiangsi hill country with an army of 400,000 to smash a stubborn Communist penetration. The Red guerrilla tactics were described as impossible to deal with, and desertions to the Soviet Chinese were reliably related to be now by the regiment.[72] One of the *Nation*'s anonymous contacts in China, writing under the pseudonym "Longbow," in August, supplied detailed praise for the growth of Communist organization in the Northwest. Here the Chinese Red Army was also estimated to be 400,000, with "vast auxiliaries," controlling a region of 250,000 square miles with a fifty million total population. "Longbow" took sides on the Chinese civil brutality, admitting and excusing the Communist executions of many thousands but condemning the Kuomintang political killings, described as "excesses." Said "Longbow," "These northwest provinces are fast being drawn within the Communist vortex," and expressed the trust that they would soon be establishing contact with Moscow.[73]

The same month, a lead *New Republic* editorial paragraph detailed new developments in the failure of Chiang's suppression of Communism. Two of his "crack divisions" had deserted en masse with all their weapons. One must remember that a fundamental approach to the Communist-Nationalist struggle by liberals was the fixation that half of the Red manpower and *all* their weapons and munitions were "furnished by the enemy," through the defection route. To allude that so much as a carbine was being supplied by Muscovite sympathizers was calumnious. For five years now, ever since the fallout between Chiang and Moscow in 1927, the Red Chinese had been at this civil war, with impressive results:[74]

During this time they have conquered about a sixth of China, dividing the land among the peasants, setting up their own schools, clubs, banks, factories, and establishing a stable government which has so far remained comparatively free from graft. Western observers of Chinese life, even those who write from a conservative point of view, are beginning to prophesy that the whole country will go Communist.

This was a preliminary report on the only war being supported by liberal pacifists in the summer of 1932. It included the strong strains of the "agrarian reformer" legend of Communist intentions in China, plus the beginnings of a serious intellectual effort to see the Russian and Chinese versions as vastly different, and to the creditable side of the Chinese. If the Red leaders could keep from being "corrupted," it was predicted that the whole Far East would be precipitated into a conflict "between communism and imperialism," implicitly a fine thing for all of Asia.

The Chiang-Moscow diplomatic reconciliation in December posed a perplexity in view of possible commitment of Russian support to the Kuomintang on interior policy, but this was quietly settled by reassurances that the Nanking government had "in recent months become only an empty shell," with Communists or "semi-Communists" in control of "a large part of Chinese territory," having won over millions to their cause. Little was expected to stand in the way of this process. Parenthetically, it was expected that the Japanese position in Manchuria would also get worse, mainly due to an expected stepping up of "bandit" activity there, a thinly-hidden euphemism for irregular Chinese troops supported by Russian aid from nearby Siberian points. These guerrilla bands were sure to find "a new position of great value" as a result of this diplomatic step. Henry Hilgard Villard, writing from Manchuria a few weeks before, had concluded that the disorder in Manchuria and in the new state of Manchukuo would continue indefinitely, because it was largely "in China's favor and of her making." [75] Japan's venture in the erecting of jerry-built states was an object of scorn among liberals, even though the "Soviet Republic" of Mongolia was taken with great seriousness and never alluded to as a Russian Trojan horse sitting on the northern outskirts of China.

As the war ground into 1933, more reports on the spread of the Reds into nine of China's eighteen provinces received prominent publicity in the liberal press.[76] Along with these developments, there began an intense attack on Chiang on the basis of his alleged unwillingness to devote determined opposition to Japan. In the *Nation* in the spring a passionate attack was conducted by Mrs. Sun Yat-sen on the Nationalist leader, and the call was echoed all down the line. Faith was expressed in a theory that there was a secret agreement between Japan and Chiang exchanging tacit consent to Japanese occupation in return for help in smashing the Communists.[77] And in

America, the pro-Communist front groups began to press this charge, coupled to an additional arraignment of American complicity. In July the *Nation* published a long communique signed by one J. Loeb, represented as the executive secretary of "The Friends of the Chinese People." He asserted that the Roosevelt Administration had made available to the Nanking government $50 millions in wheat and cotton through the Reconstruction Finance Corporation, which would be dumped on the Chinese market to further depress prices there and more deeply impoverish Chinese peasant farmers. He further maintained that these products would all be used to support Chiang's armies in their campaign to root out domestic opposition, which armies would also be detailed to collect from the peasants the original cost of the loan. Loeb protested in the name of his group the action of the United States in manipulating its "puppet government" in China, and called the entire transaction "robbery" of the Chinese by its own government. Any loans to China could not be administered fairly by Nanking, since "the whole world" recognized it as "a mere puppet in the hands of American imperialism," and urged that the "imperialist powers, including the United States," get their troops out of China. "We demand recognition of the right of the Chinese people to solve their own destiny without imperialist intervention," a delicate way of demanding that the world retire to the stands and let the two Chinese belligerents fight to a finish.[78]

Imputations of outside aid to Chiang for purposes of crushing the Communists, along with repetitions of earlier strictures upon his faintheartedness toward Japan, continued for years. An unsigned *New Republic* article late in September, 1933, purporting to be a description of the Asiatic battle at that stage, passed on the news that it was being "whispered" that the American agricultural products being shipped to Chiang were being resold to Japan at a discount to pay for "rifles and machine guns to shoot the peasants down." But after six years, "in spite of foreign help to their enemies," the Chinese "Soviets" were still in possession of their areas, and "even advancing." This report reinforced the firmly believed story that the Chinese Reds received "no foreign help, no subsidies or loans, no weapons except those captured from their enemies." This was truly the most amazing army in all history, able to satisfy its armament needs exclusively from the stores of an enemy which always succeeded in surrendering or deserting in such numbers that they provided guns enough to go around even for the originally gunless.[79] There seemed to be no limit whatever to the credulousness of a liberal reading audience.

Speaking of long-range questions, the unidentified author of "Red China" went on, "Time and again they have shown that if Western and Japanese support were withdrawn from the puppet governments of the seacoast, all China would be Communist within a few months or years." Would this be an evil thing? The same argument in favor of recognition of Russia, namely, the vast economic welfare which would befall the United States immediately thereafter, was brought out and dangled alluringly as so much bait to convince those with nationalistic tendencies: [80]

. . . if the Western powers withdrew and permitted the Soviets to fulfill their destiny, there would be a government in China which would have the allegiance of the masses of the people. War lords and landlords, the two curses of the Chinese nation, would both be abolished. There would be a new power in the Pacific strong enough to provide a counterpoise to fascist Japan. And there would, moreover, since the Communists are bent on improving the living standards of the masses, be an immense new market for Western products of all types, machinery, automobiles, oil, electrical equipment. There is a prospect here of eventual peace.

Like the faction interested in Russian welfare, the "friends" of the Chinese people were willing to work all sides of the intersection simultaneously, presenting arguments which might contradict each other but if offered in relays, might be most difficult to examine and compare. The legend of an eagerly-straining Communist world anxious to engage in stupendous trade with the capitalist West was offset by the less enthusiastic reports of the self-sufficiency strategy underlying their economic building, but consistency did not have to be a guide during this all-out propaganda campaign. The stakes were liberal sensibilities at this point.

BOOKS ON CHINA ACQUIRE
A PRO-COMMUNIST FLAVOR

An examination of the books on China gives us additional enlightenment as to the direction of prevailing winds of interpretation. From 1933 on, the volume of literature on China and its two big controversies steadily increased. The reviewers were in close accord with the editorial policy of the liberal press, examining the volumes with a sure and steady pro-Soviet hand. Isidor Schneider was slightly unhappy with R. H. Tawney's *Land and Labor in China* for the author's advice that China's transition be achieved at a cautious and measured rate, which Schneider did not think "practical or even possible." Schneider insisted that "when a civilization transforms itself it requires revolution to supply it with energy or momentum," and that "caution in political affairs" was simply "synonymous with inertia." Schneider was sure that the "red" revolution, as he consented to call it, would undoubtedly replace the "compromising" Nanking regime and continue rapidly to "Westernize" the Communists and China.[81] Schneider also found the veteran old missionary hand Kenneth Scott Latourette and his book *The Chinese: Their History and Culture* unsatisfactory, especially the latter's unfriendliness to Chinese communism, which was represented mainly as bandits and "locally independent military groups." Latourette was condemned for failing to recognize that at that date, the summer of 1933, "the Soviets in China had consolidated themselves in a vast territory with a population of seventy-five millions, where an efficient, just and orderly government has been functioning." [82]

Books by partisans were handled far differently, even if on occasion the exuberance of the author was flustering. A Chinese, Ch'ao'ting Chi, reviewed Agnes Smedley's *Chinese Destinies* in the fall of 1933 with much enthusiasm. Curiously admitting that the most impressive parts of her stories of Chinese Communism at work were fables, in defense, he apologized with some lameness: "of course, the stories cannot be true in the photographic sense. They are sometimes fictionalized, yet they are fundamentally true. . . ." [83]

Ben Dorfman, a "technical expert" to the Lytton Commission and a student of the Far East on an international relations fellowship from the University of California, praised Joseph Barnes's symposium *Empire in the East* in the summer of 1934 and recommended it "to anyone who wishes an authoritative one-volume work" dealing with Far Eastern problems, although he had to make a reservation for what he considered the book's "unwarranted Marxian tinge in spots." [84] Mauritz Hallgren harked back to his 1931 interpretation of the Japanese action in his review.[85] Barnes, who, Hallgren pointed out, had just become secretary of the American Council of the Institute of Pacific Relations, as well as Lattimore and Frederick V. Field, did a disservice to the readers by not discussing the Japanese problem from the Japanese point of view:

To survive as a nation, Japan, an insular power with no natural defenses, must follow the English pattern and either establish bridgeheads on the Asiatic mainland (Korea, Manchuria and Shanghai) or else shape its policy as to keep the mainland divided against itself.

As to China, Hallgren admitted it was still too weak to be considered an immediate threat by the Japanese,

but there is an implied threat in Chinese nationalism and a much more positive one in the growing strength of the Soviet Union in Siberia. This is a problem any Japanese government, whether ultra-militaristic or composed of internationally-minded liberals, would have to face. It is as likely to result in war as any of the other factors discussed by the authors of this book.

A sustained editorial position such as this by America's liberal press might have provided Americans a formidable service in obtaining a balanced view of the Asiatic question.

More in the usual tone was Herman Simpson's considered view of Owen Lattimore's *The Mongols of Manchuria,* "a really excellent book," predicting that it would be "read with care in the foreign offices of the Soviet Union, Japan and China." Simpson, one of the *New Republic*'s most formidable Marxists, was especially pleased with Lattimore's deflation of the merits of China's economy under "landlord exploitation" and his strong plea for belief in the viability of the usually unmentioned Communist puppet state of Outer Mongolia. Confided Simpson, "When he refers to Soviet policy in Outer Mongolia, he represents it as wise and beneficent in its effects upon the vast majority of the Mongols." [86] But the Russian absorption was not referred to in the sort of language which characterized the description of Japan in Manchuria.

T. A. Bisson, identified as "the Far Eastern expert on the staff of the Foreign Policy Association," followed a predictable trail as well. He delivered an acid lecture to the author of a biography of Henry Pu-yi, the Japanese-supported ruler of Manchukuo, which he did not like at all. In concluding this summary of *Twilight in the Forbidden City,* by Sir Reginald Johnston, whom he thought especially obtuse, Bisson said, ". . . he must be aware though he gives no intimation of it, that the Chinese workers and peasants in the Soviet areas of the south-central provinces have already begun to take their fate into their hands. When this 'mob' (as Johnston referred to the Communists) has completed its task, there will no longer be any need of a Manchu emperor—propped up on his throne by Japanese bayonets —to set China right." [87] Agnes Smedley in the *Nation* summarily dismissed Johnston's book as "500 pages of twaddle," a "trivial and vicious" volume.[88]

Bisson had a different conclusion for Victor Yakhontoff's *The Chinese Soviets.* This book, by a reputedly Russian Red Army general, mostly from material not obtained on the scene and apparently written in Moscow, was placed alongside Miss Smedley's *Chinese Destinies* of the year before as the two important books breaking through "the conspiracy of silence in the Western world" on this new Communist state, reputed now to be larger than any nation in Europe. In the New York *Herald Tribune* Miss Smedley hailed Yakhontoff's book as "a masterly summary of the Chinese movement—a rich mine of unprejudiced information and historical facts," while Bisson thought it a magnificent study of the trials and tribulations of Chu

Teh and Mao Tse-tung from the collapse of the Russian period of understanding with Chiang down to 1934. He fully concurred with Yakhontoff's assertion, very general now through the ranks of the Communists and their sympathizers, that if Western support of Chiang were withdrawn, most if not all of China would rapidly become Communist.[89]

An un-named reviewer complimented Robert T. Pollard's *China's Foreign Relations, 1917–1931* in a December, 1933 issue of the *Nation,* particularly because of the author's "moderation and impartiality" in his discussion of "Chinese relations with the Soviet Union." It was one of the few times when the fact that there were any such relations ever appeared in print in the liberal weeklies.[90] On the other hand, reviewers immediately went to work on books and authors who adopted unfriendly attitudes toward the conduct of the Communist regimes. Lewis Gannett in the same month castigated Ralph Townsend's *Ways That Are Dark—The Truth About China,* and F. R. Eldridge's *Dangerous Thoughts About the Orient.* Although atrocity story-telling about the enemies of the Soviets had been a well-respected enterprise, counter-stories were deeply resented, and Gannett was much offended by these two authors in this department, in addition to their "ignorant prejudice" about Russia and their silence about Japanese pressure on Inner Mongolia.[91] Gannett did not mention Outer Mongolia. Another book treated in this manner was Hu Shih's *The Chinese Renaissance,* flayed by Agnes Smedley in the *Nation* on August 29, 1934. She left no doubt at all that she considered Dr. Hu a reactionary of the very worst sort, and utterly unrepresentative of the "New" China.[92] When she and the liberal editors of the day used the word "renaissance" with reference to China, they were referring to the infiltration of Communism after the World War.

Miss Smedley's *China's Red Army Marches* was published too late to review in 1934, but in a brief roundup of worthwhile books on foreign affairs, the *Nation* recommended the volume as an episodic treatment of "an important movement in our era—the building of the Chinese Soviet Republic."

Still another warmly-greeted book was Sergei Tretiakov's *A Chinese Testament,* which Maxwell S. Stewart described in the *Nation* as "a page torn from life," detailing the making of a young Chinese Communist in Russia and China, who was now supposed to be "part of the forces buried somewhere in the interior of China, working underground but relentless in their operation."

With the tide of opinion on China running in this direction, it was no surprise to find the general tone of news and opinion on China following a routine pattern. The fall and winter of 1933–1934 found continual revival of the alleged Chiang-Japan secret deal against the Communists, and great praise for a Chinese Red offensive in Fukien and Kiangsi provinces, with the Nineteenth Route Army bearing the brunt. In January, reports started to filter into the editorial columns quietly announcing the collapse and defeat,[93] which was memorialized eventually late in the month in the *New Republic* by C. Frank Glass, the Russian Tass News Agency correspondent in China, in an article "An Army Betrayed." Glass identified the beaten warriors only once as "Communist" in three long columns of print, and once more reviewed the story of collaboration between Chiang and the Japanese.[94]

The Chinese Communist cause was in no sense abandoned here, however. Throughout 1934, news notes and editorials devoted to their fortunes appeared with impressive regularity. The *Nation* printed several reports by a reporter in Tientsin who used the pseudonym "Crispian Corcoran," all beaming with approval on Red activity and goals. In January, 1934, he brushed aside the idea that Chiang had won any significant victory or could expect to establish effective authority, since the tide was running with the Reds;[95]

China's salvation . . . will come only when the bankruptcy of the present rulers, both in the Kuomintang and out of it, has manifested itself in every field and a new popular movement is born out of the general disintegration. This may find its genesis in the "Soviet" districts of Kiangsi or elsewhere. There are signs of it everywhere. China awaits a moment led neither by generals nor by silk-gowned politicians. The solution of her problems can only come after a new revolutionary era.

In the lull in military activities through most of the spring and summer of the year, the *Nation's* correspondent and its editors interpreted this as partially due to Japanese fear of the Red Army and the Russians, during which interim they were presumed to be trying to make alliances with foreign powers. In May this was thought to be France, during the tenure of the liberal-execrated Doumergue regime. "Corcoran" rejoiced at this chaotic pull-and-haul and reminded the readers that as far as Russia was concerned, there should be no alarm; "Soviet Russia is fully competent to take care of her own interests and can play the diplomatic-military game as well as an imperialist Power, for an infinitely better cause."[96] Chinese affairs were never presented from the Nationalist point of view, and it was a matter of editorial policy always to apply quotations to the word "menace" when it was preceded by the word Communist in Chiang-originating reports on the contest with the Reds.

In the first week of December, 1934 came the major dividend announcement to reward the faithful adherence to the Communist cause in China, the long march into the southwestern interior and the investment of Szechuan. "Corcoran" announced a smashing Red victory in rich west-central China as well.[97] The *Nation* shouted, "The 1000-mile trek of the Red Army through the heart of China must go down as one of the heroic feats of modern history," and the *New Republic,* fully in tune with the new semantics, described this destructive odyssey as a process of "liberating all of southwestern China from its landlords and war lords." The plaudits in the *Nation* were not ended; still another rousing cheer came forth, combining not only praise for achievement but hope for even greater future victory: [98]

It is no exaggeration to say that the march of the Chinese Red Army . . . is one of the most remarkable feats of modern military history. . . . thousands of Americans will follow its struggles against overwhelming odds with keen sympathy and interest, and with confidence that the reactionary regime of Chiang Kai-shek will ultimately be overthrown.

Charges began to appear in the liberal weeklies about this time insisting that American airplanes and pilots were being furnished Chiang for use against the Communists. The *New Republic* deprecated such aid by expressing the belief that the region now controlled by Mao's Soviets was so vast no possible campaign could dislodge them.[99] The area apparently was so well-set that it was already being referred to as "Red China." In December, 1934, Harry F. Ward wrote a sizable letter addressed to the editors of the *Nation,* and protesting our furnishing of "Hessians" and aviation equipment to the Nationalists. Ward's particular complaint was that Congress had not authorized this, and the men and planes reaching Chiang were sent as the result of "arbitrary acts of executive officers," which implied the knowledge of this by President Roosevelt.[100] The editors followed Ward's letter with a scorching editorial on the same subject, charging that ex-Army and Navy fliers teaching aviation in Chiang's schools were training pilots who were flying American planes "which have been utilized exclusively in action against the population of the Soviet districts."

So the sides, having been established, continued to attract the partisans. But the liberal eye was fixed firmly and favorably on the Communists, and it became more difficult with the passing months to conceal the liberal expectations of great things from a completely communized China. An occasion was even found to speak of the growth of a "peasant" guerrilla force in Northern Korea estimated to be half a million strong, actively engaged in harassing the Japanese in Manchuria in this corner of Asia adjacent to Soviet Siberia.[101] Distracting the Japanese this way was best appreciated as a deterrent to Japanese war ambitions with Russia.

In January, 1935 following the famous and much-trumpeted-about "long march" of the Chinese Red army into the interior of China, the *New Republic* felt called upon to defend editorially various excesses of the Communists. The overrunning of the area, plus the looting and killing, were explained as "confiscation of the property of rich merchants and dividing land among the peasants." The report that two American missionaries had been apprehended and shot was waved away as of little consequence; after all, the editorial consoled the queasy, "The Red Army itself does not harm foreigners unless they are tried and found guilty of fighting against the revolution." [102] This did not absolve the Communists of responsibility for the missionaries, but it suggested that they shot their prisoners of war, since Japanese qualified as "foreigners" by any stretch of this definition.

The episode of the emergence of Communist China as a formidable force in continental Asian affairs and the liberal response to this development placed a severe strain on liberal connections with any kind of purposeful anti-war activity. But the logical absurdity of world peace proponents warmly cheering on a massive armed force of grim Asian Communist warriors was not fully realized for some time. The transformation of anti-war movements and groups into parallel anti-Fascist organizations was the death blow, but for many pacifists, the detection that they had been mobilized into another Communist front was delayed until the Second World War was well underway. Hangovers persist to this day in the form of pacifist reluctance to entertain or contemplate war against Communist regimes anywhere, though their hackles may be said to rise with ease upon hearing the word "Fascist" or "Nazi," in a case of true conditioned response.

THE PULL AND HAUL OF OPINION
ON THE FAR EAST, 1933–1935

As the Japanese pressed ahead in their campaign in Northeast Asia for the next two years, the response in the liberal ranks tended to take the various tangents already outlined. The increasing attention paid to the growth and spread of Chinese Communism under the utterly disintegrating conditions brought on by the war tended to be the main hopeful sign which liberals cared to note, although the fact that the war was its main nutrient went unobserved. But the other and conflicting policies which drew liberal advocacy remained at the top of the deck as well, shuffled into prominence as the news of the battle areas shifted from week to week. In addition to admiration for Red China, the pressure of Japan's advance induced steady calls for recognition of Russia, and United States collaboration with the Soviet against Japan, another bout of loud exhortations to the League of Nations to win another round in the field of moral disapproval of Japanese behavior, and suspicion of the Chiang Kai-shek regime's interest in driving out the Japanese, while still clinging to an anti-war attitude insofar as the white Western nations were concerned. British and American naval buildup was roundly denounced as an incitation to Japan, a strange tack in view of the fervent hoping that went on constantly that Japan would come a cropper at the hands of its Chinese and perhaps Russian antagonists. But to the other nations the "no help wanted" sign was hung out. In fact, as the naval rebuilding began, the liberal press carried overtones of pro-Japanese sentiment in its uncompromising rejection of aggressive Anglo-American gestures in the direction of the Far East.

Probably the Communist sympathizers and fellow-travelers saw with more clarity than any others the nature of the conflicting views, hopes and loyalties produced by this East Asian clash. The welfare and comfort of Communism called not only for support of the Chinese and the defeat of Japan, but at the same time the diminution of the influence of the Western powers everywhere in the Far East. They were not unaware of the mixed emotions among Westerners in Asia at that moment, either. Agnes Smedley described their position in a single sentence in her China dispatch to the *Nation* which was published on March 30, 1932: "Some of the foreigners have no desire to see the Japanese make a colony of China and usurp foreign markets and privileges; yet at the same time most of them regard Japanese imperialism as a bulwark against Soviet Russia and against Communism in Asia." The great Communist triumph of the decade was their persuasive performance in inducing the Western powers to conclude that they were the most desirable alternative in East Asia.

The liberals seemed quite satisfied to see the Western powers and the United States win a verbal contest through the ministrations of the League. Here the job was one largely consisting of proving through treaty law and international morality that Japan was wrong and the remaining nations in sole possession of rectitude. The only move which received liberal support outside the League's rhetorical offensive was a short-lived recommendation for an arms embargo to the war areas, based on the assumption that fighting could not continue without the munitions reaching Asia from the West. Liberals cooled to this when it became obvious that the Chinese would be far more seriously injured. The Japanese industrial system was deemed sufficiently well developed to keep its nationals supplied with the tools of war, while it was their opponents who were at the mercy of the arms traffic from Europe and elsewhere. The denunciation of the armament manufacturers and the traffic in arms, when placed in juxtaposition to the Red Chinese, who were in legend surviving exclusively on the arms taken from the enemy, made a cruel contradiction for the liberals. With all hope placed on the ability of forces of Mao to drive out the invader, coupled to a persistent prediction that economic collapse would soon cause Japan's war effort to founder, the other diverse and frequently not very well integrated views on the Asiatic war became largely decorative.

The extension of the war by Japan early in January, 1933 temporarily stimulated liberal anger and indignation to previous heights. The *Nation* blazed at it as a "challenge to humanity" equalling the previous ones of Japanese origin, and urged the League, President Hoover and Mr. Stimson again to make statements in disapproval. In addition to these verbal condemnations, it called upon the Hoover government to make an appeal for an embargo on all shipments of munitions to Far Eastern points.[103] The *New Republic* ventured the theory that the militarists wanted to act fast on the grounds of Japan's rapidly decomposing economic system, enjoying the dubious prosperity engendered by comprehensive wartime inflation.[104] The deep belief that such inflation had a limited future impelled the liberal papers repeatedly to predict these collapses, in line with dialectical apocalyptic treatises. That the whole world was going through the inflationary process simultaneously seemed to escape their vision during the middle and late 1930's. According to Marxian rules, it could not continue. Another thrust at Chiang's expense also resulted from Japan's Shanhaikwan venture; the same journal attacked him for his campaign to suppress Communism during the previous summer, and called upon him to bring Mao and the Soviets into a frank alliance against the Japanese. The Chinese Reds, the editorial comment confided, had "the same advantage over Chiang Kai-shek that Lenin had over Kerensky;" their policy was "single and straightforward," whereas Chiang, "in his efforts to retain power," had to "trim and tack," and "deceive his own people" as well as depend upon foreigners.[105]

Another flurry of pleas for action by the League came upon the publication of the report of the League Committee of Nineteen, a far stronger statement on the League's attitude toward Japanese action in Manchuria and China. Another committee had received and accepted Litvinov's suggestion for a bald definition of "aggression," as we have already seen, plus support of the idea of economic sanctions, all of which were considered advantageous toward eventually getting a Japanese withdrawal from the continent. Both major liberal organs printed fervent hopes that the Committee's report would get the acceptance of all members, and the collaboration of the two principal non-members, Russia and the United States.[106] The arms embargo and limited economic sanctions, "without seriously

injuring its [Japan's] population," [107] were considered effective political medicine to apply at this point. Some doubt existed as to what
the not-yet-inaugurated Mr. Roosevelt might do, although the *Nation*
was sure he would support these moves on the grounds that he had
endorsed the Stimson doctrine. The *Nation's* strong March 1, 1933
editorial, "Back The League!" [108] pointed out that Stimson had gone
"far ahead of the League in formulating the attitude of disapproval,"
and felt secure in its faith that a combination of the League, the U. S.
and the U. S. S. R. would inhibit further Japanese dreams of engulf-
ing all of North China. But just what they would do beyond issuing
new verbal chidings to Japan remained as dark and obscure as it had
from the very beginning. There did not seem to be the slightest possibility that any military action would be sanctioned, and the liberal
papers had recoiled in horror from such action, as well as refusing
to give the faintest breath of support for actual gunfire by outside
forces in Asia. Liberal policy had reconciled itself to the limited war
idea there, a consequence of the logic of its repeated assertion in those
days that a small war could not be ended to any advantage by making
it bigger.

The *New Republic* even at this stage did not share the enthusiasms
of its colleagues for sanctions, being content to forget the entire matter
after concluding the Committee of Nineteen's report with a comprehensive statement roundly condemning Japan. It also did not believe
that the two big nations outside the League would be as interested in
pushing Japan as the *Nation* anticipated: [109]

This country will be much less inclined to join in sanctions under Mr.
Roosevelt than it was under Mr. Hoover; and it is hard to imagine Russia's entering such a dangerous game at all. We hope and believe, therefore, that the world will recognize the plain truth, that the application of
sanctions is likely to lead to war; and will let the matter rest with the
present "moral judgment" against Japan the only thing now possible.

By the end of March all the glad hopes of the earlier part of the
month had vanished; the League had failed to get the cooperation of
the two big non-members, Japan had announced her coming withdrawal from the League, the nations had gone back to handling the
problem on an individual basis, and Adolf Hitler had come upon the
scene. For the next four years the Far East and the Japanese drew
steadily less attention and space in the liberal papers, being crowded
out by the volume of material on German and European affairs. In
fact, in a short time, more lineage was devoted to Germany than to
all other foreign countries combined. But the events of the day got
steady representation, even if the indignant heat of the first year and
a half of the Asiatic war managed to cool somewhat.

The arms embargo issue continued to stay hot through March and April, with the *Nation* in favor, and the *New Republic*'s frown deeper than ever on the scheme. The British application of the policy to both sides drew mixed reactions; some liberals considered that a start had to be made someplace, and that the British action was commendable. Others continued to think that such actions were dangerous proclivities, and incitations to stiffening the Japanese determination, as well as preliminaries to spreading the war. Japan's decision to cut off its participation in the Geneva Conference and its ultimate withdrawal from the League were interpreted by the *New Republic*'s editors as some of the fruit of pressure on the Japanese.[110] British sincerity came under deep suspicion as well. There even developed the theory that the British government was actually helping out Japan by this action. But the beginnings of the attack on the munitions makers and the arms trade in general in the United States were starting to take, modifying some liberal opinion. Said the *New Republic:* [111]

In the United States, there is a great deal of sentiment in favor of an arms embargo; but so far as we can judge, it is a sentiment for doing away with this unsavory trade *in toto,* and not for using the embargo to enforce moral judgments against an aggressor. For the unpalatable truth is that an arms embargo directed against Japan alone would be regarded by her as a *casus belli* quite as much as would a general economic boycott; and every argument which applies against a boycott is equally good against an arms embargo.

So, it appeared, as the editorial had admitted, all the schemes thus far advanced for checking Japan short of violence had "withered away in the bright light of public discussion," and all the optimistic guessing about Japan had not turned out to be very accurate. Robert Dell, for instance, had written to the *Nation* [112] from Geneva expressing strong hope the League would soon chide Japan sternly and that there need be no fear of Japan walking out of the League or taking any other action, as the Japanese had learned that they no longer frightened anybody, and that the Committee of Nineteen had called "the Japanese bluff." Dell exulted that "the salutary effects of its action show what would have happened if the bluff had been called in September, 1931." By the time Dell's report was published, the Japanese had walked out of Geneva and a month later had dated their withdrawal from the League. Dell's talents as a prophet suffered from the same disease of wishful thinking as marred the vision of his contemporaries.

Louis Fischer, in his periodic report from Moscow, gave a signal that Russia was beginning to back-pedal away from the collective approach to Japan and seek the best arrangement for itself. His "Russia Looks for Friends" late in March, 1933 [113] was a prelude to the new look in Soviet diplomacy brought west by Litvinov, heavily tinctured with new appeals for United States recognition and teamwork on the Japanese threat to their Far Eastern interests. Fischer was able to discuss here the Red interests in Manchuria beyond the cloud-scraping level of idealistic interests in abstract peace, and he intimated that the Russians were still looking for a non-aggression pact with Japan, and on the verge of recognizing "the new status quo in China," which also must have dismayed the liberal devout who clung tenaciously to the notion that power politics tactics of this kind were unthinkable on the part of a "workers' government." Fischer warned that the time was growing short, and that if the United States did not like this dispensation, it could prevent it from realization by recognition. If Mr. Roosevelt was "afraid to ruffle Japan by establishing relations with Moscow," then half of the fleet might be transferred back to the eastern seaboard at the same time, a maneuver which was bound to display our peaceful intentions.

From the end of March on, as the *New Republic* put it, "all the talk about forcible sanctions, embargoes and boycotts" which had dominated the scene for months "withered away to nothing," [114] and great doubt was now expressed that either the U. S. or the U.S.S.R. would have anything to do with such programs even if all the League members were in agreement. In May, the situation was re-appraised in the cold light of reality: [115]

The bitter truth is that the Western world probably has not the power and certainly has not the will to oppose the Japanese adventure by force. There is every indication that President Roosevelt, realizing the extremely dangerous situation toward which this country was drifting under Messrs. Hoover and Stimson, has altered American policy. It cannot be too often repeated that there is no hope of peace maintained through international coercion when the nations which would have to do the coercing are not genuinely desirous of preventing war, but are simply playing the old international game under a new terminology.

This was perhaps the most comprehensive repudiation of the whole line followed since September, 1931, although signs of this type of retreat had been showing for some time.

For a while after the Japanese withdrawal from the League there was no yardstick by which to gauge the week-by-week Asian war. From time to time admissions were grudgingly made that the Japanese were a cool and calculating lot. Their refusal to give up the "mandated" Pacific Islands on the grounds that their title to them dated from the pre-League secret treaties brought forth another wry comment from the *New Republic* on Woodrow Wilson's determined ignorance of these agreements,[116] while the *Nation* considered "disingenuous" but also "realistic" Foreign Minister Yosuke Matsuoka's famous remark in New York to the general effect that "formerly John Bull and Uncle Sam were engaged in an international game of poker which Japan has now begun to learn, while they, having secured all the territory they want, now desire the game to be changed to contract bridge, and complain that Japan does not understand the rules." [117]

Some of the correspondents did not adjust to this shift in emphasis and continued to castigate Japan for behaving in the tradition of the Western powers it was now tormenting. Still there was sufficient understanding of the direction in which this unrelieved moral condemnation was heading. Nathaniel Peffer, in a vast outburst against Japan in a June issue of the *New Republic,* showed great regret that "Realpolitik" was still around and bumptious in "the new international era" when all nations had presumably signed away for all time all the actions which were part of this way of national life. Still, he was satisfied that the Stimson approach had been halted: [118]

It is better that the Stimson Doctrine remain a grandiose futility than that it become a gage of battle. The cumulative hostility between Japan and America since 1905 makes the danger of war between the two likely enough without specific charges. For it must be plain now that the Stimson Doctrine could have been effectuated only by force.

Peffer now was convinced that the "international peace machinery" had failed "because there was none," and that they had all been deluding each other, thinking and talking as if there were an "international spirit" when there never was any at all. In washing his hands of the Japanese question, Peffer advised, "Before any international peace machinery can invoke any ordinance in the Far East . . . it must first have to be demonstrated that it can and will do so in Europe and North America."

In the summer of 1933, after a few months of relative sobriety, the Far East again drew liberal editorial attention, as a result of the recommendations of Roy W. Howard, the active head of the Scripps-Howard newspaper chain, who returned from an Asiatic trip with a parcel of ideas with which the liberal editors did not concur entirely. His recommendation that the 1924 Exclusion Act be repealed and that we recognize Russia were in accord with liberal policy planks of some standing, but his advice that the United States Navy be built up to full treaty limits, and beyond, if the other nations were willing to take off the bars, was roundly condemned. Howard's description of Manchuria as "another Alsace-Lorraine from which Japan would only be ousted by armed might" prompted the *Nation* to retort, "Are American Marines to recapture the Asiatic Alsace-Lorraine for the Chinese?" An angry condemnation of Howard's suggestion failed to see any reasons why the United States "should now arm to the teeth" because the Japanese had made scrap out of their treaty obligations. Howard had stated categorically that there were reasons now, to which the *Nation* tartly replied, ". . . in *The Nation*'s view, there could be no surer way of bringing about war with Japan than Mr. Howard's proposed policy." As to Howard's opinion that the Japanese did not think America willing to make the expenditure necessary to put up a competent fighting force, that was fine: "If the Japanese believe we do not want to fight, we should be highly content with that view and not attempt to prove that they are mistaken." [119]

The *New Republic* also had a question, "Just what is it that we want Japan to do, which she now refuses but would accede to if our navy consisted of a few more ships than at present?" With a campaign in full heat against munitions makers and munitions trade, a world disarmament conference going on, and harsh condemnation of elements in President Roosevelt's Administration and Congress pushing for big naval spending, Howard could not have touched a more sensitive liberal opinion nerve than this. Howard's suggestion was simply an incitation to an arms race between two "possible belligerents," and there was no evidence that relations between such nations had ever been improved through this kind of proposal. The *New Republic* concluded that with the signing of the Philippine independence bill, the United States was turning away from "imperialistic intentions in any part of the world," and that to implement this step the nation was "likely to make our foreign trade only an easily dispensable luxury." Therefore there seemed to be no earthly reason for competing with the Japanese anyway: [120]

. . . would not Mr. Howard's ends be better achieved if we said to Japan: "Under no circumstances do we propose to fight you for land, trade or opportunity for investment in Asia. In view of this fact, and since our present fleet is obviously adequate to protect our own shores from aggression—an aggression which you could not carry across the Pacific in any case—we do not propose to tax our citizens at this time for a huge, completely non-productive and wasteful expenditure on additional naval equipment?"

But the potential war that disturbed the liberal press in mid-1933 and on into the following year was not between the United States and Japan: it was between Japan and Soviet Russia. The pressure which had begun months before suggesting the worthwhile results emerging from United States recognition of Russia, closer trade relations, and an understanding on the Far East, increased in volume as the hope of collective diplomatic pressure faded. Japan's ambitions in regard to absorbing the Chinese Eastern Railway, its expressed determination at Geneva to climb into the ranks of the first-rate naval powers, as well as to stay in Manchuria, were all cited as some of "a myriad reasons why Washington should quickly get in touch with Moscow" and start drawing closer to the nations of Europe and particularly Russia. In an extended speculation on the possibility of another Russo-Japanese war, titled "Will Japan Fight Russia?" in late October, 1933, the *New Republic* continued its editorial tack established ever since Mukden by re-asserting that the Soviet Union was "the only power" that threatened "Japanese expansion in the Western Pacific." The conviction was expressed that all factions in Japan wanted war with Russia, and were only waiting for the most propitious moment to fall upon her. In view of the conflict between American interests and those of Japan, the editorial thought it highly advisable that we recognize Russia, on the grounds that "the stronger the Soviets become, the less danger there is of a war along the Amur that might involve the whole world." [121] As late as November, 1933, ominous reports of the imminent outbreak continued, even though the Russians were making "every effort to avoid it," and had already put it off by yielding to "a whole series of Japanese aggressions." [122]

With recognition by the United States achieved, in addition to the useful diplomatic shoring and patching which Maxim Litvinov managed to accomplish at Geneva and London, there was a sudden diminution of liberal accounts predicting nearly every week the mortal danger of Russia in the path of Japan. Stories of Soviet armed and aerial might replaced the picture of a conciliatory and bending Communist figure, and to the liberal pages the United States returned as the occupier of the danger spot in its relations with Nippon. In its April 18, 1934, editorial, "Japan's Blind Alley," the *New Republic* pointed out that Russia had virtually disappeared from the diplomatic talk between America and Japan, but that recognition and subsequent implications had brought America to Russia's point of view. Thus to the issues which made for economic disharmony between this country and the Japanese, now was added a political one, which imposed a much more serious barrier to Japan. In substance, it amounted to "the simple proposition that the Roosevelt Administration has said as plainly as such things can be expressed in the language of diplomacy that the United States would look with distinct disfavor upon any Japanese move against the Eastern dominions of the Soviet Union." [123] This must have made alarming reading to those who were hoping with deep conviction that the new administration would withdraw from the extended position into which the country had been pressed between 1931 and 1933. What it would amount to was admittedly a riddle, but this interpretation of the new Russo-American views on East Asia represented an amazing vault on the part of the liberal observers. Of course, their exultation at Russia's gaining such a powerful friend did not dovetail very well with the simultaneous denigration of munitions manufacture, naval rebuilding and other stirrings of American preparedness, in addition to the perennial disarmament and world peace campaigns, but very few things illustrate better the liberal conviction that a militarily strong Russia was not out of harmony with other liberal views.

Louis Fischer's "Behind Russian Recognition" in the *Nation* [124] was a long and frank display of pleasure at the Soviet's remarkable success in their recent months of playing in the game of international politics with the major league powers. American recognition was cheaper than building battleships, and more effective pressure on the Japanese, in Fischer's opinion. It was the culmination of several months of Soviet diplomatic successes over Japan, and there was little doubt now that she was in retreat before Russia on this front. He went on to list a long number of material and military advantages held by the Reds over Japan, concluding, "Japan could not win a war against the Soviet Union." But he clung to the belief that the Soviet wanted only peace with Japan, and had nothing to win and everything to lose through such a war, another way of saying that Russia was satisfied with the Far Eastern status quo, after all its display of ill will toward the Versailles settlements and its reputation as a supporter of treaty revisionism. Still another policy contradiction was involved here, the clash between the frequent assertion that preparedness and arms buildups undermined rather than guaranteed peace, contrasted to the Soviet exception, in which latter case the perfection of a formidable military machine in Asia was apparently synonymous with peace-producing circumstances. In September, upon the publication of a new incident of Soviet-Japanese bad blood, instead of another dire warning, the *Nation* confidently reported that whatever came of this new conflict, it was "reasonably clear that Japan was not prepared to attack the Soviet Union." [125] All talk of alleged Japanese plans for a "preventive war" against Russia in Siberia, as had been bruited about in January, now had evaporated, even though it was the fashion for some time to speak of Japanese military and naval leaders as "mad," and to cite the opinions of Soviet leaders as evidence for believing them to be crazy. [126]

LIBERAL COOLNESS TOWARD A JAPANESE-AMERICAN WAR IN ASIA

From the time of the recognition of the Soviet Union by the United States until well into 1935, the main liberal theme devoted to Japanese affairs was so interwoven with the problem of disarmament, the scrutiny of the past records of the munitions industry, and the quietly expanding naval building program of the Roosevelt administration, that it does not lend itself to separate treatment easily. But the stress definitely shifted from Russia to what Japanese expansion on the Asian continent meant to the United States and the "West" in terms of economic consequences. Little was to be heard now of law, morality, treaty sanctity, and the vast paraphernalia erected by the democracies to create the illusion of an international community run along the lines of a small American city. The enlarging Japanese navy and the material side of Japan's penetration in Asia shouldered these aside as topics. Thirty months after Mukden it was hard to see the relation between what was now appearing in the liberal press about Japan and what had previously dominated its pages. The likelihood of war between the United States and that country replaced the new Russo-Japanese conflict once discussed so realistically as if barely around the corner of actuality. In fact, there was an "irreconcilable conflict" flavor to the new study of Nipponese-American relations, and handled with almost a note of objectivity, in comparison with the fervent partisanship which had characterized liberal portrayal of the once strained situation with the Soviet Union. For the first time since the latter half of 1932 it was possible to learn that all Japan was not populated by bloodthirsty barbarians slavering for the opportunity to fight the world. After all the talk of Japanese Fascism, one might now learn that there were moderate elements in Japan who were earnestly seeking a way out other than through war. A faint insight into a Japan faced with large and powerful opponents everywhere might also be gleaned. But an underlying hostility toward Japan was impossible to conceal, even though liberal opposition to the United States fighting Japan in Asia was clear-cut and persistent.

One cannot readily grasp the liberal editors' strategy, unless one keeps in mind the part assigned to Russia and China in bringing about the eventual demolition of Japan and the establishment of a non-Western collectivist regime on the mainland untainted with Western capitalist imperialism and extraterritorial squatters' rights. A curious contradiction existed between the equanimity with which the liberals viewed the vicious war going on in China between the various Asiatic foes, and the approval attached to the Russian buildup in the Far East, on one hand, and the abrupt and grimly unconditional condemnation of all American moves which suggested possible United States involvement at some coming time, on the other. The strong stand for disarmament in liberal ideology did not, however, carry over to the Soviet Union and the new "Red" China.

In 1934 the liberal press saw a marked increase in the influence of anti-war moderates in Japan, partially due, they thought, to the growth of confidence in diplomatic reports that no thought of war with Japan was to be found in the United States, reinforced by the transfer of the Atlantic fleet back to the East from the Pacific by President Roosevelt. Subsequent war-scare propaganda aimed at the Japanese masses by elements interested in building military strength might be weakened, a *Nation* editorial suggested, if "tact and discretion" were practiced more effectively by United States officials, and if the "navy second to none" call "pouring from the mouths of our Swansons, Brittens, Vinsons and Admiral Standleys" was quieted. Such "moral encouragement" to the Japanese moderates would increase their strength, and their success at the expense of the militarists was given a good chance if nothing in this country was done to aggravate the situation.[127]

In actuality, even at the height of liberal excitement over League pressure on Japan in the first year after Mukden, and all the fine heat generated by the discussion of the Kellogg Pact and other paper barriers to changes in the world status quo, the liberal press and its spokesmen had never once given their approval to Western and particularly United States military action against Japan. Although the verbal abuse of the Japanese had reached riotous levels, and condemnation of the action in Manchuria had been expressed with the finesse of a blowtorch, the liberals were still able to compartmentalize themselves on Asian matters and come to a dead stop on the anti-Japan highway the minute the conversation grazed the possibility of the United States entering the picture as a participant, beyond the level of simply manning the verbal howitzers under the command of the pro-treaty protagonists. But the lack of consistency mainly cancelled out the gestures on behalf of moderation by reinvigorating the latent anti-Japanese sentiments quietly simmering in the American subconscious since 1905. While maintaining an attitude of superiority toward the common run of citizen imbibing a hate-Japan line from the despised Hearst press and other mass-circulation sources, the liberals indulged in a rarefied variety of their own, tailored to the peculiar climatic conditions prevailing on the high intellectual plateau where they spent their time. Its clash with all their other views, including that which sought to find in Japan a congenial intellectual element, simply added to the burden borne by them in a world growing increasingly complex with conflicts of interest. But the caroms of liberal opinion were most difficult to follow if one excluded the consistent approach maintained with respect to Russia and Communist China. That the opinions of 1934 and 1935 had mellowed by comparison with those of 1931 and 1932 goes without saying; still, with all the poorly-hidden hostility toward the Japanese and their threat to more-favored regimes in Asia, there was no interval here when assenting nods were given in the direction of physical participation in the struggle by the United States. All hopes were pinned on the avoidance of the outbreak of war between the two, yet the position taken by the liberal papers was one of being spectators to the approach of a catastrophe which they were powerless to prevent. When diplomatic and moral pressure failed to deter Japan from its Asiatic program, and after American recognition of Red Russia, the vogue became one of projecting the United States and Japan into an unavoidable war on the basis of their fundamentally similar economic systems and world trade policies. This gave the readers a generous variety of views on Asian problems from which they could take their choice, but which they hardly could subscribe to all at once.

At various times the liberal commentators expressed the belief that Russia or Red China would halt the Japanese and eventually drive them back to their islands. On other occasions great faith was lodged in the League of Nations sanction threats and in the moral content of the Kellogg Pact as inhibitors of Japanese expansion, while at still other times great confidence was expressed that Japan would collapse internally.[128] The theory that military expenditures would eventually pile up such a mountain of debt that the nation would no longer be able to function was repeatedly expressed, a grievous misunderstanding of the new managed currency managerial war state beginning to come into existence. It was the same kind of thinking that was supremely confident neither Japan nor Germany could possibly embark on vigorous programs because of their tiny gold reserves. The liberals assured themselves repeatedly that the Manchurian adventure was not profiting the Japanese invaders, and that the whole enterprise would surely disintegrate of its own weight.[129] There was also the variant interpretation of Japan as a Fascist imperialist order, by dialectical dictate inevitably bound to fall apart of its internal contradictions. Caught in the same "implications of capitalist industrialism" as the Western powers, Japan was expected either to be forced to abandon its drive for a controlled self-sufficiency and accept the international cooperation and trade of world capitalism, or "take as an example the methods of Soviet Russia." For this reason the liberal press hammered the Japanese schemes for a Far Eastern "Monroe Doctrine" and applied the Fascist tag continually to the Japanese regime pressing its advantage in Manchuria. According to their rule book, it was impossible to expect all this activity to have much tenure anyway.

In the weeks immediately after Mukden there had been occasional stories implying that responsibility for the outbreak of violence in Manchuria was quite mixed. There followed a spell of monolithic condemnation of Japan at the height of political and diplomatic pressure, and then from the summer of 1932 on, periodical observations of moderate nature appeared. The most reserved of all these occurred whenever the issue involved Japanese-American relations. For example, the *Nation* praised Viscount Ishii's address at that time, which warned the United States not to interfere with Japanese expansion on the Asiatic mainland, as a "courageous statement of fact," as well as doing "both countries a great service in pointing out that the conflicting policies of Japan and the United States in Asia, unless checked in time, will certainly lead to armed conflict." The *Nation* considered such warnings as valuable to this country in that it helped us to understand where our diplomacy was leading us, and thus would enable us to "shape our policies as to prevent war with Japan." There ensued an astonishing summary of the nature of American-Japanese economic conflict in China, in view of the general tone previously of condemning Japan out of hand without any redeeming reservations: [130]

Economic pressure has pushed our frontier ever westward; today our western frontier is in Asia itself. We have marked out China as an American market of immense potentialities. Under the Open Door policy, of course, we assume that we are giving all countries, and particularly Japan, an equal opportunity to do business in that market. But so vast are our natural resources, and so highly developed is our industrial system, that the real advantages are all on our side. Thus Japan is in no position to compete with us on equal terms except by pauperizing its labor, and it is the poverty of its workers that is the compelling force behind Japan's natural expansion.

Just as remarkable, and as lacking in the customary political demonology, was a late summer article in the *New Republic* by Guy Irving Burch, "Japan's Way Out," [131] which supported the views of two famous demographers that Japan be given access to Borneo, New Guinea and possibly other Pacific islands for population expansion. He was convinced Japan's foreign policy was a reflection of population pressure, and that this would be a peaceful solution. The Japanese, no more than any other people, Burch said, would prefer to sit at home and starve rather than die fighting:

Japan can lower her standard of living. But as this standard is what makes life itself worth living, most progressive nations prefer as an alternative to risk their fortunes in war, and the Japanese do not lack spirit. Furthermore, Japan has plenty of precedents in Western history and culture for protecting her standard of living with the sword, if need be.

Editorially, the journal did not agree with Burch's viewpoint, apparently, since six weeks before it had condemned Ishii's "Eastern Monroe Doctrine" approach, and flatly declared, "The answer to Japan's situation, and the only answer, is the stabilization of her population." When a Japanese correspondent objected to the editorial condemnation of this plan as "aggressive chauvinism," and called attention to the similarity of this to the stand taken by the United States in the first quarter of the nineteenth century, the editors in rebuttal discounted it by stating that they were equally opposed to the Monroe Doctrine in the Western Hemisphere.[132] Somewhat disconcerting was this same writer's recall, for the benefit of the *New Republic*'s editors, of the statement of the Senate Foreign Relations Committee at the time of the ratification of the Kellogg Pact, that each nation was free to defend itself, regardless of treaty provisions, and was the sole authority as to the definition of self-defense, as well as the necessity and extent of action to attain it. At that time, the *New Republic* had inserted the statement that the Monroe Doctrine was considered part of the "national security and defense" of the United States, and that Japan's following this course for East Asia was no more reprehensible than American persistence in following the same course in another part of the world.

Yet, there prevailed a tendency to approach balance when the subject veered to Japanese-American matters, and particularly when the threat of war between the two drew attention. Even hypothetical war drew prompt repudiation. In the fall of 1932, a Broadway play, "Men Must Fight," was built around a war between the United States and Japan and projected ahead to 1940. A *Nation* critic turned a frosty eye upon it, reserving the word "senseless" to describe the war theme.[133] The publication of a book by one T. O'Conroy in London the following year, titled *The Menace of Japan,* contained one of the clearest calls for a war at once between the West and Japan, predicting a much worse one later if force was not used then. Ben Dorfman, the *New Republic* reviewer, declared, "Mr. O'Conroy chants a disgusting and blasphemous hymn of hate. His book is decidedly unbalanced, highly colored and full of unwarranted representations." [134]

Hallgren's deprecatory review in the *Nation* for June 6, 1934 closed on a darker and even touchier note: [135]

Some day many of our prophets say the United States will fight Japan. When that day comes we shall very likely see another Committee on Public Information established in Washington to feed the American public ghastly revolting tales concerning the wickedness of the Japanese. This will be done on the theory that it is only by whipping up mob passions and mob hatred that a war can be successfully conducted.

And for that propaganda campaign, Hallgren thought, O'Conroy's book would be the source "for all the raw material any Japanese atrocity mill would ever require." Hallgren's prediction proved to be elegantly insufficient in view of what followed Pearl Harbor.

In December, 1932 the *Nation* denounced the presence of the whole American fleet in the Pacific as an incitation to hostility on the part of the Japanese. It was revealed that Japanese patriots were constantly telling their people that the United States was preparing for war, which the editors did not think was true, at least insofar as the "American public" was "aware," and that it was out of such "fears and suspicions" that war frequently emerged. In commenting on the fact that great tension already existed between the two countries, nothing was said about the Stimson pressure of the past fourteen months, with full liberal support, as an important cause. But it was admitted that we could not "possibly afford to let it increase." In reference to Japanese moderate suspicion that the motive behind our naval maneuvers in Hawaii was "to guard against a surprise attack by Japan," and that this was a mark of American distrust, the editorial felt they were justified in considering such action a cause of more ill will. The Administration's excuse that the fleets were based together as an economy move was brushed aside, and as for the defense of the country, the editorial concluded: [136]

It is even more questionable that the Japanese would dare attempt a surprise attack upon our Western shores, for no fleet can hope to operate successfully at such great distance from its coaling stations, repair depots, and normal sources of supply.

Nothing was advanced about Hawaii, nor was anything said about the mock destruction of the bases there by Admiral Yarnell's warplanes using aircraft carriers out at sea as their originating point.

In the same month, the *Nation* printed Raymond Leslie Buell's "Hypocrisy and the Philippines," [137] which recommended we abandon the islands as a naval base and open them to Japanese and Chinese trade. Buell predicted that unless we were willing to keep a quarter of a million men there as a permanent garrison, we were only creating "a dangerous source of international irritation," and that in the event of war between the United States and Japan, "should such a war unhappily occur," it was sure that "Japan would regard an attack on the Philippines as the first step to take." Compared to Buell's earlier torrid calls for economic boycott of Japan, this later position amounted to virtual capitulation. But it illustrated quite effectively the degree to which liberal concessions might be made when the whole Japanese question was framed in the context of possible warfare with America. Of course, Buell's article was in accord with the *Nation*'s existing stand in favor of Philippine independence; when Stimson had testified against the Hare bill in April, 1932, which provided for a grant of autonomy, the *Nation* grated, "Mr. Stimson was at his worst, and that means a good deal." [138]

As referred to above, the topic of Japan versus America returned to the liberal papers not long after recognition of Soviet Russia, and when liberals spoke of Japan's challenge to the "West," it was understood that the United States primarily, and Great Britain to a much smaller extent, was meant in doing so. But tying the two in a parcel became the usual manner of dealing with this problem. Diligent searching behind the ethereal language of American diplomatic reproaches to Japan as to its conduct in Asia now began to reveal things other than abstract, high-minded concern for virtue. A long unsigned editorial early in May, 1934, in the *New Republic* [139] discussed the economic implications to the United States of Japan's policies. It was flatly advanced here that the real alternative before this country was either giving up trade with China, or going to war with Japan, and the editors shrank back from the latter as if it were a recommendation to take recourse in suicide. To wage war on Japan was considered to be "insanity" and sure to result in the losing of the object sought. Our navy "could not possibly be successful in engagements with the Japanese in Asiatic waters," and even combined with the British we would have only a chance; "A world alliance against Japan would be the only means of anything like certain victory."

As the *New Republic* saw it, the competing "imperialisms" of the two countries were meeting in the last big uncaptured market left on the earth, and we stood no chance of getting it, no matter how our war fortunes with Japan fared. The economies of America and Europe had long ago passed beyond the "open door" idea into a series of highly-protected national systems, and the Japanese were now to "put the last nail in the coffin of international laissez-faire by shutting the trade door in the Far East." Japan was considered to have little hope of permanently dominating the China market, either, with internal collapse or defeat by the Chinese, and maybe the Russians, facing her. For the United States, however, with a productive system so prodigious that the producers allegedly could not buy back more than a fraction of what they produced, the hope of postponing a recourse to collectivism at home through "building up a modern industrial China" was already a lost dream. In the long run, the United States would have to "find a use for its immense productive capacity in creating plenty chiefly for its own citizens" by "installing collectivism," but the alternative facing the country in its short run problem vis-a-vis Japan was unpleasant: "Either our government must give up its traditional insistence on the open door and our industries and financiers must relinquish all thought of profits in Chinese trade, or we must go to war for these objectives." One did not need clairvoyant powers to divine which of these two alternatives the *New Republic*'s editors favored at this point.

Despite the seemingly inevitable consequences of their predictions, the liberal observers continued to search for every bit of evidence which seemed to promise the continuance of peace between the two lands, while giving occasional lip service support to the continuing diplomatic knuckle-rapping being administered by the State Department and the diplomatic corps now under the Roosevelt Administration inheritors of the headache. But the intense belief in the usefulness and effectiveness of this mode of conduct of thirty months earlier was mostly gone.

No substantial departures in the form of conciliatory moves were encouraged, however; the immediate reflection of such action upon the welfare of Soviet Russia was well understood. For example, the *Nation* experienced a brief spell of fright early in March, 1934 that President Roosevelt was about to modify the Stimson Doctrine and recognize Manchukuo. Loud editorial cries denounced this as "endangering the purpose of our recent rapprochement with the Soviet Union and support for another Japanese war of aggression," as well as "abandonment of a moral principle for the sake of political or commercial gain." [140] This was an ingenious plea from a journal which never tired of describing the methodical practical statecraft of the Marxists; the assumption of their innocent helplessness was indeed a serious retreat. When Ambassador Grew announced to the Japanese that this country was to adhere to the status quo and the open door via sustained emphasis upon respect for the treaties of the 1920's, the May *New Republic* considered the conflict merely sharpened, in view of the previous unequivocal Japanese determination to continue as before; "The controversy is made more explicit, but it has not got anywhere," was the comment. Each nation had simply told the other "in the most friendly manner possible," that it was of no mind to withdraw from its previous position.[141] Apparently an insoluble impasse was the preferred enduring situation. On occasion it appeared that editorial stands were posed to make the issues between the United States and Japan look even more insoluble. In October, 1934 the *Nation* implied that insofar as the problem of naval parity was concerned, either possibility facing this country was unthinkable; "We cannot surrender to Japanese demands for naval parity without greatly strengthening the prestige as well as prowess of Japanese militarism. Yet any effort to combat Japanese preparedness by similar action in this country is likewise bound to feed the flames of nationalism in Japan," it observed.[142].

On the other hand, this implacable insolubility did not seem to dog the footsteps of Russia and Japan in their conflicts of interest, despite the *New Republic*'s editorial observation in the same month that "Japanese and Russian interests conflict too sharply on the Asiatic continent to justify hope that permanent peace is assured." The settlement of their controversy over the Chinese Eastern Railroad came about without war, yet the same persons who lauded this action felt there was no possibility for Japan and America finding a solution to the naval and other disputes between them. Still the liberal journals had admitted their belief that Japanese offers of drastic naval reduction upon obtaining parity were genuine.

A tenderness for the possible position of Russia in Asia and the North Pacific should a general solution of Japanese-American problems come about cannot be dismissed entirely as a factor in liberal fixations on their asserted insolubility. A case in point was the *New Republic*'s mild reaction to a rumor that the Soviet Union was about to recognize the Japanese-created state of Manchukuo. Where liberal sensibilities had been outraged when such a possibility on the part of the United States had been bruited about six months before, now there was a gentle remonstration; "We hope the reports prove unfounded, not only for the reasons implicit in the foreground [the editorial claimed that it would 'set the seal of diplomatic approval upon Japanese aggression'], but because such recognition would probably be followed by other nations far less concerned than is the U.S.S.R. with the rights of helpless victims of imperialism." [143] There always appeared to be extenuating circumstances accompanying any steps projected by the Russians across the No Man's Land of Asiatic conflict.

More ominous signs of their believed correct interpretation of the nature of the situation kept appearing down into the winter of 1934–1935, on the eve of the naval conference of the latter year. More statements concerning the firmly believed irreconcilable aims of the two nations issued in editorial form. The Japanese establishment of an oil monopoly in Manchuria and the loud protests by Britain and the United States in mid-December, 1934, fell into the pattern. For a moment the *Nation* leaned back on the trusty weapon of three years earlier, suggesting an embargo on scrap iron and other materials potentially useful as war products as a substitute for war, in view of the known raw materials shortages of Japan. The possibility of Japan fighting to get what was deprived her through such action never crossed the editors' typewriters. That such a scheme was a short cut to war instead was demonstrated after July, 1941, when the Japanese drive on the raw material-rich European colonies in Asia started on the heels of being locked out of the American market. The *Nation* was unhappy over the announced military and naval budget increases in Japan as incitations to the steel and armament companies in the United States, and hoped the strategic materials embargo would be substituted as a means of maintaining "our supremacy over Japan" and gaining its subscription to "restrictions imposed by international action." [144] This language began to take on a British quality, what with the latter nation's customary reference in diplomatic language to any matter in which Britain and any other one power were in agreement upon, as "international" in nature. With reference to the complaint over the Manchurian oil monopoly, the *Nation* felt called upon to approve, although it chose in an aside to regret that the State Department had not chosen to take a firm stand until a threat had occurred to "the profits of the Standard Oil Company." [145]

As the 1935 naval talks approached, the *New Republic* concluded on the basis of the newest Japanese actions in China that Japan had not been impressed in the least by "the protests of the Western Powers," and felt even more secure in the judgment that she would not be halted by "anything short of military force." Even this was not assured beyond any doubt but would rest "upon the highly dubious outcome of a war that would itself be a world catastrophe." [146] And there was virtually no reservation observable in the editorial opinion that everything conceivable in the way of an understanding should be sought as an alternative to a war between Japan and the "West." So while the fellow-travelers in the liberal literary ranks were rejoicing over Communist military gains in China and issuing abusive broadsides directed at the United States for its alleged buttressing of the Chinese Nationalists, the editorial policy was consistently opposing American involvement in war with Japan directly, and steadily withdrawing its support from the various political stratagems used by the Western Powers ever since Mukden in an effort to soften up Japan. It was not especially evident from readers' comments that they were aware of the several aspects of liberal policy toward Far Eastern affairs. The most distressing part of this complicated situation was the impact of the liberal enthusiasts for Communism upon the reputation of the liberal press as the spearhead of pacifism. The repeated expressions of gratification with the results of comprehensive Communist bloodletting in China did not set well juxtaposed to pleas for an international community founded on the arts of conciliation, mediation and mutual compromise. The gravitation toward Communism in a substantial part explains the beginning of the collapse of the post-World War One pacifist movement.

NOTES

1 *Nation,* October 7, 1931, pp. 351–352.
2 *Nation,* October 14, 1931, p. 376.
3 *New Republic,* October 21, 1931, pp. 246–248. The *Nation* in its editorial comment of October 7 also admitted the possibility of Chinese provocation.
4 *New Republic,* October 28, 1931, p. 286.
5 *New Republic,* November 4, 1931, p. 310.
6 *New Republic,* December 2, 1931, pp. 57–58. The reference was to the famous cartoons of Rube Goldberg, which spoofed the industrialization and technicalization of

life, usually top-heavy and unworkable constructs of ingenious design for doing the simplest chores.

7   *New Republic,* December 9, 1931, p. 80.
8   *New Republic,* December 16, 1931, p. 119.
9   *Nation,* October 28, 1931, p. 449.
10 *Nation,* November 4, 1931, p. 474.
11 *Nation,* November 4, 1931, p. 475.
12 *Nation,* November 25, 1931, p. 560.
13 All above citations from Hallgren's article, *Nation,* November 11, 1931, pp. 514–516.
14 *Nation,* January 13, 1932, p. 50.
15 Hindmarsh, "Is There War In Manchuria?," *Nation,* January 6, 1932, pp. 10–13.
16 Editorial "Japan The Outlaw," *Nation,* January 6, 1932, p. 3.
17 *Nation,* December 9, 1931, pp. 633–634.
18 Editorial "Japan's 'Victory,'" *Nation,* December 2, 1931, p. 588.
19 *Nation,* December 9, 1931, p. 627; this sentiment had also been expressed in the editorial of November 25, 1931, p. 560.
20 *Nation,* December 23, 1931, p. 682.
21 *Nation,* January 20, 1932, p. 58.
22 *Nation,* February 10, 1932, p. 153.
23 Editorial "Military Peace-Makers: France and Japan," *New Republic,* February, 17, 1932, pp. 4–5.
24 *Nation,* February 24, 1932, pp. 221–222.
25 *New Republic,* February 3, 1932, p. 306.
26 See communication to *New Republic* from Felix Cohen, March 2, 1932, p. 76. In the same issue (p. 56) the editors announced, "there is a growing pressure in the United States for a boycott against Japan, either undertaken alone or in cooperation with the League. Boycott petitions have been signed by President Lowell of Harvard, Newton D. Baker, and more than one hundred and fifty other persons, including many well known educators."
27 Citations in following four paragraphs from this article, *New Republic,* February 10, 1932, pp. 334–335. On December 12, 1931 (pp. 58–59), the *New Republic* had declared, "The *New Republic* has, ever since the last war, opposed the project of attempting to maintain peace by the application of sanctions, whether military or economic."
28 Editorial "Mr. Stimson's Warning To Japan," *Nation,* March 9, 1932, p. 272.
29 March 2, 1932, pp. 58–59; citations in next three paragraphs from this source.
30 March 2, 1932, p. 245.
31 Buell, "For A Japanese Boycott," *New Republic,* March 9, 1932, pp. 100–102. For one of the more eloquent editorial disagreements see George Soule, "The Fallacy of the Boycott," *Harper's,* May, 1932, pp. 702–709.
32 Mitchell, "In re Japan vs. World," *New Republic,* February 24, 1932, pp. 38–39; "Peace In the Far East," *New Republic,* April 20, 1932, pp. 265–267.
33 Editorial "The Japanese Boycott Again," *New Republic,* April 13, 1932, pp. 221–223.
34 *New Republic,* May 18, 1932, p. 1.
35 *Nation,* May 18, 1932, p. 556.
36 Editorial "The Stimson Letter," *New Republic,* March 9, 1932, p. 86.
37 *New Republic,* March 23, 1932, pp. 145–147.
38 Editorial "The Stimson Doctrine," *Nation,* August 17, 1932, p. 137.
39 Editorial "Mr. Stimson on Peace," *Nation,* August 24, 1932, p. 158.
40 Editorial "Japan's Challenge," *Nation,* September 7, 1932, p. 203.
41 Editorial "The Threat In the Stimson Doctrine," *New Republic,* August 24, 1932, pp. 31–32.
42 Editorial "The Lytton Report," *New Republic,* October 12, 1932, pp. 219–221.
43 See in particular *Nation,* October 12, 1932, p. 319; editorial "Action Against Japan," *Nation,* October 19, 1932, p. 343; *Nation,* November 30, 1932, p. 515.
44 *New Republic,* December 21, 1932, p. 144; *Nation,* December 21, 1932, p. 599.
45 Editorial "Will Japan Destroy the League?," *New Republic,* November 30, 1932, p. 59.
46 Fischer's dispatch discussing these matters appeared in the *Nation* December 9, 1931.
47 The editors believed the Russians were indisposed to war with Japan as it "would

prove a fatal handicap to the last eight months of the Five Year Plan." *New Republic,* February 17, 1932, p. 2.

48　*New Republic,* April 27, 1932, pp. 282–283. See also May 18, 1932, p. 2.

49　Mitchell, "Catastrophe In Siberia," *New Republic,* June 8, 1932, pp. 89–91.

50　Editorial "In Time Of Peace, Prevent War," *New Republic,* June 8, 1932, p. 86.

51　*Nation,* July 20, 1932, pp. 50–51.

52　Kang review in *Nation,* August 3, 1932, p. 32.

53　*Nation,* September 28, 1932, p. 271.

54　*Nation,* November 2, 1932, pp. 419–420.

55　Editorial "The New Far Eastern Triangle," *New Republic,* December 28, 1932, p. 175.

56　*Nation,* December 28, 1932, p. 631.

57　*Nation,* March 30, 1932, pp. 369–371.

58　*Communist,* December, 1931, pp. 963–974.

59　*Communist,* April, 1932, pp. 291–294.

60　*New Masses,* April, 1932, pp. 3–6.

61　*New Masses,* June, 1932, pp. 3–4, 6.

62　*New Masses,* March, 1934, p. 11.

63　Editorial "Soviet Union In Danger," *Communist,* April, 1934, pp. 388–404 (402). See also Peffer, "If Japan and Russia Fight," *Harper's,* March, 1934, pp. 396–404.

64　*New Masses,* July 17, 1934, pp. 14–15.

65　*New Masses,* December 18, 1934, p. 8.

66　November 6, 1934, p. 5.

67　*Nation,* December 30, 1931, p. 710.

68　*New Republic,* June 22, 1932, p. 137.

69　*New Republic,* May 4, 1932, p. 309.

70　*New Republic,* June 29, 1932, pp. 171–172.

71　*Nation,* June 8, 1932, p. 637.

72　*New Republic,* July 27, 1932, pp. 271–273.

73　"A New Crisis In China," *Nation,* August 17, 1932, pp. 143–144.

74　*New Republic,* August 17, 1932, p. 2.

75　Editorial "The New Far Eastern Triangle," *New Republic,* December 28, 1932, p. 175; Villard, "This Is Manchukuo," *Nation,* November 2, 1932, pp. 421–422.

76　*New Republic,* February 15, 1933, p. 1.

77　See editorial comment, *Nation,* June 7, 1933, p. 626.

78　*New Republic,* July 26, 1933, p. 105.

79　Anonymous, "Red China," *New Republic,* September 27, 1933, pp. 171–172.

80　Above, p. 172.

81　*Nation,* March 29, 1933, p. 352.

82　*New Republic,* May 2, 1934, p. 344.

83　*Nation,* November 1, 1933, p. 518–519.

84　*New Republic,* June 6, 1934, p. 108.

85　*Nation,* July 25, 1934, p. 109.

86　*New Republic,* November 7, 1934, pp. 372–373.

87　*New Republic,* October 17, 1934, p. 288.

88　*Nation,* September 19, 1934, pp. 332–333.

89　See also brief reviews in *Nation,* December 12, 1934, p. 679.

90　*Nation,* December 6, 1933, p. 660.

91　*Nation,* December 20, 1933, p. 715.

92　*Nation,* August 29, 1934, p. 250.

93　*New Republic,* January 17, 1934, p. 267. See also editorial paragraph in issue of October 11, 1933, p. 224.

94　*New Republic,* January 31, 1934, pp. 331–332.

95　*Nation,* January 24, 1934, pp. 99–100.

96　*Nation,* June 6, 1934, p. 647; see also "Making China 'Safe,'" *Nation,* August 22, 1934, p. 201.

97　Corcoran, "The Red Army Triumph in Szechuan," *Nation,* December 5, 1934, pp. 638–639.

98　*Nation,* December 5, 1934, p. 635.

99   *New Republic*, May 16, 1934, p. 2.
100   *Nation*, December 19, 1934, pp. 712–713.
101   *New Republic*, October 10, 1934, pp. 227–228.
102   *New Republic*, January 23, 1935, p. 288.
103   Editorial "Again A Challenge To Humanity," *Nation*, January 18, 1933, p. 52.
104   *New Republic*, January 11, 1933, p. 225.
105   *New Republic*, January 25, 1933, pp. 279–280.
106   *Nation*, February 15, 1933, pp. 162–163; *New Republic*, February 15, 1933, p. 1.
107   *Nation*, February 22, 1933, pp. 189–190.
108   *Nation*, March 1, 1933, p. 221.
109   *New Republic*, March 1, 1933, p. 58.
110   *Nation*, March 8, 1933, p. 245; *New Republic*, March 8, 1933, p. 85.
111   *New Republic*, March 8, 1933, p. 91.
112   Dell, "The League Acts," *Nation*, March 8, 1933, pp. 260–261.
113   *Nation*, March 29, 1933, pp. 341–342.
114   *New Republic*, March 22, 1933, p. 143.
115   *New Republic*, May 31, 1933, pp. 55–56.
116   *New Republic*, April 5, 1933, p. 199.
117   Editorial comment, *Nation*, April 5, 1933, p. 359.
118   Peffer, "Japan in China," *New Republic*, June 14, 1933, pp. 115–117.
119   *Nation*, July 19, 1933, p. 59.
120   *New Republic*, July 19, 1933, pp. 245–246.
121   *New Republic*, October 25, 1933, pp. 295–296.
122   *New Republic*, November 22, 1933, p. 31.
123   *New Republic*, April 18, 1934, p. 258.
124   *Nation*, January 3, 1934, pp. 9–10.
125   *Nation*, September 19, 1934, p. 310.
126   *New Republic*, February 14, 1934, p. 2.
127   *Nation*, January 31, 1934, p. 114.
128   A *Nation* editorial on December 7, 1932 (p. 543) predicted that the militarists of Japan would precipitate a prompt collapse of the Japanese economy by their expenditures, bringing about an unbearable national debt. See also Dorfman's "The Manchurian 'Incident' of 1931," *Harper's*, September, 1934, pp. 449–462.
129   This was the substance of the report, "Japan's Manchurian Blunder," by Dorfman, published by the *New Republic* on December 6, 1933, pp. 91–93. Henry Hilgard Villard's "This is Manchukuo" in the *Nation* for November 2, 1932, pp. 421–422, actually found a case for Japan. See also Nathaniel Peffer, "Manchuria: A Warning to America," *Harper's*, February, 1933, pp. 301–308.
130   *Nation*, July 6, 1932, p. 2.
131   *New Republic*, August 24, 1932, pp. 39–41.
132   *New Republic*, July 6, 1932, p. 191, and exchange between editors and Yuju Yamazaki, *New Republic*, September 7, 1932, p. 102.
133   The play was authored by Reginald Lawrence and S. K. Lauren. Review in *Nation*, November 9, 1932, p. 466.
134   *New Republic*, June 6, 1934, p. 108.
135   *Nation*, June 6, 1934, p. 653.
136   *Nation*, December 14, 1932, p. 580.
137   *Nation*, December 28, 1932, pp. 639–640.
138   Editorial "Saving Our National Honor," *Nation*, April 20, 1932, p. 454.
139   "Japan's Challenge To the West," *New Republic*, May 2, 1934, pp. 322–324; citations in this and following paragraph from this source.
140   *Nation*, March 7, 1934, p. 264.
141   *New Republic*, May 9, 1934, p. 347.
142   *Nation*, October 17, 1934, pp. 425–426.
143   *New Republic*, October 3, 1934, pp. 198–199, for this and for citation in paragraph above.
144   *Nation*, December 5, 1934, p. 631.
145   *Nation*, December 12, 1934, p. 659.
146   *New Republic*, January 30, 1935, p. 316.

8

LIBERAL PACIFISM ENCOUNTERS

THE COMMUNIST MOVEMENT

O N SEPTEMBER 23, 1931, five days after Mukden, William Floyd, identifying himself as the director of an organization called "Peace Patriots," wrote a letter to the *Nation*, published in the October 14 issue, describing that journal as "the most prominent paper in America advocating pacifism," and seeking its support behind a campaign to popularize the wearing of "2% buttons." The basis of this program was a statement by Albert Einstein to the effect that if two percent of the people in each nation in the world refused military service, there would not be another war. Einstein at the moment was the most prominent figure in the world conducting a total offensive against conscription everywhere. A short time after this, in a substantial essay featured on the first page of the New York *Times* Magazine for November 22, 1931, "The Road To Peace," Einstein stated flatly, "The introduction of universal military service is the principal cause of the moral decline of the white race."

Reference has been made frequently to liberal pacifism and its related sentiments in other contexts, but a separate treatment of the organizational side of pacifism as related to the liberal press and its enthusiasts is in order. The rift between the older pacifism with its strong religious tinge and absence of class consciousness, and the new varieties, which began to trace their exotic careers in the depths of the depression, is one of the immediately observable consequences of an examination of this kind. But the most striking characteristic is the conversion of liberal pacifism into a sullen and belligerent movement with the most transparent political objectives, completely captured by Communists and breathing smoke and fire of a sort not very different from the varieties resulting from the war they professed to hate so heartily. In its excitable language and aggravated approach can be seen the warm seedbed from which sprouted the urges to participate in violence hardly a hairsbreadth removed from the sort they condemned so categorically. The Popular Front, labor warfare and Spain lead directly from it, and the taste for the class violence sampled here proved in its time to lend itself in the most enthusiastic display of willingness to march off to another big world war once the war issues and circumstances had been wheeled into a convincing and appealing series of dramatic acts. A straight line runs from the anti-conscription and anti-military training demonstrations of the early 1930's to the Lincoln Brigade and premature enlistment in the Allied armies in the two years prior to Pearl Harbor. The class warriors, in their furious assault upon the war system of the capitalist nation states, bred a type of eagerness for carnage among their zealots which made the hated militarist enemy stereotype seem rather restrained by comparison. The frightful political massacres in "liberated" Europe at the conclusion of World War Two can be said to be one of the most prominent fruits of a pacifist movement captured by a ferocious political partisanry and raised to impressive levels of savagery, by years of participation in another world war.

To be sure, the pacifist sentiments of the liberals at the start of the depression era and the war in Asia were undoubtedly genuine. But the helping hand they lent to the new type of pacifist organization by way of publicity and encouragement involved emotional attachment eventually, and alienation from the main stream of anti-war thought and action, as well as enrollment in a brand of political action which was only faintly associated with any comprehensive opposition to war. The signal for the end of unadulterated pacifist concern was the broadening of the movement to include the demolition of Fascism as well as war. The hard, bright light of Communist attachment shone through at this stage with an unmistakable gleam, and the language took on a bristling belligerent quality quite undistinguishable from that of any band of fighters.

There was never any lack of attention to literature attacking war as an institution and probing the dark corners of international intercourse, seeking for the forces which made for war and gained from it. In the comprehensive assault on the munitions trade and the disarmament struggle, much publicity was given to books written in this vein. The revisionist literature always carried within itself a strong under-current of disapprobation of war as a means of settling international conflicts of interest, and emphasizing the complex nature of the factors producing war. Arthur Ponsonby's *Falsehood in Wartime* deserves mention as an example of this. In the fall of 1931, the liberal papers were giving very sympathetic attention to such books as Esmé Wingfield-Stratford's *They That Take the Sword,* Caroline E. Playne's *The Insanity of War* (which received a two-column favorable review by C. Hartley Grattan in the *New Republic* in September) and Scott Nearing's *War: Organized Destruction and Mass Murder by Civilized Nations* (which received widespread attention from both the main liberal journals). Beverly Nichols' *Cry Havoc!,* published just as the main attack on the munitions manufacturers was beginning, some time later, was considered worthy of "high praise" as a denunciation of war and an encouragement to abstention from engaging in military service.[1] But in the main, there was a noticeable impatience with the pacifist output as the thirties wore on, if it did not stress the material side of war and the elements profiting from it. The steady gravitation toward socialist and communist theory as to the origins of war in liberal circles accounts for most of the exasperation. By the time the depression was in full flower, the politically-conscious were finding it hard to conceal their contempt for the old pacifist group and their entire outlook. The moral and religious frame of reference of these historical anti-war elements also jarred those who preferred the Marxian outlook on religion. In the main, the new liberal political pacifists did not reject their support; accepting them as allies was primarily a procedure of condescension, but it was difficult to hide a feeling that the older pacifists were babes-in-the-woods, political innocents who did not yet know from whence their obstacles derived.

Perhaps this irritation was most effectively expressed by Malcolm Cowley in the spring of 1932 when he reviewed the famous pacifist pictorial history of the World War, *The Horror Of It.* The title of the review, "Sermon Against War," [2] in one sense suffices to explain Cowley's reaction to this shocking collection of photographs, largely reprinted from previously published German works. Cowley granted that they were impressive documents, but thought the stress on death symptomatic of pacifist sentimentalism, revealing "an important weakness of many pacifists, and perhaps of the American pacifist movement;"

One can safely say that the editor of the present volume and most of his like-minded associates don't know what it's all about. They don't know what is the cause of war, or how it can be prevented, or what is its worst result.

Cowley disagreed that death in violent forms was the most appalling result of war; "War does something else. It destroys not only human lives, but human ideas, emotions, attachments, living standards, means of production, everything that unites individuals into a unity more important than themselves; war is the suicide of a civilization." From this point on, Cowley launched into a summary of war as a product of competing economic forces, and averred that a new war was nearer than at any time since 1918. He saw no evidence among pacifists that they understood this, and was convinced that the approach dominated by "noble indignation" and "Christian sentiments" made the persons of this mind easily mobilized behind another war; Cowley demonstrated remarkable prescience in declaring "uninformed hatred of war is likely to be transformed into a ferocious hatred of the Germans or the Japanese." The pacifists then calling for an anti-Japanese embargo were the new counterparts of the 1917 pacifists who "were easily convinced that our defense of the Morgan loans and the Dupont munition contracts was 'a war to end war.' " Cowley was sure such an embargo would "lead to fighting almost inevitably." He offered no solution to war himself, but felt a thorough education in the economic realities of international life indispensable to an understanding of what was going on. This he was sure would end any feeble expectations of war terminating as a result of the action of "courts, round tables, conventions and conferences," the terminology Carrie Chapman Catt had used while writing the foreword to the book under review.

It was obvious that Cowley was immensely displeased with the fortunes of the anti-war movement; the leaders, both in Europe and the United States, were these well-intentioned innocents who wasted all their energy on denunciation and moral attack, but had no idea how to realize their aims. That there was no popular basis of this pacifism was the interlinear message Cowley was sending. A mass action alone could bring the economic turmoil producing war to a halt, and the implication that a world organized along some collectivist and antinational lines would surely be war-free was not too deeply buried. Later in the year, the long article by Norman Angell criticizing Jonathan Mitchell's war theory stimulated *New Republic* readers with views such as Cowley's and Mitchell's to bring up the matter again. Only an international socialist society would lack the selfish interests which encouraged the war system as a means of realizing greedy personal ambitions, Angell was told, and the hopes of pacifists like himself to proceed along non-materialist lines were bound to remain completely ineffectual.[3]

From a strictly actionist standpoint, the liberal press did not push anti-war programs of their own, but they served as media by which actionists advertised their doings, and were launching stations for the rash of trial balloons released by the new generation of pacifist organizations which proliferated in the early depression thirties. The anti-war sentiments of the editors were only too well known, even though they lapsed into supporting schemes which the new pacifists did not approve. From the point of view of space, their sympathy with these new approaches was unimpeachable. It does not appear that they closed their columns to any of these groups, and found occasion to commend them editorially as well.

The "new pacifism" was already underway in at least two separate (for the moment) departments, one vague and not clearly outlined, involving the youth arriving at conscript age, and the other, increasingly well organized and purposeful, in the control of the previous generation. For a time they remained separate, but slowly blended and emerged in the middle '30's as a dynamic group with opposition to war still in their name but caught in the currents of Communist politics with a vengeance. The evolution of the American League Against War and Fascism reveals a process which led so far away from war and intensely against Fascism that they eventually found no objection to employing the former to annihilate the latter.

Shortly before Christmas, 1931, the *New Republic* displayed great editorial indignation over the breaking up of a pacifist congress in Paris by French patriots, which had reportedly been attended by some 1000 delegates from thirty countries. It was the first intimation in liberal pages that a great anti-war stirring was afoot, but its political texture was in no way discernible from what was occurring at hand.[4] Reports on collegiate pacifism and growing opposition to compulsory military training in the United States were billed prominently. Heavy student polls in the Ivy League institutions of Yale and Dartmouth in this same month for total disarmament and against compulsory military training were interpreted to indicate that "the next generation of students may turn out to have a different political temper."[5] Student anti-war sentiments and what appeared to be a changed temper on the American campus were looked upon as most encouraging developments. When President Nicholas Murray Butler of Columbia was awarded a co-share in the 1931 Nobel Peace prize with Jane Addams, the *Nation* lauded him for this and for his pacifist and disarmament speeches of the moment. Better days were expected at his institution insofar as student expression of the same sort was involved, but the long liberal memory of the intoxicated days of 1917–1918 prevented an unqualified acceptance of the noted Morningside Heights Francophile. The December 23, 1931 issue said, "He was a great pacifist before the war, but during the war his record was thoroughly bad; he subordinated what he knew in his heart to mob psychology." The following July, the same journal, in an editorial titled "Butler, Borah and Bunk," declared pointblank: "We expect him, should war come again, to lead the hue and cry once more, and again to drive out of his university men who had the character and conscience to stick to the beliefs that they professed before hostilities commenced." [6] The *Nation* was a better prophet than it knew, although by the time the next war did arrive, it had changed so much itself that it showed small concern for the spiritual legatees of Beard and Cattell. There was a minimum amount of dust raised the second time President Butler ordered his faculty to declare war on Germany.

As regards the academic world, far greater hopes at the moment were banked upon the new student social consciousness pertaining to military service, and the suggestions and leadership of a number of veterans of the peace movement. The *Nation* gave publicity to a contest sponsored by the *New Historian* in the winter of 1931–1932, offering a prize for an essay on "How May the Colleges Promote World Peace?" with the judges to be John Dewey, Devere Allen, William Floyd, Tucker P. Smith, James G. MacDonald and Kirby Page. In the *New Republic* the contemporary proposal which got a measure of support was the peace proposal of Albert Einstein. This involved a suggestion that an international treaty be signed, committing the signatories to the elimination of compulsory military service, conscription and draft in war time, as well as to allow any or every individual citizen to refuse to aid any or all war activities. In the hands of a correspondent, Einstein's plan received articulate and enthusiastic exposition, and he sought the active support of the *New Republic* in supporting this program, what with a major disarmament conference in the immediate offing. The *New Republic* liberals were reproached for not backing this program rather than arms reduction, which was shown to be a futile approach to the question of the elimination of war. The reductions of thirty years might easily be made up in one, with the new techniques of production. Therefore, it was far more important to legalize the rights of each individual to make his own decision in time of war rather than to chop down armaments. The establishment of legal conscientious objection would thus create the basis for an outspoken public opinion on militarism and war, which might prove to be the foundation for a substantial organization everywhere against war. As things stood, "the legal ideology of nationalistic political organizations" made declarations of refusal to participate in war "a minor form of sedition." [7] There was some spirited response to this proposal, and it was revealed shortly thereafter that the pacifist Fellowship of Reconciliation had recommended this plan to President Hoover in a letter signed by John Nevin Sayre, Devere Allen, John Dewey, John Haynes Holmes and J. B. Matthews.[8]

Related to this and occurring in the same month of February, 1932 was a study by Gardner Jackson, "Congressional Jingoes," an attack on the opponents of a bill introduced by Rep. Anthony J. Griffin of New York, which would have established the right of aliens to become citizens without promising to bear arms in all the wars the United States might join. Jackson's sympathy with the bill was transparently obvious.[9]

Evidence for the existence of a deep-rooted dissatisfaction with the anti-war movement among the political actives came forth a very short time after Cowley's reprimand to the orthodox pacifist camp, indicating that much work had been done along these lines since December of 1931. From Switzerland in June, Romain Rolland issued a comprehensive call to all the opponents of war everywhere, urging them to "attend a large congress, which will be a powerful manifestation of all parties against war;"[10]

We summon everybody, from whatever social horizon they come! Socialists, Communists, trade unionists, anarchists, republicans of every shade, Christians and free-thinkers, all the pacifist organizations, war resisters, conscientious objectors, all independent individuals and all those in France and other countries who are decided to prevent war by whatever means.

This lengthy and urgent message to anti-war people, "to come to a decision as to common action," "to raise an immense wave of opinion against war," "to enable the will of the people to roar out for all that is wholesome in humanity," had all the classic earmarks of political front, pressure group fence-building, and the closing paragraph of this manifesto, printed verbatim in the July 6 issue of the *New Republic*, coincided carefully with the strongest interpretations of the source of war emanating from the most articulate liberal opinion-makers:

Let them [the people] compel the unworthy and equivocal weaknesses of the governments to choke the monstrous instigators of wars—the profiteers of massacre, the armaments industries, the cannon merchants, their clientele of provocateurs and the unscrupulous press, and all the mob which is intriguing to fish in bloody waters.

Within less than a month, it was reported to the readers that there was already formed an "American Committee" to take part in the "World Congress Against War" called for by Rolland, headed by Theodore Dreiser, Roger Baldwin, Edward C. Lindeman, Alla Nazimova, Upton Sinclair, Lincoln Steffens and Thornton Wilder, a cast spotted with enough names outside the normal pacifist leadership to be symptomatic of the change beginning to take place. The committee announced its job to be that of assembling for the meeting place in Geneva, scheduled for August 28, "a delegation that will adequately represent this country, its leaders of thought, its veterans, its teachers, students and workers, employed and unemployed." The convention's job was to "forcibly convince" the world's statesmen, generals and munitions makers that they would be unable to make war pay again.[11] The threat of violence was most significant, and served to point up dramatically the different outlook which the "new pacifism" was adopting.

A week later an open letter in the *New Republic* by Cowley, in his new status as secretary of the American Committee, pleaded for funds from the readers to help defray the expenses of the trip overseas. He called upon the sympathizers to "join unequivocally the ranks of those who are willing to fight against war," a remarkable way of putting the question, in view of the fact that peace was considered to be the absence of fighting. But as an indication of political aspirations it could hardly have been any plainer put. Several nations involved in the fighting in the Far East as participants or suppliers of munitions were mentioned, but not Soviet Russia. As for the United States, although the fleet was "ready for action in the Pacific," and although "warmongers" were making preparations for another war which would "dwarf the horrors of the last war," he promised that the delegation being sent to Geneva would "be strong enough to mobilize the entire American people to chain the hands of the militarists," and "to muzzle the cannon of war." [12]

A preliminary meeting in the beginning of the third week of August was announced, this a congress of writers in Berlin, "Kampfcongress gegen den imperialistischen Krieg," with Rolland, Baldwin, Henri Barbusse, Einstein and George Bernard Shaw expected to take part. As it turned out, as reported by the *Nation,* the first session of the "World Congress of All Parties Against War" met in Amsterdam, and chose Rolland president, with Barbusse as secretary of the "permanent international commission"; and had in attendance, among persons not previously designated to take part, Sherwood Anderson, Henry W. L. Dana and Scott Nearing, according to still another *Nation* dispatch supplied by A. A. Heller, the treasurer of the American Committee. Rolland's address must have warmed the hearts of the assembled Communists and their sympathizers, in that his savage attack on the warmaking of Anglo-Saxons, Germans, French and Asiatics pointedly omitted the Reds from criticism. In fact, at one point in his address he took the trouble to commend the Soviet Union and reinforce the deep conviction of its friends that it alone sought peace in the world: [13]

In the midst of all these combats, a single people—more than one people, twenty peoples, a world—has constructed and constructs from day to day the proletarian state; namely, the U.S.S.R. whose very existence constitutes a defiance of the old exploiting world, a hope and an example to all exploited peoples, which it becomes our common duty to preserve against all the threats of the correlated imperialisms.

No one at any subsequent time ever explained the purpose of the "new pacifism" more eloquently or so succinctly.

Rolland had pleaded with the conference that before separating they should create "a permanent international movement" against the war "smoldering everywhere under the ashes," to be erected "upon a close union between the two great groups of confederated workers; those who are called intellectuals and those who are called hand workers." This "Animal Farm" prospectus apparently did not come about exactly as planned, because most of the year 1933 was spent in several separate appeals to those pacifists yet unregistered in the United States, at least, by both the old and the new organizations. In January, Devere Allen issued a call for more members and funds for the older War Resisters' International, of which he was the chairman in America and Arthur Ponsonby in England. His *New Republic* call, headed "Shock Troops of Peace," showed the tendency to couch their ideas in the same military terminology they despised, but was most illuminating in that the claim was made that the WRI was the real organization spirit behind the world pacifist movement, and that the other figures were "cooperating" with it.[14]

A counter-call for the anti-war folk to line up with the American Committee for Struggle Against War, as it was now being called in the post-Amsterdam time, appeared in the same journal two weeks later, signed by Oakley Johnson, of the City College of New York, involved in a bitter battle in the city on charges of Communist activity and his decisive part as an adviser to the student Liberal Club. With the pro-Soviet writers discussing endlessly the possibility of Russia being involved in war with Japan momentarily in the Far East, it was more than a coincidence that the "anti-war demonstration" which was to be called all over the country on February 4 by the Committee, in New York was to make a point of deliberately marching past the Japanese Consulate before going to Broad and South streets for the mass meeting. "The opposition of American workers and intellectuals to imperialist wars, both of their own country and Japan," it was hoped, would "exert pressure on Far Eastern opinion."

Not to be outdone in the department of mass meeting and marches, the War Resisters' League announced an extensive call in the *New Republic,* plans for a parade in Washington on April 22, to be followed by a mass meeting at which they hoped to "answer the militarists in America." This call, signed by Allen, John Haynes Holmes, Jessie Wallace Hughan and Sidney E. Goldstein, stressed the theme of individual action, especially refusal to serve in the armed forces or as an employee of a munitions company. It spoke for those who were "utterly opposed to war without reservation, compromise or condition," and wrote in no escape hatch clauses to exempt the Soviet Union or any other power.[15] That there was a fundamental clash of outlook between these two organizations could be determined simply by carefully reading their pronouncements to the public.

A student section of the new belligerent pacifist organization was inevitable. Given the furious abuse of the military training programs in the colleges, concentrated notably on the Reserve Officers' Training Corps, this loose resentment was ideal material to corral into a branch of the new anti-war offensive. Robert Wohlforth's "The R.O.T.C. as a Peace Society," in a July issue of the *Nation* at about the time the famous Rolland manifesto was being publicized about the land, was a vitriolic essay upon the program and its unpopularity, buttressed by seemingly convincing statistical evidence.[16] The *New Republic*'s contemporary "College Writing Contest," which apparently favored proletarian and anti-war themes, awarded its praise to a curious production by a University of Oklahoma student, titled "The —plus Patriot's Catechism," a merciless question-and-answer debunking of the World War.[17] In the same journal, Nathaniel Weyl sympathetically reported, in his article "A College in Rebellion," City College student demonstrations against the military training program and the anti-militarist student publication which had attacked the R.O.T.C. Manual. With Dr. Johnson[18] of the American Committee for Struggle Against War as an adviser, one could imagine without too great a strain to cerebral powers the intellectual sources of this student ferment.

The contagiousness of these political flourishes and the attempt to smother them on the part of the customarily wary school administrators did no more than to cause the trouble to get wide publicity, and the birth of another front group, the Committee for the Conference on Student Rights, which sought to air the matter on a comprehensive basis for the entire city of New York early in December. A varied group of sponsors appeared behind this new organization, with Baldwin, Dewey, and Holmes joined by Professor George S. Counts, Elliot E. Cohen, Waldo Frank, Sidney Hook, Robert Morss Lovett, Jesse H. Newlon, Mark Van Doren and Harry F. Ward.[19] This notable gesture "in defense of academic freedom," as its *New Republic* call to action on December 7, 1932 was titled, was followed two weeks later by still another revelation, that a student auxiliary to the new anti-war group was in existence: the National Committee for the Student Congress Against War. The signators did not sound like students, with the names of Barbusse, Sherwood Anderson, Counts, Dana, Corliss Lamont, and Scott Nearing prominently featured. But the roster did include Donald Henderson and Reed Harris, the recently expelled editor of a Columbia University student publication, whose case had already received generous attention in the liberal press.[20]

After a brief introduction which re-echoed the words of Romain Rolland earlier in the year, this proclamation announced that the students were joining the workers and intellectuals "to fight shoulder to shoulder against war and the preparations for war," once again underlining the easy transferability of militant language to the side of the professedly anti-militant. Following a recital of the distress in which the students of the various lands of the world were trapped by the resurgence of war, and a caustic survey of the means by which the college age generation was "being prepared mentally and physically" for another war, a call to action was issued. Largely patterned after the Amsterdam Congress, this specified a mass student descent upon Chicago on December 28–29 to a Student Congress Against War. It was hoped by the organizational committee that the protest group would be of such numbers "that the militarists and the imperialists" would "pause before the ringing protest of our Congress."

In February, 1933, the *New Republic* readers learned by way of a dispatch from one of the participants some of the infighting details of this gathering, reputedly attended by seven hundred delegates from colleges in twenty-six states and claiming to represent 10,000 students. For the first time some details were available on the creeping capture of the new pacifism by the Communists. Although the writer rejoiced that the tensions between the various ideological elements had been "happily submerged by the achievement of unity," it remained plain that a marriage of the diverse groups mentioned was a virtual impossibility. The pacifists had been reported "standing by" while Socialist and Communist factions indulged in loud and angry wrangling, and it could be well imagined that they remained "standing by" at the conclusion.[21] A student wing of the Rolland-inspired anti-war Communist-dominated movement had come into existence, close enough to the adult group to be easily recognized in all the organizational details. This fight forecast a major breakdown in its parent organization's gathering later in the next year.

Through the summer of 1933, the plans for a major gathering built up, and new committees emerged. Now that the students had taken the initiative, in New York there appeared the "Provisional Teachers' Anti-War Committee," joining its efforts to those of the American Committee for Struggle Against War and the New York Student Committee for Struggle Against War. But the big news was the projected United States Congress Against War, scheduled to meet in New York City in the last week of September. A substantial preliminary commentary on this coming event appeared in the September 6 *New Republic,* which was of importance for bits of news on this new pacifist movement not previously available. The coming Congress was billed as a united meeting of groups "all the way from the Right to the Left" to discuss a program of opposition to war. But it was actually to be the birthplace of the formidable Communist front, the American League Against War and Fascism.

A quiet statement acknowledged the withdrawal of the Socialists from the meeting, but the Communists remained, as well as groups from American Federation of Labor unions, the League for Industrial Democracy, the Civil Liberties Union, the Fellowship of Reconciliation, the Women's Peace Society, the War Resisters' League and the Women's International League for Peace and Freedom. These diverse folk were joining, it was announced, with no program in advance and no commitment to second the resolutions of the Amsterdam Congress, admittedly the "parent body" from which this American Congress stemmed. News of other Congresses in other parts of the world was advanced as evidence for a multi-national and international flavor which was now reaching the stage of a planetary agreement. That something was undesirable about the Rolland Congress was acknowledged indirectly when it was revealed that the meeting had been denied access to Geneva, London, Paris and Brussels before going to Amsterdam, and then only after the Dutch government excluded representatives attending from the Soviet Union. But from Rolland's address, it appeared that sufficient Russian patriots were present despite this barrier. It was further admitted that a large number of the delegates to Amsterdam were illegal border crossers and presumably persons without passports who had domestic records such as would have prevented their leaving their home countries legitimately.

What this New York meeting would contribute to making "a united anti-war front" all over the globe was not made clear, but high hopes were held on the basis of the "patient organizational work" which would follow to "perpetuate" the enthusiasm of the delegates. A giant front group was being forecast here as the inheritor of the programs of the diverse smaller participating elements. What had been decided upon at the other Congresses also came out, especially decisions as to actual action beyond the educational and propaganda level. The content was sufficiently unordinary to deserve more extended treatment: [22]

The means of struggle against war voted by the different congresses have centered on the simple policy of seeking to stop them, or to prevent them from occurring, from below—by stopping the transport and manufacture of munitions, by continually pointing out the dangers of war to the classes which suffer most from it, and by making war a threat, not to the ruled classes of each country, but to the rulers.

That such a program involved engagement in affairs which contained numerous ugly political overtones and indirectly suggested a worldwide conspiracy even to indulge in assassination, if necessary, seemed completely to escape the writer of this remarkable news editorial. As for the American meeting at hand, nothing was expected of it at once, but much was considered within the range of possibility in the future. That it would be clearly marked off from what previously had been traditional pacifist and anti-war action and attitudes was never in doubt. But in view of the angry tone of the liberal press toward the domestic regimes in Italy, Japan and especially Germany, the continuance of the customary pacifist approach would have been meaningless. The only logical consequence of this protracted campaign against hated political forces in power in those lands and keeping in mind the undisguised beaming sympathy for the Soviet regime, documented week after week, was a steady drift toward action. Thus liberal approval of these novelties in the anti-war "struggle" was not the least inconsistent, even if there was a reticence as to explaining the real nature of the seat of control in the new organization. But after the New York Congress, at which the American League Against War and Fascism was fabricated, there was an end to the season of vagueness. It was no longer possible, necessary or desirable to disguise the fact that the American Communist Party had taken over the driver's seat.

The details of the gathering were reported with remarkable sobriety by both the main liberal weeklies early in October. The most unpleasant fact to report was undoubtedly the deliberate absence of the Socialist Party, although the *Nation* explained that Socialists were members of other attending organizations.[23] Yet the absence of their organizational machine was a serious lacuna in this new situation. The *New Republic* admitted directly that this event alone "left the Communists in the majority among the delegates and audience." [24] Thus the meeting in the first place would have been primarily a test of strength between Socialists and Communists as to which was to take the leadership in a political front against Fascism, and not a comprehensive meeting place for the country's anti-war forces at all. Continued the *New Republic* account, "The atmosphere of the gathering was undoubtedly colored by Communist feeling and characteristic forms of expression, to such an extent indeed that representatives of pacifist societies found themselves looking at one another askance and wondering if in seeking to escape from international war they were being committed to the doctrine of the class war."

The *Nation* apparently did not see this clash. The Congress meant to them a sign of proof Communists could unite "with other groups in a common project," and that the American League Against War and Fascism which came from it was proof that such a gathering could, despite its seemingly forbidding obstacles, "work constructively" provided the purpose was "sufficiently single" and was sincerely adhered to. The top-heavy part a single numerical dominant element might play in keeping these factors intact was not considered worthy of mention.

The *New Republic* account went into greater apologetic detail on the conference, concluded that the oratory of the Communists amounted to a "good deal of wild talk," but was to be expected of a group subject to regular "repression by force," in that it "necessarily reacted by verbal violence." It suggested that those made apprehensive by this speech recognize that the outcome of the meeting was not couched in this flaming language, and was "animated by a deep resolve to do away with the economic causes of war," held in common by the attending "farmers, workers and youth." In extenuation for the name of the organization adopted, as well as all the verbal eruptions, the editorial advanced a thesis which implied that violence was the proper way to confront violence:

No one who realizes the horror and the imbecility of war among peoples can blame the bitterness with which representatives of those who bear the cost of it speak in condemnation of a social order which permits it, which expends resources in preparing for it, which refuses to renounce it even as a primary condition of the survival of what we call civilization. That this social order under direction of its ruling class tends today to assume a specifically militant form is recognized in the name adopted for the permanent organization born at the Congress—the American League Against War and Fascism.

The liberal papers did not realize their enthusiasm over the apparent blending of all the diverse anti-war camps was premature until the end of the year. When the Fellowship of Reconciliation dropped J. B. Matthews, the first editor of the League's monthly organ, *The Fight,* from his post as executive secretary of the organization for subscribing to the new notions of the licit domestic violence, it was evident that the historic pacifist groups were not going along with the American League Against War and Fascism, on the grounds that it was not enough against war, and drawing the definition of "Fascism" too broadly and loosely. Matthews' unwillingness to accept the FoR's ban on the class war as well as the international variety was considered a great dividing point in the anti-war program, as well it was. With strong anti-Communist regimes growing in power in Italy and Germany, and with Japanese statesmen issuing warnings against allowing Communism to spread in Asia, it was hardly a time for Communists and their friends to stand by the generalized position of historic pacifism. The inclusion of Fascism in their target might have been understood as a necessity. The *New Republic* reported with satisfaction that Roger Baldwin, famous for his pacifism in the First World War, and now a contributor to the League's monthly publication, had resigned from the FoR, as well as others, as a gesture of their support of Matthews, commenting at length upon the present conditions which made the older pacifism intolerable as a personal philosophy for those now anxious to "do something about it," as it might be phrased. The reason pacifists now had to don armor in the class war, Baldwin explained in the following manner: [25]

The Fellowship's action, of course, emphasizes the growing breach between conventional pacifism and radicalism, movements which once seemed to have much in common. The lessons of Italy and Germany, to name only two, show that if radicals won't fight, conservatives will—and will win. Indeed, not to fight is sometimes to take part in the struggle on the other side. To accept absolute pacifism is nowadays to retire into an ivory tower—with a good chance of finding this tower overturned ere long in the hurricane of social change by violence which is sweeping the world.

Baldwin's explanation was exceedingly charitable, compared with overt Communist views. When the *Communist* in its issue for November, 1933, printed the "Manifesto and Program of the American League Against War and Fascism" which had been adopted at the New York meeting of September 29-October 1, it appended to the Manifesto the ferocious attack on pacifism and "pacifist swindlers" made at the Sixth World Congress of the Comintern in Moscow in the summer of 1928. It left absolutely no doubt that according to Communist strategy, any collaboration with traditional pacifist groups was utterly impossible. But no liberal commentaries appeared on this issue, and only the piecemeal defections of anti-Stalin Marxists in the succeeding three years indicated that there were those who were aware that the American League was first of all a Communist front, and only in a secondary sense an anti-war organization in the accepted sense of the day.[26]

The editorial tone and the tenor of the articles in the League's monthly organ *The Fight,* from its first issue of November, 1933, onward, was sufficient evidence to underline the virtual disappearance of traditional pacifism from the League, if its membership, delegates and public pronouncements were still not convincing enough documentaries. Even though many liberals attached themselves to the new publication, its lock-step procession in the Popular Front parade was an established fact in short order. Though it subscribed to the attack on the munitions makers, castigated military training in the colleges, and talked incessantly of the evils of war and the blessings of peace, illustrated by grotesque cartooning in the manner of the *New Masses,* the orientation was impossible to miss. Conscription was attacked in all countries except Soviet Russia, which was also exempted from abuse on the subject of manufacture and stockpiling of war materials. "Russia Fights For Peace," the September, 1934 issue trumpeted. But another fight, that of the Communists in China, was cheerfully supported as well. On the European scene the readers were exposed to a continual nightmare of towering Italo-German martial strength, juxtaposed to the image of a domestically-absorbed Soviet Union barely in possession of a fowling-piece over the fireplace. By the end of the year even the most innocent and trusting liberal would have had to concede that the *Fight* was another transmission-belt publication. The Old Pacifists had been driven to cover, and whatever prestige it enjoyed as an organ of pacifism was due to what rubbed off the many eminent liberals and intellectuals who for one reason or another lent their names to the League and its pages.

There was a logic to this decay and collapse of pacifism, if one followed the virulence of the verbal attack on the Hitler regime and the indignant response to the slightest moves made in the Third Reich against the elements to which the Communists were allied philosophically, despite the fact that they amounted to a tiny fraction of the national population, even by admission of their friends such as the American liberals. When Einstein declared that despite his pacifism even he could understand "how young men might enlist in an international army to combat Hitlerism," as the *Nation* reported in its October 4, 1933 issue, the question became even more dramatic. Despite the eagerness of the new and some of the old pacifists to tangle with the Fascist states in armed combat, the *Nation* still was reluctant to support them, no matter what sympathy it was willing to cast in their direction.

Even though no publication in America exceeded the intemperance of the *Nation* in its condemnation especially of Germany and Japan, its acquired stand since the World War was still powerful enough to inhibit a gradual wandering off just yet in the direction of the forces in the process of building. Surrounded by "pacifists" who were beginning to see virtue in the flexed muscle and the gunshot, the *Nation* persisted in being an island of its own kind of pacifism. Reviewing the World War once more as the source of the then present dislocated world, it editorially warned those persons with eagerness for a large-scale Armageddon that "any attempt by the rest of the world" to meet these dictator states "with armed force can only result in an unheard-of cataclysm"; "Another, greater conflict could only multiply tenfold the injustice and misery which now oppress us." Opposition to these loathed regimes through war was the wrong course: [27]

The answer lies in the perfection of international organization, the mobilization of world opinion, the use of the boycott, and the continuance of the protests of those who know the futility of force. How can anyone in his sane senses, after the horrible futility of the World War, believe that war can produce anything but evil or fail to recognize that it rights no wrongs and rarely, if ever, settles any question aright? This is not the hour to fling our beliefs overboard, to discard for all time the Prince of Peace and his noblest teachings; it is the time to insist upon finding other ways than wholesale murder to bring outlaw nations to book.

So there continued to be two conflicting currents in the liberal journals on the new developments in pacifism, a tendency to approve the new toughness and its gradual absorption in concern over class warfare, and at the same time a hesitance to jettison the hard-earned lessons of the World War days and after. The new proletarian ideologies had not changed the spots of war, to this particular segment of liberal opinion. Furthermore, there continued to appear here and there signs of success on the part of the traditional pacifism, mostly to be seen in the behavior of the new generation of potential gunbearers. The growing belligerence of the World War generation, gradually becoming safe through the aging process from the chilling wind of the draft, was mainly evident in the leadership of the new pacifism, if the names attached to their public pronunciamentos indicated anything. The age group becoming eligible for military service took far less initiative, despite its student sections attached to the new political pacifist fronts.

The *Nation*'s January 27, 1932 editorial "Youth Votes For Peace" was an optimistic commentary on the recently-concluded Intercollegiate Disarmament Conference, and the heavy votes among undergraduates of 70 colleges of up to 90 per cent for both arms reduction and unilateral disarmament by the United States, with one out of seven voting for total disarmament and 80 per cent voting against military training in the colleges. The *Nation* described this as a "veritable cry for peace," and hoped it would spur college officials and teachers to work with more determination at "their task of freeing their institutions from the clutches of war ideology," and undergraduates to join anti-war societies such as the War Resisters' League and the Fellowship of Reconciliation.[28] It amounted to a few twittering bars in the harsh, bristling symphony called into existence by the contemporary Japanese action at Shanghai.

The *Nation* took especial comfort as well from the action of the

Oxford Union in the late winter of 1932–1933 in adopting a resolution by which they rejected the idea of fighting in another war engaged in by Great Britain. This famous "Oxford Pledge" was a subject of repeated praise and evidence of the surviving vitality of pacifism, and its duplication in virtually all the major universities in England and Wales was offered as an example to the more restrained American undergraduate.[29] Strong anti-war and anti-conscription positions taken by students at Brown, Stanford and Columbia universities in the spring of 1933 similarly aroused firm support. "When young men refuse to fight, war must cease," the *Nation* pronounced. "May our universities turn into jails when next the old men decide that 'war must come!' "[30] When the British Labor Party, led in a by-election campaign in the fall of 1933 by the pacifist Laborite George Lansbury, won an important contest over the Tories with major war preparation or pacifism the only issue, the *Nation* felt safe in recognizing this as still another sign of the vigor in the pacifist position and the continued popular rejection of war preparation in spite of all the provocation to the contrary.[31]

But the exhortatory manifestoes from the new organizations kept drifting into the rear pages of the liberal magazines, reminding the readers of yet still other reshufflings of the politically-conscious youth anxious to establish a reputation as opponents of conscription and international war. In March, 1933, under the expectable heading "Militant Students," a strong plea was made for funds for the National Student League, revealed as the band which had represented American undergraduates at the now historic Amsterdam World Congress Against War, as well as already having gotten embroiled in several instances of the domestic socio-political "fight," both on and off university campuses. The sponsoring notables were by now a familiar group of New Pacifist "elder statesmen": Sherwood Anderson, Newton Arvin, Roger Baldwin, Slater Brown, Mark Van Doren, Max Eastman, Scott Nearing, H. W. L. Dana, Theodore Dreiser, Waldo Frank, Michael Gold, John Dos Passos, Oakley Johnson and Corliss Lamont.[32]

In the columns of all the liberal papers, a steady drumfire of attack on compulsory military service accompanied the sprouting of the campus-side protestants. In August of 1933 the *Nation* roasted the trustees of Cornell University for refusing to heed a faculty recommendation that military training be made optional, and also excoriated the Wisconsin legislature for repealing its optional military training law for the University of Wisconsin. It editorially ran down the excuses offered for so doing, and charged that it was just part of a growing national sentiment, communicated here by the developments in Italy, Germany and also Japan, to "teach our young to rattle the saber." "The fact is that over Americans and their homes hang the domestic perils of destitution and foreclosure—not the threat of a foreign enemy," the editors chided the respective educational policy-makers. These latter were referred to as the "men whose hardened mentality and hardening arteries have played so large a part in bringing the world to its present crisis." They represented the forces in America which desired "to transform our country into a Fascist state." [33]

The suspension of students refusing to comply with compulsory military drill at institutions all the way from the University of Maryland to the University of California at Los Angeles drew forth an article in the *New Republic* in February, 1934 by Edwin C. Johnson, identified as the secretary of the Committee on Militarism in Education, titled "Hitlerizing American Students," and inviting the interested to inquire for more information regarding the legal and opinion fight going on about this matter. The suspension of these students "because of their refusal to join the military goose steppers" in Johnson's opinion was a forecast of "an era of regimentation from and by the right" in the United States, and was bound to become a more critical issue in view of the fact that the courts had already given support to the authorities in their efforts to entrench the tradition, begun with the creation of the land grant colleges.[34]

The same month the *Nation* warmly applauded the action of the board of trustees at De Pauw University in requesting the War Department to withdraw their ROTC unit, which presumably ended the "nine-year fight" against it carried on by students and faculty under the leadership of its President, G. Bromley Oxnam. The editorial reported that Oxnam "had been the recipient of threats from the War Department for his unpatriotic attitude," but had persevered nevertheless to a triumphant conclusion. The *Nation* concluded that the ROTC should be dropped everywhere, in consonance with the universal talk of peace, as being "highly unbecoming for such coercion to come from presumably educational institutions." [35]

When in December, 1934 the Supreme Court unanimously backed the state authorities against the conscientious objectors, the *New Republic* once more went on record in disparagement of traditional pacifism and suggested that relief from military service and war would come only on the heels of the social revolution. Franklin Roosevelt's amnesty to the World War's conscientious objectors the previous January was already forgotten. It now was naïve of objectors to war to expect to refuse to fight "with the consent or protection of the government." This very act was a type of warfare "against the existing system," a "fundamental fact" which needed emphasizing. Thus, such persons should oppose war and military service in full knowledge that they had to "accept the risks and casualties" following such choices. Large numbers of people morally opposed to war would never be able to stop a government from raising armies and stifling objectors; "The way to end war is not by a moral campaign aimed at non-participation, but by a reorganization of society such that war situations will not arise." And the journal speculated editorially that "it is more than likely that those who want such reorganization will in the end have to fight for it, if they are to get it." At this stage the editors were marching abreast of the nation's embattled social revolutionaries.[36]

The new pacifist organizations worked at full speed in 1934; even the ladies grew active and began to issue proclamations. In the *Nation* in April, the United Anti-War Association of the University of Chicago posted its petition to Senator Dieterich of Illinois, calling for his support for Senator Nye's resolution for an investigation of the war and munitions industries. Lucy Liveright, the secretary of this new organization, claimed the petition had been signed by 600 students and faculty. The petitioners referred to themselves as "the future cannon fodder for senile statesmen, capitalists and generals— all of whom die in bed." [37]

Still another reference to action by college and university alumni drew praise from Villard in the *Nation* in May, 1934 when he publicly commended Dr. Harry Emerson Fosdick's anti-war pledge. In his editorial, Villard thought it "magnificently encouraging" that 43 per cent of the Yale class of 1924 had voted that they would not take up arms to defend the United States even if attacked.[38]

In the first week of June, Margaret Forsythe, the Chairman of the American Section, International Women's Congress Against War and Fascism, announced in the *New Republic* [39] a plan to hold a World Congress of Women in Paris on July 30, "to work out plans for combatting fascism and war." The delegation was in the process of being selected and "organized" by the parent American League Against War and Fascism, which was now revealed to be under the leadership of Dr. Harry F. Ward, although the masthead of the *Fight* had carried this news for some time.

At the end of the summer the announcements of another mass meeting of the American League and its various auxiliaries began to sift into the pages of the liberal weeklies. Perhaps the most vigorous was written by James A. Wechsler, student editor of the Columbia *Daily Spectator,* speaking for the Youth Section only. Roger Baldwin and Harry F. Ward followed later with the announcement that the entire League planned to repeat its previous Chicago gathering. It was quite evident from the tone of the two open letters that the enemy now was Fascism, and that the resistance to war had become a parenthetical thesis kept primarily for the protective coloration it offered. Wechsler called for the now-familiar "genuine cross-section of America" to come to Chicago "from schools, factories, shops and farms." He offered no rebuttal to the charge that "a militant organ-

ization such as the League" was being labeled "red." "I am convinced," declared Wechsler in this statement, "that the Communists
in it [the League] are sincere, energetic, and fearless opponents of
war. I am certain that they are ready and have already demonstrated
their ability to work side by side with conservative elements—so long
as these remain sincere and courageous." Wechsler neglected to add
that the Communists, in addition to possessing these admirable qualities, were also the numerically preponderant group in the organization, and could well afford to work with virtually anybody.

Although in the name of the organization the word "war" preceded
"Fascism," from the point of view of tactics and strategy, the group
now reasoned from the reverse. While at one stage, the theory read
that war produced Fascism, this was modified to make the two allies
and contemporaries, from which point it became a simple matter to
place Fascism in the lead position and make it the principal target.
From Wechsler's prospectus, one might indeed expect that the
League Congress was to begin virtually recruiting an army of its own
to fight Fascism: [40]

To prevent war, to smash its ally—fascism—in its incipient stages, demands
immediate, widespread action. It means mobilization along non-political
[sic] lines. It is time that the young men and women of America took up
the challenge to their lives. It is time they decided to make a serious fight
for their own welfare. It is time they realize that they have to look out for
themselves. The League of Nations won't look out for them.

To such square-jawed belligerent argumentation had the new pacifism travelled. It was obviously in a world apart from the traditional
pacifist approach and no longer could be spoken of in the same context or as engaged in a task of common nature.

The Baldwin-Ward call was even more pointedly political, and
hardly found space to mention foreign affairs: [41]

The recent violence in California, the spread of Hitlerism in Europe, the
huge naval rebuilding program which President Roosevelt has launched,
make it more imperative than ever that the fight against war and fascism
should be carried on with greater determination.

In this way the call for volunteers to another Chicago Congress was
introduced. With the first big strikes of the New Deal era breaking
out on the San Francisco water front, it was obvious that the League
spokesmen and leaders were much more excited by domestic "Fascist"
trends than they were by the more generalized struggle against war.
At a later point in the prospectus, war and Fascism were reported to
be "inseparably linked by nationalism gone mad," and that every-

body, "irrespective of race or creed," was duty-bound to combat nationalism. This seemed to offer a slightly out of character solution to the twin-headed monsters of the League when compared to the tides of verbiage which had risen and fallen since the famous Rolland oration at Amsterdam. In December, when the League sponsored John Strachey in an address at Mecca Temple in New York City, speaking on the topic, "Does Fascism Breed War?" a question which appeared to have an obvious answer, the season of switching cart and horse apparently had not ended. The League was above reproach as a promulgator of monodiabolism; it had a full hall of *bêtes noires*.

In the meantime the 1934 meeting of the American League Against War and Fascism came off in Chicago in October. The *Nation*, reporting on its sessions, announced that there were 149 delegates representing the Communist Party, but caused no alarm among the pacifists for that reason. A few growls were being heard, however, not from the pacifist societies, but from Marxist opponents of the Stalinist majority position and more inclined to support the Trotsky wing. One of these, James Burnham, in a message to the *Nation* in December, openly accused the League of being a prominent gambit of "Stalinism," and doubted its sincerity as an anti-war association.[42] The momentary dabbling in domestic American political struggles did not appreciably divert the League from its Russian bent.

The persistent question mark in the tale of the birth and growth of the new pacifism is the relation of its organizational side to Russian Communism. Regardless of all subsequent maneuvering, the several groupings labored under the weight of the Rolland call to defend the Soviet Union at the very incipience of this variety of anti-war sentiment. Such quiet statements concerning the problem of Communism as did appear made it quite clear that the Communist Party had captured the organizations, and the frequent appearance of the names of known Communists and warm supporters at the bottom of the proclamations which proliferated in the early and mid-thirties did nothing to establish the theory of widely diversified foundational support.

Peculiarly enough, with all the stress being placed upon the remarkable social innovations in the Soviet Union, and with virtually all the facets of its culture gathering unqualified praise, nothing was put on record regarding the area of presumably deepest concern to the League. The silence was deafening concerning the status of Russia's draft-age youth. There were no dissertations dealing with pacifism in Russia, nor what the position of conscientious objectors to war and compulsory military service happened to be there. The enormous Red Army, which other reporters on things Russian described, and its munitions production, air force and army mechanization, all described as mighty in scope by one or another writer in the liberal press, indicated that the managers of the Soviet State were conducting an enterprise of nationhood in much the manner of the orthodox capitalist lands where Fascism lay incubating, and occasionally hatching. But "nationalism" was never referred to as a Soviet sentiment, and in like manner "patriotism" appeared not at all whenever the domestic Communist world was being described in one or another of its manifestations.

In view of the sustained efforts which had gone into building the legend of Soviet Russia as the home of world pacifism and disarmament, and in addition, the theory that only a Socialist world would lack the pressures resulting in war, the omission of the Communist military state was an expectable consequence. The only subject on which these new pacifists quoted or mentioned the Soviet Union was disarmament. The liberal press and the pacifists of the newest variety were convinced that the nations of the world were all hypocritical when the desirability of reducing arms was expressed—all except Russia. All proposals emanating from Moscow were taken at face value, accompanied at times by expressions of such faith in Communist oratory that one might have imagined the Soviet had already demolished their war stocks, and were pleading with the other powers to do the same. When the Communists published in 1933 *The Soviet's Fight For Disarmament,* which included the fantastic Litvinov speeches at the Geneva Disarmament Conference, the *New Republic* accepted it without a doubt or reservation, and repeated the Red dictum that the Western powers were to blame for the continuation of the arms race in the world for having rejected the Litvinov suggestions.[43] Virtually no one expressed the idea that Litvinov may have been just plaguing his colleagues by making proposals such as that recommending the elimination of *all* armaments everywhere by everyone. Even the tough and skeptical Oswald Garrison Villard thought these Soviet proposals sincere. Belief in the sincerity of these strange suggestions might have been diagnosed as lack of faith in the sanity and good hard common sense of the Soviet leaders, however, in view of their reputation for employing logic and practical common sense.

The utterly uncritical approach to Russia and the sanction of class warfare with no limits to the employment of violence for political objectives on intranational levels undoubtedly had much to do with the estrangement of the older pacifist movement from the new Communist-dominated and influenced pacifism or, to be more exact, anti-Fascism. Their refusal to talk of Russia as a nation state with an armed force to be used as an instrument for the promotion of its national interests did much to cast suspicion on their protestations of nonpartisan interest in world peace. After all, it was war and not parliamentary processes which launched the Bolsheviki. The failure to explain the function of the massive Red Army in a nation presumably devoted completely to the ideal of a world without organized violence did much damage to the new pacifist cause, but not as much damage as the new pacifism did to the pacifist movement. The glib excuses offered in the middle 1950's to the effect that Hitler destroyed pacifism might be re-examined, and checked against the evidence as to the part played by a vigorous and energetic pro-Soviet-oriented domestic political group, speaking in the tongues of pacifism as verbal camouflage for completely different sympathies. In America, Romain Rolland's call to defend the Soviet Union first and foremost was heeded with a vengeance. Those liberals who called such action "pacifism" performed a mighty deed in the preparation of the burial of any genuine pacifism, as well as contributing impressively to the vocabulary of belligerence for later use in different contexts. When Malcolm Cowley castigated the older pacifists for their ignorance and warned them that "uninformed hatred of war" might easily be converted into hate of Germans and Japanese, he overlooked how much more easily this could be done with the "informed" variety advanced by the new pacifists.

NOTES

1 Grattan's two-column review of Playne was published in the issue of September 23; Nearing was advertised in major format by Vanguard in the *Nation* on September 30, 1931, and a very favorable review by Winchell Taylor was published in the *New Republic* on November 18; Wingfield-Stratford was also advertised in the *New Republic* by the publisher, Morrow, on October 28, 1931. Review of *Cry Havoc!* (Doubleday, Doran) in *New Republic*, September 27, 1933, p. 193.

2 *New Republic*, May 4, 1932, p. 333.

3 Letters to *New Republic* signed by Haydn Haines and Jerome Cornfield, October 26, 1932, p. 293.

4 *New Republic*, December 9, 1931, p. 81.

5 *New Republic*, December 23, 1931, p. 147; *Nation*, December 23, 1931, p. 683.

6 *Nation*, July 6, 1932, p. 4.

7 Letter from Alexander Lesser, *New Republic*, January 13, 1932, p. 245.

8 Reprinted in *New Republic*, February 3, 1932, p. 323.

9 *New Republic*, February 17, 1932, pp. 13–14.

10 This citation and others below from letter published in *New Republic*, July 6, 1932, p. 210.

11 *New Republic*, August 3, 1932, p. 299.

12 *New Republic*, August 10, 1932, p. 346. See also the fierce approval of the World Congress in "Against Imperialist War," *New Masses*, August, 1932, p. 13.

13 *Nation*, September 21, 1932, pp. 251–252. For personnel of the committee, see *Nation*, November 30, 1932, p. 533.

14 *New Republic*, January 25, 1933, p. 298.

15 *New Republic*, April 19, 1933, p. 284.

16 *Nation*, July 6, 1932, pp. 10–11. Wohlforth cited evidence which indicated 327 educators had requested Congress to take military training out of the colleges and universities.

17 The author was Jack Fischer. Entire work reproduced in *New Republic,* October 12, 1932, p. 236.

18 See also Oakley Johnson's open letter to *New Republic,* February 8, 1933, p. 354, speaking for the American Committee For Struggle Against War.

19 *New Republic,* December 7, 1932, p. 100. The secretary of this organization was Herbert Solow.

20 *New Republic,* December 21, 1932, p. 165.

21 See report by M. B. Schnapper in *New Republic,* February 1, 1933, p. 326.

22 Editorial "A Congress Against War," *New Republic,* September 6, 1933, p. 90.

23 *Nation,* October 11, 1933, p. 394, and for subsequent citations on this matter below.

24 *New Republic,* October 11, 1933, pp. 227–228, and citations below.

25 *New Republic,* December 27, 1933, p. 180.

26 "The first duty of Communists in the fight against imperialist war is to tear down the screen by which the bourgeois conceal their preparations for war and the real state of affairs from the masses of the workers. This duty implies above all a determined political and ideological *fight against pacifism.* In this fight the Communists must take careful note of the various shades of pacifism. . . .

"In the struggle against pacifism, however, the Communists must draw a distinction between anti-war sentiments of large masses of the toilers, who are ready to fight against war, but do not as yet understand that the revolutionary way is the only proper way of combating war, and therefore become a prey to pacifist swindlers, and swindlers themselves, the pacifists of various shades. The masses must be patiently enlightened as to their error and urged to join the revolutionary united front in the struggle against war. But the pacifist swindlers must be relentlessly exposed and combated."—*The Struggle Against Imperialist War and The Tasks of The Communists:* Resolution of the Sixth World Congress of the Communist International, Moscow, July–August, 1928, in *The Communist,* volume 12, November, 1933, p. 1124; italicized words in text from the original.

27 Editorial "War Or Peace," *Nation,* October 4, 1933, p. 368; Einstein quoted here as well.

28 January 27, 1932, p. 91.

29 *Nation,* March 15, 1933, p. 275; May 17, 1933, p. 560.

30 Editorial paragraph in *Nation* on April 12, 1933.

31 *Nation,* November 8, 1933, pp. 524–525.

32 *New Republic,* March 15, 1933, p. 133.

33 *Nation,* August 9, 1933, p. 142.

34 *New Republic,* February 7, 1934, p. 366.

35 Editorial "Still the R.O.T.C.," *Nation,* February 21, 1934, pp. 207–208. See also S.L. Solon, "The American Student and the Coming War," *Common Sense,* October, 1934, pp. 14–16.

36 *New Republic,* December 12, 1934, p. 113. For editorial commendation of Roosevelt and the general amnesty to conscientious objectors, see *New Republic,* January 3, 1934, p. 207.

37 *Nation,* April 4, 1934, p. 388.

38 *Nation,* May 23, 1934, p. 581.

39 *New Republic,* June 6, 1934, p. 102.

40 *Nation,* August 29, 1934, p. 241, for this and additional citations above.

41 *New Republic,* September 19, 1934, p. 162.

42 *Nation,* October 17, 1934, p. 422. Burnham's reference in *Nation,* December 12, 1934, p. 682.

43 *New Republic,* February 1, 1933, pp. 332–333.

9

THE LONDON CONFERENCE AND
REFLECTIONS ON THE FUTURE
OF INTERNATIONALISM

LIBERAL CALCULATIONS ON THE MEANING
OF THE ECONOMIC PARLEY

IN THE post-1929 period, the liberals had available two different varieties of internationalism, so to speak, from which to choose as a personal choice for success and survival. There was the pre-World War kind, an international capitalist economic structure in which free trade, the absence of tariff barriers and hindrances to population movement, and free convertibility of currencies based on the gold standard tended to be the outstanding characteristics. This system had provided a maximum of safety and security to money, goods, and businessmen migrating across national boundaries. The Anglo-Saxon world, and particularly the British Empire, found it especially congenial, useful and comforting. But the War had dealt it a staggering blow, and in addition had spread the chaos which engulfed a sizable area in which the old system had been entrenched, and directly spawned the totalitarianism which was to become the previous order's implacable challenger. War had done more to establish Communism in three years than all the theoretical collectivist propaganda of the entire Christian era combined. Its proponents now were in the ideological market place with their attractive product, a rival brand of internationalism which ostensibly hung before the eyes of the miserable and unhappy everywhere the vision of a stateless world of global cooperative socialist societies, all fabricated in such a way that the built-in defects of the older order were completely missing.

With the older internationalism reeling from the sledge hammer blows of a planetary war and two disastrous business collapses in less than two decades, plus the growth of a vast number of artificial interferences with the relatively casual and unsupervised economic world *ante* 1914, the prospects for the Communist alternative never were better. But the development of nationalistic forms of state capitalism was to add still another ingredient to those already mentioned. And in the ensuing years the blending of all three was to create a hair-tearing set of circumstances for the descriptive economists and dealers in simplified labels for competing economic systems, as well as to convert a sizable part of the vocabulary of political propagandists of all hues into meaningless hypocrisy. The politico-economic language of the 1950's and thereafter had a snug niche in George Orwell's "Newspeak."

The liberals were torn on this controversy as they were on several other world issues. A group of liberal elders looked back on the pre-World War I times with fond memories, and in their ruminations on the grim and comfortless days which had fallen on the world since that time, were inclined to favor its restructure. It is unnecessary to recapitulate the words of most of the younger liberal generation already dealt with in other contexts, whose unhappiness with this order had edged them into the ranks of the social and economic revolutionaries clamoring for a radical change. Oswald Garrison Villard, early depression editor-in-chief of the *Nation,* perhaps typified best the first of these two sentiments. Those in opposition were numerous, and grew in voice and stature especially after the collapse of the London Economic Conference of June and July, 1933, which might be called the last effort made between the two World Wars to reach a congenial and satisfactory settlement of world economic problems on a broad international basis. The liberal press gave it a generous measure of support, and its demise was interpreted as "a deadly blow to the world's progress and international cooperation." To the liberal enemies of this program it was just another proof of the impossibility of profit-dominated national economies getting together on a plan for international cooperation. To others, it was the signal to embark on a conscious project of national self-sufficiency. And it was accompanied and followed by a vigorous controversy among various ideologues debating the likely form of the immediate future and what appeared to be the significant literary leads and theoretical essays furnishing guidance. The Communist versus Fascist struggle broke out with a vengeance at its conclusion, and the ranks of the uncommitted were sharply reduced in the ensuing contumacious wrangling.

The breakdown of the Conference in the early months of the first Administration of Franklin D. Roosevelt simply added another item to the substantial case the liberals had stacked against him in the first term of office. By the time the dust of the explosion of the Conference had settled, the liberals and their press were united in placing the greatest share of the blame for its crash directly upon the President. But from the time the United States participation at the meeting was announced, in the spring of 1932, nine months before Mr. Roosevelt had acceded to the presidential office, there had been a tendency for the liberal press to expect little from it. The reason for this was the truncated agenda. The *New Republic* had an especially damp editorial greeting: [1]

While we are warmly in favor of international cooperation by America, we must confess that we can only throw our cap a couple of inches in the air at this news. For war debts are to be excluded from discussion; so are reparations, so is the American tariff. To have an international economic conference without discussing these things is like leaving out of "Hamlet" not only the Prince but Elsinore, Ophelia and the whole second act.

The *Nation*'s June 29, 1932 editorial also pointed out that Secretary of State Stimson had ruled out all three as unacceptable subjects for the agenda when the Hoover Administration committed the United States to participating in such a conference.[2] It was the opinion of the editors that the chances of anything being done of any significant help to a crumbling system in Europe were of the ratio of one hundred to one, however desirable.

That no substantial improvement was expected of the Roosevelt administration when it inherited the commitment to attend such a conference was demonstrated in the liberal press on occasion in the first few months of 1933, at a time when foreign affairs were hardly being mentioned by the New Deal leaders. The *New Republic*'s oracular "T.R.B." did not think he was revealing confidential material in the least by stating that neither Roosevelt nor his advisers had any kind of plan for dealing with this conference at his inauguration time, and that they "had extremely hazy notions as to what the conference was about" to begin with. He further maintained that it was common knowledge that some of the President's associates were of the opinion that "no international conference yet held had really accomplished anything," that the "principal fellows around Mr. Roosevelt were frankly bored by the very mention of the 'World Economic Conference'" and "did not want to talk about it."[3] All of this had been in line with the campaign denial of Hoover's position that the depression was world-wide, and could only be brought to a halt by adjustments and cooperation on a world-wide basis.

Nevertheless, "the education of the administration" had been "as swift as it had been complete," the *New Republic* columnist now insisted, and the President and his advisers thought the Conference "the greatest opportunity" to "enact a program for recovery that will be truly effective." There was an element of the incomprehensible about the report of this miraculous conversion and a sharp flavor of politics. "T.R.B." was writing just six weeks after the inaugural, and a turnabout so fundamental on a problem this vast by a group admittedly stumbling about in the dark as to what it was even being held for, was a test to almost anyone's credulity. A *Nation* editorial of the same date (May 3, 1933) expected little to come of the Conference despite the "best efforts of President Roosevelt," and granting his "frankness and friendliness and his realization of the crucial need of agreement." Villard's signed lead editorial of the same day, "The Crucial Conferences," was the most favorable of all. "Mr. Roosevelt has a glorious chance, the world looks to him for leadership. . . . As he comes through we shall know how successful his Administration is really going to be. . . ." [4]

But the general tone of the liberal editorial comments throughout May was restrained and skeptical. Economic nationalism and the rival alliance systems being rebuilt were expected to trip up almost anything proposed at London, and American positions of resistance to tariff reduction, the adamant stand on the debt collection, and the recent departure from the gold standard were not expected to cause any substantial rise of faith in the United States on the part of the other powers attending the meeting. Nor were the President's consultations with the British and French leaders in Washington considered of much importance in altering existing national psychologies in those nations. The *New Republic* suggested that the most intelligent European response to the war debts owed to the United States would be their frank repudiation, since in this country "everyone now knows these debts will not be paid." [5] As to tariff reductions and currency stabilization, no elation of any magnitude was entertained. A full-page editorial, "What Hope for the London Conference?" [6] concluded that there was not very much. It was too much to expect the President to "persuade the world to return to international laissez-faire, where price was the only factor determining the flow of international trade." The competing national industrialisms had made the issue of low-cost production of basic importance to the customer, and every nation was now in the tariff protection field comprehensively. The only hope seen was the possibility of Roosevelt's preparation "to recommend generous, uncompensated reductions in our own tariff"; otherwise the "prospects of accomplishment" were "microscopic." And in view of what was evident, the editorial declared, "we are going to see at London the familiar, wearisome spectacle of the statesmen of the world, clad in pith helmets and put-tees, carrying elephant guns and surrounded by sweating, grinning experts, industriously engaged in hunting mosquitoes." The Euro-pean politicians showed no will to reduce tariffs anywhere, whatever the economists were saying about reduced barriers to international trade as the way out of the depression. And now with the beginning of the Hitler regime in Germany, the journal commented that it was hard to imagine the abandonment there of the "economic nation-alism which is the heart of his program." [7]

Proof of overseas opposition to tariff reduction was the unhappy comment on the denunciation of Cordell Hull's opening address at the Conference by the French press. The *Nation* was convinced at this stage that Roosevelt had undermined Hull because of opposition to the latter's low tariff ideas, and the changes made in his speech left him saying precisely nothing. Since there was to be no discussion of tariffs, war debts and currency stabilization, there was nothing left to talk about, and the journal recommended that the American repre-sentatives might just as well come home. The confusion among the prospective American delegates before the Conference met had simi-larly displeased the liberal press. The *Nation* was most unhappy about Raymond Moley's radio talk of May 20 advising the public not to expect too much from London, and saw a serious conflict here between Hull and Moley. A recommendation was made that one or the other viewpoint be silenced before going to London, as "our representatives cannot work for internationalism and talk national-ism at the same time." [8] A full-page *New Republic* editorial in the June 14 issue on the eve of the Conference was very morose, and saw little likelihood of anything substantial emerging from this preten-tious meeting. As to new rumors that Germany was to be offered a new international loan, presumably to keep up the reparations-debts farce a while longer, it was frankly expected that Hjalmar Schacht would refuse, on the grounds that he foresaw (and probably cor-rectly, admitted the editorial) that "the granting of such a loan would be used by the Powers to wring concessions from Germany on disarmament, the Polish Corridor, Danzig and a host of other questions." [9]

Nation statements throughout June continued in this black and pessimistic vein. Roosevelt was accused of having as little courage as Hoover in failing to come to terms over the war debts, even more uncollectible now than before, while Hull, "the least nationalistic among the leading members of the American delegation," did not have the boldness to come out for a tariff reduction across the board of larger than ten per cent.[10] As for currency stabilization, the only hope was seen in a return to the gold standard, but with reduced backing as compared to the pre-depression period. On June 28, the first paragraph in the issue was headed by this sentence: "The revelation of President Roosevelt's attitude on currency stabilization must come as a crushing blow to all who had looked to the London conference to put the world on the road to economic recovery." The President's refusal was seen in the report by Acting Secretary of the Treasury Dean Acheson, who had said, "We do not wish to say that any currency should be pegged at the present level on any certain date. We just have not arrived at a place where we can pick out a particular point where stabilization should take place." The *Nation* asked ironically when the President was going to decide when we had arrived at a congenial point, and how were the people to know when we had gotten there.[11]

In the *New Republic* the corrosive comments of the spokesmen in opposition to the restoration of the old internationalism were being given vent to in parenthetical comments in deprecation of the entire concept. In a commentary on a long article by the British economist J. A. Hobson on the prospects of the Conference, it declared, "A nation whose economy is run in the interest of private profit makers cannot be a cooperative part of a world economy. The London Conference is barking up the wrong tree."[12] And at the end of June, a first-page editorial comment insisted, "It has been clear for months that Mr. Roosevelt and his advisers put domestic recovery ahead of everything else." [13] Even Villard, who probably had been the most optimistic of all the liberal observers, and who was in London himself while the deliberations were in progress, began to conclude that Roosevelt and those close to him did not intend to take the sessions too seriously, and in the words of Moley, intended to "build the basis of its [the United States'] prosperity at home." He reported the evidence clear that there was no real intention of breaking down the barriers, as each nation was looking out for itself.[14] And at the end of the month, a major *Nation* editorial on the meeting stated flatly, "If, as now seems extremely probable, the World Economic Conference should end in almost complete failure, the United States will enjoy the dubious distinction of having done more to bring about its collapse than any other nation." [15]

Criticism of the Conference had largely been on the basis of what were considered incorrect policies, poorly constructed and presented in a faulty manner. But liberals were beginning to see that there had been no real will to achieve the goals announced. A *New Republic* effort at pinpointing the trouble concentrated on intentions instead of particular measures: [16]

No one measure is, in itself, either national or international. Internationalism is not a group of specific policies, but a willingness of nations to cooperate on a common program—whatever that program may be. True internationalism must therefore be based on a conviction of the nations that the program agreed upon will serve their several interests. Any other kind of internationalism, like any other kind of cooperation among individuals, is insubstantial vapor.

The degree to which the nations at London failed to qualify according to this measuring rod was left for the reader to figure.

The liberals interpreted the July 3 speech of the President as the *coup de grâce* to the Conference, and a torrent of abuse promptly issued from the *Nation* in particular.[17] On July 19, the *Nation* devoted a full page to an editorial, "Mr. Roosevelt Repudiates Himself," [18] and reached considerable peaks of eloquence in denouncing his action. The Conference was now considered "killed," and the President the "assassin." Regardless of the apologists and rationalizers who now were excusing his action, "the blunt truth," said this unsigned attack, was "that from the beginning his record in connection with the World Economic Conference has been indefensible." It was somewhat difficult to put the matter any plainer than that. He had sent over to London a delegation most of whose members were "third rate," and "with no clear instructions and no positive program of any kind." These men had made no effort to conceal their differences, and the President had repudiated their statements anyway. On top of that had come the Presidential statement of July 3, a "naïve document, badly written," with "amateurish and muddled" economic thinking its basis. To the *Nation* it sounded as if Mr. Roosevelt "had been browsing through some gay magazine article called 'If I Were World Dictator.' " It was difficult to even guess what was in the President's mind from its contents:

. . . in tone it was not only belligerent towards the conference but frankly contemptuous of those participating in it. Grave as these faults were, there was one aspect of the statement that was even more disturbing. This was the indication it gave of the emotional and intellectual instability of the President.

The President had repudiated all his delegated representatives, and now was capping this performance by "repudiating himself and all his solemn and public pre-Conference agreements." The editorial gave the air of being outrageously betrayed, and would accept no excuses for torpedoing the Conference, even FDR's statement that the changed domestic situation was responsible for the repudiation of the money and tariff policy intentions announced in May. And if this were true, the question was asked why had the President not apologized to the Conference for changing his mind, instead of issuing a condemnation to it for trying to put these policies into effect. The

Washington opinion that "international cooperation conflicts with our 'domestic' recovery program" was absolutely false, the editorial countered; "The exact opposite is the truth: unless we promptly participate in policies of international cooperation our so-called 'domestic' program must fail."

Villard's signed editorial from London, "The Roosevelt Revolution," had this to say: "His recent treatment of the World Economic Conference seems to me to have been disgraceful," and "to have discredited utterly our delegation and our country abroad." The day before the Conference was to recess, the *Nation* spoke of it becoming "more and more a pathetic spectacle," with the American delegation, in particular, "bent upon making itself seem increasingly silly." [19] And Villard capped the whole interlude with a signed page of excoriation titled "The Damage to America in London." [20] The editors of *Common Sense* were even more apprehensive than Villard; they predicted a war on the heels of the failure of the Conference.

The rumble of the critical thunder in the liberal press continued all summer. The *New Republic,* in a statement headed "London Post-Mortem," did not express the vehemence of its associate publication. Roosevelt's opposing a currency stabilization proposal was just one of a number of possible "reefs" upon which the Conference could have "foundered," and the unhappy aspect of it all was that our diplomacy allowed the nation's "opponents" to select "the precise issue which caused the failure." The French were given the credit for this, by precipitating a major opinion clash "between those who wanted recovery with rising prices and those who wanted it with existing prices, or at least wanted to maintain existing prices, whether or not recovery occurred." French vulnerability to British and German products in a market featured by rising costs had been pointed out at the start of the Conference. The United States wanted the first of these two policies, the French of course the latter, and "both were equally nationalistic." The notion that the French were the "champions of internationalism" could only be subscribed to by "soft-minded innocents" and the choice before the United States here was "between giving up her internal policy of recovery and giving up agreement with France." Where did the *New Republic* stand? [21]

Naturally, in view of its diagnosis of the depression disease, the *New Republic* supported the administration in choosing the first course. This does not mean that we do not want international cooperation. It means merely that we do not want it on a deflationary program.

To this degree one camp of liberals had decided to go along with the economic nationalism of the day despite its efforts at camouflage. The London Conference did precipitate a mighty discussion on the future economic course of the world now that return to the pre-1914 formula appeared finished for good. No clear route appeared for any-one for some time until a great deal of thought could be applied to the significance of the London meeting and its demise. With the New Deal applying most of its emphasis on the domestic scene and interest in international solution of problems sagging, the tendency to follow the impulses of the moment had its impact on the planetary-minded liberals as much as upon the self-centered nationalists held in such disfavor. But there still remained a hard, stubborn residue of attach-ment to their basic outlook.

The matter of leadership was not utterly immaterial in this situ-ation. The *Nation* had now acquired a low regard for Roosevelt, Moley, and a variety of others as directors of our affairs abroad, but the *New Republic* considered Hull just as weak. In its late August discussion, "The State Department and the Old Deal," it spoke of Hull as being dominated by the Adam Smith school of economics, "and having a slow-moving mind, Mr. Hull has little comprehension of the intricate nature of our present economic system, nor any detailed knowledge of international politics." Men like these seemed to know where they were going, but reservations of doubt about them were not hidden as the liberals tried to fathom the course ahead. It might be an appealing thing momentarily to think that foreign nations had ceased to exist and that all that mattered was the bringing back to life of material prosperity in the United States. In a major sense, the poverty and unemployment at home seemed a big enough job to conquer, let alone the Ajax-like chore which faced those anxious to solve this distress all over the globe. But the disquieting reality of the rest of the world kept being edged ahead in the liberal papers, and commented about in a way that compared with the chronic ache of a diseased tooth. "To those wrestling with the vast problem of unemployment, foreign problems may for the moment seem unimportant," the *New Republic* editors concluded, but clung to the view that "Actually the solution of our pressing domestic ques-tions may ultimately depend upon the careful readjustment of our relations with other countries." [22] Curiously enough, despite all the invective heaped on Roosevelt in the hectic criticism, no liberal spokesmen ever described his action as "isolationism."

Common Sense in August, 1933 published an even blacker picture than the weeklies in the form of eyewitness Mary Heaton Vorse's "The Gods Play Tiddlywinks," in which she dwelled on the fact that the gathering had been "nothing but sunshine for Russia," what with Litvinov stacking up non-aggression pacts and gaining a substantial loan to Amtorg from America, which she interpreted without a moment's hesitation as "no doubt the forerunner of the long-delayed Russian recognition." In her estimate the Conference proved that [23]

The countries of this civilization are not geared for cooperation. They are geared to cut each other's throats. When not actually at war, they war with economic measures, and so in the end they are doomed to murder one another. But in one way, this conference was eminently successful. In miniature it showed vividly why our economy doesn't work, for the conference was a small model of the world. Here, small enough to grasp, were all the different trends and contradictions and dissonances which ultimately make war. If one believed that the statesmen of this dying social order could come to an agreement, they had not watched the slow, agonizing course of the conference.

Mrs. Vorse spoke in the measured and confident deterministic accents of the British Marxist gravedigger of Western capitalism, Christopher Caudwell.

The turning of the Administration's back on foreign affairs on a highly-publicized level after the London Conference fiasco and the virtually complete preoccupation with home-front problems also explains in part the heavy attack on this domestic program from liberal sniping posts, as examined in an earlier chapter. But the end of the London attempt to rebuild a world laissez-faire helped to sharpen the remarks on the budding Hitler regime in Germany, and also to build a bonfire under the entire basic argument about the world order in the future, as well.

REACTION AND IDEOLOGICAL READJUSTMENT
TO THE FAILURE OF THE CONFERENCE

Why the World Economic Conference failed, and what was likely to prevail in the international politico-economic community, was interpreted variously. By the end of the conference, virtually all the voices in the liberal press were critical, but hardly agreeing as to what was expectable or desirable in the future. Barely a week before the London meeting adjourned, the *Nation* had printed a special dispatch from London by Harold J. Laski, ominously titled "Why Conferences Fail." This was one of the messages from the liberal camp which looked forward to the Socialist International, and construed what was taking place in that light. Laski told the liberal audience that "a unified and interdependent world" was impossible because that world was made up of "capitalist states," and that the "inherent logic" of their world was "inequality"; therefore it was futile to expect any significant "international planning" to come from the various interactions of such nations. Diagnosed Laski, "None is able to confront the necessary implications of economic internationalism because each confronts internal forces which are too zealous for their own chance of individual well-being to make sacrifices for the common good." Thus, the Conference was in reality a "supreme illustration of the contradiction between world needs and an institutional system" which prevented those needs from realization.[24]

The Laski approach had its enthusiastic supporters, even though it seemed to have little possibility of consummation in view of the conditions then prevailing. For this group there remained only the idealized Soviet Union as a hope, achieved only as a result of determined efforts to close eyes and ears to Russian evolution along the lines of one of these already despised selfish and egocentric national states. At this stage, in mid-1933, according to liberal opinion, the existence of the Soviet as an inspiration could hardly be over-estimated. Even when not mentioned, it was the implied model and example set up for the world to emulate, in the thinking of this camp.

The *New Republic*'s major immediate contribution to realism on the subject was one of the longest articles that they had published in years, "The End of Internationalism" [25] by Clark Foreman, a few days after the Conference had adjourned. The noise being made as the Conference collapsed, said Foreman, was caused "by the ugly birth-wails of the new world system," the various forms of national self-development as they appeared in one shape or other in Italy, Germany, Turkey, and, he instructed the Communist enthusiasts, especially Russia, if they wished to look beyond the theories they preferred to cling to instead of the economic facts of the day.

Foreman was convinced the conflict between the older economic internationalism, with its disregard for national boundaries and its facilitations of movement of money, property, business and trade across frontiers and the new tendencies represented a situation which could not be reconciled in favor of the former. The English had been the people to prosper and profit from this system the most in the past, and it was not surprising that they had taken the initiative at London to try to revive it. It was for that reason that the English at London had tried to get the others to eliminate or abate the hindrances to the "free exchange of commodities and services on the world market," products of the period especially since 1914; ferocious tariffs, war debts, interferences with free currency dealings, and the absence of a world-wide respected monetary standard.

After discussing briefly how these devices had made Britain the great industrial and financial power of the world down to the outbreak of the war, Foreman discussed the rise of the forces which challenged her leadership, and now had created "changes in the organization and control of production, exchange and distribution" which made return to the pre-war capitalist conditions impossible. The method being introduced to control the vastly increased productive capacity of industry now was the "national planned economy," instead of the theoretically self-regulating mechanisms of the international "liberal" capitalist order. One of the main features of the new system was the imposition of state control over such basic functions as banking, transport and communication, plus a steady movement into the field of all import and export business, a necessity if any internal planning was to be a success. He cited the Soviet Union's state corporations monopolizing foreign trade as one example of this, but felt that state control of foreign trade to protect home industries had as a logical consequence the state control of the industries themselves. Closely-supervised wage and price levels represented new changes in the distributive system, although the "rigid" rationing in the Soviet was largely a response to their low production and not a characteristic likely to be copied by the nations beginning their own experiments in nationally planned economies.

Foreman cited the first World War as being responsible for unleashing a large part of these pressures, what with the death, destruction and impoverishment of so many millions, the withdrawal of Russia's enormous land area and potentialities from possible capitalist expansion, the great number of new political and economic rivalries created by the peace treaty map-makers, with their multitude of "tariffs, embargoes, prohibitions and subsidies" helping to contribute strong encouragement to the deepening of nationalist sentiments. The "suppression of individual vested interests in favor of national development" was a consequence of all these, plus the contributions in the form of the crisis produced by the conflicts between the rival capitalist producers themselves in the period down to the outbreak of the war.

The "strong current" in the direction of achieving self-sufficiency in these new national-centered economies was also a consequence of the war, which had demonstrated how weak they were individually when the mechanisms of the international order were suspended. Russia was the prime example of this, insisted Foreman, and nothing better explained the great haste for industrialization, to which "the Soviet government sacrificed the principles of international socialism."

Foreman insisted that Russia represented the complete opposite of the system by which Britain "won her world position," and that there were noticeable elements of the Soviet system in the National Socialist order in Germany, regardless of their pretended ideological opposition. He also thought that Germany was faring better in world opinion because it did not pretend that its program was intended for export to the rest of the world, as did the Russians.

The clash between American and British ambitions at London was caused by the drift of the United States under the New Deal leader-

ship in the same direction away from the internationalist liberal capitalist order and the initiating of measures like those described elsewhere but tailored to American circumstances. Roosevelt's frown on
currency stabilization was symbolic of the new developments here,
which he believed clearly signified "the complete breakdown of the old
international system based upon the capitalism of private ownership
and control."

For England Foreman saw only "a slow and painful decline to a
level at which the population of the country bears a much closer relation than at present to its capacity to maintain itself out of its own
resources." But he thought this decline would be "modified and
checked" to the degree that she was able to maintain a grip on the
dominions and colonies of the Empire. For the nations not strong
enough to maintain themselves in a world of "planned and self-
sufficient states," there remained gathering in regional confedera-
tions, "mutual strengthening by combination," if they wished to
avoid being drawn into the systems of their strong neighbors.

But there was no doubt that the older pre-1914 economic order
was through: "The Conference, failing to accomplish the desired end
of setting the clock back to the period of Victorian bliss when free
trade and individualism were accepted as fundamental verities, represented the swan song of internationalism." This "enfeebled" arrangement, "speaking through its chief institution, the League of
Nations," was proving that it could not halt Japan in its acquisition
of additional territory, and no longer could be expected to have much
impact. Nor was there any substance or content to the long-propa-
gandized apocalyptic showdown between this world capitalist arrangement and Marxian world socialism: "Today the conflict is no
longer between international socialism and international capitalism,
but between national socialism and decay."

Foreman did not say at any time that he liked or preferred the
system he was describing. As to Fascism, he later expressed revulsion
for it, in a comment on a controversy over Vilfredo Pareto which
raged for a time in the *New Republic*. But he obviously did not think
that Fascism and all the hot emotional language expended upon it by
the Communists had anything to do with explaining the growth of
the new form of internally-oriented national economies in process of
fabrication all over the globe. His recommendation to the Communists that they examine the Soviet system for evidences of national
socialism obviously was unappreciated. And it did nothing to daunt
the persistence of a Communist theory based on the disintegration
of international capitalist economic discipline.

To expect Communists or Soviet apologists to admit the Soviet
Union had abandoned the dream of world socialism for the purpose
of making Russia a strong state was utterly unthinkable, and Com-

munist explanations as to the way international capitalism was giving way dwelt upon a different interpretation. The nationally-centered economies emerging everywhere were simply the last stages of a corrupt capitalism, and upon their collapse from internal stress and strain, would be swept away by domestic revolutionary socialist action and replaced by replicas of the institution that had now entrenched itself in Russia. The most effective voice in describing the future in Communist verbiage for the liberals was John Strachey, the English aristocrat-turned-intellectual proletarian, in his *The Coming Struggle For Power*. Strachey's book preceded the Conference, and received cordial reviews in March by Matthew Josephson in the *New Republic* [26] and by Lawrence Dennis in the *Nation*.[27] Josephson considered Strachey's examination accurate, and felt that his interpretation of the new national systems as "capitalism . . . in its last and most monstrous form" was correct. And "as for the emergence of a World State such as the liberal capitalists dream of, Mr. Strachey is scarcely to be blamed if he concluded . . . that the tide is running the other way," Josephson pronounced. Dennis admired the book as a piece of literature, commenting that "a well-written book by a Communist" was "a literary event." He considered Strachey's description of the Communist case for the collapse of capitalism "impressive," but he did not think him correct in assuming that Communism would replace it. Dennis considered state capitalism along other lines than the Soviet variety just as likely to be the inheritor. He also thought Strachey failed to find a place in his new proletarian classless order for people like Strachey himself who were not by any stretch of the imagination "workers," and that he had also not proved that "in the classless society of the Communist millennium, after the dictatorship of the proletariat is no longer necessary for the liquidation of the bourgeoisie, there will not remain the classes of the governing and the governed." This was a cruel observation, in view of persistent Communist testimonials to the faith they had in a society with interchangeable leaders and a total absence of a vested interest in leading. But it emphasized the double standard of the Communists, for which the liberals showed a strong leaning, judging one side of the question by the acts of the disliked, and their own by its verbal testimonials.

Strachey's post-Conference contribution was a shorter book, *The Menace of Fascism*, a revelatory title, in many respects, keeping in mind the Communist world outlook. The struggle going on in the Communist mind as to whether Fascism was really as weak and rotten as they continually told each other, or whether it represented a stiff challenge to the spread of Communism, was involved here, as well as the unwillingness to compare the Soviet with the Fascist states in terms of similarities instead of projecting them as opposites by definition. That this book received a welcome reception in the lib-

eral press was to be expected. Cowley reviewed it in two full pages of
small type in the November 1, 1933 issue of the *New Republic* [28] and
found nothing whatever to criticize or modify. It also indicated which
of the routes the world was likely now to take was preferred by some
prominent liberal spokesmen, as well as showing yet once more the
intellectual debt of depression liberalism to Communism. Strachey
had written one of the classics for future debates, and his definitions
and theories were to be detected in liberal commentaries on Fascism
thereafter. The message was not noticeably changed from the previous
book. The spread of Fascism to other countries, "a movement owned
and controlled by the very richest and biggest capitalists, who use the
lower middle class and the peasants as their indispensable instruments
for the destruction of the working class," was to be followed by wars
among the states coming forth from such a movement. Each of these
would be accompanied by extensive arming of the masses, and would
result in working class revolutions at their conclusion; and, as to their
success, Strachey said one could not doubt that for even a moment.
Strachey assured the readers that the internal mechanisms of the
national socialist states was a sham and that no possible planning
could come forth in a system where private ownership was preserved.
Cowley referred to the book as "an advanced treatise on Fascism
which reads as simply as a primer." For the wing of the liberals which
had already chosen its champion, it was a giant intellectual bulwark.

Strachey digressed for a while from the purely theoretical early in
1934, delivering a few sharp critiques of current American practices
which seemed to illustrate part of his message. In his *Nation* article,
"The Two Wings of the Blue Eagle," he insisted that the Roosevelt
Administration was conscious that its economic program was "incompatible with any form of international cooperation . . . there can
be no doubt that the exigencies of the economic situation has driven
Mr. Roosevelt and his ministers along a course which is leading them
into even more violent conflict with the rest of the world." As an example, Strachey insisted FDR "had not the slightest hesitation in
destroying all possibility of world economic cooperation in order to
push on the monetary part of the New Deal": [29]

The particular form of inflation which Mr. Roosevelt and his advisers
have adopted is of the most imperialist and aggressive type imaginable.
The forced depreciation of the dollar in terms of foreign currencies *before*
there has been any corresponding rise in the American price level is
undeniably equivalent to a pro-rata increase in the American tariff and
a pro-rata bounty on all American exports.

Strachey insisted that the New Deal in its foreign aspect was a "steadily pursued" and "virulently aggressive economic policy." Marxist

liberals now had two counts of "Fascism" against the Roosevelt regime, its domestic labor policy and its foreign economic program, as a consequence of its domestic monetary directives.

But all of this furious assault on Fascism had dangerous implications for these liberals, beyond their commitment to a particular doctrine which itself was an unliberal action. The next stage of this struggle, in which personalities were to be substituted for policies as the targets, would find the liberals in no position to resist the appeals for their partisanship. As soon as the main opposition to a program was based on hatred of the men who were leading it, the road to war was shortened and widened. By the time the complexities of Fascism had been reduced to "Hitler" it was possible to tap the hatred potential of the liberals generously, and wreck completely the insulation against being mobilized emotionally in another war which had been so slowly and painfully put together after 1919.

The combination of the Hitler regime's extended successes in fastening itself upon Germany and the London Conference break-up brought upon the liberals a sharply steepened tension on the ideological front in several particulars. The final contestants in the world arena now appeared to be even more definitely the theoretical world socialism issuing from the fount at Moscow and these disturbing national variants. Communist agitation over the latter had grown immensely especially after the German Communist organization fell apart in its tracks on the eve of Hitler's 1933 electoral victory. This greatly sharpened attack on the anti-Communist national totalitarianisms communicated itself in rapid order to the American liberal journals. Part of the intellectual war being waged upon it was a search for the ideological origins of these new political movements, and a parallel assault upon their intellectual respectability. No false gods were to be allowed to remain upright in the presence of the Marxian verities.

The first target of substance was the Italian Vilfredo Pareto. He was subjected, in the *New Republic* in July, 1933, to a scathing assault by the self-professed Marxist, George E. Novack, titled "Vilfredo Pareto, the Marx of the Middle Classes." [30] It touched off a controversy of considerable bitterness, which was heightened in September when Cowley reviewed very disparagingly in the same journal a newly published book dealing with Pareto's sociological theories. Cowley's review was titled "Handbook for Demagogues." [31] It started a vogue of linking Pareto with both the Mussolini and Hitler movements which went on for two decades, and began to be deflated in the sobered 1950's.

The major defender of Pareto from the charges of the Marxian-tinted liberals was Bernard De Voto, in a substantial article in the *Saturday Review of Literature*. De Voto maintained he was accused of heading up a Fascist penetration of America by so doing, and he and Novack traded long memoranda in the columns of the *New Republic* in October, bringing each other up on their relative shortcomings. Novack claimed De Voto did not show the slightest understanding of what Fascism was, and that the interest now being shown in Pareto in America was an index as to how imminent Fascism was in coming into existence here in "our sick society," and how amazingly it had grown in the past five years. De Voto stuck by his judgment that Pareto was a very significant thinker and a great contributor to producing "an objective description of society," and chided Novack for his obstinacy in reading Pareto through a Marxian filter: [32]

I believe that it is unwise, in discussing it [Pareto's sociology], to lay oneself open to the suspicion of arguing by accord or sentiments. Yet Mr. Novack exposes himself to that suspicion. He seems to dislike some of Pareto's conclusions (possibly because they are unfavorable to Marx?) and so he finds them unmistakably related to fascism—because he dislikes fascism and may assume that his readers do. I cannot see that the evidence bears him out. . . .

Cowley had nothing but contempt for the Paretian principles, and was especially repelled by his notions of a permanent elite leadership made vigorous and sustaining by its constantly being open to persons of quality rising from humble origins. Cowley was sure this type of government would fall before its "masses," by being unable to keep them quiet. The proletarian revolt would put a quick end to these unspeakable forms of control; "in Italy the masses are beginning to stir and in Germany they will soon be marching," Cowley confidently predicted. That the Italian and German "masses" would require a gigantic Anglo-Russo-American army to assure them success could not possibly have been anticipated in this atmosphere of expectant apocalyptic Marxian liberation. A short time later the big guns were trained on Oswald Spengler, although here again liberalism took its cue from the Communists, who had attacked him as a Hitlerian philosopher some time before Hitler came to power.[33]

Suspicion of the Fascist inclinations of some of America's more articulate intellectuals was not new in the liberal press before and during the summer of 1933; the tribulations of Archibald MacLeish have been seen in another context. There were other disquieting flutters beside those created by MacLeish and De Voto. The appearance of the journal *The American Review* in the spring, "which calls for radical reform—but inclines to the Fascist variety," according to its own prospectus, provided a new source of perturbation. A goodly sample of the new thinking could be found here, sometimes mistakenly referred to as "conservatism" by its contributors, in the opinion of the liberals. One of these allegedly deluded writers was Herbert Agar, whose 1934 Pulitzer Prize-winning book, *The People's Choice,* in addition to his *American Review* contributions, was received rather tartly. The *Nation* unleashed its fury on the Committee for having awarded this volume such high commendation. In its May 23, 1934, editorial, "Who Gives the Pulitzer Prizes?", it considered this act to be a bad blunder. It was nothing more than a reactionary book calling for rule by an oligarchy, and the editors suggested that if they could do no better job than this in selecting meritorious books, then it might be better if the awarding of the Pulitzer Prizes be abandoned.[34] "A nostalgia for the old South with its 'Greek democracy' and fixed social order also haunts Mr. Agar," the historian Edward C. Kirkland reported in his *New Republic* review; "Democracy irks him"; "he hankers for a return to the days when the educated and the privileged led the nation." Agar's message in this book, said Kirkland, was that "something must be done to meet the evils of democracy and unfettered capitalism," and he seemed to be quite certain what the "something" was. Not a Communist dictatorship: that would result in "the end of the American effort"; [35]

Mr. Agar obviously inclines to a dictatorship by conservatives, but when he scans the American horizon for acceptable ones, he seems to find only plutocrats. So he flees backward for over a century to a time "when America was young and had a soul" and knew that she must be "disciplined." It is not necessary to be a feverish left-winger to detect in such a prescription a hint of fascist rhetoric divorced from economic realities.

Kirkland was actually describing the sustained impact of the famous Twelve Southerners' *I'll Take My Stand* of 1930 upon Agar, without directly referring to this work. But there was little doubt that a wave of disquiet was washing across the liberal landscape, and the resuscitation of the old "liberal" internationalism appeared to be not only virtually impossible, but undesirable as well, if prominent judgments by all brands of liberal voices meant anything.

John Maynard Keynes rationalized another liberal case against the restoration in the *Yale Review,* which simply used milder language in coming to a viewpoint not very far from any of the other observers of the wasting away of the world economic order of the turn of the century. Nor was Keynes's study and changed attitude entirely surprising. Henry Hazlitt, reviewing Keynes's *The Means to Prosperity* in the *Nation* while the London Conference was in session, noted that Keynes was a "frank nationalist and isolationist" who lauded the employment of currency depreciation and tariffs by Great Britain ("they have served us well").[36] Late in August, the *Nation* felt sufficiently disquieted by all these attacks to post a two-page editorial, "Is

Internationalism Doomed?"[37] comparing the dissections of Strachey, Foreman and Keynes. Its description of the Foreman interpretation as "the fascist viewpoint" must have made the *New Republic* editors cringe. They had printed it without comment and without warning any reader that they were beginning the publication of subversion. But the editorial staffs of both were not above moments of similar weakness when the suggestions of the day caught their fancy as well. While the London meeting was in session and futilely handling the impasse in world trade, a *Nation* editorial had recommended the creation of a vaguely outlined "International Barter Corporation," which had the qualities of a regional grouping of government state trading monopolies.[38] In the mid-autumn, the *New Republic,* expecting an Anglo-Franco-American currency war, now that stabilization hopes had evaporated, suggested "a great non-gold currency bloc" with the British, in an editorial with a serious anti-French flavor.[39] It fitted well the journal's overall hostile attitude toward the French.

By the end of October, 1934 the *Nation* appeared to have adjusted rather well to a world moving off in other directions, and seemed to be relieved that the London Economic Conference had failed; it had been, after all, "essentially an attempt to restore an international laissez-faire economic structure such as existed prior to the World War," and now it had nothing but hostility for any international flexibility; [40]

The New Deal in the United States, the new forms of economic organization in Germany and Italy, and the planned economy of the Soviet Union are merely the latest and most extreme manifestations of a tendency which has been apparent for the greater part of a century.

A year of discussion by the searching critics since the end of the Conference seemed to have educated the editors as well as the readers.

The storm which blew up after London had other repercussions, but the immediate effect of driving a wedge between the old and the new liberalism was undeniable. The attitude of disrespect for the liberal formula that failed to respond to the ministrations of the World Economic Conference lifesavers was bluntly exemplified in the *Nation's* first issue in September, when it printed Lawrence Dennis' unusually critical review of Sir Norman Angell's *From Chaos to Control* under the title "A Dated Liberal." Dennis characterized Angell as about the most persistent voice over the years pleading the cause of the now collapsed order. It was Sir Norman's generation on trial in Dennis' review, and he heaped a chill ridicule upon all who subscribed to the principles now in disrepute. The liberals referred to throughout were held responsible for a number of shortcomings, "a lack of philosophical profundity," and the failure "to think things through" was a summary charge against all "the outstanding exponents of British and American liberalism." Dennis rejected Angell's whole basic argument as now "irrelevant," and the book "a piece of immature discussion by a dated liberal." [41] Probably nothing could have been said which more plainly marked the degree to which the earlier internationalism had been discredited among the entire spectrum of depression critics and re-thinkers which used the liberal press as the center of dispersal of their ideas. Liberalism, like pacifism, was in transition. The descriptive terminology remained, but the content was markedly altered. The London Conference was just another milepost in the departure of liberalism from known to unknown points.

NOTES

1 *New Republic*, June 15, 1932, p. 109.
2 *Nation*, June 29, 1932, p. 709.
3 *New Republic*, May 3, 1933, p. 334.
4 Lead editorial, *Nation*, May 3, 1933, p. 485; Villard's column, p. 491.
5 *New Republic*, May 10, 1933, p. 348.
6 *New Republic*, May 10, 1933, p. 351.
7 *New Republic*, May 17, 1933, p. 1.
8 *Nation*, June 7, 1933, p. 625.
9 *New Republic*, June 14, 1933, p. 114.
10 Editorial "Black Fog In London," *Nation*, June 21, 1933, p. 686.
11 *Nation*, June 28, 1933, p. 709.
12 Editorial "London: Barking Up the Wrong Tree," *New Republic*, June 21, 1933, pp. 139–140, commenting on Hobson's "Forethoughts About the Conference," pp. 143–144.
13 *New Republic*, June 28, 1933, p. 163.
14 *Nation*, July 5, 1933, pp. 12–14.
15 Editorial "To Save the Conference," *Nation*, July 5, 1933, p. 3.
16 Editorial "What Kind Of Conference?," *New Republic*, July 5, 1933, pp. 193–194.
17 *Nation*, July 12, 1933, p. 29.
18 P. 60. Citations throughout succeeding two paragraphs from this source.
19 *Nation*, July 26, 1933, p. 85.
20 *Nation*, August 2, 1933, p. 119.
21 *New Republic*, July 26, 1933, pp. 276–277, for this and preceding citations in paragraph.
22 *New Republic*, August 23, 1933, p. 35.
23 *Common Sense*, August, 1933, pp. 7–9.
24 *Nation*, July 19, 1933, pp. 65–66. See also Laski, "President Roosevelt and Foreign Opinion," *Yale Review*, June, 1933, pp. 707–713.
25 *New Republic*, August 9, 1933, pp. 332–335, for citations in subsequent nine paragraphs.
26 Josephson, "Crisis: The Communist View," *New Republic*, March 1, 1933, p. 78.
27 Dennis, "A Communistic Strachey," *Nation*, March 8, 1933, pp. 264–265. This review undoubtedly had much to do with the Communist press singling out Dennis as their most formidable ideological opponent.
28 Cowley, "A Primer Of Fascism," *New Republic*, November 1, 1933, pp. 339–340. See also comment by Foreman on page 357.
29 *Nation*, January 10, 1934, p. 43.
30 *New Republic*, July 12, 1933, pp. 258–261. The same dubious line was taken by

R. V. Worthington in the Fall, 1933, issue of *Economic Forum*, in his article "Pareto: The Karl Marx of Fascism."

31   *New Republic*, September 12, 1934, pp. 134–135.

32   *New Republic*, October 11, 1933, pp. 244–245.

33   See especially G. Vasilkovsky, "Oswald Spengler's 'Philosophy of Life,'" *The Communist*, April, 1932, pp. 371–377, a feverish official attack on Spengler's *Man and Technics* and the identification of Spengler as a Hitlerian philosopher.

34   *Nation*, May 23, 1934, p. 580.

35   Kirkland, "Democracy Slips Downward," *Nation*, September 13, 1933, p. 306.

36   *Nation*, July 5, 1933, pp. 21–22.

37   *Nation*, August 23, 1933, pp. 201–202.

38   *Nation*, July 5, 1933, p. 5.

39   *New Republic*, November 15, 1933, p. 7.

40   *Nation*, October 31, 1934, pp. 494–495.

41   *Nation*, September 6, 1933, p. 278.

10

PEACE AND NAVAL REARMAMENT: THE LIBERALS APPRAISE F.D.R., 1933–1935

THE conflict between the liberal pacifist and the liberal legalist minds as to the most desirable attitude to adopt toward the boiling world affairs of the early depression 1930's has already been examined from a number of vantage points. Still another insight is available from an examination of reactions to the major stands and actions of the Roosevelt Administration concerning foreign affairs in its first years. A set of policy circumstances had been inherited from the previous government, and a number of liberal views as to the efforts of Mr. Hoover had also been examined. Consequently, they had something to measure the new government by, both in respect to improvements upon, and instances of falling short of, its predecessor.

In the summer of 1931, the *New Republic* published "President Hoover's Foreign Policy" by John B. Whitton, an associate professor of international law at Princeton.[1] The academic liberal mind, with its firm Anglophile and Francophile commitments, was adequately revealed here on the pros and cons concerning Mr. Hoover's handling of the United States' foreign relations of then recent vintage. Great praise was accorded Hoover for beginning the policy of non-intervention in Latin American affairs, while agreement to the naval building suspension and tonnage limitations of the London Naval Treaty was referred to by Professor Whitton as "substantial gains." But it was in the areas of broader commitments that faults were found, the field of policy which went back to the emotions of the war-time alliance of 1917–1918 and which presumably was involved in the treaties and the League of Nations. The legalist liberals had never ceased lamentation over the failure of the nation to accede to these, and to join the Wilsonian collective security dream. This act alone lay at the base of all the charges of "isolation" which grew in incantation content as Europe began to slide toward another war. The key word in building this verbal wall against another war had always been the concept of aggression, vaguely understood and rarely if ever interpreted or defined. Perhaps, if probed deeply enough it would have led back to the propaganda stories of the War and the apparition of the "German Beast," easily the most formidable nightmare image of "aggression" still incubating in the academic liberal mind. Sir Gilbert Parker and Lord Northcliffe had testified on occasion to the ease with which the academic community had been taken into the British camp in the pre-1917 days, and as for a substantial portion, in the words of John Maynard Keynes in another context, they had never been "debamboozled."

Therefore, the issues that Professor Whitton brought up might be considered the main residual vexations felt in the liberal academic-legalist sector insofar as Hoover and foreign affairs were involved. The absence of action at London on collective security, sanctions and the "freedom of the seas" issue, so dear to the British, were cited as its main shortcomings. "Security" to Whitton meant the granting of concessions to the French and British—to the latter, the assurance that there would be no insistence on free navigation of the world's oceans in case the British were involved in another war, and to the former, support in the form of guaranteeing United States economic sanctions against whatever state might become its enemy. Said Whitton, "Our delegation . . . were not ready to meet the proposal . . . that in case of a collective war waged against an aggressor nation the United States should promise that after determining for itself who was the aggressor, it would not trade with the latter." The sheer arbitrariness of this approach, with its incitation to behaving in the flightiest manner imaginable as long as it was in the interests of a side toward which we were already committed in advance, is symptomatic of the persistence of the new thought on the subject of bringing into existence the reign of permanent peace. In it is the germ of the schemes proposed later by Norman H. Davis. The most desirable world was obviously one in which the British and French were supremely contented, and in which not the slightest jog in the status quo might be suffered lest the cry of "aggression" once more bring out the spears and armor plate. An eye-opening index to the new peace thought of the liberal legalists was Whitton's condemnation of Hoover's suggestions in his 1929 and 1930 Armistice Day addresses that food ships be exempt from attack in future wars. The basis for his disapproval was the alleged hostility of "public opinion generally in Europe" and especially the damage this concept did to the theory of the sanctions system. The conflict between such latent ferocity and the humanitarian over-view of Hoover hardly suggests additional comment, let alone the clash between legalist liberalism and the revisionism and pacifism of the editors.

With the outbreak of war in the Far East came the Stimson Doctrine, correctly associated by the great majority far more with Stimson than Hoover. Its approach to Japan was one of the major legacies handed on to the Roosevelt organization. A side issue of this major policy decision, partially related to the war between Bolivia and Paraguay, involved a proposal vesting the President with the power to suspend the shipment of munitions of all kinds to nations either at war or threatening to fight. The original understanding was that such products were to be made unavailable to both sides; it had no relation to the sanctions idea, a separate proposal which was part of the League of Nations' scheme aimed at pressuring Japanese compliance in Asia. The "arms embargo" notion was comprehensive, and presupposed no commitment of American preference between or among potential belligerents. This was still hanging in mid air, *i.e.* awaiting the inauguration of FDR. An unresolved disarmament conference, Soviet recognition, a projected world economic conference, action on a League Asia policy statement and a reopening of world naval strengths also remained in the heap of unsettled foreign matters in March, 1933. Liberal responses to the handling of the arms embargo, League and naval parity questions are the situations under immediate examination in view of the treatment of the other matters in prior contexts.

LIBERAL COMMENTS ON THE ROOSEVELTIANS
AS PEACEMAKERS

Insofar as foreign policy was concerned, the liberal editors and commentators during the first few months of the New Deal did not think the Roosevelt entourage had one. During the presidential campaign the Democrats had been oppressively silent on the issue of Hoover and foreign affairs; there had been no mention of the League of Nations, and the general impression gathered by the great majority had been that the New Deal physicians were going to devote all their attention to internal medicine, so to speak. The rejection of the Hoover contention that the depression was world wide, and solvable largely on international levels, helps to spread understanding of the New Deal world outlook which it was carrying into office along with its other baggage. Thus when the early Roosevelt foreign trails led down well worn and easily recognized paths, the inference was made that they were relying not only on the previous policies but the policy-makers as well. When Mr. Roosevelt, hardly in office, took what the *New Republic* described as the Administration's "first important step in foreign affairs" by issuing to the League of Nations the news that the United States would go along with the League's special committee examining the Far East situation but would reserve "independence of judgment and action," it was assumed that it was simply extending an inherited view. "The announcement of course occasions no surprise," remarked the editorial comment; "it was foreshadowed some time ago by Secretary Stimson, and it was an open secret that his statement at that time represented the views of Mr. Roosevelt and Mr. Hull." [2]

The heavy reliance upon Norman Davis for trouble-shooting chores as a kind of personal presidential envoy helped the liberal press to divine the meaning of a variety of Administration steps, especially in the area of European affairs. Like Stimson, Davis's foreign affairs actions in the Hoover government were still remembered. Davis's close sympathy with collective security notions of the Wilsonian days and his rarely-concealed gestures of support for the status quo as appreciated best by the French and British drew comment on the occasions upon which he broke into print with a speech or message. He eventually became a target for indignant liberal expostulations, and in the opinion of some was appraised as a serious obstacle to sustained American neutrality. But the liberal raking of the back room uncovered other evidence of influential holdover advice on international questions. In a June, 1933 column headed "Our Foreign Experts," the *New Republic* columnist "T.R.B." observed,[3]

. . . it may be worth mentioning that, while in his mouse-like way he keeps well under cover, the eminent Colonel E. M. House still retains the position he has had since Mr. Roosevelt's nomination, as his most trusted adviser in matters of foreign affairs. The President has a deep appreciation of the Colonel's wisdom, and, though the Colonel does not come to the White House in person, he talks on the telephone with Mr. Roosevelt with great frequency and is consulted by him before any move is made in the foreign field. The "corps of correspondents" still does not seem to know that Colonel House is one of the real inside group, but it is none the less true.

Mr. Roosevelt's inaugural month had not yet elapsed before the liberal editors began to see the outlines of the early New Deal attitude toward the increasingly unsteady world situation: the confrontation of the other powers with an olive branch in one hand and a naval gun in the other. "A desire for peace and preparations for war seem to go hand in hand in Washington," reported the *Nation* in discussing the new President's attempt to obtain from Congress the same kind of embargo power on the shipment of munitions to belligerents sought by Mr. Hoover. Furthermore, "The President also appears anxious to relieve the political tension in Europe," as Norman Davis's first pilgrimage on mollifying courier duty to the heads of European states, in the tradition of Wilson and House, was interpreted.[4] But these gestures seemed feeble when placed against the sudden interest in greatly expanding the navy, reflected in what was then a prodigious naval construction bill given to Congress for its blessing. This combination of peace moves and martial muscle-building kept the liberals in confusion for some time, but the pieces began to fall into place when a closer scrutiny of Geneva revealed a long stride taken in the direction of another war instead of any discernible disarmament. Speeches by Davis at Geneva and Roosevelt in Washington during May and June, 1933 induced liberal editors to re-check the score, and early enthusiasm over what seemed to be a repudiation of the "isolationist" caution of the preceding decade declined abruptly in temperature. The *Nation* persisted in hoping for peace out of war preparations somewhat longer than its opposite file, in the same way that it persisted in supporting the application of likely war-producing measures against Japan some time after the *New Republic* categorically rejected them as incendiary and dangerous.

A review of the ponderings over the Roosevelt-Davis messages is in order. The *Nation* went into a dizzying climb of enthusiasm which lasted three weeks, finally succumbing to the increasing volume of publicity given to the parallel inflation of the size of the American Navy, and the isolation of Germany, which the "disarmament" delegates at Geneva were quietly fabricating. The *Nation*'s disapproval of the former because of its incitatory effect upon Japan and a possible Pacific war, and of the latter because of its frown upon becoming involved in Franco-British political ambitions in Central Europe again, primarily explains the rapid cooling off. Its page editorial on May 24 read "Our New Role in Europe"; that of June 14, "Saving the World by Ballyhoo." The "new role," upon peering at it from all angles, turned out to possess some remarkably familiar qualities, and the *Nation* did not appreciate most of them. Throughout the next year and a half, the *Nation* had additional opportunities to express bewilderment at the contradictions in the President's comforting pacificatory words and the policy positions which drained them of any possible tangible result to the good.

Roosevelt's address in May got a cordial *Nation* reception. It was interpreted as a signal to the world that the United States was about "to take an active part in international arrangements to promote good relations and stability, and the President's personal determination to assume a role of leadership in world affairs." In general, the comment dressed in platitudes its survey of Roosevelt's platitudes, and referred specifically only to his support of the disarmament plan of the British Prime Minister Ramsay MacDonald, which implied involvement in "consultations" with the nations affected "in the event of a violation of the Pact of Paris," and that he had proposed "a new non-aggression pact." [5] The latter was not detailed, and the assumption was that it could be found in the daily press. As it turned out, it resembled very closely that which had been advanced by Litvinov at the then sitting Geneva Disarmament Conference, while a new *cordon sanitaire*, this time against Hitler Germany, was being sewed together.

The distressing thing about the act and the time to the *Nation* was the knowledge that a buildup against Hitler was under way, and that revision of the Versailles Treaty complex, once more described as "unjust" as well as being the reason for Hitler coming to power in Germany, was now out of the question. And with the concept of "security" once more plainly intended to mean the shoring up of all the existing treaties and the rigid maintenance of the post-1919 status quo, the hope of any other way out than of joint action with the status quo powers appeared non-existent. "Security has come to mean one thing—an agreement among the nations, including the United States, to attempt to reach some common basis for action in event of a violation of existing treaties."

As in the case of the first year and a half of the Japanese question in Asia, there was the same fond hope of some magic verbal formula emerging from such a concept which would inhibit treaty-violation and keep the existing political boundary lines of the world tranquil. There was no other way of interpreting the *Nation*, in view of its blunt stand, "The one thing that must be prevented on the face of Europe is a new resort to arms." Vast faith was placed in the antiseptic effect of American participation in joint consultation upon the occasion of a treaty violation; in fact the mere joining of such a plan by the United States "would do much to make such violations unlikely." That such an event might just as likely be interpreted by a nation as "encirclement" and call forth immediate military action was overlooked, in the same way that the call for sanctions against Japan was not recognized as an incitation to war by that country for many months. The only thing the editors saw was a painless method of preserving the Kellogg Pact.

In the midst of all their hope and joy, they did issue a sobering caution. The possibility of being used by French and British leaders in aiding them achieve un-peaceful goals of their own was admitted, and strongly warned against. Although the *Nation* was at the time publishing some of the most incendiary literature attacking Hitler that ever saw the light of day, there was not the slightest scrap of zeal for bringing him down by war. The American course by necessity should be one of considered and gingerly steps through the European underbrush: [6]

In taking these steps toward international cooperation our government should be wary lest it find itself acting as a tail to the French kite. Obviously we do not wish to join an anti-German alliance, no matter how carefully disguised it may be in garments of peace. If we oppose German aggression we should equally oppose any attempt to find in Hitlerism an excuse for French or British aggression. The peace must be kept; and the only sort of cooperation possible between the United States and Europe is cooperation in preventing the use of arms to satisfy ambitions or to settle claims.

A similar rosy view was taken of the Norman Davis commitment at Geneva, which largely repeated the President's desire to join in consultation with the nations seeking to hold all the Kellogg Pact signatories to their word in renouncing "aggressive" war. It was hoped that the Geneva powers would take heart from this guarantee of moral support and reconsider real disarmament plans once more. It was also thought that the London Economic Conference would be enabled to commence its sessions under promising and optimistic circumstances. The *Nation* liked Davis's definition of "aggression" as much as FDR's: an aggressor was "one whose armed forces are found on alien soil in violation of treaties." [7] Subscription to this curious verbal totem by persons as politically sophisticated as the *Nation* editors seemed to suggest that all that George Brandes, Victor Cherbuliez, Jacques Novikov and Alcide Ebray had written about the swift mortality of treaties throughout the ages had been written in vain. Nothing could have been more naïve than to expect a nation to abide in perpetuity by a treaty fastened upon it by force, and to stay off "alien" soil, especially if it had once been theirs.

There was one observation of great perspicacity on the part of the editors rejoicing over the Geneva statement of Norman Davis, although its full significance was to be realized in a way not intended at this time. Whatever the outcome of the policy maneuver at hand, the judgment appeared to have an enduring prophetic quality: [8]

By signing such a consultative agreement as is being drawn up at Geneva, we acknowledge officially, what has been a fact, that there can be no neutrals in the next war. The Pact of Paris made the doctrine of neutrality an anomaly; but the United States had clung passionately to its theory that we could somehow disassociate and isolate ourselves in the event of war. We cannot do so. We are now committed to give at least negative support to international action against an aggressor, if we concur in the decision to apply such action.

The view expressed was premature to a degree, in that the Senate ultimately applied a halter to the runaway in the form of an amendment to an arms embargo, specifying that arms be denied all parties to a future conflict, and thus making the joining of an aggressor-branding ceremony impossible. Denial of arms to the "aggressed" was bound to be a frosty form of sympathy. But the deeper meaning of the *Nation* commentary was to support involuntarily the view of the critics of the Kellogg Pact that its logical effect was not to generalize peace but to outlaw neutrality and guarantee a war status for all its signatories.

By mid-June, the *Nation*'s cheerful outlook on the consequences of the Roosevelt-Davis statements had begun to become overcast. The big barrier to sustained unqualified enthusiasm was the troublesome fact of the new naval buildup. But there were others. One of these was the contradiction between the President's peace call, which had strongly suggested an international non-aggression pact committing the nations to "agree that they would send no armed force of whatsoever nature across their frontiers," and the just-concluded Presidential talks with the Japanese diplomat Ishii. The President's non-aggression pact suggestion seemed aimed especially at Japan, but when the official communique announced that Roosevelt and Ishii had concluded their talks in "close agreement," it was cause for bewilderment, and induced the editorial comment to suggest that Roosevelt was adopting "a frivolous approach to complicated and grave issues."

The same thing had been noted in the case of the MacDonald visit, accompanied by loud cries of "Anglo-Saxon unity," and now represented by a fierce parrying of antagonistic ideas as to disarmament and economic recovery. It was thought symptomatic that the British delegate at Geneva, Captain Anthony Eden, had "stubbornly fought Mr. Roosevelt's, Norman H. Davis's, and the Soviet's definition of an aggressor," even though the upshot of FDR's policy was to give in to a dearly-sought British objective: "American renunciation of the principle of the freedom of the seas." But the wonderment over Eden's action was unnecessary, if any thought had been given to the British Empire and England's troop dispersals all over the planet, hardly in accord with the homeland's national boundaries.

As far as one could look, the same conflict between "pronouncements and acts" was to be seen, with "France and her vassals" talking peace and harpooning the possibility of Versailles Treaty revision, the one positive act which might guarantee a peaceful Europe. In disillusionment the statement suggested that a closer adherence to reality might be in order, and more attention given to separating talk and action about peace: [9]

Governments apparently find it necessary these days to create illusions in the minds of their citizens that something is being done in the interest of disarmament and peace. This suggests a universal mass desire for peace. But it should be the task of real pacifists to sift the wheat from the chaff, to disclose the discrepancies between ballyhooing propaganda and realities, and to continue the struggle for disarmament and peace in fact.

The *New Republic* viewed the Roosevelt-Davis statements unfavorably from the start.[10] It was unimpressed by the fervent declarations to the effect that neutrality was dead and that America was now prepared to defend the peace of the world. They were sure that even with this sort of brave language, the French would be unwilling to lay down even a single carbine. In fact, the journal took an even stronger stand toward French action at Geneva in trying to isolate Germany and blame her for the failure of the Disarmament Conference as well as for attempting to foment another war. But the *New Republic*'s principal contribution to this issue was a long article late in June, 1933, "The Wrong Road to Peace," by Edwin Borchard, the well-known professor of international law at Yale, and the academic opposite of the views expressed by Princeton's Professor Whitton and his numerous sympathetic colleagues in the Ivy League schools.

Subtitled "Dangers in the Davis Commitment at Geneva," [11] Borchard's three-page blast was a high water mark in the fight against the new diplomacy of involvement, and was an admirable recapitulation of a liberal position which had not been disturbed by the latest season of wars, as was the case of some of the more frantic seekers for world peace via another world war. But the old liberal-revisionist approach had been subject to such neglect in the past months that Borchard considered it apropos to go over the period since 1914 again and refresh the memories of those who might be inclined to date world affairs from the fall of 1931.

The threat to "enforce" peace by the wielding of the pen was more dangerous than the sword, Borchard began, and identified this gesture with the consequences of the War:

For nearly fifteen years a highly charged emotional morality has been directed toward supplying the world with what is called "peace machinery"—treaties and enforcing instruments designed, professedly, to prevent disturbance of the peace by collective intervention against the "aggressor." These ideas have their roots in the crusade of 1914–1918, followed by the vindictive treaties of 1919, which, while assuring the victors their conquests and spoils, purport to create a legal structure by which any challenger of the system thus established is to be denounced as a moral pariah and to expose himself to collective strangulation. . . .

Essentially, said Borchard, this was the foundation of the entire controversy. It was the enforcement of this policy which had "prevented that reconciliation and appeasement" which was necessary for Europe if it hoped "to live either in peace or in a capitalist economy," and it was the never-ending effort of the principal beneficiaries of the war to involve the United States as an additional guarantor. The demonstrated material strength of this country in the War began the real campaign against American "neutrality and independence," and the Davis commitment at Geneva was just another in a series of such moves to involve the United States in the chaos which the winners had made of Europe.

As long as this attitude was persevered in, that long would it take to settle the long overdue treaty problem. The threat to meet any challenger of the 1919 settlements "with obloquy, outlawry and collective war" was supplemented by consistent smashing of all the plans to alleviate the treaty pressures by any peaceful means, which Borchard considered evidence that the powers which had gained abnormal and artificial advantages from these treaties never intended to see them adjusted in any way whatsoever. So the collective security plan against "aggressors" was simply "transparent hypocrisy" and largely the remaining step needed to coop up the seekers of treaty revision permanently.

Borchard considered that in "a less confused age" the fakery of the treaty would have long ago been subjected to the "contempt and ridicule of intelligent people," but in this case the real supporters were the "intelligentsia," who persisted in considering this viewpoint sound despite the fact that armaments had ballooned in size and the political situation grown steadily more ugly around the world. No better proof of the error of this policy could be found than in its patent unworkability, but defenders increased their zeal on its behalf with each additional display of its structural deficiencies. And now the interest of the nations seeking to perpetuate this "unnatural" position coincided with those of the "pacifists," who perhaps did not realize that in their devotion to peace, they had gathered under a "benevolent" banner which covered "the Secret Treaties, and the Fourteen Points . . . the Kellogg Pact, consultative pacts, pacts of mutual assistance and guarantees of security, schemes one and all designed to preserve the 1919 status quo—a status quo more dangerous to the future of Europe and humanity than any yet invented by the ingenuity of vengeful statesmen."

Borchard read one of his strongest warnings to those who had become mesmerized by the word "aggressor" and could hardly refer to international relations without using it repeatedly:

The word aggressor has a derogatory sound. It seems simple. It is designed to stigmatize the "guilty nation." One might suppose that the United States would have learned from its last intervention against an aggressor in Europe that the word "aggressor" is a political term, fashioned to describe the enemy of the moment. It is essentially a dishonest and mischievous term, calculated to mislead the unwary and the uninformed. It cannot be satisfactorily defined. . . . It may be supposed by some that the decision as to who is the aggressor would be reached by judicial methods. But such a supposition would be false. The decision is bound to be political, informed by passion and prejudice and purveyed by propaganda, compounded especially for the consolation of the home population and for the delectation and enticement of the feebleminded outside.

But for those with the collective security mirage image shimmering on their horizons, it was consoling to cling to the notion that all wars involved "an aggressor and an innocent victim," and that therefore it was "immoral to stay out of the stranglers' union when the situation so clearly called for punishment." To these people, "the motley countries of the world are conceived as a sort of *posse comitatus,* interested only in sustaining the right against the wrong." Borchard pleaded with his liberal readers to reject this approach, and hoped that the United States would be wise enough to avoid abandoning its neutrality stand for such plausible and misleading proposals as Davis had already given preliminary support to at Geneva:

The instinct of self-preservation and the necessity of limiting the area and the destructive efforts of war are the sources of the doctrine of neutrality. It is one of the beneficent achievements of a long struggle with barbarism. Impatience with war, accompanied by provocative policies which tend to promote it, is not adequate justification for stifling a doctrine which has enabled at least some people to live and carry on the thread of civilization. Its abandonment would be likely to spell permanent chaos.

Borchard was also quite harsh with European diplomats and their ceaseless search for methods and formulas to involve the United States in power combinations and various kinds of political dead-end streets; American energy should be devoted to settling the rivalries of Europe as a mediator and peace broker, instead of making them more unbalanced by joining one side or another. And it was to every-one's good in Europe to accept America as a disinterested third party and not to commit her to one cause; "If Europe were wise, it would support American neutrality, instead of seeking to break it down. American neutrality is the best hope for European appeasement and reconciliation."

The Davis policy and the whole sanctions notion were steps "in the direction of war and destruction, both for Europe and America," charged Borchard in conclusion, and were hardly to be confused with peaceful moves:

Peace through force assures the means, but not the end. There is no short cut to peace, which must be unremittingly nurtured and cultivated. . . . Nothing can replace the time-honored peaceful policies of negotiation, simple decency, reconciliation and of live and let live, fortified, to be sure, by the instrumentalities of mediation, conciliation, conference and arbi-tration; but the threat of sanctions and the use of force arouses those human resentments which invite war rather than discourage it.

This was the voice of one of the most articulate old liberals, already becoming obsolete in a world of younger standard-bearers of liberalism who preferred clenched raised fists rather than extended arms and open palms as symbols of their ideology. But it amounted to a stern rebuke to those who were already following the sanctions train to the next stage in the war buildup. And with all the incita-tions toward raising high blood pressure over the Hitler movement which the *New Republic* was simultaneously publishing, it indi-cated that in a showdown situation, its editors were still possessed of enough residual common sense to appreciate the sobriety and firmly-entrenched wisdom of the Borchard line of reasoning. Several more years of neutrality-destroying propaganda from the creators and benefactors of Versailles were to be necessary before the *New Repub-lic* editors and its correspondents and readers would be willing to go off once more to a war which they had reassured each other for nearly two decades they would never be so simple-minded as to sub-scribe to again.

Villard, reporting to the *Nation* from London later in the sum-mer,[12] mentioned British enthusiasm over the Davis Geneva speech and that they welcomed having this country as a partner when the examination of the question of guilt arose in the case of another war. It was obvious from their cheer that there was no chance they would ever be adjudged the "aggressor," else their confidence would hardly have been so transparent. But by that time the first round was already over, and nothing had been done to support Davis along lines of actual involvement. And the Senate's comprehensive arms embargo suggested that much more pressure and "education" would be required to obtain the desired commitments.

But another series of Roosevelt-Davis statements in the early months of 1934 started the question on its rounds again. This time the editors of both the liberal journals were ready with frowns and irksome side comments. The situation this time was not as hard to judge, since the literary campaign against the munitions business was under way in a vigorous manner, and the booming naval building program, and plans for even more, set up a difficult pair of facts, one too obvious to ignore on the part even of those who wished to accept the picture of Mr. Roosevelt as a person with undivided attention applied to the problem of preserving and strengthening peace.

Roosevelt's speech before the Woodrow Wilson Foundation dinner a few days after Christmas, 1933, was the incident which took the subject back into the press. Roosevelt's declaration concerning our Latin American relations was accepted at face value as a commitment to abjure the recourse to armed intervention "south of the border," although the *Nation*'s lead editorial comment on January 10, 1934 suggested that there were just as effective and not anywhere as easily detected methods of penetration and pressure application as military invasion. As for his reiterated world peace program, exhorting each nation of the world to prohibit "offensive" weapons and to issue a "simple declaration" that each would not permit its armies "to cross its own borders into the territory of another nation," grave doubts were registered. Roosevelt's call for mass worldwide support and pressure upon political leaders everywhere to assent to this plan was not expected to produce anything. "Most of the people of Europe and Asia are ruled by dictatorships or by governments pursuing cold-blooded policies of reprisal or aggrandizement or panicky measures of self-protection," the editorial pointed out; "Nothing short of general revolution would establish in power the masses to whom Mr. Roosevelt addresses his appeal." So the only thing that the editors could do was to "enthusiastically endorse the good sense and humanity" of FDR's proposals, and expect nothing to ensue.[13]

A week later, after the New Deal President had presented his budget message, the *Nation* reviewed its position soberly, and concluded that on the basis of the requests for massive funds for naval building, Roosevelt's statement on war had been incomplete. His declaration had called for promises to prevent the movement of armies across national frontiers. In reflection, the *Nation* editorially ruminated, "Evidently Mr. Roosevelt is concerned with war on the land. On the sea it is another matter." [14] War in the Pacific might be fought without necessity of considering boundaries. However, a strong case was already being made that the President's widely publicized calls for world peace were clashing directly with the persistent interest he was simultaneously revealing in expanding the navy.

The *New Republic*'s extended editorial comment, "Uncle Sam as Good Neighbor," predicted that the new edition of the old plan would prove as empty as the previous one. Reference was made to the fact that Roosevelt's definition of aggression was the same as that produced by the Soviet Union, but that what the world needed at that moment was not more definitions of aggression, "but ways to prevent it." Practically, the European governments simply accepted Roosevelt's repeated peace plans "as supporting their present policies, whatever these may be"; certainly no energy was being expended in the interest of avoiding another war. The European view seemed to be that another war was inescapable, and the only act that amounted to anything was "to try to be on the winning side." Peace pacts were worthless unless the signers "intended to live up to them," and "the one way to have peace is not to want war." But there was no evidence of this sentiment; "Mr. Roosevelt's proposals are like a temperance sermon directed toward a drunkard who has already reached for the bottle." The continuing influence of the non-interventionists upon editorial policy was demonstrated in blunt language in closing: [15]

Over and over again, one gets from Europe the argument that it is now hopeless to expect the Great Powers to make peace through their own unaided efforts, and that the United States must intervene actively in the present quarrel. But the Europeans overlook what seem, from this side of the Atlantic, to be obvious facts: that the only permanent peace is one arranged by the conflicting nations themselves, that the United States has not the power even if it had the will to resolve Eurasia's difficulties, and that the American people are at present so overwhelmingly opposed to further direct interference in the affairs of the Old World that no American government would dare propose such interference.

The *New Republic*'s editorial, "A New Threat to Neutrality," three and a half months later, was the ultimate in unvarnished language on the early diplomatic wriggles of Mr. Roosevelt's State Department and personal envoys in the field of European affairs. It involved the latest promise by Davis to the statesmen reworking the Versailles Treaty, "presumably with the approval and advance knowledge of the State Department," to commit the United States to embargo all shipments of arms to any violator of a new proposed arms pact. Liberal zeal over arms embargoes had cooled; they now were referred to as "ex post facto methods of preventing war." The editors promptly repudiated the suggestion as "highly dangerous" and informed the readers that if concluded it meant that "the United States would in all human probability enter the next European war against the nation or nations whom Great Britain and France pronounce to be their enemy," since their enemy would "automatically" be the country which transgressed the arms pact. No time was wasted in careful study of this new recommendation: [16]

This is the same old scheme that Messrs. Stimson and Norman Davis and the misguided advocates of the League of Nations have for years been seeking to impose upon the United States. Only the words in the scheme are changed. In place of the Treaty of Versailles, the Covenant of the League of Nations and the Kellogg Pact, it is the proposed arms pact that is to be enforced. Instead of the "aggressor" who was to be strangled by the aid of the United States, we have the "violator of the arms pact." The plan is infinitely worse than last year's unilateral arms embargo. . . .

There was no escape clause in this which prevented the United States from being "subtly forced into taking sides"; the big New York daily newspapers, so loud in praise of this plan, were misleading the people by speaking as if there would be full opportunity to "retain independence of judgment." This was just "delusion":

The French and British governments would find no serious obstacle to their own course of action in any situation. Their propaganda machinery is too well oiled for them to be worried by the fear that the United States would disagree with them on any decision. And if, perchance, the United States should disagree, we should simply invite trouble with them, for they would be certain to excoriate America throughout the world for our "refusal to appreciate the moral issue." The plan of Norman Davis is on a par in its unwisdom with his proposal along the same lines at Geneva last May. . . . Such proposals have an innocuous sound, but the price paid for them would be high.

That the earnest concern over this scheme was premature in that it suffered the same fate as the previous ones was immaterial. The remarkably frank essay on the Anglo-French tactic of recruiting world opinion on its side in every clash was astounding, even in view of a consistent previous criticism of both these powers. The pain suffered by readers and members of "internationalist"-minded British and French "friendship" societies in the United States over such unconstrained bludgeoning of what was one of the most carefully protected relationships in the Western Hemisphere probably reached a dizzying zenith. A tradition had been established here for over half a century that busy concern for the welfare of a European country was considered "hyphenated Americanism" in the case of supporters of all nations except France and Great Britain. An assault of this kind came close to treason in the eyes of those who psychologically enjoyed a common moral citizenship with the two great European democracies of the West. But for the liberals who still believed that "peace" for America meant the absence of war and not perpetual treaty commitments to protect the interests of the rest of the planet, this editorial could not have been more pertinent.

F.D.R. AND THE NAVAL EXPANSIONISTS
DRAW A FROWN

Japanese penetration in Asia in the autumn of 1931 did not give birth to American naval expansion or provoke big navy enthusiasts into their first declaration of intention. But there is little doubt that immense stimulation resulted from Japanese action, and a healthy propaganda designed to intensify American fear and suspicion of Japan contributed to nourishing the campaign to extend the size of America's fleets. A similar interest group in Japan gained similar prestige and power by cultivating the identical responses to the United States. The result was a national rivalry of a peculiar sort, perhaps the most intensely hostile relationship between two states so distantly located in the political history of the race. It would have done justice to the stirring up of two peoples six miles apart, instead of six thousand. This long-distance hatred is in a class of its own, and the performers of autopsies upon propaganda have never done an adequate job of examining this case. At full bloom in the early 1940's it played an important part in sustaining one of the most brutal race wars the world has ever known.

The post-Mukden time was well beyond the halfway mark in the history of this complex racial-national antipathy. Much of the damage to enduring good will between the two countries had already been done since the Russo-Japanese war, which is not saying that a war between America and Japan was inevitable or unavoidable. There were numerous opportunities for the salvaging of peace even in the decade ending in Pearl Harbor. Yet there is plenty of evidence that policies, intentions and actions of several kinds were held and taken, the logical consequences of which screamed "war" with emphasis no one might plead inability to comprehend.

The strengthening of the American armed forces, especially the navy, during the first years of this increasingly critical period, and liberal response to it, makes an appropriate foil to match off against the promiscuous peace and disarmament proposals, conferences and manifestoes simultaneously issuing from all quarters. Given the mood of the mid-depression, with its strong overtones of pacifism and war disillusionment, due in large part to a decade of realistic writing on the causes and results of the first World War, enthusiasm over war preparations, however explained, was microscopic among the liberals. It was this reluctance to support armed preparation which made some early liberal attitudes toward Japan so difficult to understand, since the policies they pressed for adoption sooner or later called for the remedy they were most against. But liberal unhappiness over American "big navy" spokesmen and their successes outlived the interval of fascination with "sanctions."

Although the liberal editors and correspondents were not known for their moderation in speaking of Herbert Hoover, on foreign affairs and military-naval policy they were complimentary on many more occasions than they were willing to recall in later years. The *New Republic* on Armistice Day, 1931, contained one of the most sympathetic editorial commentaries ever directed at the depression President. Its subject was his proposal to cut naval appropriations deeply and his expressed willingness to have the United States participate in a one-year naval construction "holiday" dating from the first of November, despite the loud criticism of such spokesmen as William H. Gardiner of the Navy League. It was thought that the funds saved might be put to far better use, as well: [17]

Mr. Hoover stands . . . in a particularly sympathetic light. The heavy attacks on him from jingo quarters . . . only do him honor . . . his effort to reduce the American naval budget must certainly be counted among the more courageous and commendable actions of his unhappy regime. What we approve about this action, however, is not that it cuts governmental expenditures at this time, when government expenditures ought to be expanded, but that it saves money for better uses. Every dollar cut from our program of destruction ought to be put into the building of valuable and lasting wealth, into the expansion of expenditure which would help revive industry, raise prices and absorb employment.

The *Nation* [18] went on record in support of a similar paring-down of military strength, and alteration of plans for large military spending in the event of another big war, with economy a major motive, as well as making a gesture before the world as to our sincere disarmament intentions. It editorially asserted that the National Defense Act of 1920 was intended to commit the country to participation in a system of international sanctions, and contained the plans "to throw six field armies of 4,000,000 drafted men into Europe immediately upon the outbreak of war." Calling strongly for its radical amendment, on the grounds that it was inconsistent with principles of the Kellogg Pact, the editorial declared, "The American Army should be transformed into a genuine defense force, thus saving millions of dollars to the taxpayer and proving our sincerity." As a substitute for formidable armed forces to obtain national objectives, the country was advised to "work for the development of international organization based upon pacifist principles." These themes of economy and foreign relations based on other than armed strength, carried over into the next few years, and played a strong part in the attack on the naval buildup under Roosevelt.

By the end of January, 1932, the liberal critics of increased naval spending and building were aware of how the extension of the war in Asia to Shanghai had enabled the naval enthusiasts to once more push vigorously for their objectives. When even Hoover appeared to give in and give his approval to the Vinson naval arms bill, and with the entire American fleet together for the first time in history, holding winter maneuvers off Hawaii, the liberal press scolded loudly. The first of these items was compared to the comprehensive naval arms program of 1916, "when this country was preparing for war with Germany," while the second was interpreted as a direct attempt to bring armed pressure upon Japan, also a reprehensible gesture.[19] It was following this that the *New Republic* published the series of scathing attacks written by Charles A. Beard under the title "Big Navy Boys," [20] which went into unusual detail on the subject of naval armaments and who and what the main protagonists and their interests happened to be. Beard continued this offensive in *Harper's*.[21]

The zeal of the Democrat-controlled Congress in Hoover's last two years for preserving army and navy appropriations at constant levels drew a hot blast from Villard in the *Nation* early in February, 1933, titled "The Army and Navy Forever." [22] In many ways it could be considered the inception of the protracted campaign of criticism directed at the next administration and its even more cordial attitude toward spending for the army and navy, especially the latter. Villard professed to be mystified at what he called the "sacrosanct" quality of naval and military appropriations in Washington; their total had not suffered any appreciable reduction despite the other budget slashes, while it was becoming almost vulgar to even speak of them critically. A virtual "curtain of inviolability" had been drawn around them, and the *Nation*'s senior editor was puzzled as to the reason. The armed forces' political friends acted as if the country was actually in danger, and he proceeded to demolish this by taking up the instance of every possible enemy and finding no evidence in support of any alleged belligerent intentions toward this country. "The simple truth is," Villard insisted, "that there is not a nation in financial condition to undertake a struggle with the United States, and certainly not one whose military officers and financial and economic experts could hold out the slightest hope of gaining anything whatever from war with the United States, whether the war should be successful or unsuccessful."

Villard scoffed at those who justified these continued heavy expenditures on the ground of defense against a world hostile to America, but for those who argued that personnel reductions would just add to the huge unemployed totals, he saved a special rebuke. These men would be far better off living on a dole in private life than in uniform in barracks, in his opinion, and at far less expense as well. In addition, Villard considered the armed forces would be "much more efficient" if they canceled the services of thousands of officers as well. In closing, he saw no reason whatever for postponing any longer these beneficial economies; "there is today no sound reason why the army and navy appropriations should not be cut by several hundred millions of dollars."

Villard and the *Nation* took the initiative in addressing strong disapproval of the naval policy in the first few months of the Roosevelt Administration, largely overlooked by enthusiasts who were overwhelmed by the volume of domestic legislation poured out by Congress during these celebrated "One Hundred Days." The emphasis on Mr. Roosevelt as physician to domestic ailments hid from view these other facets of his program to most, but not the persistent *Nation,* which documented the state of the new naval construction plan week by week. Editorially, it was considered significant that the President had frequently gone on record in favor of an "adequate" navy, prior to his election. When the Democratic Party leaders in Congress and the Secretary of the Navy, Claude Swanson, began to champion another Vinson bill for big navy spending—from half a billion to a billion dollars was so considered in those days—the journal came to the conclusion that they had the full support of the President, otherwise they hardly would have been so intrepid in their agitation. Before the first month of FDR's presidency was over, an editorial challenged him to repudiate the Swanson-Vinson forces if it was true that they did not "accurately represent" his views.[23]

The *Nation* charged at this time that a widely circulated story in Washington predicted the President himself would come out in support of this naval expansion bill, using the excuse that the work so created would help reduce the pressure of the unemployment problem. Two weeks later, such a plan was advanced, but by the same spokesmen who had assumed the leadership before. When Representative Vinson asserted that eighty-five percent of a hoped-for $230,000,000 appropriation for building craft for the Navy would go out as wages to the labor employed in the construction, he was subjected to a brief but intense bolt of ridicule. Vinson had in the course of his explanation made the remark that the plan sounded "fantastic," and editorially the *Nation* expressed complete agreement with that; "Consider the anomaly involved," it jeered, "in spending money on engines of mass murder and destruction, on the pretext that the expenditure will serve humanitarian ends." The only "social gain" likely to follow from this activity was added profits for the munitions industry, and the President was pressed to "halt this insane plan" and devote the money to a housing project instead. At this stage the liberal critics were still willing to believe that Roosevelt had little or nothing to do with the project, and that it was being propelled along by big navy advocates as an independent undertaking. Temporarily it was not considered important to call to mind the dark campaign charges against Roosevelt as the friend of militarists, nor his part as a naval booster during the days of Woodrow Wilson. It was the Navy Department which was blamed for this, "the most absurd, and at the same time the most dangerous, unemployment relief plan yet proposed." [24]

There already was a distinct feeling of losing the propaganda battle with the naval expansionists, which was expressed in discussing the great volume of pro-big-navy sentiment which the American public was being exposed to in the newsreels, "particularly flamboyant in their militarist appeals." It was admitted that a sizable number of *Nation* readers had become incensed at a recently-shown Pathé film which had continually stressed the relative weakness of the American fleet compared to that of Japan, and in addition to claiming that the President was behind this drive to build more war ships, it had urged the viewers to write to their Congressmen in support of the pending legislation. It was conceded that nothing could be done to combat the comprehensiveness of the news pictures, but that if the one in question had misrepresented Mr. Roosevelt's views, it was up to him to force the company which had issued it to make a public retraction in every theater which had exhibited it. No retraction requests from the White House followed.

On April 19, Villard devoted his full-page personal editorial to the subject, "The President and a Big Navy." [25] It was a last-minute plea for a repudiation of the naval building, the appropriation for which was expected to be hidden in a more comprehensive Public Works Administration measure, to escape the possibility of a protest. This bill, said Villard, was expected to be "jammed through by the force of the same vote-but-don't-read-it-or-argue psychology which has resulted in driving through Congress the legislation thus far asked by the President." Villard hoped it would not eventuate, and considered the money thus spent "wasted upon a purely unproductive undertaking." He predicted that if it went through, there would follow many, many others, since this stimulus would encourage the growth of a substantial interest group anxious to extend and expand their stake; "your big-navy maniac is never satisfied."

Not much hope now remained that FDR would block it, and his background was reviewed once more to indicate why the "big-navy people" considered him a friend at court:

. . . he has been deeply interested in the navy ever since boyhood, and he pretty well soaked up the big-navy propaganda when Assistant Secretary of the Navy. His collection of prints of naval battles was for a long time considered one of the finest in the United States. He saw nothing wrong in the overseas aggressions of the Wilson Administration of which he was part. . . . Hence the big-navy people feel that he is definitely on their side.

There was an outside chance the spending might be justified if America was threatened—which the Navy talked about incessantly concerning Japan. Villard countered: "To this we reply that we are a long way from a war with Japan," and inferred that such a struggle should be the last thing anyone should seek. "The next war means suicide for our entire capitalist civilization—what is left of it; and this President Roosevelt knows, or ought to know, as well as the rest of us."

Villard was exceedingly confident that another naval race would surely end in "another terrible conflict," and recommended that if we were going to condemn German rearmament under Hitler, which had yet to get started, our standing as critics would be flimsy; "when preaching disarmament to the rest of the world, let us set the example ourselves."

But the fight was virtually lost by the time this was published, and from that point on, liberal press comments concentrated on questioning the wisdom of the policy. There still remained a considerable audience of readers who greatly disliked this step to encourage as critics. Late in June, the *Nation* fired another verbal arrow at Secretary of the Navy Swanson upon his reiteration that 85% of the appropriation for this naval expansion would go directly for labor. The comment was that this assertion would be very difficult to prove, and, if this was going to be the method of rationalizing the act, "it may be suggested that if he would pay the men to play leap frog, 100% of the money would go for labor and the consequences would be far less mischievous." [26] The *New Republic*'s full-column editorial on the same date (June 28, 1933) suggested that as soon as the new ships were built, they be towed out to the middle of the Atlantic and sunk. This would save all the expense of the upkeep, and be "a token of our pacific intentions,"

and it will be a vivid illustration of the crazy economic system under which we live, whereby men can be kept from starvation only by useless labor expended on needless instrumentalities of murder.

The *Nation* kept up a continual attack all that summer, comparing in a disparaging manner the loud peace talk at Geneva and London with the belligerent statements of the Secretary of the Navy, calling for "a navy second to none." "Mr. Swanson's program might be compatible with the ambitions of Hitlerism, but it has no place in the policy of any enlightened modern state," it pronounced in mid-July.[27] Villard's signed editorial at the end of the month was even sharper: [28]

As for the announcement of the Secretary of the Navy, with Mr. Roosevelt's approval, that we are arranging to build our fleet up to treaty limits, and our establishment of a new—and somewhat aggressive—naval policy, all I can say about that is that it is worthy of Adolf Hitler. At this stage of our own and the world's history such an action is criminal folly, indefensible from any point of view. Yet a demand for naval expansion was precisely to have been expected from Franklin Roosevelt, whose big navy proclivities he long ago sincerely and openly avowed—which is one reason why I could not vote for him for President.

By the time the London Conference crashed, not long after this, the green light for military and naval spending seemed to be gleaming all over the landscape. When the Secretary of War, George H. Dern, taking his cue from Swanson, also bid for public works funds to be used for a re-vamping of the Army, great concern was shown, and the *Nation* hoped Harold Ickes would prevent this raiding of the PWA moneys for such purposes, and that Frances Perkins would halt the exploitation of the unemployment situation as an excuse for doing the same. The fact that the Japanese were using the "Roosevelt-Swanson naval program" as the reason for stepping up naval building was considered particularly ominous, especially since for the first time in history the budget allotment for the Japanese Navy exceeded that of the Army. As the two countries were teetering "on the verge of a disastrous naval-armaments race," it was hoped that the "enlightened progressives" in the New Deal Administration would see that they had "a duty to perform," namely, to challenge the militarist proponents, and if necessary, "carry their cause to the people," in order to get public support behind a protest "to prevent the country from being plunged into an era of militarism" very likely to "lead us into new wars." [29]

At the London Economic Conference, despite the formal unpleasantries between the British and American delegations, some liberal observers thought they saw the initial stages of another Anglo-American understanding, disguised as a naval rivalry but in actuality aimed to obstruct the growth of Japanese power in the Pacific. Said the *New Republic:* [30]

America and England, in their relations to other nations, have been and are selfish, imperialistic, predatory. However, ever since the World War they have managed to maintain, between themselves, a sort of bandits' partnership, in the Far East, in Europe, and in central bank management and international lending, and in naval armaments.

It was for this reason that British excuses for new naval building, and the increased building in Japan and America, were taken lightly.[31] It was, besides, a point which Villard made in London a few days after the London Conference, that he kept hearing from highly-placed people that America and Britain were on their way to another *entente,* and that ultimately the combined American and British fleets would be used "to impose peace upon the world." He did not think this possible, in view of what he interpreted to be widespread British "distrust" of the United States, but the Roosevelt-Davis public statements on foreign policy and the "Roosevelt-Swanson" naval enlargement moves suggested this step as the first one away from the previous "isolation."

By the autumn of 1933 the liberal disparagement of military and naval spending and expansion had become interwoven with both the new pacifism and the crusade against the munitions trade. *Common Sense* delivered a blunt editorial condemnation of big-navy notions in August.[32] The *Nation* devoted considerable space to Mauritz Hallgren's "Drifting Into Militarism," [33] a concise summary of virtually all the happenings in the past eight months in these various departments. "The American people are drifting into militarism, which means, to put it bluntly, that America is drifting toward war," was Hallgren's lead sentence. He defined militarism as "a system emphasizing the military spirit and the need of constant preparation for war." He referred to the New Deal Administration as having launched, with the exception of 1916, "the biggest and most expensive peace-time preparedness program in the country's history," as well as making the assertion that the War Department was spending as much money as it ever had except during times of actual war. He compared the Administration's spending for direct relief and the armed forces in a manner which indicated the former was coming off a bad second, and expressed strong suspicions over the Civilian Conservation Camps. He thought it peculiar that the stress was upon keeping "jobless men of fighting age" "fit"; "Fit for what? it might be asked," was his rhetorical question. Hallgren compiled a bothersome collection of facts and inferences from them as to the flow of money into numerous military and naval channels, and suggested that the unwillingness of Congressmen to ask questions about these issues was the consequence of greatly increased activity on the part of interested manufacturers of the products going into the program. The first low rumbles of the renewed clash with the makers of guns, ammunition and armor plate were actually being heard, with provocative writings like this serving the purpose of stimulating readers' protests to the politicians concerned. Even the President was suspected of being circumspect when it came to ruffling the tempers of the "big navy hornets," as the *Nation* comment of January 17, 1934, indicated, on thinking over the implications of his hearty tribute to the yearnings for peace around the world before the Woodrow Wilson Foundation the previous December 28.

The running rear guard action liberalism was staging against the rehabilitation of the striking power of the armed forces involved another sharp stand not long after, when a refurbished Vinson bill calling for major naval construction beginning in 1936 made its appearance in legislative channels, on the heels of the Nye resolution recommending a comprehensive probe of the entire munitions business. The *New Republic* was especially annoyed by this, and denounced the Vinson bill as "the most indefensible naval grab in this country's history." In addition to a strong plug for the passing of the Nye resolution, its February 28, 1934 editorial urged an immediate investigation of collusive bidding made the previous year by firms seeking contracts for the construction covered by PWA funds. The Vinson bill, even if the contracts let under it were administered under the purest circumstances, was still declared to be"thoroughly bad," for other reasons: [34]

The certain fact is that the Vinson bill, if permitted to pass, will be used by ex-admirals in England and navy clansmen in Japan to inflame opinion in those countries to a point where neither the English nor Japanese governments, next year, will dare to make any concessions whatever. Its passage will doom the 1935 naval conference to futility.

The *Nation,* temporarily shaken by the complexities which had brought its Russian, Japanese and American policies into a whirlpool, suspected that there was some hidden aspect to the Roosevelt Administration's new footing with the Soviets on Japan, and that it involved the naval rebuilding program somehow. Its February 7, 1934 editorial, "War Words in the East," suspected that the new bristling note in Russian verbal attacks on Japan by Stalin and Lazar Kaganovich after a long period of moderation was a product not only of the recent American recognition but of some ominous agreement between Russia and the United States which had not been revealed, hence the haste to build battleships. The editors charged FDR with frankly aiming at Japan, and protested that the naval building program could "only add to the suspicion and tension now abroad in the world," but by far the worst in Asia; "By planning to build more and ever more warships we are simply causing Far Eastern tempers and suspicions to rise still higher." [35]

Like the *Nation* previously, the *New Republic* learned in rapid order that trying to defeat this latest move at enlarging the navy was a stupendous job, in view of the President's known support and sympathy. In a long editorial the next month, "Big-Navy Roosevelt," it ruefully admitted, "With anyone but Mr. Roosevelt at the head of the government, the task of defeating the Vinson Naval Bill . . . would be infinitely easier." In explaining the President's "sympathetic regard for the admirals," FDR's previous cabinet experience and his exploits as an "ardent amateur sailorman" were once more reviewed. The political problem posed by this issue fascinated the editors. Mr. Roosevelt was "the rare case of a big-navy man" who at the same time was "on most other questions, a liberal." The result was to place potential opponents of the bill among the old line liberal Congressmen in a bad jam, since they were supporters of his purely domestic proposals. It was realized that the "Western progressive bloc in the Senate" was quite willing to vote against the Vinson Bill, but was not of the mind to lead the fight against the Administration, regardless of the knowledge that its "chief strength" was FDR's "personal support." [36] In many ways, this new Vinson Bill was a preview of a long series of President-backed bills of similar content in the future, unopposed because of this anguished tug-of-war in the minds of liberal progressives for domestic reform, but rigidly against measures which they were convinced meant war, of some sort, somewhere.

The passage of the Vinson Bill in the spring of 1934 took place with virtually the entire liberal camp in loud disapproval and protest, as the naval arms bill of the previous year had crossed over into law. The President's supporting arguments had been punctured cruelly time after time, and the whole impact of the legislation in the making blasted as pure social loss and an incitation to all the militarists in London and Tokyo. The *Nation,* on the heels of this new defeat, considered the restoration of almost the entire budget cut in the army appropriations for 1935 another measure of salt in the liberal wounds, but blamed the Senate this time, instead of the President, for refusing to go along with the "economy program" which the President was presumably calling for. What Mr. Roosevelt's firmly backed naval expansion bills did to his cherished economy desires seemed momentarily forgotten. All that was seen now was another boost for "the American military machine, with its inevitable tendency to thrust us into war." [37]

The liberal press varied its campaign after losing the Vinson Bill redoubt. The principal reason for this was the almost simultaneous voting by the Senate of approval of the Nye-Vandenberg resolution for the arms makers investigation. The previously mentioned *New Republic* articles by Jonathan Mitchell, "The Armaments Scandal," [38] angrily hit at virtually everyone now but Roosevelt. In fact, these lengthy dissertations did not even mention the President personally as having anything to do with the souped-up activity of the gun, ship, plane, tank and armor plate producers. A whole new hierarchy of responsibles was paraded for the readers of the liberal press, with several conflicting approaches which were sure to encourage the maximum of bewilderment among those interested in fixing real responsibility. Mitchell, temporarily dazzled by the Soviet "as the only nation in the world which had made even a beginning towards coordinating its political and commercial policies," [39] and which presumably did not even dream of producing weapons for others than itself, attacked the American approach of permitting private companies to sell the implements of war anywhere a customer could be found. He was unusually indignant over the sale of military aircraft to Chiang Kai-shek's Nationalist Chinese in 1933 and up to that time in 1934, as acts which could only "alarm and infuriate Japan." He blamed the State Department for this, and insisted that the Department should have been more anxious to "appease Japanese-American relations" instead of being concerned in promoting "the sales of the Curtiss-Wright Corporation." Mitchell did not think it strange that Navy Secretary Swanson was such a dogged partisan of United States naval arms expansion. He had been known during his lengthy Senate tenure as a "big-navy" man, and on the eve of his cabinet appointment had been Chairman of the Senate Naval Appropriations Committee. But as for foreign arms selling, Mitchell had no sympathy here, especially military planes to China, which he felt sure the Japanese were "grimly determined" to terminate. It was an issue that the Roosevelt Administration would have to face, "probably in the very near future," he forecast. The expansion of the navy was having serious effect upon Japan, to be sure, but in his mind there was no reason for permitting American suppliers of munitions "to exacerbate the Japanese war psychosis." Mitchell posed an ominous rhetorical question: "Last month (April, 1934) Secretary of State Hull delivered a homily on the sacredness of the Open Door. We are entitled to know from Mr. Hull for whom he wants to keep the Open Door ajar. Is it for peaceful merchants, against whom no Japanese protest has been made, or is it for the vendors of swift, terrible death?" [40]

Villard, the same month, in his signed editorial "Coordination and Recovery," concluded that the confusion had mounted to such a point that it was now plain that the Cabinet was trying to function "without a national foreign policy or well-thought-out naval policy." The maintenance of a fleet capable of "steaming great distances" and carrying war virtually anywhere was utterly out of harmony with the President's "own proposal of defensive weapons only." For this reason he thought the billion-dollar battleship construction program which the Vinson Bill called for could be scaled down nine-tenths, and still give the country an adequate protective force, "if we were determined to abide by the President's proposal never to send an armed force across our own frontiers, that is, never to engage in a war except in actual defense at home of our country." [41]

Bruce Bliven's signed editorial, "No Santa Claus," in the *New Republic* for the same date, had even more disparaging observations to make on the President's "delusions," most of which were considered to be in the domestic arena. But Bliven in extended remarks thought it relevant to express second thoughts on the implications of the new naval biceps-flexing: [42]

One further item belongs . . . in this list of the President's delusions. He recognizes, as everyone does, that there are serious conflicts of interest between the United States and Japan. He knows, too, that a race in naval armament has never in the past led to anything but war. Yet knowing this, and sincerely desiring peace, he has pushed through a program for new naval building that will cost something between $900,000,000 and $1,250,000,000 in the next seven years. It may be said that he is only trying to put himself in a strong trading position at the naval conference of 1935; that by scrapping his new ships, he can persuade Japan to scrap her ships, also, and perhaps modify her policy on the mainland of Asia. As to this, we can only say that we hope he is more correct in his dealing with the minds of the Japanese than he has been in dealing with the minds of his fellow countrymen on a majority of his chief domestic issues. For if he is wrong, the results will indeed be tragic for the world.

It was most difficult to imagine from the context of this judgment that Bliven entertained much hope for the success of the President's big maritime gamble with Japan in the late spring of 1934. The "peace through war preparations" argument especially failed to fire him with ardor at this stage.

Bliven asserted his belief in the sincerity of the President's peace desires, but the intensity of the *New Republic*'s criticism of the navy's "new look" thereafter gave little evidence of such faith. Editorially it heaped uncomplimentary language on the subject of the strategic preparations of the War and Navy Departments in 1934. It objected to the fleet actions in the Pacific, where it was "flaunted in the face of Japan for many months," besides challenging the usefulness of the navy's decision to build a base at Dutch Harbor in the Aleutian Islands, and the sending of submarines, mine-layers and sea planes there. "All the items about the Aleutians received scant notice in the American press," said the journal, but "they made headlines in Japan." The reflection this was expected to cast upon the peaceful protestation of the Commander in Chief was undisguised. Otis Ferguson's "The Old Navy Game," published in June, was a biting satire on the navy show as a "taxpayer's plaything" and sheer economic waste.[43]

The Fourth of July issue's lengthy "Why More Battleships?" [44] went into American naval and Pacific policy with great gusto, and was not designed to comfort the New Deal Administration's strategists, long range or short. The naval expansion was condemned as indefensible from every major interest viewpoint, ranging from Asiatic trade to national defense. The decision to free the Philippines was looked upon as the act which undercut the argument that stiffening against Japan in Asia was essential to our future trade and economic growth in that part of the world. The remaining trade and investments were calculated to be worth not more than half a billion dollars, most of which Japan would not interfere with, even if completely successful in her ambitions, for "reasons of self-interest." "Suppose however that she did in fact cut off some of it—what should we do? Engage in a war which President Roosevelt himself declared, after his experience as Assistant Secretary of the Navy, was certain to result in a costly stalemate? In our judgment, there are millions of Americans who believe that such a war is unmitigated folly."

As for the three-cornered naval race, it was "absolute folly" to engage in the "international suicide pact" which the Japanese and British seemed determined to have:

If Japan and England are determined to bankrupt themselves even farther by a navy-building race, let them do so, but let us stay out of it. We have no interest in the Orient, or anywhere else, that demands that we participate in any such folly. Our present fleet is ample to protect us in any possible defensive warfare—and like every other country in the world, we have pledged ourselves, through the Kellogg Pact, to indulge henceforth in defensive warfare only. If the 1935 conference breaks down, or is not held, we shall be subjected to a flood of big-navy propaganda even worse than that of the past. We shall be told that in a world of wolves, we must not act the part of sheep; that our homes will be endangered unless we match Great Britain and Japan, ship for ship. The proper answer to such propagandists is: Whom do you propose to fight, and where, and why?

In advancing views of this kind, there was no difficulty in understanding that the editors did not support the contention that at the 1935 Naval Conference it would be pertinent or proper for FDR to insist on discussing Asian mainland political questions as a corollary to any agreement with Japan about the relative size of naval forces.

In the clangor over the ambitions of the naval expansionists, liberal editors did not entirely overlook the quiet pressure for an air buildup simultaneously under way. The *Nation* in August, 1934, discounted the talk of "an air force second to none" as another pernicious slogan, and subjected Assistant Secretary of War Woodring, General Douglas MacArthur and "ex-pacifist" Newton D. Baker, whose Aviation Committee had recommended building a great air fleet, to considerable verbal abuse. In conjunction with disparagement of American aims, it spoke of French, German, Italian and British building plans of the same kind with great disapprobation, pointedly omitting any mention whatever of the vast Russian air force already in existence.[45]

All of the pre-Conference talk contained a note of depression, as the rumor spread that the existing naval limitations were going to be repudiated with a wild-swinging naval race to begin on the heels of the Conference's adjournment. In the light of these widely-circulated suspicions, the *New Republic* suggested in September the creation of a "Futility Prize" for 1934, to be awarded to the American and British governments for their efforts in mutually agreeing to the desirability of reducing the caliber of the heaviest naval guns. A mutual understanding as to the limitation of merchant ship-building was deemed worthy, since merchant shipping business was far below the shipping capacity already in existence. But here the President disagreed with the British and the editors. Again it was thought necessary to scold the President for rejecting the suggestion of Secretary of Agriculture Wallace that American exports be increased and that foreign merchantmen be used on the grounds of economy. FDR's insistence on building more unneeded merchant vessels was also thought to be traceable to his "sentimental attachment to the sea." As for taking the other talks seriously, the conclusion was that "to talk about fourteen-inch or sixteen-inch guns is just about as helpful as suggesting to a man dying with cancer that he get his face lifted." [46]

Villard also thought the season appropriate to educate the President. In an editorial comment just prior to the sixteenth anniversary of the Armistice, he expressed his enthusiasm over the pastoral letter of the House of Bishops of the Protestant Episcopal Church which denounced armaments and war in language familiar to *Nation* readers. The letter's specific condemnation of "the building of vast armaments and the maintenance of greatly augmented forces on land and sea" impelled Villard to remark curtly, "Washington papers please copy, and Franklin D. Roosevelt please read." [47]

Comments on the Naval Conference itself revealed a tendency to view the Japanese position more sympathetically than that insisted upon by the Administration's delegates. American insistence on adhering to the 5-5-3 ratio worked out at the Washington Naval Conference, in the administration of the despised Warren G. Harding, had a hollow sound to liberal ears. It was **more widely** believed that the

grim clinging to this formula was going on largely in the hope that
Japan would in anger give up the whole situation, and bring on an
unrestricted naval building splurge, at which they would be easily
bested, in the thinking of the President. The *New Republic* considered this a very dangerous kind of "international poker game" to be
playing at that time, with the American economic situation being
what it was, let alone the provocation to Japan. Confident expectations that this enormous navy would be sufficient to cow the Japanese
into re-opening the Open Door, once more kowtow to the 5-5-3 program, and even make additional trade concessions, was looked upon
as wildly unbalanced optimism.[48]

A Japanese proposal to agree to a fifty percent reduction in all
naval strengths upon the achievement of equality with Britain and
America was met by a *New Republic* editorial declaration that "there
is no reason to doubt Japan's sincerity," while Japanese Ambassador
Saito's speech in Philadelphia in the last week of November, 1934,
in which he posted Japan's case against the implied moral superiority
of the British and Americans in insisting on this unequal relation of
naval strengths was given sober approval. This mutual reduction plan
was considered better by far than the continued efforts of Roosevelt
at trying to "outbluff" the Japanese, "a desperately dangerous expedient in a world where any spark may set off a conflagration." [49]

Equality with Japan and the cutting back of navies to the stage of
"defensive equality" was looked upon as a sure way to "greatly diminish" the possibility of war, the dominating consideration from the
liberal corner, the "practical question of the utmost moment." Again
in view of the purely defensive aspect involving the United States,
the stiff and unyielding insistence upon the old ratio needed explanation. There also was the question of framing this policy so as to make
it intelligible and comprehensible to the mass of the citizens: [50]

Just how much are Americans willing to pay to have a fleet two-thirds
larger than Japan? Just how much is it worth to them? If the purpose of
the United States government were merely to protect our shores against
a possible Japanese invasion, this supremacy would not be worth one de-
valuated cent, for naval preponderance is not necessary for this purpose.
No hostile fleet could cross the Pacific and inflict any real damage unless
it was twice as large as its opponent. What is it, then, that we need the
ratio for?

The *Nation*'s approach was not quite so conciliatory toward Japanese views, and sounded as if written by an indignant British observer
circa 1895, with its repeated invocations of international law, but it
still favored at bottom a change of American position, which could
be best realized by converting the navy to a defensive force exclu-

sively, and adopting the principle of defensive equality, so as to remove "any stigma of inferiority as far as Japan is concerned." [51]

The week before Christmas, 1934, the *New Republic* editorially answered its own questions of a month before. It amounted to as serious an indictment of the Roosevelt naval policy as a similar arraignment four months earlier of his international economic policy; Norman Davis' speech in London was interpreted to be the voice of the President demanding no other alternative than the 5-5-3 ratio. As such it signalled to the editors the end of another London Conference, which they lamented as a "disastrous failure." The President was given a stiff reproof and openly charged with dismissing the Japanese offer of drastic reduction in exchange for equal status. The possible outcome in the event Mr. Roosevelt was wrong on his guessing game with the Japanese was worded in dark, simple terms which were not in danger of being misunderstood: [52]

Our government is prepared to see the cancellation of all agreements and an unrestricted naval-building race, believing that we can outbuild Japan, can force her to sue for terms, and that among these terms will be the restoration of the so-called Open Door in the Far East for American trade and investment. This is a desperately dangerous course of procedure. It puts upon the United States the onus of making general reduction of the fleets impossible, since there is no reason to doubt Japan's sincerity in offering a reduction of 50% if given "defensive equality" and it is well known that Great Britain was willing to accept some such compromise. We should not like to be in President Roosevelt's shoes if his guess turns out to be wrong, if Japan refuses to be bluffed, and if, out of the tension created by the race in naval building, there should finally come the imminent peril of war.

NOTES

1 *New Republic,* July 1, 1931, pp. 9–10.
2 *New Republic,* March 22, 1933, p. 143.
3 *New Republic,* June 28, 1933, p. 181.
4 Citations from editorial paragraph, *Nation,* March 29, 1933, p. 331.
5 *Nation,* May 31, 1933, p. 597.
6 "Our New Role In Europe," *Nation,* May 24, 1933, p. 573, for this and citations in previous two paragraphs.
7 *Nation,* May 31, 1933, p. 597.
8 Above, p. 597.
9 *Nation,* "Saving the World By Ballyhoo," *Nation,* June 14, 1933, pp. 657–658, for this citation and those in previous two paragraphs.
10 "A Breathing Space For Europe," *New Republic,* May 31, 1933, pp. 58–60.
11 *New Republic,* June 28, 1933, pp. 171–174, for citations in following seven paragraphs.

12   Villard, "The Damage To America In London," *Nation*, August 2, 1933, p. 117.
13   *Nation*, January 10, 1934, p. 29.
14   *Nation*, January 17, 1934, p. 57.
15   *New Republic*, January 10, 1934, pp. 239–240 (239), and for quotations in paragraph preceding.
16   *New Republic*, April 18, 1934, p. 259, for this and subsequent quotation.
17   *New Republic*, November 11, 1931, p. 335.
18   Editorial "Progress At Geneva," *Nation*, August 10, 1932, p. 117.
19   *New Republic*, January 27, 1932, p. 279.
20   Beard's articles were subtitled "Selling Increased Armament To the Taxpayers," January 20, 1932, pp. 258–261: "What Is A Naval Expert and Why?" January 27, 1932, pp. 287–291; "Who Is Behind the Navy League?," February 3, 1932, pp. 314–318.
21   Beard, "Our Confusion Over National Defense," *Harper's*, February, 1932, pp. 257–267.
22   *Nation*, February 8, 1933, p. 139, for citations in following two paragraphs.
23   *Nation*, March 29, 1933, p. 331.
24   *Nation*, April 12, 1933, p. 385. For early criticism see also "Preparing For War," *Nation*, March 22, 1933, p. 307.
25   *Nation*, April 19, 1933, p. 435, for citations in following four paragraphs.
26   *Nation*, June 28, 1933, p. 709.
27   *Nation*, July 12, 1933, p. 30.
28   Villard, "The Roosevelt Revolution," *Nation*, July 26, 1933, p. 91.
29   *Nation*, August 2, 1933, p. 114. See also *Nation*, September 27, 1933, p. 338, commenting on Roosevelt's announcement of intention to close fifty army posts.
30   *New Republic*, August 30, 1933, p. 61.
31   See *Nation*, November 29, 1933, p. 608, bitterly criticizing the British decision to boost the size of battleships under construction.
32   *Common Sense*, August, 1933, p. 6.
33   *Nation*, October 4, 1933, pp. 372–374.
34   *New Republic*, February 28, 1934, p. 57.
35   *Nation*, February 7, 1934, pp. 145–146.
36   *New Republic*, March 7, 1934, pp. 89–90.
37   *Nation*, April 11, 1934, p. 399.
38   Subtitled "Lobbying For the Home Market," May 9, 1934, pp. 353–356, and "Sowing Death Abroad," May 23, 1934, pp. 37–39.
39   Mitchell, "Sowing Death Abroad," p. 39. "Today our air force ranks fourth in size in the world, being exceeded only by the fleets of Soviet Russia, France and Japan." Mitchell, "Lobbying For the Home Market," p. 355.
40   Mitchell, "Sowing Death Abroad," p. 37.
41   *Nation*, May 16, 1934, p. 553.
42   *New Republic*, May 16, 1934, pp. 12–14.
43   *New Republic*, June 13, 1934, p. 131.
44   *New Republic*, July 4, 1934, pp. 194–195, for citations in following two paragraphs.
45   *Nation*, August 15, 1934, p. 174.
46   *New Republic*, September 12, 1934, p. 114.
47   *Nation*, November 7, 1934, p. 525.
48   *New Republic*, December 5, 1934, p. 85.
49   *New Republic*, November 28, 1934, p. 57; December 19, 1934, p. 149.
50   *New Republic*, November 14, 1934, p. 3.
51   *Nation*, November 21, 1934, p. 579.
52   *New Republic*, December 19, 1934, p. 149.

11

AMERICAN LIBERALS AND GERMAN

INTERNAL POLITICS, 1931–1933

THE LIBERAL PRESS OBSERVES
THE APPROACHING END OF AN ERA

THE month of September, 1931 was not only the occasion for the detonation of the crisis of Asia in Manchuria. It was an ominous one for Central Europe as well, culminating in the celebrated 8-7 vote of the World Court on the 5th, which sank for good the tentative customs union between Germany and Austria, proposed in March of the same year. Its obvious political flavor was discerned by the liberal press at once; they were not deceived by the pomposities of the legal intricacies of the case. They also had a clear idea of the crisis this brought to the German Republican order and the government of Heinrich Brüning, now in office since March, 1930, and fighting a desperate struggle to keep German political affairs in the hands of a moderate coalition. In the eyes of a number of astute liberal commentators, the customs union suggestion was the last sane recommendation leading to the finding of a way out of the lunacies visited upon Central Europe by the amateur map-makers of Versailles, and they viewed its sinking with much agitation. No one had condemned the barbed-wire politics and the economic feudalism resulting from the Treaties more extravagantly than the American liberals, and the ultimate ill-functioning assemblage of vassal states set up by them, with their military alliances and their confusing money, tariff, customs, passport and visa barriers to the movement of men and goods.

German politics had always drawn its share of space in the liberal weeklies, but the volume took a sharp upward climb from this time on, and by the time of the rise of Adolf Hitler to power, there were sometimes three or four articles and editorials a week. In some months there was more news and opinion on the German question in the *Nation* or *New Republic* than in three or four years of one of the literary monthly or quarterly publications of good reputation. As a source of information and liberal opinion on the issue of things German, they rank among the most influential of the time. At this stage the linking of disarmament and reparations issues to German distress was omnipresent, and the liberals had little doubt as to the cause for most of the German desperation; their nearly sole culprit was France. The three months after the final turning down of the customs union saw some of the strongest writing critical of French policy in Europe ever to see print.

THE FRENCH AS CENTRAL EUROPE'S MAIN TROUBLEMAKER

Two days before Mukden the *Nation* flamed at the French government of Pierre Laval, ruling with his second ministry since June, for being at the root of the halting of the customs union. In their view the Germans and Austrians never had a chance; "The cards were irretrievably stacked against them by France," and it went on to describe the French action as "a monstrous thing, utterly unworthy of the French people, entirely inimical to the restoration of economic sanity and of intellectual amity in Europe." The innocent French pose of detachment from the World Court decision it dismissed impatiently and expressed the conviction that French behavior was an "unanswerable argument for the revision of the postwar treaties at the earliest possible moment," because "if the present economic chaos in Europe goes on much longer those treaties are likely to be abrogated by revolutionary forces before which even France will tremble." [1]

Stories and editorials critical of French actions and designs abounded in the succeeding months, and on-the-spot reports from reputable writers and journalists, such as Harry W. Laidler, John Gunther, William Harlan Hale, John Elliott, and the *New Republic*'s own editor, Bruce Bliven, detouring from his trip to Russia, gained prominent attention. Gunther's *Nation* article, "French Gold and the Balkans," described a grandiose French plan to "isolate" Germany, and its current pressure on Austria and Hungary the latest step, preceded by the military alliances with Poland, Czechoslovakia, Rumania and Jugoslavia, apparently sealed with generous French funds. "Austria and Hungary must have credits. Only France can give them. Promises of loans are dangled as bait for complete political submission." Gunther called the Court action on the customs union "an outrageously political decision." Gunther, at this time also the Chicago *Daily News* Vienna correspondent, reported in addition the alarming bit that the Austrians had been promised a goodly French loan in return for renouncing the customs union, but then did not receive it. He concluded that the next move by France would be the pushing of a Franco-Soviet non-aggression pact and an attempt to "buy off" the Italians from any participation in the German determination to revise Versailles. What France was "seeking to purchase," said Gunther, was "perpetuation of the status quo." [2]

Somewhat stronger was a long *New Republic* editorial in mid-November, "Pax Gallica," which had much the same diagnosis as Gunther's. It charged that the French were exploiting the financial crisis as "their chance to obtain hegemony of Europe for a generation to come." It described a plan to infiltrate the directorates of German industrial and business enterprises with Frenchmen and dictate policy, and described this as an effort "to muscle into German business and industry as Capone used his gunmen to muscle into the Chicago beer trade." Its purpose was far-reaching: [3]

It is obvious that if French capitalists and French bankers succeed in gaining control of any considerable portion of Germany's economic machine, the French government will be in a position to bring great pressure upon every succeeding German government for years to come. This is the classic pattern of economic imperialism.

The political concessions the French sought were reported to be principally German acquiescence to "a loose confederation of Danubian states," Austria, Hungary, Jugoslavia, Bulgaria, Rumania and Czechoslovakia, to be molded into an economic unit, supported by French funds and French supervision. "In other words," the editorial declared, "France is proposing nothing less than the re-creation, in a greatly altered form, of the old Austro-Hungarian Empire," but under its control. Its object was to place "an insuperable barrier to German eastward expansion," but capable of being used as a threat to the Soviet as well. In addition to this major scheme, the Germans were being badgered to accept the 1931 Polish-German boundary as definitive, and to give up forever their "long cherished hopes for *Anschluss* with Austria."

The editorial considered it somewhat revealing to quote Marshal Philippe Pétain's declaration, while attending the Yorktown Sesquicentennial in October, 1931, to the effect that France would never consent to the elimination of the Polish Corridor on the grounds that "If the Polish Corridor were to fall into German hands, the Red Army would have a bridge through German territory into the heart of Europe, and all civilization would be at the hands of Communism." Its implication of lack of faith in the German state was very bald, but its revelation of the encompassing French hopes of dictating to both Germany and Russia was the desired effect.

Still another indication of the expansiveness of French dreams was a report that the Laval mission then in Germany included some persons who eagerly looked forward to the victory of Hitler and his National Socialists soon, on the expectation that it would be quickly realized by him that he could expect a very short tenure without French support, and thus would be inclined to make even swifter and more comprehensive concessions than the stubborn Brüning. That the French, in their excess of unreasoning nationalism, might "resort to some mad dangerous experiment such as this," caused the editorial to conclude with a shudder, although the late fall of 1931 was still a season of scant respect for Hitler or the future of his political ambitions. But Pétain's fear of Russian engulfment of Europe via Poland and Germany was considered even more preposterous.

The occasions of the meetings of Laval with President Hoover and Brüning, and the suspension of the Weimar constitution and the ruling of Germany by decree with the approval of the Reichstag, in October and November, brought forth another series of exasperated commentaries on French obtuseness. The *Nation* was ironic over the Laval-Briand mission to Germany to begin with, reminding the French that the cordial reception they received from President von Hindenburg was at the hands of a man the French had tagged as a "war criminal" some years before. The *New Republic* expressed much hope and enthusiasm for a future "thorough-going Franco-German *Anschluss*" based on a plan by a former German cabinet member, Professor Mendelssohn Bartholdy, which suggested a customs union among France, Germany, Belgium and Austria, with a bi-lingual government to handle their mutual foreign policy, national defense and customs affairs, "the germ of an ultimate European unity." [4]

But the actual turn of events did little to infuse confidence or suggest that any way out of the impasse would come from all the talk, and the French were blamed, while Laval and Hoover were conferring, for the failure to get anywhere. And the emergency decree of the German Chancellor, suspending constitutional guarantee of inviolability of personal liberty and private property and the whole spread of civil rights, evoked black views in both liberal weekly editorial columns. The *Nation* remarked that with all the talk of a possible Hitler or Communist coup, the way "had been smoothed" by such action; "It makes such a difference how respectable the people are who do these radical things," it commented sourly, even though "the precedent created may speedily come back to challenge the originators of this decree in a way they will not like." [5]

The ensuing sharp rise of Hitler's popularity and the National Socialist Party's amazing electoral success aroused new concern. The *New Republic* flatly announced, "To a very large degree, the weakness of the Brüning cabinet, and the strength of the 'Nazis,' are a result of French foreign policy." It warned the French that its persistence in "humiliating" the Brüning government was not only destroying German faith in their hope for "independence in foreign affairs," but that it was creating "Nazi" converts "by the thousands." Through late October and early November, this same journal editorially approved of the application of stern pressures on Laval and the other obdurate French nationalists in behalf of Germany by President Hoover, to the point of threatening to isolate them in reprisal for their sabotaging of European "stability," in itself "a major objective of American foreign policy."

Laval was not to be allowed to leave Washington without being asked to make some significant concession, even if it meant the weakening of the then "dominant position" of France in Europe. If he could not be "persuaded or compelled" to do so, then the future of the German Republic was exceedingly dim. The editorial called upon the President to note that Hjalmar Schacht's anti-reparations speeches were "enormously popular," and that the Germans could not be expected to pay reparations much longer as "war tribute." It went on to suggest that the French had already displayed their terror of possible isolation by "a solid Anglo-American-German grouping" at the time the moratorium had been announced by Mr. Hoover in June, and that now was the time to impress upon them the necessity for conciliatory acts; "Ever since the days of old M. Clemenceau, French diplomats have been aware that France, in the long run, cannot hope to hold the gains it made at the Paris Peace Conference without the friendship and support of Britain and America." The end of reparations and the permission of equality of armaments were suggested as basic concessions by the *New Republic*.[6]

But two weeks later it became clear to the *New Republic* that Laval had not come to the United States to make concessions but, in his view, "to obtain a pledge that America would not, henceforth, interfere with France in Europe," and to obtain an acknowledgment that France was "entitled to settle European problems in its own way." As much blame was placed on Hoover as upon Laval; "Mr. Hoover, in his conversations with M. Laval, had an opportunity to use the influence of the United States on the side of political stability and moderation in Europe, and blithely kicked it away." Nevertheless, Laval and the French were credited with winning a "hollow victory," and would find it exceedingly difficult to use their power to any real advantage; "Unless it [France] is hardheaded enough to be satisfied with the success of prestige and to turn about and make real and rapid progress toward appeasement, any real recovery of Europe is postponed." The French were warned in addition that the obvious unhappiness in Berlin and London with the outcome of the Hoover-Laval talks was an ominous consequence, and grounds for caution; "French policy is daily pushing Germany nearer to an explosion, which, if it occurs, will wreck all hope of Europe's economic recovery for years to come." [7]

The year closed out in a welter of hostile arraignments of the French, the most violent of which was a *Nation* editorial blast in December upon the riotous breakup of a Paris peace meeting November 27, attended by several distinguished international delegates, including Viscount Cecil of England and Alanson B. Houghton of the United States, accompanied, as the editorial noted, by "the unanimous condonation of this public rowdyism and bad manners by the French press, the legal and police authorities, and the government"; [8]

It will make plain to intelligent men everywhere that it is France that blocks the way both to peace and to economic sanity in the world; we see clearly the lengths to which its officialdom is willing to go even to stop criticism of its policies. It will further open the eyes of Americans to the present French determination to rule Europe by force, to cling to a military dictatorship far more dangerous than any ambitions attributed to the German militarists.

The *Nation* also chided Professor Charles Rist, among other Frenchmen, for opposing "immediate and adequate relief from reparations" for the Brüning government, which was now admitted to be acting in open defiance of a considerable section of the German people by acceding to this policy; "To what madness has their nationalism reduced the French!" exclaimed a 1931 Christmas Week editorial.[9] The *New Republic* chose to ruminate on the impatience of the MacDonald government with all this French biceps-flexing, and British attempts to move the Hoover Administration to their side and away from the French in this season of exasperation.[10] Meanwhile many American liberals had become reconciled to Brüning's "dictatorship of the moderates," as an alternative more desirable than civil war, which at this stage was considered very likely between the Right opposition and the Socialists and/or the Communists.

EARLY EYEWITNESS COMMENTS

ON HITLER AND GERMAN POLITICS

Both liberal weeklies profited from extended reports from Germany on conditions, activities and prospects in the agitated autumn of 1931, but these voices were not very much in tune, except on one or two issues. In general the sympathies of these reporters and travellers were with the Social Democrat forces, in the bewildering collection of shadings which went to make up the German political spectrum. And there also was some agreement as to the temporary preferability of the Brüning "dictatorship" of the moment, however its non-constitutional base exasperated them. Laidler, in his commentary "German Socialism in the Balance," in the *Nation*, admitted the German Social Democrats were caught in a "grim situation"; "Slowly but steadily the Social Democrats, the great supporters of the German republic, are losing votes to both the right and left radicals," he announced. They were supporting Brüning against their better instincts out of fear that to desert him would precipitate the government "into the arms of Hitler." He noted that it was widely admitted that Brüning's government was already a dictatorship, ruling through emergency decrees issued without Reichstag support, and that on top of this, press censorship and other acts had reduced German parliamentary life to a "caricature." But with all the distress, Laidler felt that conditions were better politically in Germany than in Italy, Hungary, Poland, Jugoslavia and Finland, all in the grips of "fascist terrorism," in his view. "German Socialists have a grave responsibility to contest every step in the further advance of fascism," but cooperation with the Communists was out of the question, because the German Communists were at the mercy of "dictation from Moscow based largely on the needs of the Russian Communists at any given moment." [11]

Bliven, on his way through to the Soviet Union, sent home a fearfully depressing report, and later remarked joyfully on how much better he felt on arriving in Russia, which he contrasted with Germany as day and night. His analysis was in the current Marxian vein; but there was a bleak note of foreboding over the National Socialist movement and Hitler, a movement whose philosophy was "madness" and utterly without a plan for resuscitating the country's feeble economy. He dwelled on the Hitlerites as illegal revolutionaries, yet was obviously nonplussed by their steadily heavier vote totals in regular, unspectacular elections. The quality which Germans saw in this movement and its leader escaped him completely. Bliven was convinced that Hitler was recruiting German youth for an immediate "hopeless, suicidal war" with both Poland and France simultaneously, if not for another revolutionary attempt to uproot Brüning in the manner of the 1923 Putsch.[12]

Hale, whose work appeared during the ensuing decade in many of the most respected periodicals in America, reported to the *Nation* in the same week of November that the German economy was on the verge of collapse in two weeks should the foreign capital propping it up be withdrawn. Germany was "isolated in the midst of a hopelessly nationalist Europe," almost entirely the work of the French, who were achieving an objective not too much appreciated, the maturing of a rich harvest of militant German nationalist hate, even from the German Communists. "The Germans are not deceived," Hale pointed out; "They know perfectly well that French policy demands a supine Germany." And in his opinion, the chief fear of a Communist Germany was that "The new order would carry with it the threat of a war to the end with France." Thus Bliven was expecting Hitler to go to war with France in short order, while Hale felt such a war was first on the agenda of the German Communists, should they win.[13]

Michael Farbman, the author of a very sympathetic book on the Russian Communist Five Year Plan, in his Berlin report shared Bliven's marked distaste for the Hitlerian group, and favored the Marxian interpretation of the "Nazis" as the temporary holding company for German capitalists, and little more than tools of the industrialists and powerful nationalist figures, such as Alfred Hugenberg.[14] But the report which disclosed the most careful and searching analysis was that of Elliott, also from Berlin. "Brüning governs with dictatorial powers far exceeding anything that Bismarck ever had at the zenith of his fame and success," was Elliott's conclusion, adding that Germany was worse off than at any time since Jena, if not since the Thirty Years' War. An unemployment figure close to 7 million was officially admitted, while the streets of Berlin were filled with people hawking matches and shoestrings, begging for money, playing violins and singing in apartment courtyards, and collecting old clothes. He freely predicted Hitler would win the next election, and that the Socialists were draining away in large numbers to the Communists. In the political nightmare, the liberals were still supporting the emergency Brüning dictatorship, hoping that it would produce "a clear program of reconstruction," but nearly everyone was in agreement "on the necessity of an ultimate revision of the Reich's frontiers on the East." But Elliott did not believe a government "controlled in part by Hitlerites" would go to war with any nation.[15]

To add to the complex of amorphous and half-formed views on the political bewilderment of Germany there was the editorial opinion on Hitler, repeated in substance in both weeklies, to the effect that he was a vainglorious mountebank suffering from delusions of grandeur, pushed into prominence mostly by blind French obduracy toward Germany.[16] On other occasions there were editorial allegations that he was a product of shadowy foreign financiers, one of the *Nation's* favorite gambits for a while in 1931, and a device picked up later by Hitler to describe the backing behind his enemies. It was disconcerting for them to support the justice of Germany's strident protests against reparations, when this stand placed them in the same stall with the vociferous and detested "Nazis," who were pledged to do something about it of more substance than mere vocal remonstration, namely, outright repudiation. Here the editorial position snagged, and the till then completely frustrated action by "negotiation" for such a settlement was once more brought to the front as a proper method of ending this galling obligation. The *Nation* agreed with Hitler when he declared the defeat of the customs union was "catastrophic," as well as asserting that "his promise to pay Germany's commercial debts while ceasing the payment of reparations has behind it justice and logic," [17]

But the aftermath of a German-declared end to reparations without negotiation threatens an upheaval likely to engulf all Europe in violence and to delay economic recovery. And even the fulfillment of Hitler's rosy pledges, of which there is no guaranty, would be a dear price for the enslavement of the German people under a reactionary, bombastic, anti-Semitic militaristic dictatorship.

This editorial pronouncement of December 16, 1931, at a time when few liberals took Hitler seriously and were quite secure in their feeling that a Socialist-Communist coalition would soon head the National Socialists off, is a concise view which summarizes editorial judgment on the Hitler regime, in the making and in power, for the next ten years. But to attempt to place the onus on Germans for ending the reparations question without "negotiation" had an anticlimactic flavor, when racked against all that had been written since Versailles about the French obstinacy toward any negotiation. Thus another no-man's-land of inaction had matured; an area of conflict where the defenders of the status quo refused to listen to any suggestion for redress short of violence, accompanied by shudders of respectability when the exasperated threatened to resort to just that.

But Hitler was not in power yet, and there was still time for supplementary pleas for a conference-table settlement involving both reparations and debts as a parcel. By mid-1932, as it grew more apparent that no one, and least of all the French, was going to suggest a comprehensive program of mutual conciliation on the interlaced debt, reparations and armament questions at the Lausanne and Geneva conferences, liberal editors and correspondents grew steadily more passive toward the situation in Germany, as the ultimate victory of Hitler and National Socialism cast a larger shadow week by week. In a vague way they hoped that Brüning's alliance of Catholic Centrists and Social Democrats might yet hold off the "Nazi" surge, strengthened by Anglo-Franco-American concessions.[18] As this possibility waned, they accepted the successively sterner Papen and Schleicher governments with grave reservations, dreading the far more dynamic Hitler movement and hoping against hope for the victory of a left-of-center element in German national affairs. During this last year of Germany without Hitler, the American liberal voice wavered but little in its championing revision of the wartime treaties, concessions to Germany, and the application of brakes on French, and to some extent British, ambitions in the politics of Central Europe. But nothing along such lines was done. With the entrance of the National Socialists and the taking of unilateral steps to correct nearly fifteen years of inaction, the American liberal's general approval of treaty reform modulated to a whisper. By 1934, a thread of hostility had re-appeared, rapidly growing into a wide swath of reaction to any German attempts to alter the status quo.

LIBERALS PURSUE
THE GERMAN POLITICAL SERPENTINE
IN THE LAST YEAR BEFORE HITLER

Through January and February, 1932, the *Nation* kept up an almost weekly fire on the reparations and debt questions, accepted the German protest that they could no longer pay, and urged the Hoover Administration to consider sympathetically the cancellation of all the international financial obligations inherited from the War.[19] Great concern was expressed that otherwise the French nationalists such as Laval and Tardieu would propose a new crushing of Germany and a new Ruhr occupation, sure to ignite a German nationalist reaction, the sweeping out of the moderates, and much bloodshed.[20]

Both journals breathed editorial sighs of relief when the March 13 presidential election returned Hindenburg, which was interpreted as a decision to uphold Brüning. Even more delight and comfort were taken from Hindenburg's triumph in the April 10 runoff, but there was an air of the calm before the hurricane, since it was not lost on either that the Nazis had doubled their vote since 1930, and that Brüning, by delaying the adoption of a vigorous protest attitude toward reparations until this late hour, now lagged behind all other political groups in Germany on this issue.[21] "Fascism is not to be conquered by popular elections," warned the *New Republic;* "It will flourish so long as it is nurtured by desperate economic and social conditions." [22]

When Brüning suppressed Hitler's S.A. Brownshirt organization three days after Hindenburg's April victory, under strong pressure from the Socialists,[23] the first major stumble toward defeat took place, and the finishing touch was the abortive attempt at land redistribution in Prussia. But American liberal comment credited a promised tough foreign policy for Hitler's alarming local election victories in May. Said the *New Republic,* "While there is reason to believe that Hitler is far less anti-French than he pretends, and is not at all likely to tear up the Treaty of Versailles and throw it into the Rhine, the French conservatives have used him as a bogeyman so long that it is impossible to debamboozle the [German] voters, even if anyone wished to do so; the result is likely to be a large increase in the vote of the Right parties." The *Nation,* however, thought that Brüning and Hitler had "virtually identical" policies toward reparations by now. [24]

It is instructive to note that the Communists did not wait for Hitler to describe Germany as a "Fascist dictatorship." The Red press referred to the Brüning government as such many times two years and more before the advent of Hitler, and the German Communist leader Ernst Thaelmann wrote an extensive article on this subject for the American Communist audience in March of 1931. Thus the critics of National Socialism had a ready-made propaganda even before the latter emerged as the dominant force, as well as the contraction "Nazi" as an identification, also brought to popular use by Communist and Socialist journalism, as precise a label as the epithet "Commie" when used against the Red partisans. Thaelmann, a passionate defender of Russia, issued calls for violence against Brüning's "Fascist dictatorship" by the KPD, and Brüning by all odds was the favorite German political demon of Germany's Communists throughout the period.[25]

Great shock was expressed when the Brüning government abruptly fell on May 30, and the succession of Franz von Papen and his "reactionary regime of aristocrats, big businessmen and militarists" [26] was roundly condemned. The month of June saw article after article raking over the ashes; "Having sown the wind in Germany, the Allies (and France most of all) must now reap the whirlwind," grimly declared the *New Republic;* "the days of the Weimar Constitition are numbered." [27] Already the fact that Brüning and his predecessors had ruled via scores of decrees and had mothballed the constitution for substantial periods of time was being consigned to forgetfulness.[28] The *Nation,* in its "The German Republic Totters," preferred to recapitulate the stresses of its exasperating foreign obstacles and to apologize for the situation: [29]

. . . one must never lose sight of what has been going on in Germany during these crucial years: the economic distress, the sense of infinite wrong to Germany by the Treaty of Versailles; the false accusation of sole responsibility for the War; the Ruhr invasion; the frightful loss of wealth due both to the War and the inflation, and other factors. All these incidents, plus the weakness of the government, the failure to carry the revolution through with vigor, and the survival of many militarists and monarchists, are today why the German Republic totters.

Stories on internal German politics poured into the liberal press all summer, including reports that widespread disorder instigated by the "Nazis" was upsetting the country, involving outrages against Jews and the killing of Communists in street fights.[30] The failure of Papen to arrange a majority coalition in the Reichstag after the July 31 election and its dissolution in September kept affairs in a constant state of agitation and unrest, with repeated hopes that Hitler could be staved off by some political magic.[31] Over and over the editorials lamented the inability of the two "socialist" parties to "unite for a common goal," to block both Hitler and Papen's "monocle" government.[32] But the unsettling development on the foreign scene was the bleak challenge of Papen's minister of defense, General von Schleicher, threatening to push German rearmament if the other nations did not reduce the strength of their military and naval forces in compliance with the pledges given to the German delegation at the Paris peace conference.[33] The *Nation* was not overly sympathetic with Schleicher, but agreed in general as to the justice of the case, and indicted the French again: [34]

How derelict the League has been in performing this one of its "first duties" is all too tragically apparent. At every turn, disarmament has been sabotaged by the Powers controlling the League, particularly by France. If the change in German policy now means the end of the world disarmament effort, as seems probable, these Powers must bear their full share of the blame. Moreover, if they now retrace those "first steps" taken at the peace conference which were to lead to general disarmament, they will in effect be admitting that they never really intended to disarm, that they were simply using the pledge as a means of disguising their subjugation of Germany, and that they were finally giving in only because their hypocritical gesture at Versailles had been exposed.

But it was not expected that the French would consent, in view of the importance of French military strength as the glue holding the alliances with the succession states together; and that none of them would stand by and watch the Germans gain military equality, since that would be the end of the whole Versailles system. The *Nation* did not know what the French would do if the Germans went ahead with military enlargement on their own initiative, but they were quite sure the French "would think twice" before attempting another reprisal in the form of an occupation along the lines of that of 1923. Their main hope was that Britain's MacDonald and French figures such as Herriot and Leon Blum could still bring about disarmament.

Gunther's dispatch, "Danube Blues," published in the same journal two weeks later, exceeded the editorial heat of condemnation of the French, and the British as well, for the dolorous state of Central Europe; [35]

Having made an unfortunate omelette out of Central Europe, the so-called Great Powers are seeking to retrieve whole eggs from the mess. The badly cracked states of Austria, Hungary, Rumania, and so on are to be carefully pasted together again, in order to encourage them in the belief that they are really nations and to satisfy British financial and French political desires. The Powers made Central Europe what it is today, at Versailles, at St. Germain, and at Trianon. . . .

Gunther was vehement in his declaration that only the revival of Germany would right that tottering region, and that the approximately one per cent imports of Britain and France from the whole region of Central European Danubia hardly entitled them to exert such ponderous influence; "The spectacle of France and Britain trying to freeze Germany out of a Danube scheme is laughable." He was willing to concede the formidable Anglo-French financial interests in Central Europe, but "What one must hope for in the post-Lausanne negotiations is willingness by the French to admit Germany's commercial supremacy."

Woeful feature stories on the German scene, showing persistently strong strains of sympathy, continued to appear through the last few months of the much-pruned Weimar era. H. N. Brailsford and Lewis Mumford, a summer visitor in Germany, in the *New Republic,* lamented the striking debility of the Social Democrats and their failure to resolve the "class struggle" favorably, as had the Bolsheviki in Russia in 1920–21, with the result that hostile elements were succeeding in taking the initiative and promising to undo most of what had been put together so painfully since 1918, especially parliamentary democracy. Their tributes to German brains and ability were flattering, and their belief in Germany's capacity for instituting a vigorous collectivist society deep, but the shadow of the political deadlock of the moment depressed both. Brailsford announced, "A great nation, to which most of us look up as the possessor of the most highly trained intelligence in Europe, seems to find democracy an unworkable system," while placing most of the blame on her late enemies for the exasperation of the moment.[36] Mumford too was deeply troubled, but concluded that "At the bottom, in Germany, there is sanity and strength." [37]

In the *Nation,* Emil Ludwig and an Oberlin professor, Karl Frederick Geiser, were somewhat less hostile to Hitler. Ludwig also blamed "the shortsightedness of the peacemakers of Paris" for Germany's misfortunes, and declared that a National Socialist government would be preferable to the Papen regime. "This National Socialist movement has no real leaders, but its roots lie deep in the nation," Ludwig told his readers. He was convinced that in time "the socialistic or more modern sections of its program" would take precedence over and survive its "medieval" sections.[38] Professor Geiser also stressed Hitlerism as a "popular movement" and "a functional disorder in the heart of Europe." Hitler was a reflector of "the misery of all classes," which he understood profoundly and knew how "to express in domestic form," even though Geiser conceded that some members of Hitler's party had weakened it by excessive "acts of terrorism." [39]

There was an obvious conflict between these views and editorial opinion, since the position taken over and over up to now had conceded that Hitler in power would be a planetary catastrophe,[40] but in one way it reflected the feeling that he had little or no chance to win anyway. After the Communists precipitated a lack of confidence vote against von Papen in September, 1932, thus bringing about dissolution of the Reichstag and another election set for November 6,[41] it was expected that the "Nazis" would do poorly. An anonymous columnist in the *Nation* in October called Hitler a "has-been," and declared that he would have to take over via military overthrow, else he would have to confess himself "the most disastrous flop in postwar history," [42] while the fact that the "Nazis" lost some seats in the election compelled the *Nation* to suggest rather confidently on November 16, "The strength of the National Socialists is now definitely waning." [43] A good part of this confidence was wishful thinking, a product of the persistent hope that some kind of understanding among German leftists would emerge out of the confusion strong enough to halt the decay of Social Democrat strength and contain Hitler and replace the Papen-Schleicher forces. As the *New Republic* put it editorially, "If the process of mutual toleration between Socialists and Communists so auspiciously begun during the last campaign progresses during the next two months, it should be possible to confront the combined Fascist and Junker attack with a more powerful opposition than it has ever met before." [44]

Confusion and contradiction marked the liberal trail through the last ten weeks before the accession of Hitler, featured by consternation over Germany's internal politics, and mixed views on persisting German pressure against reparations, and for rearmament and a relaxation of world tariffs and trade restrictions which were keeping German products out of foreign countries. Von Papen's insistence on the latter the *New Republic* described as "the restatement of an economic truism;" [45] "no nation ever made net capital payments to others, whether of interest or principal, except by means of a net excess of exports over imports, visible and invisible." But the editorial position on German rearmanent was beginning to waver ever so slightly; it was now becoming suspected that German desires were for unilateral rearming. There was also a heavy feeling of helplessness, brought on by the long-standing Anglo-French temporizing. The *Nation*'s incognito column "Behind the Cables" concluded that the present crumbling of the barriers set against Germany should have been expected; "that Germany would sooner or later split the disarmament racket wide open must have been obvious to a child." [46] But others saw a new German army projected in every act of the Papen government, and especially in the announcement that vast training camps for young men for the intensive propagation of sports, gymnastics and general physical fitness were to be established shortly.[47]

Still, the increasing suspicion of Germany was insufficient to cancel out the years of bitter criticism of the French at this point. Herriot's "disarmament" plan of November, 1932 was flayed by the *Nation* as "simply another bold attempt on the part of France to extend its political control over continental Europe," and the German criticism was supported. The "international army" which Herriot proposed be placed under the authority of the League was seen at once to be a tool of the will of the majority of the League Council; "France and its satellites now dominate the League and therefore, under the Herriot scheme, would have virtual command of the international army. History records no bid for power more audacious. . . ." [48] "Behind the Cables" for November 30, 1932, seemed to sum up a substantial part of liberal opinion as of this date on the Franco-German question: "France has to face the worst problem in the world, that of adjusting itself to what eventually must be permanent inferiority to Germany." [49]

But the liberals desperately hoped that the dominant Germany which they expected to see emerging soon would be a decidedly leftist one. The fear and detestation of Hitler and the "Nazis" was reflected constantly, occasionally lighted by casual deprecations of his threat, and then quickly dispersed by newer expressions of agitation. The mercurial path traced by liberal opinion of National Socialism in the two years prior to Hitler's accession is one of dizzying fluctuations. The fear of his victory in the December 6, 1932, election elicited a disturbed *Nation* call, "Whatever the difficulties of the situation, there should be no compromise with Hitler. His becoming

Chancellor could only be a catastrophe for democratic Germany." [50] In fact this alternative even forced this journal to find previously undetected virtues in von Schleicher upon his replacement of Papen as the new Chancellor of the German Republic, despite the depressing realization that a military man of the old school had risen to power who had already declared in no uncertain terms that Germany was going to rearm, and promptly. This was viewed as another opportunity to read a reproachful text to Germany's former conquerors; "Thus do we see again how well it pays to go to war to make a people democratic and establish democracy throughout the world." [51]

But the *Nation* could not restrain the impulse to make one more corrosive comment on Hitler and his refusal to become a coalition Chancellor, one of the prodigious miscalculations of this kind for which it became noted in later years. In a bitter attack it ridiculed him as a weak vacillator, and cawed, "No Napoleon here—just a confused and weak demagogue in the process of being deflated. He now declares that he will be Chancellor within four months. But he has told his army of their impending victory so often this need alarm no one." [52] The surprise and shock when his prediction materialized in advance reflected their poorness at prognostication, but the vials of hate and denunciation were not tipped over until a complete takeover occurred just about the time Hitler had predicted his assumption of power would occur. From that time on, the liberal press, with occasional lapses, presented a common front of implacable hostility against National Socialist Germany which was exceeded in venom only by the *New Masses, The Communist* and the *Daily Worker.* From the spring of 1933 until the late summer of 1939, despite the many conflicts which separated the American liberal and Communist press on the subject of Hitler Germany, there was a community of agreement which made these two ideological impulses quite indistinguishable.

THE EVALUATION OF THE LITERATURE
ON GERMANY IN THE CRISIS PERIOD

The preliminary rumbles of the German political explosion loosed a steadily increasing volume of literature on Germany in the year before Hitler's absorption of total power. The liberal weeklies gave it the best review coverage of any literary medium in America short of the New York daily press. There were enough differences of opinion in this early dozen or so publications to provide sufficient confusion for a decade, quite apart from the tone of the prodigious flow of books on Germany after the "Nazis" were entrenched, which from that time on was uniformly hostile and quite intemperate, often out-matching the propaganda of "Nazism" in the field of invective. But the earlier vintage contained an attitude of trembling hesitancy and indecision, due to the characteristic fluidity of the German political scene. Only on Hitler was there some semblance of agreement, and here most of the observers were impressively wrong.

Dorothy Thompson wrote the first account which got any attention aimed at demolishing Hitler, *I Saw Hitler!*, closely followed by *Hitlerism: The Iron Fist in Germany*, by Louis L. Snyder, later a professor of history at City College of New York, who used the pseudonym "Nordicus." They were reviewed in the same issue of both the *Nation* and the *New Republic* the first week of April, 1932, by Mauritz Hallgren in the former, and by Mary Heaton Vorse, a contributing editor to the *New Masses*, in the latter. Hallgren was unhappy with both, on the grounds that they were excessively super-ficial, although he subscribed to both authors' contempt for Hitler. He did not know the author of *Hitlerism*, suggesting it was written by a woman on the basis of its excited and sometimes hysterical prose, and what he considered its excessive use of exclamation points. Mrs. Vorse approved both very warmly, and thought Miss Thompson had spoken a final word when the latter announced that she had de-cided in the first fifty seconds after seeing Hitler that he would never be dictator of Germany, as well as seconding the determined opinion of both authors that the "Nazis" were all impractical madmen.[53]

Journalistic accounts of Germany, which grew to mountainous proportions in the following decade, made their appearance in the form of interpretative studies by H. R. Knickerbocker, *The German Crisis;* Edgar Ansel Mowrer, *Germany Puts the Clock Back;* and Oswald Garrison Villard, *The German Phoenix*, along with George N. Shuster's *The German Crisis*, the Frenchman Pierre Vienot's *Is Germany Finished?*, two searching pamphlets by Leon Trotsky, and another by Paul Douglas, *The Economic Dilemma of Politics*, which included some serious words on the German debt situation. Shuster was reviewed by Quincy Howe, Knickerbocker by Mrs. Vorse, and the others by unidentified persons, although one of the Trotsky anal-yses was examined in the *New Republic* by Herman Simpson.[54] It was evident by the impatience shown in most of these summaries that editorial opinion which stressed the influence of the treaties on Germany was not too widely shared, and the Marxian view as pre-sented by Trotsky came closer to the point. That much exasperation with German Social Democracy existed was no longer a secret, and the Trotskyite position that a civil war was preferable to letting Hitler take over the reins was not considered improper. For such purposes Trotsky had suggested a joining of the Communist and Social Democrat forces in Germany, and the calling in of the Russian

Red Army as an emergency intervention factor if necessary. He argued this in both *Germany: The Key to the International Situation* and *What Next? Vital Questions for the German Proletariat*.[55]

Thus the readers had another source of opinion on the German question supplied by these reviews. The literature itself was uniformly hostile to the Hitlerians, but what was to be done about preventing them from taking over elicited a bewildering confusion. After March, 1933, and for almost two years, those who believed that a civil war should have been waged against him from the start had the liberal journals mostly to themselves, during which time the Social Democrats were accused of muddying the scene with ersatz Marxism and failing to collaborate with the German Communists for such purposes. For nearly two years, repeated stories of a vast underground Communist revolution in the making tripped across the pages of the liberal press, eventually petering out after conscription was restored in March, 1935 and after the Saar voted overwhelmingly to return to the Reich. But in this budding period of Popular Frontism, it was usually ignored that as Trotsky had called so urgently for civil war, he had flailed the KPD fully as severely as he had the Social Democrats, for adopting the view that Hitler should be allowed to take over and then engineer a Communist Germany after "Nazism" had been allowed to run its course. At this stage no one in the liberal left had the slightest faith in a centrist and non-Marxian solution to the grievous state of Germany's internal political impasse.

Thus, generally speaking, the liberal journals as of 1932 were badly torn by two tendencies—the impulse to defend Germany for much of its current conduct as the natural reaction to the indignities, repressions and humiliations suffered since 1918, and at the same time sponsoring a rising note of complaint, generously influenced by Marxian and pro-Russian tendencies, to castigate those who were doing the most toward changing Germany's relations with the rest of Europe. This conflict was evident month after month. Thus, in April, 1932 the *Nation* chose to present a biographical sketch of Hitler by the Russian Communist Karl Radek as an admirable portrait, even though it was an unmixed attack in fulminating language describing the Nazi leader as an "insane quack" and his whole program "social balderdash," backed only by steely-eyed "bank magnates and leaders of the metal trusts," pushing for a program to enslave the labor movement and give German capitalism another lease on life.[56] It was fully as extravagant as anything ever written by a "Nazi" about their favorite enemies, yet the *Nation* felt no obligation as a professed voice of moderation to seek elements of truth regardless of the source.

On the other hand, a few months later, both the *Nation* and *New Republic* printed hot editorials chiding the French press and the

British journalist H. Wickham Steed for their peevish commentaries upon the recently published correspondence and memoirs of Gustav Stresemann. Their discovery that Stresemann, the famous foreign minister of the 20's, had acted in Germany's interests instead of those of France and Britain was no reason for their childish anger and aspersions on his character. The *Nation* admonished, "These observers forget that there has never been any secret as to the ultimate goals of German foreign policy. Stresemann was simply using the tactics employed by every diplomat in trying to advance what he considered the best interests of his country," while the *New Republic,* noting the recent French criticism of Briand for not having been sufficiently pro-French, concluded, "Are the French really logical? Sometimes it seems doubtful, for they fail to remember their proverb: 'Ce qui est bon à prendre est bon à rendre,' which may be put down in English, as 'What is sauce for the goose is sauce for the gander.' "[57]

But the approach of Hitler and other determined nationalists who promised a number of much more rapid moves toward separating Germany from the remainder of the tangle of nagging grievances accumulated since 1918 filled these essentially liberal friends of Germany with foreboding, and the major irritant was not obscure; the warm wind of sympathy for the Germans was encountering the Soviet glacier. The suspicion of immediate trouble between a nationalist Germany seeking to recover its historic Central-East European lands and interests and influence, and the new order in Russia, for which liberals had formed a steadily increasing affection since 1919, soon was to precipitate this tugging of conflicting sympathies. The victory of the uncompromising anti-Soviet National Socialists cleared the deck in a matter of hours. Material sympathetic to objectives dear to German hearts disappeared from liberal pages in rapid order, to be replaced by an attitude as frigid as liquid helium. Within a few months a thaw toward French aspirations spread noticeably, castigations of Versailles subsided markedly, and comprehensive suspicion of German motives became the order of the day. The expansion of Germany under the auspices of Hitler ranked last on the liberal agenda of future hopes, and disappeared entirely after the fierce campaign against the German Communists, Socialists, liberals, pacifists and Jews got under way. But the stiff counter-attack by the Communists set the tone of the anti-Hitler crusade which materialized in the ranks of American liberals, at least.

What might have been Germany's foreign policy under a Socialist or Communist regime instead of Hitler's nationalists beginning in 1933 will probably always be of speculative interest. Its tenure would undoubtedly have been brief if it had followed the policies down to 1933, given the German unhappiness, unrest, distress and misery in that depression year. Whether the American liberals would have followed a Socialist or Communist Germany in a policy which also ended in war with Britain and France in the West and Poland and Russia in the East will never be known. And if a Communist Germany had linked up promptly with Russia and precipitated a showdown with France and Britain even earlier than 1939, it would have posed an even tougher choice. There is no doubt that Hitler's coming ended all deliberation as to the posting of future affections; America's liberals in large part snapped back in one year from a dozen of intensive revisionism. By 1935, with a number of exceptions and occasional atavisms, there was little evidence that American liberalism had ever championed the attainment of German goals which were now coming into realization under the most hated of sponsors. But Versailles as the hatchery of the German scourge of the Hitler movement remained in the background always; no one could conjure it away.

LAST ACT: JUDGMENTS AND PRONOUNCEMENTS IN THE FINAL WEEKS OF WEIMAR

On November 19, 1932 the London *Daily Herald* published a piece by Harold J. Laski titled "Hitler: Just a Figurehead," which dismissed the National Socialist leader with a shrug, called him "a myth without permanent foundation," and little more than a front for powerful German business, financial, commercial and national interests. This was in large part the verdict of American liberals as well, through the nearly two months of the regime of Kurt von Schleicher, ending with the ascendancy of Hitler as Chancellor on January 30, 1933, with a mixed Nationalist and National Socialist cabinet. No one expected him to forge out in front as long as men like Papen and Schleicher were available, and his emergence on this occasion was somewhat of a shock. The *New Republic* in its February 8 editorial, "Hitler Wins," rebounded rapidly, and discounted him largely by pointing to the fact that his cabinet, with only three of his own party in it, was really more "truly representative of Junkerdom at its worst," surely in the control of a lopsided coalition of Hugenberg-Papen-Schleicher figures. This unsettled situation was not considered grounds for excusing the indecision and wavering of the "labor movement," with both Communists and Social Democrats doing nothing but "assuming an attitude of watchful waiting." "Unity of action by labor, so urgently needed in this catastrophe, seems as far away as ever," it reported; "According to present indications the German labor movement will take Fascist dictatorship on the chin." [58]

A week later the *New Republic* editors were not so sure. Now they were impressed by the close similarities of Hitler's rise to Mussolini's, accompanying the same heterogeneous factors, and which were one by one dropped until only the Fascisti remained. It was now conceded that a similar series of events would happen in Germany. His invocation of a stiff censorship and the ruthless suppression of a large number of Social Democrat and Communist newspapers was the immediate source of apprehension. The foreign policy indications were an even more striking resemblance to Mussolini, however, which led to the concluding observation, "The logic of the situation leads to a new block with these Fascist states at the center, in opposition to France and the Little Entente. The traditional European balance of power is by way of being restored." [59]

The same issue contained the results of a lengthy interview between the well-known journalist H. V. Kaltenborn and Hitler, which contained lengthy passages indicating the "Nazi" leader was an astute and intelligent politician, possessing, according to Kaltenborn, "a much sounder social and economic philosophy in private conversation" than when speaking in public, on which occasions Kaltenborn considered him to be indulging in his prodigious talent for appealing to "the mob mind" with oratorical exaggeration and popularization stunts. As to political theory, he quoted Hitler as asserting,[60]

"Europe cannot maintain itself riding the uncertain currents of democracy. Europe must have authoritarian government. . . . The form which this authority takes may differ. But parliamentarism is not native to us and doesn't belong to our traditions. Yet because the parliamentary system has not functioned we cannot substitute brute force. Bayonets alone will not sustain any government for any length of time. To be viable a government must have the support of the masses. A dictatorship cannot be established in a vacuum. Any government that does not derive its strength from the people will fail the moment it confronts a crisis. The soldier and the policeman do not constitute the substance of a state. Yet dictatorship is justified if the people declare their confidence in one man and ask him to lead."

In a six-column report on his talk, Kaltenborn refrained from abuse of Hitler, but he subscribed in the end to the opinion then current among the liberals that Hitler had "lost prestige" prior to becoming Chancellor, and that in the ensuing Reichstag elections, on March 5, no matter what the result, there was to be little fear that he would have the opportunity "to establish his long-heralded Drittes Reich."

So the uneasy wishful thinking continued up to the very moment of the sensational Reichstag fire and the March 5 elections, by which time a majestic somersault was in order. The *Nation* in February watched the situation unfold with the same mixture of concern and detachment, uncertain of the full meaning to Germany but convinced that at the rate of development the German working class would "without question be reduced to a state of servitude of a sort unknown to modern industrial history." This was largely based on contemplation of Hitler's promise of a system of compulsory labor service and its likely effects on the big Marxist labor unions. The admission that no general strike was in the offing, and that the Socialists and Communists and their press had already submitted "with only a feeble murmur of protest," helped to underscore the gravity of the situation.[61] But no attention was devoted to what Germany's nearly seven millions out of work thought of the prospect. There was no hostility expressed toward the idea of compulsory labor service as such, only to its introduction "in a society based on the profit system."

The last issue of both weeklies, before the news of the fire and the repressions that followed it burst upon the startled world, contained ominous editorials which acknowledged that government by decree and suppression of criticism and opposition had already gained great headway locally in the country.[62] But restraint gradually evaporated upon receipt of the report on the most famous conflagration of the decade, followed by the outlawing of the Communist party of Germany and the feverish program of political vengeance on the part of the "Nazis," along with their hunt for Socialists, pacifists, liberals, and others, including some Jews. The New York *Herald Tribune* Berlin correspondent John Elliott's March 8 report to the *Nation* on the election, not printed until three weeks later, was written in a spirit of detachment already utterly out of style in the liberal press;[63]

Adolf Hitler on March 5 won the greatest parliamentary victory in German political history. An amazingly brilliant propaganda campaign and a well-nigh complete repression of the two principal opposition parties, the Socialist and the Communist, in part explain Hitler's triumph, but only in part. For the election, if not fair, was at least free. The Nazi leader's victory was the result of the greatest nationalist uprising in Germany since General Yorck called the German nation to arms against Napoleon in the early winter of 1813. If the elections had been held under a system like England's instead of the method of proportional representation that permits minority opinion to be registered, Hitler would have had an even more overwhelming majority than Ramsay MacDonald in Great Britain after the elections of the autumn of 1931. However vehemently liberals throughout the world may detest Hitler's political tenets and his philosophy, they are bound to recognize that he has the highest credentials any statesman can have—the mandate of his people.

Nothing quite like this ever appeared again in the liberal press on the subject of Hitler. Its effect had already been cancelled out by three weeks of vociferous attacks on him for his party's handling of the Marxist groups after the fire, blamed on the Communists. Thereafter, the language of denunciation became even more inflammable than the materials of the German Reichstag, and by the end of 1933 there was little to distinguish the American liberal press from that of the Communists or the Socialists on the subject of Hitler Germany, a matter which will be examined subsequently.

However, this indignation over the Reichstag fire and the stern treatment of the German Marxists grew slowly and required some stoking by the Communist press, which started to function at peak strength on this matter toward the end of 1933. The *New Republic* editorial comment on the fire on March 8 was matter of fact, and resigned insofar as the outcome of the election was concerned. No change was predicted, and it expected the "labor parties" to eschew "concerted mass action" in opposition in favor of "guerrilla warfare;" at this point, the victory of Hitler was presumed to be a signal for civil war, as many Communists had been saying for some time.[64] The following week a longer unsigned comment, "The Terror in Germany," went into a detailed examination of the political context of the government resulting from the March 5 election, forecast suppression of the Communists and mass pogroms against the Jewish population, the former of which materialized. But there was the same atmosphere of serene confidence in the antagonists of the regime; "But even though its leaders are exiled, imprisoned or murdered, and its organizations perhaps forbidden by decree, German labor will continue to threaten the security of the new dictatorship," it promised.[65]

Two weeks later the same publication once more suggested that a grand upheaval in Germany was just around the corner, based on a recent dispatch from Russia to the effect that the Communist International was sponsoring proposals for a united front against Hitler's regime, with provisions for extending it to many other countries "against all attacks on the working class." [66] Leon Dennen of the *New Masses* supplied the *New Republic* with a special dispatch from Hamburg printed in the same issue that supported the same line. "In no other city can one feel more definitely the approach of civil war than in Red Hamburg," declared Dennen. According to him the fighting had already broken out; "The fight seems to be mostly between the Communists and the Nazis. The Communists are fighting like lions, dozens of them are being killed every day." [67] Thus despite its own admissions that Russia was interfering in German politics, it persisted in seeing the German Communists as a domestic force only, and ultimately condemned the Hitlerian repression of the KPD in the strongest imaginable language. But this was still a premature position; at this point, as is displayed in a four-page editorial comment on March 15, "Can Hitlerism Survive?," [68] the belief was still largely in the negative. The wound-rubbing ruminations and the sulphuric attacks on the Nazis were to emerge out of the collapse of the expected united front.

The *Nation* delivered itself of one fairly restrained editorial reflection on the occasion of Hitler's electoral victory. On March 15, reporting on his entrenchment in the chancellorship, it admitted, "He has achieved his goal, and the only redeeming feature of this disaster to the democratic and liberal movements in his country is that he has won the chancellorship by constitutional methods without resorting to violence." [69] It was a great shock to see that a force identified with the Right might win over a country through the ballot box. But much was made now of the terror which had been imposed on the country through the hysteria attending the fire, and the suppression and arrest of the Left leaders. It was harder to explain why over $5\frac{1}{2}$ millions of Germans voted for him who had not done so in the previous election, almost $1\frac{1}{2}$ millions of these representing defections from the Social Democrats and Communists. Much of the editorial was devoted to castigation of Versailles and self-abuse; "Altogether the spectacle of Germany is one to make the gods weep. It is, of course, at bottom due to the folly and the wickedness of the Treaty of Versailles." For the American implications, the editorial offered, "And so another fascist dictatorship arises, to remind Americans of the complete failure of our 'victory' in the World War to achieve the ends we set ourselves."

In the ashes and ruins, there was still time and room for speculations on other foreign implications of Hitler's victory, especially the effect on the Austrians and French. An editorial paragraph on March 22 discussed the alarming rise of a "Nazi" tide in Austria and the possibility of the achievement of union with Germany, as an aftermath of the triumph there. No opinion was expressed other than the cryptic comment, "France showed in 1931 that it was ready to go to any length, even so far as to wreck Europe, to prevent the Austro-German *Anschluss* from materializing. There is no good reason to suppose that France has changed its policy in this respect." Thus, what began on a note of vigorous condemnation of France for its German policy ended in a veiled suggestion that it probably had not been such a bad policy after all, leaving unexpressed the hope that French pressure might be the damper to extinguish this latest and much more formidable German eruption.

But in a few months it shied away from this, largely because of its implications for the United States. For all their talk of moderation the liberals were shown to be as bereft of suggestions as anyone else as to how national aspirations might be achieved in a framework of peace. Hitler more than anyone exposed their devotion to the status quo as a good thing, and their helplessness before still another demonstration that no practical substitute for force as an engine of change had yet been evolved by those who professed to detest force more than anything else in the world.

NOTES

1 *Nation*, September 16, 1931, p. 267.
2 *Nation*, November 11, 1931, pp. 511–513. Gunther referred to the customs union proposal as "the first great attempt in Europe to circumvent the injustices of Versailles," p. 512.
3 *New Republic*, November 18, 1931, pp. 3–4.
4 *Nation*, October 14, 1931, p. 376; *New Republic*, November 11, 1931, p. 337.
5 Editorial "More Dictators Abroad," *Nation*, October 21, 1931, p. 420. At the same time the editors compared Ramsay MacDonald's plea for emergency powers in England to the actions of Mussolini in Italy.
6 Citations in above two paragraphs in editorial, *New Republic*, October 21, 1931, pp. 248–249.
7 *New Republic*, November 4, 1931, pp. 311–312.
8 *Nation*, December 9, 1931, p. 625. The editors recommended that Hoover and Stimson "isolate France at the Geneva disarmament conference," and create a disarmament bloc headed by the United States and England.
9 *Nation*, December 23, 1931, p. 686.
10 *New Republic*, December 30, 1931, pp. 175–176.
11 "German Socialism In the Balance," *Nation*, October 21, 1931, pp. 384–386.
12 "Germany in Fear," *New Republic*, November 18, 1931, pp. 7–8.
13 "From the Heart Of Germany," *Nation*, November 18, 1931, pp. 554–556.
14 "Deadlock In Berlin," *New Republic*, December 16, 1931, pp. 124–126.
15 "Germany In the World Crisis," *Nation*, December 16, 1931, pp. 662–663. Continuing in this vein was Henry Raymond Mussey's long, gloomy account of the German home front scene, "Patient Germany," *Nation*, January 20, 1932, pp. 64–66.
16 "Herr Hitler is beginning to show signs of delusions of grandeur," the *Nation* began an editorial on September 16, 1931. The theme of insanity became fully developed in later years. But the editorial continued, "It is a curious fact that the more France persists in her ruthless anti-German course the more she encourages and strengthens these Hitler forces which are pledged to denounce the peace treaty and to cease all payments to France and the Allies the minute they take office. Sometimes one wonders whether France is not deliberately planning anarchy for Germany," p. 269.
17 *Nation*, December 16, 1931, p. 654.
18 See especially editorials in *Nation*, October 21, 1931, p. 417 and December 30, 1931, p. 709. The editors particularly deplored Hindenburg's reception of Hitler and the adamant stand of the United States Congress toward repudiation of reparations as factors which "considerably strengthened" and "encouraged" National Socialism and its leader.
19 But the *New Republic* columnist "T.R.B." on November 11, 1931, p. 351, concluded that Hoover would bow before congressional pressure and not go through with requests for further debt and reparations reductions, suggesting "all this means that the initiative will come from Germany, and not from us." See also "End Of the Young Plan," *Nation*, January 6, 1932, p. 5; "If Germany Cannot Pay," *Nation*, January 20, 1932, p. 59.
20 The *New Republic* repeatedly predicted that Hitler would attempt to seize power, which would be followed by a general strike of organized labor in Germany. One of the latest of these editorial forecasts was that in the issue of February 3, 1932, p. 306.
21 *Nation*, March 23, 1932, p.241; April 20, 1932, p. 455.
22 *New Republic*. March 23, 1932, p. 141.
23 John Elliott, in a piece written from Berlin on June 4, 1932, published in the *Nation*, June 20, 1932, pp. 720–722, titled "How Brüning Was Overthrown," stated that

the act of suppression of Hitler's Brownshirts "was taken under strong pressure from the Socialist Party," and that this act "led directly to the Chancellor's downfall."

24 *New Republic*, May 4, 1932, pp. 314–315; *Nation*, May 4, 1932, p. 501.

25 Thaelmann, "Growth Of the Fascist Dictatorship In Germany," *The Communist*, March, 1931, pp. 219–225.

26 "Europe In Extremis," *Nation*, June 8, 1932, p. 639; "The German Peril," *Nation*, June 15, 1932, p. 667.

27 *New Republic*, June 8, 1932, p. 83; "Germany Goes Fascist," *New Republic*, June 15, 1932, p. 114.

28 See one of these early complaints against unconstitutionality under Brüning in *Nation*, October 28, 1931, pp. 446–447.

29 *Nation*, June 22, 1932, p. 695.

30 *Nation*, July 27, 1932, p. 66. Successive stories of this kind appeared all summer; on August 17, 1932, p. 134, the *Nation* again announced blandly, "Murder and terror are still the order of the day in Germany," while subsequently conceding weakly that "the vast majority of German citizens, traditionally law-abiding, desire peace and order." There was little variance between the *Nation* and the Communist press on reportage of internal German conditions during most of 1931–1933.

31 See especially the editorial "The End of Hitler?," *Nation*, August 10, 1932, p. 115, which saw an immediate demise of both National Socialism and its hated leader.

32 "Germany Clears the Decks," *New Republic*, August 3, 1932, pp. 301–302, and "Whither Germany?," *New Republic*, August 10, 1932, pp. 329–330, two important major statements. See also McAlister Coleman letter to editors, *New Republic*, August 17, 1932, pp. 20–21.

33 The *Nation* editorial of August 10, 1932, p. 114, said of this announcement by Schleicher, "This decision was bound to come not only because a militaristic regime now rules Germany, but because the German people long ago lost their faith in the hypocritical disarmament pledges of the other nations. The unceasing French cry for 'security before disarmament' has been the chief stumbling block . . . to execution of the provision in the Versailles treaty for reducing all armaments to the levels forced upon Germany by that treaty."

34 "Threatening the Peace Of Europe," *Nation*, September 14, 1932, p. 225.

35 *Nation*, September 28, 1932, pp. 275–277.

36 Brailsford, "Is German Democracy Dead?," *New Republic*, August 17, 1932, pp. 8–9. At one point Brailsford exploded angrily, "It is true that Hitler denounces class war, as Mussolini did, but that is the one joke of this solemn charlatan; he wages it relentlessly, and kills on an average three Communists daily."

37 Mumford, "Notes On Germany," *New Republic*, October 26, 1932, pp. 279–281.

38 Ludwig, "The Flight Of the German Spirit," *Nation*, October 26, 1932, pp. 391–392.

39 Geiser, "Hitler's Hold On Germany," *Nation*, November 16, 1932, pp. 474–475. Said Geiser in conclusion, "if there is one thing that is clear it is that the great majority of Germans want no more war."

40 See especially *Nation*, September 7, 1932, p. 202.

41 "Another German Election," *New Republic*, September 21, 1932, pp. 140–141.

42 "E.D.H.," "Behind the Cables," *Nation*, October 26, 1932, p. 348.

43 *Nation*, November 16, 1932, p. 468.

44 See note 41 above.

45 Editorial paragraph in *New Republic* for October 26, 1932. On suspicions of desire for unilateral rearming in Germany, see editorial, *New Republic*, September 28, 1932, p. 162.

46 "E.D.H.," "Behind the Cables," *Nation*, October 26, 1932, p. 348.

47 *New Republic*, October 12, 1932, p. 219.

48 "Another Herriot Plan," *Nation*, November 30, 1932, pp. 519–520.

49 "E.D.H.," "Behind the Cables," *Nation*, November 30, 1932, p. 531.

50 *Nation*, November 30, 1932.

51 "Von Schleicher is a remarkably able man. . . . He is not as reactionary or as stupid as most of the men whom von Papen had collected in his cabinet. Von Schleicher at least knows that things have changed in Germany. In other words he is distinctly

more pliable than the average German reactionary." *Nation,* December 14, 1932, p. 580.

52 *Nation,* December 7, 1932, p. 543.

53 *Nation,* April 6, 1932, pp. 401–402; *New Republic,* April 6, 1932, pp. 213–214.

54 Knickerbocker in *New Republic,* May 25, 1932, p. 53; Mowrer in *New Republic,* February 15, 1933, pp. 27–28, and in *Nation,* March 15, 1933, p. 295; Villard in *Nation,* February 1, 1933, pp. 125–126; Shuster and Vienot in *New Republic,* May 11, 1932, p. 358; Douglas in *New Republic,* December 7, 1932, p. 107.

55 Reviewed in *New Republic,* July 20, 1932, pp. 268–269, and December 28, 1932, p. 195, respectively.

56 Radek, "Hitler," *Nation,* April 20, 1932, pp. 462–464.

57 "Sauce For the Goose," *New Republic,* July 13, 1932, pp. 220–221; *Nation,* October 19, 1932, p. 340.

58 *New Republic,* February 8, 1933, pp. 336–337.

59 "The March On Berlin," *New Republic,* February 15, 1933, pp. 3–4. See also Ludwig Lore, "Who Stands Behind Hitler?", *Nation,* February 22, 1933, pp. 191–192.

60 Kaltenborn, "Heil Hitler!," *New Republic,* February 15, 1933, pp. 9–11.

61 "Hitler's Role," *Nation,* February 15, 1933, p. 164.

62 *New Republic,* March 1, 1933, p. 57; *Nation,* March 1, 1933, p. 219.

63 Elliott, "Hitler Takes Power," *Nation,* March 1, 1933, pp. 337–339.

64 *New Republic,* March 8, 1933, pp. 86–87.

65 *New Republic,* March 15, 1933, p. 119; see also *New Republic,* March 29, 1933, p. 170, for report on political persecutions, and the first report on the plans for concentration camps, with the prisons "overflowing with political opponents of the Hitlerites, particularly the Communists and the Republicans."

66 *New Republic,* March 29, 1933, p. 171.

67 *New Republic,* March 29, 1933, p. 188.

68 *New Republic,* March 15, 1933, pp. 120–123, especially section 6, "Seeds of Dissension."

69 "Hitler Wins," *Nation,* March 15, 1933, p. 227, and for following citations in same paragraph.

12

AMERICAN LIBERALISM REAPPRAISES

ITS VIEWS ON GERMANY, 1933–1935

THE EFFECTIVENESS OF A DOUBLE STANDARD
AS A MAKER OF OPINIONS

THE daily press discovered, during the World War and after, that foreign news and foreign policy could be made exciting news. Periodical literary organs were not far behind. But there was little if any contemplation of the consequences of exciting domestic populations into a state of sustained indignation, which much of such news succeeded in doing. A few studies of the role of news in arousing emotions in the Spanish-American War quietly made their appearance twenty-five to thirty years after that event, emphasizing the results then, and in the late '20's and the depression years many similar studies discussed the misuse of the press in the propaganda of 1914–1918, so that a feeling of sophistication in such matters was widespread by 1933. Any number of Americans promised to be invulnerable to the printed word henceforth, no matter how incitatory the subject. Perhaps under this false sense of immunity to hate via printer's ink even the sedate and established periodicals were wont to indulge in excesses of description, and the journals of American liberalism proved to be no exception. The ability of their supposedly more realistic readers to discount exaggeration proved to be largely mythical; in fact, the average citizen with far less formal education was much less easily influenced as time demonstrated. In time the willingness to believe the worst of an adversary tended to increase in direct proportion to the amount of education and literary acumen, if a cross-section of the title pages of books and the lists of contributors to periodicals published between 1939 and 1941 mean anything.

Indeed, a lengthy thesis can be prepared on the printed political language of the decade of the 1930's. The effect of the tension induced by the economic misery and the purposeful incitatory style of the radical press, especially that of the Communists, led to recklessness in print matching even the colorful excessiveness of earlier pamphleteering eras in times of few if any legal inhibitions. When added to remembrances of the inflammatory inheritance of 1917–1918, plus the ingredient of breeziness which was part of the fashion of the first post-war decade realism, there was little lacking for a grandiose plunge into printed excess. But the full effect when applied to foreign affairs and politics was never dreamed of, and by the time the brakes of discretion were applied, the headlong plunge was well out of control.

In one extremely important sense the separation of foreign from domestic affairs in the liberal press was almost impossible well before 1933. For years the "progressive" view called for stinging criticism of the whole social order, and the economic dislocations stimulated this criticism to a nearly incandescent level. Restraint here had nearly vanished. The balancing element in this picture was the image of Soviet Russia. By the time Hitler emerged in Germany there was an unbroken fifteen years of portrayal of the Soviet Union as the ideal order, whatever weaknesses might have prompted exposure from time to time. Though the vicissitudes of Marxian politics in the United States had already created a sizable collection of heretic splinter groups from the parent Communist body, even these persons were usually to be found defending Russia, or at least a hypothetical equivalent of its present regime under new management, in showdown conflicts with the capitalist democracies, or the order represented by Mussolini's Italy, a diseased breakdown of capitalist democracy in the Marxian world view. The large number of Marxist writers who had access to the pages of the liberal weeklies and to a somewhat less degree to a dozen other eminent periodicals, ensured the posing of rivals to Russia in a much less flattering light for some years; the stresses and strains in the Soviet in the last five years before the Second World War reduced the zeal of many of its well-wishers, but at no time did their defection or reduced affection lead them to adopt Russian enemies. The Communists alone remained with dedication unshaken.

Thus during this ominous decade the breakdown of the domestic scene provided the foreign side of the picture with its counterbalance; for the panorama of unbroken disintegration in the old order there was the compensatory vision of Socialism of one variety or another: Russia when it was serene; some yet unrealized form when Communist life showed less edifying aspects behind its monolithic facade. On the home front this was not always easy, especially when caught in the ripsaw of the violent factionalisms of the Marxist-Socialist spectrum. Liberal editorial pages on more than one occasion writhed from the blows of heated sectarians whose affront at some heresy knew no bounds. This edginess encouraged support for a grand semi-planned drift toward government control if not operation, though few details were given that might have stimulated factionalism. But in the foreign affairs field this necessity for circumspect behavior was less pressing. Straight black and white were more easily used here, and were also more acceptable. The arranging of the nations into "good" and "bad" parcels was made much easier, as we have seen earlier, by the fundamental assumptions that liberals believed should underlie a world order in which they could have faith.

As "journals of opinion" the liberal weeklies felt no responsibility for adopting postures of objectivity, no commitment to present a detached picture of anything on which they already had opinions, views or attitudes. Since it is impossible to tell how another policy might have worked other than the one which was adopted, and since only one program can be put into operation at a time, it is futile to debate what might have happened had American liberalism chosen a different course than that which it pursued relative to the world in the fateful ten years before Pearl Harbor. All that can be done is to chart its course by way of its documented pronouncements in this era. Of immediate concern is the poverty of judgment on the liberals' part due to the application of a double standard of measurement to foreign politics and its overall consequences on opinion, and the two-faced approach to German and Russian affairs was by far the most obvious. The coming of Hitler brought about a change in liberal attitudes toward Germany equivalent to the changing of the scenery in a theater upon the billing of a new production. In time every adversary of Hitler Germany gained liberal support, and although there developed much difference of opinion among liberals as to the decision to engage the Germans in war, as there was in the case of Japan as well, by 1939 a majority had taken stands which logically left no other course possible.

The impulses and beliefs and convictions which led American liberalism to see in the new Soviet state the coming form of the new society have already been discussed. Such a state of mind was subject to much modification by the time World War Two broke out, but in 1933 it was probably at its peak. The continuation of the splintering process in American Marxist groups and the successive uproars brought about by the 1934–1938 purge trial series in the Soviet did much to moderate the enthusiasm over socialism in its Russian form, even though this repression had little effect in quelling the enthusiasm over Soviet foreign policy objectives and Communist activity in other countries. International Communism received its first serious setback in the liberal press upon the Russian invasion of Finland. The liberals were a persistent source of irritation to the Communists. The Communist press in the United States was repeatedly engaged in belaboring liberal editorial judgment for its doubting and hesitant attitude toward some aspects of the domestic Soviet scene between 1934 and 1941, while at the same time neglecting to admit that liberal support for Communist stands on Germany, Spain, China, Italy, and most other countries whose foreign policy and fate were linked in some manner to those of Russia, was most comforting. The only time they were in general conflict was in the 22 months of 1939–1941 during the life of the Russo-German agreement, and even during this time American liberal publications took part in the domestic anti-Communist hostility with considerable hesitance.

Had there been no disposition to regard Russia with genial approbation, one might have expected the liberal press and its impressive list of contributors to present the European scene by (1) admitting that Russia did not differ in any appreciable manner from the regimes held up to group detestation and scorn, thus eliminating it as a liberal safety-valve and consolation prize as the one safe repository of their hopes for Europe's future, and (2) admitting that the pictures of Italy, Japan and Germany were substantially overdrawn, thus depriving themselves of the nightmare materials used to frighten the readers for a decade and driving them by default to embrace another European rival as the nearest expectable approximation to Utopia, on the grounds that its sympathetic interpretation by Americans with a reputation for moderate reformist and pacific views testified to its qualitative superiority. On the contrary, this traditional reputation was sacrificed by their reporting of foreign news in such a way that political regimes whose ideology they did not appreciate were described in an unrestrainedly emotional style. And a readership brought up on such fare could not be expected to cherish peace, conciliation and compromise very long. By the end of the decade there was little to choose between the extremity of the daily commercial press and that of the liberals, by and large. Emotional exaggeration and hysteria-producing overstatement had captured them all. American liberals were effective intellectual recruiting sergeants to a degree far surpassing the much less sophisticated special pleading of the First World War. Disillusionment with their part then raised up a crop of repudiations within five years, but in the case of the Second World War, the process of self-deception was so thorough that after twenty years liberal views on the second pre-war period had hardly been jostled.

The liberal writers did an impressive job of decking the revival of the European power struggle in ideological and moral dress. The heroes and villains acquired different clothing, and the situation promoted the adoption of more and more un-realistic judgments which led to the posing of the struggle as a conflict between mighty spiritual absolutes versus depravity of a depth never before plumbed by the human race. It took war to expose the utterly synthetic structure of this apocalyptic vision.

In the immediate period after Hitler's March, 1933 climb to power, it was a practice in the liberal press to bill the situation as the German "tragedy," "disaster," "catastrophe," and so forth. Inflammatory one-dimensional portraits of Germany were soon the order, unrelieved by any conditioning factors. When juxtaposed to denunciations of similar criticisms of Russia, and accompanied by *ad hominem* attacks on authors hostile to the Soviet, the side-taking left no doubt in anyone's mind, nor was it supposed to do otherwise. Frequently the anti-German editorial or article included a spirited defense of the Soviet, so the reader rarely had a need to make up his mind. By mid-year the staple was the terror story, which averaged one a week for months, the author frequently writing under a pseudonym. Others were the product of *émigrés* of a considerable variety, often self-imposed exiles. The less easily identified, the more the author tended to extreme abuse and vilification. This form of irresponsibility toward the readers was explained as care for the safety of the writer or relatives still in Germany. There was a tendency to treat such retaliation as a "Nazi" invention, ignoring the similar Soviet tactics of long standing, documented by many splinter-left escapees since the Revolution. In many ways this was the most dishonest aspect of the presentation of Russo-German affairs in the liberal press. The use of terror and violence for the purpose of suppressing dissenters was presented in different lights in the respective cases. That of Germany, involving a somewhat smaller number of people, was unspeakable; that of Russia, glanced over or even ignored, was brushed aside as "the heavy price any nation pays for revolution," the standard excuse in the Communist press also. German internal politics, whatever their severity were never reported in proportion to those of Russia. And it is of note that the liberals implored Americans and others to form their views on Germany and fashion their foreign policy views insofar as this country was involved to a great extent on the basis of German *internal* policy for over two years.

The policy of interpreting a nation's internal order through the eyes of a refugee minority did much to form the lopsided view characteristic of liberal opinion, but it posed some unanswered questions.

No explanation was advanced to account for the stories of the incredible efficiency of the Hitler regime in hunting down and killing or incarcerating its political opponents, when so many prominent enemies were able to escape the Reich in excellent health and voice, to wage a ferocious counter-propaganda from foreign rostrums and publishing offices. Even more astounding were those who claimed to be escapees from the new concentration camps, an increasing number as time went on, whose every word was accepted as certain fact. On the other hand, a trickle of survivors from the vast Soviet forced labor camps had for years been greeted with incredulous snorts and guffaws of ridicule. A sign of the times was the angry cry of Granville Hicks of the *New Masses* at the New York *Times* for giving so much space to a review of Chapin Huntington's *The Homesick Million: Russia-out-of-Russia,* published just about at the start of the Hitler regime. This description of the vast number of non-Red Russians scattered over the world, the predecessors and counterparts of the new German homeless, was savagely attacked.[1]

However, there was a significant difference in the quality and character of the two refugee groups. The fact that so many of the expellees or escapees from Russia were inarticulate while so many of those from Germany were remarkably active politically suggested the Russians were much more effective in silencing the potentially damaging, with such exceptions as Leon Trotsky. The existence of such a legion of Hitler's enemies abroad testified either to Hitler's preference to let his opponents live, or to the atrociously poor security measures existing in the Reich that permitted many vigorous and articulate critics to escape. This did great damage to the liberal specter of Germany as a vast barbed-wire prison, unless one wished to adopt as a consolation the view that Hitler's antagonists were more resourceful than the opponents of Communism in Russia. In a way this approach was unconsciously adopted, but the view that few wanted to leave the Soviet Union had been standard belief for so long at the time this matching of Germany and Russia on the subject of their refugees occurred that it did not present itself as a problem to most liberals. It also accounts in part for the grim and merciless treatment accorded the few anti-Soviet books appearing at this time, such as those by Max Eastman, Tatiana Tchernavina, Alan Monkhouse and Malcolm Muggeridge.

It is true that liberal criticism of the British and French for suppressing internal dissenters in their colonies occasionally was voiced, but policy in such places was rarely presented through the eyes of *émigrés* representing a small fraction of the total population. That their misery and resentment were real, was not the issue. The fact that there was a persistent effort to identify the whole country with themselves emerges as the most clear-cut consequence of their special appeals. This tactic reversed that employed with respect to Soviet Russia, always seen through the official eyes of a four or five per cent Communist Party minority or a slightly larger group of sympathizers outside of Russia, purporting to represent the views of a majority of all Russians.

Thus the liberals rationalized a most unusual campaign of concerted attacks on the regime of a foreign country, on behalf of the tiny percentage of this state's total population who were the victims of its internal policies. As time wore on, this generalized attack approached crusade proportions, and foremost among the most vociferous were the German *émigrés* of all varieties. In the history of national states, there has never been one which produced so many *émigrés* to other lands who devoted themselves to calling so implacably for a war against their estranged homeland as did the Germany of 1933–1941. The Huguenots of France of an earlier age provide a pale comparison. The full effect of this upon American liberal opinion can hardly be overestimated. Rarely has there been such a drastic display of how domestic policy may form someone else's foreign policy. This concentrated belligerence toward National Socialist Germany was bound to lead to war, and the wonder is that American liberalism debated the issue so long before deciding; its anti-war positions melted one by one like ice under the impact of a tropical sun. From spirited insistence that Hitlerism was unrepresentative of the Germans to a call for a war against all Germans took some time, but the course was set from the very beginning. At first the editorial policy remained cool while two dozen correspondents raged at the new German order over a period of two years. By the time the foreign policy of this new Germany began to result in movements disturbing to the post-1918 status quo, all the basic attitudes had been formed. The Soviet Union's Popular Front gesture recruited no candidates more eager and enthusiastic than the American liberal, on the whole, a recruit so devoted that he clung to the creature even after it had been repudiated and discarded by its creator. The seething resentment against Russia on the part of so many American liberals between August, 1939 and June, 1941 was more the wrath of a scorned and betrayed compatriot than anything else.

THE LIBERAL ROLE IN EARLY MARXIST DREAMS
OF A NEW GERMANY

The death of the Weimar Republic led to an extremely short period of mourning in the American liberal press, and almost no expressions of sorrow or regret came from its spokesmen at the time. The sides began to form for the next contest, already expected and partially prepared for by Hitler's formidable opponents in German Marxist politics, the Social Democrats and the Communists. Although they devoted much time to intemperate abuse of each other as the ladder upon which Hitler's party had climbed into office, they busied themselves with bright plans and hopes for an early dethroning of the "Nazis," and their cheerfulness had a contagious effect upon the favorably-disposed everywhere, and Americans were no exception. The American Communist press had been at war with Hitler some time before the liberal contingent also bloomed into the full flower of aggressiveness. The foundations of the American League Against War and Fascism were laid as early as May and June, 1932, with the delegation to the John Reed Clubs of the objective of forming "Anti-Imperialist War Councils" of the intellectuals, and with the publication of the "Draft Manifesto of the John Reed Clubs," which latter were assigned the task of building the superstructure of a World Congress Against War, announced the following August.[2] This had a theme of implacable hostility toward "imperialist" war, and was supported by a seemingly substantial organization, of which Theodore Dreiser was chairman and Malcolm Cowley of the *New Republic* was secretary. This distinction was necessary since the stamp of approval had been applied to the Communist war against both Chiang and the Japanese in China. It took most of the non-Marxist pacifist and anti-militarist organizations several years to discover the Communist dichotomy between good and bad wars.

With respect to Germany, Hitler was hardly invested in the Chancellery before the *New Masses* began the recruitment of liberals behind their orthodox line. As Joseph Freeman, later editor of this trim Communist monthly (and weekly, subsequently) declared, "the Fascist terror is directed first and foremost against the revolutionary vanguard of the working class, against the Communist Party." The April, 1933 issue contained an impressive list of condemnatory statements from persons familiar to the readers of the liberal magazines as well, including Newton Arvin, Roger Baldwin, Heywood Broun, Lewis Corey, Waldo Frank, Horace Gregory, Sidney Hook, Scott Nearing, James Rorty, Isidor Schneider, and Edwin Seaver, in addition to Michael Gold and Granville Hicks. Some of them displayed substantial impatience with liberal editorial policy; Nearing's response was a good barometer of the extra belligerence some of them harbored: [3]

There are two things we can do about the experience of the last six months in Germany. One is to scream like the *Nation*. The other is to study the situation from every angle, to see where our comrades have blundered and to avoid making the same mistakes when *our* turn comes.

And come it will. The struggle for power in Germany is merely a prelude to a class conflict that will be fought out across the entire capitalist world.

This vision of a global war, with Communism the defender of virtue, was widespread, and the Communist press indulged in no hesitant obscurity about it. As the issue was put by the then editor of the *Daily Worker,* Clarence Hathaway, "Between a Fascist and a Communist nothing can be settled by debate. This issue will be decided on the barricades." Given the large number of writers who had access to the pages of both liberal and Communist publications, the message of imminent revolt spread rapidly through the former as well as the latter.

At the bottom of the Communist rage at Hitler was the conviction that he had robbed them in Germany of a chance to make Germany into a Communist state. That they got liberal allies in this early period was of slight interest, at a time when liberals were classed with all non-party leftists as "social fascists." The Communists scorned them as political incompetents, subjected them to scathing abuse, and accepted their support in anti-"Nazi" fervor as if there was nothing else for them to do. Not until the "Popular Front" of two years later was it considered desirable to be polite to liberals in Communist ranks. And in truth the Communists taught them valuable lessons in the preparation of inflammatory material on Hitler Germany, with the accent in the first two years on the beatings, jailings and killings of Communists. One of the most impressive documents of this order, *The Brown Book of the Hitler Terror,* a volume prepared under the direction of Willi Muenzenberg, for nine years a Communist deputy in the Reichstag and one of the chief workers in the creation of the German Communist Party, had none but Communists as heroes throughout. Liberals praised this book without stint or reservation, but never alluded to its origin. This was just one of several very influential opinion-makers in this early stage. Where Muenzenberg and his compatriots were headed was not in doubt; as he said in the title of a *New Masses* article of July 31, 1934, "After Hitler—A Soviet Germany." Muenzenberg also shared the amused contempt for the liberal camp followers so widespread among the American adherents of Communism. It was he who was credited with inventing the term "innocents' club" to designate a front group consisting mainly of sympathizers under Communist leadership, of which there were some 300 in the United States alone within five years of Hitler's rise in Germany. An intensive investigator of American liberal hostility to Hitlerism must necessarily spend long hours among the Communists to trace one rich source of their inspiration.[4]

In the liberal press itself, however, the commentators on Germany were not frequently those of Communist circles. Fully as hostile, many liberal writers shared a closer affection for the Social Democrats. In 1933 a substantial number of voices that spoke their piece on Germany were all condemnatory. Among those were several refugees and a goodly sprinkling of anonymous and never identified people, but most of them were travelers, professsors, or journalists. These included Ludwig Lore, Reinhold Niebuhr, John Gunther, Ludwig Lewisohn, Waldo Frank, Robert Dell, Frederick L. Schuman, Louis Fischer, Verne Andrews, Joseph P. Lash, Richard L. Neuberger (then a law student at the University of Oregon), Mary Heaton Vorse, also of the *New Masses,* the British Socialist H. N. Brailsford, and, among the recognizable refugees, the famous Communist heretic Leon Trotsky, then in hiding in Turkey, Ernst Oberfohren, an anti-Hitler Nationalist of the Hugenberg camp, Johannes Steel, and a Czech named Egon Erwin Kisch, held in high esteem by the Communists at that time.

The bill of particulars against the Hitlerites was almost entirely a consequence of the "Nazi" internal policies; the suppression of the Marxist parties vied with the persecution of the Jews as the most serious charge. When on the personality level a Marxist target turned out to be also a Jew, the propaganda against the "Nazis" was given an added lift. The liberals were badly torn during the first two years between the Socialists and Communists, each accusing the other of having done the most to aid Hitler's climb into the saddle. "Nazi" Party acquisitions of millions of supporters from both embarrassed the entire Left except the anarchists. In the earliest weeks the editorial policy of both the *Nation* and *New Republic* tended to accept the Communist position, and were loudly condemned by vigorous Socialist letter-writers for doing so. But by 1934 the majority of the contributors on German affairs were identified with Socialist politics in the United States, or were German left-Socialist *émigrés.* Nevertheless, Communist literature on Hitler Germany continued to be warmly received and reviewed.

One astute propaganda success on the part of the special pleaders for a Marxian socialist Germany of some sort was the capture of the word "democratic" which soon was a synonym for their own particular brand of collectivism. Hardly a spokesman for moderate centrist republicanism got the floor in this period, and the key to understanding the position of any attacker of Hitler at this time was to follow his argument to his own recommendations for a substitute for Hitlerism. Even the most passionate pleaders for freedom, liberty, and similar undefined values usually came forth with a program of forced nationalization and confiscation of property and rigidity of rule that in essence provided no alternative. Much was made of the fact that Hitler's government monopolized the press and public communications, as if this were a striking innovation. But nobody considered it significant to compare this with Russian policy, where the denial of communications media to enemies was considered as natural as breathing, and no more worthy of notice than the passing of the hours of the day.

The impotence of Social Democracy and the German unions alarmed and vexed many liberal surveyors of German politics in Hitler's first six months. The remarkable lack of militancy and the complete failure of any general strike to materialize were also topics of wonderment. The fact that they were more numerous than National Socialists tended to incline liberals toward the Red position, namely, that the Socialists were more responsible for the survival of "capitalism" in Germany for *not* joining the Communists in doing it to death at once, hoping that it would expire naturally while they were at the bedside ready to snatch power.[5] About the only voice of German moderation who believed in saving capitalism from all dictatorships who got to say anything on this struggle, M. J. Bonn, former rector of the Berlin Academy of Commerce, was violently condemned editorially in the *New Republic* for having the audacity to declare that "the Communists were responsible for introducing physical violence into German home politics." After the hundreds of dispatches and reports which uniformly blamed the "Nazis" for it all, this smacked of the most outrageous type of heresy.[6] Now that Hitler had triumphed no one wanted to remember that violence had been rather widespread, and yet the logic of the new positions pointed to a return to violence as soon as the anti-Hitler forces could be reorganized. When International Publishers released Hans Marchwitza's novel *Storm Over the Ruhr*, built around a fictitious Ruhr strike which was betrayed by the Social Democrats, Granville Hicks, reviewing it for the *Nation* in June, 1933, saw in it the promise of a mighty class struggle renewal in Germany, as well as the fore-runner of a "rich, vigorous, many-sided literature of the working class." [7] The Communists had far from given up. Indeed, Lore, more a spokesman for the genteel reformists among the Social Democrats, at the end of the summer of 1933 declared in a *New Republic* article that "Communist party underground apparatus was in operation before the Hitler regime was twenty-four hours old," and in a tone which was far from hostile.[8]

But by now the romantic concept of a Paris Commune type of resistance, so evident earlier in the year, was no longer dominant in left thinking. The longest critique on what had happened in Germany on March 5, 1933 and after which appeared in the liberal press was, strangely enough, written in Turkey by Leon Trotsky, and translated by Max Schachtman, the head of a Marxist splinter of his own and not dependent on other organs as a means of getting his views publicized. The *New Republic* printed this, "The German Catastrophe," on July 5;[9] Trotsky antagonized both the main groups of sympathizers by indicting both, with a tendency to hold the Communists in special disrepute for failing to create a common front before 1932 by gradually taking over the Social Democrats while stifling National Socialism. It was Trotsky who first pointed out that no official Russian Communist organ "uttered a word" for a month on the official position on the German political events after March 5, not even *Pravda,* which then on April 7 announced that the action of the KPD and its Central Committee under Ernst Thaelmann "was completely correct up to and during Hitler's coup d'etat."[10] Trotsky condemned this strongly while bestowing no bouquets on the Social Democrats; he found the leadership of both extremely inept, and the strategy of the Communist International in denouncing the Socialists as "social Fascists" and in staying aloof to the idea of a united front up to the last moment as the fatal step. According to Trotsky, "The masses wanted to fight, but they were obstinately prevented from doing so by their leaders," and Hitler had really backed into power, when he should have been halted by the precipitation of a bitter and comprehensive Marxist-led civil war. So the readers had two main arguments to balance, with their variations, in seeking to get a clear view of what had happened in Germany; the Social Democrats had failed to join with the Communists, as opposed to the view that the Communists had failed to join with the Social Democrats.

"One cannot, unfortunately, deny the superiority of the Fascist over the proletarian leadership," Trotsky had declared in the *New Republic,* "But it is only out of an unbecoming modesty that the beaten chiefs keep silent about their own part in the victory of Hitler." This paralysis of leadership and the dazed months immediately after the "Nazi" win helped to sprout a confusing number of views not only as to what had happened but as to what effect National Socialism was having on the German people as a whole. A *New Republic* story the second week of May, one of the several anonymous reports published in the excited days of 1933–1934, asserted that the "great mass" of the German people were already either fully in harmony with the nationalist revolution, or "benevolently neutral," and that the great stir abroad about the ill fortune of the Socialists, Communists and Jews was not reflected among the populace; "Aside from the Communists, Socialists, Jews and foreign-newspaper correspondents, no one chooses to think about the matter at all." This observer noted that the foreign press was most outraged by the "mishandling" of the Jews, but he was firmly convinced that the Communists had been far worse treated as far as physical violence was concerned, and that Jewish troubles were mostly caused by "economic persecution." This on-the-spot report conveyed the over-all view that most people thought the stern treatment of the Communists was fully merited, and hardly subscribed to the position that a Communist reaction was imminent.[11] And in this period of shock and amidst the agitated babble of contradictory voices, despite the loud and extreme condemnations of editorial statements, the situation was conducive to encouraging views of this sort, among others. It was not until late in the summer that a strong and clear position began to take shape.[12]

Late in June, in the same source, Reinhold Niebuhr described things similarly in his article "The Opposition in Germany"; [13] thousands of Socialists and Communists were entering the "Nazi" Party, the Communists could not be expected to be a virile element in German politics for some time to come. The Socialist cause was "even more hopeless." Although he conceded that there was a widespread underground Communist press, its effectiveness was largely discounted. Niebuhr was inclined to credit Hitler's success in large measure to his foreign stand, especially the attack on "the policy of trusting the Allies to be reasonable if Germany fulfilled the conditions of the Treaty of Versailles"; "This policy is discredited in every rank and class of Germany today," Niebuhr observed, with no rancor or reproach. In his opinion the radical movement's future lay mostly in the ranks of the Storm Troopers, who he thought were "on the whole on the side of radicalism." A titanic struggle between the radical and conservative elements behind Hitler was expected soon, one which would wreck the "Nazis" completely. Hitler's regime had "no real stability," and he predicted "its ultimate disintegration will come from within and not by attack from without." Much was expected from these "beefsteak Nazis," described as "Brown outside, Red inside," a comparison of the color of the Party uniform with that of their political convictions.

Niebuhr was just one of scores of liberals whose bad judgment on Nazi Germany had to be underlined by the war of 1939–1945; six years of wistful dreaming for Hitler to collapse had to be followed by six brutal years of war against him by a large part of the world to bring him down. Their gradually changing views on the strength of Hitler and the weakness of his main opponents testified to a growing lack of liberal faith in the cheerful optimism on the future of a Marxist Germany found in the Communist papers. But the tenacious belief in the approaching fall of the "Nazis," as predicted by a legion of Marxist economic soothsayers, kept alive the hope that signs of his overthrow would soon appear, no matter how black things looked at the midyear.

Late in the summer, stories began to come forth breathing confidence in a coming uprising against Hitler, and they continued through 1934. Countless cells of Reds in groups of five, the "fünfergruppen," were said to exist, supplying the leadership cadre for the upheaval just around the corner. Ernst Henri's description of this coming Marxian uprising, "The Revolution Lives and Grows in Germany," in the September, 1933, *New Masses* dwelt heavily on the major part being played by these "groups of Five." [14] Liberals were much influenced by such writing. Furthermore, it was evident to all that the National Socialists were incompetent to solve the pressure of Germany's economic problems. As John Strachey, in his *The Menace of Fascism,* so calmly pointed out, this was guaranteed. The central aim of this Hitler group was no more than a "movement for the preservation by violence, and at all costs, of the private ownership of the means of production," [15] and this was an impossibility. Through the fall and winter the stories of a vast underground in the making continued. One such report, in the *Nation* in December, even implicated the Soviet Union in such activities in Germany, but consisted more of wishful thinking than anything else, in view of the Russian aloofness to Communist problems in Germany, plus the existence of normal diplomatic and commercial relations between the two.[16]

After the February, 1934, Left uprising in France and the threat of a general strike this tactic gained repute as the ultimate weapon against Fascism. A *New Republic* editorial on February 21 supported it warmly,[17] and reviving Communist combativeness encouraged more such thinking. When Alter Brody reviewed the German refugee Ernst Toller's *I Was a German* in the *Nation,* he rejoiced in the author's new belligerence and his recovery from the "pacifist Nirvana" in which he had been lying since Hitler's rise.[18] No conflict was felt in urging toughness in the internal political situations of Germany, France and Spain while simultaneously pressing a loud anti-militarist, anti-munitions and anti-war propaganda on the international level; they were utterly separate programs in the eyes of the Communists, and liberals unconsciously accepted this as the correct attitude. It was expertly summarized by a *New Masses* writer, who in part quoted Lenin's *War and the Second International* verbatim: [19]

> The fight against war by the workers and exploited classes in all imperialist countries is fundamentally the same; organize against war by supporting the militant anti-war program of the revolutionary movement —then, if efforts to stop war fail, turn imperialist war into civil war, under the slogan of Soviet power to the masses.

This homogenizing of domestic and foreign policy and affairs satisfactorily blurred all dividing lines, making acceptance or rejection of the entire package the issue and rendering discrimination on specific issues a virtual impossibility. Liberals slowly drifted into this position, and it took a number of them over a decade to get out of it by the time they decided that it was imperative that they do so.

But in 1933–1934 it appeared to be the correct strategy to apply to Germany. All manner of wishful thinking and gossip on the alleged German underground circulated widely into the summer of 1934, to finally quiet down and blend into the beginnings of the Popular Front, with the spread of propaganda toward that goal across the national frontiers of France, Austria, Germany, and the Low Countries in the latter months of 1934 and early 1935. By this latter date, all ideas of an internal apocalyptic showdown with Hitler's forces in Germany were hardly to be heard; the impulse behind the Popular Front was the stirring of German rearmament and the first steps of a foreign policy which promised to do something besides talk in obliterating the territorial settlements of Versailles. The rapid spread of authoritarian regimes in Central Europe began to bring home to the supporters of the Soviet Union everywhere that it was approaching a season of threatening influences; warned the *New Masses* in an editorial on November 6, 1934, "The danger of war against the Soviet Union is graver now than at any time in recent months." And the liberals, already leaning in this direction, began to discuss war as the means of stopping Hitler, while lightly ignoring their parallel crusade against munitions makers, militarism, school and college military education and allied subjects which formed part of the war on war. The state of mind which embraced war so enthusiastically in 1939–1941 was already being formed in 1934; the attitudes required to accept the unicorn of left liberalism, a "good" war, grew rapidly and healthily under tillage in the Communist truck garden.

So the year 1934 closed out with the controversy over which Marxist group had done the most to ensure Hitler's victory still ringing noisily, set off by the undertones of the new schemes for the revival of left Socialism both in Germany and as a joint effort of interested groups among her close neighbors. It was now being admitted that Hitler had "a safe majority" backing him up; a *New Republic* correspondent supported the view that his "popularity" had been appreciably heightened by "the disillusionment of the workers with the weak and cowardly Social Democratic government." [20] Lore, in a palpitating piece in December in the *Nation* on the growth of the "United Front" also was in a mood of this sort as far as the past was concerned; the German labor movement had submitted to "the National Socialist offensive" without a show of resistance.[21] Schuman, in his *New Republic* piece "The Road to Hitler," had similarly poured invective upon "the shameless cowardice and treachery of the Social Democratic leaders." The Communists were getting the benefit of the doubt at this point in one sense, along with the bitter attack on Hitler for having doped the German laboring masses with his "sham socialist propaganda." [22] In 1936 a new Communist version appeared: "We were taken by surprise in January, 1933."

An occasional voice in opposition was heard. James Burnham, reviewing *Fascism and Social Revolution* by R. Palme Dutt, editor of the British *Labor Monthly* and a leading Communist Party theorist in England, in the *Nation* in December, 1934, took the Social Democrat point of view, repelled by Dutt's wholesale attack in which he repeated the charge that they were to blame for the Fascist victories. Burnham denied that the Social Democrats were responsible for the demise of the "united front" with the Communists in Germany and elsewhere, and admonished Dutt in Trotskyist tones to abandon Stalinist withdrawal and "exclusive preoccupation with building socialism in the Soviet Union," and concentrate again "on the real fight against Fascism which can only be the determined advance to revolution." [23] But this was minority opinion in liberal centers in these times.

Yet all was not thought lost. The publication of an anonymously written pamphlet, *Socialism's New Beginning,* stirred animated responses from several who were still hoping against hope. Lore, in a *New Republic* article, "German Socialism Underground," still stunned and bewildered by Hitler's victory, thought this prospectus the most heartening and constructive development since, particularly its counsel to abandon the eager wait for the Fascist debacle which had not yet materialized, and prepare a slow, patient reconstruction through small underground cells.[24] Niebuhr, in the *Nation,* was similarly impressed: [25]

This secret manifesto . . . is first of all a passionate reaffirmation of Marxist faith and an expression of confidence in the possibility of ultimately establishing a socialist society upon the ruins of fascism. As a declaration of faith it is a symbol of the fact that Nazi terror may have silenced the voices but has not changed the loyalties of the real Marxists of Germany.

Joseph P. Lash, then editor of the *Student Outlook* and a delegate of the League for Industrial Democracy at the congress of the Socialist Student International at Liége, Belgium, reached heights of grandeur describing the sanction by the Congress of an "Einheitsfront" against Fascism, and waxed enthusiastic in the *Nation* on the *Neu Beginnen* movement in Germany. He subscribed to its theory that the Hitler regime would be maintained for a long time, and that their devotion to creating "a disciplined, conspiratorial organization" with a program looking toward "revolutionary seizure of power followed by the installation of a 'mixed economy' of socialism and capitalism" was very sound.[26] In general these well-wishers for the revival of Marxian Socialism in Germany did not distinguish too closely between what Germany already had and what this new order would provide; the main quarrel seemed to be over who would run German affairs and not particularly over what kind of system would prevail.

Although the last four months of 1934 found the liberal papers boiling with articles, editorials and special communications on the subject of the growing rapprochement between the Socialists and Communists of six countries south and west of Germany, and the cessation of the vitriolic "social Fascist" catcalls of the latter aimed at the former in the interests of "anti-Fascist unity," there was no notice of the significance of the admission of Soviet Russia to the League of Nations and this sudden spurt of international understandings among the major Marxian collectivist parties. Although the anniversary of Mukden, September 18, continued to draw baleful editorial reminders in successive years, this date in 1934, on which the Soviet entered the League, might have been advanced in other circumstances to be as fateful a day for Europe as Japan's Far Eastern action of three years earlier. As "the thieves' kitchen" of Lenin, once it incorporated Russia, began to function in part as a world-wide Communist front, there was a steadily accumulating heap of evidence of Russian interest in this resurgence of the clenched fist and the belligerent slogan outside its boundaries and particularly within the neighbors of Germany. And this time an ideological *cordon sanitaire* against Hitler was to gain powerful liberal support, where the earlier military-financial program of similar intent on the part of France only roused liberal reproach and abuse.

All manner of other reasons were seen for this activity by most liberals who followed it in high excitement. In France the "cooperation" of the Socialists and Communists "in the struggle against Fascism and for the defense of working-class and democratic liberties" was explained by the *New Republic* as a consequence of the February, 1934 explosion of the French Right and "the increasingly reactionary attitude of the Doumergue government." [27] The same journal in November saw the Belgian Socialists' "De Man Plan" for promoting joint "united-front activities" with the Communists there as a product of local political developments.[28] The *Nation* also reported an "anti-fascist phalanx" formed out of French Socialists and Communists, uniting on "a non-aggression pact for mutual protection and defense," on the twentieth anniversary of the outbreak of the First World War.[29] In October, A. Fenner Brockway of the Independent Labor Party in England reported to the *New Republic* on similar understandings taking place in Austria, Italy and Spain, as well as England, and suggested in an open letter addressed to the Socialist and Communist parties in all these states the desirability of an international congress of all these parties of all countries "for the purpose of obtaining united action against fascism, the war struggle against fascism."[30]

Yet it was not easy for liberals to assess the elements in the picture correctly. The sudden about-face of the Communists, after a campaign of ridicule of Socialists and Left liberals through the summer of 1934, accompanied by the heaping of endless blame for the debacle in Germany, did puzzle the liberals somewhat. But the age of innocence was to last long after, and the work of Maxim Litvinov in using the League marketplace to advance the interests of Soviet Russia, disguised as a world crusade on behalf of virtue, was perceived only in the dimmest manner even at the conclusion of the titanic war which all reasoning pointed to as its only logical consequence. But if this was not noticed in the context discussed above, it was no better seen in the liberal press's voluminous attention to foreign affairs *per se,* unrelated to the purely political hopes and wishes for the future.

GERMAN DOMESTIC POLICIES
AND DEVELOPMENTS UNDER ATTACK

Nothing quite compared with German politics and actions in the first two years of Hitler as a producer of news in the American liberal-left-labor press. Every move in the country was given the benefit of searching examination, during which time Soviet Russia was attracting restrained and respectful attention on specific issues, and the other great powers of the West all but being neglected in the meanwhile. A great chorus of confused counsel on things German rose in the liberal ranks, accompanying hurried and hysterical judgments on Germany and Germans under Hitler in general; the great majority of them turned out to be false or wrong. German censorship was used as an excuse for the frequent publication of exaggerated and distorted stories, on occasion editorially admitted, several of them by people who were never identified. Predictions of all kinds flowed freely, and practically none of them came within miles of realization while judgments of the most ponderous sort were handed down to the readers, resulting in little more than the confirming of the readers in views which had already been assumed.

The liberals leaped into the arena at once on the matter of the sensational Reichstag fire trial. This was covered in much greater detail by the Communists, in view of the fact that Communists were indicted for this offense. But their enterprise in pleading innocence and their zeal in fixing the blame on prominent Hitlerites instead did not exceed that of the liberals fighting alongside. Imaginations began to run wild: the *New Republic* reported as facts the beat-

ing to death of Socialist mayors, the killing of Jewish rabbis in the
gutters, and the shooting of hundreds of Communists and Socialists
after their arrest, along with the jailing and torture of thousands of
people.[31] The jailing and trial of the German Communist Ernst
Torgler and the Bulgarian Communists Dimitroff, Taneff, and
Popoff for responsibility for the fire touched off demonstrations on
their behalf everywhere, at which time the loud charges that the
"Nazis" had done it themselves began to issue from Communist ac-
cusers. The liberals gave wide circulation to these accusations, along
with others from different sources. The *New Republic* printed a
lengthy account charging Goebbels and Goering with having staged
the whole affair, written by Ernst Oberfohren, chairman of the parliamentary group of the German Nationalist (Hugenberg) Party, which
had been opposed to alliance with Hitler's NSDAP. "The Nazis
Burned the Reichstag," charged Oberfohren, and the journal followed it up with other allegations that the "Nazis" killed him to
prevent his testimony from being heard in court.[32] The lack of evidence against the "Nazis" for either offense did not bother liberal editorial scruple in this hectic moment. But the Germans conducting the
trials were expected to keep their heads. The *Nation* and the *Manchester Guardian* supported the *New Republic*-Oberfohren thesis, but it
was the Communists who brought up the heavy artillery against the
"Nazis" in the fall.

The American League Against War and Fascism and a battery of
widely-known French Communists and sympathizers, headed by
Henri Barbusse and Romain Rolland, issued fiery protests against
the Communist trial which the liberal weeklies advertised,[33] although the big blow struck on behalf of the defense was the Communist propaganda volume *The Brown Book of the Hitler Terror*,
reviewed with high praise in the *New Republic* by Herbert Klein
on October 25, 1933.[34] The *Nation*'s editorial response a few weeks
later was to disparage the whole proceeding as "an alarming farce." [35]
In retrospect, however, the discomfiture of the German court conducting the Reichstag sabotage fire trial was a reflection on German
inexperience in conducting public political trials, as well as a commentary in comparison with similar spectacles in Russia, the most
recent having been the Metro-Vickers British engineers case a few
months earlier. There had been no tender solicitude for the welfare
of the accused here, and the conduct of the trial, as if degree of guilt,
and not guilt or innocence, were the issue, had been taken for granted.

When the Soviet conducted trials, including the Shakhty (1927–
1928), Ramzin (1930), and Groman-Sukhanov (1931) stagings, as well
as that mentioned above, no lawyers pleaded for them or sought acquittal, nor was the lack of such provisions thought unusual. Yet in
the German case, the German lawyers sought to get the accused ac-

quitted, and succeeded, while the defendants Torgler and Dimitroff even used the court as an opportunity to deliver stirring Communist political speeches. Nothing proved the rank amateur status of the "Nazis" more than this trial; the liberals shouted their praise of the successful fight against the prosecution by the Communists for months after acquittal. The reputation for restraint and suspended judgment among liberals suffered serious damage as a result of the prompt side-taking in this sorry spectacle, in which the object of both accuser and accused was the making of political capital and not seeing that justice was done.

What most liberals who became incensed over the Reichstag fire trial did not see was that from the point of view of international Communism the fate of the accused was secondary to the arousing of the world against Germany. The Leipzig trial was conceived as only a supporting device for freeing the defendants, while its purpose as a funnel for the distribution of hate of Russia's German enemies all over the world was emphasized. The *Communist* for December, 1933 heatedly shouted, "Around the Leipzig trial we must arouse the hatred of the toilers of the whole world for the Fascist provocateurs." [36] As it turned out, a great many of those who were aroused were toilers in the literary fields of American liberalism.

The liberal journals reverberated with editorials and special pieces on the trial by Gunther, Lore, Trotsky and Malcolm Cowley for weeks after the trial had cleared all the accused but the Dutch Communist Marinus van der Lubbe, for whom, strangely enough, almost no words of sympathy were expressed whatever. The heroes were Torgler and Dimitroff, propaganda figures of high repute at that time in the Communist International. But the main lesson was the comparison of the cautious and moderate language used in examining the Russian case against the British engineers, with the scorching, indignant reporting of the Leipzig proceedings against the alleged Red arsonists. Gunther made a passing reference to this in a *Nation* report in December, 1933; both he and the editorial statement a short time later commented on the courage of the lawyers for the defense of the Communists, an amazing fact when compared with traditional practice of Soviet defense lawyers to assume guilt of the accused, and to act accordingly.[37] Lore, reviewing Douglas Reed's flatly partisan book *The Burning of the Reichstag* ("Douglas Reed is a man without political or national bias") crowed especially over the acquittal of Dimitroff; "Here, in the person of an unknown Bulgarian revolutionist, is the mighty force that will yet encompass the downfall of the Nazi horror," he promised loudly. That it was to be at the hands of a well-known Russian one instead may be beside the point, but no one ever expressed in more forceful terms the eagerness for an apocalyptic Marxist finish.

The German National Socialist internal policy which drew the hottest fire from the liberal-left was the season of violence which ensued in the first three months of Hitler's regime. The "Nazis" received in the English speaking world a reputation so bad that they never really recovered from its hostility-producing effects. Although there was to be a substantial period of quiet in the era of 1935–1938 on the internal program, there was a latent unfriendliness which needed little agitation to whip it into flaming heat again. The Communist press ran the liberals a stiff contest as to which could print the most unfounded atrocity stories, and they lacked the capacity of the latter for stock-taking, for the liberals on several occasions admitted that some of their stories might be incorrect. The liberal weeklies also printed letters from readers protesting the unqualified withering attack on every and all National Socialist actions, but they eventually found a way to pin even the responsibility for their liberties with the truth upon Hitlerian policy, especially the press censorship. This had never been used as an excuse to accept sensational stories from Communist Russia, which hardly could have been referred to as a nation with a free press, but the Germans found themselves the targets of another double-faced set of measuring sticks.

The *Nation,* in extenuation of its repeated inflammatory stories with titles such as "Back to Barbarism," editorialized in April, 1933, "Under rigid censorship, and with complete suppression of the freedom of speech, press and assembly, it is impossible to get all the facts. Some exaggerations, some false stories are inevitable." [38] However, its own part in abetting this, such as the publication of second-, third- and fourth-hand accounts of physical violence, repeated alarming reports by un-named correspondents "of unimpeachable character and intelligence," plus inferences that all Germany had become a bleak madhouse in which most of the population were in jail or dead, hardly merited blaming their enemies for their own culpability in transmitting false stories. That there was violence was not the issue, but proper respect for their readers' intelligence required some attention to the matter of correctness, balance and proportion. However, the liberals in general were medal-winners compared to the Communist press. No Communist had a right to complain about the ugly excesses taken by Julius Streicher's *Der Stürmer* after matching this periodical with the caricature fantasies of the Red artists attached to the *New Masses,* for instance. Comic books had just started three or four years earlier, and their appeal to an audience not yet accustomed to reading or thinking was no excuse for following their leadership on the part of serious weeklies of comment on the public scene, whose readers hardly deserved to have their minds made up by the tasteless distortions which passed as political cartooning of that time.

One of the earliest and most extravagant attackers of Hitlerian violence was Villard in his signed weekly page in the *Nation*. His April 12, 1933 comment, "The Folly of Adolf Hitler," asserted that Hitler had already admitted borrowing many of his ideas from America; his Aryan race doctrines from Madison Grant, his crusade on the Jews from a book by Henry Ford, his technique of raising funds from both our major political parties, and his exclusionist views of Germany for the Germans from American immigration laws. He bitterly criticized Hitler for trying to rehabilitate industrialists and financiers as leaders, on the grounds that they had been "utterly discredited" for all time by the world depression, and chided him for not having taken advantage of the opportunity to learn something from the history of Russia. But his "greatest folly" undoubtedly was his estranging the good will of Americans, Frenchmen and Britons by allowing his followers to victimize their defeated enemies.[39]

In many ways this was one of the best summaries of liberal opinion on Germany, and helps to explain why most of it was so futile, as well as failing to explain anything. Liberals such as Villard seemed to think that Hitler had come to power solely for the purpose of vexing Britain, France and the United States with his unpopular domestic policies. That he was speaking to an internal audience and to a surrounding region of Central and Eastern Europe which did not share most Western views never seemed to enter the American liberal consciousness. Thus they never understood the waxing of his power and the entrenchment and growing popularity of his program. They dutifully predicted his collapse several hundred times on every issue imaginable, told the world his regime was the shakiest and weakest in the memory of man, encouraged their readers to expect all manner of swift revolutionary uprisings, including mass popular rejection, none of which was justified by the facts. Once these brave oracular excesses had all failed to materialize, they substituted a picture fully as false, the specter of an irresistible, all-powerful, all-encompassing evil genius of power, capable of obtaining mastery of the planet. This was the frightful apparition which was used at the end of the decade to mobilize American liberalism for a showdown war, and it was as untruthful as the prior image of laughable debility and bungling incompetence.

Within five weeks of Hitler's emergence there appeared a "Provisional Committee for Protest Against German Fascist Atrocities" in New York City, enrolling among its members *New Republic* editors Robert Morss Lovett, Niebuhr, and John Dewey, along with John Haynes Holmes, Roger Baldwin, Lincoln Steffens, Alvin Johnson and James T. Shotwell.[40] Tempers were rising steadily; the *New Republic* had declared, "The Hitlerites are crazy fanatics—almost as crazy and fanatical as were the Moslems of a century or two ago." [41] An unsigned full-page editorial had furiously attacked "Nazi" internal policies and presented an unrelieved portrait of gloom, with the entire German working class in chains, and highlighting especially the predicament of several world-famous Jews. Mary Heaton Vorse rose to equal heights in her piece "Germany: Twilight of Reason," which dwelled mainly on the famous book-burning incident but was much more exercised over the "filthy terror" perpetrated on the Berlin "liberals and radicals," spiced with unsupported but amazing statistics of numbers killed and imprisoned.[42]

From June until the end of the year these stories continued, with the unsigned and anonymous articles marked by the least sobriety and the most emotional appeals; the journals which had done the most to deflate the atrocity stories of 1914–1918 were well in the lead in giving credence to every story of this type that appeared. There is no record of either world-famous liberal weekly ever questioning in print an atrocity story coming from Germany after March, 1933. The reports in the autumn by Neuberger were in the new tradition, ugly accounts of violence reported in great detail but not a single instance of which he himself saw take place.[43] Several pieces exceeded his for incendiary gossip and sinister innuendo [44] of the type which had never been permitted for an instant in their pages when made about the Soviet Union.

There were plausible excuses to explain why large numbers of tourists were returning from Germany with accounts of the apparent peace and contentment which they found prevailing there. Neuberger laid it entirely to airtight "Nazi" control of the press and other media of public communication, a story which did not coincide at all with other stories, that of Niebuhr in particular, to the effect that underground Communist publications, one with an alleged circulation of 700,000 copies, were abounding.[45] In the meantime, press reports from Germany which did not coincide with those of the liberal and left were placed under strong suspicion; the motives even of publishers who featured "colorless" reports from Germany were questioned, as in the case of the German-language press of the Ridder family.[46] Journalists such as George Sylvester Viereck once more came under severe attack, although in his case there was much perplexity. The *Nation*, in an exasperated comment on his expressed sympathy for both Germany and the Jews, decided to classify him as "a prominent and indeed well-nigh unique example of the pro-Jewish Nazi," and chided him for not protesting to the German authorities in Leipzig when they confiscated his novel *My First Two Thousand Years*.[47]

Yet despite this unqualified side-taking, there were editorial protests when publications without a trace of detachment were banned in Germany. Villard was incensed that the *Nation* was barred from entry, and seemed hurt that he and his associates could not print a totally hostile journal advocating revolutionary tactics and circulate it freely in the area against which the hostility was directed. His pride in noting that it was the first such American journal so treated there was misplaced,[48] however, since the *New Masses* was banned beginning April 29, 1933. The *Manchester Guardian* was to join them soon, in turn denounced, and when the expulsion of individual journalists began on the grounds of their anti-German slant, even more comfort was extracted from the situation.[49]

The heavy accent on the debilitating effects of internal repression and indiscriminate terrorism was linked to steady reports of political struggles and dissension, and as the Marxian parties, despite their ballooned reputation, displayed less vigor by the week, every imaginable political splinter gained plaudits as a focus for unhorsing the "Nazis." The tempo of these increased as the November, 1933, plebiscite on the withdrawal from the League and election for the Reichstag approached. The Catholics, the Centrists, the splintered Hugenberg Nationalists, the Junkers and the Steel Helmet veterans' organization had all been looked upon as the forces likely to disintegrate the National Socialist spell.[50] Many liberals were now striving to pin the tag of illegitimacy on Hitler, a little over six months after admitting his victory through constitutional procedure.[51]

As the election drew near, it was announced editorially in the *New Republic* that fear would prevent large numbers from voting against the Nazis. But no one was prepared for the staggering 93% vote of approval of the action of withdrawal from the League on October 14, nor for the almost identical percentage which voted for the "Nazi" list of candidates. The fact that 3 million people spoiled their ballots was interpreted as a gesture of protest, but hardly as significant as it was made out to be in view of the positive vote. This acceptance by Germans did not reconcile any American liberal or radical; there was a tendency to grow more intemperate instead. Schuman, in his *New Republic* article "The Third Reich Votes," set a new high for condemnatory emotional reporting on German conditions. Both he and the editorial staff agreed that brutal individual coercion accounted for this towering majority, and that in reality it could be assumed that Hitler Germany was one vast prison camp. An aggressive undertone accompanied Schuman's piece, amounting to an early call to war to prevent a menace to peace.[52]

There was one curious consequence of Hitler's demonstration of political sagacity upon the liberals at this time. *Common Sense* had become involved in third-party politics on the domestic level as a result of deep dissatisfaction with the New Deal and all the collectivist parties still in existence, and in the summer of 1933 joined hands with the League for Independent Political Action, which then had among its sponsors John Dewey, Paul H. Douglas, Emil Rieve,

Villard and others, aiming at creating a vigorous farmer-labor party on a new basis. Although this monthly had printed practically no foreign news in its first year, it gave notice of its awareness of Hitler by devoting the back cover of its August, 1933 issue to a sketch of the rise of Nazism from nothing to full national power in 14 years. After conceding that this form of political action was "the great menace" of their time, the statement went on to advise the LIPA that "we can learn a great deal that is valuable about the techniques of political organization from a study of the development of the National Socialist Party." If a person with "so few of the qualities of a great leader" and with a negative program could defeat all the opposition parties so completely, it concluded, "it is reasonable to assume that a new party in America builded along sound organizational lines, with a positive program and with intelligent propaganda based on education and not prejudice, can achieve far more rapid success." Despite the nobility of the conception, few ventures of the depression decade collapsed so abjectly as this new third party adventure.

The growing tension in the National Socialist Party which resulted in the eruption of bloodletting on June 30, 1934, was mostly misinterpreted both before and after its occurrence. Prior to this occasion it was asserted that Hitler's most formidable enemies and the ones most likely to do something about it were the monarchists in the Nationalist camp. "Hitler is determined to have it out with these reactionaries," the *New Republic* editorialized early in February, 1934.[53] When the "Purge" struck, it was followed with a breathless fascination and horror, and long columns of speculation on its meaning appeared for months. The *Nation* misread this political civil war to a greater degree than their younger partner in weekly liberal journalism.[54] This was to some extent due to the influence of Villard, who saw Hitler's resort to summary executions a grave sign of weakness, and he freely predicted that the Nazi chief was a man with a brief future. All through 1934 he and others predicted catastrophe for National Socialism as a result of internal upheaval. In Villard's eyes, the killings now seemed "to justify the wartime atrocity propaganda stories of the Allies," evidence that the revisionism of the previous fifteen years was little more than a thin veneer covering a basic attitude of mainly unchanged proportions. In August he felt moved to qualify his judgments by charging that the Russians had killed more persons connected with their contemporary crisis following the assassination of Kirov, although he rightly insisted that this did not mitigate the guilt of Hitler and his associates. This brief essay in objectivity was uncharacteristic of the liberal and left; the Kirov purges literally vanished from consideration as news while the German bloodletting went on. But in one sense this was a grave defect of the largest part of the American press in 1934; their partiality helped create the conviction that political assassination was a purely German trait, and their silence or restraint as to similar conditions in the Soviet helped along the great Communist myth of ponderous mono-lithic stability and prosperity as a socialist island in a world of insane capitalist decay.

Political guessing continued wildly up to the day of the August 19 plebiscite which installed Hitler in exclusive executive power in Germany, seventeen days after the death of President von Hinden-burg. In the second week of July the *New Republic* still believed the purge had been intended to "nip in the bud the impending monarch-ist uprising," [55] while the following week it reversed its field and interpreted it as a turn to the right, and a sign of impending over-throw. "Hitler's overthrow will not come as soon as many persons hope and expect," a July 18 editorial testified, "but it is likely to come more rapidly than any but extreme optimists believed a year ago." [56] This soothsaying matched the wishful thinking of Villard. A month later, as the plebiscite approached, the *New Republic* was not so confident; Hindenburg's departure from the scene changed everything: "One may take it for granted that the German people will give Hitler the power he demands and would do so, even in a free and unrestricted election," it declared, rather astonishingly, four days before the event. It went on to undermine all its previous stories of debility; "On the whole Hitler's position at this moment seems firmer than before June 30. Certainly the outlook for a speedy end to his regime is far from rosy." [57] However, this pessimism did not diminish its powerful yearning to see Hitler's movement demolished.

By the end of the winter of 1934–1935 there were still occasional rumbles of comment over the sensational intra-party explosion, matched now by occasional anguished commentaries on the Kirov case. Unlike Villard and the *Nation,* which expressed strong views on the handling of the Kirov suspects, the *New Republic* was still trying desperately to believe the official reasons given by the Stalin govern-ment for executing 117 persons for Kirov's assassination, a most un-likely number of individuals to be involved in such a personal act. Though this was many more than the number killed in Germany, the junior liberal weekly grimly editorialized, "Russia's right to crush Nazi-White Guard conspiracies or other plots of murder and arson no one questions; few have anything but approval of it." [58] Despite its plaintive reservation due to the fact that no court had established the guilt of any of the executed, this expression of faith in Commu-nist probity could hardly be bettered from any source as a means of understanding the double standard prevailing for the weighing of political killing in these extraordinary days.

There was a wavering note of defeat in the August editorial com-mentaries on the nearly 90% approval of the recent Hitler moves by the German electorate. The *Nation* stressed the significance of the total number of those in opposition rather than its tiny percentage weight,[59] and the *New Republic*, still portraying the domestic scene as the "Hitler Terror" of the stock Communist press leaders on all news of Germany, concluded a hostile August 29 editorial with the lame admission, "For after all is said and done, Hitler still has the support of the vast mass of the German people." [60] A month later, in a scathing commentary on Hitler's promise at Nuremberg of a thousand years of National Socialist rule, the *New Republic* reproached those Germans who had voted for him the previous month in expectation of a mitigation of the repressiveness of the policies aimed at the Jews and the trade unions. Here it chose to identify these programs as "stage props" perpetuated by Hitler "lest he lose his still widespread popularity among the younger element and the thoughtless masses." [61] The latter observation was not very creditable to that part of the social order in which all virtue had presumably been lodged since the days of its discovery by Marx. The *Nation* was, if anything, even more puzzled and chagrined by Hitler's towering plebiscite majority. Accustomed to parliamentary circumstances where even a minority of the popular votes for the winning candidate was not uncommon, there was something almost indecent and immoral about this vast total. It alone indulged in innuendo as to the honesty of the election, and hinted that as many as 10 to 11 million of the votes had been faked.[62] It produced no proof or semblance of proof to substantiate this allegation.

An even more false note was struck in the succeeding months by the liberals who began to see encouraging signs of revolt against Hitler's regime in the behavior of the German churches, which were presumably venturing into "an open and organized opposition to Nazi tyranny." [63] It was a lame tack for those who had bristled with confidence in "the revolutionary militancy of the workers" and "the angry masses." Organized religion had never gained much support in the liberal ranks as a political force, and Hitler's attempt to get the churches out of politics had involved him in a number of serious ecclesiastical controversies as well, in which the churchmen held their own. For the next three years there were intermittent reports of churchmen in defiance of the Nazis on one matter or another, all conceived as heartening evidence of a substantial island of antagonism to the German total state. Had the German churches not been receiving state subsidies, their cause would have been somewhat more convincing. But this spot of infection was slim consolation for the abject defeat suffered by the forces most depended upon to wrest German political power away from this hated Brown Shirt group.

There were other grounds on which American liberals expected the Nationalist Socialist state to collapse shortly in addition to those of political partisanship. Its specific policies were expected to fall apart, leading to big changes on this evidence of incompetence. The suppression of the labor unions and the substitution of government arbitrators to negotiate agreements between the labor bureaus and the employers was conceived of as the very essence and distillation of Fascism; on the domestic scene, while attacking General Hugh S. Johnson and the NRA in 1934, the *New Republic* had insisted that the entry of a third-party mediator between workers and employers was the most outstanding characteristic of a Fascist economic order. This barrier to the maturation of the class struggle, and its arbitrary maintenance of order, was felt to be unbearably stifling. The introduction of compulsory labor service for the unemployed youth was also bitterly condemned, even if there was a trend toward such practice in several countries.[64] Lore's attack on the German program did not question its social utility, but simply opposed those who would be operating it, "a Fascist dictatorship from which all progressive elements have been ruthlessly expelled." [65] The *New Republic* was convinced in May, 1933 that Germany was already bankrupt, that Hitler's days were numbered by the sure collapse of his public works, labor service and farm aid plans, in addition to the question of exports and foreign exchange, two other assumed insolubles.[66] Obsessed by the idea of a gold standard world money system as a sure barrier to the achievement of Nazi goals, the liberal economic experts were never psychologically prepared for the phenomenal German recovery of 1933–1938, and the impressive expansion of its foreign trade. A special propaganda was perfected later on to account for all this and to attach to it a most condemnatory flavor and color.

But in these early years, when a long succession of cheerful predictions of sudden doom to National Socialism appeared among the liberals, it was customary to attach the blame for their sure demise to the financial and industrial barons, who were assumed to be utterly incompetent as proved by the massive depression in Germany. The economic and political aberrations of the leaders were credited with the rise of "the perversions of Hitlerism," as Mauritz Hallgren suggested, not "irremediable defects in the German character." [67] This latter diagnosis did not gain widespread credence until Germany had regained its dominant position in the affairs of Central Europe. As James Burnham, deep in his "Trotskyite" period, put it, "Hitler is no Teutonic accident. He is the cultural price we pay for the preservation of the rights of private property. And black Germany is an early twilight to the darkness that lies in the capitalist future." [68] Such announcements of swiftly approaching doom from internal collapse were constantly appearing in Hitler's first two and a half years, and they continued with some modification until the outbreak of the war in 1939. In March, 1935, another in the stream of refugee economic experts from Germany, Paul Crosser, announced, "Nazi Germany is sinking farther and farther into the economic quicksand." He purported to describe a comprehensive economic decline across the board, with severe unemployment, a badly deteriorated standard of living, and disaster everywhere except in the armaments industries.[69] It was one of dozens of similar predictions which helped to keep the readers in an utter state of unpreparedness for the change of tune some while later, to that of an invincible and omnipresent Nazi economic colossus astride the world.

In the field of foreign trade, liberal economists, amateur or otherwise, sought to locate definite proof of approaching German desperation and prostration. As an international debtor with a heavy concentration in industry, under Hitler it was assumed that Germany would continue to depress wages still further downward, as had been going on since the Brüning emergency decrees of 1930, accompanied by a serious attempt to further undercut the world prices for manufactured goods, while maintaining a stern control of imports, since only in this way was it expected to pay off its private external debts. For this reason, no one expected any significant reductions of tariffs at the London Economic Conference, barring a substantial reduction of the debt burden on Germany, which might effect an easing of the wage level there as well as a relaxation on imports, stimulating world trade all around.[70]

As if this inheritance of the strait jacket woven at Versailles were not enough, the boycott of German goods in the Anglo-Saxon countries which was stimulated by the anti-Jewish measures was expected to wreak additional damage. Both liberal editorial comments assumed that the country would suffer terribly from world Jewish boycotts, leading to suspension of foreign debt payment, increased unemployment and a further depressed standard of living. Grim comments piled up all the first year, but the "Nazi" economy refused to take the final fatal nosedive. Such steps as leaving the gold standard bloc, the development of autarchic programs of self-sufficiency and the ingenious multi-valued currencies to accommodate foreign commerce, as well as subsidies to the export trade, all postponed the final reckoning which orthodox Marxist theory had plotted out for some time.[71] The *Nation* in its January 3, 1934 editorial doggedly insisted the extinction of Germany was still approaching in seven league boots, to be followed by the continuation of economic life "on a comparatively low plane." [72] When matched against the flood of accounts of stunning economic prosperity in Soviet Russia during this time, Hitler Germany in the liberal journals was one vast poor house and slum. These reports did not help support the growing apprehension over its foreign plans and ambitions, since a nation as weak as Germany was being portrayed scarcely could entertain a foreign policy at all. But ways were found to rationalize this as well as other contradictions. The relation between Hitlerian autarchic measures and the world boycott was not often explored, but this German economic nationalism drove out of mind, especially in the *Nation,* the wrath it had strewn upon Britain, France and the United States in 1932 for their "Buy-British," "Buy-French," and "Buy-American" campaigns of the same sort.

The German government's decision to repudiate its financial obligations under the Treaty was not handled as roughly as a later one to interpret the long term foreign debt as commercialized political obligations which Germans were also not morally compelled to pay. Both weeklies denounced these steps in the spring and summer of 1934,[73] and went on record a little later recommending that the Roosevelt Administration "forbid all further loans to the Reich or its industries," not only because of previous repudiation of debt obligations but also because it would be exceedingly difficult to obtain adequate guarantee that new loans would be dependable, safe investments; "Conditions there are going from bad to worse with progressive rapidity," a *New Republic* editorial of August 1, 1934 warned.[74]

By this time domestic and foreign affairs with respect to German economic activities were starting to blend, and the full consequences of the acts of the National Socialists were beginning to be assessed in more than simply home front significance, as will be seen later. There was for instance bitter comment on German rearmament on the grounds that resources were being diverted from the standard of living necessities of the German masses, in addition to the political portent to France and Russia, the two nations which American liberals began to champion actively by early 1935 against waxing German strength. This argument was never employed against Russia, however, and the massive Red military and aerial buildup was never estimated in its cost as represented by the deprivations of ordinary Russian citizens. When Louis Fischer in a Moscow dispatch to the *Nation* January 2, 1935, announced that bread rationing in Russia was scheduled to terminate as of the first of the year as if this were a great achievement,[75] it was not found necessary to reveal that Germany in its lowest depths had never had to resort to issuing bread cards. But this did not jog the fixation of Russia as the great bastion of economic strength as opposed to a desperate and chronic near-bankrupt Hitler Germany. A lengthy list of experts and on-the-spot journalist-observers poured these stories of German economic prostration into the weekly liberal press to the very eve of World War Two.

TRUMP CARD AGAINST HITLER:
RACIAL PERSECUTIONS AND
THE CONCENTRATION CAMPS

When World War Two finally began, in the English-speaking world there probably was hardly a person in ten thousand who could have recited in a coherent manner the economic, social and political policies of Germany under Hitler. But from the ocean of words which had fallen on him in six years about Germany, the ordinary citizen might be expected to have gleaned two facts: there were concentration camps for various persons declared untrustworthy by the regime, and it was conducting an anti-Jewish policy of discrimination and persecution. Those who could identify more than these actions were part of a small minority. But the fact that such understandings were so widespread testifies to the effectiveness of repetition in the press in a simplified manner; few other media of communication bothered to publicize these events with such undeterred constancy and simplicity. How these two policies were reported in the liberal press and by liberals for a much higher than average level of political sophistication is a revealing incident in the history of opinion-making in the pre-war decade.

Neither concentration camps nor Jewish persecutions were novelties in the English-language press when they began to draw comment and condemnation for their appearance in Germany in the spring of 1933. In what was referred to as the "commercial press" by liberal intellectuals, the story of the massive camps for varied elements in the Russian Soviet had been repeated for several years, while outrages committed on the persons of Jews had been the subject for a flood of print especially since the great post-Russo-Japanese War pogroms in Russia, the numerous massacres in Poland and in Central Europe at the end of World War One, and up to the latest season of violence in depression-struck Central and Eastern Europe. As to Russian concentration camps, this was a tender subject among left-inclined liberals. Such stories were subject to a massive discount among them, and rarely treated with credibility in the main liberal organs. Such persons as claimed to have escaped from them were rarely believed, and in the early 1930's they were often dismissed as sensation-mongers and reactionary cranks trying to bring discredit upon what was deeply believed to be the only significant social reconstruction experiment taking place in the whole world. With respect to the Jews, the liberal friends of Russia felt themselves on much sounder ground, and developed a deep ritualistic respect for the Communist dogma that a fundamental change had been brought about in Russian minds, resulting in the "outlawing" of all anti-Jewish thought, talk and action.

This was repeated over and over, and with extra emphasis after Jewish repression became a quasi-state policy in Germany. It helped liberals to reassure themselves that their position on Hitler Germany had a sturdy basis, as well as confirming them in their conviction as to the immensely superior morality of the Communists. When paired with their strong leanings toward a Marxian socialist and anti-nationalist society, it gave extra stimulus to their hatred of the "Nazis" on account of their overt and blatant nationalism. In addition, by concentrating on the German scene it became possible to draw attention from whatever aspects of Russian society they felt were not particularly conducive to good relations with that part of the American world still not inclined to accept the Communists without reservations. With one exception, from the accession of Hitler until the Russo-Finnish war of 1939–1940, the liberal attention to concentration camps in Russia hardly produced a column of print, and the Jewish policy of Russia was reflected as an untarnished spectacle of glory, while reserving a few sedate and restrained comments on Communism's deep hostility to Zionism, an attitude they did not criticize.

American liberals had already built up a culprit on the issue of excesses against Jews long before the accession of Hitler. In the early depression years it had been Poland which drew the scorn and despising for its numerous harsh policies, an attack renewed in 1937–1938 upon the renewed outbreak of Polish assaults on Jews.[76]

Of special importance in the pre-Hitler bitterness felt toward the Poles was Michael Farbman's extended dispatch from Poland published by the *New Republic* in early January, 1932. In a long critique of Polish nationalism and the spirit of expansionism sweeping the younger generation, and a revived militarism which led him to remark that he saw more officers in uniform in Poland than anywhere else in Europe except Rumania and Bulgaria, Farbman spoke of anti-Jewish riots in Cracow, Warsaw and Vilna. His critique of the "racial supremacy" ideas of "resurrected Poland" was as sharp as his discussion of Polish territorial aims at the expense of their neighbors.

In 1931 and 1932 Austria and Rumania had also been censured for the occurrence of beatings and belligerent demonstrations, which seemed to be part of a spreading practice all over Central and Eastern Europe at that time,[77] excluding of course Russia, in liberal minds. The great Communist propaganda victory of the moment, in the spring and summer of 1932, as the German National Socialists began to forecast the more ominous moves of the future by decrees against Jews in Prussia,[78] was the announcement of the creation of the district of Biro-Bidjan in Siberia exclusively for the immigration of Jews from outside the Soviet Union who were anxious to leave where they were. William Zukerman accorded this high praise in a *Nation* article, "A Jewish Home in Russia,"[79] although Fischer in his regular dispatch from Moscow two weeks later, "The Jews and the Five Year Plan," delivered himself of a lengthy tribute to the Reds for the admirable way in which they had incorporated the "declassed" Jews who had been uprooted from capitalism and placed in industrial, technical and mechanical positions of prominence, while gaining full political, educational and social stature thanks to the total suppression of anti-Jewish prejudices among non-Jewish Russians. Fischer was particularly cool toward the Biro-Bidjan project, however, as an encouragement to the resurgence of Jewish particularism. He believed that Bolshevik success in undermining Zionism without diminishing Jewish culture should be extended toward eliminating "Jewish nationalism," that through "intermarriage on a large scale" and "the gradual disappearance of religion," the "rapid assimilation of Soviet Jewry" was now a fact. For this reason he suspected that such distractions as this Soviet adventure would encourage the persistence of "Jewish consciousness," something that was extremely tenacious and largely due to the efforts of "the prejudices of vested Jewish interests." [80]

Coming as it did in 1932, the most obvious beneficiaries of Biro-Bidjan were expected to be Polish Jews, as few others were spoken of in relation to it, and Polish hostility toward Jews drew repeated broadsides, even well after the introduction of the German repressions. Early in October, 1933, Fischer ridiculed Polish protests of German action in sharp manner: [81]

A Poland protesting against anti-Jewish persecutions [in Germany] is a comic anomaly. Other states have ground down national minorities and disaffected colonial peoples no less ruthlessly than has the Germany of the hooked cross. The white terror in China is probably as shocking as the brown terror in Germany. Yet popular movements do not thunder against Chiang Kai-shek. Much of the emotion in Western lands against Hitler is a carefully nursed preparation for government moves should German rearmament warrant forcible Allied intervention. Much anti-Nazi propaganda is at bottom anti-German and smacks of wartime psychology and of hypocrisy.

Such blunt language indicated that even the Hitlerian measures had not succeeded in erasing the memories of Polish and other indignities from liberal minds at this point, when it might have been quite simple to join in the barrage against the Germans. Even the *Nation*'s editorial policy had a long memory. Late in September, 1934, there was a curt sally against the Poles for their treatment of their minorities, successfully shielded from widespread view because of their ties with the French; "So long as France dominated the League and Poland was the ward of France, complaints against Poland could easily be muffled at Geneva," this critique explained.[82] The occasion was a late-season British and French reaction to a Polish attempt to unilaterally denounce the treaty which gave the League supervisory powers in the administration of racial minorities. Such occasions were not aberrations but part of a persistent fire directed at the Poles which was still vigorous in 1938, and taken up the following year with great gusto by the Communists after the celebrated non-aggression pact between Russia and Germany.

However, the German actions against Jews led to a substantial diminution of the criticisms of the Poles and others for doing likewise; in fact, in the four or five years after Hitler's rise to power, a sizable segment of the readership of the liberal press grew to identify Germany and anti-Jewish programs as complements. Even though an impressive number of books by travelers and journalists during the period underlined hostility toward Jews as endemic in Central and Eastern Europe, and even though a newspaper or two such as the *Jewish Daily Forward* were so bold as to assert that even in Russia Jews were still victimized in a variety of ways, the overall stereotypes of Russia as the benefactor of the Jewish people and Germany as their nemesis gained wide credence. Liberals in general accepted the Communist attitude of implacability toward Zionism, and persisted in instructing Jews in America and elsewhere that their salvation lay in acceding to the class conflict thesis, despite the fact that by and large the Jewish community even in Germany contained only a minority of the left-inclined.

But there is little doubt as to the German National Socialists taking the lead in the hall of villains on this question, and before the era was over, the Germans were also credited with the concentration camp as a social innovation. By 1939, the similar institutions of the British in the Boer War, the Spanish in Cuba, the Russians and others might just as well not have once existed in the popular mind, let alone America's Indian "reservations" of the era prior to the reorganization of the Indian Bureau. Both liberal weeklies editorialized on the subject with intense heat, and indiscriminately blended the Hitlerian repressions of the Marxist political opposition parties and the Jewish crack-downs, especially after 1933, creating the impression that most Jewish victims were also leftist political enemies of Hitler. Only by carefully reading the reports of special correspondents was it possible to discover that this was far from the truth.

In the beginning the indignation against Jewish repressions reached a sudden peak in April, 1933, just at the time the early hysteria in Germany was subsiding and when such outrages were quietly tapering off. The *Nation* was more incensed than the *New Republic,* and implied that Hitler's regime had mortally wounded itself before the opinion of the world for permitting such behavior, although it really amounted to the opinion of Britain **and America.** There never was a study of the effect of Hitlerian hostility toward Jews among Germany's Central European neighbors, and nothing was ever printed which indicated that the populace of any other country in the world reacted with such deep affront as those of the British and American audiences. One of the most marked innings of quiet was that which occurred in the Soviet Union. When the angry *Nation* editorial "Nazis Against the World" appeared on April 5, 1933, it might best have been qualified by the insertion of the word "Anglo-American" since no reference was made to any other part of the planet objecting to the German behavior. In fact, the liberals themselves served as documentors of the continued contagious spread of anti-Jewish measures all over Europe after 1933, rather than outraged protest over its eruption among the Germans. There was undoubtedly a great amount of injustice in this program as carried out in Germany, but the liberals did immense damage to the truth by concentrating on the purely German aspect and poisoning the world indiscriminately against Germans whether they sympathized with anti-Jewish measures or not, rather than dealing with it as a long-standing fact of European society. In America especially, the effect was profound and cumulative. When its soldiers waded ashore in France in the summer of 1944, it was a rare fighting man who could state any fact about their adversary's socio-economic order other than that they had instituted some vague program for eliminating the Jews from their country, even though the ending of this state of affairs was the least important of all Allied war aims by that time.

The liberal attack on German anti-Jewish measures was varied. *Nation* editors such as Villard and Freda Kirchwey spoke as outraged persons of German descent from the days of the Forty-Eighters, migrants to America from a Germany of an earlier day. Many of the assailants were of German or Jewish extraction, an increasing number of them exiles or refugees from the Hitler regime themselves. In most cases they championed Hitler's political enemies in Germany more than they defended Jewish rights, often for Socialist or Communist causes, although there were occasional contributions from Jews who promoted no particular cause; notable among the latter was an unusually eloquent piece by Ludwig Lewisohn in the *Nation* in May, 1933,[83] which suffered from the defects of many of the communications of that time in that it was prepared outside Germany and yet purported to describe intimate scenes in that country. It was noteworthy for its impatience with the German Jews themselves for trying to adjust to their unusual predicament as Germans. It also was less effective as a consequence of being late, since it described situations already in decline by the time it was published.

After the first few weeks there was a tendency for a while to stress the material and related distress of Germany's Jews rather than incidents of violence against their persons, and their tiny numbers as compared to the total population of the country as evidence that their alleged inordinate influence in the country was largely imaginary. Ludwig Lore in his *New Republic* essay "The Jews in Fascist Germany" on April 12, 1933 sought to get at the source of this nationalist hostility, concluded that anti-Jewish programs were "not an essential of Fascist philosophy," an observation based on the experience of Mussolini Italy, a regime in which many Jews were known to hold prominent posts. Lore interpreted it as a product of the nationalist reaction to internationalism of all kinds, and resulting in the coupling of Marxism to the Jews by Fascist nationalists in Germany, to which he did not object. In his view, the Hitlerians were more hostile to Marx on account of the internationalist character of his philosophy than because of his Jewish heritage. [84]

Such analysis was not uncommon from those writers like Lore whose affection for Marxism was demonstrably warm. Their most telling blows were struck against those in Germany who expected the material lot of the non-Jewish element to improve markedly merely by the suppression of Jews in business and the professions.[85] A *New Republic* editorial of April 19 observed, "While the atrocity campaign against the Jews seems to have subsided, at least temporarily, discrimination against them is merciless and systematic." Two reasons were advanced to explain this diminution of physical humiliation and injury: a "world boycott" of German products and the bringing up of the question of mistreatment of Jews in Silesia before the League of Nations, on the grounds of being a violation of a 1922 treaty with Poland respecting all Silesian inhabitants "without distinction as to race, language or religion." When the "Nazi" anti-Jewish laws were suspended there late in the spring, the same journal announced, "The Jews have won what may prove to be an important victory over the Hitler government in Germany." [86] But the possibility of Silesia becoming a Jewish sanctuary within the Reich was considered to be of definitely second rank compared to the economic boycott, which was freely predicted to be capable of bringing Hitler's regime to its knees.

Enthusiasm for the boycott, led in America by the well-known New York attorney Samuel Untermyer, and pressed elsewhere by an international Jewish congress held in Amsterdam and by the National Joint Council of the labor unions in England, was one of the ways in which liberal energies were mobilized against Hitler Germany in the summer of 1933,[87] in addition to the wide publicity given to atrocity stories, too often based on hearsay. Other projects gained ground: the "University-in-Exile," under the direction of Alvin Johnson, and supported by a formidable group of intellectual and academic liberal figures, which sought to gather together some day a total of 300 exiled Germans of minority racial or political sentiments,[88] and the newest of the relief organizations, the International Relief Association, under the leadership of Freda Kirchwey and Sterling D. Spero, all received strong support.[89] It was obvious that these groups were interested in particular Germans, not the rank and file of those who might want to leave for various reasons. The figures who received the widest attention were renowned personalities of the academic, artistic and literary worlds, although it was not often shown that they were suffering from personal indignities or physical want. Insofar as Jews were concerned, no indication was ever shown that they had the slightest interest in taking advantage of the Soviet invitation to Biro-Bidjan. The Germans who went there in the next six years were an infinitesimal trickle, and in all the subsequent propaganda against the "Nazis," no issue was made of the Communists succeeeding in making any headway through attracting unhappy Germans to Russia. But there was no let-up in the liberal circles on the shamefulness of the Jewish persecutions, with tendencies for this to blend into the attack on Hitler for the comprehensive penalties being inflicted on German Marxist radicalism. In the later 1930's every element which felt the pressure of Nazi curbs came in for its share of praise as well: pacifists, "republicans," churchmen, Jehovah's Witnesses, and others. But in no case did another German minority as small as the Jews gain the support the latter did in the American liberal press. It was probably the most remarkable campaign ever conducted in the interests of such a small minority group of citizens of a foreign state by any segment of American public opinion-making media in the nation's history.

Late in September, 1933, the *New Republic* pronounced, "The world-wide boycott of German goods, shipping and services of all kinds which is being organized by prominent Jewish bodies seems to us the only way of impressing upon those responsible for the present regime in Germany the detestation with which its persecutions are regarded." It repeated its stand of having "steadfastly opposed governmentally authorized boycotts" yet admitted that private boycotts were a type of war measure nevertheless. However, it excused the Jewish retaliation on the grounds that Hitler had declared war on them first, and even though many innocent Germans were likely to suffer from the effects of a global ban on German products and services, it would be justified if it hurried the end of the Hitler regime.[90] The distinction between the "Nazis" and other elements in Germany was starting to disappear even at this early date; the fate of the millions of Socialist and Communist opponents in Germany was already becoming a minor detail.

When Richard Neuberger returned to the United States in the fall of 1933, he wrote additional *Nation* dispatches elaborating on Jewish distress in Germany, but he confessed to being more depressed upon learning that such a firm as the R. H. Macy Company, "chiefly owned and operated by Jews," should be disregarding the Jewish boycott and buying large quantities of German products. He urged Jesse I. Straus, Ambassador to France and one of the company's principal owners, to heed the stand taken by Macy's "Christian competitor," Lord & Taylor, which had terminated buying in Germany immediately upon the beginning of the Hitler "reign of terror." When Macy's and the Untermyer American League for the Defense of Jewish Rights became engaged in a hot exchange of charges shortly after, during which the three New York morning newspapers all refused to print one of Untermyer's open letters to Macy's president, the *Nation* took Untermyer's side and published the controversial advertisement and the correspondence between him and Percy S. Straus.[91]

The more belligerent supporters of the boycott among liberals used this and other incidents as opportunities to flay the "bourgeois" Jews for their reluctance to make a flaming fight out of the boycott, and some of the most aggressive were not Jews. No one exceeded Villard, who was still writing energetic editorials in the late fall expressing his conviction that it was still possible to crush Hitler under an economic boycott administered by volunteer independents all over the world.[92] Few matched him in ability to produce anti-German invective; in retrospect, Cold War anti-Soviet polemics have an air of restraint compared with the more flowery of the Villard attacks. It may be questioned how anyone could avoid shaking with rage after reading them, and in the light of his diligent stand against going to war against Germany six years later, one must still accord his work a high rank in the mobilizing of liberal enmity toward Germans in this important formative period.

By the winter of 1933–1934 the attention to the boycott began to wane, as it became evident that the National Socialists were displaying a tenacious will to survive despite its partially crippling effects. More and more emphasis began to be devoted to rescue of those anxious to leave, admittedly a tiny part of Germandom still. Here and there the counselors of resistance and class warfare pounded liberals for not keeping up a full-throated roar over the persecutions and indignities to Germany's Jews and harassed intellectuals,[93] while Waldo Frank, in an extremely provoking *New Republic* article in December, "Should the Jews Survive?", suggested that Jewry was suffering a deserved fate for having become "bourgeois" and seeking to become indistinguishable from other Germans, and recommended the adoption of the Marxian class struggle as a tactic for group survival. No other theoretical article on the Jews in Germany drew as many reader responses to the editors as this, up to this time, and a torrid and recriminatory exchange went on for weeks.[94]

In truth, the campaign to help beleaguered Jews could not be kept distinct from the several organizations whose interest in German affairs extended to a variety of elements, most of them readily discernible political adversaries of the Hitler group. There grew out of the intermixing and conflicts of these groups arguments as to who deserved support first, and technical distinctions between a "refugee" and an "exile" evolved, which led to questioning the political pedigree of some of the more prominent Germans now disaffected from National Socialism. Herbert Solow and Harry Slochower found it necessary to chastise Thomas Mann for his restrained behavior in *New Republic* broadsides in 1934, Solow for Mann's failure to write for determined anti-Hitler publications, Slochower, as the agent for a committee of noted writers, for Mann's failure to come to the support of imprisoned German Communists such as Torgler, Thaelmann and Ludwig Renn, and Karl von Ossietsky, former editor of the German liberal weekly *Weltbühne,* the nearest equivalent to the American weekly organs of liberalism. Solow did not believe a "refugee" as such deserved the sympathy of active anti-Hitler people, since he might even be "a Jewish millionaire who now rides around the Riviera in a Rolls Royce," and was not absent from Germany by choice, whereas the "exile" was defined as a person who fled because he would not be "coordinated" by the regime, and furthermore was one who "used his freedom outside Germany to carry on the fight against Hitler." Mann, Stefan Zweig and others were subject to sharp critiques for failing to come up to this latter definition.[95]

Some of the liberals, Jews and non-Jews alike, were not entirely pleased or convinced by the politicalization of refugee-exile relief. Some suspected the International Relief Association and the World Committee for the Relief of Victims of German Fascism of being too tenderly concerned for the welfare of Communists, to the exclusion of others, although the ostensible leadership seemed detached from such goals. In the case of the latter, its moving spirit was the British Laborite Socialist Lord Marley. Both organizations pleaded for nonpartisan interest in Germany. But branches of the IRA in 22 countries in the spring of 1934 caused suspicion to brew in the minds of some liberals, who knew of no group in Germany in opposition to Hitler which could lay claim to such international sympathy other than the Communists.

There were other uneasy discussions over the matter of the emotional publicity given to the Jewish tribulations in Germany, as well as the persistence of unreconstructed views of non-Communist and non-radical Jews, which often touched off fiery fulminations from those of far more leftist inclination. Nathan Asch in a *New Republic* book review in the issue of April 18, 1934, quietly reminded the readers that "not all Jews are liberals or radicals," and there were even expressions of fear that the liberal journals might import anti-Jewish views to America by unintentionally presenting an exaggerated notion of the virtues of Jews and the depravity of Germans in general. Defensive books written by Jews which recited reservations about Russia and overlooked Jewish financial support to Hitler incited angry remarks at intervals, which revealed much impatience with what was considered an outmoded form of instruction for survival in an increasingly hostile world.

One of the sharpest of these was a reproach delivered by Norbert Guterman, previously cited editor of a French review *Avant-Poste,* and quondam contributor to the *New Masses* as well as the liberal weeklies, in reviewing Rabbi Mordecai M. Kaplan's *Judaism as a Civilization* for the *New Republic* in October, 1934: [96]

> Look at the situation in Germany, where even in the face of such policies of downright persecution as Hitler's, the opposition is divided by the fact that Jewish capital is thrown to the support of Nazism. And see how easy it always is to find, in Germany or anywhere else, certain conservative elements of the race fishing around in the muddy puddle of nationalism. Rabbi Kaplan, for one, is doing precisely this sort of thing. . . .

Guterman was bitterly opposed to Kaplan's insistence on "Jewish racial and national peculiarities," and he denounced the repetition of such themes as having about them "the unmistakable smell of Nazism dressed in Jewish fringes."

This was, of course, another appearance of the anti-Zionist predisposition on the part of one who was convinced the Communist solution of the dissolving of Jewish distinctiveness in the "classless society" was immensely superior to trying to "assimilate" in the capitalist nationalist state, or segregation into the purely Jewish state of the Zionists. As late as February, 1935, Ernest Sutherland Bates was chiding Robert Nathan for emphasizing Russian brutality toward Jewish exiles in his book *Road of Ages.* Bates exploded that this was "an inexcusable attitude, in view of the Soviet record in the matter of racial persecution," another in the long line of fervent testimonials to belief that the Russians had succeeded in outlawing all discrimination of a racial or ethnic sort.[97]

But the liberals and their press in general did not reach the dizzying peaks of scorn for Zionism attained by such devotedly pro-Communist publications as the *New Masses.* A sensational series of nine articles by John L. Spivak in this weekly in the latter part of 1934, which purported to establish that America's Jews were in mortal danger of a comprehensive assault by anti-Jewish zealots everywhere in the United States, led up to a climax editorial in the issue of December 4, 1934, titled "Anti-Semitism: What to Do About It." [98] It called upon American Jews to adopt Communism as in Russia, where Jewish persecution had ceased due to the evolution of the "classless society," excoriated Zionism, and dismissed the reformism of the American Jewish Congress and the American Jewish Committee as "two reactionary nationalist organizations seeking hegemony over the Jewish masses." It did not reach quite the vitriolic level of Robert Gessner's onslaught on Zionism and its leader Vladimir Jabotinsky two months later, "Brown Shirts in Zion: Jabotinsky—the Jewish Hitler," [99] but its message was just as clear: "The only safety for the Jew, his only tactic, can be his alliance with the working class." The *Nation* praised Spivak's articles, and agreed that American Jews were in danger of their lives as a consequence of a massive movement in imitation of Hitler Germany, but it did not support the editorial stand which the *New Masses* believed Spivak's reporting logically pointed to for the future. [100] But by this time the Popular Front era was upon liberalism, and the blending of the defense of the Jews with its dynamics will be dealt with subsequently.

In its first issue in January, 1934, the *Nation* editorially noted that it was being taken to task periodically for its "intemperate condemnation of the Nazi government in Germany," one of the rare occasions when either it or its junior opposite file admitted such charges were being made by readers. [101] That no admissions of this failing were made goes without saying, since the political commitments of the editorial staff placed the matter beyond discussion. Exaggeration of the plight of some Jews and Communists undoubtedly accounted for some of the protests, but the astonishing portrayal of the German concentration camps played a part in the registering of this minority opinion. The failure to put on record a factually faithful picture of this particular political institution left the door open for the appearance of a flock of sensational reports, and the sum of them after two years of National Socialism still amounted to controversial confusion. Who were committed to these penal colonies within the Reich, what for, for how long, and what their condition was while incarcerated were essentially factual matters that were handled in the most unfactual manner. But what did gain credence in liberal channels hardly supported the imaginative atrocity picture conjured up for the general public.

Given the stubborn refusal to believe in the existence of similar prison camps in Soviet Russia and hardly to allude to the possibility of their reality for the better part of two decades helps to explain why the liberal weeklies and numerous writers of liberal persuasion could reach such heights of indignation over the German variety. It especially might be cited in extenuation of the *Nation*'s publication in August, 1933 of Harrison Brown's assault on this emergency institution of Hitler's: "For the first time in history in time of peace a government has imprisoned numbers of its own nationals on no other grounds than that their opinions are objectionable," Brown reported in his "Six Months of Hitlerism." [102] This of course ignored the decades of Siberian exile in Russian Czarist times, and the well-established Communist successors, which certainly anteceded the Nazi stockades. It also failed to achieve the level of fact in neglecting to note that there were persons imprisoned there whose detention had little or nothing to do with their opinions, barring the intention of establishing the elastic view that all action contrary to law was originally due to a difference of opinion, in which case the entire prison population everywhere might have been said to be jailed on the grounds of entertaining "objectionable opinions."

That Brown's piece performed no service at all in helping to understand this issue may be peripheral. However, it was one of the first to try to estimate the number of those who had been apprehended by the authorities. He estimated that there were "at least" 30,000 men in these camps "doing forced labor." In itself this estimate, made with no intention to understate the case, made a shambles of six months of liberal reporting on the German concentration camps. As a report that Hitler had imprisoned an infinitesimal fraction of one per cent of the German people, it hardly could have been released in expectation of rousing much new concern. But it was indicative of the manner in which the subject was handled for years. Brown confessed that "not a great deal" was known about the administration of the camps, supplied no facts other than hearsay, and appeared to be most agitated by the incarceration of German pacifists. Later writers stressed the detention of Communists, Socialists, liberals, Jews, religious dissenters and so forth. But this report made a strange contrast to the *Nation*'s nearly contemporary editorial which recited "the horrors of the overcrowded German prison camps."

In a similar manner the *Nation* undermined the widespread belief that those sentenced to such camps were there for indefinite periods and were the victims of arbitrary imprisonment, not legal proceedings. In July, 1933 it printed a report by one R. S. Wheeler, "In a Nazi Court of Justice," a baleful commentary on "Nazi" political trials by an actual eyewitness.[103] His attempt to paint the picture in the darkest hue fell wide of the intended mark, since he reported that the great majority of persons whom he saw sentenced for acts against the regime received sentences of from two to six months. Even compared to the actions of American courts in the days of high hysteria in 1917–1918, these were remarkably mild; one did not have to call to mind the Soviet practices at all here.

By October, 1933 the total had risen sharply. Robert Dell, the *Nation*'s Geneva correspondent, a devoted partisan of the French and one of the first liberal journalists to frankly suggest a coalition war against Germany in Hitler's first year, was the author of the figure 80,000.[104] This was admittedly an approximation, and nobody ever expressed any sureness in advancing these figures; that they might have been set higher for effect cannot be utterly dismissed. This figure lasted for several months, without confirmation. Villard, in a signed editorial in March, 1934, repeated it but admitted it was a rumor.[105] He attacked this program with great gusto, however, with the same lack of logic characteristic of American liberalism in this era of good feeling toward Russian Communism. The time for criticism of Russian domestic policies still lay in the future.

Stories of persons claiming to know of concentration camps from first-hand acquaintance were not too common, but imagination made up for what was missing. A variety of such accounts appeared in both weeklies from time to time, with some degree of contradictory comment. Those of 1934 and 1935 exceeded even the earliest in dramatic content, but one constant was the sparse number of eyewitness relations of violence committed on the persons of the prisoners. In the first two years there was but one outstanding account of any one camp in the *New Republic,* an August, 1934 narrative by an anonymous author relating in amazing detail the interior of Dachau, probably the most notorious of the sites in Germany proper. This went into revolting descriptions of the treatment meted out there, with a startling statement as to the constitution of its population as of that summer. According to this source there were about 1700 persons in Dachau, "the majority of whom are either Communists or members of organizations known as sympathetic," with Jews constituting only about 40 of the entire number.[106]

It seemed on occasion that the editors did not read these stories very carefully, because editorial comment inclined toward believing that the entire anti- or non-Nazi element in Germany were in these internment areas. But as long as these institutions were palpitating news, there was a dominant trend toward following the *Brown Book* pattern and identifying the majority of this concentration camp element as Communist party personnel. In the late summer of 1934, as the rumors of a coming gigantic Marxist upheaval reached their peak, there was a similar upward climb of stories relating the affairs of these impromptu prisons. Evelyn Lawrence's "The Hitler Terror Mounts" in the September 5, 1934 *Nation* was perhaps the most persuasive of the reports which related the influx of prisoners with the sharp increase of "underground and revolutionary movements" in Germany and Austria.[107] But the overthrow of Hitler did not come.

During the Popular Front period, there was a diminution of accounts stressing the Communists in the camps, and added attention to other elements, especially the Jews, liberals and pacifists. Perhaps the single individual intellectual who aroused the greatest concern as an internee was Karl von Ossietsky; there can be little doubt that the publicity he received as a special prisoner of Hitler led to his being awarded the Nobel Peace Prize in 1936. But while he was languishing in the Hitler prisons it was not considered important to point out that this ex-editor of *Die Weltbühne* had also been sentenced to 18 months in jail in the Weimar regime.[108] Yet, until the outbreak of war, the most numerous group of prisoners in these dreaded prisons continued to be political opponents of the National Socialists, with "work dodgers," the shirkers of assigned tasks, and those classed as habitual criminals, close behind. Although there was a tendency for the casual person subject to a maximum of propaganda to assume that the entire German Jewish community had been sentenced to permanent residence, they never constituted as high as 15 per cent of the total, in the view of one of the most diligent and hostile liberal students of the government of National Socialist Germany, Professor Karl Loewenstein. But first impressions were impossible to erase; liberals persisted in the belief that the largest part of Germany's radicals, intellectuals, artists, writers and Jews were dead, incarcerated in the concentration camps or *émigrés* to other lands by the end of 1935. When the 1935 edition of the Degener *Wer Ist's* was published late in the autumn, this 1900-page German *Who's Who* was hardly evidence that any vast number of learned and scholarly Germans had found the country as impossible to live in as the *émigrés*, exiles, and refugees maintained.

For the Communists, two objectives were made possible of achievement by the attack on the anti-Jewish tenets of National Socialism in Germany. A blow was struck at Hitler's regime which redounded to Russian benefit, while at the same time focusing attention on Germany as the alleged fountainhead of European hatred of Jewry and permitting Russia, the home of the pogrom, to escape criticism under the wearily repeated fiction that the Classless State of the Soviet had eliminated the "Jewish Question."

As for official British, French and American expressions of horror and alarm at the racist policy of National Socialist Germany, there was a distinctly hypocritical odor accompanying this protest, in view of widespread traditional American attitudes toward Indians and Negroes, and subsequent excesses toward the Japanese, let alone the known views and behavior of the British toward non-whites in many colonial lands, probably best exemplified by the signs "Chinese and Dogs Not Allowed" which hung over the entrances to parks attached to British consulates in China even into the twentieth century.

Hitler Germany was a literary, artistic, scientific, cultural and intellectual desert, nevertheless, in American liberal minds, if the commentaries and the controversies spread before the readers of the liberal press meant anything. Press censorship and the inhibitions and suspensions visited upon publishers, and the daily and periodical press, as well as the world-propagandized "book-burning" incident of May 10, 1933, were exploited to the full. It was ironic that the *New Republic* published two substantial critiques of literature under the Nazis in their issue of this same date, one in exhaustive detail by the *New Masses* regular, Harry Slochower, which developed the theme that German literary standards had descended precipitously and that the vast majority of Germans with talent had already become exiles, while the *Nation* on this same date also foresaw the extension of political interference in related areas in their page editorial, "Putting Art in Its Place." [109] Stories of the demotion or removal of composers, musicians and conductors were not unusual at this time, but the peak of criticism in these areas was reached in 1934, when famous American academic figures became involved in a number of acrimonious tilts fought out in the correspondence pages of these journals.

Few American academic figures held the Nazi regime in more contempt than Charles A. Beard, and Beard spoke out witheringly against German and American educators alike who he thought were providing decorative services during this period. It was he who exposed to ridicule a professor of the University of Berlin named Frederick Schonemann, who was on an itinerary in the United States delivering lectures sympathetic to the new German government, as well as sharply condemning Dean Roscoe Pound of the Harvard Law School for accepting an honorary degree from the same German university. Dean Pound's expression of kind words about Germany stimulated Beard to question his probity, and in this the *New Republic* warmly supported Beard editorially. When Professor William A. Orton of Smith College came to Pound's defense and corroborated his views on Germany and Austria on the basis of personal on-the-spot observation, the *New Republic* chided both Pound and Orton as "bad" reporters of what was going on in Germany and Central Europe.[110]

In October, 1934 the *Nation* wrote a stirring editorial commendation of Harvard President James B. Conant's vigorous refusal of an offer of a travelling fellowship to Germany from Harvard graduate Ernst Hänfstangl, on the grounds of the latter's close association to the leadership of a political party which had "inflicted damage in the universities of Germany through measures which have struck at principles we believe to be fundamental to universities throughout the world." [111] The inference of approval of the standards of the Russian Communist higher educational system was not concealed whatever here. But in a large part of the academic world at the time, this was a basic assumption. A few weeks before, the *New Republic* had published a furious three-column manifesto attacking German policies with respect to science, signed by fifteen persons, including Sir Basil Blackett, Harold J. Laski, J. B. S. Haldane, Hyman Levy and Julian Huxley. It predicted that the Nazis would put scientific research back in the Middle Ages, and it especially condemned the mobilization of science for military and political purposes, concluding with an exhortation to scientists everywhere to join them in "the maintenance and protection of free science, as one of the most essential elements of international culture and peaceful cooperation." [112]

As in the case of Italy, liberals showered abuse on the loyalty oaths of Hitler Germany. In the *New Republic* of May 4, 1932, Roger Baldwin, speaking in his capacity as chairman of the International Committee for Political Prisoners, had proclaimed, "No act of compulsion by the Fascist regime in Italy seems to have aroused such worldwide indignation among intellectuals as the decree of last summer [1931] imposing an oath of loyalty on all university professors." [113] The *Nation* was in the forefront of the attack on this procedure in Germany also, and in December, 1934 gave wide publicity to the dismissal of Professor Karl Barth from the faculty of the University of Bonn as a result of insisting on "qualifying the oath of loyalty of all university teachers." References to this incident kept appearing for months, excoriating the organized churches for not challenging the regime. "The church . . . ," the *Nation* trumpeted, "has probably sunk to a lower level of authority and moral prestige in Germany than in any other nation of the Western world." [114] But again, partiality toward the new world in the making in Russia precluded expressions of distaste for the peculiar forms of restraint placed upon academic and ecclesiastical figures in that country.

All in all, even though it has been the tendency to ignore the internal history of Germany between 1933 and 1938, in which year its success in creating a powerful Teutonic Central Europe induced widespread hysteria and panic in liberal ranks, as well as the Anglo-Saxon world generally, the events of this period, particularly the first two years of National Socialist tenure, form a powerful part of the whole leading to the formation of the impression of the German society which grew under Hitler, helping to support the remarkable change of views this impression made inevitable.

NOTES

1   Boston: Stratford, 1933. Hicks' denunciation in *New Masses*, October 2, 1934, p. 17.
2   See "To All Intellectuals," *New Masses*, May, 1932, p. 3.
3   In symposium headed by Freeman, "The Background of German Fascism," *New Masses*, April, 1933, pp. 3–9.
4   Muenzenberg's article in *New Masses*, July 31, 1934, pp. 14–17. On front groups see

also C. A. Hathaway, "On the Use of 'Transmission Belts' In Our Struggle For the Masses," *The Communist*, May, 1931, pp. 409–423.

5   See exchange in *Nation* between J. Bornstein and Abraham Bluestone, April 5 and April 26, 1933, p. 375 and p. 475, and the communication by Travers Clement in *New Republic*, May 31, 1933, p. 76, critical of the *New Republic* for siding with the Communist position in attacking the Social Democrats as responsible for the success of Hitler. The *New Masses* continued to laugh at liberals deploring Fascism for well over a year, repeatedly accusing them of trying to hide the part of the Social Democrats in the National Socialist victory. *New Masses*, March 27, 1934, p. 26.

6   Bonn made this observation in his review of Oswald Garrison Villard's book *The German Phoenix* in *New Republic*, May 10, 1933, pp. 370–371. Editorial rebuff of Bonn on p. 349 of same issue.

7   *Nation*, June 21, 1933, p. 703.

8   *New Republic*, September 27, 1933, pp. 174–176.

9   This major essay was datelined Prinkipo, Turkey and appeared on pages 200–203. Citations below from this source.

10   The official organ of the CPUSA, *The Communist*, published no material at all on Hitler in the January through March issues in 1933. The first reference to German politics was an editorial "For United Action Against Fascism", April, 1933, pp. 323–326.

11   "Kicking Hitler Upstairs," *New Republic*, May 10, 1933, p. 358.

12   For other views see Kisch, "Under the Whip In Germany," *New Republic*, April 26, 1933, pp. 306–308; Gunther, "Who Killed the German Republic?," *Nation*, May 10, 1933, pp. 526–528; the anonymous stories signed "Y.K.W." in *New Republic*, "Eye-Witness in Berlin," April 5, 1933, p. 207, and "The Nazi Terror," April 12, 1933, p. 235, as well as *Nation* editorial, May 24, 1933, p. 570. The emphasis on atrocities is preponderant.

13   *New Republic*, June 28, 1933, pp. 169–171. The editors admitted later that a "not inconsiderable number of leading Social Democrats and Communists" had gone over to the National Socialists. April 11, 1934, pp. 227–228.

14   Henri, "The Revolution Lives and Grows in Germany," *New Masses*, September, 1933, pp. 10–11. See also *Nation* editorial on "Fünfergruppen," August 30, 1933, p. 227, and *New Republic*, September 13, 1933, p. 113.

15   Review by Henry Hazlitt, *Nation*, October 11, 1933, pp. 413–414.

16   Roger B. Nelson, "Underground Germany," *Nation*, December 6, 1933, pp. 647–649. Herbert Solow in the *Nation* for February 7, 1934, described the Hitler movement as a "reaction" which "crushed the suffering rebel peasants of Germany."

17   *New Republic*, February 21, 1934, p. 29.

18   *Nation*, April 4, 1934, p. 391.

19   Seymour Woldman, "Roosevelt and the Next War," *New Masses*, December 11, 1934, p. 19.

20   Augustus Bauer, "The Threats to Hitler's Rule," *New Republic*, May 9, 1934, pp. 356–357.

21   Lore, "The United Front Gains Ground," *Nation*, December 19, 1934, pp. 714–716.

22   *New Republic*, July 4, 1934, p. 215.

23   *Nation*, December 12, 1934, pp. 681–682.

24   *New Republic*, August 15, 1934, pp. 8–9.

25   Niebuhr, "German Socialism Still Lives," *Nation*, August 1, 1934, p. 135.

26   Lash, "Socialism's New Beginning," *Nation*, December 5, 1934, pp. 650–652. On Lash as a new expert on French politics and his Belgian experiences, see his article "The United Front In France," *New Republic*, September 19, 1934, pp. 153–155 and 168, the follow-up commentary in *New Republic*, October 3, 1934, p. 217, and the rhapsodic description of the sanction of the "Einheitsfront" against Fascism at Liège in *Nation*, September 12, 1934, pp. 297–297.

27   *New Republic*, August 1, 1934, p. 302.

28   *New Republic*, November 7, 1934, p. 354.

29   *Nation*, August 1, 1934, p. 115.

30   *New Republic*, October 24, 1934, pp. 312–313.

31   See especially "Terrorism Rules Germany," *Nation*, March 29, 1933, p. 332, and "Who Burned the Reichstag?," *New Republic*, April 5, 1933, p. 203. The former edi-

torial credited Edward Dahlberg as a source for some of their atrocity reports. For a sample of Dahlberg's reportage on Germany, see "I Saw the Nazis," *New Masses*, May, 1933, pp. 13–14. The largest number of the specific cases mentioned involving mistreatment or flight from the country concerned persons active in Marxist political organizations.

32   *New Republic*, August 23, 1933, pp. 36–38; "The Reichstag Fire," *Nation*, September 6, p. 256.

33   See for example open letter in *New Republic*, October 18, 1933, p. 282.

34   *New Republic*, October 25, 1933, p. 314.

35   *Nation*, November 15, 1933, pp. 556–557.

36   "Leipzig—A Grandiose Provocation Of the Bloody Fascist Dictatorship," *The Communist*, December, 1933, pp. 1201–1212 (p. 1211).

37   Gunther, "The Reichstag Fire Still Burns," *Nation*, December 13, 1933, pp. 674–675. Also of importance in comments on the trial are an editorial in *Nation*, January 3, 1934, pp. 2–3, and the statements of Malcolm Cowley and Romain Rolland, "To Save Ernst Torgler's Life," *New Republic*, January 10, 1934, pp. 255–256, as part of the efforts of the American Committee To Aid Victims of German Fascism. Trotsky's interpretation, written from the vantage point of Turkey, "Politics In the Reichstag Trial," appeared in the *New Republic*, January 3, 1934, pp. 214–216.

38   *Nation*, April 12, 1933, p. 388.

39   *Nation*, April 12, 1933, p. 392.

40   *New Republic*, April 19, 1933, p. 284.

41   *New Republic*, May 17, 1933, p. 3.

42   Vorse, "Germany: The Twilight Of Reason," *New Republic*, June 14, 1933, pp. 117–119; the unsigned "The Arts Under Hitlerism" had been published in April, anticipating much of what appeared in her article.

43   Neuberger, "The New Germany," *Nation*, October 4, 1933, pp. 376–379, and "Germany Under the Choke-Bit," *New Republic*, November 15, 1933, pp. 13–15. These appeared to be part of the propaganda for the support of a boycott of German goods in the United States.

44   See especially the anonymous "The Nazi Hexenkessel," *Nation*, September 6, 1933, p. 269.

45   Niebuhr, "The Opposition In Germany," *New Republic*, June 28, 1933, p. 170.

46   *New Republic*, June 4, 1933, p. 111.

47   *Nation*, April 25, 1934, p. 461.

48   *Nation*, March 7, 1934, p. 265. A *Nation* editorial on October 18, 1933, p. 422, spoke of its being under ban in Germany at that time.

49   See comment on expulsion of Dorothy Thompson, *Nation*, September 5, 1934, p. 255, and the tribulations of the Berlin correspondent of the London *Times* in *New Republic* November 15, 1933, p. 2. The expulsion of hostile journalists was handled as a Hitlerian innovation in international politics.

50   See especially *New Republic* editorials, June 21, 1933, p. 137, and February 7, 1934, p. 348, Ludwig Lore, "The Last Stand Of the Junkers," *New Republic*, September 27, 1933, pp. 174–176, and editorial "Nazi Unification," *Nation*, July 18, 1933, pp. 33–34.

51   *New Republic*, November 22, 1933, p. 30.

52   *New Republic*, November 22, 1933, pp. 38–40.

53   *New Republic*, February 7, 1934, p. 348.

54   Editorial, *Nation*, July 18, 1934, p. 63; "Carnival Of Murder," *Nation*, August 1, 1934, p. 114; editorial, *Nation*, August 1, 1934, p. 119. See also editorial "Hitler Coordinates" which the *Nation* published on August 15, 1934.

55   "Revolt In Germany," *New Republic*, July 11, 1934, pp. 222–223.

56   "Hitler Turns To the Right," *New Republic*, July 18, 1934, pp. 251–252.

57   *New Republic*, August 15, 1934, pp. 6–7.

58   *New Republic*, January 9, 1935, p. 233.

59   *Nation*, August 29, 1934, p. 225.

60   *New Republic*, August 29, 1934, pp. 57–58.

61   *New Republic*, September 26, 1934, p. 171.

62   *Nation*, September 26, 1934, p. 339.

63   *Nation*, October 3, 1934, pp. 365–366. See also *Nation* editorial, November 14, 1934,

p. 549, on more news of friction between Hitler and Protestant church leaders. The *New Republic* had hoped Hitler would encounter internal checks from all the churches earlier; see editorial, August 2, 1933, pp. 299–300.

64 *New Republic,* April 5, 1933, p. 197; June 14, 1933, p. 110; "Hitler Crushes the Labor Unions," *New Republic,* May 17, 1933, pp. 4–5.

65 Lore, "Compulsory Labor In Germany," *New Republic,* June 7, 1933, pp. 89–90.

66 *New Republic,* May 10, 1933, p. 349.

67 *Nation,* June 6, 1934, p. 653.

68 *Nation,* October 3, 1934, p. 375.

69 *New Republic,* March 6, 1935, pp. 96–98.

70 *New Republic,* May 10, 1933, p. 352.

71 *New Republic,* May 17, 1933, p. 1; "German Realities," *Nation,* June 14, 1933; *New Republic,* October 11, 1933, p. 224.

72 "Hitler's Economics," *Nation,* January 3, 1934, p. 7.

73 See especially "Exit, Versailles," *New Republic,* May 2, 1934, pp. 324–325; "Germany Decides Not To Pay," *Nation,* June 27, 1934, pp. 718–719.

74 *New Republic,* August 1, 1934, pp. 302–303; see also "The New Fascism In Germany," July 25, 1934, pp. 278–279, for extended unfavorable comments on the survival power of Hitler's regime.

75 Fischer, "Russia Abolishes Bread Cards," *Nation,* January 2, 1935, pp. 11–12.

76 Farbman, "Poland: An Empire On the Make," *New Republic,* January 13, 1932, pp. 237–239. Farbman's hostility toward the Pilsudski government and his constant comparisons of repression, arrests, police torture and the like in Poland with "old Russia" indicated his basic political orientation. It stimulated a vigorous rejoinder from Arthur P. Coleman, published by the *New Republic* on February 24, 1932, in which he denounced Farbman's insinuation of a policy of "deliberate anti-Semitism" on the part of Poland and went on to say, "The delicate balance that enables Jews and Poles to live peaceably together in normal times is continually being upset by the agitation of foreign Jews, especially American, whose misguided meddling is resented by the Poles as intensely as Americans would resent investigation of a foreign commission of the lynching of Negroes or the treatment of the Japanese in California." p. 49. See also Boris Smolar, "What Polish Jews Are Facing," *Nation,* January 27, 1932, pp. 99–100.

77 Noah Fabricant, "Intolerance In Vienna," *Nation,* October 21, 1931, pp. 442–444. This described among other things the beatings inflicted upon Jews on June 23, 1931, the day the Rotary International Convention opened.

78 *New Republic,* July 13, 1932, pp. 218–219.

79 *Nation,* May 11, 1932, pp. 340–341.

80 *Nation,* May 25, 1932, pp. 597–599.

81 Fischer, "Russia: Fear and Foreign Policy," *Nation,* October 11, 1933, pp. 403–405 (p. 404).

82 *Nation,* September 26, 1934, p. 339.

83 *Nation,* May 3, 1933, pp. 493–494. Lewisohn's article was dated Paris, April 14.

84 *New Republic,* April 12, 1933, pp. 236–238.

85 *Nation,* April 19, 1933, p. 430; July 19, 1933, p. 59; *New Republic,* April 12, 1933, p. 226; April 19, 1933, pp. 264, 266. The *New Republic* was especially incensed at Hitlerian efforts to reduce the number of Jews in the professions to the same proportion as Jews in general in the total population, roughly one percent. It alleged in its April 19 editorial that "everything possible is being done to destroy the economic life of all Jews except the bankers—a discrimination which is highly significant." p. 264. See also review of Frederick L. Nussbaum's *A History of Economic Institutions of Modern Europe* by Herman Simpson, *New Republic,* August 30, 1933, p. 80, and editorial, *Nation,* June 21, 1933, p. 682.

86 *New Republic,* May 31, 1933, pp. 55–56; June 7, 1933, p. 84.

87 *Nation,* August 2, 1933, p. 115.

88 "Meeting the Nazi Threat," *Nation,* July 26, 1933, pp. 89–90.

89 *Nation,* February 21, 1934, p. 223.

90 *New Republic,* September 20, 1933, p. 139. On the establishment of the boycott see *New Republic,* August 2, 1933, p. 300; *Nation,* August 9, 1933, p. 142. In its editorial of August 2, the *New Republic* had declared that "President Roosevelt was dis-

suaded from intervening in Berlin against Jewish persecution by Mr. Felix Warburg, who warned him that such a step on the part of the American government would harm rather than help the German Jews." Warburg subsequently wrote the editors to the effect that they were wrong, and that, on the contrary, he had been "in constant consultation with the American Jewish Committee and approve of their consistently expressed hope that our government would exert its utmost influence through diplomatic channels to deter the wretched persecution of Jews in Germany." Warburg's letter to editors, *New Republic*, September 6, 1933, p. 104.

91 Neuberger, "The New Germany," *Nation*, October 4, 1933, pp. 376–379; *Nation*, October 18, 1933, p. 423; *New Republic*, November 1, 1933, p. 320.

92 *Nation*, November 29, 1933, pp. 614–615.

93 See in particular Johan J. Smertenko's "J'Accuse" in the *New Republic* for May 31, 1933, and Annie Nathan Meyer, "The Bewildered Liberal," *Nation*, February 28, 1934, pp. 243–244.

94 Frank's famous article ran nearly ten columns in the *New Republic*, December 13, 1933, pp. 121–125. For criticisms, see especially *New Republic*, January 31, 1934, pp. 337–338. The editors admitted receiving many letters they could not find room to publish.

95 Solow, "Thomas Mann: Exile Or Refugee?," *New Republic*, February 21, 1934, pp. 48–49; Slochower, "An Open Letter To Thomas Mann," *New Republic*, June 27, 1934, p. 185.

96 *New Republic*, October 24, 1934, pp. 317–318.

97 *New Republic*, February 20, 1935, p. 52.

98 *New Masses*, December 4, 1934, pp. 11–13.

99 *New Masses*, February 19, 1935, pp. 11–13.

100 *Nation*, October 31, 1934, pp. 492–493. The editors thought that the Congressional Committee on Un-American Activities should have hired Spivak as a special investigator.

101 *Nation*, January 3, 1934, p. 3.

102 *Nation*, August 2, 1933, pp. 121–124. The *Nation* had just published an editorial on July 5 complaining bitterly of the "horrors of the overcrowded German prison camps," p. 3.

103 *Nation*, July 12, 1933, p. 45.

104 *Nation*, October 18, 1933, p. 434.

105 *Nation*, March 7, 1934, p. 265.

106 Anonymous, "Prisoner Of the Nazis," *New Republic*, August 8, 1934, pp. 337–339.

107 *Nation*, September 5, 1934, p. 261. See also Verne Andrews, "Off To A Concentration Camp," *New Republic*, March 21, 1934, pp. 155–157.

108 The campaign on behalf of the German Communist leader Thaelmann sagged during this period, though occasional attention was directed to the persisting Communist efforts on his behalf. The frequent contributor to the liberal press, Albert Viton, devoted some attention to this subject in his *New Masses* article of March, 1935, "The Fight For Thaelmann."

109 Editorial "A Clue To Hitlerism," *New Republic*, May 10, 1933, pp. 352–353; Slochower, "Literature In Exile," *New Republic*, January 31, 1934, pp. 340–341; editorial "Putting Art In Its Place," *Nation*, May 10, 1933, p. 519.

110 Letters of Beard, Homer G. Richey and Orton, plus appended editorial comment to latter, in *New Republic*, January 3, 1934, p. 227; March 21, 1934, p. 161; November 14, 1934, p. 19. Also editorial September 26, 1934, p. 170.

111 *Nation*, October 17, 1934, p. 423. Three Communist front groups led the aggravated protest over Hänfstangl's presence in Boston in September, 1934. The *Nation* sided with the demonstrators and their denunciation of the jailing of Communists in Germany. *Nation*, October 24, 1934, p. 480.

112 *New Republic*, August 29, 1934, pp. 76–77.

113 *New Republic*, May 4, 1932, p. 329.

114 *Nation*, December 12, 1934, p. 660.

13

EARLY HITLERIAN FOREIGN POLICY
AND THE NEW LIBERAL IMAGE
OF GERMANY, 1933–1935

THE CONFLICTS AND CONTRADICTIONS
PRECEDING THE SOMERSAULT

THE new Germany's foreign relations, especially those with the rest of Europe and the United States, amounted to a general topic of almost equal interest to American liberals as the startling domestic affairs in the budding National Socialist era. Editorial policy frequently and voluminously documented this interest, while the commentaries of a sizable contingent of contributors were accorded prominent space in the liberal weeklies. As the tempo of European affairs began to quicken after the spring of 1935, the volume of print on Germany increased, along with a marked heightening of the temperature of opinion and emotion, and a noticeable hardening of lines of sympathy.

Germany's first two years under Hitler did not spark any substantial switch in editorial stands of either the *Nation* or *New Republic,* insofar as America's relations with Germany were involved. *Common Sense,* confined almost entirely to the field of domestic politics, rarely went beyond detached and brief editorial comments, while the *New Masses,* with its exclusively Marxist view and strong pro-Russian stand, found occasional room for the work of liberals whose overall approach did not do any damage to these set courses. Despite the heat which invariably marked liberal comment on German affairs, the editorial opinion of the liberal press in the early years was notable for its consistency in shying away from suggestions of a test of arms between its champions and Germany. The *New Republic* differed from its senior associate in adhering to a policy which was more frankly "isolationist," using the word in the sense of frowning on collective security agreements. No matter how the sense of outrage against the "Nazis" welled up, it was late in the season of the 1930's before the journal headed by Bruce Bliven came around to supporting once more the idea embodied in the League of Nations, and then in a much modified sense. The *Nation* was much more sympathetic, and at a somewhat earlier occasion, to the idea of a pooling of strength against the slowly expanding power of the Germans in Central Europe. It advocated the principle of collective security with France, Britain and the Soviet Union, a stand also backed to the hilt by the *New Masses*. But neither editorial staff of the liberal weeklies reflected the belligerence of many of their contributors and book reviewers; a clear call to war against Germany came from such avenues of expression years before war occurred, and long before editorial policy reluctantly fell in behind their recruiting and mobilization calls. Journalists such as Robert Dell and Ludwig Lore and professors such as Frederick L. Schuman issued blunt personal declarations of war on Germany within a year of Hitler's ascendancy, and the eagerness of some of the *émigré* reporters for a martial showdown was even less well-concealed. The conflict between the editors and the contributors' staff on Germany is one of the most interesting aspects of opinion-making in the confines of American liberal journalism between 1933 and 1939–1941.

The most belligerent liberals never made clear just in whose interests another war with Germany might be fought, a difficult matter perhaps because of the numerous frontiers of Germany and the crisscross of conflicts among its potential opponents: Russia, Poland, France, England, and Central Europe generally. In addition, although the bitterest anti-Hitler liberals never entertained the slightest doubt that Hitler was preparing for a war from the start, they were in confusion as to whom *he* would fight. Communists with access to liberal publications played a one-note foreign policy symphony, posing a Russo-German conflict exclusively before and during the Popular Front, but others suspected the "Nazis" of contemplating other enemies, even while debilitated, in the period prior to the re-introduction of conscription, while Germany's neighbors held a staggering margin of armed might against her. Hitler's writings were useful here; a selective employment of these, applying the rule that anything of discredit from his pen was to be believed to the letter while any modifying declarations were to be held in perpetual suspicion, made this attitude appear reasonable. It helped to prepare the way for the abandonment of the vision of France as the martial trouble-maker of Europe and its replacement by the brave and defenseless feminine image so popular in the World War. Its corollary was the revival of the wartime slavering Teutonic beast embarking on a world conquest spree once again. Nor did this interfere with the new tradition of posing Russia as the sole world power with a sincere interest in peace, its vast arms buildup, conscription, and near-million-man standing army explained away as a completely defensive precaution.

The unbounded personal hate toward Hitler is perhaps a matter which clinical psychology may unravel, in view of the remoteness of those who expressed such furious sentiments from the object of their distaste. But its effect upon their judgment as makers of public opinion is a matter of record. That Hitler as a German statesman was a master bluffer was not in consideration in the early years, and taking his every word literally and seriously helped undermine liberal criticism progressively. The antidote to this some years later was the characterization of his diplomatic coups as "gangster diplomacy," as if bluff had no prior part in statecraft in the era of national states, and the dangerous culmination was the creation of the view that Hitler was all bluff, which could easily be proved by the exercise of a strong counter-bluff. The two years prior to the outbreak of hostilities in 1939 was the period when this theory enjoyed maximum liberal endorsement.

In the field of foreign policy and relations, the liberal journals and many of their contributors were thus involved in two strange contradictory processes. While still fighting the 1918–1921 period on behalf of Germany in 1933–1935, they were simultaneously active in publishing inflammatory attacks on the contemporary Germany, thus assuring the creation of a reservoir of hate and hostility to throw to the support of another anti-German combine. And, while expressing the conviction frequently that the foreign policies of all the major world states and their conductors deserved scrupulous examination for evidences of defection from probity, an exception was made for Communist Russia, whose goals were considered so transparently progressive and pure as to be above suspicion. There was never an article by a liberal titled "Can Stalin Be Trusted?" in any of the printed sources read by people of liberal bent in the decade before Russia abandoned its collective security plank in favor of a "go-it-alone" position. The absence of any feeling that it might occur some day helps to explain why American liberals took the Russo-German pact of August, 1939 as an insulting slap in the face to each personally, and turned on the Russians with such venom in the next two years.

The danger of becoming hopelessly involved emotionally in another European situation leading directly to war was not utterly unanticipated in 1933. A two-page unsigned *New Republic* editorial May 24, "Europe: On the Brink of Catastrophe," reviewed the essentials of the new situation with remarkable sobriety, in view of the tone of what it was printing on German internal happenings. It began by reiterating its charge that "the Allies, and France in particular, are more responsible than anyone else for the rise to power of the swashbuckling Hitler regime," having "subjected the Germans to intolerable humiliation and unendurable economic distress, all excused by clauses of the peace treaty which Germany signed with a pistol to her head, and erected upon a false historical thesis of her sole war guilt." It promptly discounted this gesture toward objectivity by denouncing the whole Hitler regime bitterly, then lapsing once more by describing the existing European situation as "strikingly analogous" to that in April, 1917, suggesting that the "anti-Jewish campaign" was the equivalent of the unrestricted submarine warfare of the earlier date in alarming and arousing American sentiment. Its conclusion was anything but an exhortation to repeat the course of that time: [1]

It is to be hoped that America will have the wisdom not to repeat the frightful mistake made sixteen years ago. Nothing that we can do now will help to resolve the European quarrel. No matter how many consultative pacts we might sign, we would become only one more pawn in the European game. Sixteen years ago we helped to give France a mastery of Europe which she has used to bring ruin to the whole Continent; if we came to her aid again we should only help to perpetuate the evils of the Versailles system. This is not the dictate of selfish isolationism; . . . It is merely a frank facing of the realities, undeceived by any delusions of grandeur about the might and power of America. There can be no peace in Europe until the people . . . are at last prepared to accept justice as its base.

The occasion for this editorial was the preliminary discussions on the famous Four Power Pact proposed by Mussolini (suggesting a bloc of the four big powers of Western Europe as a realistic substitute for the League with its tangled intrigue of small states), and the imminent collapse of the Geneva Disarmament Conference. Powerful propaganda had already been made against the Germans by the agitated French, who were shouting about "crushing" them "by peaceful means," especially through Foreign Minister Paul-Boncour; and the German insistence on the right to rearm was all the additional fuel the touchy situation needed to induce hysteria.

The *Nation* felt impelled to comment also, in a somewhat similar vein, perhaps subdued by comparison, as a consequence of the fierce anti-German dispatches it was publishing from its Geneva correspondent, Dell, a vehement French protagonist in this and almost all other issues involving French interests. Three weeks earlier Dell had sent an agitated piece in which he imagined the relatively unarmed Germans already masters of Europe, and announced that insofar as German internal affairs were concerned, "The most charitable explanation" was "that half the German people have gone mad." He implored the world to make not the slightest concession to Hitler, since he was "clearly a criminal lunatic," urging upon all the European powers "any action that may be necessary to prevent Germany from rearming." [2] The editorial position was caught midway between Dell's and that of the *New Republic*. Taking seriously Dell's unconditional pronouncement that the "whole of Europe" had "suddenly become anti-German," its May 24 statement declared, "Revision is for the present inconceivable." The *Nation* seemed to wriggle in an unendurable predicament in its observation that "A change in the unjust treaties that doubtless brought Hitler into power must now, ironically enough, be delayed until Hitler is eliminated." But like the *New Republic* it recommended a careful, sober tread for American policy, in view of Roosevelt's recent address which indicated vague leanings toward willingness to participate in extended talks: [3]

In taking these steps toward international cooperation our government should be wary lest it find itself acting as a tail to the French kite. Obviously we do not wish to join any anti-German alliance, no matter how carefully disguised it may be in garments of peace. If we oppose German aggression we should equally oppose any attempt to find in Hitlerism an excuse for French or British aggression. The peace must be kept; and the only sort of cooperation possible between the United States and Europe is cooperation in preventing the use of arms to satisfy ambitions or to settle claims.

Despite all this, no restraint was felt necessarily applicable to commentaries on the subject of Germany. Anonymous *émigrés* continued to tell incoherent tales of massive German arms and manpower buildups preparatory for general war for two years before the National Socialists denounced the Versailles treaty limitations and commenced conscription, took the storm troopers and the Hitler Jugend youth movements seriously as armed forces, and reported wholesale German industrial conversion to munitions and gun production. [4] At the height of the "merchants of death" agitation these accounts attained substantial influence, supplemented by the war-scare stories of journalists such as Johannes Steel, Dell and Fischer, and reports on sensational books by German authors of varied backgrounds which strongly pointed in the same direction. Early in February, 1934, Professor Schuman in the *New Republic* described a Germany already mobilized on the home front for a long war, and frankly advised "France and her allies" that they had better not wait any longer before interfering in German affairs.[5] Two weeks later in the *Nation* Dell issued a hectic call for an economic blockade or military occupation of Germany at once to save "European civilization." His description of France and Russia as the sole powers in the world that had shown "any inclination to renounce national sovereignty and to sacrifice national egoism to the general interest" flatly contradicted liberal editorial picturization of the former, at least, even though he presented no evidence for this astounding turnabout other than citing the numerous French pleas at Geneva for international armed forces, ignoring their potential usefulness to the French as an international insurance company to bail them out of their Central European difficulties.[6]

Thus the friendliness toward France and the Soviet plus the hate of Hitler was aiding the establishment of hate of Germany as a respectable attitude once more, by almost imperceptible weekly edging movements. Steel's [7] five long articles in the *Nation* at the height of the furor caused by the *Fortune* assault on the munitions business had as their theme the charge that "international capitalism" was fomenting trouble all over the European continent in the hope of profiting from the hostile reactions thus provoked. By the late spring the pressure on editorial views had increased to the point where the *Nation* condemned the Germans almost exclusively for the breakdown of the disarmament proceedings, while urging President Roosevelt to alter the situation by making substantial disarmament proposals in imitation of Secretary Hughes at the outset of the Washington Conference of 1922.[8]

By the end of the summer, liberal editorial policy noticeably quieted down criticism of Versailles, issued occasional plaintive notes addressed to the French asking why they were not applying strong pressure to Germany for its rearming in violation of the treaty provisions, and continuing to publish articles by unabashedly pro-French and pro-Russian contributors peddling a persuasive preventive war remedy. The revived sloganeering of 1914–1918 accompanied all this, providing appealing dressing rather than clashing contradiction; "saving civilization" was by far the favorite objective. But the somewhat more prosaic realities of the "Nazi" attempt to take over Austria into the Reich and the incredible growth of their strength in the Saar on the eve of the plebiscite deciding its permanent future lay behind much of this flustered agitation. The failure of the first moves to isolate Hitler Germany, followed by the breakdown of disarmament talk, and Hitler's sensational decisions to repudiate the disarmament restraints on Germany and to re-introduce conscription, finished this early "quarantine" gesture on the part of the powerful but disorganized states ringing the German periphery. The evidence of Hitler's entrenchment in Germany in addition to his growing influence in the area contiguous to Germany brought the wave of hopefulness in his early overthrow to an end in the liberal view generally, but did not terminate their persistent attack. This took a somewhat different route in 1935, a phase which continued in one way or another until August, 1939.

In fact, the hostility of American liberalism toward Hitler Germany gave way for a time to the older position again, bitter castigation of the Allies for never having had the enterprise to adjust the inequities in the Versailles Treaty. In comments upon Hitler's strategy of rebuffing attempts to bring him back into the League, plus his initiative in repudiating rearmament hobbles and commencing conscription once more, there was a thinly disguised note of vindictive reproach to the British and French in particular. The *Nation* connected Hitler's growing confidence in his foreign policy moves to realization of security at home. In its commentary on the second anniversary of Hitler's establishment, it struck down all the talk of a coming upheaval in Germany by admitting that the Nazis had consolidated power remarkably and effected "a coordination of all existing social institutions which have apparently made the Nazis secure from internal attack for a number of years to come." [9]

Both journals expressed dark views on the Anglo-French diplomacy of February, 1935 and saw no hope of their influencing Germany now. The *Nation* declared that the offer to abrogate the military clauses of Part V of the Treaty was three years too late, credited the German reply to the February 3 note a "masterpiece of skilful diplomacy," and interpreted the German support of Hitler's "secret" rearming as a product of their "resentment against the stigma of inferiority imposed by the Versailles Treaty, especially the war-guilt, reparations and armament provisions." [10] The *New Republic*'s editorial, "A Last Gasp From Versailles," took about the same position, adding further that the French had now failed to find anyone to help them in preventing German resurgence by force, "obviously the only means by which Germany could be stopped." Now, "Her right to equality is again recognized, as it was in the compact at Versailles. At that time the Allies promised that they would disarm down to her level—a promise they have grotesquely failed to keep."

Both journals were close in their interpretation of the subsequent steps as well. As the talks between Hitler and Lord Simon of Britain were about to begin, the *New Republic* had the following observation to make as to the ultimate goal of German ambitions: [11]

Germany under Hitler is still determined to be the dominant power in Central and Eastern Europe; France is still determined to prevent this.

. . . Perhaps it is true, that neither of these countries wants war, but certainly each of them wants things that, in the long run, the other will fight to prevent.

The *Nation* added an amplification not long after: [12]

Nazi tactics have been directed toward winning the sympathy of the British in the hope of breaking the iron ring which Soviet-French diplomacy has built around the Reich,

and it suggested that if the London *Times* was any indication, such sympathy already existed in some volume. Thus, despite the comprehensive denunciation of Hitler Germany which characterized liberal editorial policy, there tended to appear marked reserve toward the Reich when the subject involved German diplomatic interplay with the other powers, and it was far from a menace to the world in their editorial eyes, whatever may have been the sentiments of several contributors in favor of such interpretation. The *Nation* described Hitler's rearmament plan as "bold," offering a veritable apology for it in an editorial paragraph on March 27, 1935; "Surrounded by an ever-tightening ring of hostile nations, Germany's own need for security has obviously increased." [13] And its full-page commentary, "Hitler Liquidates Versailles," was a stiff rebuke to the Allies accompanied by heaping abuse on the Versailles Treaty once more. A *New Republic* editorial of the same date, "Europe's Tragedy," had an almost identical orientation. The *Nation* described Hitler's dramatic announcement as a *"coup de grâce"* to what remained of the League, and suggested that he had not only "thrilled the German people and fortified himself more strongly than ever" but had "administered a bitter dose of humiliation to the former Allies and victors" since he had "exhibited anew their failure to live up to their own promises to disarm." [14] The junior liberal weekly also summarized its reasons for this latest crevasse opening in the peace of Europe: [15]

If the Allies had not forced on Germany the iniquitous Versailles Treaty, or if they had kept their own mutual promise to disarm, or if they had not tried to collect the impossible sum of reparations, or if they had been able to implement that section of the Treaty making possible peaceable readjustment of its terms, or if they had known how to maintain international prosperity in which Germany had a full share, they probably never would have had a Hitler to deal with. He was made nearly inevitable by their own acts.

Thus another point of conflict between editorial and contributor points of view was laid bare; the relatively detached editors shared the enthusiasm for a crusade against Germany in the faintest manner, if at all, when the foreign situation in Europe was seen in its totality. The weakness in editorial reasoning displayed itself when the relations of each of the potential antagonists of Germany with that country were examined. On such occasions there appeared a uniform sympathy with the anti-German position, thus placing liberal editorial policy in the curious contradictory spot of supporting a group of individual state policies, the logical collective results of which it sharply disapproved. As an example of this we have the *Nation* expressing the blackest of doubts as to the trustworthiness of Germany in its individual relations with France, Poland and Soviet Russia, in turn. Yet in its editorial of April 3, 1935 it rejoiced that a "preventive war" against Germany seemed already ruled out of consideration, and warned the major powers to abandon their *cordon-sanitaire* psychology and desist from building grandiose alliances against the Reich, since such actions would only serve to aggravate German defensiveness and aid Hitler in intrenching himself deeper. It favored the acceptance of German rearmament as a *fait accompli* and urged work toward the creation of a system of European security in which Germany might be a member in full equality.[16]

But the very next week this attitude of conciliation melted before the portent of Hitler using his rearmament to adjust some of the galling territorial hangovers of Versailles, and its likely consequences especially in the East brought a chill. Liberals rejoiced that the Simon-Hitler talks had been fruitless, since this gave new life to the Soviet proposals for collective security against Hitler on the part of Russia, France and Britain.[17] The week before, such understandings had been disparaged as incitations to German defensiveness, and productive only of more hate and suspicion. Now it was credited with being a wise idea and the only sure barrier to another European war. The *New Republic* was no more logical. After blaming the Allies for bringing about the impatient reaction of Hitler's Reich to their hypocrisy over the rearmament question, in the same breath it placed on Hitler the responsibility for British, French and Russian plans to increase *their* armed forces, neglecting to mention the formidable conscript armies of the two latter powers already in existence.

At the bottom of the liberals' anguish of indecision was a serious lacuna in their ideological stand; eager and willing for change, convinced that it was necessary, yet emotionally bound to interests which were adamant against considering it unless subjected to force. The mere mention of force threw liberals into agitation and prompt support of any measures seeming likely to inhibit the application of force on an international level. Part of the explanation lies in their having already accepted the Communist application of force to political theory, as a transfer of the methods of warfare from the foreign to the domestic sphere, which accounts for the ability of many liberals to deplore war between nations with such detestation while spiritedly supporting civil wars which purported to have a class basis. Hence the curious campaign against war and munitions while paying rousing tribute to the Communists fighting Chiang Kai-shek in China, and the subsequent fervor for collective security as a barrier to international war while encouraging the enlistment of pacifists in the irregulars fighting in Spain against Francisco Franco.

The picture of Germany during these two years as revealed in the literature which the liberal journals chose to review also showed a distinct penchant for ascribing bellicose propensities to the new regime, despite its admitted weakness in this pre-armament-and-conscription time. The sensational *Germany Prepares For War* by Ewald Banse was given chapter-and-verse credence by the *Nation* as an accurate reflection of German policy, although the review written by the veteran publicist Frank H. Simonds calmly stated, "Germany will, of course, lose the next war just as she did the last, because she is bound to end by driving the whole world into another combination against her." Simonds pleaded innocent of the charge that he might be trying to inspire "a new wave of anti-German sentiment" into existence by his declarations on Germany, and went on to state that German imperialistic dreams were no more wicked than those of other powers, but just that they were a century too late. He was referring to Banse's discussion of German plans to incorporate the small nations on her frontiers,[18] along with other alleged National Socialist goals, of which Simonds asserted 90 per cent of the Germans were unaware. The *Nation* warned its readers not to believe the "Nazis" when they repudiated this book as no reflection of their official policy.[19]

A similar lesson to Banse was derived from *The Berlin Diaries*, purporting to be the legendary memoirs of an anonymous German general as edited by one Helmut Klotz, reviewed in both journals, and with especial warmth in the *Nation* by Steel. Its gossipy innuendo concerning future war plans aroused shrill alarm.[20] Still another was Ernst Henri's *Hitler Over Europe*, reviewed by Ludwig Lore and H. N. Brailsford. This was one of the first extended treatises reviving the allegation of German plans to conquer the world, so painfully familiar to those who remembered the hyperthyroid efforts of 1914–1918. Its firm Marxist point of view was accepted by both reviewers, and its basic thesis was unquestioned. Lore admitted that the "best parts" of the book were "exceptionally able Communist propaganda," while Brailsford described it as "a daring application to current events of the Marxist canons for the interpretation of history." Henri's home front picture of a Germany in an abandoned riot of war goods production expansion under the leadership of bloated industrialists who were simultaneously "sentencing millions of men and women to hopeless and unrelieved unemployment" received Brailsford's enthusiastic approval, even though it presented a substantial contradiction; the expansion of German industry to achieve such goals must have involved sizable re-hiring of German unemployed.[21] But details of this kind, plus the discussion of the workers' stake in a war industry job, obtained no space.

However, 1934 was the year of according credence to rumors, no matter whence derived. In England, Wickham Steed even claimed to have discovered documents whose validity he never questioned purporting to give details on coming massive German gas and bacterial warfare against London and Paris via their subway systems, and plans for gas attacks on an additional twenty French cities. The *Nation* calmly commented that "there is a very good chance that the documents are genuine." [22]

Not all of the literature on Germany chosen for review dwelled on "Nazi" propensities for war planning or concentrated on Marxian evaluations. A few titles even offered mild apology and shunned diabolism in explaining the rise of Hitlerism, which reviewers sometimes expressed irritation about; the anonymous *Germany: Twilight or New Dawn?;* [23] Prince Hubertus zu Loewenstein's *The Tragedy of a Nation,*[24] which Lore found bothersome for its criticism of the Communists and its failure to exempt the German Jews from all responsibility for the state of Germany; George N. Shuster's *Strong Man Rules,*[25] which irked Emil Ludwig because it did not follow the trend of the day by failing to lambaste intemperately all the new German leaders, and Villard's *The German Phoenix* [26] stood out as volumes which dealt at least in part with matters not wholly to German discredit. M. J. Bonn, in reviewing the last for the rival *New Republic,* praised it so warmly and added so much additional material highly critical of the Communists for their special contribution in making the rise of the Hitlerites a successful one, that he succeeded in arousing a special editorial critique of his review, one of the few occasions when this happened. The same weekly even deplored the appearance of the abridged Dugdale translation of *Mein Kampf,* which apparently was published to capitalize on the sensation and interest created by the novelty of the National Socialist system, leaving little doubt that in its editorial opinion it was a thoroughly evil and worthless book written in "hysterical German." [27]

Around 1935 a new trend in books on Germany made its appearance, lacking almost entirely the detachment of some earlier commentators, as well as some of the loudness of alarmed persons remote from the scene. There was a grim, implacable tone to the newer products, the majority containing a moral and sometimes suggestions for action. Perhaps the best model at the beginning was Konrad Heiden's

A History of National Socialism, blandly sanctioned by Lore in the *Nation* as the product of "an unprejudiced German's eye," after which he calmly described the author's political pedigree as an active fighter against Hitler since the early post-war period.[28] This was an important opinion-forming book, but the presentation of its writer as an uncommitted and detached chronicler was an indication of things to come. In the succeeding five years, as book after book written by *émigré* political enemies of the "Nazis" poured out, liberals found less and less time and reason to explain their backgrounds to the reader audience. And by the time the war broke out, a book on Germany which was not totally condemnatory was a rarity, regardless of the national origin of the author, while the persistence of the "Nazi" regime and its continued increase in strength acted as a goad to its critics, so that one may notice a direct correlation between the waxing of Hitler's Reich and the extravagance of the printed condemnations of it and predictions of its early demise.

THE LIBERAL OPINION BAROMETER REFLECTS
THE FIRST TWO YEARS
OF HITLERIAN FOREIGN POLICY

Hitler's two-year delay in denouncing the Versailles arms limitations on Germany and in adopting conscription gave his critics a leisurely opportunity for speculation as to his plans. His success was sometimes dreaded as the opening step in the gradual spread of his system via contagion, during which the Germans were expected to perform passive roles, while on other occasions the more implacable of his liberal enemies charged him with grandiose plots involving the subversion of the political systems of the world. British writers were, with a few exceptions such as Dell, less disturbed than others as to what Hitler might achieve immediately, though they were no less hostile to the entire National Socialist movement. Brailsford, reporting in the *New Republic* after a visit to Germany in June, was sure that Englishmen were utterly opposed to the ending of reparations, German unity with Austria or even moderate rearmament, but he frankly admitted that British concern was not "so wholly disinterested" as the superficial were inclined to think: [29]

We do not wish to disarm Italians, or Poles, or Jugoslavs, nor do we talk in their case of "sanctions," though their governments are not less brutal, less nationalist, less militarist, less autocratic than that of Germany. But Germany can upset, as they cannot, the balance of power that we adjusted to suit our interests at Versailles.

Brailsford did not oppose German rearmament at this time, but he was utterly at a loss to suggest a policy to replace that now unbalanced by the emergence of this truculent German regime, whose state of mind he described as an "inferiority complex," brought on by its wartime enemies; "We made this state of mind, all we victors." He charged Wilson with being "as benighted as his colleagues" in approving such policies as reparations, the separation of Danzig from Germany and the creation of the Polish Corridor, all of which he believed to be bad mistakes. And topping it off, he summed up, "The two settlements that wrought the final mischief were sponsored by the great American capitalists," an oblique reference to the Dawes and Young Plans of 1924 and 1929 for perpetuating the reparations system under less galling circumstances to the Germans. But for the agitated calls of the moment for a cure-all he had no suggestion to make; "If we were worthy of the healer's duty, we should have assumed it fourteen years ago," was his resigned conclusion, accompanied by cautious observations as to the healing properties of the passage of time.

Villard, in a cable to the *Nation* while visiting England at about the same time, spoke with strong emotions on the vigorous anti-Germanism of the British press, which he approved *in toto*. Villard laid it almost entirely to anger over the German policies of repression of the Jews and academic personalities as well as to indignant response to the banning of books and papers critical of the government's programs, not to concern over high matters of state. He cheered the Conservative politicians who had already delivered condemnatory orations, and expected this type of abuse to bring rapid modification of actions by a chastened Hitler. On the eve of the London Economic Conference he told his readers in America that "there is no let-up whatever in the daily attacks upon Hitler and all that he stands for," as well as giving a few details on an economic boycott already in full swing against German products being carried out by British businessmen. An implacable England converted overnight from a pro-German to a pro-French country emerged from his excited four-column report.[30]

The existence of neutral Britons such as Lloyd George or Lord Rothermere in high places in subsequent months was not expected to be of great significance, and only Strachey went so far as to deal directly with the subject in his May, 1934 *New Republic* article, "Fascism in Great Britain," which showed him completely absorbed with the activities of Sir Oswald Mosley's group. Strachey, clinging to the orthodox Marxian definition of Fascism as "the praetorian guard of monopoly capitalism," saw little danger of Mosley's movement succeeding in England.[31] In fact, no British correspondent to the American liberal press exceeded the concern of Villard for many months, and rarely did they discuss British hostility to the new German system in the same way; matters of serious national interest rather than the unpleasant fate of German minorities were of more interest to them. Ultimately the editorial position in America drew around to this as well, in essence getting back to the method by which foreign news had been commented upon prior to the emergence of German National Socialism. But it was not until the stirring events of 1935 that British concern began to reflect itself in American liberal sensibility, by which time the strain of American liberalism critical of British policy had regained its vigor. Yet at no time did the liberals in America conceive of the German system as one interested in gaining or able to gain headway within Great Britain.

Of Germany's neighbors to the West liberals were less sure, especially after the eruption of French politics on February 6–7, 1934 and the coming to power of the Doumergue regime, with its ban on Socialists and Communists as partners. A series of palpitating editorials and articles followed this event, that of March 14 in the *New Republic* reflecting best the changing image of France. "Will France Go Fascist?" went so far as to concede that "the bourgeoisie in France" might soon "apply fascist methods" in the effort to retain control and presumably move toward war with the Germans, since it suggested reassuringly that "in spite of the chauvinistic Parisian press, the general pacific and liberal spirit of the French nation is still one of the most effective brakes in the present European race to war." As if this breath-taking somersault were not enough, the editorial expressed such faint faith in parliamentary processes as a bulwark of the French Left as to recommend a revolutionary coup; "only by . . . creating socialism instead of hopelessly defending a parliamentary democracy that seems fatally to turn against its own ideals, can they stop the reactionary tides." [32] The *Nation* more or less answered its compatriot with a substantial article early in May written by a journalist who concealed his name, titled "France Is Still a Republic," emphasizing especially the French Left's stiff resistance to additional war expenditures and its clamor for substantial military reductions.[33] It appeared at this point at least that Left outrage over Hitler did not yet subscribe to international war to bring him to a halt. Again, in the fall, a scant two weeks before the fall of the Doumergue ministry, the *New Republic* conceded that on the basis of some local election victories the French people had taken an even longer step in preparing a French counterpart of the Hitler system by underscoring the very element which this journal had expected to be capable of revolution, and which it now dismissed airily as merely a distant possibility: [34]

In France, as elsewhere in Europe, the cry of "Red Terror" has done its work. The French middle class, panic-stricken by the remote danger of a proletarian dictatorship, was not frightened enough of fascism to rebuke the conservative elements that are consciously and deliberately paving the way for it.

This was the contagion theory again, reinforced by the charge of copying of Hitler's method of allegedly emphasizing unduly the Communist menace in order to break down resistance to the gathering of total power by the most implacable of Communism's enemies. But apparently France going Fascist did not in the least mean teamwork with Germany; in view of its vast activity on the foreign diplomatic field, quite the contrary. The alarm over the possibility of a new Austro-German union in the summer of 1933, the feverish fence-building of Foreign Secretary Jean Louis Barthou in southeastern Europe the following year, French support behind Soviet Russia's bid for entry into the heretofore off-limits League of Nations, and the proposal of two grandiose regional pacts in east-central Europe and in the Mediterranean area to supplement Locarno, all this was hardly evidence that whatever the direction of their internal politics, the French were going to make any concessions to the Germans, except under duress. Nor did this conflict with the new pro-French orientation of American liberal thinking. But editorial policy of warmth toward a Left France internally and a resistant France toward Germany externally did not attain the vehemence of the *Nation*'s Geneva correspondent Dell, who from 1934 on incessantly preached the necessity of a military smashing of Hitler as an act of "defending European civilization" against a "barbarian invasion." Dell used the term "preventive war" repeatedly, by which he meant quite frankly the desirability of an invasion of Germany before it got very strong. He urged the French to insist steadfastly on maintaining the Versailles Treaty limitations on German armament, and was further convinced that the German grievances were unlikely to be abated by France or any other nation, thus inciting German action. For this reason he advocated the strongest possible alliance against Germany, resigning himself to a future of unlimited and endless spreadeagling of Germany as an alternative to just settlement of her claims. It was axiomatic to him that close Franco-Russian ties and a complete rejection of any kind of consideration of German requests or demands were absolutely necessary, and he repeatedly called to the French from the pages of the *Nation* to follow such a path, as well as recommending to the French long before it became reality that they strive to get Russia into the League and into occupation of the seat on the League Council vacated by Germany's withdrawal from that body.[35]

In the summer of 1934, nothing hopeful to French ambitions seemed to be appearing, however. A June 6 *New Republic* editorial remarked sorrowfully, "French hegemony in Central Europe is slipping fast and Gallic diplomacy seems to be helpless to prevent it." [36] Only in the immediate environs did French interests prevail. On the coming of Leopold to the kingship of Belgium the same journal frankly described the situation thusly; "Leopold," it observed, "pledged himself to keep Belgium what it has always been: a buffer state between France, Germany and England, dominated by French interests and French foreign policy." [37] But this was small consolation for the sagging scene in the Central European preserves marked out in 1919.

French gropings toward an understanding with Mussolini Italy as a hedge against German movements southward and with Stalin Russia to bar German expansion eastward were received with sympathetic approval in both liberal editorial departments. The day after Russia entered the League the *New Republic* hopefully suggested, "Cooperation between France and Italy, together with Russia's entrance into the League of Nations, would give Europe for a time a new system of international relations. It would be a system of everybody against Hitler." [38] This was another way of unconsciously describing the capture of all of the "everybody against Hitler" camp by ultimate Soviet foreign policy.

Some idea of the turnabout on France which had taken place among American liberals can be gathered from the *Nation's* editorial of October 24, 1934 titled "The Aftermath of Marseilles," inspired by the sensational assassination in that city of Barthou and King Alexander of Jugoslavia. Barthou, trumpeted the *Nation,* "had made a greater contribution to peace than any other statesman in Europe, save possibly Litvinov." Although the editorial admitted that Barthou had broken up the Disarmament Conference in June with a "particularly tactless speech," he had made up for that by working so hard for the admission of the Soviet Union into the League of Nations; in fact, he was largely responsible for this event, the editorial asserted. The big fear now was the possibility of "a serious breach in the iron ring which by Barthou's diplomacy had all but encircled the Third Reich." [39] In a few short months this major organ of liberal opinion was pulling hard for what it had hardly finished denouncing, this forging of "iron rings" around Germany, and in addition had heaped plaudits on a diplomat who would undoubtedly have been held up to loathing and contempt as one of the most sinister of warmongers before March, 1933. The security of the Soviet Union led to few more obvious somersaults than this one.

In December, 1934, the *Nation* was softening up to the acceptance of a new alliance system against Hitler headed up by the French and Russians. Its policy statement "Security or War in Europe" expressed some sadness at the similarity of this new line-up to the Entente of pre-1914, and although it had on scores of occasions denounced the pre-1914 alliance of these two powers as helping to make war inevitable, now it blandly posted this diplomatic event as a means of preventing war.[40]

In reality, there was no subject discussed in the liberal press during 1933–1934 which gave more evidence of the terrible stress and turmoil of conflicting positions than France. The years of viewing France as the militarist troublemaker of Europe in collision with the frantic scurrying around of the French for new positions upon the emergence of Hitler indeed created an agonized literature. And the *New Republic* and its foreign correspondents were as disturbed as the *Nation*. In May, 1933, after months of aggravated attacks on Hitler, the journal still retained enough of its former coolness toward the French to say, "If the public opinion of most of the world must henceforth support France, then another war is inevitable and will not be long in coming," [41] but in August it was rationalizing an anti-German, French-led combine against Germany in Central Europe to prevent the latter's establishing an economic order "which would mean the end of the valuable French trade connections in the Balkan States." [42] This, after having told its readers not many months before that the French part in the economy of Central and Eastern Europe was a trifling affair.

The explanation of Russo-German relations between the accession of Hitler and the Stresa conference was similarly a carnival of speculation and often outright guesswork, and went through several clear stages. Down to the London Conference, whence Litvinov was to come away with his glittering diplomatic victories, the liberals were most vexed by Soviet silence on the stern repression of the Communists in Germany and even more so by the renewal in Moscow in May, 1933 of the Berlin agreements of 1924 and 1926, as well as the arbitration treaty between the two nations of 1929. The *New Republic* connected this with the boycott on Russian imports clamped down by Britain after the conviction of the British Metro-Vickers engineers in the famous Russian spy trial ending on April 19, and professed to see the Russian behavior in all clearness: [43]

In the first place, the Russians believe in economic determinism; they need their German trade, and all the more desperately now that the Anglo-Russian reciprocal boycotts are in effect. In the second place, the Stalinist policy is to let the Communist movements in other countries than Russia get along as best they can. In the third place, Russia is the most anxiously pacifist country in the world today; she knows that a war will ruin all her plans and perhaps put an end to the entire Communist experiment. Since she cannot and will not fight Germany, she will be friends. We wish there were more nations which took such a rigidly realistic view of international relations.

This attempt to divine the Russian mind was not especially comprehensive, since it did not explain why the Communists did not look upon the vast war in China as a roadblock to Communist goals, and fought there with substantial enthusiasm. Nor did it suggest why the vast disparity between a powerful armed force such as that of Russia and a yet un-rearmed Germany should arouse such strong sentiments in favor of protectiveness on the part of the far superior Russians.

A month later the *New Republic* circulated the summary of a report by a French journalist named Jules Sauerwein, who had charged that Hitler had secretly proposed turning the projected Four Power Pact of Mussolini into a coalition directed against Soviet Russia, in order to take advantage of the new official coolness between Russia and England. This was presented as an explanation of recent Anglo-German and Polish-German diplomatic conversations, and it was further asserted that Mussolini was in full accord, hoping to profit by getting Hungary's frontiers restored at the expense of Rumania, which in turn was to be compensated by confirmation of its hold on Bessarabia, still disputed by the Russians. Poland was alleged to have been offered portions of the Russian Ukraine in the direction of the Black Sea in return for the ceding to Germany of portions of the Corridor, thus extending Italo-German influence into the Black Sea through their various allies. The reasons for the failure of the British or French to respond to Hitler's suggestions were given to be the suspicion on their part that Hitler could not be trusted, plus the fact that neither France nor Britain had a fully rightist government. "With a Right government in France, a Right government in England and Hitler in Germany, the possibility of a capitalist war against Soviet Russia will be nearer than at any time in the last decade," was the concluding sentence of this long editorial "Hitler's Anti-Russian Plot," [44] one which ended on a note extremely familiar to regular readers of the *New Masses* as well.

The melody quickly changed after the collapse of the London Conference, from which Russia emerged not as the shrinking friend of peace come what may to the other states in their dealings with Germany but as a powerful and vigorous state, "the honored friend of half the governments of Europe," in the *New Republic*'s fond prose, spoken in the tone of a protagonist's sturdy pride in the success of a protégé.[45] The reason for this sudden reversal was alleged to be the realization among its likely enemies such as Poland that "counterrevolution" against the Communists was now considered quite improbable, although it was conceded that primarily the coming of Hitler was responsible for "Russia's new international popularity." The pro-Russian tide was still running strong in November, shortly before United States recognition, when the same journal's editors suggested among other reasons for recognition by Mr. Roosevelt the issue of bettered world prospects for peace by bolstering Russia against Germany and Japan.[46] From this major launching to admission into the League ten months later the steady emergence of Russia as the natural leader of an anti-German coalition, by slow and easy stages, was an expectable consequence, chronicled at every juncture of importance by American liberals with the full sanction of approval besides.[47]

But among Germany's near neighbors, the contagion theory persisted as an explanation for their steady orientation toward the Hitler regime. In the *Nation* the Czech reporter Egon Erwin Kisch, noted for his extremely cordial views toward Soviet Russia, described the reaction of the Czech government as one of middle-of-the-road detachment, but consequently playing into the hands of a similar situation at home. By suppressing Czech Socialist and Communist "self-protective organizations" gathering to resist the spirit of German Fascism seeping across the border, it was encouraging a dangerous home-front situation; "Actually the Czech democracy is helping Fascism into the saddle." [48]

The first real German break-through in the French alliance system by virtue of the German-Polish treaty of January 26, 1934 stimulated an extended alarm in the *Nation* over this specter of creeping Fascism. Coming after several months of tension as a consequence of the Russo-Polish cordiality after the London Conference, it left the liberals somewhat shaken in their confidence in a solidifying ring of states isolating Germany. But looking beyond this fact, the editors saw the whole French system sagging, and the increasing anti-French or pro-German gravitation of the Rumanians, Hungarians and Czechs as well signalled to them that the Polish-German treaty meant more than just the coming to terms of two old enemies; all these states were moving "within the German-Austrian-Hungarian economic orbit," and the fifteen-year period of French hegemony in Central Europe was about to end.[49] On May 30 the *Nation* made sad note of the emergence of Right regimes in Latvia and Bulgaria too, adding the comment, "The most disheartening note in both episodes is that apparently no resistance was offered to the Fascist seizures." [50] In none of these instances had an allegation of direct German interference been made; it seemed that the failure of the vaunted Social Democratic underground uprisings to materialize in the slightest was so crushing that momentarily there was no broadcasting of alarms of assiduous German fostering of treason and subversion. This was brought to the fore when the first steps were taken toward the actual increase of the Reich's territory, the premature putsch in Austria and the Saar plebiscite preliminaries.

"AUSTRIA: THE HEART OF THE STORM"

Bruce Bliven thus titled a piece written from Europe which appeared in the January 20, 1932 issue of the *New Republic,* demonstrating fine political awareness of European realities with respect to this unhappy surgical patient surviving the Versailles field hospital emergency operation. His fervent pro-Soviet sympathies at this time prevented him from understanding its internal politics, in view of the fact that he thought there was little chance of Austria being taken over by a National Socialist regime, although Vienna's vigorous Marxian Social Democrat organizations undoubtedly had a part to play in forming this view of immunity to such possibilities.[51]

But the following year, after Hitler's victory in Germany, such blithe confidence thinned out and diminished to smoke-like wisps. John Gunther, one of the veteran reporters on Central European affairs to the *Nation* and one of the most frank Socialist sympathizers, displayed serious concern in April, 1933. He expressed profound conviction that the Socialist achievements in Austria deserved the support and respect of "friends of liberty and progress the world over," as well as deep sorrow that they appeared to be already outmaneuvered by both the political forces of Chancellor Engelbert Dollfuss, whose coalition government had been in power since May 20, 1932, and the burgeoning Austrian National Socialist forces, which had upset the tenor of affairs with a long series of hectic demonstrations all during the month of March.[52]

In the next few months liberal editorial opinion established a queasy truce with Dollfuss on the basis of his repression of "Nazi" activities in May and June, 1933, which was followed by a period of quivering tension with the neighboring Hitler regime.[53] Even as late as October the *Nation* advanced an exploratory editorial probe according very reserved approval of Dollfuss. In the issue which appeared on the 4th, the day after an unsuccessful assassination attempt on the chancellor's life, the senior liberal weekly declared, "Fighting fire with fire is dangerous technique, but sometimes there is no alternative, and in creating his new 'fatherland front' Chancellor Dollfuss has not only added to his personal prestige but probably extended the life of Austria as an independent nation."[54] It then went on to qualify this with a somber comparison of the mobilization of nationalism and the political moves undertaken by Dollfuss with those of Germany under Hitler in a manner which left little doubt that it did not especially relish these tactics, even when introduced to hold off the hated Hitler. H. N. Brailsford in the *New Republic*'s issue of the same date also displayed the orthodox Socialist anguish, and shuddered at the possibility of either Germany or Italy taking over Austria and dissolving the Socialists. In this sentimentality there was a curious strain of realism, however; the *Nation* freely admitted that "the desperate economic plight of the country" was at the base of the "Nazi" "demand for change," and Brailsford similarly conceded that the impossible economics forced on the Versailles-truncated state and the rejection of *Anschluss* played the major part in the trouble. Even now Brailsford had no hostile feeling toward Austro-German union, partially a reflection of his embarrassed recollection that even the Marxian Socialists had been enthusiastic for *Anschluss* before Hitler's victory. But his major energies were now being devoted to visioning the ancient liberal mirage of a United States of Europe as a solution to Austrian frustrations.[55]

As in the case of Germany, American liberals were unable to explain why the unions and the Social Democrats failed to head off National Socialism's meteoric rise in Austria. They were astounded by "Nazi" growth in the October, 1933 elections, and heartily condemned the Socialist leaders, but what they could have done about it was never made evident, while the moral collapse of the Austrian proletariat found them in such a state of shock that they barely found it possible to record it. In a November 22 editorial the *New Republic* announced in limp despair, "Today the Austrian worker is looking forward to the coming of Fascism with fatalistic indifference." [56]

But this attitude of resignation concealed a substantial vessel of indignation, which overflowed in February, 1934 when the Dollfuss Christian Socialists crushed Austrian Marxian Socialism and concluded its suppression with the spectacular and astounding bombardment with artillery of the Marxist housing units, the Karl Marx Hof. The *Nation* to the end hoped that Socialism would triumph in its civil war with Dollfuss, and Gunther's on-the-spot report conveyed the idea of hope to the end as well, even though he admitted distorting what he was witnessing and confessed to strong partisanship; "I should like extremely to see a Social Democratic Austria," he reported in a February 14 article titled "Keeping Hitler Out of Austria." [57]

Two weeks later, the issue seemed settled beyond any doubt, and the concluding judgments started to come in. A long *New Republic* editorial denounced the Austrian Chancellor thusly: "Chancellor Dollfuss of Austria will go down in history as one of the arch-fiends of the class war," but distinguished between his regime and that of Hitler rather sharply, even if in considerable bad grace, and ended on a closed-fist note of defiance; [58]

The meaning of the Austrian tragedy, beneath all the surface complications, emerges. It is but a step in the preparation of a new European holocaust, in which the workers, having been defeated at home and absorbed into capitalist states, will be set murdering one another across national boundaries. The only true force of internationalism is an independent workers' movement strong enough to build and maintain international socialism.

There were powerful liberal attacks launched against nearly every important European state except Soviet Russia for complicity in this debacle, with the bitterness being particularly vehement against Britain, France and Italy. The *New Republic* maintained that Anglo-French intervention might have prevented this, conceding that French preoccupation with an internal crisis caused by the Stavisky scandal might have substantially impeded her freedom of movement in the affair.[59] Querulous outcries against both continued in the post-mortem period, deepened by conclusions to the effect that if Dollfuss was unable to establish a regime with strong Italian instead of German leanings, there would still be danger of war between Mussolini and the French, a likely consequence of a pro-Italian Austria, since the former was determined to break the French "hegemony over Central Europe." Hitler was exempted from major criticism for a short while. In fact it was assumed that Mussolini's Italy was the critical element in this new foreign situation, and that an Austria oriented toward him would diminish his fear of a "Teutonized" Austria, leading to his willingness to aid Hitler against France and her remaining Central European allies such as Czechoslovakia and Russia, a calamitous consequence.[60] On the other hand the *Nation* felt that this was simply a stage in a coming Austro-German *Anschluss,* which neither the French nor Italians would be able to prevent: "The Germany of Hitler, who has won the support of a large part of the Austrian population, is stronger than any other single Power," it warned; "The differences between the various groups opposed to his rule are too deep to be bridged for a common front against Nazi Germany." [61]

A later *Nation* editorial of considerable length on the Italo-Franco-German struggle for "lasting influence in Central Europe" charged that Britain had played the part of "the laughing bystander, not at all averse to the spectacle of its chief competitors at each other's throats." [62] Gunther even found a reason for Austrian warmth for National Socialism in that Austria was fighting the peace treaties of 1919–1921 as much as Hitler was, and that the vast poverty of its people made "Nazi" promises sound appealing. He took almost grim satisfaction in suggesting that if Austria did end up in the "Nazi" camp, it would just be "another item in retribution—another answer of revengeful Germany to the injustices of the Treaty of Versailles." [63]

Other verdicts running on into midsummer, 1934, reinforced these views, and also underlined growing hostility toward Hitler as an agent in the Austrian political explosion. A *New Republic* editorial

"Europe Marches" concluded that the victory of "Fascism in Austria" meant that "Hitler's Germany is today the most important factor in European politics," [64] and Edmund Stevens' article "Austria After the Terror" in May confirmed that "Such nationalist sentiment as does exist in Austria is German nationalism and flows in Nazi channels"; in his opinion, "The attempt to dream up an Austrian nationalism evokes no response." [65]

The liberal cannonade of Dollfuss continued with slight lessening for the next five months, with Dell, Gunther and Schuman vying for top honors in preparing incendiary accounts on Austro-German affairs. Gunther, who could blandly write in May, 1934 that the whole Jewish population of Germany was already a victim of "mass execution," reached new heights in his excoriation of Dollfuss as well.[66] However, in detailing his bitter hatred for the Austrian leader Gunther admitted that the contacts on whose confidential reports he depended were Socialists, Communists, Jews, and foreign diplomats who also were furiously against this new Austrian order.

All proved to be poor prophets, down to the moment of the assassination of Dollfuss in the abortive Nazi putsch of July 25. Gunther and Dell predicted that war would promptly break out, and for over a month Gunther prophesied that Mussolini would invade Austria,[67] while liberal editorial policy trembled for weeks over this startling development. Faint traces of the pre-February 1934 sympathy or detachment toward the murdered Dollfuss returned to their columns as a consequence of this outrage, and vast abuse was heaped on Hitler and Nazi Germany for a long time. The dreaded war failed to make its appearance, however, but this did not stem the quivering expectancy appreciably.

Weeks after the establishment of Dollfuss' intimate associate Kurt Schuschnigg in executive power in Austria, the liberal press announced in somber tones the likelihood of a Hitlerian sally into Austria.[68] The *New Republic* especially cautioned its readers to take no stock in Hitler's interview in the London *Daily Mail* in which he volubly stressed his intention to keep Germany at peace, since in their judgment it was assumed that everyone realized that "peace and National Socialism are incompatible." The failure of anything exciting to follow in the wake of all the terror did not diminish the volume of expectation. In Austria the liberals had their prime case in support of their theory of the contagious extension of National Socialism out of Germany into its neighbors, which was supported by far more evidence than they were able to advance as documentation of the situation in other areas contiguous with Germany. The failure of a German follow-through did not provoke any significant feeling of disappointment,[69] and in fact a new focus of infection rapidly replaced Austria as news in the press. This was the knotty question of the Saar, as the 1935 deadline for its League of Nations-prescribed plebiscite approached. In a slightly milder way the furor raised over Austria was repeated here, but with drastically different consequences. The German victory with ballots here was more of a surprise than the Austrian "Nazi" failure with bullets in Vienna.

THE VEXATIOUS QUESTION OF THE SAAR

Prior to 1933 it was not uncommon to see American liberal expressions of sympathy with the case for Germany in the Saar, which was in harmony with liberal conviction that the territorial settlements of the war were almost without exception prime examples of poor judgment and obtuseness, if not outright brigandage. In fact, the topic of the territorial loppings and grabbings after 1918 was a perennial in American liberal journalism. As late as the third week of February, 1932 the *Nation* was still finding it pertinent to reprimand the Lithuanian government with considerable briskness for its swift snatch of the Versailles-decreed international autonomous territory of Memel from French control in 1923, after it had been wrested from Germany. At a time of loud lament over Japanese action in Asia, the editors considered this as serious an act of contempt for the League of Nations as anything Japan had done in Manchuria. Again, in October, 1935, when a new season of outrage over the behavior of a power toward the League broke out, this time over Italy in Ethiopia, H. N. Brailsford brought up in the *New Republic* the case of Lithuania in Memel with considerable heated disapprobation. "Memel is a solidly German town," he protested.[70]

That the Saar belonged back in the German state was rarely questioned. The ascendance of Adolf Hitler stopped most of this, and in place of castigations of France one now began to observe cautious, exploratory statements reflecting good will toward the French. As early as September, 1933 the *New Republic* was of the opinion that the plebiscite which was to take place on January 13, 1935 would result in an undoubted vote for return to Germany.[71] But now this was no longer looked upon as a desirable eventuality, and dark reservations began to appear on the record, gaining scope and momentum in the early autumn of the following year, as the election date drew nearer. A substantial part of this new alarm was a product of the stunning developments in Austria, particularly those of July, when most liberal commentators had predicted an imminent German takeover following the assassination of Dollfuss. Now they were not so sure, and increasing reports of "Nazi" activity in the Saar made possible the loosing of the suggestion that a *putsch* along the lines which had been expected but which had not materialized in the former might very likely occur in the latter.

Beginning in September, 1934 both liberal weeklies began to let up trial balloon editorials suggesting now that there was a good chance the Saarlanders might reject reunion with Germany, and that consequently Germany might "resort to force in an effort to sustain its national prestige," as the *New Republic* put it. Part of this new wave of hope was a reflection of the budding Popular Front-*Neu Beginnen* sentiments all over Western Europe, plus the added comfort derived from the admission of Communist Russia to the League of Nations. The Saar was now supposed to harbor a formidable "Liberty Front," consisting of an alliance of Socialists, Communists and Catholics which was alleged to be bitterly against the "Nazis" and in a position to do something about it.[72] A war cry went up also from the *Nation*'s Geneva correspondent, Dell,[73] who expressed his confidence in a coming military invasion of the Saar by Hitler, which he implored the British and French to be prepared to take immediate countermeasures against and to abruptly turn their backs on "sentimental pacifism" in their lands, which he considered "the greatest danger to European peace." Dell's transparent sympathy with the Reds in this period now was in conflict with his verdict that "Mussolini deserves our gratitude" for having in his opinion prevented Hitlerian intervention in Austria by moving troops to the Brenner frontier. He was urgently of the opinion that the British and French should emulate his example by being ready for the similarly-expected thrust at the Saar.

The bank account of good will which had slowly accumulated for the French in the American liberal press promptly vanished late in September, when the French announced that in the event of a proGerman vote in the Saar, the Hitler government would be expected to pay for the French-owned mines at once, *in toto* and in cash. The *New Republic* denounced this as a most unwise act which was part of a French "propaganda that consistently played into Hitler's hands," and that "nothing less than madness" on the part of the French leaders could excuse it. All hope was now given up that a vote in favor of remaining under the League could occur, and that Hitler's enemies in the Saar could be expected to go along with return to Germany "simply as an act of fundamental national justice," because of this unreasonable French stipulation. The junior liberal weekly even fell back on its pre-Hitler language by announcing grimly, "The stupidity of the peace dictators of Versailles, who cut off from the mother country for a period of twenty years a district almost exclusively German, is now bearing fruit." [74]

Still again, in November, the *New Republic* found reason to issue a massive rebuke to the French; "If the Germans win an imposing victory in the Saar plebiscite of January 13," it warned editorially, "they will have Paris with its hysterical alarms about a Putsch and an invasion to thank for it." [75] In barely two months a propaganda in which they themselves had once cheerfully participated had become so obsolete that the French could be excoriated for using it now. Nothing testified so conclusively to the growth of a deep pessimism over the chances of the Saar remaining out of Hitler's Germany. The *Nation* retained a more sanguine view of the issue, and deprecated "Nazi" predictions on the Saar vote until the end.

A *New Statesman* and *Nation* reporter, Jack Fischer, cabled the results of the vote to the *Nation* from Saarbrücken on January 15, 1935 and the *Nation* recoiled editorially in deep shock. "The plebiscite was absolutely fair and peaceful despite extreme Nazi moral pressure," Fischer announced; "Ninety-seven per cent of the eligible voters balloted—the most complete expression of public opinion on record." [76] And with reunion with Germany gaining 91% of this vote, there was almost nothing to take comfort in, but a few scraps were salvaged. To solace the readers Fischer and the editors announced that the Saarland's Socialists and Communists were not going to submit to Hitler but would go underground and continue the political struggle, while by some statistical legerdemain it was now considered grounds for consolation that the slightly more than 5% vote against reunion constituted "a thumping vote of censure against Hitler by loyal Germans." [77] This, after having calmly supported the position on a number of occasions that there was a strong possibility of defeating Hitler.

This brief wave of bravado passed rapidly, and the *Nation* soon felt constrained to adopt the position that there was nothing for the League to do other than to "restore the territory to Germany at an early date." In the numb period of wound-licking that ensued a significant change of tune took place, and much of the alarm of the kind displayed during the Austrian crisis evaporated. Villard in his February 13 column estimated that Hitler had emerged from the Saar test "much strengthened," and felt that the absorption of Austria might follow anyway, since there was evidence of increasing enthusiasm there for Hitler as he proceeded in creating his Central European German power.[78] And a season of calm settled on the liberal press in a not completely tranquil setting, to end in short order in shouts and gesticulations as Hitler proceeded with the demolition of the Versailles straitjacket by repudiating the arms limitations and announcing the resumption of conscription. But the coming to full flower of the pro-Russian Popular Front and the immense agitation stimulated by Mussolini's ambitions in Northeast Africa had fully as much to do with a new wave of American liberal trepidation and vociferous opinion-influencing action. The Spanish Civil War, which broke out a few weeks after the Ethiopian adventure ended in Mussolini's favor, mobilized those who had managed to maintain their aloofness through the other disturbing events.

NOTES

1 "Europe: On the Brink of Catastrophe," *New Republic*, May 24, 1933, pp. 31–32.
2 Dell, "Hitler Over Europe," *Nation*, May 3, 1933, pp. 407–408.
3 "Our New Role In Europe," *Nation*, May 24, 1933, p. 573.
4 See especially the article "Germany Prepares For War," published by the *Nation* under the pseudonym "Ernst Schulz," September 27, 1933, p. 353, and the editorial "Educating For War," *New Republic*, November 8, 1933, pp. 351–352.
5 Schuman, "Germany Prepares Fear," *New Republic*, February 7, 1934, pp. 353–355. See also Lore, "How Germany Arms," *Harper's*, April, 1934, pp. 505–517.
6 Dell, "Can The League Be Saved?", *Nation*, February 21, 1934, pp. 211–213.
7 "Johannes Steel is the pseudonym of a German refugee now in the United States." *Nation*, March 7, 1934, p. 286. Steel was further identified as a contributor to British periodicals and the author of the book *Hitler As Frankenstein*, published in England. His series was titled "Europe Moves Toward War."
8 "Disarmament Retreats," *Nation*, May 2, 1934, p. 495.
9 "Two Years Of Hitler," *Nation*, February 6, 1935, pp. 145–146. The editors were convinced that foreign hostility would weaken Hitler's hold on the people extremely.
10 *Nation*, February 13, 1935, p. 170. On the regret over failure to get Germany back into the League, see editorial in issue of February 27, 1935, p. 233.
11 "A Last Gasp From Versailles," *New Republic*, February 13, 1935, p. 5.
12 *Nation*, March 20, 1935, p. 318.
13 *Nation*, March 27, 1935, p. 345.
14 "Hitler Liquidates Versailles," *Nation*, March 27, 1935, p. 348.
15 *New Republic*, March 27, 1935, p. 169.
16 "Europe Must Choose," *Nation*, April 3, 1935, p. 376.
17 *Nation*, April 10, 1935, p. 401.
18 Simonds' review in *Nation*, March 14, 1934, pp. 305–306.
19 Editorial, *Nation*, March 14, 1934, p. 289.
20 *Nation*, June 20, 1934, p. 710. It was also reviewed in *New Republic*, July 4, 1934, p. 215. The foreword was written by Edgar Ansel Mowrer.
21 Lore's review in *Nation*, July 25, 1934, p. 107; Brailsford's in *New Republic*, August 15, 1934, pp. 25–26.
22 *New Republic*, July 25, 1934, pp. 275–276.
23 *New Republic*, February 7, 1934, p. 374. Reviewed with this was Paul Kosok's *Modern Germany*, of which the reviewer said that Kosok, "by employing the Marxian method of analyzing a given society into its constituent social-economic classes," had produced "a most lucid exposition of present-day Germany." See also the brief review by George E. Novack of *The Rationalization Movement In German Industry* by Robert A. Brady, *New Republic*, March 21, 1934, pp. 164–165.
24 *Nation*, January 16, 1935, p. 29.
25 *New Republic*, November 28, 1934, pp. 81–82.
26 Bonn's review in *New Republic*, May 10, 1933, pp. 370–371.
27 See also the criticism of this review by F. P. Magoun, Jr., in *New Republic*, February 21, 1934, p. 49.
28 *Nation*, February 20, 1935, p. 227. This could be compared to the *Nation's* review

of Hamilton Fish Armstrong's *Hitler's Reich,* in the issue for August 30, 1933, p. 248.

29 Brailsford, "A German Sunday," *New Republic,* June 21, 1933, pp. 145–146.

30 Villard, "Hitler and England," *Nation,* June 28, 1933, pp. 718–719.

31 *New Republic,* May 2, 1934, pp. 331–332. The *New Republic* considered Rothermere a partisan of Hitler's plans for reorganizing East-central Europe. Editorial, December 13, 1933, p. 114.

32 *New Republic,* March 14, 1934, p. 117.

33 *Nation,* May 9, 1934, pp. 532–533. The author used the name "Donald Barrett."

34 *New Republic,* October 17, 1934, p. 254.

35 Dell, "Will Germany Conquer France?," *Nation,* April 18, 1934, pp. 440–442.

36 *New Republic,* June 6, 1934, p. 89.

37 "Crisis In Belgium," *New Republic,* June 6, 1934, pp. 88–89.

38 *New Republic,* September 19, 1934, p. 312.

39 "The Aftermath of Marseilles," *Nation,* October 24, 1934, p. 466. See also the *New Republic*'s favorable view of Barthou's diplomacy in editorial on July 18, 1934, p. 247.

40 *Nation,* December 12, 1934, pp. 663–664.

41 "Europe: On the Brink of Catastrophe," *New Republic,* May 24, 1933, pp. 31–32.

42 *New Republic,* August 30, 1933, p. 57.

43 *New Republic,* May 17, 1933, p. 1. Louis Fischer had precisely this kind of interpretation to make in his "Russia: Fear and Foreign Policy," *Nation,* October 11, 1933, pp. 403–405; "Russia's economic relations with Germany help the Nazis. But those relations are maintained because they help the Bolsheviks . . . The Kremlin's first concern is the progress of the Revolution. . . . The triumph of agrarian collectivization in the U.S.S.R. is far more important for the world revolution than making faces at Hitler or calling him names. There ought to be a division of labor; those condemned to sterile anger in bourgeois countries can stick to the faces and names while the Bolsheviks continue on their difficult climb toward a socialist state."

44 *New Republic,* June 21, 1933, pp. 140–141.

45 *New Republic,* August 2, 1933, p. 304.

46 "The Bear and the Eagle," *New Republic,* November 1, 1933, pp. 323–324.

47 See especially "The New Pattern in Europe," *New Republic,* September 26, 1934, p. 173.

48 Kisch, "Czecho-Slovakia's Nazi Neighbors," *Nation,* July 26, 1933, pp. 99–100.

49 *Nation,* February 7, 1934, p. 142.

50 *Nation,* May 30, 1934, p. 605.

51 *New Republic,* January 20, 1932, pp. 264–266.

52 Gunther, "Will Austria Go Fascist?," *Nation,* April 12, 1933, pp. 393–395.

53 *New Republic,* May 3, 1933, p. 325.

54 *Nation,* October 4, 1933, p. 366.

55 Brailsford, "Austria Confronts Fascism," *New Republic,* October 4, 1933, pp. 202–204.

56 *New Republic,* November 22, 1933, p. 32.

57 *Nation,* February 14, 1934, pp. 180–181.

58 *New Republic,* February 28, 1934, pp. 60–61.

59 *New Republic,* February 14, 1934, pp. 1–2.

60 See note 58, above.

61 *Nation,* February 21, 1934, p. 203.

62 "The Death Of Austrian Democracy," *Nation,* February 28, 1934.

63 Gunther, "Keeping Hitler Out Of Austria," *Nation,* February 14, 1934, pp. 180–181.

64 *New Republic,* February 21, 1934, pp. 32–33.

65 *New Republic,* May 9, 1934, pp. 359–360.

66 Gunther, "The Struggle For Power In Austria," *Nation,* May 16, 1934, pp. 557–559.

67 Gunther, "After the Dollfuss Murder," *Nation,* August 22, 1934, pp. 204–205.

68 *New Republic,* August 15, 1934, p. 2.

69 "What Next In Germany?," *New Republic,* August 15, 1934, p. 7.

70 *Nation,* February 17, 1932, p. 183; Brailsford, "The League In Action," *New Republic,* October 30, 1935, pp. 324–326.

71 *New Republic,* September 6, 1933, p. 86.

72 *Nation,* September 19, 1934, p. 310.

73 Dell, "The Future Of Hitler," *Nation*, September 19, 1934, pp. 320–322.
74 *New Republic*, September 26, 1934, pp. 171–172.
75 *New Republic*, November 14, 1934, p. 4.
76 *Nation*, January 23, 1935, pp. 96–98.
77 *Nation*, January 23, 1935, p. 85.
78 Villard, "Hitler After the Saar," *Nation*, February 13, 1935, p. 175.

14

ITALIANS IN ETHIOPIA : FIRST
LIBERAL BUGLE CALL, 1935–1936

THE immense impact of Adolf Hitler upon liberal America did not completely erase Benito Mussolini from their hall of demons. He had for some time been in the shadows, since their case against him and the Fascisti had been spoken with much reiteration long before 1931. In the period while Dino Grandi held forth at the Disarmament Conference, as we have seen, they were even inclined to issue reports which contained traces of restrained praise and expressions of belief in Italian sincerity for world peace. With the blooming of Hitler, the atmosphere warmed a bit more, partially a consequence of the casting of Mussolini as a sure opponent of German expansionism and German influence toward the south and southeast of Europe. Bright little pieces dealing with the surety of Italo-French understandings were not uncommon products of liberal writers on foreign politics. But just as this seemed to be even more certain of maturation than ever, especially as a consequence of the stirring events in Austria and the Saar, the Stresa meeting and the revival of conscription in Germany, the sky darkened as a result of Italian moves in northeast Africa, adding unpleasant complications in the form of agitated British reaction. The struggle over Ethiopia not only wrecked the iron-ring-around-Germany movement, but started the first steps leading to the riveting of the so-called Berlin-Rome Axis.

The fundamental enmity of most American liberals toward Mussolini Italy never was more than briefly masked at any time, nevertheless. The orthodox Marxian prediction of dire internal revolt and collapse of Fascist Italy was steady liberal press fare. Grim attack and refusal to admit anything of substance and consequence had ever been performed by the regime continued to be liberal dogma, and any kind words spoken on behalf of Mussolini's internal order were bitterly resented.

A few incidents of the period just past may be reviewed for background purposes. The year 1932, it will be recalled, was a time of renewed attention to Mussolini and Italian Fascism, largely due to the activities of Grandi at the international conferences discussing war debts, reparations and disarmament. The *New Republic* did not hesitate to refer to Grandi's ideas as "sound sense." [1] Though liberals were subdued by this, loath to comfort themselves that the Italian efforts were insincere, they did not suspend their condemnation of the regime despite its obvious gain in stature through championing reform in the above matters. Though one might find an Edmund Wilson referring to Mussolini as "a first-rate intelligence embodied in the clever politician," [2] it was no sign that detachment was about to become the characteristic of liberal approach to Il Duce.

For one thing, the liberal press and many writers were already committed to the support of various Italian political refugees and their campaign to bring about Mussolini's downfall. Particularly esteemed were the *émigré* academic coterie ostensibly led by Gaetano Salvemini, a frankly collectivist group known as "Giustizia e Libertà," which yearned to confiscate land wholesale for distribution to the peasantry, and nationalize broad bands of the country's industry upon taking over, if successful in smashing the Fascists, which they bluntly expected to achieve by a "violent overturn." [3] Hence no amount of creditable behavior in efforts at international understanding was bound to jog the ideological commitment against Mussolini significantly. And even here there was room for the publication of pseudonymous attacks, when done within the context of controversy over internal Italian politics. [4]

There was such a thing as going too far here, however. In January, 1932 there was a wave of bomb-mailings to representatives of the Italian government in the United States and to prominent Italo-Americans known to be friendly to Mussolini's regime. Three men were killed by explosions, and four wounded. This led to a hasty repudiation by the *New Republic* in particular, which sought at once to dissociate Salvemini and its other favorite anti-Fascists from the charge of implication; "Their act is a dreadful crime," the editorial

of January 13, 1932 said of the bomb-senders.[5] And it sharply rebuked A. J. Muste, who was the chairman of the Committee for International Anti-Fascist Protest, and Carlo Tresca for trying to insin-
uate that the bombs had been mailed by the Fascists themselves to
discredit the anti-Fascist movement. Said the editorial of January 27,
"To suppose that the Fascists would try to murder half a dozen of
their leading representatives in America in order to discredit the anti-
Fascists here seems to us to strain the limits of common sense." [6]
Though the *New Republic* did not mind a "violent overturn" of
Mussolini in Italy, it did not think that the proper place to start
was in the United States through utilizing the facilities of the Post
Office Department.

In the fall of 1932 the liberals were reminded of their ten-year-old
feud with the Mussolini regime when several of its political prisoners
were granted amnesty on this anniversary of the inauguration of the
Fascist government. It was an occasion for a blistering condemnation of Mussolini for having imprisoned anyone, by the editors of
the *Nation*,[7] presented in the usual context of overlooking the Russian Communist achievements in this field, and for that matter ignoring that Il Duce had rather effectively blotted out Communism from
Italy during the decade under review. Yet one of its anonymous overseas contributors in a satirical commentary on Mussolini a month
later could not find it possible to deny that some tangible gains in
Italy were evident: [8]

Domestically, things are going smoothly. Anyone who talks of impending civil trouble is 'way off. . . . Mussolini is at the very height of his
health, his career, and his power, and nothing is going to end his regime
except his death or, conceivably, a war. You should have seen that tour of
his through the North to celebrate the tenth anniversary of Fascismo. I
find my liberal principles making me regret a little that it was so impressive, but impressive it certainly was.

Compared with the solemn, respectful reports of Soviet Russia by
Louis Fischer appearing simultaneously, it was not too noteworthy
a tribute, yet worthy of note because of the rarity with which this sort
of balancing the foreign scene was noted in these times.

Basically, however, the conviction that the Mussolini order was but
a momentary irritation in the way of Marxism on the march remained unruffled just below the surface of liberal consciousness.
Orthodox Marxists with a close affinity to Russian Communism were
accepted as the authorities on Italy, and the theory of the Marxists of
the moment, that Fascism and National Socialism represented the
final phase of a collapsing capitalism, was confidently broadcast. John
Strachey's famous book on Fascism held the status of a political bible

after it appeared, and his conviction that the entire Mussolini order was a sham and a façade received wide acceptance.[9] The curious result of this was the simultaneous viewing of Mussolini as a potent statesman who was making Italy the dominant state in the Mediterranean and about to create an ominous "Balkan league of states," gaining the upper hand in the direction of Austria's future and pushing Britain and France into the status of "bystanders" in the Danubian region, and yet the shaky leader of a domestic order which was already displaying the evidences of rot and dissolution. When the *New Republic* printed Strachey's special dispatch on the Italian internal order on March 7, 1934 and followed it with an editorial "Mussolini Challenges Europe" three weeks later it unconsciously posed diametrically opposed pictures of Italy.[10] But it seems, in the light of the arguments advanced during the ensuing Italo-Ethiopian war, that the vision of a feeble Italy had become the most firmly entrenched in American liberal imaginations; economic warfare as a means of bringing about Mussolini's collapse would hardly have been proposed so often and so attractively had this not been the case.

The later months of this same year immediately preceding the expansionist adventure in Africa had been featured in the liberal weeklies by a tempestuous controversy over a matter related to those immediately above; Columbia University had been charged flatly with providing a shelter for Fascist intellectuals in its Italian Department and with permitting a campus organization, the Casa Italiana, to become a center of Fascist propaganda, in the liberal view. Italian refugees such as Max Ascoli warmly praised the *Nation* especially for the large amount of space it devoted to this affair, the editors being especially incensed because the Casa had not asked fierce *émigré* enemies of the Mussolini regime such as Salvemini and Carlo Sforza to speak before their meetings.

The sparks flew back and forth on this issue for weeks, with no particular outcome becoming evident, and it was still in flame in November, 1934.[11] It accompanied the bitterly hostile reports coming from overseas correspondents, part of which were rumbling rumors of internal disaffection again. Robert Dell, in his "Impressions of Italy," a catalog of predictions which never did materialize, capped it with the following: "The chances are that Mussolini will be assassinated some day. If he is, his assassin will be a man in a black shirt."[12] No one took notice of the color of the shirts of Mussolini's Communist murderers in 1945, but that they definitely were not members of Mussolini's Black Shirts is a fact of the most unshakable sort.

Both weeklies took editorial notice with different accents that all was not well between the Italians in their African colony in Eritrea and adjoining Ethiopia in their issues of the day after Christmas of 1934. The *New Republic*'s comment was quite calm, found room to attack French and British policies there as well, and observed in summation, "the great imperialists of Europe are again dividing the African continent." The *Nation* spoke up sharply and called upon the League of Nations to step in at once and give its "peace machinery" a real test in settling this dispute, not unlike its reaction to Japan three years before, the fruitlessness of which had apparently made no impression at all.[13]

The tempo picked up sharply after the Ual-Ual incident, featured by the customary contradictions among liberal views as various complexities of the situation unrolled. As the British began to bridle the most obviously of all, liberal invocation of the League unconsciously called upon them to make the strongest efforts to halt Italian movements at the expense of Ethiopia, although the *Nation,* far more devoted to the ceremonies of League incantations, on a few occasions even appealed to the Roosevelt Administration to blunt Mussolini's ambitions. A February 27, 1935 editorial, "Italian Sword-Rattling," was strongly for the United States assumption of responsibility in discouraging the litigants from using force, and for American leadership in "forcing a discussion," since it was felt that this country was in a peculiarly favorable position "to exert moral influence against the sort of territorial brigandage which all nations have renounced in principle." [14] Of course, all nations had not renounced the changing of things by force, but the tone of the editorial cancelled out the implication that there was a mediable dispute here by baldly assuming that territorial aggrandizement was the issue unconditionally.

The *New Republic* was far less fearful for the welfare of the Ethiopians. In its editorial comment of the same date it expressed confidence that the country could easily field an army of two million out of a population of seven million, and that it could hold the line "against all comers for a considerable period." It poked derision at Mussolini and denied that there was the slightest case for Italy in this affair whatsoever.[15] In July it backed up this estimate of the fighting potential of the African opponent of the Fascisti: "The Ethiopian army," it advised, "is not composed solely of wooly-headed tribesmen with spears. It is equipped with modern guns, rifles and a few tanks and airplanes," equipment which it believed had been obtained from Japan.[16]

Still in these early months of 1935 the total picture was exceedingly cloudy. Italian remonstrance in Africa scrambled completely the comforting hope of mustering Mussolini as an anti-Hitler barrier, and this was made still worse by the German decisions to rearm and conscript. The *Nation*'s editorial of April 17 writhed with discomfort over all this. The tough policy toward Germany required "Anglo-Italian cooperation," yet the two were on the verge of serious disagreement over Africa. A morsel of consolation was extracted from it all on the basis of allegedly detecting that German rearmament had led to "the complete conversion of Mussolini to cooperation with France." Thus the muddled ingredients were assembled; a France inclined to be conciliatory to Mussolini in exchange for his support versus Germany, and a truculent England, bridling at Italian pretensions to a greater African empire and increased influence in Britain's Mediterranean lake.[17]

In the first months of 1935, the liberal voices were not entirely entranced with British poses of moral superiority. In the *New Republic* and elsewhere, Bruce Bliven and others entertained the notion that British outbursts of concern over Ethiopia were not motivated by concern for the welfare of world peace, but out of fear for the future of the Empire, and that the English were seeking to use the moral weight of the League once again to support their goals. The League might be considered a chain, these Americans said, but there appeared to be little evidence that even in this touchy situation there was any real intention to use it as "a set of handcuffs for Mars." Subsequently there was much liberal shrilling about Ethiopia's "inviolability," a rather empty assertion in view of the rather professional way African real estate had been absorbed by the British, French, Belgians, Portuguese and Spanish since the 1870's, made even more obvious by the new deathly silence over the manner in which the German colonies had been parcelled out after 1918.

But the new vogue of substituting contract bridge for the everything-wild form of colonial poker was gaining strength, and the pose of moral superiority on the part of the Anglo-French combine, with nearly all of Africa in their control, was gradually accepted by American liberals, as much as it pained some of them in the early stages of this controversy. Bit by bit the Ethiopian crisis furnished them with the makings of an ethical wrestling match. Over and over prior to the actual shooting stage it was thought necessary to note that the moral powers and the pleaders for "sanctions" had some questionable linen of their own to hide. But the counterbalance was the reiteration that the League's existence still promised a new day, "a deliberate effort to substitute law for anarchy in the international sphere." This led to the annunciation of complete faith in the success of a policy of denying to Italy the trade of the League's members.

There were moments of subdued disturbance because certain voices in Britain such as George Lansbury and Stafford Cripps, and Americans like Frank Simonds, advanced objections to the sanctions process. And there was a solid front, among even the wildest liberal supporters of sanctions, against American involvement in the politics of the Ethiopian struggle, beyond such legal steps as the Congress might take to place the United States alongside the League sanctioneers. At still another occasion the Franco-British concern over Mussolini in Ethiopia was interpreted, in the *New Republic,* as the result not of a sentiment of outrage, but of their fear that Il Duce would send out too many troops from Europe and thus increase the likelihood that Hitler might expand into Austria in their absence. To quiet the sentimental who might have been ready to admit the British had little compunction about destroying the lives of Asians and Africans but who tended to idealize the French, the *New Republic* May 22 published Raymond Postgate's "Echoes of a Revolt," an account of current ugly French atrocities against the Viet Nam in Annam, Cochin China and Tonkin, which stressed among other things French wholesale shooting of prisoners.[18] So close readers need not have developed any lopsided fixations about the state of virtue among some colonials.

But the British government seemed to be having some success in getting the League in position to wheel up its moral artillery, and the *Nation* of the same date, commenting on the meeting of the League Council on May 20, put all its emphasis on the hope that it could head off an Italo-Ethiopian war, quivering with anxiety and fear that failure to do so "would destroy the moral basis for possible future punitive measures against German aggression." [19] The *Nation* apparently was already looking well ahead, hoping the League machinery would survive in healthy enough condition to be wheeled into action against the much more formidable threat to the status quo represented by the ambitions of Hitler Germany. And by the end of the month of May it did not look the least bit hopeful, in the *Nation*'s editorial opinion, since Mussolini seemed to be edging toward a showdown with Emperor Haile Selassie and Ethiopia despite the fact that the League had gotten around to appointing arbitrators. "The one hope of arresting war," it said, "is that the League will be forced into a position where it must act to save its very existence." [20]

By July, 1935 the *Nation* had moved almost entirely into a moral position on the question. The usual astute comments on the clash of rival imperialisms and the material stakes involved had mainly vanished. It agonized with Britain's effort to try to get the League to "curb" Italy, blamed the French for refusing to "collaborate," stood adamantly against recognizing any Italian advances in Africa whatever and argued that Mussolini's adventure was proof that "Fascism means war." [21] No explanation was given how the absence of "Fascism" had nevertheless led to the long string of African wars for territorial aggrandizement in the 60 or so years before. At the moment the stress was being placed on the virtues of maintaining the League as a disciplinary machine, and Mussolini's criminality in wrecking it by his defiance.

The one bit of heartening evidence to the *Nation* was the strange "Peace Ballot" in England which it reported on July 10. In this il-

logical demonstration, participated in by 40% of the British electorate, some 11 millions voted in the affirmative on remaining in the
League, 10½ millions voted for "all-round reduction of armaments"
and against the manufacture and sale of munitions "for private
profit," but nearly 6,800,000 voted for the application of economic
sanctions against Italy. The *Nation* found nothing contradictory in
the British voting for a get-tough policy while simultaneously voting
even more emphatically in favor of getting rid of the things to get
tough with.[22] At this stage, it appeared that liberals thought economic warfare was a device which had the qualities of perpetual motion and needed no propulsion or dynamic help. This kind of ill-
digested view, that sanctions were a means of obtaining the objectives
of war without fighting, persisted well into the next year, even after
the African campaigns of Mussolini had ended in swift military success.

When the new Tory government assumed power under Stanley
Baldwin, the *Nation* persisted in its view that the Peace Ballot was
"a mandate for applying sanctions to Italy," as well as a signal for "the
revival of the League to meet the rising menace of Hitlerism." [23]
However, when the Tories began to push for rearmament as the basis
for stronger defenses in support of the League, as the logic of the
Peace Ballot called for, the *Nation* denounced them as "reactionary."
And when President Roosevelt responded with the determination to
run in the naval armament race, now under way, the *Nation* cawed
in derision, "our naval strength has been determined by voters in a
foreign land," and it was a good thing for it discomfited the "isolationists." [24] But it obviously discomfited the *Nation* too. Thus Liberals following the *Nation* at this point were in approval of just half
a policy; voting economic warfare via sanctions was fine, but the approval of the navy and the guns to back up such a policy was un-
speakably evil. One might push for the enforcement of the League,
but it was immoral to do anything about it except apply economic
restrictions on paper. The conviction was undislodged that no nation
would be proud enough to fight because of this kind of discrimination, and that opponents of League righteousness were basically cow-
ards. But through all the *Nation*'s agitation over Italy and the League
there ran the argument that the League should be kept in health especially for future use against Germany.

By the end of July the *Nation* had just about given up on the
hope that the League might inhibit Mussolini and deter him from
seeking an advantage in Ethiopia. In its editorial of the 24th, "The
Wolf and the Lamb," it concluded disconsolately that "not only is
the League of Nations shown—one may hope for the last time—to be
hopelessly inadequate to deal with international disputes when those
are projected by a determined and predatory government, but trea-

ties to 'outlaw war' are equally displayed to the world in all their futility." [25] From this time until the outbreak of the shooting its advice to the country was to "face the issue realistically and decide upon a strong and consistent peace policy," on the expectation that the war might not be localized in Africa,[26] while in the department of supplying embarrassment to Italy it placed its hope on sanctions: "An embargo on loans, credits, and essential war materials imposed by the League of Nations and supported as far as the law allows by the United States would check if it did not prevent Italy's aggression in Ethiopia and would end the immediate threat to the peace of Europe." [27] The relation of this struggle to the United States and the neutrality controversy will be discussed at length subsequently. The fundamental assumption behind faith in economic pressure however was the belief that Italy was the least self-sufficient of all major nations, and that furthermore Fascism had made a shambles of the Italian economic system. Marxists had been bellowing this for a dozen years, and it was a firm article of liberal faith. Villard in September, 1935 predicted the war would be a very long and terribly costly war to Mussolini if he persisted in it,[28] while the *New Republic* a few weeks earlier also fell in line with a prediction that the whole Ethiopian affair was the last gasp of a bankrupt adventurer, boasting that it had predicted as far back as 1927 that Mussolini's program was sure to collapse internally from the stresses of economic nationalism.[29] No group of people on earth were more enraged than American liberals when the war ended in Italian victory after hardly six months of engagement.

The *New Republic* and *Common Sense* were far less perturbed than the *Nation* over the effect of this crisis upon the League, whatever their antipathy to Mussolini. Both were far less interested in this phase of the matter, and both far exceeded the *Nation* in criticisms of the other colonial powers and the United States, urging a total hands-off position for this country. In an editorial comment on Secretary of State Hull's note to Haile Selassie of Ethiopia in July, the *New Republic* acidly observed, "For the present the United States will probably content itself with giving support to the fumbling peace efforts of England, whose motives, it may be added, are even more obviously self-seeking than ours." [30] In August, when mediation was totally broken down, the same journal recalled that the League's failure was as complete as it had been in the case of Japan and China, and it bridled at the charges of some Englishmen that it was all America's fault because this country had abstained from joining the League in the first place. The editorial flamed back at these English critics by insisting point-blank that the real reason for the League's ineffectiveness was that "the Great Powers that dominate its membership continue more concerned with their own na-

tional advantage than they are with preventing injustice and maintaining peace." [31] And in late September 1935 the *New Republic*
summed up its case and policy in even less equivocal terms: [32]

The *New Republic* believes that wisdom and ultimate justice are with
the "tide of sentiment" that says that "America should remain aloof at
all hazards." For 15 years this paper has pointed out that the Great Powers
were following courses of which the final outcome could only be war.
We have repeatedly argued that no one of them could come into court
with clean hands, so far as judgment against an aggressor was concerned.
We have said that sanctions inevitably lead to war and may actually be
as disastrous in their effects as war itself.

The editorial concluded with sympathetic words for Ethiopia but
insisted, "we still feel that . . . the way to abstain is to abstain.
Our present neutrality legislation wisely . . . makes no distinction
between the belligerents in any conflict," and that it was "better to
attempt neutrality, however heavy the cost, than to join an effort to
prevent a war that is almost certain to be the first chapter in a new
conflict."

Common Sense in its September issue devoted a fiercely critical
editorial attack on both France and England in the Ethiopian crisis;
in part the denunciation observed, "Although they have enjoyed for
years the exploitation of colonial peoples, they . . . point a smug
finger at Mussolini and cry 'unclean, unclean.' " [33]

In truth, the sentimentalizing over Ethiopia and its emperor came
a little later for all liberals, whether in favor of the League and
sanctions or not. A note of harsh attack on colonialism persisted even
in the *Nation,* in addition to suspicion that even the cause of Mussolini's enemy was not utterly untarnished. The *New Republic* on
October 2 did not think it uncharitable to comment, "Haile Selassie
and his Amharic nobles wish to continue to exploit the Ethiopian
peasant farmers unmolested by white men," [34] a forbidding view expressed months earlier by the *Nation,* which on July 31 stated its
basic opinion, contrary to a sentimental portrait of the region slowly
building up in the emotion factories of the daily press: [35]

For our part we shall not be naive about Abyssinia. The country is deep
in the dark ages, its millions of blacks are kept in bitter subjection by
their ruthless masters. Our indignation over the policy of Mussolini, and
the final collapse of all international morals at Geneva, does not make us
defenders of the feudalism of Abyssinia. The best we can say for the
country is that it has a right to lift itself from the depths under the protection of the League.

The other two liberal organs, having identified the League with France and England, did not permit themselves to take the latter part of this position; they reserved for themselves the right to blister Anglo-French action as well, and not to discriminate among them. Their view was best expressed by Lamar Middleton's book *The Rape of Africa,* reviewed in the *New Republic* by W. E. B. DuBois,[36] which included no specific European nation in its title. At the moment when anger at Mussolini was boiling over, the *New Republic* published the bomb-like article by Leslie Reade, "Ethiopia and Kenya," which roasted British policy in the latter country unmercifully. Reade insisted that the "new virtue found in the League" by the English and the enlarged British Mediterranean fleet were really responses to the Italian threat to their "Kenya slave state" adjoining Ethiopia and their "equally disinterested empire-builders" in Egypt, and not tender concern for the independence of the government of Haile Selassie.[37]

To be sure, the American liberal press had never been known for its evasion or soft-pedalling of the situation in British or French colonies prior to these days. India had always been a favorite topic, and even in the year just prior to the Italian penetration of Ethiopia, the *Nation* had printed a number of serious indictments of English policy, some of them written by major figures in the nationalist forces. In April, 1934 there had been the solid page-and-a-half smash by Jawaharlal Nehru, "The Humiliation of India," describing the campaign of repression, "detention camps" and penal colony on the Andaman Islands for resistants to British rule. A nice note had been missed by the liberals who foamed at the German book-burnings a few months earlier for failing to respond to Nehru's comments on similar British policy in India: "We have long been used to the proscription of certain books. But that was not enough. In the future not merely individual books but whole classes of literature specified by the [British] government are to be proscribed." [38] This quite exceeded any of the publicity stunts of the German propaganda ministry, and it was interesting that liberals made no demonstration over this revelation by Nehru, "the intelligent Marxist," as Shaemas O'Sheel of the *New Masses* was wont to refer to him in later years on the publication of his biography by Anup Singh.[39]

In September, 1934 there had been the follow-up story "Labor Militancy Spreads in India," by V. K. Krishna Menon, who told *Nation* readers that India was rejecting "Gandhian pacifism and the politics of loving one's enemy," and that the proletariat of India was responding "to an unexpected degree" in the new fight for "emerging Indian nationalism" against British repression.[40] In December the *Nation* aimed a hot editorial at British policy in India in general and at Winston Churchill in particular, the "diehard Tory" whose element was accused of refusing to make the slightest concession what-ever.[41] No Englishman was so little respected between the wars in the American liberal press as Churchill, and none more contemptuously handled until the rise of Neville Chamberlain. Churchill's trans-formation from the personification of the worst traits of Englishmen to a figure surpassing Charles Martel in a single year, that of 1940–1941, is the most stunning propaganda re-creation in the history of English-language journalism.

In fact, during the *Nation*'s hottest concern for the sins of Italy in Africa it was simultaneously engaged in publishing one hostile story after another on Britain in India; in its opinion, English policy in 1934–1935 reached new plateaus of sheer reaction, which Harold Laski's *Nation* piece of January 2, 1935, "The India Report," under-scored in the most blunt language.[42] And hardly a month before hos-tilities began in Ethiopia, accompanied by moral ejaculatory explo-sions among the English, the *Nation* published a lengthy report by T. A. Bisson, "Britain Tightens Control in India," [43] still another indication that even at this point there was enough realism among American liberals to prevent their enrolling *en masse* in the Brit-ish propaganda corps.

And after the shooting began, the suspension of full commitment persisted. On October 16 the *New Republic* changed its once confi-dent picture of Ethiopian military puissance and declared that the Italian campaign was "a spectacle of half-naked, practically unarmed semi-savages, men, women, and children, being mowed down by ma-chine guns, tanks and aerial bombardment," an amazingly rapid about-face. But it admitted editorially that Italian action there was no worse than British bombing of various Arabian tribesmen, and defiant elements in the northwest frontier of India, or even the American action against Sandino in Nicaragua a few years earlier. And in addition, it expressed the view that despite its belief that no war was justifiable on moral grounds, the conversion of Ethiopia into another African colony would be preferable to an extension of the struggle into a general war spreading over the whole world; "a little war is less evil than a big one," concluded this unusual essay in realism.[44]

Common Sense, after a brief season of support for sanctions, quickly adopted a position similar to the *New Republic*'s. In Novem-ber it sized up the situation thusly: "England will neither brook colonial rivalry at the headwaters of the Nile, nor will she allow the continued growth of Italian seapower in *her* Mediterranean. So much for idealism." [45]

The strident theme of anti-colonialism persisted in liberal writing on the Italo-Ethiopian war, and it did not subside until the fighting was over and a wave of fierce anti-Italian books began to appear, amounting to the real legacy of liberal and left rage at Mussolini's successes. In March 1936 Villard poured more vitriol on colonialism as the impetus behind Mussolini's interest in Ethiopia. It amounted to support for a *Harper's* article by Nathaniel Peffer two months earlier, although both writers were much more wroth at current Italo-German demands to get into the game than they were at the major beneficiaries of the moment. Villard was sure that the man-power of the areas must have been the real desire, since he thought it was amply proven by Peffer and many others that the economic gains to be derived had otherwise been grossly over-rated. Still, neither Villard nor Peffer, in proving that colonialism did not pay, could think of any nation which had become so disgusted with the spare returns from its colonies as to induce it to cede them voluntarily. This did not inhibit Villard from sternly chiding the Italians for their attempt to repeat the story of colony-making in Ethiopian lands, and he consoled himself that if the case against it could not be made in one way, it certainly could in another; "The current jest that if there had been wealth in Ethiopia, England would have stolen it years ago is altogether justified." [46]

In May, with Italian victory an accomplished fact, Villard still argued that this conquest was a long nail driven into the coffin of colonialism, that it would surely spur the whole of Asia and Africa into determined efforts to unhinge all the European colonial regimes.[47] A major roundup of sentiments supporting this view especially with reference to British decline was published in the *Nation* on August 15, 1936, in an article by the journalist "Albert Viton," writing from Jerusalem: [48]

> The most important aspect of Il Duce's recent *coup de théâtre* in Ethiopia is that without firing a single round of ammunition, he defeated the greatest imperial and naval power in the world. . . . A statistical analysis of the Arabic press of the last eight months . . . would show that the greatest number of articles were written on The Decline and Fall of the British Empire. Even in the Zionist movement a very important group is already turning to Mussolini.

Viton declared that India and the whole Arab world were seething, and that England could look forward to an early expulsion from both. Speaking particularly of the latter, Viton announced, "The feeling among the Arab masses is that all imperialisms are essentially alike, however different their outward appearance. England will some day be told with hot lead that she is not wanted here, and that day, I am convinced, is not so far away."

CONSOLATION PRIZE IN RE MUSSOLINI
AND ETHIOPIA: SANCTIONS

When the League failed to blunt Mussolini or to find a suitable solution to the Italo-Ethiopian dispute, and the two conflicting parties drew near to gunfire, the action thought next best was the application of economic sanctions by the other states against the recalcitrant Fascisti. This was economic war spelled in small letters and spoken *sotto voce*. And because it involved no noticeable display of armed might and because its effects were theoretically hidden, slow and deteriorative, liberals with a sensitive side toward the more spectacular methods of killing one's opponents found it possible to subscribe to this less bloody method of disposing of them. Starving the non-combatants did give the illusion of being more charitable than shooting the men in uniform. Some liberals were realistic enough to see it in this light, but the blinding sun of collective security kept most of them from observing this likely result, providing that the policy was introduced and kept in force, like the post-World War I blockade of Germany, although, as we shall see, it was not to be the case in the matter of Italy in 1935–1936.

The *Nation* enrolled most of the ardent sanctionists among American liberals. From September to Christmas Day, 1935 there was an almost weekly editorial of great urgency on this subject. The overall import was the spreading of the confident view that economic strangulation would bring Italy to its knees if there was a widespread consonance among the other states desiring this result.[49] The growing reluctance of the governments of the major states, with the verbal exception of Soviet Russia, to pursue this end had little effect in changing the *Nation*'s editorial policy, and with a Mussolini triumph imminent in the spring of 1936, it was still being advanced to readers that sanctions could bring about different results.

The positions of the Communists and other Marxists on this matter may be given an examination here. It was the thesis of these groups that because Russia and the various Socialist parties of Europe warmly favored sanctions Mussolini's imperialists had actually suffered a serious propaganda defeat even before the outbreak of hostilities. Laski tried to explain this to the *Nation* readers at the end of October in his long essay "England Faces War," and this he said was the reason why the Labor Party had rejected Lansbury and Cripps at their 1935 Brighton Conference; their lukewarm-to-cool stand on this one issue.[50] In fact, liberals might have profited by investigation of the motivation behind this seeming European Socialist front unity on the beauties of applying sanctions to Italy. But given their wish-thoughts and preconceptions about the Communists, it was unlikely that they could detect the concert already gained by Russia behind its foreign policy. This might have been illuminated by a more critical look at Soviet behavior at Geneva. Liberals gave no publicity to the statement of the Ethiopian delegate there praising Litvinov's activities on Ethiopian behalf, and though Communists were among the noisiest in their build-up of Haile Selassie to the point where he became almost overnight a towering hero in the fight for freedom, they were not the least inhibited in giving wide publicity to the prevalence of slavery in this noble democrat's kingdom.[51]

But the existing fixations of liberals toward Communist virtues excluded the possibility of thinking that the Russians were playing a double game here too, and that their ostensible subscription to what appeared to be liberal goals was hardly of the same political order. The *New Masses* of November 12, 1935 went further in posting Russia on the side of those who wanted this conflict localized by announcing, "Among the League nations only the Soviet Union is sincerely interested in preventing the war from spreading into another world conflagration. The big imperialist powers like Britain and France are only concerned with making Mussolini submit to a deal that will protect their vested interests in Africa." [52] Thus no element in the picture claimed sincere Russian support. The Reds favored sanctions on Mussolini, Earl Browder making one of the strongest pleas for it in his book *What Is Communism?* but at the same time disparaging both the Haile Selassie regime in Ethiopia and Mussolini's French and English opponents. They were not averse to spreading atrocity stories about the Italians after the fighting began there,[53] yet, even after the English succeeded in getting the League to vote sanctions against Italy with reference to sale of petroleum products, Russian sale of oil to Italy continued, while Italian shipyards kept building ships for the Soviet fleet. The liberals did not seem to learn about this until World War II was under way. Nevertheless, it cannot be dismissed that a substantial part of the feeling of security and of being on the right side experienced by American liberals favoring sanctions was derived from the knowledge that Russia and European Marxian Socialist parties were formally lined up behind this stand as well. Why or for what purposes seemed to be too obvious to bother investigating.

By no means were all liberal spokesmen in agreement on sanctions, as some of the best known ones were quite unfriendly to this policy. Frank Simonds, highly respected in the *Nation,* was allowed to speak his piece in opposition at great length in two long communications in October and December, 1935. Simonds declared that the world was really witnessing a clash between a sated and an unsated imperialism, not a showdown between sin and virtue. He pointed out that the British Labor Party, by supporting sanctions so vigorously, completely undermined their companion policy of opposition to English armament expansion, that the form of sanctions advocated was identical to the post-1918 blockade on Germany, "the most devastating detail of the most devastating war in history," and that instead of starving Italians into submission this policy would simply ignite nationalistic elements there and provoke them into pressing ahead for more armaments of their own. Thus sanctions would blast forever any hope of disarmament. Simonds tried to point out the illogical and contradictory side of this in summary: [54]

The League of Nations is being employed as the weapon of the satisfied powers. What in effect liberals and Socialists are now asked to do is to defend an old imperialism against a new. Because the new cannot realize its aims save by war, the old is able to mobilize to its own ends, which have nothing whatever to do with real peace, the thoughtless friends of peace all over the world. And because the present aggression is the work of fascists, there is an additional incentive to liberals and Socialists to join in the effort to restrain Italy.

This was essentially the message of Brailsford to the *New Republic* from England itself. He was immeasurably milder toward Mussolini than the editors, praised the new Tory Foreign Secretary Hoare's "elastic" interpretation of treaties and his "degrees of aggression" doctrine, all sound common sense to Brailsford. Nothing appeared more sensible than the observation that "some aggressions, to be plain, are relatively excusable." [55] On the League he nearly echoed Simonds: [56]

. . . even for the British Tory government, and still more for the French, the League has a certain political value. It can be used, and in fact always has been used, to give to the actual status quo a moral and legal sanctity. All liberals and most Socialists regard it with superstitious veneration. Even the Communists have now rallied to it. If ever it is necessary in England and France to call the workers into another war against Germany a reference to the sublime abstraction in Geneva will suffice to answer the argument that this is but another imperialist struggle to maintain the gains won at Versailles.

New Republic editorial positions were not exactly in tune with Brailsford, but in the issue of October 23, 1935, six weeks after Brailsford's long article, it did observe that the paralysis of the League was evidence that it had no independent life of its own but acted "purely as the instrument of self-regarding policies of the Great Powers." [57] And on November 27 the issue was made even sharper: "If the chief American aim is to keep out of another world war, rather than embarking on the almost desperate attempt to preserve general peace, that aim cannot be served by associating ourselves with the League and its sanctions. Neutrality is possible only if we embargo virtually all trade with both parties." [58]

Common Sense underwent a sudden change of heart on the question of sanctions. In its October, 1935 issue, it was firmly in favor of them as action most likely to head off American involvement should the war spread: [59]

If this dispute spreads, as it is capable of doing, the United States may well be bulldozed into taking sides in another world conflict, and the neutrality resolutions will be so many scraps of paper. Under the circumstances, we must cling to any straw, the straw in this case being the hope that the members of the League, particularly Great Britain and France, will have the courage to censure Italy not only with words, but with the cold fact of an economic boycott.

But the wind shifted almost at once in this quarter. The very next month it editorially censured the Labor Party and its "peace" poll, with its pro-sanctions vote, for playing "right into the hands of the Tories and the imperialist interests." And in December it gave its enthusiastic support for American neutrality without reservation, and encouraged, like the *New Republic,* an embargo on both Italians and Ethiopians, which they fervently hoped would sink "the hopes of the Geneva sentimentalists that the United States will line up with the League powers in condemning Italy." And in a final word in the issue for May, 1936 the editors hoped that the evidence of Ethiopia's rapid surrender had destroyed the theory "that economic and moral sanctions can stop war," since despite the half-hearted impositions placed on her, "Italy's fighting strength and her fabricated war hysteria have never faltered." [60]

Of course, it was not all clear that such avoidance of involvement was possible in October. With the voting of sanctions against Italy, the *New Republic's* "T.R.B." observed, in a piece somewhat longer than usual for news from Washington, "the British propaganda organization in Washington went swiftly and smoothly into action." All considerations of England acting in her imperial interests were no longer evident; one was "entreated to believe," he said, that these were all irrelevant, and that now the case was simply that "England is standing for peace by collective action." Americans were getting a preview of 1939, but by that time most liberals were shucking off the skepticism of "T.R.B." in 1935, including "T.R.B." himself.

At this stage the anonymous columnist was not so sure we might not buy this case outright, what with Stimson's 2½ column letter to the New York *Times* and Norman Davis's dispatch to the *Herald*

Tribune voicing the case for Britain better than her own propagandists. They were symptomatic of a much larger community in actuality; remarked "T.R.B.," "The task of British propaganda in this country is comparatively easy, since many of our so-called community leaders—corporation lawyers, industrialists, professors in Eastern universities—are already committed to collective action." He noted a strong tendency to appeal to businessmen, and wryly observed that "While it is doubtful that prosperity seeps from the top downwards, it is certain that propaganda does." [61] But for the businessmen and financiers now possibly leaning to a hostile position toward Mussolini, John T. Flynn, also in the *New Republic,* furnished some embarrassing reminiscences on Il Duce's enthusiastic endorsement by them in New York in 1925 and the financing furnished his regime from Wall Street.[62]

Left-liberals and Socialists were not particularly interested in the campaign being laid against Mussolini by English propagandists and their faithful echoes such as Stimson and Davis. Among the liberals, talk was already spreading as to the likely consequences in Italy should the sanctions be successful and Fascism be toppled. The consensus seemed to be a definitely leftist government, perhaps very close to the Communist model in the Soviet Union. And no liberal voice in American journalism came forth at this point to doubt that this would be a good thing. In December, 1935 the *Nation* editorially surmised that such a government would be "the inevitable consequence of Mussolini's overthrow," and there was no talk of any mild, centerish, semi-Social Democrat group stepping in as Mussolini's replacement. The admission was made however that as of that time the Italian people were "still solidly behind Mussolini," but that this solidarity might easily "melt away" on the application of tough economic sanctions, which might be materially aided by a few setbacks at the hands of the Ethiopians in Africa.[63]

In March and April of 1936 both the liberals and the crustiest of pro-British Empire pleaders had the same theory on Mussolini's future; both were predicting a devastating and early collapse, using different evidence and hoping it would happen for different goals. The news of Il Duce's announced intention of nationalizing many of Italy's key industries during its war in Africa brought from the *Nation* on April 8 an incredible admission: "Italian fascism is not as completely reactionary as it is sometimes pictured in the *émigré* press; if it were, Mussolini would not have been able to hold popular support for as long as he has." [64] This news was also the signal for *Common Sense* similarly to announce grounds for a shift in liberal articles of faith. The theory that Fascism was a tool of big capitalists was no longer credible; "Fascism has been steadily moving toward a form of collectivism," [65] it sagely pronounced. And Louis Fischer in a *Nation* piece in late May, 1936 had long and detailed remarks on the socialist tendencies there.[66] But even in victory, faith remained undimmed that the Fascisti were hardly intelligent and competent enough to operate a really significant collectivism, if that was the path Italy was taking, and liberals were cautioned against taking seriously a regime whose economy was on the edge of total breakdown. Thus while Anglo-American financiers may have desired a change in Italy which resulted in their gaining a much enhanced position in influencing policy, American and British liberals were hoping for a comprehensive Italian collapse as a prelude to profound political upheaval.

HOSTILITY TOWARD ITALY GOES UP
AS THE LEAGUE GOES DOWN

Pro-sanctionist liberals enjoyed a brief moment of seeming success at the end of 1935 with the scrapping of the peace proposal discussed by the British Foreign Secretary Sir Samuel Hoare and the French Foreign Minister Pierre Laval, a proposal which became a liberal and left symbol for the darkest act of infamy known until the Munich agreement of September, 1938. Most bitterly resented in this quiet discussion had been the assumption that Italy had a case of some kind in its dispute in Africa, when the liberal-left standing doctrine was that there was not the faintest sort of case; the Ethiopian affair represented an entirely right versus wrong situation, with Mussolini obviously in the wrong.

The *Nation*'s New Year's Day, 1936 issue rejoiced loudly at the Hoare-Laval defeat, and credited it entirely to the small states among the League membership. The editors were now satisfied that the League was "at last more than a mere tool of British and French imperialism." Now that nothing had replaced something, it was a rather odd moment to celebrate, although the expectation was that the economic freeze-out of Italy all over the world was ready to start. The big obstacle to this was now the non-member United States, and a bitter attack on the American business boom in trade with Italy since hostilities had begun was assured. The editorial also attacked the Roosevelt Administration for maintaining that it was helpless to prevent American businessmen "from aiding Mussolini in his illegal war." And as long as the United States persisted in sabotaging the League's working out of "the only substitute for armed coercion," the embargo on war materials, there were grounds for doubting that this country was sincerely trying to avoid war; "If the past has taught us anything, it is that peace and war profits are mutually incompatible." [67] A signed editorial by Villard, "A World Public Opinion Exists," in the same issue, expressed the same sentiments.

Laski's "What Remains of the League?" three weeks later consisted of an even more serious attack on the entire Baldwin Tory government for the Hoare negotiations, now a standard piece of British left invective, in which Hoare had attained the apparition-proportions of another Machiavelli, although Laski also heaped much criticism on Vansittart, who many leftist journalists believed had actually drafted the plan which had gotten Hoare's name. Until his death in 1940, Robert Dell, especially, lost no opportunity to ascribe to Vansittart the whole scheme which left-liberals thought they had scotched single-handedly on the publicity level. Laski was in a much blacker mood than the *Nation*. He considered that the League of Nations was "incompatible with an imperialist system"; "the contradictions between imperialist purposes and the League remain; in a society of capitalist states they appear incapable of solution." [68]

A week later the *Nation* agreed with Laski in blaming the Baldwin government for the failure to apply pressure on Mussolini, but still held out the hope that "public opinion" could force the League to strengthen the movement toward sanctions. The editors were completely convinced the Italians could be bluffed, even though Fischer's sizable article from Rome in the same issue was titled "Mussolini Outbluffs England." And even as late as mid-March, 1936 an editorial commendation was accorded the Sanctions Committee of the League for announcing that an oil embargo would be employed on Italy if she did not discuss peace terms within the week.[69] When this was not done, nothing was said.

With Italy sweeping ahead in Ethiopia late in April, the *Nation* editorial view was still that League sanctions could make Mussolini quit, and that now it was the French who were responsible for the impending collapse of that "fundamental principle" of collective security.[70] The May 13 editorial, "Ethiopia's Collapse and Europe's Peril," rounded up all the views of the past five months in an omnibus parcel, with denunciations of England and France, secondary elements of blame being assigned to the United States. In spite of all the heated condemnation of England, the editorial concluded with the prediction that the League of Nations would be bolstered by the British in the immediate future. "The very existence of the British Empire depends upon preserving the League," the explanation went on; "This is not only because Britain is one of the chief beneficiaries of the status quo and would suffer heavily if it were disturbed, but because the British Empire can exist only in a world in which effective international organization is possible." [71]

The only break in this adamant preaching of a pressure campaign against Italy occurred in February, when in its lead editorial paragraph on the 19th it had violently condemned the Baldwin Cabinet for rejecting a Labor Party motion calling for "an international conference on the distribution of raw materials." This was somewhat out of character, in one sense, for the implication that the nations might have been disputing about other things than which ones were the most morally pure was evident, and that there were issues and cases on all sides. The current wave of discussions based on catalogs of "have" and "have-not" nations was obviously responsible for this register of impression. As the editorial went on, the suggested Laborite conference had a vital part to play in the whole world scene; "if collective security is to have any permanence, it must involve something more than mere defense of the status quo. War cannot be eliminated unless some machinery is created for meeting the legitimate complaints of the 'have-nots' among nations." [72] But the tone of this statement was so out of step with the editorial position over the past six months as to intimate that the writer had not been reading the editorials very carefully during that time.

In actuality, from March 7 on, any action of conciliatory capacity, no matter how mild and weak, had been out of the question, for the German announcement that the limitations of the 1925 Locarno treaty were no longer to be respected and that Germany was going to re-militarize its lands west of the Rhine even pushed the Ethiopian war into the wings for a spell. The consternation and agitation which this signalled brought Hitler and Mussolini together as twin demons, almost for the first time. The lingering sentiment which still envisaged Il Duce as a likely associate of France and England in posing an obstacle to asserted Hitlerian goals started to evaporate at about this time, not because of anything the Italian said or did in defense of the German move, but because they were both involved in enterprises which were causing a maximum of anxiety and aggravation. It thus appeared logical to denounce both of them in the same breath thenceforth.

The *New Republic* editors were about equally divided over which was the worst portent for the future of the world they wished to see evolve. In their May 13, 1936 issue it was fervently hoped that now that the Ethiopian war was over, Britain might gather together its divided strands and "take a firm line against Hitler," and they entreated England and France in the name of peace to oppose both "the Fascist and Nazi dictatorships," to give them no aid and sternly and resolutely to resist them, because "to make terms with them, to strengthen them, is to make war inevitable." [73] The recommended policy made the war even more "inevitable," unfortunately. Villard, in the *Nation* for this same issue, was for shooting the works on the hopes of an eventual Franco-British-led economic boycott on both Hitler and Mussolini to stop their continuing disturbance of the status quo; this he was sure would halt the "drifting into another world war." [74] Behind all the talk of extended grim resistance and economic pressure was the persistent Marxian theorizing that both the Italian and German regimes were in sheer economic desperation, and in danger of weekly dissolution. No other theory could have been adhered to and still have made any sense, for if the liberals thought both were vigorous, then it would be sheer incitation to badger them with economic harassment. Since the professed goal of the get-tough policy in the liberal view was the *prevention* of a general war, then their advocacy of economic constriction implied their belief in the inability of either hated regime to conduct a comprehensive military campaign. And in this theory of the deathly economic illness of both Hitler Germany and Mussolini Italy is to be found the essence of liberal sanctioneers' vast faith in the positive efficacy of mere *economic* war to bring about their destruction. Occasional liberal voices, as we shall see, did not share this approach, and called loudly for the hottest kind of military war against Germany, especially, four to six years before the war finally came. But editorial positions of even the pro-sanctions elements did not go anywhere near as far as that in the Italo-Ethiopian war days.

The *New Republic* on July 8, on the eve of another League Assembly meeting which was to put the concluding damper on the half-hearted sanctions experiment, could not help taking another sharp thrust at the organization's origins, again showing more concern for its relations to Hitler than to Mussolini, the new post-Rhineland gambit: [75]

> It is not necessary, at this late date, to preach another funeral oration over the League. Everyone knows by now that from the beginning it never lived up to the idealistic visions of Woodrow Wilson and of the lesser folk throughout the world who pinned their hopes to it. It was made a part of an iniquitous peace treaty and its machinery was used to perpetuate the unjust terms of that treaty. . . . the injustices have helped to create a Europe that has all but destroyed the remnants of the League idea. No one will ever be able to say just how much the attitude of the Allies, partly expressed through the League, helped to bring Hitler into power, but the share of the responsibility must certainly be heavy.

Mussolini and the feverish emotionalism over Ethiopia were apparently already forgotten.

In May the *New Republic* had maintained that the League was not dead, because it had "not been born." As liberals became more and more aware of the fact that diplomacy, bargaining and intrigue were still very much a part of the intercourse of states and in no danger of unemployment at the hands of "collective security," there crept back into their analyses the vision of the Soviet Union as the dependable champion of the peace which did not seem to be attainable through their joint endeavors. Despite the fact that they had blamed every major Western state for the collapse of sanctions and the campaign of pressure against Italy, strangely enough there had never been any harsh words of this sort aimed at Russia. Its established membership in the League and its repeatedly publicized gestures on behalf of their oft-repeated slogan, "Peace is indivisible," apparently built up a bank account of good will so large that they were not held culpable to the slightest degree. In fact, the Ethiopia debacle and the Rhineland surprise brought Russia an even larger measure of favor and good will. And in addition to castigation for the downfall of sanctions, Stanley Baldwin's Tory British government was charged with deliberately going easy on the German situation in the hope of steering them to the East by placation and soft judgment, despite the "Britain's frontier is on the Rhine" talk. Bit by bit the point was made clear that the failure of the League was simultaneously the signal for a reorganization, to be followed by a grouping behind Russia as a champion. Both liberal weeklies stressed the renewed importance of the Soviet. The *New Republic,* although it had no faith in the League from the beginning by its own admission, still felt that the Ethiopian situation and the brief bristling at Germany over the Rhineland had been tests which it failed; hence its recommendation of the Left road to Russia once more. Its editorial of May 20 put it most plainly: [76]

The best hope for peace in Europe continues to be the coming to power of Left governments in the greatest possible number of countries and the shortest possible period of time. The reason Soviet Russia today represents the smallest threat to peace of all the great powers of the world is because there is no powerful individual or group [in Russia] that has anything to gain from aggression.

The *Nation* was even more emphatic in condemning what happened on the grounds of the threat to Russia. A June 27, 1936 editorial, "Making the World Safe for Aggressors," commenting on "Mr. Eden's ignominious surrender on sanctions," for Anthony Eden had replaced the much-maligned Hoare as Foreign Secretary, not only accused Baldwin of trying to make the bigger struggle of "collective security versus aggression" into an exclusively Anglo-Italian conflict by sending the British fleet into the Mediterranean, but declared that he was "no longer interested in preventing a Nazi attack so long as it is directed toward the East." [77] And on July 18, commenting on the final abandonment of sanctions by the League on July 15 in an editorial headed "Retreat to the Old Diplomacy," a statement was

made which sounded almost exactly that of its junior liberal partner
two months earlier except that it preferred the word "democratic"
to "left": [78]

There is one new element of importance in the European situation.
That is a growing recognition that if the old diplomacy is ever to be
broken down and collective security achieved, the foundation of that
security must first be laid by democratic movements in each of the important countries of Europe. Russia, in her own fashion, has led the way.
Spain and France, however imperfectly in their own fashion, are following. Every victory of the organized forces of labor and the common man
within each European country must prove a nail driven into the coffin of
the old diplomacy, and eventually of the war system in Europe.

Apparently, however, it did not matter how many wars resulted from
these developments, for the belief ran high that there was no cure for
war quite like war, conducted on a local, class, or civil level.

Villard's signed editorial in the same issue exceeded the unsigned
one in vituperation, but did not contain the unmistakable concern
for the welfare of Russia in the European jungle, made worse, presumably, by the defeat of the League. Again the liberal double image
surfaced; in the first place denial that the League was moral because
of its relation to the "iniquitous" Versailles Treaty and second,
criticism because it was not proving workable in achieving the towering goals set up before it. To this now was attached its trailer, condemnation of the Versailles settlements, but matched by an almost
uncontrolled agitation over something being done about these settlements in a unilateral manner by the admitted major victim of
them.[79]

The hostility to the "old diplomacy" was well illustrated by the
New Republic's comment early in September on a suggestion by
President Roosevelt for what has since been called a "top level" conference involving himself, King Edward VIII of England, President
LeBrun of France, Hitler, Mussolini and Stalin. The front page story
on this reported in the New York *Times* drew an incredulous and
condemnatory, if not contemptuous, hoot; its concluding message
was not very comforting: [80]

The idea seemed to be the simple, not to say naïve, one that if these
worthies saw one another across the table they could settle their differences in an amicable spirit. Not since [Henry] Ford's peace ship has a
project for international accord appeared so humanly attractive and so
utterly innocent of political and economic realities.

Thus did the junior liberal voice greet the suggestion of what has
since become the perennially recommended and on occasion par-

tially met nostrum for the conflicts between nations in the last twenty years.

The outbreak of the Spanish Civil War, a few hours after the final League of Nations act calling off of the sanctions hounds, gave the liberal press a much more highly seasoned fare than the wobbling of the League, of course. There was a sharp drop-off of attention as the scene shifted a little nearer home, to the opposite, western end of the Mediterranean. Books by devout League partisans such as Raymond Leslie Buell's *The Dangerous Year* and James T. Shotwell's *On the Rim of the Abyss* drew the faintest of praise in the late summer of 1936 from the reviewers, Jonathan Mitchell and Devere Allen.[81] And the *Nation* even interrupted momentarily its one-dimensional portrait of Mussolini following his fiery anti-Communist and anti-League speech on November 1 by commenting,[82]

. . . it must be admitted that determination, recklessness, and a fair number of grievances are ranged on the side of the Fascist bloc; while Britain and France are bogged down by vacillation and an unwillingness to right, or even recognize, existing wrongs.

How much of this startling statement was due to a desire to balance the picture and how much was due to vexation with Britain and France over their wallowing policy toward the Spanish government in its fight against Franco cannot be known.

There can be little doubt that this savage and bloody struggle in Spain did a massive job in diverting American liberals to the barricades, figuratively and otherwise. Most peace talk withered in the face of it, and so did the speakers. Nine months of this fierce affair undoubtedly was the key factor behind *New Republic* editor Bruce Bliven's grim-jawed editorial "open letter" to Marshal Rodolfo Graziani, the Italian commander in conquered Ethiopia, in the issue for March 31, 1937, upon the report that hundreds of natives had been shot following a near-successful assassination attempt upon him. The concluding paragraph was not only a major break in Bliven's peaceful front, but practically a nutshell commentary on the path scores of other prominent liberals were to take in joining hands with the belligerents: [83]

In the days before you and others like you came to power . . . I believed with my whole heart in peace. I held that there was never any dispute between human beings that could not and should not be settled by an appeal to reason. I felt that a resort to arms, even in order to redress a wrong, was a mistake, that it dragged the champion of right down to the level of his adversary, that, in the old saying, there was never a bad peace or a good war. Today, I find myself shaken in this former view. It begins to seem to me that to change you and your kind, to stamp out forever your doctrines and practices, may be worth any sacrifice however great. I realize the danger that such an effort would simply make me and my kind more like you and yours, and in the final crisis I have no doubt that I should recoil against my feeling that brutality must be answered with brutality. But what concerns me now in my present state of mind, is the fact that you and your masters have forced me into such alien thoughts and feelings. I protest.

Bliven's eloquence admittedly did not stir many readers to a favorable reaction, largely a consequence of his selectivity in denouncing brutality. He admitted getting several sharply satirical and critical letters, attacking him for reaching such heights of indignation over this incident, while failing to recall similar Anglo-Saxon butcheries in America and India in the past, also as reprisals for native uprisings. This partially cooled him off. No one bothered to recall the aplomb of Bliven's journal three years earlier when scores lost their lives in Russia after the assassination of Sergei Kirov. But the main impact of this incident was to remind liberals that the Ethiopian war was an unsettled score and that they still had a day of reckoning appointed on the calendar, even though no one was sure what month or year it would be consummated.

Perhaps the last scene of the Italo-Ethiopian war act was the withdrawal of Italy from the League of Nations in December, 1937, bringing to a conclusion the exacerbated conflict between the two. Liberal press editorial comments were remarkably restrained. The *New Republic* observed, "Italy's announcement that she is leaving the League of Nations is like the revelation of a divorce between people who have been separated for years and who have fought in public every time they met." There was an ironic flavor in the chuckle over the futility of the British effort to placate and conciliate both Italy and Germany separately or together. The *Nation* did not consider Italy's withdrawal of immediate importance, although it expressed regret that Italy was "forced into a position where it represents one of two conflicting factions." [84] This was rather anticlimactic, in view of the three previous years of propaganda, which never tried to do anything but present Italy as an extreme faction in its dispute with the League. The fact of the matter at this moment however was that Japan and Germany had taken the frontrunning positions as the terrors of the liberals, and although sentiment against Italy was running very strong for its participation indirectly in the Spanish Civil War on the side of the left-liberals' hated adversary Francisco Franco, the heat of the Ethiopian war period seemed to have dissipated. But liberal spokesmen were much too perturbed by the fate of the Spanish "Loyalists" and the Chinese Communists in their respective wars to bother about making too much of an issue out of Italy temporarily. Added to the Stalinist-Trotskyist struggle which had broken out and which was contributory to the figurative mauling of a substantial number of American liberal partisans of both, and the renewed concern over American foreign policy as a result of the new neutrality fight and the alarming Japanese aerial foray on American ships far up the Yang-tze in China, liberals had too much demanding their attention now to return to the events of 1935–1936 with the same merciless quality in their criticisms.

POST-ETHIOPIAN HERITAGE:
THE WAR OF THE BOOKS

When the Italo-Ethiopian war ended in Africa in the spring of 1936, it continued on another front, in the book sections of the liberal periodicals. After a number of uneventful years, things Italian got a sharp boost late in 1935 as a result of Italy's furious controversy with the League of Nations' major members and the war in Africa. The result was, among other things, a flurry of books on Italy and Mussolini, written by bitter opponents for the most part, and reviewed by other enemies of Il Duce and the Fascisti no less implacable, sometimes by each other. A steady fare of these undoubtedly firmed the views of any liberal whose mind may not have been fully made up as a result of the conflicting ideas, influences and interests which the news and editorials reflected.

Three especially hostile books dealing with Mussolini and Italy were published and reviewed while the war was in progress: *Mussolini's Italy,* by Herman Finer, *Sawdust Caesar,* by George Seldes, and *Under the Axe of Fascism,* by Gaetano Salvemini. The politics of none of the authors was left in doubt regardless of their subjects. Finer's book was reviewed by Vera Micheles Dean in the *Nation* on Christmas Day, 1935. She approved of its almost unrelieved and violent condemnation of Italian Fascism, the abandonment of parliamentary democracy and the institution of the one-party state being especially emphasized. As in most other books condemning the Italian and German systems, most all of the criticisms advanced applied equally to Russia, their precedent in most all their innovations. But the lack of representative parliamentary rule in Italy, which inspired yards of fiery liberal prose, rarely if ever brought more than a quietly apologetic and evasive footnote when related to the similar situation in the Soviet Union. Miss Dean gobbled a bit at the publisher's boosting of this book on the grounds that it was not fair to the author, then a professor of public administration at the University of London: "The publisher's blurb is decidedly misleading in describing it as 'strictly objective reporting,' " she pointed out. "Objectivity can hardly be called the hallmark of a book permeated by the honest anti-Fascist indignation of a firm believer in democracy and peppered with often violent personal attacks on various aspects of Fascism." But she was even more puzzled by Finer's apparently "sincere respect and even admiration of Mussolini." [85]

Seldes took care of that category with his totally destructive portrait of Il Duce, a tale which had no extenuating observations. Quincy Howe was not too impressed with it in his *New Republic* review, but it drew unqualified praise from Salvemini, the most ferocious of Mussolini's refugee critics in America, in the *Nation* six weeks later, on January 22, 1936. The reviewer's own book was about to appear, but he described Seldes' as "the best comprehensive work on Fascist Italy which thus far has been published in the English language." It was written without an ounce of impartiality, but the only thing Salvemini objected to was the fact that the author could have cited his sources "with greater care." [86] In this book Seldes revived the story of the death of Il Duce's Socialist opponent, Giacomo Matteotti, in 1924, with such vividly dramatic accents that it was picked up and repeated almost verbatim scores of times in the next ten years, an act which most of the American liberal-left felt justified the murder of Mussolini at the earliest opportunity.

Salvemini did not disappear from the book sections with this contribution. His own book was followed by his repeated return, attacking with great gusto every book on Italy in the following years prior to the war which did not take a completely antagonistic position on Mussolini and Italy. The liberal press never featured a writer so completely hostile, on some occasions even exceeding their requirements. In May, 1936 the *New Republic* was even driven to declare editorially that his loud shout of disgust over the behavior of the American foreign correspondents reporting the war from Italy was unrealistic.[87] Salvemini fervently believed that they should all have attacked Mussolini personally and have gladly suffered expulsion for it. His unrelieved paean of praise for the Socialist and Communist targets of Mussolini was too obviously his primary concern.

The domestic liberal who matched Salvemini in intemperateness toward Italy was Paul H. Douglas, who blossomed in the spring of 1936 as an expert on Italy after a long *New Republic* article on March 4, "Mussolini and the Workers." [88] This vastly more incitatory specialty replaced the careful, sober publishings on wages, social security and unemployment relief which had been his academic trademark heretofore. On some occasions his excoriations of Mussolini even exceeded those of Salvemini, and his review of Salvemini's contribution in the *New Republic* in October rejoiced in the drastic estimate meted out by the author, as had Oscar Jaszi in the *Nation* four months earlier. Both felt Salvemini eminently correct in failing to find a single thing done by the Mussolini regime worth commending, but neither of them was made curious by his failure to explain the regime's continuity.[89]

A year later Douglas delivered a similarly elegant piece in praise of G. A. Borghese's *Goliath: The March of Fascism,* in which he again displayed his main irritation, Il Duce's crushing of the "radical Left," although he firmly believed that Borghese had proved that Mussolini was neither a nationalist nor a Socialist but an anarchist, and that his ideas were a distillate of Nietzsche, Sorel, Marinetti, Max Stirner and D'Annunzio. Douglas expressed the view that Mussolini was merely blackmailing Italy's conservatives by threatening a proletarian takeover there if he were to be removed from the scene; Communism in Italy was hardly more than a wisp of a possibility in Douglas' view in the fall of 1937. William Yandell Elliott of Harvard reviewed this book in the *Nation* the same month, and he also was captivated by the author's imaginative treatment explaining the origins of both Mussolini and Fascism. Although not a refugee, Elliott was even more fulsome in his commendation, and highly recommended Borghese's type of historical acrobatics, which found Fascism rooted "in Dante and the myths of Rome, Machiavelli, and the peculiar frustration complex of the Italian tradition." [90] In a few years this same treatment was to be applied to Hitler and National Socialism, with half a dozen authors seeking to trace Der Führer almost as far back in Teutonic history as Herman the German.

All the Italian refugees did not share the same almost automatic approval by American liberals when they chose to write a book. Max Ascoli's *Intelligence in Politics,* published after the Ethiopian campaigns had ended, was treated with coolness and even disparagement in reviews by Frederick Schuman and Matthew Josephson in the winter of 1936–1937. But his *Fascism For Whom?* which he wrote in collaboration with Arthur Feiler received an echoing cheer from fellow-refugee (from Austria) Albert Lauterbach in the *Nation* on December 24, 1938. It was notable for a new definition of Fascism which Ascoli contributed to the many shouting, confused definitions left-liberals had devised since 1933, "the anti-capitalist revolt of pre-capitalistic masses coupled with the financial support of big capitalistic forces, with racial nationalism as its flag." It probably was no more confusing than the previous ones. Ascoli, at this late date, was not so sure as his predecessors had been in predicting Fascism's collapse from internal weakness and debility; his book was more a quiet, polite entreaty of the United States to get prepared to fight it.[91]

About the last book in the first series of studies probably calculated to capitalize on the Italo-Ethiopian situation while it was still newsworthy was a volume titled *The Plough and the Sword,* by Carl T. Schmidt. The author was severely criticized in the New York *Times* for tailoring the facts on Italian agriculture to fit his Marxian assumptions. Paul Douglas's review in the *New Republic* for July 13, 1937 praised the book highly and supported his thesis that the agricultural policy of the Fascist regime was a total and unqualified failure. While abjuring himself of any possible connection with Marxist doctrines, Douglas denied that the *Times*'s review was right in charging the book had a Marxian bias, and supported Schmidt in his conclusions to the hilt. With the controversy between the Stalinists and Trotskyists racking each issue of the liberal weeklies now, Douglas chose to skirt this whole matter carefully, but his hostility to Mussolini was so powerful that he even preferred risking giving aid and comfort to the Communists than appear to be even minutely noncommittal on a book attacking Fascist Italy. Salvemini was unbothered by these scruples while giving the book unreserved recommendation in the *Nation* six months later.[92]

Salvemini had other opportunities to issue admiring résumés of anti-Fascist books, which did not diminish because Italy temporarily drifted off the front pages. He was most enthusiastic over G. Lowell Field's *The Syndical and Corporative Institutions of Italian Fascism,* a destructive attack on all of the labor policies of the Mussolini government, and he bestowed unrestrained admiration for still another personal assault on Il Duce himself, Gaudens Megaro's *Mussolini in the Making,* although this did not reach the limits of Seldes' earlier incendiary work.[93]

Salvemini's major sphere of action was the attack on books which portrayed anything about Italy in a favorable light, and in the three years prior to Italy's entry into World War Two he brought this talent to an exceedingly sharp point. He was enraged by George Martelli's *Italy Against the World,* which he fulminated against as a whitewash of Mussolini because of its impartiality. "The author is English to his fingertips," fumed Salvemini, "and is therefore a master of the gentle art of misinforming the reader by telling him the truth, but not the whole truth." [94] Salvemini had plenty of opportunity a few years later to castigate the English again, this time his erstwhile friends among them, whose wholesale attacks on Italian character as part of the wartime propaganda so antagonized him and provoked his angry accusations of bad faith in his 1943 book, *What To Do With Italy.* Long before 1945 Salvemini discovered that bleak dividends awaited those who attacked their homeland for the edification and comfort of foreigners.

Another book on Italy which Salvemini hammered in 1938 in the *Nation,* along with that by Martelli, was H. Arthur Steiner's *Government in Fascist Italy,* also convicted of excessive detachment. He was deeply offended by Steiner's "objective realities," mainly his failure to condemn summarily the Mussolini regime in blunt language. The same fate befell other books which reflected some degree of detached attitude, such as *Fascist Economic Policy* by William G. Welk, *Fascist Italy* by William Ebenstein and *Price Control in Fascist Italy* by Henry S. Miller. The war was six months under way by the time he denounced these volumes, and there was little hope of making American liberals more hostile toward Italy than they already were, even though Mussolini had not yet committed his country to military action. But as demonstrations of sustained commitment to purpose they amply illustrated the issue.[95]

Salvemini and other ideological refugees were successful in establishing the view among American liberals that their homeland was a nightmare state which nearly everyone but Fascist party members would gladly flee if they could, and that no one of their predisposition was to be found in that barren land of conformity to reaction. An embarrassing exception appeared in the *Nation* for April 19, 1941 with the publication of "Liberty and Action," an article by another famous Italian dissident Benedetto Croce. It was taken from his *History As the Story of Liberty,* a volume which was wildly hailed by liberals in America. When Reinhold Niebuhr generously reviewed this book two months later, he pointed out that Croce was not an exiled refugee but was writing in Mussolini's Naples.[96] But with the liberal press and a solid contingent of their contributors clamoring for a declaration of war upon Germany and Italy, it hardly was the time to bring up a discordant note in the propaganda symphony which had been put together in all its movements since the Ethiopian war and to expect a hearing. This struggle, and the closely following one in Spain, exerted great strain on American liberal stands on peace, neutrality, disarmament and allied positions, a strain which contributed heavily to the pressures which cracked them into fragments and overwhelmed them with utterly opposing stands. It may be appropriate to examine some of these home-front stands against this backdrop of world events.

NOTES

1 *New Republic,* July 13, 1932, p. 217.

2 In review of Emil Ludwig's *Talks With Mussolini* in *New Republic,* March 15, 1933.

3 See *New Republic,* June 8, 1932, p. 85, for comments on Mussolini's opponents and their doctrinal differences.

4 In particular "Mussolini In Sheep's Clothing," *New Republic,* February 24, 1932, pp. 36–37, by "Pasquino Ianchi," identified as a pseudonym by the editors. Though the author claimed to be an Italian, the context of the remarks suggested a fervent Francophile.

5   *New Republic,* January 13, 1932, p. 227.

6   *New Republic,* January 27, 1932, pp. 297–298.

7   *Nation,* November 11, 1932, p. 469.

8   "E.D.H." (pseudonym), "Behind the Cables," *Nation,* December 21, 1932, p. 607.

9   *New Republic,* November 22, 1933, p. 32.

10 Strachey, "Has Mussolini Gone To the Left?," *New Republic,* March 7, 1934, pp. 96–98; editorial "Mussolini Challenges Europe," *New Republic,* March 28, 1934, pp. 173–174.

11 *Nation,* November 14, 1934, p. 565.

12 *Nation,* June 13, 1934, p. 672.

13 *New Republic,* December 26, 1934, pp. 177–178; *Nation,* December 26, 1934, p. 724.

14 *Nation,* February 27, 1935, p. 237.

15 *New Republic,* February 27, 1935, pp. 58–59.

16 *New Republic,* July 10, 1935, pp. 238–239.

17 *Nation,* April 17, 1935, pp. 428–429. See also full page editorial, *New Republic,* September 19, 1934, p. 143, which closed, "Mussolini realizes that he will be able to maintain his influence in Albania . . . only with the consent and assistance of France. In Geneva several days ago Louis Barthou, the French Minister of Foreign Affairs, warned that the Franco-Italian understanding is not yet complete. But it will come because it must, because without it there can be no united defense against the German aggressor—that need which at this juncture overshadows all other issues in continental politics."

18 *New Republic,* May 22, 1935, pp. 44–45.

19 *Nation,* May 22, 1935, pp. 585–586.

20 *Nation,* May 29, 1935, p. 614.

21 *Nation,* July 17, 1935, p. 58.

22 *Nation,* July 10, 1935, p. 30.

23 "The Tories Apply A Lesson," *Nation,* November 27, 1935, pp. 609–610.

24 See note 23.

25 *Nation,* July 24, 1935, p. 89.

26 *Nation,* August 14, 1935, p. 169.

27 "Can Italy Defy Sanctions?," *Nation,* September 11, 1935, p. 283.

28 Villard, "War in Ethiopia," *Nation,* September 11, 1935, p. 287.

29 "Italy's Economic Crisis" and "Mussolini's Red-Ink Imperialism," *New Republic,* August 7, 1935, pp. 347–349.

30 *New Republic,* August 14, 1935, p. 262.

31 *New Republic,* August 14, 1935, p. 1.

32 *New Republic,* September 25, 1935, pp. 171–172.

33 *Common Sense,* September, 1935, p. 5.

34 *New Republic,* October 2, 1935, p. 202.

35 *Nation,* July 31, 1935, p. 115.

36 *New Republic,* June 24, 1936, p. 210.

37 *New Republic,* October 2, 1935, p. 211.

38 Nehru, "The Humiliation Of India," *Nation,* April 11, 1934, pp. 410–411.

39 The Nehru biography by Anup Singh was published by John Day, reviewed by O'Sheel in *New Masses,* January 30, 1940, pp. 26–27.

40 Krishna Menon, "Labor Militancy Spreads In India," *Nation,* September 12, 1934, p. 293.

41 *Nation,* December 5, 1934, p. 632.

42 *Nation,* January 2, 1935, pp. 14–15.

43 *Nation,* August 21, 1935, pp. 210–212.

44 *New Republic,* October 16, 1935, p. 253.

45 *Common Sense,* November, 1935, p. 4.

46 *Nation,* March 11, 1936, p. 319; Peffer, "The Fallacy Of Conquest," *Harper's,* January, 1936, pp. 129–136.

47 *Nation,* May 20, 1936, p. 646.

48 Viton, "Italy Challenges Britain," *Nation,* August 15, 1936, pp. 182–184. ("Albert Viton is the pseudonym of an American correspondent in Italy." *Nation,* October 16, 1935, p. 439.)

49 See especially "Geneva Stands Firm," September 18, p. 312; "The League United Against Italy," p. 340; "On the Brink Of War," October 2, p. 368; "Will Sanctions Lead To War?," October 9, p. 396; "The Outlook For A League Success," October 16, p. 424; "What Does Britain Want?," October 23, p. 452; "Can Laval Make the Peace?," October 30, p. 497; "We Must Enforce the Kellogg Pact," November 6, p. 524; "Britain Holds Its Ground," November 6, p. 525; "The Revival Of British Jingoism," November 13, p. 552; "Helping Mussolini Win His War," November 20, p. 580; "The League's Hour Of Trial," December 25, p. 728.

50 *Nation*, October 30, 1935, pp. 509–510.

51 See especially editorial "Imperialism, Not a Race War," *New Masses*, October 22, 1935, p. 7.

52 *New Masses*, November 12, 1935, p. 4.

53 The *New Masses*, January 21, 1936, p. 5, revived one of the most sensational of the World War One atrocity stories, claiming reception of a letter from Ethiopia with a note written under the postage stamp in which the author alleged the Italians had cut out his tongue. After World War Two began, the liberal press repeated this story a number of times, with the Germans substituted for the Italians as the villains.

54 See Simonds' full remarks in *Nation*, October 9, 1935, pp. 408–409 and December 18, 1935, pp. 710–711.

55 Brailsford, "The League In Action," *New Republic*, October 30, 1935, pp. 324–326.

56 Brailsford, "Mussolini Goes To War," *New Republic*, September 11, 1935, pp. 119–121.

57 "The League Hesitates," *New Republic*, October 23, 1935, pp. 285–286.

58 "The Meaning Of Sanctions," *New Republic*, November 27, 1935, p. 60.

59 *Common Sense*, October, 1935, p. 5.

60 *Common Sense*, November, 1935, p. 4; December, 1935, p. 4; May, 1936, p. 6.

61 *New Republic*, October 30, 1935, pp. 332–333, for quotations here and in above paragraph as well.

62 *New Republic*, April 29, 1936, pp. 344–345.

63 "The League's Hour Of Trial," *Nation*, December 25, 1935, p. 728.

64 "Is Mussolini Moving Toward Socialism?," *Nation*, April 8, 1936, pp. 438–439.

65 *Common Sense*, May, 1936, p. 6.

66 Fischer, "Can Italy Make Peace With Europe?," *Nation*, May 20, 1936, pp. 643–645.

67 "The League Struggles On," *Nation*, January 1, 1936, p. 4.

68 *Nation*, January 22, 1936, pp. 102–103.

69 "The League Falters," *Nation*, January 29, 1936, p. 117; Fischer, "Mussolini Out-bluffs England," *Nation*, January 29, 1936, pp. 123–124; *Nation*, March 11, 1936, p. 297.

70 *Nation*, April 29, 1936, p. 533.

71 *Nation*, May 13, 1936, pp. 599–600.

72 *Nation*, February 19, 1936, p. 205.

73 *New Republic*, May 13, 1936, pp. 1, 5–6.

74 *Nation*, May 13, 1936, p. 614.

75 "The League's Dark Hour," *New Republic*, July 8, 1936, p. 255.

76 "Can the League Survive?," *New Republic*, May 20, 1936, pp. 33–34.

77 *Nation*, June 27, 1936, p. 829.

78 *Nation*, July 18, 1936, p. 74.

79 *Nation*, July 18, 1936, p. 74.

80 *New Republic*, September 2, 1936, p. 114.

81 Mitchell review of Buell in *New Republic*, August 5, 1936, p. 390; Devere review of Shotwell in *New Republic*, September 9, 1936, pp. 136–137.

82 *Nation*, November 7, 1936, p. 535.

83 Bliven, "The Marshal and I," *New Republic*, March 31, 1937, pp. 236–237.

84 *New Republic*, December 22, 1937, p. 181; *Nation*, December 18, 1937, p. 673.

85 *Nation*, December 25, 1935, pp. 746–747.

86 Howe review of Seldes in *New Republic*, December 11, 1935, p. 137; Salvemini review of Seldes in *Nation*, January 22, 1936, pp. 108–109. Salvemini predicted that economic collapse at home would force Mussolini to give up the war in Ethiopia before June, 1936. "Economic Forces In Italy," *Yale Review*, March, 1936, pp. 553–572.

87 *New Republic*, May 6, 1936, pp. 370–371.

88 *New Republic,* March 4, 1936, pp. 103–105.

89 Douglas review of Salvemini in *New Republic,* October 14, 1936, p. 287; Jaszi review of Salvemini in *Nation,* June 3, 1936, pp. 716–717.

90 Douglas review of Borghese in *New Republic,* October 13, 1937, pp. 275–276; Elliott review of Borghese in *Nation,* October 23, 1937, pp. 443–444.

91 Schuman review of Ascoli in *Nation,* November 21, 1936, p. 611; Josephson review of Ascoli in *New Republic,* March 3, 1937, p. 117. Lauterbach review of Ascoli and Feiler in *Nation,* December 24, 1938, pp. 696–697.

92 Douglas review of Schmidt in *New Republic,* July 13, 1938, pp. 286–287; Salvemini review of Schmidt in *Nation,* January 22, 1938. Douglas remained outside the raging battle between the Stalinists and Trotskyists at that moment, choosing to criticize both freely in his review of Angelica Balabanoff's *My Life As A Rebel.*

93 Salvemini review of Field in *Nation,* June 11, 1938, pp. 676–677; his review of Megaro in *Nation,* July 2, 1938, pp. 19–21.

94 *Nation,* May 14, 1938, pp. 564–565.

95 Salvemini review of Steiner in *Nation,* October 15, 1938, pp. 386–387; his reviews of Welk, Ebenstein and Miller in *Nation,* February 3, 1940, pp. 134–135.

96 Niebuhr review of Croce in *Nation,* June 14, 1941, pp. 699–700. Part of Croce's book appeared as a separate article, "Liberty and Action," in *Nation,* April 19, 1941, pp. 467–470.

15

THE INFLUENCE AND CONSEQUENCES
OF THE NYE COMMITTEE HEARINGS
ON AMERICAN LIBERALISM, 1934–1940

THE LIBERAL CASE AGAINST
THE PRIVATE MANUFACTURE
OF MUNITIONS

THE sources of the attack on the manufacture of munitions of war as a perpetual aggravation and incitation to more war are varied, and there is no necessity to examine the entire episode exhaustively here. Part of the attention devoted to the topic grew out of World War revisionism, which among other things focused a spotlight on the enormous paper profits made by the industries furnishing the basic necessities for an industrial and technical "total war" involving the entire community. This was a major social aspect of the Great War, and cast an ominous shadow as to what was to prevail thereafter should another eventuate. Conscription and industrial technicalism fundamentally changed the conditions under which fighting had customarily taken place. And from a financial angle, such a war was bound to heap up fabulous wealth at the doors of those whose products had become absolute necessities for continued fighting under the new circumstances. That these same interests might also engage in a few activities to aid in boosting their fortunes was revealed incidentally in the diplomatic studies of the coming of the war. The interlocked and international aspect of these businesses for a time brought upon them a great deal of public attention, thanks to a number of books written primarily for that purpose. Private international organization had been the businessman's answer to nationalism and its tendency to produce exclusiveness for some time before the war; to a large extent the novelty now was due to the special nature of the firms involved and the peculiar services they supplied.

Criticism had slowly mounted in the post-war decade, reaching one peak after the 1927 naval conference. The unsavory details involving the lobbyists for warship builders sparked an even more vigorous era of remonstration, and for the first time a wide audience was invited into the private workings of the business side of war. Wartime propaganda, with its unity appeal and collective adjectives and nouns, by definition calls no attention to the various segments of a social system at war. The leisurely examination of subjects of this sort was bound to occur if at all in a period of no war, and also in a period marked by much unhappiness and disillusion over a previous war. But even the Civil War, the greatest war in modern times until that of 1914–1918, did not hatch the literature of criticism which the latter unloosed. It goes without saying that liberals and their radical allies had a conspicuous place at the head of the column of critics. No program dovetailed better with the overall denigration of the war in all its aspects and the peace and disarmament appeals which formed such substantial portions of the liberal outlook at this time.

But a sizable part of the volume of complaint came from other sources. One with which the liberals had little if any contact, and not much desire to establish any was the veterans' organizations. In the later 1920's and the early depression years, the American Legion had conducted a vigorous propaganda to "take the profits out of war," reflected in politics by the proposed Capper-Johnson Universal Draft Bill. One of its main results would have been the establishment of the privilege of the federal government to "conscript capital" as well as young men on the outbreak of war. Expectations from such a move were based on the notion that by establishing very high taxes and even taking property over for the government use in wartime, the material burdens and deprivations would be more evenly spread out over the whole community. It was still possible to make reunion groups of veterans boil by calling to mind the high wage rates of the home front in 1917–1918, as compared to the very meager pay of the "dough." A populistic flavor tempered a large part of this hostile literature and talk on the subject of war profiteering, more concerned with a rough kind of equity than any serious desire to make the likelihood of war remote.

On the other hand, liberals with a habit of sampling Communist literature here and abroad must have been aware that the attack on munitions manufacturers was in full bloom in such circles by at least 1928, and that several Marxist writers had brought the "merchants-of-death" theme to ripe development years before its 1933–1938 vogue among American liberal publicists.[1]

One fruit of this seething contention was the series of hearings before a special body, the War Policies Commission, held in March, April and May of 1931. Congress had directed it to consider the advisability of amending the Constitution for the purpose of taking private property for public use during war and of equalizing the burdens and removing the profits of war. There was a sharp upswing in the volume of favorable comment on this from that point on. No analysis of the hearings was published before early in 1933, but that did not inhibit the increase of dis- and anti-armament calls.[2] Liberal enthusiasm for disarmament and zeal for exposure of war profiteering probably was never higher than in the summer of 1931, although new heights were to be attained by 1935. The most sympathetic allies of those with liberal tendencies were the peace societies, which had for years been convinced that the ultimate solution to war was the making of a state monopoly in every country out of the manufacture of arms and ammunition of every kind, followed by national control of the traffic of such products. This was expected to abolish one of the most powerful pressures leading to war. Socialistic tendencies among liberals responded most favorably to this approach, and not the slightest breath was expended on the possibility of a war between national states with nationalized arms factories.

Liberal response to President Hoover's moratorium in June, 1931, on the heels of the conclusion of the hearings of the War Policies Commission, was most favorable, and this gesture was figured out to be an ideal point at which to open up the peace-disarmament-anti-munitions case. A week after applauding Hoover for the moratorium on the war debts, the *Nation* ran an exhortatory editorial, "Now Mr. Hoover, Disarm!" [3] "The swollen armaments of Europe have contributed not one whit to its safety or peace," it charged; "On the contrary, they are one of the potent reasons why fear stalks abroad in all the lands touched by the World War." "The way to disarm is to disarm," it advised Mr. Hoover; armaments were simply "criminal waste," protecting nobody and "merely guarantees of the continuance of war." Pointing to United States history prior to 1900 it went on:

There is no prouder chapter in the history of the United States than the fact that during the first 111 years of our national history our regular army never rose above the figure of 25,000 men, and our fleet was negligible save during the Civil War; during this long period we never had a foreign war that was not of our own seeking.

When Under-Secretary William R. Castle delivered his speech denouncing the competitive arms race in October, the *Nation* showed great enthusiasm over this, as it had over any and all gestures toward disarmament made in both the Coolidge and Hoover Administrations. Coolidge, target of multitudinous liberal criticisms on grounds of intellectual vacuity, was quoted by Villard as having made the observation that armaments never yet kept any country out of war nor insured its victory after one began, a view which the *Nation's* senior editor shared *in toto*. Hoover's insistence on budget cuts for naval spending was vigorously applauded. No reason could be seen for maintaining such a large fleet anyway; only the British, "on the verge of bankruptcy," had a comparable one. There were no nations menacing us; "Not Japan certainly; not Russia, which has no fleet, not Italy or France." This huge fleet was in existence "because our armament profiteers, Navy League, and naval officers, with their vested interest in maintaining a fleet, are constantly propagandizing for it." [4]

Various evidences are to be found in the liberal press that it eagerly looked forward to government intervention and control of munitions making. In this same month the *Nation* suggested an international treaty limiting arms manufacturing by private industry, and insisted that the general war powers of Congress already were sufficient to make possible the enactment of legislation placing all armament firms under federal control.[5] In January, 1933 it gave its sanction to a proposal which favored Hoover's using an executive order to prohibit the shipping of munitions to Japan and to the warring areas of South America. It also came out openly in favor of "nationalizing our own munitions industry," [6] which put it on the same stage as the peace societies.

Substantial sustenance was obtained from a speech delivered by retired Marine Major General Smedley D. Butler in New York City in mid-January in which he referred to the United States military forces as "a glorified bill-collecting agency." It reviewed the whole Haitian affair from 1915 until the time General Butler was dismissed from his command there, claiming it was an object lesson in how the national armed forces were used to buttress foreign investments, a kind of protection no investor in domestic enterprises was entitled to or received.[7] But much greater satisfaction was to be obtained from General Butler when his sensational little book, *War Is A Racket*, was published in 1935.

In the Washington's Birthday issue, 1933, Villard reviewed Seymour Waldman's *Death and Profits*, the first comprehensive report on the hearings before the War Policies Commission. He regretted that the Commission had only one "liberal-minded and anti-militaristic person" on it, and spoke very disparagingly about its recommendations, even if a number of the statistics of the profits made out of the last war was considered clear gain on the educational side for the anti-war people. Villard noted that the Commission did not recommend anything to the President except that he be empowered "to stabilize prices at a level which would minimize inflation" in the event of another war. "The report gives complete security to the profiteers in the next war," Villard summarized, but he still insisted that the book belonged "in every library in this country as proof of the alliance of big business with the warmaking forces. It is as melancholy a record of a completely abortive effort to make the next war unsafe from the profit standpoint for munitions makers, bankers, and other big business men as could possibly be imagined." [8]

THE "MERCHANTS OF DEATH" THEME
BEGINS TO TAKE FULL SHAPE

Actually the situation was not in the least as desolate as Villard pictured it for the forces seeking munitions making controls. Numerous commentaries, articles and other literature poured out through 1933, focussing attention on the international aspects of the manufacture of the tools of war. Overseas liberal allies, such as the Union of Democratic Control, were responsible for searching studies on what was now being called the "Secret International," [9] and a *New Republic* editorial devoted some space to a fascinating story based on a French magazine which revealed the Frenchmen who came into possession of German heavy industry in Alsace and Lorraine after Versailles.[10]

The tempo picked up abruptly in the late winter of 1933–1934. The naval building and expansion ambitions of Roosevelt had a prominent part in stimulating the political controversy out of which came Senator Gerald P. Nye's resolution calling for an investigation of munitions manufacture in the United States. The *Nation*'s February 28 editorial "A Navy For War" hit the President and Admiral William H. Standley, Chief of Naval Operations, hard upon the preliminary release of long-range expenditures for the Navy as outlined by the latter and provided for in the Vinson Bill, calling for a rate of expansion annually which was three times as large as the pre-World War annual expansion rate. Queried the editorial,[11]

Can the Roosevelt Administration really justify this enormous expenditure? Before acting on the Vinson Bill, the Senate should demand a straightforward explanation from the White House and Navy Department. Before all else it should insist upon a sweeping investigation of the munitions industry as provided in a resolution introduced by Senator Nye.

The *Nation* hailed the establishment of the investigation; "The Senate's acceptance of Senator Nye's proposal for an investigation of the manufacture of munitions in the United States is most gratifying. . . . If the right man heads this committee and it means business, we shall have astounding revelations as to the character of the munitions trade and its menace to the peace of the world and to the United States." [12]

On May 9 it followed up with a tribute to the aroused public interest: [13]

We are glad that the public is taking a keen if belated interest in the activities of the international armament ring during and between wars. It becomes peculiarly relevant to American young men, any one of whom faces the fantastic but real possibility of being killed in the Far East by a bit of shrapnel that was originally part of his mother's kitchen stove. We hope the Senate Committee's investigation of the munitions racket will be thorough.

But there were occasional puzzlers in the almost universal acceptance of this Senate query. The *Nation*'s Memorial Day issue editorial was nonplussed at FDR's unconditional approval of the Nye investigation, which went out simultaneously with allotment of millions of dollars of PWA funds for naval building and his signing of the Vinson Bill providing for a billion of additional naval spending. The President's castigation of "the manufacturers and merchants of engines of destruction," language which sounded like material from the Seldes and Engelbrecht-Hanighen volumes, led to a certain amount of editorial head-scratching and the laboriously obvious conclusion that "he is open to the charge of being on both sides of the fence." [14]

In September the *Nation* devoted a full page editorial on the 12th commending Senator Nye for his timeliness in setting off the munitions investigation at a time when military budgets were ballooning, and heaped praise on his chief investigator Stephen Raushenbush as well.[15] The following week, in its editorial "The Death Business," it announced, "The Senate inquiry into the munitions of war which is at present being conducted in Washington under the chairmanship of Senator Nye has shaken out more lightning than has any other government investigation in years." [16]

The week before Christmas the *Nation* was still defending the Nye investigation against all comers, and summarily opposed any move on the part of anyone from preventing it "from carrying the investigation to its full completion." Its expense was not to be considered, "as even partial insurance against another holocaust like the World War it is cheap indeed." [17]

The *New Republic* also came forward promptly, pleading the case for the continuation of the Committee, praising its chairman and urging the appropriation of the necessary funds to keep it in existence in a fervent editorial on January 16, 1935: [18]

No senatorial committee has ever performed a more useful public work than the one investigating the munitions business. Its funds are now exhausted, while much of its important work is still to come. Senator Nye has asked for another $100,000 to continue the work, and we trust Congress will promptly grant his plea. No Congressman can vote against the appropriation without putting himself under the suspicion of benefiting, directly or indirectly, from the munitions business—surely one of the foulest that ever encumbered the earth.

The *Nation* thought it detected a move to squelch the Nye hearings with premature plans to satisfy the critics. Its editorial three weeks earlier demanded that Nye and his Committee get more money for a deeper probe, on the grounds that it had just scratched the surface, and that before any proposals for action be made the Committee be allowed to get much more factual material on the record; "The inquiry must not be allowed to lag," it warned. The editorial also condemned Roosevelt's action in summoning a special committee to prepare legislation for "equalizing the burdens of war" as "untimely and ill-advised." [19]

But by this time, a sensational year of exposures had already elapsed. The first prominent fruit of the uproar over the Nye recommendations was an article in *Fortune* in March, 1934, "Arms and the Men," during the editorship of Archibald MacLeish. This exposé of the munitions makers, which Dwight MacDonald, on the editorial staff of this journal from March, 1929 until June, 1936, described as "the most famous liberal gesture *Fortune* ever made," although comprehensive in sound, actually devoted only 350 of its 10,000 words to the sins of American traffickers in munitions. But it stimulated a reading public for much more extended fare.[20] John Gunther kept up the momentum in the prestige journals with his May, 1934 *Harper's* piece, "Slaughter For Sale." [21]

Two widely-read books were published almost simultaneously with the creation of the Nye Committee, *Merchants of Death*, by H. C. Engelbrecht and Frank C. Hanighen, and *Iron, Blood and Profits*, by George Seldes. Quincy Howe reviewed both for the *New Republic* in May, 1934 with substantial sympathy, and lauded the Nye investigation in the process. Howe expressed the hope that it would check the progress of the new naval race already under way, despite the pious and reserved language still being spoken by politicians about the desirability of disarmament.[22] The same two books were reviewed by MacLeish for the *Nation*, and apparently he suffered from feelings that the famous article he had published was creating the impression that only businessmen were at fault in the production and trade of war goods. MacLeish disparaged this approach and widened the circle of the accused. He did not think singling out the business community exclusively would do much to aid the struggle against war; "The world can only be turned against war by teaching. Teaching requires the use of the radio and the press. So far efforts to use the press to that end have failed, and have failed largely because of a counterpropaganda of fear." He concluded from this that the problem of peace propaganda could be attacked intelligently only by the "cleansing of the press" which largely promoted the manufacturing of munitions "through subsidized and dishonest mediums of news." Failing this, said the editor of *Fortune,* there was little to be gained in promoting peace by the "crucifixion" of the munitions makers.[23] Archibald MacLeish had become a partial penitent in two months.

MacLeish's incrimination of the press as equally guilty in war promotion along with the makers of fighting equipment did bear some fruit for a short season. A furious attack on William Randolph Hearst and his newspaper chain brewed in the following year, carried on with equal vigor in the liberal press and the pro-Communist sources. *Common Sense,* which supported the liberal weeklies in backing the Nye investigation, as well as attacking FDR's "big navy" views, did its part by printing elaborations on General Butler's book *War Is A Racket* prepared by Butler himself, and also by serializing the first five chapters of Oliver Carlson's and Ernest Sutherland Bates's *Hearst, Lord of San Simeon,* stressing his part as a fomenter of war scares and war propaganda.[24]

The *New Republic* was as earnest and eager in its support of the Nye hearings as any other liberal force. Its May, 1934 issue carrying the reviews of the Seldes and Engelbrecht-Hanighen exposés displayed a long unsigned editorial, "The Munitions Revelations," which took unconcealed pleasure in the incriminating material being paraded before Nye and the committee. Another long editorial in the issue for May 23 engaged in a detailed comparison between the tension in the world of 1913 and of 1934, and found a remarkable analogy. The sharp upturn in business activities concerned with the building of military and naval might around the world drew much attention, mostly blaming the armament makers, and accusing them of persisting in "resort to the foulest possible means, bribery, corruption, and the dissemination of faked reports concerning military expenditures of other nations," simply in order to produce a "scare." [25] William T. Stone, Washington representative of the Foreign Policy Association, in a long *Nation* article, "Exposing the Death Business," on October 3, 1934, concluded in calm satisfaction that the Nye hearings had proved without a doubt that the armament industry had been expert in launching war scares.[26]

No recognition was made of the possible part the devoted anti-war liberal and allied groups were playing in aiding such a course by their consistently loud and abusive charges against the Japanese, Italian and German regimes, as these hearings went on. The *bête noire* was the capitalist order, hoping to "get a new lease on life by an economic revival artificially produced by an increase in the output of those industries that manufacture instruments for the destruction of human lives." So "subtle propaganda" and the "skillful creation of war psychology," international capital in general and the international arms trade in particular had once more stimulated the "Great Powers" into another war-breeding armament race.

The liberal press had launched their own armament makers' probe some time before the Nye Committee became activated, so the Senate Committee investigation caught them in full stride. Anticipating intrigue by American "big-navy" enthusiasts at the Geneva Disarmament Conference early in 1932, the *New Republic* had turned the full force of one of the most persuasive historical voices in America, Charles A. Beard, directly upon the purely American part. Beard's previously mentioned three long articles in January and February, 1932 titled "Big Navy Boys" were a most embarrassing trio of treatments of the forces pressing for increased naval armaments for the United States Navy, stressing especially the 1927 Geneva "cruiser" Conference. Walter Millis' June, 1932 *Atlantic* article, "Prepare, Prepare, Prepare!",[27] continued this caustic attack on "big-navyism." And in its June, 1932 issue the *Nation* launched one of the earliest attacks on the international arms trade with its substantial editorial titled "Profits In Blood." [28] Most of the key words and trigger slogans were in existence well before the major assault began in 1934.

In 1934, as a prelude to the Nye hearings, the same publication ran another series, this time by Jonathan Mitchell, titled "The Armaments Scandal," which went deeply into the situation as it was taking shape in that stage of Mr. Roosevelt's New Deal. It did not handle the Administration with the slightest charity. Mitchell clung to this theme with considerable tenacity. One of his summaries of the Nye investigation, published in September and titled "Mass Murderers in Person," probably was his peak contribution to the hostile case being compiled against the entire part of the business community that had anything to do with munitions or armament from World War days to that moment. His particular favorite among the investigators was Senator Bone, "an instinctive scientist," who was patiently "bringing up into the light a fundamental part of our present system" so that everyone might see it.[29] Mitchell was equally perturbed by both the naval vessel and aircraft proponents, although he was more mystified by the air buildup, he admitted. It was interesting to note that in listing the major air forces in the world, he let it drop casually that the Soviet Union had the largest as of that writing, in May, 1934. This had no influence in other departments of the liberal papers, where the presentation of Red Russia as the only power in the world sincerely interested in peace proceeded without a break in stride. In like manner, a few months earlier, when the Soviet Commissar for War announced that the Red Army was more thoroughly mechanized than most others of Western Europe, no special comment was considered necessary.

Robert Wohlforth's "Armament Profiteers: 1934" in the March 14, 1934 issue of the *Nation* was the counterpart to the Mitchell articles in the *New Republic,* written with some heat, disapproving of armed service condemnation of the Nye resolution and ending with a plea for a government-owned armament business as a solution.[30] Almost all the liberals who took part in this controversy adopted this same approach, a view heartily supported by the editors and writers in the *New Masses.*[31] But this journal showed no more alacrity than the liberal press for discussing the state of war implements in Russia. Of the major nations who were subjected to the searchlight of investigation on this subject, only the Soviet Union was exempted from publicity and criticism. The basic premise appeared to be that no one gained from the manufacture of arms in a Communist country, and that it had no intention of using them anyway.

Indeed, the logic of the liberal pursuit of the subject called for the conclusion that federal armament factories were the answer to the evils and grievances which they believed were being piled at private industry's door by the Nye investigation. Special reports and editorials alike, when they took up the subject of alternative action, invariably came around to nationalization. Johannes Steel, Marxist refugee from Germany, took time out from his attack on Hitler to write "The World's Greatest Racket" for the *Nation* in June, 1934, and arrived at this conclusion. He deplored the effect of ballyhooed crises and border clashes and incidents in raising the prices of armament stocks, castigated every nation but Soviet Russia for its arms industries, and released the slogan, "There would be fewer wars if there were fewer armament makers." [32]

Editorially, both weeklies agreed with this position. On November 28 the *Nation* stated, "We know of no cure of the armament evil short of the absolute abolition of the industry," [33] and in the *New Republic*'s December editorial "The du Ponts Testify," there was a vigorous call for the nationalization of the armaments industry, at least in "peacetime," when such production it was felt should surely be a government monopoly.[34] The *Nation*'s post-Christmas issue was not so conditional; its editorial on the subject was headed "Nationalize the Arms Industry!"

The *Nation* expressed considerable impatience with Bernard Baruch in July, when, speaking at a commencement, he reacted to the spirit of the moment by issuing a testimonial critical of "big war profits"; Baruch's plan was one for "making war safe for capitalism," not promoting peace. The editorial comment doubted that he had the slightest interest in that in view of his preoccupation with the "preparedness" theme, and his audience, which happened to be the Army Industrial College. Baruch's scheme, it was averred, was an attempt to escape the "dilemma" of all states with a profit economy, and it reasoned thus: [35]

> . . . the uncontrolled profit motive drives these competing capitalist states into war; but during the war, the profit motive must be controlled so that capitalism may not destroy itself during and after the war which it has made.

Baruch, then, was simply proposing a plan which actually was a phase of "realpolitik," since his concern was saving the system from the wrath of a presumptive hostile home front, angered by the inflation and the vast gains made by the war suppliers, in addition to the fear that debts contracted in wartime inflationary times would bring about a collapse if required to be paid back in post-war, presumably deflationary times. Neither Baruch nor the *Nation* discussed the possibility of permanent inflation. In December the *Nation* had less patience with the Baruch and du Pont plans for "taking the profits out of war," and equated them with a situation if "Dillinger and Capone should recommend plans for combating crime." [36]

So the campaign against the munitions makers and for the nationalization of all arms manufacture went on into 1935, with the liberal papers occasionally chiding the daily press for its inadequate publicity to various disclosures of the Nye hearings. A pre-Christmas, 1934 release by the Committee of a telegram from Ambassador Walter Hines Page to President Wilson dated March 5, 1917 received considerable attention in both the prominent liberal weeklies, although the claim was made that only a small sample of the nation's largest papers printed the text of this message.[37] This wire predicted a crisis in the United States if the Allies failed to make their payments on a large Morgan loan then outstanding, ending with the judgment that "it is not improbable that the only way of maintaining our present pre-eminent trade position and averting a panic is by declaring war on Germany." The *New Republic* especially rejoiced at this revelation in its December 26 issue, and it went on to report, "The Nye Committee is planning to study the whole question of our financial relationships with the Allies, and it could do no more useful service in the cause of peace." [38]

This disclosure fitted in closely with the revisionism on war guilt during the fifteen years past, pieced together arduously from scraps of information of this kind. The liberal press considered it very significant. With the disarmament, reparations and munitions investigation activities now upon the heels one of the other, and complicated by the happenings in East Asia and Central Europe, still another circumstance began to shoulder its way into the arena of daily events and stir up comment. This concerned the foreign policy actions and statements of the new national Administration, which came upon the scene with all these developments already in motion. The Roosevelt camp was to conduct a tortuous journey during these years in liberal estimation. The attempt to follow all the twists and turns frequently resulted in their getting lost, but on one phase of behavior, they maintained excellent contact, namely, the increasing national rearmament.

LIBERALS APPLAUD AS
THE NYE HEARINGS GAIN MOMENTUM

On January 30, 1935 the *Nation*'s editorial voice announced triumphantly, "All friends of peace will rejoice that the munitions investigation is to continue," on the news that sufficient funds would be available. In this commentary it was especially congratulatory to Raushenbush, the Nye Committee's chief investigator, although it hurried to point out that it had not intended to "minimize our admiration for the signal ability with which Senators Nye, Clark, and Bone, in particular, have used the material and conducted the inquiry." And it was even more emphatic in asserting its belief that the revelations to come would only "illuminate the dire need for nationalizing the munitions industry." [39] But as subsequent hearings involved finance more than industry, the logic of the *Nation*'s position seemed to suggest that it urge the nationalizing of the country's banks instead.

In truth, the hearings were approaching the harvest stage, which in the field of congressional investigations usually meant recommendations for legislation to apply to the particular grievance under scrutiny. With a furor over neutrality going on currently, there was time to note the relationship between the investigation and immediate policy suggestions. The *New Republic* sharply disapproved Roosevelt's views on a pending arms embargo move because of its basic approach, which involved the revival of the "aggressor" concept to give it meaning. It backed Senate thinking of the moment instead, which felt that it was not the business of anyone in the United States to seek to establish the relative sinfulness of two or more states at war, and favored the application of an impartial, across-the-board arms embargo on all warring nations in any putative international conflict. It advanced this view as part of a commentary on the Nye hearings in the third week of February, 1935 at which time it expressed the view that this investigation was not producing the proper legislative proposals for curtailing the arms business, and thought the comprehensive arms embargo a suitable temporary solution.[40]

Of course, the hearings were far from over, even though the Committee was on the verge of presenting a substantial recommendation. Jonathan Mitchell's long article in the February 27 *New Republic*, "Senator Nye Hunts Big Game," established that rather than winding up, it was about to extend its operations to a much broader field; "After months of poking around in the underbrush of the munitions industry, Senator Nye and his committee have started up two large, important animals," he revealed. "One of them is named War; the other, which bears a marked resemblance to the first, is called Imperialism in the Orient." Mitchell used this approach to introduce the subject of Nye's head-on collision with the Roosevelt Administration, and cited several bits of evidence to support this contention. The fact that the President had Bernard Baruch and General Hugh S. Johnson conducting a private investigation of the munitions business, and that there were already two rival diversionary House investigations was enough to convince Mitchell that the President was most unhappy over Nye's work. And if that were not enough there were FDR's request of $700 million from Congress "for military purposes" and Norman Davis's rejection at London in December, 1934 of the Japanese offer to reduce their fleet by one half if the United States did the same, as well as suggesting the mutual abolition of carriers and capital ships. Mitchell was not only perturbed at these developments, but felt strongly enough to suggest that the rival investigations were intended to "shield" the munitions makers from Nye, and that the Administration was declining to do anything to prevent profit-making by the munitions companies or to consider nationalizing them, which was just as serious an omission. Pronounced Mitchell, "In its investigation the [Nye] Committee has proved the worst that anyone suspected about the munitions makers," but concluded in despair that in view of current developments, it was likely that "In the event of another war, I believe that it will be impossible to prevent the same sordid swindling of the government that occurred in 1917–1918." Mitchell thought that Nye had proved that the Wilson Administration was the "original advocate of preventing wartime profits," but had knuckled under in order to get its army supplied, and that it was unlikely that another administration would do any better. For this reason he thought that the Roosevelt policies of building up the fleet and spending for "war preparations" needed to be repudiated before anyone could look forward to the future with comfort, no matter what the Nye hearings were likely to turn up henceforth. And as long as these policies were unquestioned, the President was likely to obstruct the Nye Committee more.[41]

Mitchell's hope that a plan to tax munitions company profits 98% would be adopted was almost realized at least on the level of recommendations, as a result of John T. Flynn's plan for "taking the profits out of war" projected before the Nye Committee in March. The *New Republic* endorsed it fully, while expressing great pride that Flynn was one of its contributing editors, concluding grimly: "It would be an excellent thing if some such plan as that of Mr. Flynn could be adopted. If it did nothing else, it would check the prosperous loungers in clubs who keep saying that 'a good war would end the depression.' "[42]

The *Nation* was no less firm in its espousal of the Flynn proposal, which specified that 3% was to be the maximum profit allowed in wartime, and $10,000 the maximum annual wartime income; in its April 3 editorial, "Abolishing War Profits," it declared bluntly, "We unreservedly subscribe to the principles underlying the plan presented by John T. Flynn to the Senate Munitions Committee for taking the profits out of war. . . . The generation which waged the war would pay for it as it fought," another way of saying that "the nation would take a vow of poverty as long as its youth served on the battlefield."[43] At the same time both journals condemned the plan proposed by Baruch, and Benjamin Stolberg, reviewing General Johnson's book on the NRA, *The Blue Eagle from Egg to Earth,* two weeks later in the *Nation,* took advantage of the immediate prominence of the author and his wealthy associate to wither both. To Stolberg, Baruch was "the Wall Street gambler who got out with enough to become one of our Great Economic Thinkers," and Johnson was his "glorified economic research valet."[44] *Common Sense* also warmly endorsed the bill drafted by Flynn, and praised its partner, the McSwain Bill, as amended by Maury Maverick, because it called for the elimination of universal conscription.

Imaginations began to get out of hand with this early proposal and various schemes began to appear which went far beyond suggestions for paring down the profits of the arms trade in the event of war. The *Nation* felt called to chide the Committee late in April, 1935 for discussing plans for conscripting wealth and manpower in case of American involvement in another military adventure. In an editorial which took pains to praise Nye and his associates and commended them for "educating the country on the meaning of modern war," it soberly advised that the newer avenues of investigation were a "blind alley," and that any conscription plan, no matter how it was intended to distribute the costs and burdens of fighting, was really sinister, and indirectly played into the hands of the War Department people who were expecting "to use it in another overseas war fought on the same scale as the last war." In the *Nation*'s considered view, there was no need to envisage any kind of conscription of anything in any putative war conducted purely in the defense of the United States, by which it obviously meant a war fought to preserve the territorial integrity of the country.[45] But the Communists, dead-set against manpower conscription,[46] were not hostile to a conscription of "capital" in 1935.

WATERSHED OF THE NYE HEARINGS:
THE MORGAN PROBE

The May Day, 1935 issues of both liberal weeklies contained generous stories on the newest development in the Nye hearings, the decision to examine the relations which existed between the Wilson Administration and the banking firm of J. P. Morgan during the entire World War. The political repercussions had immediately rolled to London and promptly reverberated, and it was obvious to all observers that the agitation and concern excited in Washington indicated a serious crisis had arrived for all concerned. Raymond Gram Swing in his extended *Nation* piece "The Morgan Nerve Begins to Jump," flatly charged that the Baldwin Government was deliberately trying to hide from all eyes something connected with the British part in the mysterious financial history of the World War and that it was able "to enlist the services of President Roosevelt in trying, insofar as diplomacy was able, to keep it hidden." The *New Republic*'s editorial went over the same material, asserting that several "desperate attempts" had already been made to keep pertinent facts hidden from public disclosure during the Nye hearings, and thought it most unusual for Baldwin to speak in the House of Commons and express his personal view that "the British government hoped nothing would be made public that would upset the present friendly relations among the Powers." It went on to describe the agitated messages that followed, including FDR's call upon Nye, who had thereupon stated that nothing would be made public that would upset international amity. This annoyed the *New Republic* visibly: "We hope it does not mean the committee intends to pull its punch, or that the President wishes it to do so," it concluded fervently.[47] But something seemed afoot, and an uneasy feeling started to grow that even under attack the arms companies enjoyed the eye-winking patronage of the Administration, especially after the testimony of Donald Richberg the next week under the cross-examination of Alger Hiss for the Committee, seeking to establish that the Colt Patent Fire Arms Company had been violating Section 7a of the

National Labor Relations Act with the presumable tacit permission of Mr. Roosevelt.[48]

The *New Republic* had appealed at the conclusion of the previous week's editorial comment that "it would surely be better for all concerned to have the facts established in definitive form," because it maintained that "To all Americans the matter is of overwhelming importance at the present time." But even it was not prepared for some of the subsequent disclosures. Late in the summer Nye and Clark revealed a letter written by Secretary of State Lansing to Wilson on September 6, 1915, which explained that the Allies were paying for munitions from America by mobilizing the securities which their citizens owned in American companies, and that this means of payment would be exhausted by the end of the year, which would be catastrophic to American export trade if they could not float loans here thereafter. Lansing's implicit approval of their doing so was accompanied by the bland prediction that Anglo-French bond flotations here would have no material effect on United States sentiments on the outcome of the war; he neglected to point out the possible exception of the American owners of such bonds and their emotions on contemplation of their becoming worthless should the issuing nation lose the war. The *New Republic* commented loudly on this exposure, and wondered how Mr. Lansing could have expected the buyers of these foreign bonds not to develop a bias in favor of the issuing country.[49]

But the really incendiary part of this phase of the hearings occurred early in 1936 when the Committee released information indicating that Wilson had been in full knowledge of the secret treaties among the Allies which committed them to a round of territorial grabbing quite in contradiction to their noble formal war aims. This news came just as the Committee's appropriations were running short, and a powerful group in the Senate led by Senator Carter Glass of Virginia bitterly denounced this action and threatened to block any further appropriations. The editorial opinion of all three of the chief liberal journals promptly descended upon Glass like a ton of lead, and for the next six months he continued to receive their scorn and contempt. The *New Republic* flamed at Glass and his supporters and ridiculed their indignation at "the alleged besmirching of the memory of President Wilson"; "Neither Senator Glass nor any of the other Democrats who rushed to the defense of President Wilson's memory knows what he is talking about." It also thought it somewhat suspicious for Glass to become concerned over the hearings at this late date, and only when the Morgan interests were being investigated, and his own relationships to the banking business were caustically reviewed. But most of all it called upon the Congress to vote Nye more money to pursue the hearings: [50]

So far as the Senate Committee's investigation is concerned, Mr. Wilson's relation to the treaties is a minor matter of hardly any importance compared with the whole story of international banking and its relation to war. That story has not yet been told in full. If it cost the United States $100,000,000, and if it helped keep us out of another war, it would be the best investment the Senate had made in many a day; but actually it will cost but a few thousands. The investigation should go on. The Senate should vote the necessary funds.

The *Nation* began headlining the findings of the Nye Committee before the others on the banking question. On January 22, 1936 it printed Walter Millis' exhaustive article, "The Last War and the Next: Morgan, Money and War," [51] which supported Nye to the hilt and added a few new bits of information as well. Millis was enjoying unbounded acclaim at the time as a result of his immensely popular book *Road to War*, by far the most critical work published describing America's slide into the world conflict in 1917. Editorially the *Nation* backed Nye and Millis but not without reservation on their black view of the part played by the Morgan financial interests and their involvement in the British cause. Its editorial "War Profits and Personal Devils" denied that this course was one of following a "narrow economic determinism" or of seeking to pin it all on "a single cause for our entrance into war," but in reality one of seeking to outline the "dynamic" of it all, which it found to be "the quest of American business for profits." It concluded, "The Nye Committee has rendered great service in verifying and publicizing this position," although it expressed unwillingness to accept Nye's seeming "attempt to establish a personal complicity of the Morgans in America's entrance into war." It thought that Millis had put it better, that the onus for precipitating the country into the war could not rightly be put upon "the House of Morgan," despite the fact that it was "almost fanatically pro-Ally," but "on our whole business system, caught as it was in the obscene scramble for war profits." [52]

Nation suspicions were boiling by this time that a concerted move was on to throttle the whole investigation. The contemporary publication of Charles Seymour's *American Neutrality, 1914–1917*, which again revived the wartime interpretation of blaming United States entry entirely upon the submarine warfare, and which surprisingly got the warm endorsement of Sidney B. Fay, the erstwhile academic leader of the revisionist history view which had always sniffed at this simple explanation, was one bit of evidence that a counter-movement was under way. [53] But the explosion of the Democratic Senators upon Nye's placing on the record Wilson's knowledge of the secret treaties was even better and more surprising evidence. In its January 29 editorial, "The Uses of Woodrow Wilson," it denounced the

attack on Nye led by Glass and Senator Tom Connally as a thinly disguised preface to a drive to stop the entire procedure. The editors
believed that Nye had committed a serious tactical mistake, but
refused to concede a jot to the forces wishing to end the inquiry; [54]

The Nye investigation must proceed on a broadened base of investigation—*but it must proceed.* If the Senators carry out Senator Glass's threat
of cutting off the funds of the Committee they will show that they are
motivated more by fear of disclosures than by reverence for the dead.

Villard's "A Measure of America's Betrayal" in the same issue put
his contempt for Glass and the other defenders of Wilson on the
record. He went into a detailed account of the wide contemporary
knowledge of the secret treaties which Glass and others were now
claiming that Wilson did not know about, and insisted that the
wartime President had not revealed his awareness of them for fear
of being denounced. For their placing of this incident on the record,
Villard stirringly commended the Munitions Investigating Committee, and insisted that Nye and Clark should be awarded the Newman
Foundation's gold medal "for the most outstanding and distinguished
service rendered to our country and to humanity" during 1935.[55]

In February the *New Republic*'s widely-quoted "T.R.B." and
Flynn columns spent extended space on the topic and vigorously
defended Nye and just as energetically attacked Morgan and Nye's
congressional opponents. "T.R.B." thought it especially ironic that
the Congress should be considering at that moment a neutrality law
for the country designed to prevent American involvement in a
future war, a distinct possibility then, in view of the ominous situation in Europe over the Italo-Ethiopian crisis. From his point of view
all this legislative effort seemed quite superfluous and irrelevant,
when placed alongside what Nye was dredging up on the last war
involving the United States: [56]

The reason for the Nye investigation, and for the neutrality bill now
before Congress, is to prevent us from being drawn into a future foreign
war. . . . If the Nye Committee has made anything clear, it is that
American business men do not think that war trade is wrong, and are
prepared to accept as much of it as they can get. As long as men with such
a feeling about war are in control of the jobs and incomes of most of the
people of the country it is rash to believe that legislative safeguards can
protect us.

Flynn's double-length commentary two weeks later expressed vast
sympathy toward Nye and much hostility toward the bankers,[57] but
neither he nor his anonymous fellow-columnist approached the qual-

ity of praise for Nye which Charles A. Beard poured into a series of three articles in the *New Republic* beginning on March 4, 1936; nobody in the liberal journalistic field hailed the Committee so massively. Beard compared their revelations to the post-1917 diplomatic exposés in Eastern and Central Europe, and in some respects he thought the Nye findings even more informing on what had happened; in his view they had "made the files of contemporary newspapers look like superficial scribblings of ten year old children as far as actuality was concerned." [58] In the second of the series, Beard concluded that,[59]

it may be said that from the Nye papers we can know something about the history of 1914–1917 and the eminent gentlemen who played such a large part in making it. And the American people did not have to wait a hundred years to obtain this knowledge.

Common Sense gave full editorial stamp of approval to all phases of the Nye investigation, including the Morgan inquiry, and thought that the attack on Nye by Glass and other Democrats was a serious discredit to them. It pointed out that Nye had been corroborated by the recently published memoirs of Colonel House and Lloyd George, which none of the Senators seemed to have read, and could not discern what the meaning of this blow at Nye amounted to: [60]

The eleventh hour defense of the late President Wilson seems absurd on the face of the documentary evidence, which proves that he knew full well, though unofficially, of the London treaties of 1915. And pure sentimentality seems hardly reason for raising such a rumpus.

Common Sense hoped that the hearings would result in neutrality legislation which "would demand absolute isolation," and in April, 1936 strongly attacked FDR for not championing such a program. The relationship of the neutrality fight to the Nye hearings will be examined at length in a subsequent chapter.

The week the *New Republic* began publishing Beard's glowing acclaim of the Nye Committee findings, the *Nation* printed a generous dispatch by Harold Laski on the analogous situation in England, and he could find nothing complimentary to say. Laski was utterly opposed to the Baldwin government's conducting such an investigation, because he thought it would result in a total whitewash of the British record. "We shall have to wait until after the next war to get at the facts," he morosely concluded.[61] It goes without saying that in Britain no investigation followed the "next war," the unsullied "people's war" which obtained Laski's complete and vociferous support.

As for the revival of the single-causation school of history which blamed United States entry upon the German submarine warfare, the *New Republic* in mid-May, 1936 thought that Nye had quite well punctured that by reproducing the files of the post-war Senate Foreign Relations Committee, which contained Wilson's declaration upon a question by Senator McCumber that he thought the United States would have gotten into the war regardless of submarines or even the most blameless German behavior toward United States citizens.[62]

Throughout the late spring and early summer of 1936 material in support of Nye and critical of his targets regularly appeared in the *New Republic*. A May 13 editorial demolished the Morgan defense against the Nye accusations; although agreeing that the United States entered the World War for complex reasons, it refused to discount the financial circumstances, "among which was undoubtedly the fact that our commercial and financial interests were inextricably bound up with the cause of the Allies." [63] When the Committee's report was issued in June, a full editorial commendation promptly appeared, supporting its chastisement of the Morgan interests, which obviously had not dragged the country into war but had used their position "to steer us bit by bit to a situation from which there was no way out but war," as well as expressing full agreement with the Committee's conclusion that Wilson "as early as 1916 had determined to bring this country into war." [64]

It no longer considered the case of Senator Glass against the Committee worth a particle, especially after the publication in the London *Telegraph* of a biography of Lord Balfour by his niece, a Mrs. Blanche E. C. Dugdale, in which the fact that Balfour had told Wilson about the secret treaties was established in painful detail. In its editorial view Glass had done Nye an injury by denouncing him for insisting on this before and for maintaining that Wilson had not told a post-war Senate Committee the truth, and it did not spare Glass in the least: [65]

It is easy to understand the attitude of Senator Glass and other followers of President Wilson. Loyalty to a dead friend is certainly an admirable trait. That loyalty, however, should not be carried to the length of flying in the face of historical facts and denying the testimony of every witness qualified to comment. Sooner or later, Senator Glass will be forced to make either tacit or open retractions. Meanwhile his effort to halt the munitions enquiry must remain an ineradicable blot upon his record.

At this moment, with liberals of all hues in general agreement with the worthiness of the Nye Committee and in accord that its revelations were of first-rank importance to the nation, the feeling could not be dismissed that powerful opposition existed, and that a goodly portion of it rested within the Roosevelt Administration and the Democratic Party and not just in the beleaguered heavy industries businesses. Thus, while all the superficial signs of victory waved, underneath the vague presentiment of coming defeat could not be entirely smothered.

FROM HEROES TO ''SUBVERSIVES'':
THE DENOUEMENT OF THE NYE INVESTIGATIONS

Despite the sensational changes of scenery in the Nye agenda, the liberal press did not lose sight of their major objective and contention. The expectation that the arms business would either be nationalized or surrounded by stern governmental controls was never far below the surface of all discussions of the munitions investigation. However, a bad traffic jam eventually ensued on the recommendation thoroughfare, and it was soon obvious that no real foresight had been made recourse to by the liberal reformers. With rival investigators releasing their legislative suggestions and with Congress fabricating a variety of bills which all went far beyond what the opponents of the arms trade had originally envisioned, it began to dawn upon some of the most enthusiastic that out of all this uproar might come plans for a national regulation and mobilization in case of another war that would render the previous circumstances ideal by comparison. Each new suggestion of production, profit or income control related to war and war goods making invariably led to the addition of objectionable riders taking action far beyond where it had been expected to be concentrated. And the rising concern over the foreign policy actions of Germany, Italy and Japan did not result in a climate of opinion where what was wanted as future policy could be soberly discussed. So the Nye recommendations were eventually subjected to such a number of ingenious turnings and polishings that the final product was all but unrecognizable when matched with the early depression liberal asseverations.

In the New Year's Day, 1936 issue of the *Nation,* Engelbrecht published a generous article outlining a separate and independent plan for the control of the sale of arms in advance of an expectedly significant majority recommendation of the Nye Committee, with the objectives of bringing "the arms industry into line with national policy" and also to police the industry internally.[66] With a great commotion loose over the possibility of United States aid getting into the hands of Italy in its war in Ethiopia, there was an immediate as well as a remote goal in the minds of some of the builders of putative fences around America's war materials potential. But this plan did not rouse up anywhere near the enthusiasm of the Committee majority recommendation in April for nationalizing munitions manufacturing and naval construction, which the *Nation* described in enthusiastic editorial endorsement as "an event of the first importance." [67]

The next month, during debate on the Administration's current tax measure, there was another occasion to praise Nye, when his Committee prepared a wartime tax-on-income bill which it hoped to attach to the over-all bill, calling among other things for a 90% tax in wartime on incomes larger than $10,000. "T.R.B." in the June 3, 1936 *New Republic* exclaimed vehemently that "If this bill can be passed—and if industrialists can be made to believe that it will be enforced—it ought to serve permanently to diminish propaganda for war." [68] This preceded by a few weeks the report to the Senate by the Munitions Investigating Committee, which the *New Republic* on July 1 warmly praised, while uttering the marginal comment that "The Committee is dealing with the realities of government, not its surface trifles."

But other centers of recommendation activity were alerted by now, and a defensive note was soon to be heard, presaging an almost entirely protective approach within a year. Liberals were diverted from their own campaigning against the untrammelled "merchants of death" to a fight against a concept of socio-politico-military mobilization and regulation growing up alongside it which shocked them profoundly. Of first rank here was the Industrial Mobilization Plan of the War Department, reported on for the Nye Committee by Senator Bennett Champ Clark unfavorably, and similarly condemned by the *New Republic* early in January 1937. Its editorial was sure that its adoption would result in "the people of the country being hogtied by industry during a war," and expressed the conviction that the War Department was "showing industry how to tie the strongest possible knots." It applauded Senator Clark's observation that in the light of this plan, should America become involved in another conflict, "the price of war may be actual operating dictatorship, under military control." [69]

The next month the *Nation* gave extended space to Raushenbush's disconcerted article "Kill the Conscription Bill," a bitter attack on the proposed Hill-Sheppard Bill calling for conscription of manpower and several comprehensive economic restraints in time of war. He maintained the bill would make the President "an absolute monarch" in time of war, which he quoted Irénée du Pont as recommending, and he denounced Baruch for supporting this measure. The Nye Committee's chief counsel was convinced the Hill-Sheppard Bill would have absolutely no effect on curbing war profits in any event.[70]

Editorially the *Nation* rejected the bill as a "blueprint for fascism," but it similarly described and turned down a parallel bill proposed by Nye and Maverick, and felt that if either were adopted, it would not take the profits out of war but would serve as efficient vehicles to make it possible for the country "to pass promptly and smoothly to a war footing."

In early March, 1937 the *New Republic* commented on the latest proposal to emerge from the Nye Committee, a variant of its previous proposal of a year before, a declaration that the United States build its own factories and shipyards for the production of the military supplies and naval vessels it would find necessary. The editorial did not discuss the implication that the privately owned firms in America might still manufacture such products for foreign customers, and that public ownership of arms factories for domestic use was no automatic guarantee that war would not occur, but it approved such a course and declared that there were "great advantages" in it, and no discernible objections; "If there is any valid argument against the Nye proposal, we do not know what it is." [71]

The offensive against the "merchants of death" was nearing its peak among liberals by this time, and although there appeared to be a diminution in the amount of material devoted to it, this was not so.[72] The stifling of the drive against the private manufacture of arms among liberals was not to begin until the end of 1937, achieved not so much by the resourcefulness of the opposition as by the self-applied chokers of Communist-oriented "Popular Front" propaganda and the growth of militant concern for the safety of Soviet Russia and the Communist-led wars in Spain and China.

Senator Nye was still a highly preferred person to the *Nation* at the end of 1936. He was prominently enshrined in its "Honor Roll for 1936" in the issue of January 2, 1937 [73] and was one of a dozen well-known public figures asked to contribute to a symposium titled "What I Expect of Roosevelt," after FDR's re-election in November. On the subject of arms limitation and the likely course in foreign affairs, Nye wrote,[74]

The largest field for progressive action is offered by the prevention of war. America must not be drawn into other people's wars, to the destruction of whatever economic balance may have been restored after the last war. A strict neutrality policy of a mandatory rather than discretionary type must be resorted to if we would avoid seeing our appetite for trade outweigh our appetite for neutrality and peace. While the maintenance of an adequate national defense is essential, Americans must now realize it as the cloak of interests profiting from mad armament races. Strong legislation against the influence of profit both in war and in preparation for it is very necessary, but I fear that in these fields the Administration will be found painfully compromising.

Nye was able to spell this out a few months later when the *Nation* published his review of the just-issued book *The Tragic Fallacy* by Mauritz Hallgren. Hallgren's main thesis was that United States military policy was almost entirely unconcerned with home defense or the fear of invasion, but was really being built around a plan for "another holy war," "a swift expedition to war abroad." Hallgren, in his bitter attack on the Roosevelt Administration's rearmament-defense program, boldly charged that this war was to be fought in Asia, that Japan had already been selected as the enemy, and that although it was going to be fought in the guise of "another crusade to save democracy," it might likely end up in dictatorship in America. Both the reviews by Nye and by William T. Stone of the Foreign Policy Association in the *New Republic* were unreservedly laudatory; said Nye, "Never was a finer job of debunking our so-called national defense policy done than that undertaken and completed by the author of this work." [75]

A short time before, Nye had reviewed for the *New Republic* the ponderous book by Philip Noël-Baker, *The Private Manufacture of Armaments,* the most thoroughly documented attack published in the entire period. Nye's extended review described it as the best single book on the subject, and was equalled in his endorsement only by Raushenbush, who reviewed it for the *Nation.*[76] Thus, less than six months before the Chicago Bridge speech of the President, the principal liberal publications were still whole-heartedly in support of the principles of the Nye recommendations, and the theory that the Administration was not following a candid course of seeking no involvement in future wars abroad.

A querulous note shimmered through both journals in the summer of 1937 on the subject of Nye and domestic affairs, especially after his reference in July to the National Labor Relations Board as "a C.I.O. adjunct." The *Nation* took quick exception to this, while "T.R.B." spoke hesitatingly of him as having "the reputation of being liberal" and a friend "of the common voter"; there seemed to be grounds for doubt now.[77] But liberal sensitiveness toward any criticism of the President on domestic issues had grown prodigiously in the past six months, especially since the brassy wrangle over the Supreme Court "packing" plan and the plummeting of the economy again, even though there were voices of dissent still about. The combination of this, the growing commitment to Popular Front "collective security" and the President's radical turn of foreign policy direction in October, 1937 more or less ended the *Nation*'s four-year comradeship with Nye, but in the *New Republic,* which did not follow this change of line, he remained a respected figure. The only exception in the *Nation* was Villard, who did not agree with editorial policy, and who retained an unchanged attitude of high regard for Nye, even though there appeared to be dwindling hope for the eventual success of his aims.

Villard's February 26, 1938 column contained a warm plea to all American liberals to work to get Nye re-elected to the Senate. It was his view that the whole country had a stake in his return to another term in the fall, because he had been and was still "a great leader in the fight for peace." [78] Despite the growing split among the liberals on the merits of the "Popular Front" and the Administration's adventuresome edging toward active intervention in world affairs, the work of the Nye Committee had not entirely sunk out of sight. When Nye was successful in getting the nomination in the summer, defeating William L. Langer, the Governor of North Dakota, Villard exulted, and suggested that the event "ought to be a cause of widespread rejoicing," admitting that he had gained the distrust and dislike of "those liberals who regard him as a dangerous isolationist," which was a delicate way of describing what the pro-Soviet collective security drive had done to the once-solid liberal position on Nye and non-involvement in war.[79] In 1935 the liberal press had scorned Nye's enemies as hated "economic royalists." The exigencies of Russian security had now furnished them with a band of odd allies from the heart of the very camp which had once comprised their most implacable opponents.

The full measure of this was realized already by that part of the liberal sector which for some time was aware that the strongest pressure for American involvement in a new war now came not from the group of the business and financial community which had been so drastically keelhauled by the Nye Committee but from the elements of the left which had become so desperately attached emotionally to Russian Communism. And it was displayed in the *New Republic* in the summer of 1938 in unmistakable clarity. Popular Frontism was to prevent the possibility of a "merchants-of-death" explanation of the coming of World War Two among liberals, nor have any of them attempted such an analysis in the two decades since it began.

The incident which led to the *New Republic*'s new look at the causes and likely adherents of a new war was John T. Flynn's April 6, 1938 column, devoted to a reminiscence of his part as chairman of a committee which drew up an anti-war-profits measure for the Nye Committee as it was closing out its investigation. Flynn contrasted his bill with one credited to Baruch, which had proposed a price ceiling at the start of the war, plus widespread governmental powers to commandeer industries and furnish preferential priorities to industries in "essential war production," and so forth. Flynn pointed out that this was strongly inflationary, and that as the government borrowed and farmed out the funds to its favored war industries, these funds would filter from them to the buyers of the products of peace industries, resulting in comprehensive price climbs.

Flynn explained that his plan was based on the refusal to pay for a war with borrowed funds but to "pay for it as we fight it," out of steeply increased taxes. Price control would be no good if at the same time the government flooded the economy with vast purchasing power from borrowed origins. Such a bill as his for the Nye Committee he thought was currently being sponsored by Senator Connally, which would establish "a set of tax rates which will make it impossible for any man to prosper during the war." [80] Editorially the *New Republic* approved of Flynn's bill to finance new wars entirely out of taxes, but doubted seriously that adoption of such a program by law would have any effect on *avoiding* war. And in a comment on June 8, 1938 on Flynn's proposal and on a new bill reported by the Senate Finance Committee which would have *required* people to loan their money to the government in proportion to their wealth at 1½ per cent interest and in non-tax-exempt bonds, its realization of the immediate political realities and the change of wind since 1934 was made extremely plain. Beside the fact that this latter proposal of forced loans was in fact a capital levy, there was a now-untenable thesis behind it; such measures, the editorial went on,[81]

rest on the supposition that war is caused in large measure by the pressure of those who expect to make money out of it. This thesis is a tremendous oversimplification, as may be seen when we remember that one of the strongest influences in the direction of possible participation in war at present is exerted by those pacifists who favor collective action against aggressors. Among these no group is more active than the Communists, who cannot be accused of seeking profits.

Other than completely missing the point of the American Communist eagerness for war with Russia's most threatening enemies, the *New Republic* had in three sentences utterly smashed nearly a decade of liberal theorizing on the origins of modern war. Its only remaining act was conversion to the new course itself, which was a fact upon the elapsing of two more years.

But in the meantime the "merchants-of-death" proposition enjoyed moments of indulgence, albeit brief ones, even in the *Nation,* which soon found Senator Nye almost unbearable, and which sounded more and more like a recruiting bulletin as 1939 wore on and the war approached with calm steady tread. Frank Hanighen, whose famous book written in conjunction with Engelbrecht in 1934 had started the wide use of the term, wrote on the subject repeatedly, startling the *Nation* in February, 1939 with a revealing article on the hustling Franco-German trade in metals and munitions at that moment, as well as documenting that the Hitler and Mussolini regimes had been and were still shipping arms to both sides in the Spanish Civil War, still in progress.[82] Such pesky journalism did great damage to the sharp ideological portraits which the Popular Front exigencies had forced upon liberal thinking, but it was not intended to produce any significant re-thinking of positions, since a substantial part of American liberalism had all the intellectual ammunition it needed to see it through an extended war as long as it was fought on left versus right stereotypes prepared long before.

On February 28, 1939 Nye expressed a statement to the press that he was convinced there would be no war in Europe "unless and until one side in Europe can have assurance that the United States is going to stand ready to assist them in that war," and that if the "democracies" got hope of United States support they would refuse further concessions and war would result. This infuriated the *Nation,* which denounced him in an angry editorial on March 11, particularly for his suggesting that any further cessions, revisions or boundary adjustments were necessary.[83] The *Nation* had been exceeded by no paper in the Western Hemisphere in its explosive language over the Munich agreement of the previous September, and with the Germans now seeking an adjustment of their boundary grievances with Poland, it seemed too much for anyone as prominent as Nye to remark in America that this process might go on another step. In addition, immediately to the east of Poland was Communist Russia.

The scrambling of liberal America by the Russo-German Pact of August, 1939, from which it has not yet recovered, will be examined in detail elsewhere, but with the coming of war and the two-year battle between interventionists and non-interventionists for the allegiance of the mass of Americans, the era of under-the-surface investigations of tendencies toward war involvement abruptly ended for liberals and disappeared from their publications as if they were the prefaces of obscene jokes. The simple and superficial reasons for fighting returned to vogue with a vengeance, and have luxuriated ever since.

On July 10, 1940, with the war well under way, with the German armies in possession of Western Europe and a stunning campaign of sentimentalism for France and England sweeping the United States, and with a large part of the most articulate of American liberals more eager to fight than almost any other segment of the populace, a bit of news seeped into the daily press: the Federal Bureau of Investigation was said to be investigating Senator Gerald P. Nye for alleged "pro-Nazi leanings." The *New Republic,* still not entirely intellectually convinced of the necessity of American involvement, apparently was struck by a pang of remembrance of more congenial days, and commented on this adversely and angrily; [84]

> This is indeed an odd piece of business. . . . He is of course one of the chief isolationists in the Senate who has bitterly opposed Mr. Roosevelt's foreign policy; but it is a big jump from the fact to an accusation of lack of patriotism. . . . Somebody owes Mr. Nye and the country an explanation of the whole affair.

The subject got no further than this, and there was no subsequent raking over of this incident. But the transformation of the decade could not have been made more dramatically conspicuous.

But the next year, with the *New Republic* more anxious for war between the United States and Germany than three-quarters of the New York daily newspapers, came the last bit of the arc describing a one hundred and eighty degree turn since the investigation of America's entry into the World War in 1917 began. Senator Homer Bone of Washington, once the most highly praised member of the Nye Committee in its heyday, by the entire liberal press, was now savagely blistered as a "fervid isolationist" in the course of a comprehensive attack on the Senate Interstate Commerce Committee for investigating charges that the moving pictures and radio were being used as instruments of propaganda to get the United States involved in the war actively.

The demise of the "merchants-of-death" theory among liberals as a prominent cause of war was due to a variety of factors, undoubtedly, but three stand out especially in the 1937–1939 and 1939–1941 periods: the function performed by the Communist-directed Chinese and Spanish Civil Wars, which softened up the "imperialist war" slogans and posed the vision of an idealistic, altruistic "people's war"; the fright and alarm over what was interpreted as a steady worsening of the cause of the Soviet Union due to its internal purges and the repeated diplomatic triumphs of Germany, which indicated that fighting on Russia's behalf might be necessary in the near future; and after the war had gotten under way, the conviction that the political ascendancy of British Left-Laborites in the Churchill war government in England gave promise of a Marxian Socialist regime at the end of a putative successful war over Germany. These will be submitted to extended review in subsequent chapters, but the subjects immediately related to the Nye Committee, the flowering and eclipse of the revisionist history of the First World War and the installation of the respectability of armament, come next under purview.

NOTES

1 Jan Relling, "The Political Connections Of the International Armament Firms," *The Communist,* June, 1933, pp. 583–589, was one of the first revivals of the arms story since 1927, even though several books and articles had been published overseas in the interval, as Relling's bibliographical references indicate. Much of the flavor of *Merchants Of Death* and *"Arms and the Men"* can be discerned in this path-breaking article.

2 See Seymour Waldman, *Death and Profits: A Study Of the War Policies Commission* (Brewer, Warren and Putnam), reviewed by Oswald Garrison Villard in *Nation,* February 22, 1933, p. 212.

3 *Nation,* July 8, 1931, p. 28, for citations in paragraph below.

4 *Nation,* October 14, 1931, p. 378.

5 *Nation,* October 26, 1932, pp. 384–385.

6 "Munitions and Peace," *Nation,* January 4, 1933, p. 5.

7 *Nation,* January 18, 1933, p. 48.

8 See note 2, above.

9 *Nation,* May 31, 1933, p. 600.

10 *New Republic,* February 21, 1934, pp. 30–31.

11 *Nation,* February 28, 1934, p. 236.

12 *Nation,* April 25, 1934, p. 455.

13 *Nation,* May 9, 1934, p. 519.

14 "The Munitions Message," *Nation,* May 30, 1934, p. 607.

15 "The Munitions Investigation," *Nation,* September 12, 1934, p. 284.

16 *Nation,* September 19, 1934, p. 313.

17 "Death Business Again," *Nation,* December 19, 1934, p. 699. The editors were especially angered by reports that ex-Army and Navy officers were in China teaching aviation to Chinese in Chiang Kai-shek's army and that American planes were going there, reportedly being utilized exclusively against the population of the Soviet districts.

18 *New Republic,* January 16, 1935, p. 259.

19 "Nationalize the Arms Industry!," *Nation,* December 26, 1934, p. 726.

20 MacDonald, "Fortune Magazine," *Nation,* May 8, 1937, pp. 527–530.

21 Pp. 649–659.

22 Howe review of Engelbrecht and Hanighen titled "Government By Ghouls," *New Republic,* May 2, 1934, p. 342; his review of Seldes titled "The Secret International," *New Republic,* May 16, 1934, p. 24.

23 *Nation,* May 23, 1934, p. 597.

24 The Carlson-Bates chapters appeared in the May, June and August, 1935 issues. See also comment on British rearmament in *Common Sense,* June, 1935, p. 5.

25 *New Republic,* May 23, 1934, pp. 32–33.

26 Stone, "Exposing the Death Business," *Nation,* October 3, 1934, pp. 376–378.

27 June 1932, pp. 753–769.

28 *Nation,* June 29, 1932, pp. 713–714.

29 *New Republic,* September 26, 1934, p. 180.

30 *Nation,* March 14, 1934, pp. 299–301.

31 See report of Second United States Congress Against War and Fascism, *New Masses,* October 2, 1934, p. 3.

32 *Nation,* June 6, 1934, pp. 646–648.

33 *Nation,* November 28, 1934, p. 604.

34 *New Republic,* December 19, 1934, p. 152.

35 *Nation,* July 4, 1934, pp. 2–3.

36 See note 19, above.

37 *New Republic,* January 2, 1935, pp. 204–205.

38 *New Republic,* December 26, 1934, p. 175.

39 *Nation,* January 30, 1935, p. 113.

40 *New Republic,* February 20, 1935, p. 34; for an earlier suggestion of similar content see *New Republic,* May 30, 1934, p. 57.

41 *New Republic,* February 27, 1935, pp. 64–66, for citations in above paragraph.

42 *New Republic,* April 3, 1935, p. 198.
43 *Nation,* April 3, 1935, p. 377.
44 *Nation,* April 17, 1935, p. 456.
45 "Should Wealth Be Conscripted?," *Nation,* April 24, 1935, p. 469.
46 See Walter Wilson, "Capital's Fight Against A Draft Law," *New Masses,* August 27, 1935, pp. 14–17.
47 *Nation,* May 1, 1935, pp. 504–505; *New Republic,* May 1, 1935, p. 324.
48 "Bigger Than the Government," *Nation,* May 8, 1935, p. 524.
49 "Mr. Lansing's Unneutrality," *New Republic,* September 4, 1935, p. 90.
50 "President Wilson Stops An Inquiry," *New Republic,* January 29, 1936, pp. 326–327; see also editorial in same issue, p. 321.
51 *Nation,* January 22, 1936, pp. 95–98.
52 *Nation,* January 22, 1936, p. 89.
53 *Nation,* January 22, 1936, pp. 109–110.
54 *Nation,* January 29, 1936, p. 116.
55 *Nation,* January 29, 1936, p. 119.
56 *New Republic,* February 5, 1936, pp. 363–365.
57 Flynn's remarks in column, *New Republic,* February 19, 1936, pp. 46–47; "T.R.B.", "The Nye Committee Points The Way," p. 45 of same issue.
58 Beard, "Peace For America," *New Republic,* March 4, 1936, pp. 100–103.
59 Beard, "Solving Domestic Crisis By War," *New Republic,* March 11, 1936, pp. 127–129. Beard put this in classic form just before the outbreak of the war in his "Giddy Minds and Foreign Quarrels," *Harper's,* September, 1939, pp. 337–351. See also Hubert Herring, "Charles A. Beard," *Harper's,* May, 1939, pp. 629–652.
60 *Common Sense,* March, 1936, p. 4.
61 Laski, "The British Arms Inquiry," *Nation,* March 4, 1936, pp. 272–273.
62 *New Republic,* May 13, 1936, p. 19.
63 *New Republic,* May 13, 1936, p. 6.
64 "The Munitions Committee Reports," *New Republic,* July 1, 1936, p. 229.
65 "Balfour On the Secret Treaties," *New Republic,* June 10, 1936, p. 117.
66 Engelbrecht, "How to Control the Sale Of Arms," *Nation,* January 1, 1936, pp. 10–12.
67 *Nation,* April 29, 1936, p. 533.
68 "Nye's War On War," *New Republic,* June 3, 1936, p. 101.
69 *New Republic,* January 13, 1937, p. 312.
70 *Nation,* February 27, 1937, pp. 236–238.
71 *New Republic,* March 10, 1937, p. 150.
72 See Hanighen, "Arming the Industrialists," *Nation,* August 22, 1936, pp. 209–210.
73 "Honor Roll For 1936," *Nation,* January 2, 1937, p. 7.
74 *Nation,* November 28, 1936, p. 627.
75 Nye review of Hallgren in *Nation,* April 24, 1937, p. 479; Stone review of Hallgren in *New Republic,* May 12, 1937, pp. 25–26.
76 Nye review of Noël-Baker in *New Republic,* March 24, 1937, p. 216; Raushenbush review of Noël-Baker in *Nation,* April 17, 1937, p. 439.
77 *Nation,* July 31, 1937, p. 114; *New Republic,* August 18, 1937, p. 45.
78 *Nation,* February 26, 1938, p. 245.
79 *Nation,* July 23, 1938, p. 89.
80 Flynn, "A Bill To Dull the Appetite For War," *New Republic,* April 6, 1938, p. 274.
81 *New Republic,* June 8, 1938, p. 114.
82 Hanighen, "Arms-Makers' Holiday," *Nation,* February 18, 1939, pp. 199–201.
83 "Arms and Isolation," *Nation,* March 11, 1939, p. 280.
84 *New Republic,* July 22, 1940, p. 101.

16

THE FATE OF REVISIONIST HISTORY DURING THE GREAT LIBERAL TRANSFORMATION, 1935–1941

THE revision of the story of how the First World War came about and how the United States became involved in it has been described briefly elsewhere, with special emphasis on the health and progress of this literary enterprise at the time the structure of the world which grew out of its settlements began to crumble in 1931 and for a few years thereafter. Its steady growth and vogue paralleled the Nye Committee, and in many ways the two shared fortunes and misfortunes, and their dizzying rises and precipitous declines took place in virtually simultaneous relation to each other. Both took nourishment and buttressing from each other, and they shared alike the tumultuous liberal acceptance and the sudden liberal repudiation. In the case of revision, there has never been in American experience a school of historical interpretation more seemingly incapable of being dislodged which went into such swift oblivion. Its quick death by the strangulation of silence, mainly at the hands of the very group which had done by far the most to establish its intellectual respectability, makes it a worthy case study to accompany the saga of the Nye hearings as beacons to light the path American liberalism took on its road back to war.

In many ways the re-opening of the whole agenda of 1914–1918 by Senator Nye and his colleagues paved the way for a number of fresh studies of the period especially from the angle of American experiences. Their main impact was to imprint more firmly the impressions which the fifteen years between the Armistice and the Nye hearings had already well burned into the literate consciousness. Much new evidence, ably placed on the record by the employment of the dramatic novelties which had been adopted by American journalism in the interim, gave it a somewhat wider audience, and, aided by the pocket magazines and the innovations of public opinion polls, seemed to guarantee the permanent survival of revisionist findings in the national intellectual arsenal. But the two-year assault on the consciousness of the American public prior to December 7, 1941 is a glowing testament to the proposition that public opinion is a product of propaganda, in demonstrating so dramatically how quickly an image could be erased from consideration.

The last stage of revisionist scholarship and writing, between the Nye hearings and the involvement of the United States in the Second World War, dwelled heavily on the thesis of mixed reasons for American involvement in the First, with heavy emphasis on economic factors as a substantial source of influence in edging the United States toward ultimate participation, along with added stress on the propaganda of the Allied countries and other tangible factors, and the disparagement or dismissal of previous explanations, especially the enlistment-poster idealism and the German submarines, which had served as contemporary interpretation. A second major aspect of revisionism in this time was related to one of its earliest themes, the responsibility of the treaties ending the war for the greatest part of the melancholy state of affairs which had promptly ensued everywhere. This latter thesis, emphasizing the injustice of the treaties and implying the necessity of their revision if pressures leading to new wars were to be drawn off, was the one which became most unpalatable to the pro-involvement portion of articulate liberalism as a new war approached between practically the same lineup of nations as before. Its dismissal in order to make the new war appear to be a unique and utterly unrelated event was imperative, and in the effort, a large part of the entire liberal rationale on war in the generic sense was obliterated. The delicate treading of liberals through the battlefields of the world since 1945, applying a weak pragmatic yardstick to new conflicts and groping for the long-lost pre-1937 position, has indeed been a distressing sight when compared with the two decades of open-eyed, adamantine sureness which followed 1917.

At the zenith of the Nye Committee's popularity in the spring of 1935 there appeared what is probably the most widely distributed and read revisionist book ever published, Walter Millis' *Road to War. Nation* editor Charles Angoff's adulatory review was headed "Road to National Insanity," a paraphrase of William Allen White's tribute quoted by the publishers, Houghton Mifflin; "This is a story of a nation that went mad," said Angoff without qualification. "His book forms a valuable record of one of the most insane periods in our national history." [1] The same exceedingly high praise appeared in *Common Sense*,[2] while the book drew a full-page two-column review in the May 8, 1935 *New Republic* by C. Hartley Grattan, a first-rank revisionist writer himself, who added this observation: [3]

> It will not, however, have its full possible effect if its readers do not apply the ideas it suggests to the contemporary scene. Today while Congress is talking more and more about measures to preserve our neutrality, it is also voting bigger and bigger appropriations for the army and navy. Only the pro-war aspects of Roosevelt's program seem to be a howling success. As the world approaches the rapids, the American people find themselves in charge of men hardly more fitted to keep them out of war than the rulers of 1914–1917.

But at this date a warning of this kind still seemed far more Cassandra-like than the circumstances tended to indicate.

Very little literary evidence existed or was contemporarily appearing which suggested anything but a deepening of the spirit of skepticism, and liberal writers, reviewers and publications showed a unanimity here which appeared in few if any other contexts. Harry Elmer Barnes, reviewing G. Bernard Noble's *Policies and Opinions at Paris, 1919,* stressed the other main point in the revisionist case. His May 1, 1935 *Nation* review described the mellowing of one of the American academic participants at the despised Versailles Treaty proceedings: [4]

> Professor Noble had many advantages in writing a book on the Versailles settlement. He possessed full knowledge of the facts and was sufficiently removed from the events to have the perspective that was denied the authors of the crop of books that appeared from 1919 to 1921. And while he was one of the shipload of "performing professors" who went to Paris with Wilson after the war, there is little evidence in the book that he still points with pride in the classroom to his part in making the treaty. . . . He ascribes the moral and diplomatic debacle partially to selfish patriotism of the European peacemakers and partly to the necessity of "pacifying the animals" in a democratic system. War propaganda of years' standing had created a mass savagery and greed that had to be appeased. . . .

Other memoirs by more prominent figures furnished material for successive piling up of corroborative evidence. Villard later in the month hailed Frederick Palmer's book on General Tasker Bliss, *Bliss, Peacemaker,* and described the subject as "a really humane man who truly hated the war business." [5] Others did not share this reception but their revelations were accepted in the same spirit. An example of this was the reaction to the publication in the fall of 1935 of the long-awaited *War Memoirs of Robert Lansing;* Grattan poured vitriol on Lansing in the *New Republic,* holding up to special scorn his admitted unneutral and pro-British position, and his persistence in dwelling on idealistic explanations for American fighting after twenty years of exposure of other motives.[6] By far the blackest reception was that of Villard in the *Nation,* who fumed at Lansing's unconscious disclosure of "deceit and double dealing" upon issue after issue. He especially resented Wilson's second Secretary of State for his concealing the strong American case against England between 1914 and 1916, charging that he had done this in order that American public opinion might have more time to get inflamed at Germany, and that Wilson might have kept the United States out by revealing this "to balance the injury done to us by the Germans." [7] With Congress just passing a neutrality bill, Villard thought this was an appropriate and timely publication, underlining congressional insistence during the just-broken-out Italo-Ethiopian war on American neutrality as proof that "some Americans in official life are determined not to have the wool pulled over their eyes again."

A week later Villard added to the impressive pile of tributes paid to Millis' work, which he referred to as "that extraordinarily useful and truthful book," and described as "an absolute justification of the pacifist position." [8] When Thomas W. Lamont of the Morgan banking interests protested to the New York *Times* over a review of Millis written by R. L. Duffus which Lamont considered an unfair reflection on the firm and its part in the War, Villard counterattacked at once, and took especial umbrage at Lamont's justification of the Morgan part in ultimately bringing about Anglo-American accord on the war. He returned to this subject again later in the year, chastising Lamont and others for speaking of their efforts as "serving humanity" and supporting "Good against Evil": [9]

Unfortunately for this argument, time, the remorseless, has passed judgment. We know that humanity was not served, and if the members of the House of Morgan had had vision at the time, they would have known that you cannot advance the welfare of the world by wholesale slaughter; that you cannot cure war by war, or do else than debase all mankind in the futile effort to shoot goodness and virtue and your point of view into those whom you consider erring human beings.

Still another opportunity was offered for Villard to press to the front in this peak period of criticism of America's having gone into the War when Professor Borchard of Yale testified before the Nye

Committee's rival House Committee on Foreign Affairs in January, 1936 and placed responsibility for American entry into the hostilities in 1917 on Wilson and his cabinet "because of their utter incompetence in handling the international situation"; Villard found it difficult to praise Borchard highly enough.[10]

In the opinion of some liberals, however, the most eloquent short summary of the revisionist position on United States entry into World War I ever published anywhere was Millis' *New Republic* article on July 31, 1935, a review which headed a series titled "Will We Stay Out of the Next War?" Millis maintained that we were fully in the war by 1915, by which time our economic power had been wholly devoted to it and the President emotionally enlisted on the side of the Allies, with the populace at large and the Administration no longer neutral either in sentiment or policy.[11]

The literary barrage grew in 1936, and liberal acceptance even strengthened. Grattan, reviewing the fifth volume of Ray Stannard Baker's *Life and Letters of Woodrow Wilson* in the January 22 *New Republic* announced, "the book is an explicit, extensive and forthright document of the 'revisionist' school of thought about our entrance into the World War. It takes into account all of the arguments advanced by the revisionists and sustains most of them." [12] The following month Bliven contributed a commendation of Will Irwin's *Propaganda and the News,* selecting for extra praise the latter part which discussed the lies of the propagandists in the World War. "It seems to me that all governments and all other power groups lie, consciously or unconsciously, all the time," the *New Republic*'s senior editor protested.[13] And Max Lerner, in his lead review in the *Nation* for April 29, 1936 of Granville Hicks's *John Reed: The Making of a Revolutionary,* even found a revisionist lesson here. Of Reed, Lerner declared, "Part of his genius lay in his being so terribly unfooled. 'This is not our War,' he kept saying, when everyone else was getting lost in a maze of sophistry and propaganda." Then in *Common Sense* for June, Richard L. Neuberger's "Integrity" paid high honor to Senator Harry Lane of Oregon for being one of the six senators to vote against a declaration of war in April, 1917, of which contingent only Norris of Nebraska survived at that moment.[14]

A new rash of disillusionist and revelatory books streamed out in the autumn. Early in September Martha Gruening called attention to Mary Master Needham's *Tomorrow To Fresh Fields,* a pacifist critique by a repentant believer in wartime propaganda,[15] but the most substantial book in this series was Alex Mathews Arnett's *Claude Kitchin and the Wilson War Policies,* which although it did not come out until 1937 was summarized in advance by Arnett for the *Nation* on September 26, 1936 in an article titled "The Sunrise Conference." [16] Arnett described an early morning conference in April

1916 between Wilson and Representatives Champ Clark, Claude Kitchin and Harold Flood at which Wilson was reputed to have pounded the table and urged them to use their influence to obtain an immediate declaration of war on Germany. Arnett credited these men with cooling Wilson off, and the article and the book created a substantial uproar among liberals, despite their long-accustomed attitude toward exposés of this kind. When Villard reviewed this book in June, 1937 he spared few superlatives; "No book we have had since Walter Millis' *Road to War* has brought out more clearly how a country may be misled into a war with which it has no concern," was part of his extended greeting to *Claude Kitchin*.[17]

The year was not without its vote of protests. Two principal objections to the revisionist tidal wave were Professor Seymour's *American Neutrality* and an 86-page article in *Foreign Affairs* by Newton D. Baker, two notable efforts to re-establish the official historiography on the War and the theory of sole causation via the German resumption of submarine warfare in January, 1917. Their deprecation of the recent emphasis on the economic pressures leading to entry and Baker's defense of Wilson as an innocent in the "sunrise conference" and their re-assertion of the validity of the submarine theory led to a flaying at the hands of the *Nation*,[18] while the *New Republic,* unintimidated by the eminence of the authors, summoned Grattan and Charles A. Beard to deal with both. Grattan charged Seymour with trying to dismiss the revisionist case "by resorting to verbal trickery," and wrote off Seymour and the now-converted Sidney B. Fay, who had reviewed this book most sympathetically, as a pair of "special pleaders" who had been very roughly handled by the evidence cited by Ray Stannard Baker.[19] Beard's "Five Pages From Newton D. Baker" in the October 7, 1936 *New Republic* reached a new high in attack-via-rebuttal in the struggle over revisionist history entrenchment. It was a straightforward and unyielding insistence on accepting the evidence presented by Nye, Ray Stannard Baker and Millis, among others.[20]

By the end of 1937, with the *Nation* fully caught up in the swelling Popular Front-collective security drive, and quite satisfied with the righteousness of the wars in Spain and China, it still retained enough of the animosity and recriminatory residues of the revisionist antagonism to Newton D. Baker to review his World War One record on the occasion of his death. An editorial on New Year's Day, 1938 described him as a "tired liberal" whose liberalism had not been "anchored in a continuing social movement," and commented unkindly on his part as a "pacifist and humanitarian" carrying through "a vast conscription drive" and ultimately jailing "hundreds of conscientious objectors"; "having accepted Wilson's approach toward an undemocratic war for democracy, he was caught in its logic." And to make it worse, the editorial concluded, he had clung to the Wilsonian tradition after the war where it was weakest, "in the field of international liberalism." [21]

The presence of academic notables such as Seymour and Fay returning to the wartime interpretation of American entry into the War was no indication of the general trend in professional circles. A substantial number of academic writers resisted this trend entirely. When Professor Bruce W. Knight of Dartmouth published his searingly satirical history of American conduct in the World War titled *How To Run a War* in the autumn of 1936, it was given the warmest of receptions by Maxwell S. Stewart in the *Nation,* in which he averred that the volume "should be compulsory reading for all Veterans of Foreign Wars." [22] The index of academic history writing on the War and American foreign policy was Seymour's Yale colleague Samuel F. Bemis' fiercely critical *Diplomatic History of the United States,* destined to be a most successful textbook. The review by Princeton Professor Edward Meade Earle, titled "Uncle Sam Belongs At Home," was a feature of the April 14, 1937 *New Republic,* and was an essay of unstinted admiration and approval. Earle warned the reader not to expect a stodgy and fence-straddling "moss-grown" history; "The author has a thesis to defend, and he defends it with spirit and vigor," and that more than half of the big volume was a critical account, verging on a virtual "indictment" of American foreign policy since the time of the Spanish American War. The kernel of the Bemis approach was outlined thusly: [23]

Like many others surveying the scene here and abroad, Professor Bemis believes that the continental foreign policy of Washington and the other Founding Fathers was and is fundamentally sound. To depart from it is to invite trouble. Professor Bemis is more than a little impatient with those who, with seductive phrases like "world power" and "coming of age," urge the United States to take its "proper place" in international affairs. He believes that our "proper place," to the exclusion of all others, is the continent of North America, and that we occupied it with notable success from colonial times until, roughly, 1898. Since then have occurred our most egregious, perhaps our only, mistakes in foreign policy.

Among the severe judgments by Bemis mentioned in the review were his views of the Spanish American War, an episode of "adolescent irresponsibility" and a "great aberration"; "the whole grandiose and sentimental floriation of the Open Door"; the "irresponsible" foreign policy of Theodore Roosevelt, who enjoyed the "exhilaration of mounting the new American steed of World Power," and whose actions, along with "vainglorious boasts *ex post facto,* destroyed the good reputation of the United States in Latin America and elsewhere." As for World War One, Earle observed, Bemis especially stressed the "diplomatic ineptitude" of *unconditional* entry into the conflict, at a time when the Allies could have been required to "pay almost any price" that Wilson might have chosen to name. Earle thought Bemis unusually charitable to refer to this only in the way he had, but felt he had condemned sufficiently "the blundering and insulting Immigration Act of 1924," which had "poisoned our relations with Japan."

When Raymond Leslie Buell reviewed Bemis with hostility and rancor in the *Yale Review*, Earle was incensed enough to write a lengthy letter in protest, which said in part,[24]

I find it difficult to resist the conclusion that Mr. Buell's real issue with Mr. Bemis arises out of two fundamentally different conceptions of sound American diplomacy. Mr. Buell believes passionately in internationalism and world organization. Mr. Bemis looks back regretfully on what he considers the failure of the League of Nations and other similar machinery. Mr. Bemis also thinks there is a good deal of loose thinking obscured by such phrases as "world power," "taking our place in the international community," and the like. Because Mr. Buell does not like Mr. Bemis's general approach to the problem he naturally finds fault with some of the conclusions.

In December, Earle reviewed the sixth volume of Baker's weighty work on Wilson, and found himself in agreement with the author's dark commentaries on Wilson and what he agreed were political errors in risking and losing America's neutrality in 1915 and 1916. Earle was in full sympathy with the efforts of Secretary of State Bryan, Senator Stone, and the Gore-McLemore resolution seeking to prevent the passage of United States citizens on belligerent ships, all of which Wilson was able to defeat.[25] Thus, although FDR had already signalled a possible foreign policy somersault of momentous proportions, a substantial number of academic notables were and continued to be deeply grounded in revisionism, and there were others to come. There was no rigid uniformity among them, and more than a number of minor heresies: Beard, for instance, in a *New Republic* article on March 10, 1937, "Why Did We Go To War?," made an issue out of denying that either unsullied noble ideals or dark economic greed were primarily responsible, attitudes held by superficial samplers of the literature on the subject. But his article was largely a listing of the main revisionist points on Wilson and 1917, while agreeing that they were correct. But he insisted despite this that "I am not able to take any absolutist position on it." Its complexity barred an approach of "omniscient certitude," abhorrent to him as "an old-fashioned liberal." [26] But the next month, on the occasion of the twentieth anniversary of American entry, the *New Republic* in a three-column editorial commended the sober good sense reflected by the 70% of those responding to an Institute of Public Opinion poll who felt that American entry into the first World War had been a mistake. The revisionist case had not only been accepted on the past war, the editorial stated, but "the people of the United States are almost unanimous in their desire to stay out of another." [27] Many indications pointed to the fact that American disillusion with World War One was at an all-time high-water mark six months before the President's Chicago Bridge speech.

Although what Cecil Driver once described as "the heaving moods and slow drifts of sentiment which constitute public opinion" was decidedly in this camp in America as far as the first World War was concerned, the tensions of 1937–1938 were exerting serious strain in many places, and liberals were not excepted. The enormous impetus the Roosevelt speech of October, 1937 gave to the growing Communist-propelled collective security program of the moment has not often been dwelled upon. Among the liberal journalists and writers there began to grow as a consequence a feeling that the logic of this made another war likely, and as a result it was concluded reasonably that deep skepticism on the fruits of the last war was hardly the correct spiritual armor to have to don at the start of the next. Despite the towering preponderant disposition to continue in the paths of revisionism, a slowly growing strain of resistance and hostility can be seen taking shape in 1938, undermining it in tiny sectors and tilling the liberal field of receptivity for a comprehensive rejection and the consequent substitution of almost all the once-repudiated views. To a remarkable degree the propaganda of the First World War proved to have the right cut and shape so as to be fashionable for re-use prior to and during the Second. Germanophobia was undoubtedly the most useful of these resurrected propaganda garments, but casting the war like its predecessor as a noble encounter once more to generalize virtue over the planet came close to matching it in effectiveness.

But throughout 1938, scraps of opinion and news boiled up to the top in the liberal press which fell into place in the revisionist orientation. For some it was an exercise in schizoid tendencies, but for others attacking the rationale of the last war and developing a quiet receptiveness to another simultaneously it offered no problem. In the area of editorial policy, only the *Nation* leaned strongly in the direction of supporting the collective security drive, in which campaign it was hardly exceeded by the *New Masses*. But the *New Republic* and *Common Sense* were utterly unsympathetic, and liberal writers began to polarize now as a consequence. At the same time the *Nation* began to attract a band of fellow travelers as deeply committed to the welfare of the Soviet Union as they were to favorable views of Marxist

Socialism and the progress of Communism in Spain and China. Gaining moral and possibly combative support for these ends made sense. But it made the strain on the *Nation* transparently evident.

When Ludwig Lore reviewed George Sylvester Viereck's *The Kaiser on Trial* in mid-December 1937 for the *Nation,* an imaginative hypothetical trial conducted in the spirit of paragraph 227 of the Versailles Treaty which specified that he be so dealt with, Lore could not resist remarking that "to the younger generation the idea that one could force an aggressor to face an international tribunal may be slightly comic." [28] This was in reference to the staggering mountain of scorn which revisionism had heaped on the "aggressor" concept to begin with, since its core contention was that all the participants in the war had been responsible in varying degrees. The following February the *New Republic* exulted upon the news that the 1917 head of the political science department at the University of Minnesota, Dr. William A. Schaper, had his wartime dismissal rescinded and was paid a partial money compensation for the interim period. "Dr. Schaper had opposed American entry into the World War, and personal enemies, masking themselves as 'patriots,' succeeded in forcing him out," the editorial explained, presumably for the benefit of readers who had come of age since this incident. The editorial praised this action as "a blow struck for freedom and integrity at a time when these qualities are at a discount over large areas of the earth." [29]

But the main staple of revisionism insofar as it pertained to the United States did not lack for emphasis, whatever the nature of the newest gathering grimness. Villard in January, 1938 harshly treated James T. Shotwell's *At the Paris Peace Conference,* the latest and most persuasive trial balloon aimed at refurbishing Wilson and downgrading the estimate made by John Maynard Keynes, long a standard book in the revisionist case against the Versailles settlements.[30] And Villard drew up even more powerful verbal weapons in the April 2 *Nation,* which happened to coincide with the date of Wilson's war message 21 years before. He especially attacked this address and the President's speech of November 12, 1917 before the American Federation of Labor at Buffalo, in which he had seriously criticized American pacifists. Villard exuded contempt for Wilson in this essay, underlining the point that the war President's inability to get peace was fully as futile a gesture as that of pacifists in preventing the war from coming, and described Wilson's failure to understand the forces "which made a catspaw of him" as evidence of his "absolute stupidity." The undoing of his whole program and the now-growing belief in the likelihood of yet another war was proof enough of his lack of wisdom and farsightedness, Villard proposed.[31] The following week Villard urgently called for another close look at Colonel House and his diplomatic contributions to the steady slide of the United

States into war in 1917, in view of the crisis which had blown up between this country and Japan as a result of the Panay bombing in December, 1937. He was convinced that the same process was at work, and did not think it would be a total surprise to see April, 1917 repeated in April, 1938: "Strong forces in and out of the government are at work to put this country into war with Japan as a prelude to our going to the rescue of the democracies in Europe," he cautioned.[32]

In this same month, the latest volume to appear on the revisionist bookshelf, Charles Callan Tansill's *America Goes To War*, was reviewed, and that it was done by Reinhold Niebuhr instead of Villard or any other veteran critic in sympathy with it was perhaps a signal that the conflict on the *Nation* between the two major contending tendencies was warming up. Niebuhr had no established place of any kind as a serious student of the war, but he was gaining stature as one of the most articulate pleaders for a new American get-tough attitude in foreign affairs, as well as revealing an undisguised Marxist propensity. He was not especially pleased with the book, and was most unhappy with Tansill's dismissal of economic influences in this country in the last one hundred days prior to the declaration of war.[33] But Niebuhr's frown certainly was not a liberal consensus; Tansill's historical colleague Henry Steele Commager, a growing liberal pundit, had said in a review that Tansill's book was "far and away the best analysis of American neutrality and the road to war that has ever been written," and that it was "distinguished by every quality which should command the attention of the scholar and the interests of the general reader," a reception of the warmest sort indeed.

With the Munich conference already history and the collective security and interventionist waves already breaking with loud roars on American liberalism, and a concerted move under way to refurbish the images of 1914–1919 which had been so brusquely treated since, nothing better illustrated the tenacity of the critical tradition than the *Nation*'s editorial on December 24, 1938 which noted the passing of William MacDonald, the first editor of its International Relations Section and author of "the most remarkable editorial which appeared in the *Nation* in the post-war period," on May 17, 1919. Titled "The Madness at Versailles," at a time when the country was absorbed in a deep act of faith in everything transpiring there, it had been considered "crazy," but it was fully vindicated in short order, this newest reminiscence reminded the readers. Although unsigned, it might have been written by Villard because of its implacability toward Wilson.[34]

By this time a rival view was quietly asserting itself, growing louder and louder in the following year, and in the case of the *Nation* achieving almost total domination after war broke out in September,

1939. It was not successful in the *New Republic* until the winter of 1940–1941, while it gained hardly a nod of recognition at any time in *Common Sense,* which became more and more an organ of refuge for anti-war liberals in the two years prior to American involvement. As will be shown in other chapters, there was at all times, and especially after 1933, a view that Versailles and its works had little if anything to do with the political disorder which swept Europe, Asia and Africa after 1919. This view looked on Hitler's rise imperturbably, and denied that he and his program were related to it year after year, while the Versailles-created territorial and boundary problems of the Saar, Rhineland, Austria, Czechoslovakia, Danzig, Memel and the Polish Corridor paraded down through the 1930s in a series of Hitler-determined or influenced solutions.

After September, 1939, this opinion grew to a thunderous chorus, which not only insisted that the First World War was all the contemporary propaganda said it was, but added a few elaborations. One of these was a positive-good theory of Versailles rather than a view that it was the mother of world disorder. Another was a quasi-deification of Wilson, accompanied by a savage attack on all the revisionist efforts of 1920–1935 and after as profoundly immoral efforts to destroy the fabric of Western civilization. A clear, bright view of granitic, implacable Germanophobia illustrated its outlines, part of which was furnished by political refugees and other enemies of the Hitler government who had quickly joined the opinion-making activities upon arriving in America. The prominent members of the academic world who provided leadership were headed above all by Hans Kohn, and ably supported by Albert Guérard and Frederick L. Schuman, among others. James T. Shotwell, Paul Birdsall, and John Wheeler-Bennett were among the authors who made most significant literary contributions to this comprehensive reprisal. The rehabilitation of the First War and its chief personalities on the Allied side fitted in especially well as another Anglo-Franco-American alliance began to take shape at least psychically in the six months or so following the concessions to Germany at Munich in September, 1938. It continued, and at an accelerated clip, down into the late spring of 1940, when the German breakthrough in France let loose the torrent of fear that engulfed American liberals, smothering virtually all detached discussion of war.

Kohn's reviews of the seventh volume of Baker's *Woodrow Wilson* and Lloyd George's *Memoirs of the Peace Conference* in the April 8, 1939 *Nation,* and of the eighth volume of Baker in July, would have been unthinkable in this journal even one and a half years before. Upon comparison with the reviews of the same books in the *New Republic* it would have been difficult for readers unaware of the change of emphasis taking place not to believe that these were different works by the same authors.[35] No more enthusiastic supporter than Kohn of what had taken place at Versailles broke into print in this period, and his eulogies of Wilson sounded lame and self-conscious in a journal which had conducted a twenty-year attack on almost everything that Wilson ever said or stood for in the field of war, peace and foreign relations.

Although the *Nation*'s editorial commitments made the bitter blasts of Villard and other supporters of World War One revisionism too embarrassing to print any longer, a few traces of the older views persisted in seeping into its pages despite all the evidences of closer editing in order to present a uniform and consistent ideological position. The most amazing of these was the long review-article by I. F. Stone on James R. Mock's and Cedric Larson's *Words That Won The War,* a sobering and revealing study of the nation's wartime propaganda agency, the Committee on Public Information, and its director, George Creel. Stone's review was as enthusiastic as anything Villard or anyone else had ever written in the *Nation* in the previous two decades, and contained an especially portentous paragraph that all the liberals anxious for war should have pondered for some time, including Stone himself, in view of his own enlistment in the type-writer brigades within a year: [36]

One learns from Creel's story that idealists are as necessary as brass bands in war time. One also learns that the idealists tend to suffer from the delusion that they are running the war, when it is the war that is running them. This becomes clearest when the victors meet to divide the spoils; eloquence and idealism then rate as highly as they do in other forms of poker. Creel's story warns of the organized mass idiocy that will become a necessity if we are again drawn into war, and of the difficulties liberals will encounter in trying to make a decent peace when it is over. New Creels may be in the making.

Still another reflection of the long-ingrained pro-revisionist sentiment made its way into this journal late in January, 1940, upon the occasion of the death of Senator William E. Borah. The editorial comment stated flatly that "Senator Borah was intellectually the ablest man in the Congress of the United States," and in the course of a startling eulogy, threw him a bouquet for his anti-Versailles Treaty fight of twenty years before: "He had statesmanship, and his leadership of the fight against the United States's putting its name to the iniquitous Treaty of Versailles was of the highest order." [37]

In the meantime, the anti-collective-security, but increasingly uneasy *New Republic* did not have a conflict to reconcile between rival views on the past war. Its editorials and book reviews clung to the established critical course, regardless of the new pressures to forget the early clash, and the enlistment of several of its editors and contributors on the side of a pro-involvement position, an account of which will be examined in detail later. The first revisionist book of consequence published in 1939, H. C. Peterson's *Propaganda For War*, received a lengthy and approving review in the May 17 issue by Professor Clyde R. Miller of Columbia, the director of the Institute for Propaganda Analysis and a repentant World War One journalist whose story of a Debs speech in Ohio had led to Debs' arrest and conviction in 1917. His concluding remarks were some hard-headed advice of a sort that even *New Republic* readers were not accustomed to getting, although it was also available in other sources, such as in Quincy Howe's books, *Blood Is Cheaper Than Water* and *England Expects Every American To Do His Duty:* [38]

Mr. Peterson's book is not an argument for pacifism or for neutrality. If one is to draw any conclusion, it is that Americans ought to safeguard their own interests by coolly determining what those interests are, what facts are relevant to them, and to what extent propaganda may be distorting the picture of the facts. Because the most educated, moral, respectable and influential citizens were the biggest suckers for British propaganda in 1914–1917, it may be pertinent to conclude too that Mr. Peterson's account of how they were fooled might be read with peculiar profit by today's most influential citizens. . . .

In the tense moments of the late summer, with another general European war about to break out, the *New Republic* changed step disconcertingly long enough to call attention to the 25th anniversary of the outbreak of the war of 1914, in a bruising editorial titled "A Quarter Century of Folly," which clung to the revisionist position, and which said in part,[39]

If there was ever an anniversary that the world would like to pass over in shamefaced silence, it is the quarter-century mark since the beginning of the "Great War." (What was great about it, we have never understood.) . . . The peace which followed was almost as reactionary and destructive as the war itself had been.

Long-established contributors such as Grattan kept a flow of commentary appearing, if anything more firm in its tone. His review of Frederic L. Paxson's subdued *America At War, 1917–1918* shortly after the war broke out was in a substantially revisionist vein. "In a sense Professor Paxson's book is an ironic commentary on the values for which American democracy is prepared to sacrifice itself . . . all this lavish pouring out of men, money and materials was for a socially destructive purpose." There was a Beardian quality to his regretful rumination, "As we who came to maturity after the War have learned, it is just about impossible to direct a similar loyalty toward socially constructive tasks." [40] And in November, when the sides began to form on the issue of American entry into or abstention from this new struggle, Grattan thought it worthwhile to issue another strong endorsement of the Mock and Larson book dealing with the "emotional engineering" of 1914–1918; valuable reading—"If you want to know how you came to hold those odd, inaccurate notions about America and the First World War and understand how you were led to believe that the end of the war would usher in Utopia," he suggested.[41] The last observation might have been more intentional than literary, in view of the fact that a hefty contingent of the most eloquent liberal voices in the land were already suggesting that such a situation was likely to emerge from another war in which Americans participated, even if the previous one had not done so.

And the following spring, as the German offensive was about to mount in Scandinavia and the Lowlands prior to the promenade through France, the *New Republic,* still firmly attached to the foreign policy position and actions of the Roosevelt Administration as of 1934 and 1935, and unaware of how quickly it was all to be undone via the ministry of executive agreements and a panicky Congress, devoted an extended editorial comment on the second volume of the papers of World War One Secretary of State Lansing, just published by the State Department, entirely in the older vein; "Almost every page of the Lansing letters forms an endorsement of the wisdom of our existing neutrality code," it observed at the beginning of "Lansing's Road To War"; "Like earlier documents, the Lansing papers show that the munitions industry was more important than any other single factor in pushing the United States into the 1914–1918 war." [42] This sounded like an echo of the Nye Committee, an amazing thing in that at this late time the "defense" drive was under way, and even liberals were deploring attacks on the arms business. But the editorial went on to rejoice that the Johnson Act was still on the statute books, and that it tended "to minimize the unseen pressure of a domestic munitions industry dependent on belligerent orders." A closing observation, "Of all American officials, Bryan [Lansing's predecessor] comes off best, as he has in previous compilations of documents," was thought amply supported by the way Lansing documents illustrated "the importance of the present prohibition against American citizens and merchant vessels entering the North Atlantic war zone," a policy Bryan had fought for so tenaciously before resigning.

By this time the *Nation* had quite well silenced revisionist propensities, and with major editorial policy steadily moving toward American interference, aid to the French and British enemies of Germany, and ultimately for a declaration of war itself, the situation was self-explanatory. A new thesis appeared, that the criticism of Versailles was German-inspired propaganda, and that actually it had been a kindly peace, by far more gentle and less austere than that of Brest-Litovsk which the Germans had imposed upon the Russian Communists in 1918. James T. Shotwell dwelled on this in his *What Germany Forgot,* reviewed on March 30, 1940 with acclaim by a Hungarian refugee, Rustem Vambery.[43] The following month, in a review of Sir Nevile Henderson's *Failure of a Mission,* a defense of British action prior to the outbreak of the Second World War, Kohn put forth the anti-revisionist view in its strongest form, stressing the idea that Versailles was a merciful peace, that its so-called "wrongs" were just "alleged," that explanations of Hitler in terms of reaction to Versailles were simply "blatant pieces of propaganda," that the Weimar Republic of the 1920s was a German golden age, and that Fascism was buried deep in German thought and history, unrelated to any modern consequences at all. Kohn was to summarize the situation a number of times before and after this date, but as a succinct statement in a minimum of space this was probably the most concise.[44]

And with a Villard no longer on the staff to challenge him, Guérard, reviewing Albert Carr's frank call to war, *America's Last Chance,* exclaimed,[45]

"End War! Save Democracy!" We have sneered for twenty years at these premises. Even today the anti-Wilsonian bias is the chief obstacle to clear thinking and determined action. We must first confess that our cynicism was wrong, and that the despised "idealists" were the only true realists.

The somersault was about complete, and the liberals of the Kohn-Guérard persuasion, rapidly increasing in numbers, had performed the self-convincing achievement that "ending war" and "saving democracy" were still within the grasp of Americans, through the simple procedure of fighting another war while suspending democracy.

Editorial sanction was placed on the record most unequivocally in the foreword to a special supplement of the *Nation* for March 22, 1941 written by Robert Bendiner, now the managing editor of this senior liberal weekly. The foreword heaped scorn on the group of revisionists which it now called "the look-at-the-last-war-school," without the faintest allusion to the fact that the *Nation* had been an original senior partner in the architectural firm that designed it.[46] But the wholesale change of personnel which had taken place, dominated now by a group which eagerly looked forward to the next war, made this casual but gigantic shift of emphasis understandable.

The rehabilitation of Woodrow Wilson, which the turnabout on Versailles presaged, was not long in coming. Early in 1941 Paul Birdsall's *Versailles Twenty Years After* was published. Birdsall, a colleague of fiercely pro-war Frederick L. Schuman at Williams College, attempted to make Wilson emerge as "the only man of real stature" at the Peace Conference and described the events of that time in accord with the new dispensation at this war-bound moment. It was frankly intended as a contribution to the pamphleteering aiming to further undermine isolationist strength and sentiment, which Birdsall declared threatened "to paralyze American foreign policy in the present increasingly critical world situation." Kohn's enthusiasm for this book almost escaped dimensions, and in his *Nation* review he suggested that "It may be called a scholarly revindication of Woodrow Wilson and his policies." [47] The *Nation* had now completed its one hundred eighty-degree turn in the ten years since Mukden by giving its editorial sanction to the critical revision of revisionism.

The mysterious change of heart which the *New Republic* underwent in the winter of 1940–1941 placed it in line with the *Nation* on foreign policy for the first time in several years. But, even with a pro-interventionist editorial line saturating each issue, there was apparently an atavistic tremor in April, 1941. It consisted of a review of Birdsall by Columbia Professor Lindsay Rogers. Rogers' review was antagonistic throughout, its flavor sharply reminiscent of the most cutting products of Villard or of Robert Morss Lovett of ten years earlier, right down to directly connecting the conflagration then blazing luridly in Europe with the end of the previous one; [48]

The political children of Versailles got thousands of miles or kilometers of new customs frontiers along with their economic independence to play with. They at once began the game of commercial warfare, and produced such chaos in two decades that the whole nightmare, including the straitjacket treaties binding it together, had to be burst apart by war.

Completely in accord with the liberal view of 1935, or even 1937, Rogers' review was utterly out of harmony with the new liberal line, which had started to harden into shape in February and March, 1940, that the European upheaval was not due to Versailles but to *not enough* of Versailles. The precipitate retreat from the leanings of the period 1919–1939 on the question of "war guilt" was met by the original simplistic conclusions and the emotional confusion coming back from the other direction, and the question of responsibility for the World War performed a complete circle in twenty years. Frenzied moral clichés and rhetorical panic replaced analysis almost entirely from that point on, resulting in a propaganda which was so vast and enveloping that no liberal who participated in it could ever breathe a word of criticism of George Creel again with any sense of guiltlessness.

As will be seen in the account of the ideological contest about whether or not the United States should enter the war, in most of 1941 a qualification entered into the picture, but in a very quiet and restrained manner. The Kohn wing, inclined to deprive the earlier revisionism of all its laurels, was motivated by a fierce anti-German implacability to write it all off as mainly Germanophile special pleading. But others who stressed the approach of leftist internationalism, especially after Russia entered the war in late June, were inclined to respect the position of those who continued to denounce the First World War, and to accept revisionist debunking on the grounds that the war had been a "reactionary, imperialist struggle." Yet they insisted that it was not inconsistent to support the Second, since this was one of the "people" against "reaction," and that its outcome, contrary to the dreary denouement of the 1918 Armistice, was sure to end in the advancement of democratic, anti-nationalistic Socialism.

NOTES

1 *Nation,* May 8, 1935, pp. 550–552.
2 *Common Sense,* June, 1935, pp. 27–28.
3 *New Republic,* May 8, 1935, p. 372.
4 *Nation,* May 1, 1935, p. 515.
5 *Nation,* May 29, 1935, pp. 635–636.
6 *New Republic,* October 16, 1935, p. 276.
7 *Nation,* October 16, 1935, p. 427.
8 Villard, "The War and the Pacifists," *Nation,* October 23, 1935, p. 455.
9 Villard, "Neutrality and the House Of Morgan," *Nation,* November 13, 1935, p. 555.
10 *Nation,* January 29, 1936, p. 119.
11 Millis's article was subtitled "How We Entered the Last One," *New Republic,* July 31, 1935, pp. 325–326.
12 Grattan, "The Road To Revision," *New Republic,* January 22, 1936, pp. 9–10.
13 *New Republic,* February 12, 1936, p. 23.
14 Neuberger, "Integrity—A Story," *Common Sense,* June, 1936, pp. 9–10. Lerner review of Hicks in *Nation,* April 29, 1936, pp. 552–553.
15 *New Republic,* September 2, 1936, p. 112.
16 P. 363. Arnett's book was published by Little, Brown.
17 *Nation,* June 19, 1937, pp. 709–710.
18 *Nation,* September 26, 1936, p. 353.
19 Grattan review of Seymour in *New Republic,* March 11, 1936, pp. 144–145. See also comments by Grattan on Seymour and Fay in issue of January 22, 1936 (note 12, above).
20 *New Republic,* October 7, 1936, pp. 247–248. Beard paid the Nye Committee high praise in this article.
21 *Nation,* January 1, 1938, p. 3.
22 *Nation,* October 31, 1936, p. 526. Knight also received a sympathetic review in the *New Republic* from Ralph Rutenber, January 20, 1937, pp. 364–365.
23 *New Republic,* April 14, 1937, pp. 302–303.
24 *Yale Review,* June, 1937, pp. 863–864. Buell's review appeared in the March issue.
25 *New Republic,* December 8, 1937, pp. 142–144.
26 *New Republic,* March 10, 1937, p. 129. Beard defined "an old-fashioned liberal" as "merely a person who does not imagine himself to be God."

27   "The War Reconsidered," *New Republic*, April 14, 1937, pp. 279–280.
28   *Nation*, December 18, 1937, pp. 691–692.
29   *New Republic*, February 9, 1938, p. 3.
30   *Nation*, January 29, 1938, pp. 131–132.
31   *Nation*, April 2, 1938, p. 388.
32   *Nation*, April 9, 1938, p. 414.
33   *Nation*, April 23, 1938, pp. 479–480.
34   *Nation*, December 24, 1938, p. 679.
35   Kohn reviews of Lloyd George and Baker in *Nation*, April 8, 1939, pp. 405–407, and July 22, 1939, pp. 105–106. No attention was drawn to the fact that Kohn was a recent emigrant from Czechoslovakia, where Wilson was virtually a political saint on the basis of his part at Versailles in bringing the Czech state into existence.
36   Stone, "Creel's Crusade," *Nation*, December 9, 1939, pp. 647–649.
37   *Nation*, January 27, 1940, p. 87.
38   *New Republic*, May 17, 1939, p. 51.
39   *New Republic*, August 9, 1939, p. 1.
40   *New Republic*, August 30, 1939, p. 111.
41   *New Republic*, November 15, 1939, p. 118.
42   *New Republic*, April 1, 1940, pp. 428–429.
43   *Nation*, March 30, 1940, pp. 425–426.
44   *Nation*, April 20, 1940, pp. 515–517.
45   *Nation*, December 21, 1940, p. 637.
46   *Nation*, March 22, 1941, pp. 333–334.
47   Kohn review of Birdsall in *Nation*, March 29, 1941, pp. 383–384.
48   *New Republic*, April 14, 1941, pp. 508–509.

17

THE NIGHTMARE RIDE ON THE WAR
CHARIOT IN THE SPANISH COCKPIT,
1936–1939

THE FORTUITOUS MATURATION OF SPAIN
AS A WORLD WAR TRIAL SITE

THE Spanish crisis which exploded in the bloody civil war on
July 18, 1936 was not related to the First War, although its
timing and location seemed tailor-made as an arena for the extension
of the clash between the rival political tendencies in Europe and the
conflicting national ambitions and interests. Conditions in Spain had
been growing progressively more ominous ever since the disastrous
conclusion of its war with the Riffs in Spanish Morocco in 1921
and the massacre and dispersion of its fighting forces by Abdel-Krim
at Anual. At home the uproar which followed this catastrophe led
eventually to an emergency political regime headed by Primo de
Rivera (in 1923) which managed to survive, at times precariously,
until January 28, 1930. Liberal republican and leftist elements which
had been simmering with discontent started to grow extremely active
thereafter, and their intrigues shot forward at an accelerated pace
when King Alfonso left Spain on April 14, 1931, with the apparent
intention of not returning.

Out of these developments came the liberal-left-republican-socialist
coalition regimes of Alcalá Zamora and Manuel Azaña, functioning
under a new left-leaning constitution, which among other things
actually suppressed in August, 1932 the first attempt at revolution

headed by General José Sanjurjo, a member of the three-general junta which eventually sparked the uprising of 1936. The early 1930s brought much grief to this coalition of Spanish politicians, not only from the Right which deeply opposed much of its radical legislation, but from the Anarcho-Syndicalist Left, an anti-statist radical libertarian movement which enjoyed enormous support in Spain, and was stronger there than anywhere else in Latin Europe, its general center of major concentration. Thus the Government was not only forced to put down Sanjurjo's attempted coup but in January, 1933 also used strong repressive measures to smother an Anarcho-Syndicalist uprising in Barcelona. These latter forces deserve remembrance here, because of the important part they were to play in the big explosion of 1936. Although they shared a number of views held by some of the elements composing the Government coalition, their rejection of the State and their insistence on a sweeping socio-economic reorganization of Spain, which would have found it composed mainly of decentralized cooperative communes on a local control basis at the end, involved an outlook as forbidding to the Government as the Right. And after the Communists gained the upper hand in the former, it was hard to say which group was more repelled by Anarcho-Syndicalism.

The immediate concern to the Government, however, was the gathering strength of various Right influences through most of Spain except in the Left stronghold of Catalonia, in the northeast, and its big center of Barcelona. The tension swelled as the *Partida Acción Popular* headed by Gil Robles continued to gain strength. In the election to the national legislature, or Cortes, of November 19, 1933, Right groups won more than two-fifths of the seats, and a succession of weak and uneasy coalition ministries followed, their actions inciting first an Anarchist (December, 1933) and then a Socialist (April, 1934) uprising in Barcelona, where matters had gotten extremely delicate and complicated. Situated in Catalonia, it was a natural center for trouble, especially since this region of Spain had wrung a home rule concession from the Central Government on September 25, 1932, entitling it to consider itself autonomous, with its own independent government, flag and powers in virtually all areas except foreign affairs. An extremely jealous people, who did not consider themselves Spanish any more than did the Basques of the opposite side of Spain, they had even succeeded in getting Catalan recognized as their official language.

But things got much worse later in the year, after the formation on October 4, 1934 of a government by Alejandro Lerroux which included a goodly number of Right members. The Spanish Left promptly called for a general strike the next day, and the day after that the President of the autonomous state of Catalonia proclaimed its independence, a much more radical step. In addition, a formidable strike broke out in the mining industries of the province of Asturias, in the northwest, the center of Spanish Communists; though not especially numerous they obviously hoped to capture this valuable part of the country. All of these were put down, and a reprisal was undertaken against the Catalonians, suspending the statute which had granted them autonomy.

Now things began to hurry to a showdown. The Lerroux ministry collapsed in September 1935, to be succeeded by a series of ineffectual governments which contained too much Right strength to please the now storming Left. On January 6, 1936 the Cortes was dissolved, and on February 16 there was elected the newest republican-left-socialist radical coalition in the latest fashion of the Popular Front, as seen in France at the moment and pressing to the fore in several other countries, aided by a generous push from behind by the Communists. The vote of November 19, 1933 had been reversed. The stage was set for another Right uprising in the manner of Sanjurjo, and five months later it came, beginning with a coup by military commanders in Melilla in Spanish Morocco, the famous regrouping center after the rout at Anual, which had been so dramatically described in Ramón Sender's *Pro Patria*. The army chiefs Franco, Mola and Sanjurjo organized the revolt against the Republican or "Loyalist" government, as it was to be known in the liberal and Left papers thereafter, and were followed by the bulk of the army and air force, the navy remaining faithful to the hardly installed *Frente Popular*. It was soon established on the mainland of Spain, however, after its spread to most of the cities with substantial armed forces garrisoned there, and the revolt set up a junta at Burgos to direct the attack; the Spanish Civil War was on.

Spain was off the beaten track of Europe, and although it was not entirely forgotten, it hardly compared with other countries when it came to attention from the American liberal press, or from American liberal writers as a group. Even during the Civil War itself, an alarmingly small volume of comment on it by established liberal authors or journalists took place; outside the established liberal organs a new group with powerful attachment to international Communism usurped and dominated this subject. But news from Spain did seep into the main liberal papers on occasion prior to the Civil War, although it became a major topic in them thereafter. A substantial flurry of news and comment appeared during the minor crises prior to that of 1936, the most important of which was the suppression of the Communist miners' uprising in the Asturias in October, 1934. This was at the height of the *Neu Beginnen* propaganda and the vague stirrings of the Marxist-led left revival which was to have unseated Hitler, but which led into the creation of the Popular Front machinery. In a long lament over this affair in Spain, the *New Republic* in a characteristic semantic act of the time titled it "The Last Stand of Spanish Democracy." [1]

The swiftness of the 1936 uprising caught a large part of America's liberals quite by surprise, since the new government, which had hardly started to exercise power, was ideologically very much in harmony with them, and with the neighboring Popular Front government of Blum in France as well. Great hopes had been expressed for the further pushing of left-aimed goals, but not all believed it was going to be an unhindered parade. One of the more astute observers of Spanish politics, Anita Brenner, in a long article, "Spain Mobilizes For Revolution," in the *Nation* of April 29, 1936 professed to see coming there another upheaval similar to that which shook Russia in 1917 not only in total effect but in most ideological outlines as well. [2] It was obvious to her and others that the new government was anything but satisfactory to a sizable number of Spaniards, but the prevailing consensus of opinion was that the new regime could be expected to extend its influence and fasten its program upon the country in spite of its internal opposition. Thus the rapidity, boldness and daring of the uprising headed by Francisco Franco produced more confusion than consternation at the very beginning, and few American liberals could take it seriously, in this brief breathing spell which had followed the Italian crisis in Ethiopia and that of Germany in retaking its Rhineland region a few weeks before. Symptomatic of liberal faith in the ability of the government to handle the situation was the *Nation* editorial of August 1, two weeks after the original blow had been struck in Melilla, "The Spanish Workers See It Through"; "Through the fog of conflicting reports from Spain it becomes increasingly clear that the Fascist insurrections will not succeed." [3] Two weeks later the Franco forces won a major victory in capturing the city of Badajoz.

Two new issues promptly forced their way to the front row, the problem of foreign intervention and the internal struggle among the factions making up the Government opposition to Franco's rebels. Intervention became intimately wound up with the issue of American neutrality, and eventually grew into a long and bitter fight carried on for the purpose of involving the United States on the side of the Government, or "Loyalists." It became obvious to all within a few weeks that purely Spanish factions would not be let alone to settle this conflict, any more than purely German or Chinese elements were involved in the political upheavals in those countries. But in the early weeks of the civil war certain inferences were made that this would be a good thing. Both the *Nation* and *New Republic* editorial positions on the question favored neutrality proposals leading to a general European policy of non-interference in Spain, but both expected that it was most likely to occur nevertheless. The *Nation* frankly suggested that it was sure to be one-sided and that it would come from Hitler Germany and Mussolini Italy for Franco exclusively. The *New Republic* endorsed the view that there would be intervention on behalf of both the contenders. After commending Roosevelt for declaring that this country would remain completely neutral and for recommending to Americans as individuals that they do the same, its editorial of August 26, "Publicity For Spanish Interventionists," announced what it felt to be a desirable policy; [4]

> As long as intervention is certain, let us do everything possible to make interveners on both sides lay their cards on the table. If that were done, the public opinion of the world would have a far better chance to know the facts and exert an influence. Such a course from 1914 to 1917 might have done much to check our drift into the World War. If it could now be adopted by international agreement in relation to Spain, the more reckless forces behind the aggression might be curbed. But in any case, we should like to see it enforced in the United States.

But the worsening of the fortunes of war for the Loyalists soon undermined this gesture at objectivity, despite its thinly-veiled insinuation that the interveners in Spain were surely to be largely on one side, anyway. And the reporters and interpreters of the war in both weeklies assumed a monolithic quality of devoted partisanship which in its wishful thinking and hoping for the success of the anti-Franco cause performed one of the least objective jobs of reporting a war in the history of American journalism. At the height of the fighting, the reports and commentaries of Ralph Bates in the *New Republic,* Louis Fischer in the *Nation* and James Hawthorne in the *New Masses* could best be analyzed by comparison of their similarities. Bates was launched as probably the top *New Republic* observer, commentator, book reviewer and critic of the Spanish war by a cordial full-page review of his book *The Olive Field* by Cowley in the issue of September 2,[5] two days before the Franco forces took the city of Irun and the Loyalist side emerged under a reorganized Popular Front government under Largo Caballero. Bates's book dealt with the struggles of 1931–1934 in Spain, and its orientation left no doubt that he would be watching Spain through Marxian proletarian binoculars. Fischer went to Spain from his post as regular *Nation* correspondent from Moscow, and spent most of the war on the spot, which makes his dispatches the sustained liberal eye-witness running commentary on Spanish affairs throughout the almost three years of fighting there.

The tempo of the reporting in Spain took a sharp spurt ahead in September, what with a new Franco victory, a fundamental governmental shakeup on the favored side, and a dramatic siege, that of

Toledo, to report home on for most of the month. Liberal pretensions to detachment started to vanish almost at once, when bad news started to build up. On September 9 the *New Republic* groaned editorially that the "democratic government" was "fighting for life against a band of barbarian chiefs in uniform," and that "a victory for General Franco's forces would be a major disaster to the whole world." [6]

Furious charges of comprehensive misreporting of the war were aimed at the commercial press in America. A hot open letter from the League of American Writers to the *New Masses* of September 8 accused the American newspapers of presenting "an utterly false and misleading picture" of the military revolt in Spain, signed among others by *New Republic* editors Bliven, Cowley, Frank and Soule, as well as John Chamberlain, Max Lerner, Herman Simpson and *New Masses* stalwarts Joseph Freeman, Michael Gold, Granville Hicks and Isidor Schneider.[7] A steady flow of atrocity stories which charged the Loyalists with a wide number of shocking acts was appearing regularly in the majority of the New York City dailies by the end of the fall of 1936, and they continued to be published. The *Nation,* which had published third-hand and fourth-hand charges of this type about Hitler Germany without the slightest hesitation or reservation, grew dark with anger about far less cloudy accounts being charged to its favored side in Spain, and quickly trundled its double standard into view again. In a September 19 piece titled "Faking the Spanish News," it commented, "One would have thought that credulity regarding atrocity stories had ended with the last war. But all the hoary anecdotes are with us again." [8] The editors might have contributed a valuable service by comparing the new crop with its own sown since 1931, allegedly committed on the persons of Marxists in Germany and China at the hands of German National Socialists and Japanese.

The swamping offensive eastward through the Tagus River valley, capped by the successful siege of Toledo, captured by Franco on September 28, 1936, was not noticed too widely, as a new problem confronted American liberals: the reconciliation of the matter of substantial Soviet Russian penetration of the anti-Franco side and a bitter intramural fight among the left factions as a consequence. Cheerful pro-Communist partisanship by the American liberal press was a tactical mistake, as supporters of the anarchists, syndicalists and independent Marxists made life miserable with their testy communications and charges of prior devotion to the welfare of Russian Communism rather than of Spaniards. This war-within-a-war grew much hotter and more rancorous as it became intermingled and intertwined with the uncommonly bitter controversy which grew out of the contemporaneous "purge" trials in Russia. For some months in 1937 and

1938 it was not easy to make out the nature of the contesting forces in the Spanish revolution.

THE SPANISH LEFT CONTROVERSY SPREADS TO THE AMERICAN LIBERAL PRESS

It may possibly have been expected that in view of the German and Russian policies of the liberal press, and the ideological situation in Spain, that as soon as the issue of outside intervention warmed up, there would be a reflection of the consequences among American liberals. The waxing of the Popular Front at the height of the Spanish struggle was especially unfortunate for them, in particular, since it created a deep crevasse which no amount of reconciliation was able to bridge. And the entire effort vanished in a puff of smoke when the Russians abandoned this gambit with summary haste in August 1939, a few short weeks after its deflation in Spain.

Maxwell S. Stewart's *Nation* editorial of August 29, 1936, "Inside Spain," more or less signalled his journal's position on the factions in the Government, or Loyalist, or anti-Franco coalition.[9] He left little doubt in proclaiming the superiority in all respects of the Communist and pro-Popular Front forces, mainly of one or another variety of Socialists, while denigrating their traditional Left enemies, the anarcho-syndicalists, mainly the CNT (*Confederación Nacional del Trabajo*) and FAI (*Federación Anarquista Iberica*), plus the independent Marxist group known as the POUM (*Partido Obrero de Unificación Marxista*) the body with which George Orwell fought, memorialized in his *Homage to Catalonia*. The intra-civil war which these elements fought in Spain while jointly opposing Franco is one of the most fascinating episodes in the history of the twentieth century. We can for specialized reasons deal with only a small part of it here.

This liberal affection for the Communists and those allied to them had a close relation to the issue of Russian intervention in Spain on behalf of the Government side. The entry of Hitler and Mussolini support on the side of Franco was cited as the reason for the Russian decision to become involved unofficially as well, although the evidence supplied makes it evident that such interventions were decided upon first, and then blamed on each other to make the action appear spontaneous. But the American liberal press never expressed the slightest doubt in 1936 that Russia was in Spain because the Italians and Germans had provoked the action through prior entrance. The *Nation*'s October 31 editorial "The Soviets Accept a Challenge" succinctly stated this case, and doled out high praise to the Russians for furnishing support to Franco's enemies.[10] It closely paralleled Louis Fischer's Madrid dispatch of October 25, "Will Moscow Save Madrid?",[11] which flatly asserted that the Soviets were "compelled to seize the initiative and point the way." By this time Franco had captured San Sebastian (September 12) and become the *Jefe del Estado* of the rebel side, and a wide movement had begun leading to the gigantic assault on Madrid. Although the Caballero government slipped away to Valencia, the defense of Madrid became the symbol to the Republican "Loyalists" that Richmond was to the Confederacy in the American Civil War. The siege set in in November, and the city held out until March 1939.

If there was any substance to Communist pretensions to pacifism after 1935, it shortly vanished after the Spanish War erupted. A rather sudden change came over the illustrations in the *New Masses* when it treated with the subject of war now. The "merchants of death" mysteriously evaporated, and the astoundingly grotesque caricatures of military men similarly disappeared. Still another casualty, so to speak, of the rebuilding of the integrity of war among Communists, was the ending of the depressing photographs of World War One carnage and hostile pictorial representations of war in general. With the coming of Communist intervention in Spain, a note of heroism crept back, and in a short while pictures began to proliferate *sans* butchery and destruction. The portrait of the clean, quick hero's death began to be a staple, and the gray, depressing observations of armed combat found in the postwar novels and memoirs which they once praised without stint were no longer to be found.

Instead there was now an excited tingle of anticipation, a feeling that participation in a grand historical rendezvous awaited the "progressive," in some ways almost indescribably stimulating. Combat was no longer ugly; a classical heroic touch had returned to fighting and dying in the class struggle and the international offensive against Fascism. John Sommerfield's *Volunteer in Spain*, published in the fall of 1937 and reviewed in the *New Republic* in the same breathless style by Bates, a fellow Englishman and veteran by now of the International Brigades fighting in Spain, was an excellent example of this turnabout. An even better barometer than the liberal journals or even the frankly Communist-partisan press during the first heady months of the war in Spain was the organ of the American League Against War and Fascism, *The Fight,* while it still enjoyed wide liberal support and direction from some of the liberal editorial staff members. It was among the earliest to document the existence of the International Brigades, and to glorify the war they were fighting against Franco, unaccompanied by the horrifying pictures of war damage to men and property. And its portraits of men in action would have pleased any devotee of the hero cult. James Lerner's

"I Was In Spain" in the November, 1936 issue and Alvah Bessie's turgid eulogy of the American aviator Ben Leider, killed while on a combat mission, "An American Flier In Spain," in the July, 1937 issue, were affirmative cries in support of the values to be found in warfare in the classical tradition.[12]

The April 1938 issue of *The Fight* was in a special class, rivalling any recruiting propaganda ever published in the twentieth century. It is little wonder that the cross-effect of these relatives of the liberal papers was to erase steadily the difference between war and peace, to pose no contradiction between opposition to fighting in an "imperialist" war and eagerly joining in a civil fracas such as went on in Spain. War truly became peace now; when the *New Republic* on May 5, 1937 boasted that "some of these young American pacifists, hating war bitterly, have gone to Spain to fight for democracy, and a few of them have died in the trenches," there was hardly anything that might be added to this which would be a more revealing illustration.[13]

The stir over these International Brigades partially accounts for the outbreak of bad blood in America over the reporting on the war and the giving of credit where credit was properly due in the anti-Franco fight. Although it was liberal belief that Franco had received foreign help first, it was not long before admissions began to be made by the partisans of the Loyalists that they were getting outside support as well. But a halo of righteousness hovered over the elements appearing in Spain fighting on the side of the Caballero government. Louis Fischer, now in Spain and sending to the *Nation* the only frequent and sustained eye-witness reports published in the liberal press during this struggle, cabled from Alicante on December 7, 1936 the first report of the volunteers from "the world anti-fascist front" now on the scene, preparing to leave for the besieged Madrid lines. Among the "volunteers" Fischer named was the German, Ludwig Renn, long sold to the Left and radical world as a great pacifist and writer of more effective anti-war words than those of Erich Maria Remarque. In this sensational story, titled "Spain's 'Red' Foreign Legion," he emerged as Chief of Staff on the First or Thaelmann International Brigade, being one of a considerable number who all seemed to have escaped from a Hitler concentration camp, as these narratives insisted. But in Fischer's description, Renn emerged as a pacifist only in the sense that Romain Rolland had meant it—one who was against fighting the Soviet Union anywhere. The report on this group was dramatic, closing with a description of the Second Brigade's departure for Madrid, soldiers standing in the railroad cars with raised clenched fists and singing the International. In a five-column article, Fischer chose to use the word "Communist" just once.[14] Hawthorne's piece in the *New Masses*, published three days later, repeated much of this material, adding the assertion that even Winston Churchill's nephew was fighting with the Reds in Spain, although Hawthorne showed even greater aversion for the word "Communist" than Fischer.[15] Until the fratricidal battle broke out in the Left camp, the generic term "anti-Fascist" identified Communist, Socialist, Syndicalist, Anarchist, pacifist and independent Marxist alike.

A hint of the bitter wrangling ahead was contained in Anita Brenner's extremely hostile review in the *Nation* for October 17, 1936 of the vigorously pro-Communist book *Spain in Revolt* by the *Daily Worker* international events columnist Harry Gannes, written with the assistance of another familiar figure, Theodore Repard. The reviewer took sharp exception to its pro-Soviet tone and its repeating of the now familiar Popular Front line that the Spanish war was merely another facet of the only world issue of the moment, the fight of representative democracy against international Fascism.[16] This increasingly tense situation at the *Nation,* with its book review section completely at odds with its news, columnist and editorial position, will draw additional attention when the subject of Russia is taken up. But it became increasingly a factor in the Spanish war issue too.

There was little doubt that for several months the liberal press reflected Communist ambitions in their best light, while referring to all the other factions in opposition to Franco with faint admiration, if at all. And in the same spirit the part played by Russian intervention was idealized, "helping out" with detached and purely benevolent motives on behalf of Spanish Republican fortunes. The emphasis was established especially after the Hitler and Mussolini regimes recognized Franco on November 18, 1936, with the assault on Madrid already under way. When the French and British efforts at getting an agreement on mutual non-intervention in Spain fell through, not long after, the prior hesitancy about discussing Russian participation and influence broke down, and frank discussion followed. Fischer's January 16, 1937 *Nation* piece, "Can Madrid Hold On?", announced, "The [Spanish] Republic's resources in the form of Russian aid and domestic supplies are far from exhausted. Indeed, both sources are just being scratched." Russian cotton and grain were arriving in large quantities, he recounted and had no misgivings in confidently announcing, "Industrially and financially, the Republic is infinitely more powerful than the rebels." He was sure that if supplies coming to Franco via coastal Spain and Portugal were stopped, the Caballero government would win in six months.[17] A *Nation* editorial a week later loudly condemned the stepped-up entry of Italian and German forces and help, and suggested that there was no civil war going on, but really a "definite invasion" of Spain by these countries. The editorial went on to disparage Germans using the presence of the international "volunteers" on the Loyalist side as an excuse, and took the position that there were no Russian military men in Spain at all.[18] This was actually a tribute to the superior Russian tactics of sending in their men from various parts of the world in plain clothes, instead of directly from the homeland in uniform. *Common Sense,* on the other hand, in the same month made the frank charge that the Spanish left was being organized by the Soviet ambassador and by generals of the Russian army, and contrary to opinion in the weeklies, did not rule out the possibility of an imminent Communist dictatorship in Spain.[19]

Nor were other voices entirely placated by the widening liberal acceptance of the situation. A number of pro-anarchist and anti-Communist leftists of note in New York, including Max Nomad, Carlo Tresca and Anita Brenner, bitterly attacked Fischer's dispatches from Spain as a reflection of the *New Masses'* hostility toward the Spanish anarchists and as the orthodox Communist approach in general, in a letter published in the *Nation* in December. A month later they were answered by Joseph Freeman, who came to the defense of the *New Masses,* of which he had been an editorial-board member since 1933 and was to become editor.[20] His *An American Testament,* hailed by Marxists as a book comparable to the *Education of Henry Adams,* and one of the most persuasive books ever published describing a conversion to Communism, had just been published, and his prestige was added in the old Communist-Anarchist fight which had once more broken out after a long lull following the bitter struggle in Russia after 1917. Now, with the trial in the Soviet Union of another group of old-line revolutionaries by the Stalin regime, defenders of Russian Communism temporarily became more sensitive to criticism from the Left than the Right, and overlooked no opportunity to subject the former to scathing insults if undisposed to mellowness toward Communists. Editorially the *Nation* took the position that the Communists in Spain were an innocent factor, and on February 13 it declared that "Moscow's support of the Loyalist cause does not imply a Communist Spain," but left the implication that the destruction of Franco would make it an appealing possibility.[21] The chances of that had taken another bad dip however; less than a week earlier his forces had captured Malaga, two days after the *Nation* had reported a Loyalist victory over two Franco armies.

As 1937 wore on it became obvious that the twin issues of the trials of the "Trotskyite wreckers" in Moscow and the survival of the Popular Front in Madrid were going to require the trundling up of the biggest artillery in the Popular Front arsenal. And it automatically signaled the breaking out of a raging fire all across the liberal front lines as well. The *Nation* helped contribute to this when it published on March 20 the revised version of a speech given in New York by

André Malraux, at a dinner tendered in his honor by them and Fischer. Although "Forging Man's Fate in Spain" appeared to be a contribution to the Spanish Loyalist cause, Malraux's devotion to the superiority of the Soviet Union was so transparent as to impel the suspicion that he believed the fighting was going on so that Spain might at least become a cultural colony of the Soviet Union.[22] There were several rancorous outbursts protesting this, the highlight of which was an ill-tempered exchange between Malraux and Trotsky himself which the *Nation* published as a trailer to the original address in the following issue. Trotsky attacked Malraux as really being in New York to defend the Stalin-Vishinsky trials, and that he was, as far as Spain was concerned, acting as a Comintern agent there as he had been in China ten years earlier.[23]

It was obvious from the converging forces that a substantial eruption was bound to occur, although the full force of it was partially deflected by the fact that the Writers Congress was held in Madrid beginning in July. The flurry of apologetics from the liberal fellow travelers accompanying this event took much of the sting out of the charges of excessive zeal on behalf of Communism in Spain. In the spring, both the liberal weeklies expressed their feeling of outrage at the difficulty of showing an especially bitter anti-Franco film taken in and around Madrid by one Joris Ivens, with dialogue written by Archibald MacLeish, Ernest Hemingway and John Dos Passos. This "socially conscious" picture, "Spain in Flames," was hailed in high terms, and the *Nation* could hardly express its contempt for Governor Earle of Pennsylvania when he dismissed it with a wave as "pure Communistic propaganda." [24]

With the emergence of a new Popular Front government under the leadership of Juan Negrin on May 17, 1937 the controversy among the left groups broke out again. Brailsford, in his *New Republic* "Impressions of Spain" on June 9, precipitated another round of criticism with his quiet conclusion that "To grasp the situation one must realize that the Communists now constitute the moderate center party in Republican Spain." [25] It did not help to see the CNT-FAI, POUM, Socialists and other left groups disparaged again, but this view persisted despite the heavy adverse criticism. Cowley's piece from Spain on July 1, "To Madrid," which did not appear in the *New Republic* until August 25, continued this form of apologetic, and castigated the anti-Communist left even more strongly.[26] Other prominent members of the Writers Congress took a similar position, doing their best to keep this intramural squabble muffled in essays describing the larger issue of the war against Franco. MacLeish's "The War Is Ours" in the June 22 *New Masses*, an urgent call to enlist in the war against Franco at least morally, took this tack.

But this solid front became ever more difficult to maintain, strained as it was by the rancorousness of the parallel upheaval over the Trotsky trials. Rather loud statements began to come from previous relatively-dependables. One of the most positive came from disenchanted Dos Passos in the July, 1937 *Common Sense*, "Farewell to Europe." He did not hesitate to credit the Communists with the major share of the organization of Spain against Franco, and with recruiting help and money from Communists all over the world, to which he could not resist appending an ominous sentence indicating that Spain was getting along with it something else that had not been ordered; the Communists, pointed out eye-witness Dos Passos, had also "brought into Spain along with their enthusiasm and their munitions, the secret Jesuitical methods, the Trotskyist witch-hunt and all the intricate and bloody machinery of Kremlin policy." Dos Passos' advice to American liberals was to avoid the involvement talk by fellow travelers, stay home, and concern themselves with domestic reform. He brushed aside the hysterical talk already building up among Communist propagandists in America about the possibility of American invasion by some putative Fascist force; "The Atlantic is a good wide ocean," he comforted the readers.[27] Editorially, *Common Sense* predicted in June that as far as the Spanish war was concerned, "in *no* case will the outcome of the war be a democratic government," and that the Loyalist side was emerging as a steadily-growing Communist Party-dominated military Socialism. Its editorial policy did not waver from this conviction thereafter.[28]

In November, 1937 Felix Morrow dispatched to the *New Republic* a much harsher charge, that the Stalinists in Spain were conducting large-scale assassinations of the non-Stalin Left, which was bitterly contested by Bates, the journal's most articulate apologist for the Popular Front. It was in the *Nation* two weeks later that Bates was identified as an officer in the Fifteenth International Brigade in Spain, a fact which might have been of significance if more widely known at the moment of his argument with Morrow.[29]

But by far the more acrimonious was the running fight between Fischer and his critics in the *Nation* all during the spring and summer of 1937. An uprising in Catalonia a few days before the formation of the Negrin government by the CNT-FAI and POUM groups was admittedly put down with great severity by the Loyalist regime. The *Nation*'s May 22 issue contained a rather queasy report of the "carefully selected Socialists" and Communists who smashed this syndicalist-anarchist-"Trotskyite" eruption; the uneasiness and discomfort were transparently evident, despite the sympathy with the Government. This led to a contentious debate of more than six columns in length in the issue for June 5 between Fischer and Bertram D. Wolfe, who spiritedly defended the Government's left opposition. The fact that they were both eyewitnesses to the struggle meant nothing, as they did not agree on anything of importance in this quarrel within the anti-Franco coalition.[30]

Fischer reopened the subject in a dispatch sent from Valencia June 28, "Loyalist Spain Gathers Its Strength," which reported that its forces were getting over their early "amateurishness," and were being whipped into crack shape by many new commanders; "the bulk of fresh talent is Communist," he flatly stated. But the larger part of the story was devoted to the infighting among the various factions, rather than against the Franco forces. In America this appeared on July 3 along with a blistering three-column letter by Anita Brenner which charged Fischer with getting his material on the Catalonian uprising wholly from the Spanish Communist press. She further charged that the CNT-FAI-POUM leaders had been arrested and were being held for Moscow-type trials, by Communists in Madrid, and that a string of assassinations of anti-Communist Left persons had already been perpetrated.[31]

Fischer's July 17 report, "Loyalist Spain Takes the Offensive," just after they had lost Bilbao to Franco and just before they also lost Brunete, further documented the bloodletting which was wracking the "Republican" side; "The line of demarcation in Loyalist politics is becoming clearer," he announced, to an audience to which it hardly could be any clearer. One camp consisted of "the Communist Party and groups of individuals who are ready to cooperate with it," the other a collection of factions hostile to the Communists.[32] Fischer's support did not dim appreciably for some time; his August 7 dispatch, "Franco Cannot Win," was almost entirely devoted to an account of the systematic uprooting of other left groups by the Communists with Socialist support, and the consequent extension of Communist Party political monopoly. Two weeks later, "planes and technicians from Soviet Russia and the disciplined valor of the Volunteer International Brigades" were given full credit for preventing the swamping of Madrid following the Brunete collapse.[33]

Editorially the *Nation* cheered this, but an unhappy note began to be sounded now, as the battering from the readers not enchanted with Communism was obviously having an effect. It was now admitted that the help extended the Negrin Government by the Soviet Union gave the Communists an upper hand in the left front, and increased the growth and influence of Spain's Communist Party, which the *Nation* felt now threatened "the democracy which exists in Spain today." It was underscored by the publication in the same issue of another long letter from Anita Brenner, urging the *Nation* to expose the trials of the anti-Communist left leaders going on in Madrid, conducted by "a special Stalinist Cheka," and using the threat of withdrawal of Russian aid if the Republican Government officials did not go along.

"It is time for the *Nation* to break its silence on this story," she shouted.[34]

But the defense of Communist infiltration and overall strategy continued, except that the disintegrating effects of the struggle in the left family were now de-emphasized for a while. For the most part this fight was forgotten or suppressed until the spring of 1939 when the violence exploded again, this time resulting in a massacre of Communists, which the *Nation* and other liberal voices deeply deplored. In April, 1938 Fischer insisted that the Loyalist forces owed their improved unity and resistance to the decision on the part of the Government to restore the political commissars, a signal that the Communists had won this stage of their dual battle for control of Spain. Said Fischer in apologetic explanation: [35]

This is a political war, and the army must be kept politically alert. Otherwise it should be a regular army. Caballero, even more than Prieto [Indalecio Prieto, Minister of Defense], made the mistake of crippling the institution of political commissars because they objected to too many Communist commissars. I think Negrin's instincts will prevent him from falling into this error. The political commissars are the agents on the battlefield of the civilian population. This explains the tremendous tenacity, despite unprecedented punishment, of the Republican armed forces.

Although this did not focus much light on the question in terms of justification, the comment was one of the best short statements of the new Communist concept of war as a totalitarian affair which recognized no distinction between civilian and military, and which fought for total obliteration or absorption rather than limited goals in the manner of traditional warfare as an adjunct to specific national policy. Fischer's approval here hardly needed to be implied.

The final result of the overplaying of their hand by the Communists, in addition to further light on the International Brigades and Russian help, will be taken up in the context of the reporting on the war, in the concluding section. But the over-all effect on American liberals of the re-vindication of war, the interchange of the supposedly morally superior anti-Franco side by Russian arms, military and political personnel and their foreign sympathizers and the vicious intra-civil war which was fought against their own political opponents simultaneously with the war against their nominal Franco enemy is extremely significant. This situation, as much as disillusionment with Soviet Russia, contributed to the undermining of the Soviet Dream among liberals, and left them in the morally destitute condition in which they were awash at the time of the Russo-German Pact of August, 1939.

THE LIBERAL CAMPAIGN
FOR AMERICAN INVOLVEMENT
IN THE SPANISH WAR

The belief that the Franco rebel uprising would turn out abortively in a short while undoubtedly had a strong part to play in confident liberal attitudes toward the situation in Spain in the late summer of 1936, and also accounted for its position on foreign intervention. But the defeats of the Government forces in August and September brought a chilling sobriety to those who awaited the collapse and flight of the junta. And as interveners piled into Spain, it began to be evident to the onlookers who wished a triumph of the Left that it was going to be anything but a summer war, conducted in the manner of a gay adventure. The liberal positions began to change forthwith, in adjustment to the new realities, and various comprehensive stands acquired ideological and strategic clothing. One of the earliest things to go under was the attitude of detachment toward outside participants.

In the case of the *New Republic,* the editorial policy clutched to neutrality after some of its editors and correspondents had abandoned it individually. Brailsford, just before the crushing Loyalist defeat at Toledo, called distractedly for a stand against the Franco advance; "Unless at some point the Western democracies will make a stand," he wailed, "nothing will remain of civilization." He did not explain this grandiose vision, but made it quite plain that he favored the formation at once of "an international Peoples' Front," beginning by including "in a firm defensive alliance England, France and the Soviet Union." [36] Popular Front terminology had long established that Russia, for its purposes, was a "democracy," but Brailsford did not explain by what geographical magic it had become "Western." Editorial position, however, insisted that a comprehensive neutral attitude on Spain was imperative, although in its "One-Way Neutrality" on September 30, it showed evidence of growing restive over increasing reports of aid reaching Franco via Portugal and the island of Majorca from the Italian and German regimes.[37] It was still many months too early to reveal that the International Brigades had also started to appear to buttress the Loyalist cause.

The siege of Madrid, beginning on November 6, properly ended the period of suspended judgment and "watchful waiting" by American liberals on the outcome of the Spanish war. It was now evident that not only was a quick Loyalist mop-up exceedingly unlikely; a swift defeat was a much more likely possibility instead. The tidal wave of pro-Loyalist and anti-Franco opinion-making properly began with the hectic emotionalizing during the first weeks of the ordeal of

Madrid, and the tempo rose rapidly after the Franco regime received Italian and German recognition on November 18, 1936. This made it exceedingly plain that a long, hard struggle lay ahead, and that it did not behoove the friends of the Loyalists to disdain support from any quarter. When the Baldwin and Blum governments of England and France persisted in trying to make an overall non-intervention policy viable in the face of these events, vast abuse was soon forthcoming. The *New Republic* at once adopted the view that the two should be furnishing aid to the Loyalist side, since this was the authority they had recognized in Spain, and that furthermore they should be entertaining a mutual comprehensive support plan. When Anthony Eden remarked, concerning the subject of foreign interference, "I think there are other governments more to blame than either Germany or Italy," a *New Republic* editorial on December 2 vigorously condemned him, swept by a feeling of outrage that he had deliberately referred to the Soviet Union. It went on to a comprehensive attack on the Tory English government, accused them of wishing that Franco's side would win, and even of having supported Mussolini in Italy because "they preferred Mussolini to a possible radical government in his place." [38] But there was no encouragement to President Roosevelt to abandon the American neutrality stand yet.

In January 1937 the position thawed a bit. The *New Republic*'s editorial of the 13th, "Shipping Arms to Spain," showed some of the effects of the Popular Front chorus by suggesting that the Loyalists be permitted to make use of a special "cash and carry plan," enabling them to buy munitions free on board the port of shipment, and to carry them back in any ships as long as they were not flying the American flag. This was a most worthy exception, it was emphasized: [39]

We do not want to discriminate against the Spaniards who are defending themselves from foreign intervention. We also want to stay out of war ourselves. We can quite easily do both, without tying our hands in the future. Let us not entangle this instance with general neutrality policy in a general war.

But "this instance" had already entangled the *New Republic* and most other liberals into a tangled knot in which the other strains were the munitions industry investigation, the neutrality program, the assault on rearmament, and the general peace drive. The consequences of making an exception in such a little, and righteous, war were most imperceptible. The full accumulated consequences by 1939 fitted in most admirably with the new and much bigger war drive which had blotted out the horizon in the meantime.

The *Nation* was much less inhibited in its position. Never having been excessively pleased with the neutrality concept anyway, and now finding its prior championship of pacifism a nagging irritation, its editors and correspondents were able to urge United States aid to Franco's enemies with robustness and substance. "Neutrality Makes Wars," its editorial for February 20 stated pointblank. It backed the view that both neutrality and non-intervention were strengthening the Franco cause, and that if the nations which supported his opposition would make forthright declarations on this, the Italian and German forces there would retire from Spain and the revolt would deflate.[40] Its faith in unsupported verbal protestations apparently was based on the theory of the cowardly character of the enemy, a theory which was stated hundreds of times in the many crises of the decade. It is unfortunate that in its two big tests, the challenge to Hitler in the summer of 1939 on the part of Britain and France, and to Japan on the part of the United States in 1941, both proved it to be lamentably incorrect.

From this position in the general, the *Nation* soon traveled to the specific. In March it accused Roosevelt, Hull and the State Department of being responsible for the inert state of mind prevailing on the matter of aid to the Loyalists. The State Department was categorically charged with hindering the departure of medical personnel from America for the Spanish front.[41] A prompt followup came from Fischer; his sustained criticism of March 27, 1937, "Keeping America Out of War," consisted of a comprehensive denunciation of pacifism and neutrality as war-breeders, the "best encouragement to aggressors," as he put it. In his fervid plea for the letting down of the bars against shipment of munitions to Spain, he selected the President as the individual who could stop the Spanish war if he chose to do so, but was enmeshed in the muddled state of domestic politics: [42]

Foreign policy . . . is always the exact reflection of domestic policy and domestic social conditions. If the great democracies of the world were firmly anti-fascist it would be easy for them to have a firm anti-fascist foreign policy. That is why the Soviet Union experiences no difficulty in formulating an anti-fascist foreign policy. The Russian social system is by its very nature anti-fascist. The U.S.S.R. has therefore been the strongest pillar of European peace, and the policies of Litvinov as he eloquently expounded them at Geneva and elsewhere have won ringing applause throughout the world. Russia is not neutral, for Russia is anti-fascist; we are playing around with neutrality, for we don't know what we are doing.

In August, 1939, Russia "played around with neutrality," but no one charged them with not knowing what they were doing then. Fischer gave liberals much to chew on in this piece, however, regardless of his incredible interpretation of Communist foreign policy. In addition to asserting the Popular Front doctrine that becoming anti-Fascist was the only true way of being peaceful, he declared that Italy was responsible for having "launched" the war in Spain, thus disagreeing with John Gunther, who was telling liberals everywhere that Germany had done so. But the main message Fischer conveyed between the lines of his earnest entreaty for American aid to the Russian-supported Loyalist cause was that the disturbance in domestic Russian politics caused by the purge trial disaffection was making it too difficult for the Soviet to supply all the needs of the anti-Franco war machine alone. William Mangold of the *New Republic* rang the anvil with the same theme as Fischer in a turgid piece in *The Fight*, in the same month, in which he titled his ferocious attack on American neutrality, "Betraying Spanish Democracy." [43] In a few short months, America had moved from a spot of remote detachment to one of individual responsibility for everything that was going wrong in Spain, in the eyes of fellow-traveling liberals.

Although the *Nation* was beginning to cool noticeably toward the Nye investigation, it found room to exploit Senator Nye personally at this time, as did the pro-Loyalist group in general. A March 5 editorial announced that it was according him support in his pending resolution calling on the State Department to give an official opinion whether Germany and Italy were in a state of war with Spain as a consequence of their support of the rebel side, which fitted in with its thesis that the Neutrality Act was being unfairly applied. As it explained to those readers who might have been puzzled by this gesture, "We do not happen to share Senator Nye's faith in an isolationist neutrality as a means of keeping us out of war. But it is important to prevent a measure designed to maintain peace from becoming a screen behind which the United States is covertly aiding the Fascist powers." [44] Nye still had usefulness, regardless of the clumsiness of the "merchants-of-death" approach in this moment of crying need of killing tools for the Red-backed Government of Spain; the next month he was the guest speaker at the American League Against War and Fascism's dinner in New York commemorating the twentieth anniversary of American entry into the First World War.[45] The incongruousness of decrying one war while working diligently to intensify and spread another was not apparent to such liberals as found these enterprises on the agenda simultaneously. And it may be assumed that Nye was much impressed with his new contacts. On May 19 the *New Republic* announced its earnest support behind Nye's demand for a congressional investigation of alleged agents of the Franco cause in the United States; "The desirability of an exhaustive congressional investigation seems clear," it expounded in most certain tones.[46] What might have been the reaction to a call for a combing of Communist pressure groups seeking the involvement of Americans on the opposite side was learned two years later when the Dies Committee began to examine the circumstances under which the Abraham Lincoln International Brigade had been recruited in the United States for service under Communist officers on the Madrid front; rarely has any government action in America been so roundly excoriated.

While some liberals were drumming on the thesis of American "betrayal" of Spain, others had not forgotten the English, the original scapegoats. Ludwig Lore joined Brailsford in the *New Republic* in charging this in March, 1937 in his piece "Has Britain Betrayed Spain?" Lore, absorbed with Germany, and reflecting the unnerved fright of German refugees whose stories had convinced him and others that Hitler was everywhere, ascribed the aversion of the Baldwin Government to aiding Loyalist Spain to "England's almost servile affability toward the Reich." [47] Brailsford saw little hope from others sharing Tory views; King Edward, and the Churchill faction as well, were also Fascist-tinged, according to him. The implication was that only a Labor government held out any hope for official aid to the *Frente Popular*.

When the Baldwin Government changed its policy late in April, favoring the establishment of a naval blockade of the Spanish coast and a border patrol, the *New Republic* displayed great restlessness and anxiety, and described such actions as "criminally dangerous." The war was sure to go on to a knockout, it maintained, and it was sheer delusion to try to stop it now. The Baldwin policy was a frank encouragement to a rebel victory with the aid of Italy and Germany, leading to "the encouragement of the aggressive powers in Europe and a heightened danger to peace and democracy everywhere." [48] It was an unconvincing case, since both sides were being aided substantially by seaborne supplies.

The suspicion that powerful elements in England were anxious to bring about a negotiated settlement in Spain, with a "peace without victory" conclusion, was verified in June, with a suggestion by the Tory government of a truce to be engineered by the Non-Intervention Committee still acting in a more or less shadow capacity, followed by the setting up of a "neutral" regime headed up by Salvador de Madariaga. The *New Republic* pounded this violently in June and July, 1937. This was merely evidence that the rebels were in a very feeble state, and that with both Hitler and Mussolini under fierce criticism at home and with both anxious to pull out of Spain entirely, an attempt was being made to set up under de Madariaga, ("a safe conservative,") "a regime that would be the equivalent to Fascism without the Fascists." [49] The former reference was to the denunciation of the large numbers of Italian troops reputedly in Spain, and also the shelling of the Spanish city of Almeria on May 31 by the German warship *Deutschland,* after it had been bombed by Loyalist planes.

Others were less restrained in their comments on de Madariaga's politics, while Lewis Mumford contributed his bit with a foaming review of his just-published book *Anarchy and Hierarchy,* described by Mumford as a "scientific wishful hodge-podge," suffering from "political rigor mortis." [50] Especially selected for attack editorially and by others was a projected world association which de Madariaga had outlined, charged with being just another Fascist scheme; de Madariaga exploded angrily at the *New Republic* on account of these charges, insisted his views were "wholly incompatible with fascism," countercharging that although he had been in New York City for six months, no attempt had been made by the liberal press to obtain his views on the matter. He concluded his protest against the "arbitrary and capricious labelling" to which he had been subjected by asking sharply, "Are you also afflicted with the mental color-blindness that is making millions of morons in our dismal world unable to see anything that is neither red nor brown"? [51]

But liberal harshness to de Madariaga was as much motivated by the desire to spike any serious possibility of a consideration anywhere for ending the Spanish Civil War in any way except by total victory, and in mid-1937, depite all the adversity, the liberal-Popular Front factions were firmly convinced that Franco's hopes were extremely small. While the truculent liberal exchange with de Madariaga was going on, Franco captured the Loyalist strong point of Bilbao. But it did not halt the abuse of the Spanish target. Frank Hanighen, a fierce enemy of Franco, supported the *New Republic* in its charges against de Madariaga in a communication in late July: "Every friend of Franco and fascism should be grateful to Señor de Madariaga for his splendid work in their behalf," Hanighen declared contemptuously.[52] Still another recommendation for a termination of the war on other terms than saturation victory came from Winston Churchill in the London *Evening Standard* at the end of the year, a suggestion that both Spanish factions ought to unite under a king. In the New Year's Day, 1938 issue of the *Nation,* Fischer ridiculed this; "Churchill's genius ruins his common sense."

Common Sense, no longer entranced with Popular Frontism and in loud outcry editorially over the fierce desires for war among its erstwhile liberal associates in various circles, had other explanations for British indecision and seeming ability to keep on tiptoe with held breath indefinitely. Its December, 1937 issue insisted that there were two main motives for British reluctance to assist the Loyalists. The first of these was the fear that upon doing so, the Mussolini regime's navy, operating as it had been doing, might dominate the imperial traffic route through the Mediterranean and apply immense pressure,

while the second involved their fear that should their aid be extensive and tip the balance in Loyalist favor, "Stalin might dominate a
victorious Madrid." If the latter were the case, British loss of fear of
Stalin in the next two years represented one of the grandest changes
of national psychology in recorded history.

In the meantime the effort either to stimulate the flow of war goods
to Loyalist Spain or to choke off the supply reaching Franco went on.
In July, 1937 a group of twenty persons described by the *New Republic* as "well-known American progressives," including MacLeish,
Donald Ogden Stewart, Harry F. Ward, Corliss Lamont and Rockwell Kent, requested an interview with FDR in order to urge him to
extend the embargo against the shipment of arms to the "Fascist
powers" as well as the Spanish Government.[53] The decision to hold
the Writers Congress in Madrid the same month was a dramatic
demonstration of the politics of these authors, and the occasion was
one on which attending members, like Malcolm Cowley and left
political hopefuls fighting in the International Brigades, such as
Joseph P. Lash, could use their talents to cry out for American action
benefiting the Loyalist cause, but from the actual scene of combat
instead of from the United States.

Nor was the circumspect Anglo-French hands-off policy ignored;
there were frequent exhortations to abandon this stand and participate wholeheartedly in the business of furnishing the anti-Franco
cause with war *matériel.* To the objection being made in some quarters that to do so might invite war with Italy and Germany, Louis
Fischer retorted in his *Nation* dispatch "A Lesson For the Democracies," on October 16, that "Ever since October, 1936 the Soviet
Union has been sending arms in large quantities to the legal Spanish
government," but that neither Italy nor Germany had gone to war
with Russia for that reason.[54] In this serious critique of the Anglo-
French abstention policy he insisted that the most remote consequence of their becoming actively engaged in the war goods supply
business was war with Hitler or Mussolini.

The liberal castigation of the Administration's embargo stand
stepped up sharply in March, 1938, partially a consequence of the
grave alarm over the Hitler regime's easy annexation of Austria and
probably as much a product of consternation over the fortunes of the
Spanish war. Franco's swift counter-attack had recaptured Teruel
from the Government, its only significant previous triumph over the
rebels, and a massive drive was on toward the Mediterranean in the
manner of the march of Sherman in an earlier civil war. The easy
confidence in a cataclysmic victory over Franco had vanished, and
the hysteria season had replaced it. Faith in the Soviet's ability to
supply the Negrin Government adequately had drooped to the point
of prostration. The *Nation*'s March 26 "End the Embargo on Spain!"

attacked France for not coming to the Loyalists' support, but for the first time a violent attack was levelled against the Roosevelt Administration. The editorial urgently requested readers to pressure their congressmen to revise or repeal the Neutrality Act and to repeal the Embargo resolution of January 8, 1937, in order to permit immediate and massive aid to the force against Franco. And this appeal was prefaced with the grim prognostication that future historians would hold the United States largely responsible for the outbreak of a new war in Europe, in view of our foreign policy since 1919, from the time of "American acquiescence in the shameless farce of Versailles" through the more current "failures" *in re* Ethiopia, Spain and China. This was Popular Front politics conducted in white-hot heat and at top velocity, with a few overtones of the old revisionism woven in.

The attack was pin-pointed on the State Department in the next few weeks, and in the third week of May, similar-sounding editorial assaults on Secretary Hull and unnamed associates appeared a few days apart in the *Nation* and *New Masses;* the former's "Hull of Downing Street" and the latter's "The Smelly State Department" could hardly have been more extreme. The *Nation,* in its frustration and despair over Hull's letter to Senator Pittman turning the visage of uncompromising disapproval on a Senate gesture toward repeal of the embargo, delivered the bitterest attack made on him in the liberal press by anyone since Paul Ward's sulphurous blow of some three years earlier, and bluntly declared that the letter itself "in its direction and consequences" was "one of the most reactionary state papers in the history of American foreign policy." In its rancor the journal even forgot its growing sensitiveness toward criticism of England by "isolationist" liberals to indulge in a bit itself. Its theory on Hull's action was that he was tailoring American policy in Spanish matters to suit the desires of the government of Neville Chamberlain, who had replaced Baldwin on May 28, 1937 and had promptly incurred the wrath of Leftists and liberals to a degree previously never encountered by any English politician. It was Chamberlain's fate to become responsible at the high-water mark of their concern for the welfare of Russia, and to be pressing a policy of compromise which created a maximum of discomfort for the Russians as a consequence of its side-effect of encouraging Germany. It is one of the ironies of the history of public opinion-making that the Communist fabrication of the whole "appeasement" smear on Chamberlain should go through to conclusion without any serious or significant recognition of it on the part of those caught up in its fulminating consequences. The *Nation* concluded, "The sum of the matter is that the State Department has become an annex of the British Foreign Office in a sense to a degree that has not been true since 1917," [55] and Max Lerner went into an extended treatment of this in his long essay "Behind Hull's Embargo" a week later.[56] This was hardly more than an aberration, of course, and not a shift in policy or emphasis; in the two years prior to American involvement in the next big war, the *Nation* rarely was able to detect the slightest sign of British Foreign Office influence or personnel anywhere in the United States, and bristled ominously at the inference of such activity.

Despite the shift in foreign policy which the issue of the President's famous "quarantine" speech of October, 1937 presaged, and which obviously gave great heart to the Popular Front forces everywhere, with the Communists in the very foremost rank in loud praise of its implications and connotations, there seemed to be a strange unwillingness to implement it with tangible gestures such as ending the embargo and pitching in with substantial arms for Franco's fading Loyalist opponents. This contradiction was especially enraging to liberals, tantalized by the vision of America abandoning its neutrality under Roosevelt and swarming over the world achieving the goals of Popular Frontism while under the impression of following the dictates of American interest. But it was not yet to be, and undoubtedly the sagging performance of the Loyalists, wracked by internal problems and a vicious struggle for power within, had a substantial part to play in the waning interest in the Spanish war. The protagonists of the Loyalists in America kept pounding away, while entreaty after entreaty arrived from Spain, especially from Fischer for prominent display in the *Nation,* to which attention will be paid subsequently.

When Franco triumphed in April, 1939 the post-mortems began. For months the same charges which had rocked the liberal press all through 1938 reappeared again and again. As late as August 16, a week away from the Russo-German pact, the *New Republic* was insisting that "Franco's stunning victory" could be attributed to "the little pro-Fascist and Catholic group in the American State Department." [57] But by far the most eloquent statement on the situation came in the *Nation* just two weeks after the collapse of the Loyalists, a comprehensive condemnation of President Roosevelt personally as being responsible for the maintenance of the Spanish embargo and the victory of Franco's rebellion. In a long discussion and literary criticism of the work of the Spanish poet Antonio Machado, a Loyalist protagonist and casualty of the war, Waldo Frank thundered that "all of us are accomplices" in his death, and promptly became more specific: [58]

The workers of France and England are among his murderers because they lacked in their good-will the audacity, the purity, the power which their foes have displayed in serving evil. Franklin D. Roosevelt is among the murderers. Mr. President: men and women throughout the world, seduced by your power and your honeyed words, have flattered you. Know the truth. As the stricken poet goes his last journey through the dolorous night which is our night also, under the planes of Fascists who make a sport of spraying with machine gun fire the fleeing men and women, you are among the murderers. Even as late as last summer the lifting of the illegal American embargo against Spain would have turned the tide in Europe; the peoples of France and Britain were rising against their rulers; the Chamberlains and Daladiers were wavering; a word from you would have been irresistible. Yet with the full knowledge of the facts, with avowed love of the faith for which Spain bled, with none of the overwhelming obstacles to action which stultified France and England, you did not lift a finger to implement your pleasant phrases about democracy and justice.

The drive to get American tools of war to Loyalist Spain had failed, but its contribution to entrenching the views of the virtuousness of pro-Russian Popular Front politics and the ineffable evil of the enemies of Russia, Communism and Communists could hardly be exaggerated. Part of the crest of the wave which American liberals rode into the Second World War upon had built up during the last two years of the Spanish Civil War.

REPORTAGE OF A WAR: A CASE STUDY

In its April 10, 1937 issue the *Nation* editorially accused William P. Carney of the New York *Times* of writing untrue accounts of the Spanish Civil War from his vantage-point behind the Franco lines.[59] A furious controversy had been raging as to who was telling the truth about the action there, and it was to go on for two more years. It may be instructive to examine the way in which the war was presented in the liberal journal which found the *Times* coverage from the anti-Loyalist side so offensively untruthful. Although the positions of the two liberal weeklies were for all practical purposes identical, the *Nation* devoted much more space to this conflict, and in addition profited from the regular reports of its ex-Moscow correspondent Fischer, supplementing other special features. And its deep emotional commitment to the Loyalist cause guaranteed a lively interpretation of the news which arrived in non-editorial form.

Several references have already been made in prior contexts to the military events of the early part of the war, the string of Franco victories from the formation of the rebel *Junta* at Burgos down through the beginning of the siege of Madrid, to the capture of Bilbao, on June 18, 1937. During this period of flushed confidence in a rapidly-approaching Franco annihilation, we have seen that there was a lamentable tendency to report Loyalist victories just before or just after they suffered a serious setback. When these occurred, excuses usually were found to explain them, but often other matters of importance at the same time led to the attachment of less significance to the immediate military scene, as was the case with the bitter struggle for recognition and control among the Left factions in the face of their common enemy. And though there was no hesitation to boast of Russian Communist aid to the Caballero and Negrin Governments, it was a practice to stress that which was coming to Franco from Italo-German sources, and to give them the credit for the lion's share of the successes enjoyed at Loyalist expense.

For a brief moment in the spring of 1937, while the "merchants-of-death" exposés and disillusion with World War One and the Nye disclosures enjoyed peak popularity, it was considered fashionable to apply this approach to Spain. Hanighen, the veteran writer on the sins of the arms makers and the economic drives hidden in war, interpreted the Spanish war thusly. For a moment Hitler and Mussolini were not monotonously disparaged as "madmen"; in Spain they were credited with impressive calculating craftiness. Hanighen scoffed at their claims that they were in Spain to defeat Communism; he saw them there far more because of the valuable Spanish mineral deposits, and in a long *Nation* article late in April, 1937 expressed the conviction that the multi-national interests engaged in the contest for these minerals was proof that the war was simply "an extension of the world-wide struggle for raw materials." This line was taken up by the *New Republic* which in a later editorial, "Foreign Stakes In Spain," sounded like the opening statement of a 1935 Nye hearing; "No war goes on very long without the discovery of substantial economic interests behind the slogans and high principles." [60]

But this brief spell was one of the most quickly forgotten episodes of war interpretation. With the fuller commitment of the Soviet strength to the Loyalist side, liberals perfected an idealistic frame of reference for the Spanish Civil War which made the much-reviled idealistic propaganda of 1914–1918 seem very faint by comparison. And liberal rejoicing in the smoke and blood and destruction surpassed the crude recruitment literature of the World War in much the same proportion. Before a year had elapsed, American liberals to a large degree had accepted the Communist dichotomy on war and applied it assiduously to the Spanish situation. The big difficulty came when "imperialist" war and the "people's" or civil war began to merge and blend; there were few spiritual or other resources at the command of most liberals to make recourse to at that stage, and once having gotten a taste of righteousness, the impulse to sanction the much bigger bloodletting of 1939 and thereafter proved overpowering. In view of the lengthy course of disillusionment over the First

World War, it is unlikely that so many of those who were involved in this would have adjusted to the Second with so little friction, had it not been for the conditioning of the Spanish Civil War. The transition from one to the other was achieved in the quiet manner of the shifting of speeds in a well-made motor. Far closer to the theme which would dominate the interpretation of the Spanish War than Hanighen's investigation of its "imperialistic" aspect was the new, shining idealistic reaffirmation of violence in Thomas Mann's "I Stand With The Spanish People" of a week earlier. Mann chose to stand with specific Spanish Leftist people.[61]

This spirit was reflected in the *Nation*'s editorial upon the Bilbao and Almeria bombings and shellings in May and June, 1937 prior to the taking of the former by Franco on June 18. The one-sided picturings of the air bombings during World War Two received adequate preparation in the reporting of this element of the struggle in Spain. It was not until the war was over that any substantial stories of Russian air power and achievements in Spain began to receive attention, and largely because the Communists considered it important for the purpose of gaining faith in the Soviet's military and aerial prowess, both in 1939 and 1941.

The summer of 1937 was not a particularly fortunate time for the Loyalist cause, despite the whistling in the dark on the *Nation,* both editorially and from Fischer in Madrid. While the Nyon Conference was going on, at which the French, English, Italians and Germans shadow-boxed while pretending to seek the identity of the mystery submarines conducting "piratical" operations in the Mediterranean, mostly at English expense, the Franco forces continued to move. On July 17 Fischer's dispatch was joyfully captioned, "Loyalist Spain Takes the Offensive," which presumably signalled that the string of Franco victories over the past year were about to be stemmed, and matched by Government triumphs. Fischer's reservation on the future vigor of the Loyalists was the fear that the high-flying Communist Party's "new-found ambition to dominate" had "unhealthy possibilities," but he did not explain why it had taken so long to discern the Communist goal.[62] Two weeks later Franco took Brunete, smashing the Loyalist hopes of causing a diversion and thus lifting the siege of Madrid. A note of perplexed indecision now entered the *Nation;* it was at this time, late in August, that it became practical to admit that the Communists, both Russian and in the International Brigades, were the force which not only dominated the anti-Franco side, but were keeping it fighting. The pulverizing of Spain in a dogged street-by-street struggle tilled the land for the sowing of more Communism as effectively as such a war was doing in China. Sensitiveness about the composition of the Brigades was abating; the *New Masses* of August 24, 1937 could hardly suppress a quiet note of pride in its declaration, "It will be recalled that Earl Browder recently stated that the majority of the Abraham Lincoln [U.S.A.] Battalion was recruited from the Communist Party. It will be obvious from this that the remainder of the battalion consisted mainly of non-Communists who accepted the leadership of the Communist Party." [63] There were occasional moments of reluctance, as on the occasion of the sensational assassination of the Rosselli brothers in France in June, largely used as an occasion to blame the Mussolini regime, since one of the two, Carlo, was the editor of an anti-Mussolini paper. The fact that he was just back from Spain and that he was a member of an International Brigade did not get as much publicity.[64]

The first substantial account of the record of the Brigades in the strictly liberal press came from Fischer ten days later, just after the Loyalists had lost Santander to Franco. "Madrid's Foreign Defenders" described the International Brigades as a force of some 23,000 men, a figure which was adjusted upward later in the war, and the *Nation*'s correspondent identified a variety of Americans, some of whom were not entirely unknown to readers, whom he had personally met, including Sam Romer, Lash and an ex-University of California-at-Berkeley lecturer named Robert Merriman. Part of Fischer's dispatch dealt with the Lincoln Brigade's armament: [65]

The men were firing from rifles and a light machine gun. I asked what kind of a machine-gun it was. The reply was "Mexican," but the characters on the gun were Russian. "Mexican" is a formula, and the word is never pronounced without a wink. I prefer my facts straight.

For a journal as sophisticated as the *Nation,* the last sentence was probably the most naïve *non-sequitur* published in the entire decade of the explosive and effulgent 1930's.

Reverses and disasters did not jog liberal reporting out of its calm and confident expectation of great things to come and its sure faith in the eventual success of the chosen side. When the Franco rebels captured Gijon in October and for all practical purposes ended the fighting in Asturias and northwestern Spain, it was an occasion for little or no concern. On Christmas Day, 1937 Mangold, of the *New Republic*'s editorial staff, assured the readers that the Spanish Civil War was just beginning, not about to end, and that the Loyalists were about to demonstrate their superiority. The event which provoked this gesture of buoyancy was the first substantial, and last, Loyalist victory, the capture of Teruel, on December 19. The *Nation* resounded with praise of this feat, and almost a month later was still hailing it in the most flattering terms. The New Year's Day, 1938 issue featured Fischer's dispatch, "The Loyalists Push Ahead," which declared in part with great vehemence,

Actually, the Spanish Republic is fighting half of Spain, Germany and Italy singlehanded. The U.S.S.R. saved it between October, 1936 and May, 1937, when, deserted by its armed forces and caught unprepared, it would but for foreign aid have fallen an easy prey to world Fascism.

The danger of it falling to world Communism was considered too slight to even mention in these halcyon days.

On February 15, 1938 the Franco forces re-took Teruel, and began their spectacular drive which aimed at cutting off Barcelona and Catalonia from the rest of Spain. It took nearly six weeks before the *Nation* became worried over this offensive. Leigh White's "Barcelona Faces Front" on March 5 imperturbably announced that "only the captious still regard the defense of Loyalist Spain as the expression of revolutionary ardor; the war is being won." [66] Fischer three weeks later was writing in a minor key. His "What Can Save Spain" of March 26 reflected the desperation of the Loyalist cause in the face of imminent Franco saturation of Catalonia. He announced that Soviet artillery and pursuit bombers were coming in in greater numbers, but were still not enough. He pleaded dramatically that "heavy war material be sent to the assistance of the Loyalists," and aimed this particular appeal at Blum and the French Socialist-Popular Front regime.[67] Two weeks before the collapse Fischer's "Barcelona Holds Out" contained a note of previously undiscernible panic: "Without foreign help the cause is desperate," he agonized. This obviously meant more foreign help than had already been tendered. Yet he was still optimistic; "The true revolutionist and anti-fascist never gives up the struggle. Spain is part of a war against the universal enemy of humanity." [68] The superb long-view concept of Marxist revolutionary demolition was rarely better expressed in so few words.

By April 9, the week before the isolation of Barcelona and Catalonia, the dispatches from Spain coincided with the immense pressures being applied in America for the suspension of the embargo. The editorial "The President Must Act!" asked rhetorically what happened to this political drive, but did not blame Roosevelt and Hull now; "friends of Franco in the State Department" have overridden their chiefs by means of dubious legal opinions." [69] On the 15th, Franco's forces took Viñaroz, effecting the split of Catalonia and Barcelona from Madrid and Castile. In a rueful glance and critique in its lead editorial paragraph of the 23rd, the *Nation* once more credited Franco with victory as a consequence of the failure of significant help to reach the Loyalists from the outside, this time from the United States; "pro-Catholic, pro-Fascist influences seem to have had things their own way again." [70] But even in defeat there were bits of satisfaction to be gleaned; in the same issue Leland Stowe, in a long dispatch titled "Spain's Shirt-Sleeve Heroes," issued a stirring tribute to five Communist generals, although in five long columns he failed to use the word "Communist" once.[71] This was Popular Front reporting with a vengeance.

For a short time thereafter, a measure of confidence returned. By the end of April, 1938 the *Nation* declared that the Loyalists were now recovered from their recent set-backs, although an editorial on the 30th fumed that the embargo was still in effect in the United States, despite Senator Nye's plea for lifting it. Roosevelt's stubborn refusal to act evoked acidic and irritated criticism.[72] But from Spain Fischer's communiqué radiated confidence; "Spain Won't Surrender," he trumpeted. It was in this dispatch that the stiffening of resistance as a consequence of the re-introduction of the political commissars in the line organizations received so much credit,[73] although a thorough explanation of the full role they played in Spain was not to appear in print until the late winter of 1938–1939 in the *New Masses*.

The lull during the sieges of the Loyalist strongholds produced little new comment or news from the spot, although in July, 1938 on the second anniversary of the war a variety of new developments, as well as old ones, brought Spain back into prominence. The Czechoslovak crisis with Germany tended to saturate liberal attention at this moment, but there was ample room to take up this still very important issue. The mysterious silence over the apparent sharp slowdown of Soviet help after the agreement on the withdrawal of "volunteers" was balanced off by reiterations of charges that the Loyalist cause was being "sold out" by the English. And editorial approval had already been given to a threat of the Barcelona Loyalist enclave to "open" the French-Spanish frontier by bombing Italy, with the implication that a retaliatory attack on Russia by Franco would not be unwelcome; the spreading of the war was an obvious last hope as a chance to snap the tightening grip of Franco on the last major Loyalist centers of resistance.[74]

A big Loyalist diversionary drive along the Ebro River in August changed the defensive and apologetic tone of the reporting on the war. Although Italian soldiers had started leaving Spain in mid-April, and the International Brigades presumably were to have withdrawn from the Loyalist side, it seemed that foreign intervention was still a factor. During the Ebro drive, Fischer reported that the Brigades had lost their identitiy but not their substance, "having been merged with the Spanish brigades." And the course of this assault gave every indication of success and reason for confidence. Fischer, early in September, describing the appearance of the Loyalist side, observed that "In no way do they behave like a nation on its back. I have seen worse conditions in Soviet Russia during peace years." [75] Stowe in the *New Republic* for August 31, in a report which would have satisfied the editors of any militant patriotic journal of any nation in the world, confidently predicted, "The Loyalists Can Still Win." [76] The collapse of the anti-Franco cause was just eight months away. But Stowe was exceeded by the complacency of Lawrence A. Fernsworth, the Spanish correspondent to the London *Times,* whose authoritative-sounding major report to the *Nation* on October 29, 1938, five months before utter Loyalist prostration, assured the readers that the Loyalists had "excellent chances of victory." [77]

The drive to bring about the suspension of the embargo accelerated in the fall of 1938, in a campaign which now was considered desperate enough to tie it into American internal politics. The Munich settlement had undoubtedly done much to bring about this situation, and the restraints of former days were being thrown to all corners, as the stakes began to loom larger and larger against the backdrop of planetary affairs. On October 15, an urgent editorial announced, "As the *Nation* has repeatedly pointed out, the embargo against Spain can be lifted by the President without Congressional action," and as a tactical move it recommended, "The President and the State Department must be made to feel, in these pre-election days, the full force of American public opinion." Other urgent recommendations of this sort occurred until after election, and the heat continued to be applied into the early weeks of 1939.[78] When the big rebel assault on Barcelona began in January, 1939 the *Nation* insisted that "it seems certain that the Spanish war will go on for many months," and suggested more agitation in the United States for abrogation of the embargo, arguing that chances of success were very high because five-sixths of the American people were in favor of such a policy change, in their opinion.[79]

In its December 31, 1938 editorial the *Nation* had underlined its firmness of belief in ultimate Loyalist victory, despite the failure of the big Ebro campaign and the tightening of the noose around Barcelona. "Our task for 1939 is to shake off defeatism, to take our part in the active defense of democracy" in Spain, "Europe's brightest hope." There was a wry flavor to this tribute; after having admitted the steady capture of the Loyalist side by the Communists during 1937, there was no hesitation in making a categorical assertion now that "democracy is more alive in Spain than at the beginning of the war." [80] Fischer's dispatch of January 7 similarly radiated with confidence in the Loyalists' ability to hold off Franco. Part of his assurance admittedly came from the words of Eden, Churchill and Duff Cooper, whose growing truculence since Munich was gaining favor, and who had, as Fischer put it, "been convinced by events that a Fascist Spain would be a disaster." [81] He did not describe what political order these agitated English spokesmen now preferred for Spain, but it was obvious that Churchill's suggestion of a year before, of union under a king, was impossible. In their vision of Fascism they had apparently not seen any sign of the looming political commissars behind the backdrop of the smashed cities of Madrid and Barcelona.

There was a pathetic quality to the *Nation's* editorial paragraph of January 28, "The military situation in Catalonia, as we go to press, is almost desperate." [82] It was actually much worse than that; Franco had taken Barcelona two days before, after less than a month of fighting. By February 4, the spirit of optimism had bounced back; "It is not too late to save Spain," the extended editorial "After Barcelona" announced.[83] But there was no Loyalist recovery from this blow, conceded to be a "major setback, second only to Munich." On February 11 came the shocking admission, "The collapse of Loyalist resistance in Catalonia came with such tragic suddenness that it is impossible to guess what the next few days will bring in Spain." [84] Part of the shock obviously came from the refusal to see the real situation, and to persist, despite an almost unbroken series of bad defeats, to see the rainbow of final victory hanging behind Loyalist fortunes. In a way, reporting the Spanish debacle was preparation for another war which was apparently being won until the day it was lost, the war of Finland against Russia a year later, at a time when the Soviet had fallen grievously from liberal favor.

The incredible thing about the *Nation* even at this moment *in extremis* was its flourish of the following week, "The War Goes On," in which it coupled an expectation of ultimate victory over Franco with the strong hope of ending the American embargo:[85]

It is not too late for action. It is still possible to preserve an island of democracy in Europe if we will but grant Spain the rights to which it is entitled as a sovereign state. But this will not be done unless the President displays new understanding and courage.

Some idea of how grievously the *Nation* had misread the temper of the Administration in Washington was made evident just over four weeks later, when the Franco regime was given formal recognition by Roosevelt, the champion-in-waiting of liberal hopes for over two years, the ace in the hole, so to speak, which was never there in the first place.

But before this transpired there were the last bitter and confused weeks of fighting, punctuated by French and British recognition of Franco's insurgents, insistence by Franco on a Loyalist unconditional surrender, and the renewed murderous infighting among the Loyalists themselves once more. Deep despair shimmered from the *Nation's* February 25 issue, as it reported in anguish that "The end of Loyalist resistance seems in sight." [86] Through the next two weeks it harshly denounced the French and British recognitions, deplored

Franco's insistence on unconditional surrender as an unspeakable demand,[87] and, sensing the leanings toward American repetition of the recognition action, suggested with great emphasis that the Stimson Doctrine be wheeled out instead, and that we apply it here as had been the case in Manchuria and Ethiopia. "Our government did enough to help France and Britain to help the Fascists to help him [Franco] win. Let us not hasten to crown him before his triumph is complete," advised an editorial paragraph on March 11.[88]

But Franco's "triumph" was "complete," and the final touches were applied by his erstwhile enemies, fighting among themselves. A *Nation* editorial paragraph on March 18 admitted the Communists had over-extended themselves with their towering greed for power, and that growing hate for them had touched off serious fighting and stimulated plans for overthrow of the Negrin government. In a hand-wringing commentary the liberal journal concluded, "That these comrades should have turned to slaughtering each other in their hour of defeat is a tragedy almost as great as the defeat itself." [89] The vicious infighting of the previous two years and the Communists' private war within the Loyalist ranks against ideological enemies was already forgotten. Fischer could not be held back from a personal observation; [90]

It is all very sad. This bloodshed in Madrid is senseless. The very officers and soldiers who saw Communists die in thousands at their side are shooting down the Communist executives.

But he volunteered in a consoling tone, "The Communists are putting up a swell fight." Stunned by the strength of the anti-Communist forces on the Loyalist side, Fischer's was a confused and uninformative explanation of this intra-Loyalist war. Part of his belated and stammering analysis of the source of this pent-up hostility tenaciously clung to the thesis that it was a lamentable misunderstanding:

The longer the war lasted, the more some Loyalists despaired of a successful conclusion; therefore they abhorred the Communists, who had faith and tenacity. The Soviet Union's failure to send as many munitions as Germany and Italy sent was booked to the discredit of the Spanish Communists. Besides, the Communists made many enemies by their irritating attempts . . . to control important institutions.

By this time, Negrin had been toppled and had fled to France, and a National Defense Council had emerged out of the consequent smashing of Negrin's Communist allies, headed by Generals Segismundo Casado and José Miaja. But its failure to keep the fighting going against Franco and to get terms short of unconditional surrender led to the finish of resistance on March 28, 1939. On April 1, the day on which United States recognition of Franco occurred, the *Nation* dolefully announced that Madrid had capitulated and that the efforts "to arrange an honorable peace" had come to naught.[91]

Postmortems on the Spanish War and the case of the Communists continued for many months, subject to fundamental revision by the subsequent developments in 1939 and 1941. The precipitate Roosevelt recognition of Franco drew a signed editorial rebuke from Freda Kirchwey a week later, in addition to a charge that Franco was continuing the war through the medium of his "Law of Political Responsibilities." She heaped ridicule on his designation of defeated leaders as "war criminals" and the bringing of them to trial under this law, while urging generous support of the six relief agencies already administering help to Loyalist refugees, most of whom had been incarcerated in special concentration camps in the South of France. The *New Republic* was fully as indignant over the issue of recognition of Franco. Its "Don't Recognize Franco" editorial late in March advanced the thesis that his victory was "in essence the conquest of the Spanish people by foreign powers, and according to the Stimson doctrine we should not recognize unlawful conquest." There was no discussion of what "lawful" conquest might be. A subsequent editorial on April 12 simmered with rage over the decision to recognize the new regime, which action was asserted to be "contrary to every public declaration of the President" on the Spanish situation. "Mr. Roosevelt owes his bewildered and shocked supporters an explanation," it seethed.[92] There was an outraged cry in the *Nation* later in the summer when the Import-Export Bank extended a $13,750,000 cotton credit to the Franco regime in the week before the Stalin-Hitler Pact. "Nothing could do more to undermine the Administration's foreign policy," and it went on, "How can Mr. Roosevelt aspire to be the leader of the democratic forces against the Axis when he rushes forward to bolster its Spanish puppet?"[93] The mysterious ways of statecraft still seemed to puzzle the liberals with their inscrutability, in their ideological world which had emerged with its brilliant blacks and whites in such rapidity.

As for the issue of Communism in Spain, the verdict was subject to the fluctuating of world political fortunes. Despite all the revelations about the Communists in general and the Soviet Union in particular during the Spanish war, there was a certain amount of resentment toward exposés in hostile sources, such as the disclosures by General Krivitsky which were published by the *Saturday Evening Post* in the spring of 1939. His story of overall Red penetration of the Loyalist side was responded to with some fury, especially by the *New Republic*,[94] although the supreme counter to Krivitsky was moved into play by the *New Masses*, which denied that he was an ex-Russian general but was really an Austrian citizen named Schmelka Ginsberg and that his stories had been ghost-written by Isaac Don Levine.

About the only time a serious postwar examination of the part played by Communists in the anti-Franco coalition took place occurred after World War Two was on, in the months immediately following the outbreak of hostilities. With American liberalism in a state of profound prostration as a consequence of Stalin's demolition of the Popular Front and his non-aggression pact with the long-hated Hitler regime of Germany, it was even appropriate for a while to assume unfriendly postures toward Communism, at least as far as it was represented by Russia and its influences elsewhere. The occasion which led to some realistic evaluation was the publication of two books dealing with the role of the International Brigades in Spain: *Men in Battle* by Alvah Bessie and *The Lincoln Battalion* by Edwin Rolfe, both veterans of these detachments and the latter author a correspondent to the *Daily Worker* besides. Cowley's review of Bessie in the *New Republic* on October 25, 1939 was most unhappy with the soft-pedalling of attention to these organizations and the source of their dynamism; "not nearly enough attention is given to the part played by the Communists in the International Brigades," asserted the reviewer; "It was, after all, the decisive part." Cowley was still firmly convinced that the Communists in Spain had had no further objective in fighting other than "to save and strengthen the Western democracies against Fascism," thus repeating Brailsford's memorable geographical stunt of landing Russia well out of its historical location. He was quite agitated and offended that now that Russia no longer appeared to be an element in the war picture the charge was abroad that the Reds had been "engaged in a great plot to set up a Red Republic in Western Europe." Cowley charged that this was gross ingratitude, since he thought it was amply proved now that without the enormous part played by Russian tanks and planes, the whole anti-Franco fight would have collapsed as early as 1936, which in itself was a remarkable commentary on the reliability and honesty of liberal reportage of the war. In his conclusion Cowley tried to make an agonized differentiation between the Kremlin and the Comintern, to the credit of the latter, for there was no doubt in his mind that the two were quite distinct and that the non-Russian Communists fighting in Spain had actually been fighting there "to keep Russia in the democratic front," and had been "betrayed by Eden and Blum, by Chamberlain and Daladier, and even by Roosevelt." [95]

This position was possible to present in the *New Republic*, since it was quite in opposition to the war-bent of the moment in the circles of liberal thought, and clung to its established attitude of withdrawal from participation in pro-war propaganda. The *Nation* on the other hand had gone to war with Germany long before the invasion of

Poland, and its attitude toward Russia now already had performed a majestic circling movement. Bessie and Rolfe were reviewed there in November 18 by Samuel Romer, which gave the picture an unusual quality, with two books written by Lincoln Brigade veterans being reviewed by a veteran of the MacKenzie-Papineau Canadian Brigade. But his assay of their import was in no way comparable or complementary to Cowley. Romer criticized them for their reluctance to mention the part played by Communism, and their references to Spanish politics he identified as "always faulty and partisan." And for Rolfe, Romer had the supreme thrust; "Rolfe succeeds, incidentally, in telling his story without a single reference to the Soviet Union, whose officers trained the Loyalist army, whose arms enabled it to fight, and whose foreign policy forced it into suicide." [96] Such a slight to Russia before August 23, 1939 would have been utterly out of the question in the *Nation;* the fortunes of world politics had made it possible. And the following January, in the course of the third of a series of bitterly disillusionist pieces on his Russian experiences which he was writing for the *Nation,* Fischer, no longer under any compulsion to present the Soviet Union's stand in Spain in the best light possible, made the amazing admission that a sizable number of top-level Russian officers and officials had been sent to Spain beginning as early as October, 1936, including five Red Army generals.[97]

It is to be noted that the Communist press in America in the two years after the end of the Spanish war did not hesitate in the slightest to take pride in Russian performances in Spain, especially its air force. Both the *New Masses* and the *Communist* described great air battles around Madrid in which out-numbered Soviet fliers were supposed to have knocked down scores of German planes with trifling losses to themselves.[98] Robert Minor in the *Communist* in May 1939 maintained that it was Hitler's fear of the Soviet air power as demonstrated in Spain which had made him confine his program of German expansion in areas other than in Eastern Europe. The hesitation by liberals to make such exposures, however, was not due to bashfulness or protectiveness necessarily, as it was the pressure to keep its account of the Spanish fighting within the context of the Popular Front. And when there was no longer a Popular Front, its momentum kept liberal reportage from completely reversing the story they had adhered to so stubbornly for so long a period of time. The spreading of the Second World War loosened things, but by the time liberals had mounted a serious anti-Soviet propaganda barrage on account of Russia's war with the Finns, the war in Spain no longer seemed so important, and as a special subject it no longer merited comprehensive attention. But the Spanish Civil War, a thumping, bruising trip for American liberals, had salutary contributions to make to those who followed its every jolt to the painful end; it provided the conditioning and emotional cushioning which made it ever so much easier to accept the rationale of a much bigger, bloodier and more destructive struggle later on with an absolute minimum of spiritual anguish. The Spanish Civil War was the basic training center for American liberals prior to their generous enlistment in the Second World War, but, as will be seen, extended field problems worked out with the Communists in China during the same time helped to contribute immensely to the hardening of their intellectual muscles.

N O T E S

1 *New Republic,* October 17, 1934, pp. 256–257.
2 *Nation,* April 29, 1936, pp. 546–548.
3 *Nation,* August 1, 1936, p. 116.
4 *New Republic,* August 26, 1936, p. 62. On the *Nation's* position see editorial "Civil War and Intervention," *Nation,* August 29, 1936, pp. 228–229.
5 *New Republic,* September 2, 1936, p. 107.
6 *New Republic,* September 9, 1936, p. 118.
7 *New Masses,* September 8, 1936, p. 12.
8 *Nation,* September 19, 1936, p. 322.
9 *Nation,* August 29, 1936, pp. 233–236.
10 *Nation,* October 31, 1936, p. 507.
11 *Nation,* October 31, 1936, p. 511
12 Lerner, "I Was In Spain," *The Fight,* November, 1936, pp. 40–41; Bessie, "An American Flier In Spain," *The Fight,* July, 1937, pp. 8–9. Cowley was no longer identified with this magazine, but Lovett was with it to the end. Bates's review of Sommerfield in *Nation,* November 27, 1937, pp. 593–594.
13 *New Republic,* May 5, 1937, p. 371.
14 Fischer, "Spain's 'Red' Foreign Legion," *Nation,* January 9, 1937, pp. 36–38. Fischer reported meeting Renn in a town near Albacete.
15 Hawthorne, "Madrid's International Volunteers," *New Masses,* January 12, 1937, pp. 3–5.
16 *Nation,* October 17, 1936, pp. 453–454. The Gannes-Repard book was published by Knopf.
17 *Nation,* January 16, 1937, p. 62.
18 "The Fascist Front Holds," *Nation,* January 23, 1937, p. 88.
19 *Common Sense,* January, 1937, p. 5.
20 *Nation,* December 26, 1936, p. 771; Freeman's defense in *Nation,* January 30, 1937, p. 139.
21 "Spain Is the Key," *Nation,* February 13, 1937, p. 172.
22 Malraux speech in *Nation,* March 20, 1937, pp. 315–316.
23 Trotsky-Malraux exchange published in *Nation,* March 27, 1937, p. 351.
24 "Spain In Flames," *Nation,* March 27, 1937, pp. 340–341. On the part played by MacLeish, Dos Passos and Hemingway see *New Republic,* June 2, 1937, p. 88.
25 *New Republic,* June 9, 1937, pp. 119–121.
26 *New Republic,* August 25, 1937, p. 63. Cowley was published by the *New Masses* two weeks before this; see his "A Congress In Madrid," *New Masses,* August 10, 1937, p. 16. See also Joseph P. Lash, "Time Works For US—In Spain," *New Masses,* October 19, 1937, pp. 6–8. John Chamberlain, in his *"Was It A Congress Of American Writers?,"* *Common Sense,* June, 1937, pp. 14–16, charged that the Americans who attended as delegates were more anxious to denounce American neutrality in Spain and to take the

stump for Soviet foreign policy objectives. He especially reproached MacLeish for trying to prove the United States belonged in the Spanish Civil War. Of the Madrid Congress as a whole Chamberlain declared, "it looks as if the Congress had been organized and run by people who did not want certain things discussed—and those things happen to be things that interfere with the conduct of Russian foreign policy."

27 *Common Sense,* July, 1937, pp. 8–10.

28 *Common Sense,* June, 1937, p. 7.

29 Morrow in *New Republic,* November 10, 1937, p. 19; Bates identified in *Nation,* November 27, 1937, p. 600.

30 Fischer-Wolfe debate in *Nation,* June 5, 1937, pp. 657–660.

31 Fischer report in *Nation,* July 3, 1937, pp. 7–8; Brenner letter in same issue, pp. 26–27. The Catalonian uprising had been reported in the *Nation* issue of May 15.

32 *Nation,* July 17, 1937, p. 62.

33 *Nation,* August 7, 1937, pp. 148–150; "The Loyalist Dilemma," *Nation,* August 21, 1937.

34 Brenner letter in *Nation,* August 21, 1937, p. 206.

35 Fischer, "Spain Won't Surrender," *Nation,* April 30, 1938, pp. 495–497.

36 *New Republic,* September 23, 1936, pp. 175–176.

37 *New Republic,* September 30, 1936, pp. 212–213.

38 *New Republic,* December 2, 1936, p. 128.

39 *New Republic,* January 13, 1937, pp. 315–316.

40 *Nation,* February 20, 1937, p. 200.

41 "Is the State Department Favoring Franco?," *Nation,* March 13, 1937, pp. 285–286.

42 *Nation,* March 27, 1937, pp. 347–349.

43 *The Fight,* March, 1937, pp. 8–9, 24.

44 *Nation,* March 5, 1937, pp. 266–267.

45 See advance report in *Nation,* April 3, 1937, p. 389.

46 *New Republic,* May 19, 1937, p. 30.

47 *New Republic,* March 3, 1937, pp. 99–100.

48 *New Republic,* April 28, 1937, pp. 344–345.

49 *New Republic,* June 2, 1937, p. 90.

50 *New Republic,* June 9, 1937, pp. 135–136.

51 *New Republic,* July 7, 1937, p. 253.

52 *New Republic,* July 28, 1937, p. 336.

53 *New Republic,* July 14, 1937, p. 262.

54 *Nation,* October 16, 1937, pp. 395–396.

55 "Hull Of Downing Street," *Nation,* May 21, 1938, p. 576. See also "The Smelly State Department," *New Masses,* May 24, 1938, p. 11, and "State Department and Strachey," *New Masses,* October 18, 1938, p. 12.

56 *Nation,* May 28, 1938, pp. 607–610.

57 *New Republic,* August 16, 1939, p. 30.

58 Frank, "Death Of Spain's Poet—Antonio Machado," *Nation,* April 15, 1939, pp. 433–436.

59 *Nation,* April 10, 1937, p. 394.

60 Hanighen, "The War For Raw Materials In Spain," *Nation,* April 24, 1937, pp. 456–458; *New Republic,* June 9, 1937, p. 117.

61 *Nation,* April 17, 1937, pp. 424–425.

62 *Nation,* July 17, 1937, p. 62.

63 *New Masses,* August 24, 1937, p. 22.

64 *Nation,* June 19, 1937, p. 696.

65 Fischer, "Madrid's Foreign Defenders," *Nation,* September 4, 1937, pp. 235–237. According to Fischer, these "volunteers" started appearing in Spain in September, 1936. Fischer related that Merriman had been in Moscow in the fall of 1936, and that his wife had come all the way to join him in Valencia from Moscow; Merriman had been fighting in Spain since February, and Fischer vouched for the fact that he belonged to "no political party." On the loss of Santander see also editorial, *Nation,* September 4, 1937, pp. 230–231.

66 *Nation,* March 5, 1938, pp. 266–268. See also editorial, *Nation,* March 19, 1938, p. 313.

67   *Nation*, March 26, 1938, pp. 348–349.

68   *Nation*, April 2, 1938, pp. 374–375.

69   *Nation*, April 9, 1938, p. 399.

70   *Nation*, April 23, 1938, p. 453.

71   Stowe, "Spain's Shirt-sleeve Heroes," *Nation*, April 23, 1938, pp. 467–469.

72   *Nation*, April 30, 1938, p. 489.

73   *Nation*, April 30, 1938, pp. 495–497. On the political commissars, see note 35 and also R. Luc, "The Political Commissar In Spain," *New Masses*, February 14, 1939, pp. 12–13; February 21, 1939, pp. 12–13. The author was in the Thaelmann International Brigade.

74   Editorials "A Bomb From Barcelona," *Nation*, July 2, 1938, p. 5, and " 'Realism' In Extremis," *Nation*, July 23, 1938, p. 80; Fischer, "Spain's Tragic Anniversary," *Nation*, July 30, 1938, pp. 103–105.

75   *Nation*, August 6, 1938, p. 118; Fischer, "The Drive Along the Ebro," *Nation*, September 3, 1938, pp. 219–221.

76   *New Republic*, August 31, 1938, pp. 93–95. On the other hand, the editors of the *Nation* for the first time talked of a possible stalemate. "Beyond the Ebro," *Nation*, August 20, 1938, pp. 168–169.

77   Fernsworth, "Next Round In Spain," *Nation*, October 29, 1938, pp. 448–450.

78   *Nation*, October 15, 1938, p. 369. See also *Nation*, November 5, 1938, p. 465, and editorial "Spain Must Be Fed," *Nation*, December 10, 1938, p. 611.

79   "Franco's 'Final Drive,' " *Nation*, January 7, 1939, pp. 23–24.

80   "Hope For 1939," *Nation*, December 31, 1938, p. 5.

81   Fischer, "Thirty Months Of War In Spain," *Nation*, January 7, 1939, pp. 28–30.

82   *Nation*, January 28, 1939, pp. 105–106.

83   *Nation*, February 4, 1939, pp. 135–136.

84   *Nation*, February 11, 1939, p. 161.

85   "The War Goes On," *Nation*, February 18, 1939, pp. 191–192.

86   *Nation*, February 25, 1939, p. 217.

87   *Nation*, March 4, 1939, p. 249.

88   *Nation*, March 11, 1939, p. 279.

89   *Nation*, March 18, 1939, pp. 305–306.

90   Fischer, "Spain's Final Tragedy," *Nation*, March 18, 1939, pp. 312–313, for this and citations below.

91   *Nation*, April 1, 1939, p. 362.

92   Kirchwey, "Peace In Spain," *Nation*, April 8, 1939, pp. 393–394; "Don't Recognize Franco," *New Republic*, March 29, 1939, p. 205; *New Republic*, April 12, 1939, p. 261.

93   *Nation*, August 19, 1939, p. 182.

94   *New Republic*, May 10, 1939, p. 2.

95   Cowley review of Bessie in *New Republic*, October 25, 1939, pp. 345–346. The publisher was Scribners.

96   Romer review of Bessie and Rolfe in *Nation*, November 18, 1939, p. 557. Romer was the managing editor of *The Voice*, official organ of the Mechanics' Educational Society of America and a contributor to the liberal journals on labor unrest prior to his departure for Spain. See his *Nation* article "That Automobile Strike," February 6, 1935, pp. 162–163. On his war record see his article "I Was Franco's Prisoner," *Nation*, November 19, 1938, pp. 529–533. He claimed to have reached Spain on May 4, 1937 and after fighting with the Canadian International Brigade was captured March 12, 1938, being released in October.

97   Fischer, "Death Of A Revolution," *Nation*, January 13, 1940, pp. 37–41.

98   See especially *New Masses*, July 1, 1941, p. 14, and Minor, "The Second Imperialist War," *The Communist*, May, 1939, pp. 407–434.

18

PRO-COMMUNISM AND ANTI-JAPANISM SHARPEN THE OUTLINE IN CHINA, 1935–1938

THE EXPANSION OF CHINESE COMMUNIST PRESTIGE AFTER THE "LONG TREK"

CHINESE Communism had always enjoyed a favorable press as far as American liberalism was concerned, but it was unlikely that the rousing welcome that it received upon the successful march into the western reaches of China was ever expected. Its dove-tailing into the Popular Front undoubtedly had much to do with the vast wave of friendly propaganda promptly forthcoming, the obverse of which was an increasing volume of invective fired at the Japanese. The waxing of Communist strength made defensive gestures largely unnecessary hereafter, and there was a noticeable rise in the amount of comment and the number of friendly commentators. Liberals had chosen sides long before 1935 on the struggle in the Far East; in the period after 1935 it was a matter of signifying a somewhat deeper commitment. It was accompanied by a steeply-rising rigidity toward Japan, and a reversal of attitudes which had by and large been found acceptable in 1931–1933. Behind the grand panorama of the three-cornered Asian controversy stood a possible fourth formal participant, Soviet Russia—as involved and real a participator as any, regardless of the absence of the formal niceties signifying such involvement. No intelligible view of liberal opinion on the Far East could possibly emerge without a careful look at the impact of concern for Communist health and comfort as an integral part of the liberal position. Since no other force which continued activity in East Asia had its approval, it cannot be denied that by 1935 American liberalism had become a Communist rooting squad. Since liberals despised Chiang Kai-shek, deplored the existence of any colonial strength, especially that of the French and British, and heartily hoped to see the United States withdraw physically from the entire region, while portraying Japan as a land of devils incarnate, there was no element with any significant vitality in it left other than Russo-Chinese Communism. Had American liberals never uttered a word in praise or defense of Communism in the entire two decades prior to V-J Day, it would still have been their only sanctioned protagonist by default.

The survival of Chinese Communism in good health and voice in early 1935 hardly indicated that its triumph was imminent, of course. Although there had been a substantial lull in the war with Japan, the Chinese Nationalist forces had not been resting, but using the time to propel campaign after campaign at the Communists, a matter which had aroused progressive thinking to several successive highs of flaming indignation. And furthermore, the Japanese were still very much on the premises. With a firm foothold in Korea and Manchuria, they had begun to move southwest from the latter region, now the new state of Manchukuo, into the province of Jehol, and in a westerly direction as well, which took them into the lower tier of provinces of Inner Mongolia, first Chahar, with Suiyuan and Ningsia lying beyond. North of this was the vast confine of Outer Mongolia, long organized as a Communist state. It is a mark of the innocence of this Popular Front era that Japan's creation of the state of Manchukuo out of Manchuria was always greeted with gales of scornful laughter, but Communist representation of Outer Mongolia as the "Mongolian People's Republic" was always followed by an interval of pious silence. It was an article of faith among many that it enjoyed utter independence from Soviet Russia, and that its common border with Siberia had no significance worth mentioning. However, the emergence of Chinese Communism in 1935 as a more formidable force than ever before had considerable effect on the situation that followed, as it seemed that Japanese plans envisioned a substantial penetration of Mongolia as well as northern China, the former amounting to a first-class gesture of threat to Soviet Russia. It is little wonder that tempers and emotions on the Far East began to rise suddenly, and the views on the struggle started taking on sharp, bright hues and edges. Increased truculence toward the Japanese was not the only dividend of the heightened prestige of Chinese Communism; it also signalled stepping up the attack on the Reds' domestic enemy, Chiang and the Nationalists. It had been the line since 1932 that Chiang preferred partnership with the Japanese to a similar relationship with the Communists, and the notion had grown that he was less interested in the welfare of China than the Reds were. Once the latter had fashioned out for themselves a substantial preserve in the Chinese interior, the allegations against Chiang grew markedly. And they proliferated after the Japanese began their Mongolian campaigns early in 1935. On February 6, the *Nation* declared editorially that [1]

The Japanese invasion of Chahar is ominous, not as a further attack on China but as an indication of a Sino-Japanese alliance directed against the Chinese Communists and the Soviet Union. . . . For despite the optimistic bulletins issued periodically by Chiang Kai-shek's press agents, it is evident that both Nanking and Tokyo are seriously concerned over the success of the Chinese Red Army's westward march.

"Has Chiang Kai-shek Sold Out?", an editorial screamed a week later, in which it was stated as a bare fact that "Chiang Kai-shek has worked hand-in-glove with the Japanese at every opportunity." [2]

There was one approach of Japanese apologetics which touched off the liberal press like a roman candle, and that was the plea that the aim of Japan was to combat and halt Communist expansion on the mainland of Asia. There was an occasion to explode on this subject again in this same month, when Ambassador Saito, in his Council of Foreign Relations speech in Chicago, insisted once more that the Manchuria action was provoked by Communist propaganda which had created an anti-foreign and anti-capitalist environment and sentiment there, threatening Japan's raw material resources. The *Nation* refused to accept this, heaped ridicule on the speech in general, and while admitting that "there was a powerful Chinese Communist movement in China in 1931," counter-charged that Communism had been practically absent in the three Northern Provinces and Manchuria at that time, and its alleged existence was merely a Japanese invention.[3] Liberals were warned about accepting even an iota of the Japanese case now; as the *New Republic* countered on March 13, "Everyone in the world above the age of ten must know by now that Japan intends to dominate all the Eastern Asia, including China." [4]

In mid-April, 1935 a pleased commentary appeared in the *Nation* on the progress of the main force of the Chinese Communist army under Chu Teh and Mao Tse-tung into Kweichow province in the southcentral-southwest part of the country, while making moves toward extending their strength by joining it to Szechuan province as "a base for permanent Communist activity." [5] This devotion of prior interest to the deep south of China did not fit well with what was taking place in the north, where the Japanese steadily edged west into Inner Mongolia, against faint resistance. Chiang was held deliberately to blame, although the liberals did not go so far as the *New*

Masses, which yelled sensationally on June 18, "Chiang Kai-shek Sells China." [6] Readers thus got a divided picture of the Chinese scene, a North mortally in danger of Japanese saturation, and a South steadily becoming a Communist sphere of influence. The *Nation* insisted that Chiang's weak response to the Japanese was directly related to the latter event, since Red concentration so close to the home bases of the Nationalists made it imperative that he devote his major energies toward fending them off, just at the time when it appeared that he was of the disposition "to make at least a show of resistance" to the Japanese.[7] Barring interference from the West, which was conceived as most unlikely, the *New Republic* in June felt that the only ultimate barrier to Japan was China's Communists: [8]

An Anglo-American stand might halt the advance of this Japanese juggernaut, but only at great risk. The Soviet Union will maintain absolute neutrality, short of the violation of its frontiers. This leaves one alternative. A national-revolutionary war of the Chinese masses, following upon the overthrow of Chiang Kai-shek, may yet face Japan with a military problem which will dwarf that presented by the Shanghai hostilities of 1931–32.

This appeared to be materializing, what with the announcement the following week that the main Red army had joined with the Red army in Szechuan not far from Chengtu, in what the *Nation* called "the completion of one of the most dramatic military maneuvers in history." With a force "said to be 200,000 strong," the Communists were now a much more serious threat to Chiang than ever,[9] and the sharp drop-off of his resistance to Japan could not be explained in any other way than his fear of this new development. New opprobrium was heaped on him all during the summer, and an upheaval in his cabinet in August brought forth the editorial comment that his resignation would soon be forthcoming, or else he would have to "establish a personal dictatorship based on Japanese arms." "In either event," it concluded smoothly, "the end of Chiang's long reign is probably in sight." [10] Press reports that the situation was not as grave as all this were hooted at, and Agnes Smedley, in a *Nation* article, "The Corrupt Press in China," conducted a lengthy assault on the credibility of every newspaper and magazine in China not sponsored by the Communists. Recalling Lenin's epithet "the reptile press" when referring to non-Communist newspapers, she ended her diatribe in high indignation, "All the above explains why I have become a defender of reptiles when I hear them compared to the capitalist press in China. It's utterly unfair to the reptiles." [11] There was no disguising the fact that liberal opinion in the late summer of 1935 was convinced that the days of "the most slippery ruler of any country in the world today" [12] were limited and numbered by his growing internal Communist adversary.

THE JAPANESE THREAT TO RUSSIA VIA MONGOLIA PRE-EMPTS THE SCENE

But the showdown did not come. Instead, the focus of attention shifted in a few weeks to the northwest, for two reasons. One of these was the change in the direction of Communist movement itself toward this region, and the other was the growing expansion of Japan aimed in the same general location. There for a time the dissimilar enterprises seemed to merge. In September and October there was a rash of reports that the Communists now intended to spread into the five northernmost provinces of China and probably split them off from China and form a new state out of these,[13] while strengthening their grip in western China.

At the end of October the *Nation* announced editorially that this northern penetration was going on according to schedule, and that the Chinese Reds had reached the point of establishing "a direct line of communication with the Soviet Union either by way of Outer Mongolia or Sinkiang." Much comfort was derived from this. Though liberal faith in the unswerving devotion of the Russians to peace was unchecked and unmodified, there was never a moment's doubt that war between the Soviets and Japan was almost guaranteed as a consequence of Japanese actions alone—the most likely of all the potential wars which came up for periodic discussion. It is ironic that it was the only war which did not break out until the fighting had all but ceased, after all the "peaceful" countries had long resorted to arms. But in 1935 it was a brooding expectable event, and the arrival of reinforcements from the south was appreciated as a further aid to Russia in fending off the future Japanese invasion. But just for the moment; it was not expected that the Japanese would be deterred long by this act, and the general outbreak of fighting was still contemplated at an early date. "It is conceivable that the world-wide struggle between Communism and Fascism may be settled by the developments in this remote region," predicted the *Nation* in its "Japan Presses On." [14]

It is not that Japan was thought invincible or even likely to win a partial victory. The interpretation of Japanese action followed previous theories. The invasion of the North China-Mongolia region was a compensatory move to salvage something from the overall Asian "incident" since Manchuria-Manchukuo had proved to be a "bitter disappointment" economically for Japanese business groups. The

Nation found comfort when this was thoroughly explained by the American Council of the Institute of Pacific Relations in its *Far Eastern Survey,* at the end of the year.[15] It fitted in perfectly with the Marxian prediction of swift internal collapse in Japan, which got still another popular exposition in two long articles in the Christmas, 1935 and New Year's Day, 1936 issues of the *New Republic* by T. A. Bisson and Guenther Stein, titled "Will Japan Crack Up?" But in the meantime the situation hardly called for inaction while the inexorability of Marxist economic analysis ground its way along. Japan appeared to be ready to thrust its troops into Outer Mongolia, the "Mongolian People's Republic," itself.

The *Nation* interpreted Japanese "sorties" into this region from western Manchuria and the edges of Chahar in January, 1936 as a test of Soviet Russian reaction to a possible full-scale invasion, and it replied with heat, "it is difficult to see how the Soviet government can stand idly by when its Communist sister-state is being attacked by the Japanese." [16] The only thing wrong with this was its statement of the relation, since by the terms of the 1921 treaty and the circumstances of the MPR's evolution, it perhaps deserved to be identified more as a child than as a "sister" of the Soviet Union.

The *New Republic*'s editorial position was identical. In its issue of July 24, 1935 it held that Outer Mongolia was not "technically" part of the USSR, but on January 22 it defended Soviet action in Outer Mongolia as an act of "protecting" its "territorial integrity," once more denouncing Japanese talk of the "Communist menace" as a pretext for "aggression." When the Russians announced the following week that their standing army now numbered 1,300,000 men, the *New Republic* took it not only as evidence that war in the Far East was a closer danger, but suggested implicitly that fear for the Communists need not be unbounded, in view of this formidable force.[17]

In March the *Nation* tied in Japanese actions in Outer Mongolia against Russia with German political intrigue, suggesting that Japan was working with Germany to pre-occupy the Soviet and bring about hesitation in France as to entering into an alliance between the two which was up for ratification. It was suggested editorially that any fears in France about future Russian military performance should be dismissed, in view of the "glowing reports of the efficiency of the Red Army." [18] Although it was not considered proper to refer to Soviet troops fighting Japan directly in Mongolia, this sort of indirect reference was evidence enough that it was believed such fighting was going on.

The *Nation* misread the events in Japan which began with the assassination of Saito and Takahashi, among others, by a conspiracy of younger army officers, on February 26, and the emergence of the army-dominated Hirota regime. "Japanese Fascism Misses Fire," its March 11 editorial ran, a peculiar heading, since it had insisted for several years that the Japanese already had Fascism. However, the pertinent comment was the allegation that had the assassins succeeded in taking over the government themselves, the immediate result would have been "a more aggressive policy in North China and Mongolia, culminating in an attack on Soviet Siberia." [19] The confusion continued into the next months, the *Nation*'s editorial position representing Russo-Japanese relations as improving steadily while at the same time reporting that the Japanese attacks on the MPR outposts had not diminished, indicating that the Hirota government had hardly changed Japan's Asian policy.[20] But the Mongolian People's Republic was not represented as in any serious trouble; Bisson's "Conflict in Outer Mongolia" in the April 22 *Nation,* which read like three pages from a Soviet encyclopedia, described a situation well in hand.[21]

Furthermore, the champions from the south were arriving. On March 18 the *Nation* told its readers, to balance off a disconcerting report of Chiang-Japanese "cooperation" against the Communists, that [22]

The appearance of a considerable Red force in the North along the borders of Inner Mongolia has given Japan real cause for concern. From their new base the Chinese Soviet troops could easily cut the Japanese lines of communication at Kalgan, the gateway to Outer Mongolia, and could probably establish communications with the Sovietized Mongolian People's Republic.

This appearance, balancing off the threatened outflanking of the forces in Soviet Siberia, provided opportunity once more to hail "the brilliant strategy of the Chinese Red Army" and to give wide publicity to another "2000-mile trek through the heart of China," to northern Shansi.[23] But it was not until the first week of December, 1936 that any substantial action was reported effectively halting the Japanese westward push, the capture of Pailingmiao, the headquarters of the Japanese-supported Inner Mongolian Prince Teh. The December 5 *Nation* editorial exulting over this contained an exuberant slip which momentarily let down the veil previously held over the Mongolian scene. In describing what would have been had Japanese tactics worked, it admitted: "Thus a Japanese wedge would have separated China from Outer Mongolia, that is to say, from Soviet Russia, since Outer Mongolia is a Soviet province in all but name." [24] This amazing bit of frankness, in view of the careful previous presentation of the MPR as a separate and distinct state, could hardly have been due to anything except a momentary ingenuous exhilaration over the Popular Front, since there was not the slightest intent to embarrass or injure the Communists by the statement.

THE GREAT KIDNAPPING:
ITS PRELUDE AND CONSEQUENCES

Despite the considerable space devoted to the matter of Japan and its threatened full-scale war with Russia in Mongolia, Inner and Outer, the amount of actual action in 1935 and 1936 was not alarming. The waxing of Chinese Communist strength was a much more significant subject, hardly neglected by American liberals. But over the whole area of Asian relations hung a sort of breathless expectancy of much more dramatic events in the offing. The prodigious expansion of Communism and its enormous energies hardly suggested that several more years of muffled semi-combat were in store for China. And enough notices of this vague and disturbing sentiment were recorded to justify a feeling of foreboding that some kind of fundamental dislocation was in store for the relations existing among China's major factions.

Predictions of darker days ahead for Chiang abounded during this time, of course, along with repeated charges of cowardliness, hesitancy, or outright collaborationist intents in the matter of Japan. When the *Nation* interpreted the December, 1935 student uprisings in China it appended still another of its predictions of calamity coming for Chiang: [25]

Communism has become the sole alternative to Japanese domination to thousands of Chinese. Moreover, it is clear that no effective opposition to Japan can be achieved without the overthrow of Chiang Kai-shek, which, again, would have revolutionary implications.

Nor was the resulting situation necessarily going to be a localized matter. When the arrival of the Communists into Shansi in April, 1936 drew another round of applause the *Nation* had extrapolated a situation possibly resulting from a showdown dictated by Chinese Communist strength which promised far-reaching reverberations; [26]

The possibility that the strength of anti-Japanese feeling in China may yet force Chiang to enter a united front with the Communists leaves Tokyo in a most unenviable position. Driven by internal pressure, the Japanese are almost certain to advance farther. Chiang may not fight; in which case the Communists are likely to gain in power. But if he chooses to resist, the chances are that the Soviet Union and possibly the whole of Europe will ultimately be involved.

A *New Republic* editorial comment in September came much more
to the point. In its editorial "Will China Start War?" it advanced the
view that a great expansion of the war was dearly desired by various
Chinese, irritated and frustrated by the very limited character of Japanese actions in the north, and their Mongolian-Siberian confinement,
and for reasons which were not concealed in the slightest: [27]

Numerous Chinese leaders . . . seem to have come to the conclusion
that they could cause enough trouble to invading armies so that they
could hold out for a year, and that by that time other nations would be
certain to be involved. They are counting, in fact, on a world war, which
would give China a strong government and powerful allies, would smash
Japanese imperialism, and would put an end to their present intolerable
situation.

There were no cries of dissent from the peace-loving liberal journal
upon weighing this possible eventuality, either.

The makings of this Chinese resistance in the event of the unleashing of general war were everywhere apparent. Norman D. Hanwell's
Nation eyewitness piece of September 26, 1936, "Red China on the
March," described the poorly stifled impatience of the three big Red
armies now in western China, and expressed wonderment at the
failure of the daily press in America to pay attention to this Red
increase of strength, "wandering at will" in the western provinces.
This bright report of sustained Communist success described "a new
generation of communized youth" in the region, working with the
peasantry acting in guerrilla capacity, which had frequently am-
bushed Chiang's Nationalist troops and had destroyed "whole divisions" of them.[28] A *Nation* editorial the following week, "Will China
Fight Back?," mentioned along with the heightened Red strength the
sensational increase of political assassinations in China in recent
months. "Until recently political murder was practically unknown in
China," the editorial went on in bafflement.[29] But it found no relation between these facts, and the growing pent-up energy seeking
diversion toward spectacular military explosion.

Maxwell S. Stewart went this one or two better in his "Who's Who
in China," declaring bluntly that there were Chinese Communist
armies in 12 of China's 18 provinces as of the end of the year, and
even describing Mao Tse-tung as "President of the Chinese Soviet
Republic," although he did not trace the boundaries of this new state
announced so dramatically as a recent addition to the family of
nations.[30] The actors were hurrying to their places on the Asian stage,
and the first crash of cymbals from the pit soon announced the commencement of the overture.

The pre-Christmas, 1936 issues of both liberal weeklies contained excited editorial explanations of the sensational kidnapping of Chiang by Chang Hsueh-liang; the *New Republic* in its zeal even reported at first that Chiang had been killed by this kidnapper. The *Nation* expressed the hope this would be the signal for the end of the lamentable anti-Red drives, and a prelude to a unified drive on Japan, the Communist goal. Chang, they thought, showed wisdom in realizing that it could not be done without the Reds and their vast armies in the northwest, close to the Japanese areas. His collaboration with the Reds and their use of this means of action to impress Chiang with the necessity of closing ranks were hailed as a direct result of the Third International's "United Front" tactics, the *Nation* declared; a deliberate attempt to restore the status as of 1926.[31]

The *New Republic* quickly spread the scope of this alarming event. "Soviet Russia wants peace beyond anything else," it insisted, but also was now ready to move with Chiang against the Japanese. The reason it gave was a close understanding which presumably had come into existence between the Japanese and Hitler Germany, involving a mutual commitment to a joint invasion of Russia and Siberia as soon as was feasible. The impression was given that the sudden shaping up of the unified drive on Japan in Asia was part of a plan to saturate Japanese attention and cancel out its influence. The key to the changed conditions was the enormously increased Red Chinese power, controlling a larger area than ever before, and headed by leaders who were "hard to frighten and impossible to buy," who were also in "complete unity." It quoted with approval an interview between Edgar Snow and Mao Tse-tung, chairman of the Central Soviet Committee, one of many between the two which were reported in the London *Daily Herald*, in which the Red Chinese chief expressed his confidence in China's ability to defeat Japan.[32] The editors of *Common Sense* also praised the kidnapping of Chiang, and hoped that as a result of the discussions between him and the Chang-Red leaders, the Kuomintang would admit to union of all Chinese, including the Communists, now reputed to be 70 million strong, and that the reconciliation would mean "an end of the futile wars against the Red Chinese that have wasted so much of China's energy for ten years."[33]

For liberals, this stunt was a simple, forthright action in good faith on the part of the Communists, intending nothing but the furtherance of the welfare of China. The willingness of the Reds to join with the other elements in China for the comprehensive assault on Japan was not interpreted in any other way. Agnes Smedley's "How Chiang Was Captured" in the February 13, 1937 *Nation* was the epitome of this appealing and persuasive explanation; illustrated by Gropper cartoons, it accounted for the abduction of Chiang as a product of action by Red soldiers forced upon their commanders and about to do it themselves if they had not been ordered to do it by Chang and others. Her guileless reportage of the fraternizing which supposedly followed among the once-rival troops sounded like the stories of the camaraderie in the trenches during Christmas of 1914.[34]

The smooth and even working of this momentous event into the machinery of the Popular Front of 1937 matched what was occurring in Spain, but in view of what the Communist-line press chose to say, was hardly of the order of mere fortuitousness, as was developed in Theodore Draper's "The Chinese Chessboard," in the last issue of the *New Masses* for 1936. Draper explained the behavior of the Chinese Communists prior to this time and after the achievement of substantial strength in early 1935 thusly; "for the time being, the sharp antagonisms among the imperialist powers could be utilized to greater advantage than ever before to further the Chinese unification and liberation movement." Then the change of emphasis to the United Popular Front, but with the objective still clearly in mind.[35] Closely tied in with the 'unity' movement was the sharp step-up of anti-Japanese attitudes [36] and the broadest of charges that Japan was embarked upon a program of world conquest, remarkably similar to those fed into liberal channels about Germany and repeated loudly and interminably on all occasions when Russo-Japanese or Russo-German relations had become seriously strained. Early 1937 was the occasion for repetition of these allegations against the Japanese. Communists, and their well-wishers felt themselves on the edge of especially advantageous events; either a Japanese collapse or a much-expanded war with the odds on Communist enhancement and aggrandizement regardless of which eventuality. The appearance of the first issue of *Amerasia* in February, 1937 was a harbinger of the coming barrage of pro-Chinese Communist material, and a similar flood of sentiments designed to stir hostility and anti-Japanese hysteria.

A long editorial in the *Nation* on January 30, 1937, "Japan's Fatal Dilemma," seemed to express the situation best.[37] Whether the now-released Chiang would come through on a stiffened anti-Japanese position which would undoubtedly spread the war was a secondary factor; "It happens that the Communists hold the key to the situation, regardless of what happens at Nanking," the editorial explained indulgently. It was now felt with immense confidence that the Chinese Reds were fully capable of opening up a full-scale attack on the Japanese strong points in Chahar even if Chiang did not wish to do so. Communist perturbation over the Japanese pressure upon Red-held Mongolia was such that they would not hesitate to spread the war to China proper as a diversion. In the *Nation*'s opinion the Communists not only could relieve this pressure and involve other parts of East Asia, increasing Japan's enemies and immeasurably extending its difficulties and military perplexities; should Chiang decide to desist or hesitate, the Communists would also score a gigantic propaganda scoop by turning to the uncommitted and presenting themselves as the only true patriots of China, in their devotion to driving Japan off the mainland, and a belated entry would place him in a secondary and auxiliary position to Mao Tse-tung during the anti-Japanese stage of the "liberation."

THE WAR BETWEEN THE INCIDENTS: PEKING TO PANAY

The incident which reopened and spread the Sino-Japanese war, the clash between Japanese and Chinese forces near Peking on July 7, 1937, was blamed on Japan without reservation, although there were some mysterious attending circumstances. Incitation of the Japanese was a tactic of many years' standing, everywhere where their outposts touched those of the Communists in particular. The Manchuria-Siberia sector was a well-established battleground, and in the *Nation* on July 10, a notable prelude to the Peking incident was reported between Soviet and Japanese elements along the Amur River, illustrated with the following: [38]

Each year, during the late summer and fall, Manchurian patriotic organizations, bandits and small bands of Communists make use of the cover afforded by the vast fields of *kaoliang* to launch attacks on Japanese outposts and lines of communication. Recent reports indicate that these illegal groups are more numerous and powerful than ever before.

Another dispatch in the same issue added that "scores of pitched battles have been fought along this frontier during the past few years." Regardless of the number of synonyms which might be found to use instead of monotonously repeating the word "Communist," it was quite apparent that the raw material for extended incidents had long been present. The shock and simulated outrage over that of Lukou-chiao carried a hollow, ungenuine ring.

And in the same journal's editorial "War In The East?" two weeks later, speculation on the outcome of the flareup between the Japanese and Chinese contained a significant sentence which indicated that there was far more to this event than the propaganda version being paid out for world consumption. It contained a note of interest not only on the immediate issue, but on the long-standing struggle between the two main Chinese groups, whose conflict since 1927 had been posed by American liberals as one aggressively waged by the

Nationalists against an always defensive, counterpunching Communist force. This show of hostility toward Japan seemed at last to be the gesture which had been awaited since the Great Kidnapping, for, as the *Nation* put it now, "It is not likely that anything could have persuaded the Communists to suspend their ten-year war against Nanking except a definite promise of resistance to Japan." For the first time the Chinese Communists were portrayed as carrying the fight to Chiang, instead of the reverse.

Signs of a Nanking-Communist alliance seemed to be multiplying; the furnishing of arms, munitions, food and supplies to the Reds by Chiang and the inclusion of Communists in the Kuomintang Congress were cited as some of the evidence for this. The odd note of this editorial, however, was a quiet aside to the effect that the renewed conflict and the Chinese alliance materially increased the chance of it developing into a world war, but that it would be Japan's fault, for by trying to make it "part of a holy crusade against communism," Japan might pressure the Soviet Union to reluctantly enter "against its will." The apparent logic of this was recommendation to the Japanese that they refuse to recognize persistent incitation by Communists as an excuse for fighting.[39]

Maxwell S. Stewart's "Behind China's Conflict" in the same issue contained the same sort of interpretation, a Japanese provocation as a reaction to the Communist-Chiang alliance.[40] Now that hostilities were under way, it apparently was thought best for propaganda purposes to ascribe initial action to the enemy, despite eight months of constant prediction that it would be the Chinese who would take the initiative, probably decided by a recognition of American *mores* when thinking about the subject of international affairs. The legend of unprovoked attack was always the best means for gaining sentimental support.

The Peking incident also touched off a long controversy among American liberals as to what should be the policy of the United States toward this expanded war, for a time paralleling the Spanish War directly. General sympathy with the Communists in both spheres did not extend to agreement on what American action should be. A fuller treatment of the problem of American neutrality or intervention will be made subsequently on a general level, but some attention can be advanced to the particular issue immediately at hand. The Roosevelt Administration's very thinly concealed antipathy toward Japanese expansion in Asia had, as we have seen, attracted much liberal comment prior to 1937, of a mixed quality, partly approval and partly condemnation. The *New Republic*, in the period of Chinese maturation, since early 1935, was the least enthused over the continuation of a strong attitude toward Japan. It showed much editorial disquiet in December of that year when simultaneous Anglo-American notes had been dispatched to Japan expressing unhappiness over their action in Mongolia and North China. "It is obvious that the United States and Great Britain are acting in concert in the Far East, for ends that are not stated," it complained, and went on to state that it was thought that the Stimson policy of sending notes to Japan had been ended, suggesting that it seemed that British interests must have been more seriously threatened than they thought. But there was little doubt about their anxiety over the part this country would "ultimately" play in "the Far Eastern mess." [41]

In June, 1936 the *New Republic*'s "T.R.B." expressed the view that the Buenos Aires "peace conference" would take up the idea of a world boycott on Japan to discourage its moves on the Asian mainland, again taking up the previous view that the reason was that Japan by its actions was jeopardizing "very large British, American and French business interests." He was sure that such action "would almost certainly lead" to Japanese expansion swiftly southward to seize the Philippines, Hong Kong, the Dutch East Indies, India and Siam, to get the resources which would be denied them through normal trade channels, and did not show much sympathy for such a boycott.[42] Many liberals shared his hesitance for this kind of economic warfare; there was little of the enthusiasm for this which existed five years later.

The *Nation* supported other kinds of resistance to Japan, however, especially the hostility toward the Japanese position at the London Naval Conference earlier in this year. It now tacitly approved the major Western powers rejecting her naval parity position, and hoped that Japanese insistence on it would lead to a Far East collective security move through the agency of the Far East Advisory Commission set up in 1933 at the time of the Manchurian controversy.[43] And this approach grew stronger as the months went by, especially among the Popular Front's pro-Soviet sympathizers. As Chinese Communist strength waxed, the Popular Front spokesmen grew more vocal in their approval of an active United States in Asia. A pro-China and anti-Japan position on the part of America was diagnosed as ultimately of grave harm to both Japan and the United States, to the ultimate advantage of the Soviet Union. American barriers to Japanese expansion left the field to the Communists by default, they reasoned, hence the tactical wisdom of plugging away at the menace of Japan to America. This view was brought out markedly by General Victor A. Yakhontoff in his book *Eyes on Japan,* reviewed by Barbara Wertheim in the *Nation* on August 22, 1936. Yakhontoff, a minor twentieth century Talleyrand, who had been an officer in the Czar's army, military attaché to the Russian imperial embassy in Tokyo during the first world war, assistant secretary of war under Kerensky and now a Soviet protagonist with experience working in the Tokyo branch of the Institute of Pacific Relations,[44] stated the case with great persuasive appeal, and in view of the *Nation*'s growing orientation, it was puzzling that his view should be treated coolly. The reviewer for sure took umbrage at the motivation: [45]

Nor does it help us toward a solution to insist that the United States has so vital an interest in China that it must at all costs keep its hold there, which, in other words, is to insist that we must ultimately come into active conflict with Japan. Out of his sympathy with the Soviet Union, which wants us to stay active in Asia as an obstacle in the way of further Japanese aggression, it is but natural that General Yakhontoff should adopt this thesis.

This and other expressions of deep doubt about the wisdom of profound American involvement in Asian affairs persisted in the mainstream of liberal thinking on foreign policy despite the direction its constant pro-Chinese Communist position pointed. But both the involvement and anti-involvement attitudes existed at the time of the massive 1937 outbreak. As in Spain, the majority of the exponents of involvement talked of a form of participation without the pain of actual presence in belligerent form, mainly economic pressure.

The *Nation*'s immediate reaction in July was to note that essentially the Neutrality and Johnson Acts worked for the benefit of Japan, putting America into a virtual economic alliance with Japan against China, and expressed the firm conviction that at the end of the month the Administration was "seriously worried by the consequences that loom in the Far East." Its advice to the President on August 7 was to "ignore the [Neutrality] law as long as possible," and to go on trading with both sides, since there was no need for him to invoke the law until war was declared. Its editorial "Neutrality in the Far East" seemed to exude confidence in Japan's being provoked into going to war with Russia at an early moment, if Russia kept furnishing supplies to China, of which there seemed to be every hope of expecting indefinitely.[46] Two weeks later it brought up the boycott for the first time in this new round of Asian troubles, recommending it as an anti-Japanese gesture only in the United States. A significant turn had been taken since the Ethiopian war; it now considered sanctions and embargoes "unneutral and dangerous." [47]

In these last two weeks of August, 1937, the *Nation* began to return to form. Like its slow start in the Spanish war a year earlier, Asian affairs unfolded hurriedly in its pages. After charging that Japan's offensive was aimed at capturing the coal and iron resources of North China, "and even more important, preparation for war with the Soviet Union," [48] it shouted editorially on August 28, "Boycott Japanese Goods!" Its appeal was in the correct Popular Front form, as the "people's non-violent technique against aggression," and urged that the United States keep its business interests and missionaries in China, even if they were "of questionable value in the long run," as "stabilizing influences." [49] Their potential as propaganda material should they suffer harm at the hands of any of the combatants was obviously more important, even if unexpressed in such terms. A hint as to the most desirable conduct was contained in the September 4 editorial, "Can Japan Be Stopped?," suggesting that other States follow the example of the Soviet Union in signing a non-aggression pact with China, Russian non-aggression pacts being the finest flower of the Popular Front era, in actuality, along with furnishing "concrete economic assistance," as Russia was doing.[50]

When the Administration established a partial embargo on munitions late in the same month, the *Nation* was obviously nettled. It insisted that it was a blow to China only, that American trade with Japan would be unaffected, and urged Roosevelt to stop such tactics and collaborate with the League of Nations as a member of the FEAC, once again returning to the Ethiopia days of expressed faith in its ability to conduct economic warfare better than its component members, a position which was in logical harmony with its current stand on Spain and the same problem of munitions.[51] Villard, in his signed column of September 18, added several other ingredients into as potent a package of hostility-breeding as anyone suggested in the whole period. He looked upon this Asian crisis as "a magnificent opportunity for moral leadership" on the part of the United States, and suggested that Americans withdraw entirely from China, boycott Japan, pass a non-intercourse act, and withdraw our ambassador from Japan. These were not in any sense warlike acts, Villard insisted, and as supplements to other American actions, they should make clear that this country did not have the slightest intention of becoming involved in the war.[52]

The *Nation* began its serious championship of a Japanese boycott in October, 1937. "Don't Buy Silk!," it exclaimed to the readers on the 2nd, but urged a comprehensive refusal to buy *all* Japanese goods, which were "mostly of inferior quality" anyway, it consoled the potential liberal shoppers. The same issue contained a firm and excitedly confident article by Freda Utley, "Japan Fears a Boycott," and the next week it announced editorially, "The Boycott Grows." On the 16th it hailed Stimson's letter to the New York *Times* in defense of the boycott as valuable support, although the *Nation* made no comment to the effect that their goals and those of Stimson were a light year apart.[53] The ancient Anglo-American statesmen and "Old China Hands" still were not too aware of the fact that a new group was active in China, unwilling to consider the Boxer-Rebellion-days' picture of their land which still bemused the former, and aiming at creating a land with no "foreign dogs" in it at all, barring those of Communist persuasion. But they showed no reluctance toward using them against each other in effectuating this latter goal. Stimson urging stiff resistance to Japan could hardly have furnished better unconscious assistance.

The boycott drive quickly blended into the hope for a formal pronouncement of sanctions of some sort from the Nine Power meeting at Brussels, but Popular Front recruits kept the former in progress separately. The *New Masses* began a vigorous "boycott Japan" in its issue of October 2. By the end of October the American League Against War and Fascism was in full shout in the *Fight* and in separate advertisements in the liberal press,[54] by which time it had received an immense propulsion from Roosevelt as a consequence of the famous "quarantine speech" earlier in the month in Chicago. No words spoken since 1931 contributed so much spiritual ammunition to the complex of forces which was gathering to frustrate Japan and at the same time make the mainland of China safe for Communism. "Quick Action Needed," the *Nation* called on October 23. And the action it called for was from the United States and Britain, with whom three-fifths of Japan's trade was still going on. The editors still thought seriously that the two countries would injure themselves voluntarily for the benefit of China by cutting it all out, a conclusion which even the quarantine speech did not suggest was reasonable, however.[55]

The *Nation*'s editorial position and that of Villard differed sharply on the possible efficacy of the Brussels meeting of the Nine Power states, less Japan, to consider a reproach to the latter for alleged violations of the agreements of 1921. Although it promised to be nothing more than a talkfest over Japan's sins, Villard suggested that it was "the rallying of what is left of the moral opinion of mankind against at least one aggressor state," and grimly hoped the Powers would not make the slightest concession to Japan in China, feeling that his position was a reflection of theirs, "those who stand with the angels and have an abiding faith in human nature and a better world." "I have not lost faith in the power of moral indignation to limit and control international wrongdoing if it is properly directed and adequately expressed," Villard intoned.[56]

The editors were somewhat less sanguine. They held out faint hope from the beginning, and on November 20, 1937 expressed the conviction that whatever came out of this gathering, a vote for sanctions against Japan was out of the question, "presumably because of the pressure of business interests within the democracies." What was far more distasteful was the conclusion that the possibility of America aiding China by credits and supplies, in the manner of the Soviet Union, was effectively blocked, and that the "main obstacle" was the

Neutrality Act. After expressing much irritation with the way non-interventionist liberal forces had rallied to the Act ("befogging the minds of the members of the organized peace movement"), the editorial bitterly complained that "this unfortunate law has come to stand directly in the way of the one type of collective action which might check the threat of world-wide aggression," in reality an extension of the area of controversy to a somewhat larger sphere, but still making sense in view of the *Nation*'s Spanish policy. And on November 27 came the last shovel of earth burying the Nine Power meeting. "The Brussels Conference will now be added to the long list of futile attempts to stem the tide of international anarchy;" "That it has failed is beyond dispute." To the editors, momentarily in a high state of anger, it showed up the transparency of the Chicago Bridge speech sentiment when put to a serious test.[57]

The *New Republic* embraced a difficult stand during this tumultuous summer and fall of 1937. Fully as enthusiastic over the emergence of Communist strength as the center of anti-Japanese resistance in China, and in accord with the peripheral policies and consequences which supporting this resistance involved, despite all this it firmly opposed the Popular Front drive for a statement of economic policy intention in America. Its August 25 editorial "America and the Far Eastern War" saw some hopeful consequences coming from it; the healing of the Red-Chiang split, an increase of the economic plight of Japan, and in its opinion most important of all a contribution to "keep peace in Europe" by "lessening the danger of an attack by Japan upon the U.S.S.R.," which it was thought was within a hairline of taking place, thus starting "a general European conflagration." But any underlining of the situation by Americans with anything except verbal testimony was held to be utterly unwarranted:[58]

Every available indication shows that American public opinion strongly sympathizes with China, as of course it should. The question is whether there should be any attempt to implement that sympathy, and if so, by what means. . . . Every attempt at neutrality, in this complicated modern world, influences all combatant nations. The real question is how best to keep ourselves out of war. There is nothing in the Far Eastern situation that warrants the entanglement of this country.

The United States had no imperial ambitions, we had already committed ourselves to Philippine independence, and, furthermore, "our investments in the Orient are so small *in toto* that it would be far cheaper for us to buy out their American owners than to fight, even for a few weeks, in their defense." The editorial closed with the earnest hope that Roosevelt would invoke the Neutrality Act at his earliest opportunity.

As the pro-Chinese propaganda stimulated towering percentage proportions of American sympathy to China in public opinion polls, occasional restrained and cautioned statements appeared which suggested that maybe the job of emotional engineering was being overdone.[59] Bruce Bliven apparently was so disturbed that he published a major signed article on September 22, "On Hating the Japanese," which he said had become a "new occupation" in America, although it struck a serious note to see such a late-season commentary on this tendency in a journal which had done an exceedingly small amount of work to inhibit its gaining industrial status since the days of Mukden, in particular. He took this occasion to deplore talk of an Anglo-American blockade of Japan; "In cold English, that means making war on an entire population," he warned now, and expressed full belief that if Japan were smashed by the West, it would not be long before she emerged, nursing a deep grudge and a desire for revenge. Besides, he was not sure democracy as he understood it would survive such a war; "If I know the temper of this country, we should be in a grave danger of emerging from such a struggle with a permanent Fascist regime of our own." But what irked him most of all was the superior moral posing which exuded from public pronouncements both in England and America: [60]

Could England and America fight Japan with clean hands? The great democracies have an invincible flair for self-righteousness; but even they must remember that they have a heavy share of responsibility for the situation in China. What Japan is doing is merely to continue on a larger scale and with more brutal candor what the Great Powers did in China for a hundred years. The British are not so far from the Amritsar massacre that they can afford very much righteous wrath about the bombing of Shanghai. Americans who are today only in middle age participated in the extermination of Filipino leaders at the turn of the century. Both countries still stand subject to a Japanese charge of *tu quoque.*

Bliven preferred to cling to dialectical materialistic interpretations and let Japanese "Fascism" fall apart from its own "internal economic contradictions," in which he had the greatest confidence as of this moment.

There was a warm, favorable response to Bliven's out-of-the-ordinary article on the part of the *New Republic*'s readers. It was evident that a sizable proportion were aware of the consequences of stirring up comprehensive anti-Japanese sentiments and arousing the always-latent anti-Oriental racism which had been a part of America since the aftermath of the building of the Central Pacific Railroad and the Exclusion Act of 1882, in a country not noted for its ability to discriminate among Asian peoples. But Bliven was not to get too much cooperation from others on this program. And after Japan joined hands with Hitler Germany in the Anti-Communist Pact of November 6, some six weeks later, even the *New Masses* showed that it was not utterly unaffected by racialist weaknesses, in view of the vicious cartoon caricatures which it published of Japanese, fully as ugly as those defaming Jews, which it rightly condemned when published in Julius Streicher's *Der Stürmer*. But the *New Republic* had already become *persona non grata* to the *New Masses* over its neutrality position, and was attacked several times during the autumn of 1937. The editorial in the latter on November 30, "Is the *New Republic* 'Neutral'?" went so far as to charge the liberal weekly with being responsible for furnishing aid and comfort to Japan.[61]

In addition to the intemperate stimulation of race hate accompanying the intensification of the Asian war, the *New Republic* also sharply denounced the talk of international embargo when it began to take flight in October; "Embargo Means War," its strident message announced: [62]

If the Far East war goes on, Japan will break; and it now looks as though it would continue for months. With peace maintained so precariously in Western Europe, it would be inconceivable folly for us to allow our moral indignation to sweep us off our feet. Private boycott is a legitimate expression of private opinion; but public boycott, in the form of concerted international action, can only mean war.

But it did not think too much even of private boycotts in some cases, as when it discounted the possible effectiveness of a boycott of Japanese silk after the cry had been taken up and pushed by the AFL, CIO and other organizations. An editorial on November 11 pointed out that silk was a sagging factor in the entire Japanese economy, while suggesting that a crisis produced by boycotts was not likely to have any significant effect in Japan other than to wire in the militarists more firmly and put Japan more extensively in their grip.[63] But a sizable number of liberals continued to think of Japan in the setting of a *Mikado*-image, rather than as a tough industrial state with a capacity for reacting to outside hostility in other ways than helpless prostration. Miriam S. Farley, acting editor of *The Far Eastern Survey*, promptly dispatched an open letter praising the *New Republic*'s stand against racialist propaganda, which contained a dark warning on a consequence of liberal excitement not receiving much attention in these hyperthyroid Popular Front times: [64]

There is grave danger that American liberals who condemn the present policies of the Japanese Government may unwittingly aid in stirring up a wave of jingoistic emotion directed indiscriminately against everything

Japanese. . . . It is difficult to see what long-run benefit China would derive from a change of masters. Liberals and imperialists make strange bedfellows, and though there may be circumstances in which it is expedient and even necessary for the angels of light to accept aid from the powers of darkness, liberals who delude themselves that this is possible in the present situation may wake up some morning to find that they have joined the other fellow's parade instead of vice-versa—just as in 1917.

As for the Brussels Conference, the *New Republic* editorial position was hostile from the time it was broached; it could find no evidence that there was any support for action behind the Roosevelt position as outlined in his Chicago speech. In "Brussels—The Test of Chicago" on November 10 it advised, "If the Nine-Power Conference will content itself with mere disapproval of what Japan has done, it may be a brilliant success in the eyes of those who think this way. . . . It will scarcely be a success of any other kind." [65] Events proved its prediction on this issue to be air-tight.

The war news during this hectic period of opinion matching and forming continued to be uniformly bad from the anti-Japanese point of view. A series of slashing campaigns drew the Japanese deeply into Inner Mongolia, and southward into China, the features of which in 1937 were the disastrous Chinese defeats at Shanghai in November and Nanking in December. The easy confidence in pushing out Japan once Chiang and the Communists had joined hands fluttered away. The *Nation* grew apprehensive over Chiang after the Japanese landings at Shanghai on August 11, intimating that he was unlikely to put up the major resistance all had been expecting and counting on.[66]

With both northern and southern campaigns going badly against the Chinese in September, the *Nation* conceded that they were losing, but took comfort in the political situation, "the final settlement of the long struggle between Nanking and the Chinese Communists;" [67]

For this not only brings 200,000 veterans of the Chinese Red Army into the struggle on a front where their guerrilla tactics are likely to show up to the best advantage but provides full assurance that there will be no compromise with Japan.

There was much significance to the stressing of guerrilla warfare and the political climate. Little evidence existed that the Communists wanted or expected an early victory. For the purposes of solidifying a political position, a long grinding war fought over an immense front with irregular troops and armed civilians had the dual purpose of wrecking the old order as well as injuring the foreign enemy. Recovery from the destruction of house-to-house and farm-to-farm fighting was not likely to occur in an accelerated fashion, and in the nest of comprehensive destruction lay the seedbed for the reconstruction of the New Order. A guerrilla war fought to the finish with nothing short of unconditional surrender, which was what the Communists really were saying now, guaranteed changes of a far more sweeping sort than the orthodox observers were inclined to see. The obsession with Japan made anything else very difficult to see. Furthermore, the Communist tactic of arming civilians for wholesale guerrilla warfare had a built-in propaganda compensation with a delayed-action mechanism. When reprisals against civilian populations took place, Communists and their well-wishers were enabled to shout about "wanton brutality toward non-combatants," and the Japanese were especially vulnerable to this in China. Undoubtedly there were numerous civilians innocent of participating in the fighting, but the careful dispersal of disguised guerrilla fighters among them made it especially difficult to separate one from the other. Enormous propaganda capital was made of this, but there was no appreciable moral difference between Japanese actions in China on the question of civilian participation in the fighting and Anglo-French behavior in various parts of their colonial world.

The consolation in the liberal press for the long string of defeats suffered at the hands of the Japanese was compensatory praise of the growth of the Chinese Communists, and their professed goals. In August, 1937, between the loss of Tientsin and the opening of the assault on Shanghai, the *New Republic* published two major reports on the Reds by Edgar Snow, now doing for China what Walter Duranty had been doing in the same weekly for Russia. The first in the series titled "Soviet China" contained long excerpts from an interview between Snow and Mao Tse-tung, a sympathetic report on the Communist Party in China and its gains and programs. The second brought up for memorialization once more the famous "Long March" into the interior and the subsequent expansion, between October 1934 and October 1935, called by Snow "the biggest armed propaganda tour in history." From this point on it was advanced as a feat exceeding that of Hannibal's march through the Alps, and became the foremost legend associated with the growth of Communism in China.[68] Of even greater import, although it appeared in the *New Masses,* was the stunning story of Philip J. Jaffe, "China's Communists Told Me," which this journal published on October 12. Accompanied by Owen Lattimore and T. A. Bisson, Jaffe succeeded in obtaining verbatim material from Communist leaders which was one of the most important articles published on China in the entire decade, and one of the most influential, as far as its spreading effect on American liberals was concerned.[69]

The loss of Kalgan and Paoting in September did not discommode the *Nation.* On the 18th it announced with pride that "The Red

Army, known as the most efficient military force in China, has been re-christened the Chinese Eighth Route Army." Maxwell S. Stewart also blandly ignored defeat in the field in his essay "What Chance Has China Today?" to report a bright outlook for eventual Chinese victory, which the Chinese Communists, Soviet supplies, the Red Army and credits from the democracies would bring about. The latter he felt sure would eventuate, because their right to trade in China was at stake, and they would hardly let this go into default via Japanese control. Stewart's views on China were much respected and carried great weight among liberals, as the *Nation* publicized the fact that he had lived there six years. But on the whole, reportage of the war in China did not exceed that of Spain in accuracy; the *Nation* hailed successful maneuvers of the Chinese Red Army in North China the day before the Japanese took Paoting.[70]

As the situation became increasingly grave for the anti-Japanese coalition in the fall of 1937, the dependence on the ultimate power of the Communist guerrilla warfare increased. The *Nation* even discounted the importance of the Japanese capture of Shanghai in November as no proof of their abilities, a matter which would not be settled until they reached the interior and the Communists went to work on their extended supply lines.[71] Prior to this, as the northern Japanese armies pushed deeper westward, there was some expectation that the Soviet Union might enter the war. Nathaniel Peffer, whose frequent writings on the Far East appeared in *Harper's* and the *New Republic,* confidently predicted this would happen very soon, in the October 13 issue of the latter journal. Peffer, whose views on Asian and world affairs went through one of the most unusual series of gyrations seen in the entire pre-war decade, was in a momentary pro-war mood at this time, as were others who had gotten deeply attached to the Popular Front and the Rooseveltian "quarantine the aggressors" doctrine enunciated at Chicago on October 5. He predicted that other nations would soon be making this choice which he thought so likely on the part of the Russian Communists: [72]

However horrible the war may be in itself and however dangerous to the peace of the world, no intervention is practicable or even possible except by force. The only way to stop Japan now is with an army and navy.

Peffer was apparently referring to the joint condemnation of Japan by the League of Nations and the United States on October 5 and 6, and the proposal for a formal condemnation by the Nine Power countries at a projected Brussels meeting. He was correct in his declaration that this would be futile, but much too anticipatory on Russian intervention, a matter which may have been responsible for subduing his preliminary belligerence, for in the December *Harper's* he had performed a complete rightabout: [73]

> We are left then with no alternative but to wait and hope, letting the war take its course, in apparent callousness, but only with the kind of callousness that decrees isolation for a plague victim, to die if necessary, lest others be fatally afflicted.

By December, 1937, liberal confidence was somewhat shaken everywhere. The collapse of Chiang after a three months fight quite alarmed the *Nation*, and between the Shanghai and Nanking disasters liberals returned to an earlier allegation, that Chiang's weakness was a deliberate consequence of a secret deal with the Japanese, pressured upon him by "the machinations of the pro-Fascist clique" which surrounded him in leadership and advisory positions, a group "that would rather sell out than see the country come increasingly under the influence of the Soviet Union," as the *Nation*'s editorial "Is China Beaten?" of December 4 put it. Its only consolation was the reported wide activity of the Eighth Route Army.[74]

The bombing by Japanese planes of the *Panay* and other American and British ships near Nanking on December 12 and the collapse of the city before Japanese attack the next day were blows of such consequence as to leave opinion in staggered inarticulation. The opportunity to play on the atrocity organ for a world-wide audience, on the basis of Japanese behavior in Nanking after sweeping into the city, was balanced off by apprehension over the impact on Americans of possible inflammation resulting from dramatization of the *Panay* incident. The *Nation* reached out a restraining hand toward Roosevelt, and implored him to ignore both the "isolationist" Neutrality Act supporters, and the belligerent "professional patriots" urging a get-tough policy in China. The editorial advice was to refuse to apply the Neutrality Act, which would only be a sign of "abject surrender to Japanese arms," and to also make no moves toward military reprisal, as war was "not only unthinkable but would be the height of folly;" [75]

> Instead of provoking the growth of either isolationist or war sentiment, the Nanking incident should serve to arouse American public opinion to the need for joining the other powers in collective economic action to restrain aggression.

The fiasco of the Brussels meeting had not jogged the *Nation*'s deep Popular Front conviction that some formula for conducting economic warfare still existed, and could be found if only the United States joined in a serious hunt for it. But its weight was thrown in on behalf of de-emphasizing the *Panay* incident in America, and it sharply denounced the extensive newsreel exploitation of the event as an effort to obtain a belligerent response from the country's ordinary citizens.[76]

As for Nanking, the *Nation* excoriated the Japanese, charging them with wholesale commissions of "atrocities and vandalism," and was especially sickened by a New York *Times* report, which it did not bother to confirm, that the Japanese were shooting all men "suspected of being soldiers," which it considered a particularly ugly act. But at the same time it thought the Communist tactic of "guerrilla resistance" of arming civilians was quite correct, and that prisoners taken against such forces should be treated as civilian non-combatants. The ancient practice of treating *franc-tireurs* had apparently slipped from their mind in the zealous concern for China's Communist "progressives." Chiang Kai-shek's flight from Nanking was thought to be worthy of comment only because it had been accompanied by "rising prestige of the Communist leaders," who were now giving the Japanese a taste of "resistance" warfare via guerrilla raids and stratagems. Its December 18 editorial "China's Hope" still hoped that it could "rid itself of traitors and settle down to a war of endurance, in which it will have every reason to hope for ultimate success." [77]

The *New Republic* in its editorial statements in the two subsequent weeks to Nanking was especially restrained, and showed little animus toward Japan. In a restatement of its support of complete American neutrality, it flatly assigned the responsibility for the persistence of United States citizens and interests in the war zones, inviting incidents such as *Panay*, to President Roosevelt alone; "Responsibility for preserving the anomalous situation in which these regrettable incidents are bound to happen rests squarely upon President Roosevelt and those who support him in refusing to fulfill the will of Congress by invoking the Neutrality Act." Comparing the *Panay* case with the *Lusitania* sinking in 1915 as far as incitatory value was involved, it implored FDR to put a stop to the shipping of petroleum products and planes to both Japan and China, to evacuate all United States citizens from China and to forbid American merchant ships to carry arms to either belligerent; "Why should we supply to warring nations the resources that enable them to entangle us?", it asked. In its year-end issue the junior liberal weekly returned to the theme of the Neutrality Act, and declared that the President's failure to apply it to the Far East was "incomprehensible," and that the continuation of our trade in raw materials and war goods to Japan, which thus remained unimpeded, guaranteed that Japan would go on in its China campaign indefinitely.[78]

The feature of the December 29, 1937 issue of the *New Republic* was a letter from Henry L. Stimson, urging that liberals continue their moral condemnation of Japan begun in 1932, which he considered "of marked value in the future after the present period of international dislocation is ended and the world's march toward a reign of law is resumed." His personal attitude on the rising note of belligerence about the land was in accord with the *New Republic* as well; "I regard any suggestion of sending armies to Asia or attempting to blockade Asiatic ports or any other warlike action as not only politically impossible but as a futile and wrong method of procedure." [79]

LITERATURE ON THE FAR EAST IN REVIEW:
THE COMMUNISTS DRAW THE NOD

No account of the interpretation of events in the Far East between the Great Trek and *Panay* by America's liberal press and writers would be complete without a glance at the books chosen for special notice during the period and those whose judgment was accepted in evaluating their contents. In a sense, there was no break in continuity from the years since Mukden, but the steadily rising fortunes of Chinese Communism show the greatest reflection in this middle period of the decade of the fateful 1930's. To be sure, there were other issues and subjects, with Japan drawing a healthy amount of completely hostile attention, but Chinese Communism steadily moved into the forefront with the spreading of the war in 1937. The sense of electric anticipation which the books and reviewers of books strongly oriented toward the Chinese Soviets revealed was a factor of great significance in helping to create the fund of good will which the Reds of China were still drawing on from American intellectuals at the time the war in Korea expanded in the winter of 1950.

The books on Japan selected for publicity followed the Popular Front-Marxist approach for the most part, stressing the "internal contradictions" which guaranteed a collapse from within shortly, and the inevitability of a new Russo-Japanese war, the outcome of which was confidently expressed in terms of a sure Soviet triumph. Such books as *Militarism and Fascism In Japan* and *When Japan Goes To War,* published in 1935 and 1936, followed this approach closely. Both written by O. Tanin and E. Yohan, the first title with a foreword by the Communist journalist Karl Radek, they were reviewed with firm sympathy in the *New Republic* by T. A. Bisson and Victor Yakhontoff. The second volume's strong point, that it would be impossible for Japan to fight more than a very short time against any opponent, received Yakhontoff's full agreement.[80]

The same approach could be seen in two other pro-Communist

books on the Far East, *The Problem Of the Far East* by Sobei Mogi and H. Vere Redman, and Tatsuji Takeuchi's *War and Diplomacy In the Japanese Empire*. Reviewed in the spring of 1936 in the *New Republic* by one Bunji Omura, who expressed his fervent hope for a sovietized federal republic for China, the cheering for the downfall of the Japanese continued.[81] And for most of the writers and reviewers, there was not much doubt in their minds as to what they preferred as the dominant force in Asia upon the Japanese defeat.

This was not expected to be long in coming, after the war spread in the summer of 1937, and the fear of a Japanese smash at Russia declined as a consequence. The message of expectable debacle for Japan was that conveyed by Bisson in his *Japan In China,* reviewed in the late spring of 1938 in the *Nation* by Maxwell S. Stewart, who referred to it as "an invaluable study," its "facts" being "a useful antidote for propaganda." This book was considered to contain the essential facts for understanding why the two Asiatic powers were at war. Bisson's thesis that the Japanese case had no good side at all, that Japanese rule was insecure and challenged everywhere and that its Manchurian policy was a total failure fitted in perfectly with *Nation* policy toward the Far East.[82]

In the fall Bisson reviewed A. Morgan Young's *Imperial Japan* for the *Nation,* and voted for Young's conclusion that "no enduring peace can be established in the Far East" which did not follow after the "complete overthrow of the military-Fascist clique which has fastened its rule on Japan." [83] Both author and reviewer had voted for a Communist political revolution in subdued terms.

The entry of the United States in the equation was another matter. The two important books of the period which touched on this, Nathaniel Peffer's *Must We Fight In Asia?* and Freda Utley's *Japan's Feet of Clay,* brought this out rather clearly. Stewart, reviewing Peffer in the *Nation* in April, 1935, dwelled on the author's prediction that the "capitalist" and "imperialist" forces of this country and Japan would bring us into conflict eventually; if not directly, then as a consequence of a Japanese victory over Soviet Russia. For both author and reviewer the alternative for the United States was either Japanese hegemony over the Far East or an all-Communist China as a result of a Russian victory. We would fight Japan if the former threatened, but if the latter situation prevailed, Peffer, according to Stewart, merely suggested that it would be a source of "great embarrassment." In reality, therefore, there was no alternative at all; Peffer was simply saying that the United States would fight only if the Japanese threatened to dominate East Asia, not if the Communists did.[84]

Villard devoted a full-page column to this book a week before Stewart reviewed it, and disagreed with Peffer strongly, expressing great faith in popular resistance to hypothetical Presidential and economic pressures for war in Asia, refusing to consider Peffer's insistence that indifference or hostility to war on the part of Americans could be easily overcome by government progapanda. As Peffer put it, "No people can resist the compulsion of propaganda created and disseminated by a government or compact ruling group which knows what it wants and has command of the channels of opinion." [85] But as comforting as most of this book was to the anti-Japanese Popular Front thinkers, there was still a strong resistance to his firm conviction of inevitable war between Japan and the United States; even the *New Masses* reviewer, though conceding Peffer to be an admirable Marxian scholar, found this objectionable.[86] The hope of keeping America out of Asia, in view of the predictions for the future growth of Communism, hardly involved tender feelings for the welfare of the United States, however.

The reception given the Utley volume in April, 1937 was more unfriendly but for different reasons. In the *Nation*, Barbara Wertheim expressed her revulsion at Miss Utley's anti-Japanese ferocity and disagreed that an Anglo-American economic blockade could "destroy Japan at a stroke"; she thought it "astonishingly naïve" of the author, "particularly in view of her orthodox Marxism," even to seriously suggest that "capitalist England and America should sacrifice a valuable trade for the sake of a revolution in Japan," since Miss Utley's totally black picture of internal Japan was one which she thought would be relieved only by a Marxian civil revolt.[87]

Helen Mears in the *New Republic* also found room for much criticism of the Utley thesis of the desirability of Anglo-American economic warfare, but chose to use as her major point of objection that the book tended to buttress "those numerous folk who believe that the function of America is to make the world safe for the British Empire." All this did, according to the reviewer, was to accentuate Japanese fears of colonialism, with the result that they were unlikely to throttle their efforts in Asia as long as they were taunted by reminders that United States-British collaboration might suffice to make them collapse in a few weeks. With the internal revolt idea Miss Mears apparently had no quarrel, since she suggested that instead of Anglo-American intervention the problem of the Far East might best be left with "the masses of the Japanese and Chinese, where it belongs." [88]

The China picture was a much clearer and straighter story, uncomplicated by the presence of Anglo-Russo-American conflicting interests and the sub-policies and sub-theories which were made necessary to prepare to make the Far East struggle understandable in the context of Popular Front hopes and the future of Communism. And the flow of books with a bow in the direction of Chinese Communism was unabated at this time. In the spring of 1935, Bisson reviewed nearly a dozen books on the Far East in the *New Republic,* five at one time in the issue of April 17. He praised Grover Clark's *The Great Wall Tumbles* for "its reasonable and objective analysis of the Chinese Communist movement," and considered the book's estimate of industrialism in China in accord with that of Leonard Wu in the Institute of Pacific Relations' *Far Eastern Survey.* But he was irked by "the ill-concealed anti-Soviet bias" of the three chapters added to the revised edition of William Elliott Griffis's *China's Story,*[89] in the same way as he was somewhat later displeased with Peter Fleming's *News From Tartary;* "It is unfortunate that Fleming felt called upon to crusade against the Bolshevik menace in Sinkiang," Bisson lamented in the *New Republic* on February 3, 1937. He much preferred Sven Hedin's "moderate" treatment of the same area in his book *The Flight Of "Big Horse"* which he reviewed at the same time, for Hedin stated that Russian policy did not contemplate physical occupation but economic and commercial control.[90]

With the Great Kidnapping, the stress no longer was in doubt. Ranging from the *New Masses* contributor James M. Bertram's account of the event itself, *First Act In China,*[91] and *Daily Worker* correspondent Harry Gannes's *When China Unites,* (published by Knopf and reviewed by Ch'ao-ting Chi for the *New Republic*) [92] to the books by Edgar Snow and Agnes Smedley, there was not to be much hesitation as to where the emphasis was to be laid. The three years prior to Pearl Harbor were to see an impressive continuation of this trend.

It is probable that Snow's *Red Star Over China,* issued at the time Americans were undergoing the agitation over the *Panay* bombing, was the most persuasive volume of the Popular Front period, and set the pace for all subsequent books which gradually enshrined Chinese Communism as a veritable cult well before the United States became its unofficial partner in the war against Japan. Eliot Janeway gave it most impressive billing in the *Nation,* commenting extensively on Snow's portraits of the Red leaders, Mao Tse-tung, Chu Teh, P'eng Teh-huai, Hsu Hui-tang, and his description of the "new spirit" moving across China's peasantry. Malcolm Cowley greeted it no less enthusiastically in the *New Republic.* For many it was also a welcome respite from the ugly controversy over the Russian purge trials and served as a factor tending to promote unity again, for no Stalin-Trotsky rift existed to mar the cohesiveness of Chinese Marxism. Cowley predicted that "the Chinese Reds will be the national heroes" in the event of victory over Japan, or even an inconclusive stalemate.[93]

The follow-up for those who wanted an authoritative account of the rise of the already legendary Eighth Route Army was Miss Smedley's *China Fights Back.* Despite its title, it was almost exclusively a chronicle of the movements of this Red fighting force between August

1937 and January 1938, during which time she was accompanying them. The substantial review by Bisson in the *Nation* in July was somewhat exceeded by the glowing reception of Robert Morss Lovett in the *New Republic,* Lovett declaring that it was a more reliable book than her previous volumes *Chinese Destinies* and *The Red Army Marches.* Both reviewers were awed by her descriptions of the Red leaders, whom she approached at close hand, as well as her accounts of Red training of civilian "partisan units" and the guerrilla tactics, including the raids on Japanese convoys, and destruction of communications, particularly railroads. Lovett exclaimed, "No one can help feeling that in spirit and skill the Communists have made themselves invincible," but his relation of the fact that her trip ended in Hankow with a reception by the United States ambassador to the Chiang government provided a curious coda for his review.[94]

The Nanking-*Panay* events were the dividing line and watershed in many respects on the Far East war. All the moderate talk and restraining arm motions to the contrary, emotional and psychological enlistment had already captured many minds in a way some liberals did not approve. To be sure, the liberal press and many of its editors and writers were as spiritually enlisted in the China war as they were in that going on simultaneously in Spain, but in Asia they were not as concerned with the physical fighting aspect as such. There were few American Chinese likely to be involved in Chinese Lincoln Brigades for service with the armies of Mao Tse-tung and Chu Teh. The emphasis in the Orient was on economic warfare conducted as an emanation of "collective security." Even the *New Republic,* with its hard-headed neutrality-for-the-United-States stand, in essence supported this program, since stoppage of vital forms of war trade were basic elements of the law which it dearly hoped the President would invoke, war declaration not yet made notwithstanding. The end product of this "collective security" was advanced repetitiously as the preservation and advancement of "democracy," but only the editors of *Common Sense* were blunt enough at this moment to insist that the "democracies" were not democracies at all in their foreign policies, but "rival imperialisms," and that China was not a democracy in any sense. Their position was that Chiang was a dictator with an army trained by hundreds of military experts from Hitler Germany, and that the Red Armies were hardly fighting as they were to bring China a different system. "It cannot be too often reiterated that 'democracy' is not the real issue in either [Chinese or Spanish] war," its December, 1937 editorial policy statement concluded.

Piecemeal liberal enlistment in these two wars had serious effects on a number of other positions and views. The liberals' previous stands on disarmament, pacifism, neutrality, and war responsibility all underwent fundamental change. And a complex of new issues which were a product of the slow and silent embarking on the Popular Front soon put in their appearance, forcing adjustments, back-trackings and internal conflicts which tore up the liberal scene until it was scarcely recognizable. But of all these, none caused the disorder and agony produced by the twists and turns of Russian policy. The majority of America's liberals were to learn in the most painful way imaginable that what they had believed to be the promotion of classless international socialism and the joint solidarity of mankind was in fact revealed to be little more than a temporary phase of Russian foreign policy.

N O T E S

1 *Nation,* February 6, 1935, pp. 141–142.
2 *Nation,* February 13, 1935, pp. 173–174.
3 *Nation,* February 20, 1935, p. 206.
4 *New Republic,* March 13, 1935, p. 114.
5 *Nation,* April 17, 1935, p. 431.
6 *New Masses,* June 18, 1935, p. 7.
7 *Nation,* July 3, 1935, p. 2.
8 "Japan Devours China," *New Republic,* June 26, 1935, p. 182.
9 See note 7, above.
10 *Nation,* August 28, 1935, p. 226.
11 *Nation,* July 3, 1935, pp. 8–10.
12 *Nation,* August 1, 1936, p. 115.
13 *Nation,* September 25, 1935, p. 338; October 16, 1935, p. 423.
14 Citations in this paragraph from editorial mentioned, *Nation,* October 30, 1935, pp. 497–498.
15 "Japan's New Lifeline," *Nation,* January 1, 1936, p. 5.
16 *Nation,* January 8, 1936, p. 29.
17 *New Republic,* July 24, 1935, pp. 290–291; January 22, 1936, pp. 297–298; January 29, 1936, p. 321.
18 *Nation,* March 4, 1936, p. 263.
19 *Nation,* March 11, 1936, p. 301.
20 *Nation,* April 8, 1936, p. 435.
21 *Nation,* April 22, 1936, p. 507.
22 *Nation,* March 18, 1936, p. 335.
23 "Mongolia—Red Or White?," *Nation,* April 22, 1936, p. 502.
24 *Nation,* December 5, 1936, pp. 646–647.
25 *Nation,* January 8, 1936, p. 30.
26 See note 23, above.
27 *New Republic,* September 30, 1936, p. 214.
28 *Nation,* September 26, 1936, pp. 359–360.
29 *Nation,* October 3, 1936, p. 380.
30 *Nation,* December 26, 1936, pp. 754–755.
31 "Kidnapping A Dictator," *Nation,* December 19, 1936, p. 721. See also "Behind the Scenes In China," *Nation,* December 26, 1936, pp. 748–749.
32 "The Far East Boils Over," *New Republic,* December 23, 1936, pp. 231–232.
33 *Common Sense,* January, 1937, p. 5; February, 1937, p. 7.
34 *Nation,* February 13, 1937, pp. 80–82.
35 *New Masses,* December 29, 1936, pp. 3–6.

36 The *Nation* editors were sure a stepped-up anti-Japanese campaign was coming soon upon the "pardon" of Chang Hsueh-liang by Chiang Kai-shek, and that the anti-Communist campaign was apparently out now; *Nation,* January 9, 1937, p. 30.

37 *Nation,* January 30, 1937, pp. 117–118.

38 *Nation,* July 10, 1937, pp. 30–31, 34.

39 Citations in above two paragraphs from editorial "War In the East?," *Nation,* July 24, 1937, p. 89.

40 *Nation,* July 24, 1937, p. 100.

41 *New Republic,* December 18, 1935, p. 156.

42 "A World Boycott Of Japan?," *New Republic,* June 24, 1936, pp. 203–204.

43 *Nation,* January 22, 1936, p. 86.

44 When Yakhontoff's memoirs, *Over the Divide,* were published in 1939, the *New Republic* review on November 29, 1939, p. 178, described his going over from the Czar to the Bolsheviks as a process "helped by his unswerving Russian patriotism."

45 *Nation,* August 22, 1936, pp. 219–220.

46 *Nation,* August 7, 1937, pp. 144–145.

47 *Nation,* August 21, 1937, pp. 181–182.

48 "What Japan Wants," *Nation,* August 21, 1937, p. 185.

49 *Nation,* August 28, 1937, pp. 211–212.

50 *Nation,* September 4, 1937, pp. 231–232.

51 "Embargo vs. China?," *Nation,* September 25, 1937, p. 309.

52 *Nation,* September 18, 1937, p. 292.

53 *Nation,* October 2, 1937, pp. 335–336; October 9, 1937, pp. 364–365. Utley article in issue of October 2, pp. 341–342. Editorial praise of Stimson's letter to the *Times* in issue for October 16, 1937, p. 389.

54 See example in *Nation,* October 23, 1937, p. 447.

55 *Nation,* October 23, 1937, p. 421.

56 *Nation,* November 6, 1937, p. 505.

57 "Case For the Boycott," *Nation,* November 6, 1937, pp. 492–493; November 20, 1937, p. 546; November 27, 1937, pp. 574–575.

58 *New Republic,* August 25, 1937, pp. 60–61.

59 See especially report on American Institute of Public Opinion polls in *Nation,* October 30, 1937, p. 402. According to the AIPO the least sympathetic portion of the American public toward Japan was the sector on public relief.

60 *New Republic,* September 22, 1937, pp. 177–178.

61 *New Masses,* November 30, 1937, p. 10. See also "China and the Neutrality Issue," *New Masses,* September 28, 1937, p. 12, in which the *New Republic* was singled out for serious special criticism.

62 *New Republic,* October 6, 1937, p. 230.

63 *New Republic,* November 24, 1937, p. 61.

64 *New Republic,* October 13, 1937, p. 273.

65 *New Republic,* November 10, 1937, pp. 3–4.

66 "Will Chiang Fight?," *Nation,* August 14, 1937, p. 164.

67 *Nation,* September 18, 1937, p. 278.

68 Snow's articles in *New Republic,* August 4, 1937, pp. 351–354 and August 11, 1937, pp. 9–11, titled "Soviet China: I—What the Chinese Communists Want," and "Soviet China: II—The Long March."

69 Jaffe, "China's Communists Told Me," *New Masses,* October 12, 1937, pp. 3–10. The article was illustrated with striking photographs of the Red leaders and part of their army, as well as pictures of Jaffe, and Owen Lattimore, who accompanied Jaffe on the trip along with T. A. Bisson.

70 *Nation,* September 18, 1937, p. 280; October 23, 1937, p. 418. Stewart's article in *Nation,* September 11, 1937, pp. 262–264; editorial identification on his tenure in China same issue, p. 276.

71 *Nation,* November 20, 1937, p. 546.

72 Peffer, "What's Ahead In the Far East?," *New Republic,* October 13, 1937, pp. 258–259.

73 Peffer, "Convulsion In the Orient," *Harper's,* December, 1937, pp. 1–9 (p. 9). Peffer here seemed to have returned to his views in his *Harpers* article "Too Late For World

Peace?" of June, 1936, pp. 23–32, in which he declared, "The hope of contemporary man is to prolong the interval in which the process of time can work, to prolong the peace, however artificial and unhealthy and irrational a peace it may be, by whatever means, however illogical and superficial they may be." pp. 31–32.

74 *Nation*, December 4, 1937, p. 605.

75 *Nation*, December 18, 1937, p. 673.

76 *Nation*, January 8, 1938, pp. 30–31. This was a theme which had appeared on several occasions in the *Nation*, especially in the 1933–35 period of attack on militaristic tendencies. Villard's December 12, 1934 column, p. 665, "Propaganda In the Movies," was one of the most comprehensive criticisms of this kind.

77 On the atrocities, *Nation*, December 25, 1937, p. 701; on Chiang's flight, "China's Hope," *Nation*, December 18, 1937, pp. 677–678.

78 "From Lusitania To Panay," *New Republic*, December 22, 1937, p. 183; "Second Phase in China," *New Republic*, December 29, 1937, p. 214.

79 Stimson letter on p. 230.

80 Bisson's Review of *Militarism and Fascism in Japan* in *New Republic* for March 27, 1935; Yakhontoff review in *New Republic*, September 18, 1936, p. 163.

81 *New Republic*, April 29, 1936, pp. 350–351.

82 *Nation*, June 18, 1938, pp. 704–705.

83 *Nation*, October 29, 1938, pp. 457–458.

84 *Nation*, April 17, 1935, pp. 462–463.

85 Villard, "Must We Fight Japan?," *Nation*, April 10, 1935, p. 407.

86 Donald Hemsley, reviewing Peffer in the *New Masses*, May 21, 1935, declared, "Nathaniel Peffer stands head and shoulders above the normal run of American students of Far East politics. Grounded in the main on a Marxian analysis of politico-economic factors, his writings are distinguished by a clarity of style and cogency of reasoning." But Hemsley did not like Peffer's "unconvincing brief for the inevitability of a Japanese-American conflict."

87 *Nation*, April 24, 1937, pp. 476–478.

88 *New Republic*, April 14, 1937, pp. 298–299.

89 Bisson group review in *New Republic*, April 17, 1935, pp. 211–212.

90 Bisson review of Fleming and Hedin in *New Republic*, February 3, 1937, pp. 417–418.

91 See Bertram's article "The Strategy Of the Eighth Route Army," *New Masses*, February 8, 1938, pp. 5–6, largely an interview with Mao Tse-tung.

92 *New Republic*, November 10, 1937, pp. 24–25.

93 Janeway review of Snow in *Nation*, January 8, 1938, pp. 47–48; Cowley review of Snow in *New Republic*, January 12, 1938, p. 287.

94 Bisson review of Smedley in *Nation*, July 9, 1938, p. 48; Lovett review of Smedley in *New Republic*, August 31, 1938, p. 108.

19

LIBERALISM'S RUSSIAN ORDEAL : ON
AND OFF THE MOSCOW EXPRESS
FROM POPULAR FRONT TO THE
RUSSO-GERMAN WAR, 1935–1941

LIBERAL RECEPTIVITY TOWARD THE SOVIET HOME
EXPERIMENT PEAKS, AND PLUNGES

As HAS been shown, the single bright beacon shining through the unrelieved picture of graying bleakness which was the liberal outlook on the international scene especially after 1929 was Communist Russia. In the important opinion-forming years prior to the Popular Front it was a steadily growing factor, achieving a vantage-point of towering eminence notably between 1935–1937. The forbidding commentaries on the rest of the foreign scene, and on a substantial part of America as well, for that matter, can hardly be understood except within the context of this grand political amour, which began to disintegrate along the edges in 1935, accelerated its decline in 1936 and 1937, and collapsed in 1938 and 1939. The two years of estrangement thereafter were followed by a reconciliation which lasted well after the Second World War, followed by another scission at the time the Korean War began. But the project at hand is an examination of some aspects of the pre-war halcyon days.

One of the most persistent and tenaciously clung-to liberal positions was the conviction that the world depression had hit all the nations except Soviet Russia. The perpetual production and consumption shortage crisis of the Communists was not examined from an economic point of view, since the fact that everyone seemed to be employed determined this viewpoint more than anything else. The acceptance of official Soviet statistics, claims and promises at face value stood out in marked and pathetic contrast to the suspicion which greeted the emergence of almost any kind of similar reports, even from nations which were not conducting obvious anti-Soviet-or-Communist foreign policies. The easy adoption of the views of Marxian theory on the short-lived nature of all other systems helped prepare liberals for a season of difficulty in understanding the persistent refusal of anti-Soviet systems to expire, which in turn helped feed their anxiety and then hysteria when they blossomed out in stages of vigor matching anything that had been imagined as the real state of conditions in Russia.

All the liberal organs had a hand in the advertising of Russia as the land of plenty and the only land worth a liberal's effort to visit, and a dozen publishers, including most of the most influential, did their part in issuing books expanding on the views which were compressed in weekly or monthly journalism. The *Nation* probably exceeded the others in zeal. And the publicity attending Russian economic health did not abate substantially until the civil war among the liberals themselves broke out on the subject of the new wave of purge trials which racked the Soviet, especially that of 1937.

In July, 1935 the *Nation,* back in stride after the lamentable nervous shock of the Kirov trials and their contentious aftermath, announced to its readers, still awash in the depression despite the New Deal, that "Barring the occurrence of unforeseen difficulties, Soviet Russia is expected to harvest the greatest crop in history this year." The "problems of organization and discipline on the collective farms," a new euphemism for the breakdowns, sabotage and mass starvation of the 1931–1932 period, seemed to have been "completely solved," it thought, and followed this with a recital of Soviet statistics presented without a shred of dubiety, which it clinched by a casual statement, "Food prices in the cities are approximately one-half of what they were a year ago," and terminated this triumphant present-tion by chiding the Hearst newspapers for not having published any of these "facts" in its current series of bitter criticism.[1]

Villard, a skeptic on many things going on in Russia, did not number Communist statistics among them. His July 10 essay, "Russian Progress At Home—Enmity Abroad," expressed the actual belief that the Soviet iron and steel industry had already exceeded that of Germany, and that the Communists were just a few short years from being the largest producers in the world, and he now seemed to be repenting the harsh words spoken on the Kirov mass reprisals: [2]

However one may feel about the Soviet system and however high seems the price that has been paid in human lives for this forced industrialization of Russia in the less than 20 years since the revolution, it remains a stupendous record. Looked at simply as an engineering and industrial feat, it stands without parallel.

Villard cautioned everyone that as the Soviet enjoyed further success "in establishing the Communist state," there would be a more concerted attack from the "conservatives and reactionaries" of Europe for a "holy war" to crush it, since they could not afford to have their masses learn that those of Russia were living in a state where "there is a greater diffusion of wealth and comfort and a greater security of living for the masses than elsewhere." He expected these unnamed persons to be about to back Hitler and the Japanese in a two-front war against Russia in the very near future.

A further contribution toward dispelling hostility was Anna Louise Strong's August 7 *New Republic* article "Searching Out the Soviets," which took up eleven counts involving charges being made against Communist Russia elsewhere in the world, including the United States. She denounced in particular the charge that Russia was ruled by one man, and advanced a thumb-nail definition to provide an understanding of the basic conflict in the world as of 1935; "Power resides in ownership of the means of production—by private capitalists in Italy, Germany, America, by all productive workers jointly in the U.S.S.R. This is the real difference that today divides the world into two systems." The Popular Front forced a slight adjustment in this alignment when the Communists elected America to the "anti-Fascist democracies." [3]

In October, the *Nation* editorially chided Roosevelt for listening to the "price-raising school of economists," fostering recovery schemes such as the AAA and NRA, and exhorted him to observe the example of the Soviet Union, where, it was claimed, they had "recklessly cut prices on all their products, boosted the retail turnover of goods by 34% over 1934 and abolished the ration system," in addition to several other astonishing achievements. No source was cited for these statistical wonders, but of course, the striking thing about this was the casual way in which the admission was made that food rationing on even the most common foods had persisted all through this period of supposedly peerless economic growth. It had an uncommonly close flavor to that of Joshua Kunitz' *New Masses* acclaim a few weeks later, "U.S.S.R.—Land of Plenty: Abolition of the Food Card," a giant among *non-sequiturs* as titles of the period were wont to be.[4]

Fischer's on-the-spot report, "The Russian Giant in 1935" in the *Nation* for October 23 supported this view with a long list of statistics bristling with tribute to Soviet productiveness, up 25% per man in one year. Having just gotten back to Moscow from a trip which reportedly covered 5000 miles, he announced as a side-issue to his observations that as far as the ordinary Russian resident was concerned, "This time there were no complaints, there was no discontent." For the unconvinced, Fischer had this rebuke: [5]

The Soviet Union is on the way to becoming Europe's greatest economic power. The enemies of Bolshevism are guilty of a serious tactical blunder; they should not worry over Russia's shortcomings and mistakes, whether alleged or real. They should yell about its rising might. Foreign critics have consistently made the mistake of underestimating the Bolsheviki.

George Soule, back at his editorial post on the *New Republic* after an extensive trip through the Soviet, had much the same report to make to liberal America. He prepared a series of articles titled "Does Socialism Work?" based on his Russian observations, and the answer to his rhetorical question really did not have to be made by anyone who read this series. They were considered so significant as to be collected and published as a pamphlet in 1936. His earliest report had included an intense hope that Hitler and Mussolini might be overthrown soon, so that "In an atmosphere of peace and prosperity, the U.S.S.R. can continue her development, and the left forces in France and Italy can go on to build their strength by democratic means." [6]

Even *Common Sense,* with its position of criticism toward Communism in America, was just as receptive to stories of sensational economic progress in Russia in 1935. Despite bitter hostility toward the "dogmatic intellectual discipline" of the Communists, it accepted its statistics without question. The December, 1935 editorial "Russian Progress" expressed the conviction that the Soviet industrial complex was second in size and productivity to that of the United States and climbing fast, and that the Communists already had the shortest working day in the world.[7] In such high esteem was Russia held at this point, for this was "collectivism" in action, as Louis Hacker pointed out when reviewing Stuart Chase's *Government In Business* in the *New Republic* for November 27, 1935, and was not to be confused with the developments in all the other countries Chase discussed, where the tendency was merely "toward a growing extension of state capitalism." [8]

But it could hardly be said that the liberals of the United States were encouraged to stay at home and take the word of their respected writers on the subject. Advertisements urging them to visit and see the wonders for themselves proliferated down to the very outbreak of war in 1939, including a number of special tours directed by persons whose acceptance of Russia was universally known. John Rothschild's feature "The Intelligent Traveler" in the May 1, 1935 *Nation* listed 15 "outstanding trips to the Soviet Union" conducted by various groups and under varied direction for the spring and summer of that year.[9] The standout seemed to be that conducted by the *Open Road,* its "Second Soviet Union Travel Seminar," under the leadership of the *Nation's* own Moscow correspondent, Fischer, already hailed in advance in the *New Republic* at the end of May as "The Outstanding Russian Tour of 1935." [10] The following year the *Open Road's* choice of guide was Kunitz, although the number of total trips leaped upward. Rothschild's directory of Soviet travel tours in the April 29, 1936 *Nation* had risen to 26.[11] The feature trip this year was a joint enterprise sponsored on a bargain basis by the *Open Road* and Intourist, the Soviet foreign travel agency, which offered passage to Russia and back, plus a month in the Soviet, under tour conductors such as Fischer, Kunitz, Julien Bryan, Colston Warne, Maxwell S. Stewart, and Henry Shapiro, for just $372. An unkind commentator might have noted that the largest part of the population which worked at manual labor in the United States was fortunate to gross $700 for the entire year, thus it seemed that the trip was hardly being scheduled to enable American workers to visit the "workers' fatherland." Of course, the majority of these trips involved costs exceeding the income of most American laborers for the entire year.

In May, 1937 another series of directed tours received wide publicity in the liberal weeklies, and in view of the volcano which had erupted in the midst of liberal America on the subject of the Stalin purges, the directors were somewhat more selective. With Fischer no longer in Moscow, having left quietly and taken up as the reporter from Madrid on the Loyalist side of the Spanish Civil War,[12] other faces began to make headway; the travelers in 1937 were promised the assistance of Langston Hughes, Jerome Davis, Anna Louis Strong, John L. Spivak and Kunitz in the preliminary advertising,[13] all known for their devotion to the Stalin side in the current death-grip struggle with the "Trotskyites."

By 1938 the rush had subsided, but some tours still were offered. On April 6 the *New Republic* carried the advertisement of the Bureau of University Travel, announcing its "Sixth Russian Seminar," conducted by Jerome Davis, who "KNOWS RUSSIA," the readers were assured; "Again he will lead his group of specially privileged travellers through the thrilling experience of a full month in the 'new world' of the Soviet Union. See this breathless, on-marching land of stupendous planning." [14] A week later the *Open Road* announced its "Fourth Annual Travel Collective" to the Soviet, under the leadership of Kunitz. And in the war-threatened year of 1939, with full-scale confusion now at large, parcelling liberals into segments as a consequence of the ferocity of the fratricidal fight over the merits of Communism and Communists as the Russian record displayed them, the urge to "see for yourself" persisted. *Intourist's* smiling babushka-clad women were still gazing at the readers from the pages of the *New Republic* as late as May, while the *Nation* carried news of Soviet tours scheduled virtually down to the outbreak of the war. A trip to Russia was offered to liberal readers leaving New York on the *Batory* as late as August 5, 1939.[15] There was no other nation on the planet which even approached Russia as a second choice in the department of foreign travel inducement.

An *Intourist* advertisement in the *Nation* in February, 1936 had included as an extra inducement a picture of Alexei Stakhanov, "a coal miner in the Donbas," who had recently "begun a movement that has vibrated through all the sinews of the new Soviet industry and agriculture," readers were told, while being exhorted to visit and "witness at first hand the great progress being made in a sixth of the world." [16] Other than using a reference to Russia which had become a cliché even among liberals of the day, this bit of news which spotlighted the originator of a system of speed-up in Russian industry which would have been scorchingly denounced by every labor spokesman in the Western Hemisphere had it been introduced here, was indicative of something of importance already noted. The celebrated double standard which had long been developed to praise or excuse practices and actions in the Soviet while condemning the same things when seen elsewhere was merely being given another exercise. If it drew no liberal condemnation, its repeated practice of it by their own writers and spokesmen helped to explain the inability to notice contradictions of this sort. Some examples from this period may suffice.

When Kunitz' book *Dawn Over Samarkand* was published in the summer of 1935, it received warm liberal acceptance. The book described the communization of Turkestan by the Russians with great skill and with "a minimum of brutality," as Selden Rodman put it in his *Common Sense* review, in July. Robert Morss Lovett far exceeded him in praise in the *New Republic,* compared it favorably to Anna Louise Strong's *The Red Star of Samarkand,* and accepted their stories as ponderous evidence that the Communists had "achieved in Central Asia their most complete success in building socialism." [17] Kunitz' book actually followed that of the Czech critic of and refugee from Germany, Egon Erwin Kisch, *Changing Asia,* spiritedly reviewed by Anna Louise Strong in the *New Republic* and by Maxwell S. Stewart in the *Nation*. Stewart expressed the belief that this book, by an enthusiastic Soviet sympathizer and zealot for Communist conversion of Central Asia, was the ideal book for "those who have time to read only one book on Russia." [18] Two years later the same tendency in the same journal was to be noted in Milton Rugoff's review of *Prometheus and the Bolsheviks,* by John Lehmann, a warmly favorable account of the Soviet saturation of the ancient lands of the

South Caucasus, the people of which were presumably deprived of their longstanding fratricidal propensities by being incorporated into the Soviet system "with a future of unlimited promise." Rugoff, apologizing gently for the processes employed, declared, "The abrogation of their right to criticize—which has evoked such condescending pity from Western democracies—they consider temporary, and compared to other advantages, trivial." [19]

In large part it was such strong-arm tactics as these which liberals had turned purple over for many decades when employed by Western colonial powers in Asia and Africa, and it was "the abrogation of the right to criticize" which was at the very core of the Red case against Hitler and Mussolini, let alone the new Japanese regime. In these lands Communism had spared no effort or expense to stir up the "condescending pity of the Western democracies," and had actually made most liberals their partisans. Yet liberals themselves found it exceedingly hard to apply the same standard to the Russians on occasions of the same order.

An even more striking case was the manner in which the book *Belomor* by Maxim Gorky was received, a prideful strut of the OGPU achievement in building the White Sea Canal as slave drivers of political prisoners or "enemies of the State," as they were described in the fulsome half-page advertisement in the *New Republic* of December 11, 1935. The book received an unbelievably kind review by Edwin Seaver in the same journal six months later, reiterating support for the claim made earlier that "The Belomor Canal is the first triumph of the Soviet penal system, the most humane in all the world." [20] Had Hitler built an autobahn with part of the personnel incarcerated in the German concentration camps in 1935, it would not have been surprising to see a liberal journal issue a special supplement in color denouncing it as the supreme crime committed in the modern era. But no molten abuse greeted the Communists on announcing how they had built the Belomor canal.

Liberals followed a sympathetic course on other aspects of the Soviet internal social policy. For some time it followed the Communist position on the Jews, accepting as fact the assertion that the Soviet had made anti-Jewish sentiment or action a "crime against the state," that Jews were fully integrated into the Soviet system, that only old Jewish "men of property" still hated the Soviet, and that Zionism was a despicable solution for the Jewish predicament anywhere when there was the Soviet Union ready to take them. This approach was to be seen in the reviews of Leon Dennen's *Where The Ghetto Ends* by Louis Adamic and of David Goldberg's *Sussman Sees It Through* by Herman Simpson in the *New Republic*, and the contemptuous snort in the *Nation* in January, 1935 at a New York *Times* story that anti-Jewish riots had broken out in Russia.[21] The *New*

Masses and the *Communist* were preferred sources to the liberal papers on the state of Jewish affairs.[22] Despite Russia's ancient reputation as the home of the pogrom, the firm confidence of liberals and others inclined to sympathy in the ability of the Soviet regime to make "sudden changes of direction," in the words of André Gide, was largely responsible for their sticking to the view that no anti-Jewish feeling was left in the Soviet Union.

In accordance with liberal fixations that the Soviet Union was a land which had banned all racial and socio-cultural distinctions and merged them all in a common socialism was the announcement of the creation of a Jewish refuge in the Siberian district of Biro-Bidjan. This action obtained much editorial applause and commendation, while Villard devoted his page essay on August 28, 1935 to the subject ("Russia Aids the Jews"). "Setting this tract aside for the ill-treated Jews is a magnificent deed, and history will so proclaim it," [23] Villard promised fervently. An "American Committee for the Settlement of Jews in Biro-Bidjan" was promptly formed,[24] and soon stated that "thousands of Jews in Poland and contiguous countries" were applying to go there, although it was the seriously-pressed Jews of Germany who were originally being worried about, and expected to go. The Committee did not release subsequent information indicating that any Jews from Germany had the slightest interest in migrating to Biro-Bidjan, and on February 5. 1936 the *Nation* published an editorial stating that the whole project was now considered a failure; "to the deeply middle-class minds of the German Jews it looks stark and uninviting," was the way it explained the neglect of this Siberian preserve.[25]

The entire project caught the liberal press in a crossfire between American Communists and various Jewish individuals and groups who felt that Jews were being unfairly accused of Communist affiliation because of this and other incidents, but this war was largely fought in the Communist press,[26] although Ludwig Lewisohn had issued a scornful reference to Biro-Bidjan as "a new exile." And the episode disappeared from discussion in a welter of attacks and counter-attacks, capped by a sensational switch of attention by the *New Masses,* which predicted a wave of massacres of Jews in the United States in the late summer of 1936, mainly the work of John L. Spivak, whom the logrollers among the Communist and liberal journals had tabbed as "America's greatest reporter" in that year. But the nature of his charges led to a reaction among more critical liberals, the feature of which was a fierce piece of debunking of Spivak by Dwight MacDonald in *Common Sense.* Spivak's wild stories had gained much credence while they were devoted entirely to the European, especially the German, scene. A collection of them published as a book titled *Europe Under the Terror* received an unqualified acceptance in review by Frederick Schuman in the *Nation* late in June, 1936, when the author's reliability was already at serious discount among liberals.[27]

Probably the high-water mark of uncritical indulgence of Communist Russia by liberal editors occurred in the late spring of 1936, when the Soviets announced the promulgation of a new constitution. The *Nation's* June 17 editorial was a piece of unbroken flamboyant praise, which accepted its ideals as already actual realization. The new document was a vindication of the assertion of Sidney and Beatrice Webb, that the U.S.S.R. was not a dictatorship but "a government by a whole series of committees;"[28]

What we have here . . . is a liquidation of the dictatorship of the proletariat in the civil sphere and its replacement by constitutional democracy. . . . Of course the Soviet system has always contained far more genuine democracy than outsiders have realized. . . . But the essential power in the Soviet Union has never rested entirely with the government.

The authoritative commentary of course was from Fischer in Moscow in the same issue. According to him, "The dictatorship is not retreating under pressure," by adopting a constitutional form of government. "It is voluntarily abdicating." He went on to illustrate this:[29]

Stalin is the chairman of the government committee which drafted the constitution and the task, undertaken upon his initiative, had his minute guidance from start to finish. Collectivization, industrialization, and now the launching of democracy—with these remarkable achievements to his credit, Stalin's place in history is secure.

In a separate letter to the editors from Moscow six weeks later, Fischer added that "The presumption of the new constitution is that the whole nation is loyal. I think this is the fact." He added that there was no inherent conflict between democracy and dictatorship, because the Soviet Union had both, and he was convinced that the Communist Party would disappear shortly in Russia.[30] Unfortunately for Fischer and the *Nation* editors, just a little over two weeks later, a battalion of grizzled veteran Communists were on public trial in Russia for "terrorism and conspiracy against the State." Another astoundingly bad prediction and colossal liberal misjudgment of the situation was on the record. The painful wriggling of both Fischer and his editorial superiors thereafter remains distressing to read to this day.

But of course they were not alone. The *New Republic* on June 24 applied a cordial and sympathetic evaluation of the news, adding,

"The suggested plan, ratification of which is a foregone conclusion, is a vast step toward political democracy without, however, altering the economic democracy which the Russian leaders of course regard as being far more important." [31] Six months later, with a group of liberals critical of the persistence of dictatorship and the new purge trials in full cry, the editorial position stubbornly clung to its faith in eventual realization of announced Communist goals: [32]

> During a conflict on the modern scale, any country must necessarily be governed on a dictatorial basis. The degree of centralized control in Soviet Russia has never been so great as its enemies have maintained. . . . That is why those individuals go seriously astray who announce that they are opposed to the dictatorships both of Fascism and Communism. The fascist dictatorship is an end in itself; the dictatorship of the proletariat is a means to a very different end.

And the editors held out hope that the new constitution might yet prove to be "a remarkable achievement."

But neither editorial staff quite equalled the obtuse aplomb of Sidney Webb, whose *Nation* article on November 21, 1936, "Soviet Russia's New Deal" hailed the coming ratification, and its enfranchisement of an electorate of "just over 91,000,000" gave him cause for modestly suggesting that this document, "which embodies an effective socialism, will be regarded by the future historian as even more momentous than the American Constitution of 1787 or that of the French Republic of 1793." [33] The absence of a possible slate of rival candidates to contest Communists in future elections, and the contemporary purge trials, which were certainly out of harmony with the constitution's "provisions safeguarding the liberty of the person against unauthorized arrest and imprisonment by the police or by arbitrary action of the executive government unsanctioned by the judiciary," went unnoticed in Webb's beaming greeting.

The *Nation's* editorial tribute on the occasion of the twentieth anniversary of the Bolshevik revolution in November, 1937 was a veritable apotheosis. It contained no criticism, praised its "impressive gains" internally, despite simultaneous pre-occupation with building "the largest standing army in Europe," and declared that [34]

> Above all the people and their government are united in two things: a passionate opposition to war, knowing well that the future of socialism in Russia depends on continued peace—and a still stronger determination to resist Fascism even if resistance means war—for the success of Fascism would spell the end of socialism and the Soviet Government and the essence of Western Civilization as well.

Stewart's companion piece in the same issue (November 13) took care of those troubled by the purges by discounting Russian political problems of the moment, asserting that most Soviet citizens were unruffled by them, the vast internal gains having taken their attention away from them.[35] In his proud summary of the expansion of Russia in world affairs, he emphasized that United States recognition in 1933 was the first step in ending "Soviet isolation," and with respect to recent announced Comintern policy shifts, there was no evidence that it would diminish in any way the continued expansion of the Communist Party in Japan, France and China.

But beginning in the late winter of 1937–1938, news on Russian internal affairs began to diminish noticeably, to the point where in the following year, except for persistent pieces on the new series of purges, there were six-to-eight-week intervals with no news from Russia. One of the main reasons as far as the *Nation* was concerned was the departure of Fischer from Moscow. His last dispatch from Russia came from Kiev in September, 1936, and the following month he started reporting the Spanish Civil War, from Madrid. But his last Russian dispatch gave no hint of the disillusionment which he confessed to in his autobiography a few years later. His economic comparison of the Soviet system was still with Russia in 1914 and not the Western countries, and his general tone after 14 years' eyewitness observations was still warm and favorable. He did not mention the purge trials, and praised the Stakhanov speedup "movement" as a factor in high incomes and more employment in the Russian economy of 1936.[36]

But the steady decline of material adulatory of the Soviet Union's internal order continued down to the outbreak of the war in 1939. An underlying favorable commitment was easily uncovered, however, which was accompanied by a hectic resistance to anything even remotely suggesting a "Red-baiting" in the United States. Some liberal journalists, such as Broun and Cowley, remained transparently sympathetic with the Stalin majority, although their big battle did not occur until after the 1938 purge trials of the "Trotskyites" and the exoneration of Trotsky of any responsibility as charged by the John Dewey committee, which will be treated subsequently.

If this diminution of news was interpreted as signs that liberal credulity on Russia had also diminished, *New Republic* and *Nation* editorials in January and February, 1939 were an answer to the contrary. The former, titled "Free Bread for the Bear," announced,[37]

The Soviet Union is seriously considering the distribution of free bread on the same basis as it now supplies water. According to *The Week,* the confidential London newsletter, the plan may be put into effect before the end of 1939. The practical details have been worked out, although they have not been made public. . . . The most striking feature of *The Week*'s report is the statement that the proposal—which will certainly startle public opinion in most other countries—has been taken by the Russians in a most matter-of-fact way. They are accustomed to think about possibilities such as this as logical probabilities in the course of the Soviet Union's development. And already a number of public services are offered virtually without charge. So the basic idea of free bread excites little comment.

That stories of this sort could be swallowed whole even as late as January 25, 1939 is a good index to the orientation of a good part of the liberal mind. Its pro-Soviet basis and strong will to believe could scarcely be more effectively demonstrated although two weeks later the same journal's editors took the Soviet Third Five Year Plan announcement to raise production by 62% between 1937 and 1942 as "a statement of the progress that may be reasonably attained." [38]

The *Nation*'s February 11 commentary also concerned the Five Year Plan, and took its announcement of determination to concentrate on consumer's goods at a time when arms buildups were becoming of first-rank importance around the world as having "struck a blow for sanity in a world rapidly going mad," but agreed that it was expected, anyway; [39]

By now we have become so accustomed to the Soviet's spectacular economic growth that it is no longer news. But it is a testimony to the Soviet Union's growing sense of security that for the first time a significant degree of attention is to be given to the light industries as well as to those turning out producers' goods.

It was impossible to miss the note of quiet pride in the *New Republic*'s editorial comment on the opening of the Soviet Pavilion at the New York World's Fair in May. The description compared to a parent's pride in a son's athletic trophies, boasting that it was the highest and most expensive object of the Fair: [40]

It is simple, it is imposing, and it cost a lot of money. . . . On top of the tower is the 79-foot stainless steel statue of a young Soviet worker. Gleaming above the statue is a twelve-foot red Soviet star. . . . The impression conveyed by the whole is that of power—the rather boastful but candid and friendly power of a young man showing his muscles, not looking for trouble but not running away from it either.

The deep freeze which set in on liberal-Soviet relations after the *Pakt* of August 1939 was accompanied by a prodigious shucking-off of many years of self-applied blinders as far as the reality of the Russian scene was concerned, much of it by those who had spent much effort in fixing these illusions in the first place. The *Nation* especially indulged in a debunking mood, and did not bother to discuss the pedigree of its most effective debunkers. About the most critical thing it printed in a decade on the conditions of internal Russia was Joachim Joesten's lengthy "Russia Revisited" on December 21, 1940. Joesten's pro-Communist reports on Scandinavia had been previous features in the liberal weeklies, but this story involved his observations as he was crossing the Worker's Fatherland on his way to refuge in the Western Hemisphere via Vladivostok. Comparing what he had seen in 1932 on the occasion of a visit then with the most recent time, he admitted, "By and large, things looked pretty much as they did eight years ago." [41] A decade of feverish buildup of the Soviet Union in hundreds of pages of liberal rhetorical prose was demolished by a single sentence.

THE ORIGINS OF THE GREAT LIBERAL FREEZE ON COMMUNIST RUSSIA

America's liberals had little trouble finding where they stood on the first of Europe's great political civil wars in the 1930's: the combat of the Left against Hitler and Mussolini. This partisanship had direct bearing on their attitude toward the other: the conflict between the rival Marxist and Left protagonists of Stalin and Trotsky, which performed the function of wrecking beyond all repair the laboriously constructed Popular Front. Only the most deeply committed were prepared for the debilitating effects of this long wrangle; a substantial contingent were caught in distressed indecision midway between them. By and large the editorial staffs of the liberal weeklies clung to their established faith in the going order of Stalin to the outbreak of the war of 1939, discommoded though they were by defections as the struggle reached its peak. Not until Stalin deserted the common war front against Hitler Germany did a comprehensive re-evaluation of the Soviet Union take place, followed by 22 months of chilly separation. A rapprochement occurred in June, 1941 which lasted until the setting in of the "Cold War" in 1947.

Fierce criticism of Stalinist Russia from the Left was not a novelty, of course. Anarchists such as Emma Goldman and Alexander Berkman, as we have seen, wrote indignant books between 1923 and 1925 which still rank near the top of anti-Soviet critiques. A small periodical press flourished throughout this period and later, expressing the views of a bewildering spectrum of Marxist splinter factions united only in their implacability toward the Stalin system. But they

enjoyed scant respect among established liberal organs, which preferred to see a noble and untarnished vision being made a reality in
Russia. Their hostility to all manner of attacks on the Communists
was largely indistinguishable from the same stylized resentment of
the *New Masses, Daily Worker,* and *Communist,* often a consequence
of the traffic of writers from one to the other, bringing their views
with them. Some idea of liberal asperity toward these unreconstructed enemies of Communist Russia can be seen in the *Nation*'s
editorial obituary comment upon the death of Berkman by his own
hand in Nice, France, in July, 1936, during the peak month of Soviet
prestige. Referring contemptuously to his having authored *The
Bolshevik Myth,* it volunteered now that in the light of the grandeur
which Communism had attained, "The monograph in which he gave
vent to his indignation against the Soviet government is one of the
most pathetic and unintentionally funny social writings of modern
times." [42]

The cooling process had however already set in within by this time.
The first notable editorial skeptic was Edmund Wilson, who along
with the French writer André Gide shared the honors of being subjected to serious reproach for their critical second thoughts on Russia.
Wilson's April 29, 1936 *New Republic* essay contained a very sober
study of Soviet shortcomings, including the first realistic examination
by a liberal of the aftermath of the Kirov repressions of 1934 and
after. Said Wilson of the Communist reprisals, "they still carry over
from the tsarist regime a good share of plain medieval cruelty." And
he went into detail in his soon-published *Travels in Two Democracies,* which was not quite as enthusiastic over the U.S.S.R. as he had
been in 1932, nor as condemnatory of the United States. Wilson was
subjected to violent abuse in the *New Republic*'s letters columns, and
his new thoughts were assaulted as "anti-Soviet abuse." Robert Cant-
well nevertheless appraised him still as "a middle class intellectual
who is sympathetic to Communism." [43]

Gide took a short fall from favor with the publication of his sec-
ond-look via travel as well, although *Retour de l'URSS,* despite its
many critical remarks about the Reds, revealed him to be still a
vivacious fellow traveler; M. E. Ravage's Paris-written review established that.[44] But the majority of the Communist press was upon his
back regardless. Wilson was far more an object of liberal castigation,
especially after his comprehensive critique of American left-wing
writers for their heavy "infection" by "Russian factional politics,"
and his advice to them to withdraw from the new belligerence and
look at American problems and write their own answers to them
"without trying to copy them from the bright boys in Moscow." Cowley's long *New Republic* critique of January 20, 1937, "Stalin or
Satan?," took violent exception to a number of Wilson's stands, but

was especially affronted by Wilson's term "Stalinist criticism." Cowley retorted, " 'Stalinist' is really an epithet, of vague but highly emotional and invidious meaning, invented by Stalin's enemies partly as a means of confusing the issue." [45] Of course, "Trotskyite" and "Nazi" were similarly epithets, of "Stalinist" origin for the very large part, but it was not considered a worthy matter to make an issue out of the entire subject of political criticism via epithets, already a major intellectual industry. But the stage was now dressed for a stupendous clash, brought about almost entirely by the new wave of trials in Russia, which began in August, 1936, and continued the next two years.

On August 22, 1936 the *Nation* published a rhapsodical memoir from Moscow by Fischer of Red achievements which the new constitution acknowledged as *faits accomplis* instead of yet-to-be-realized aims. Half of the article was devoted to a discussion of the eclipse of the Communist secret police, and the establishment of the new era of enthronement of civil liberties and the demise of dictatorship. Of the political structure now emerging Fischer exclaimed, "This Soviet phenomenon of democracy succeeding dictatorship is therefore unique in history and may remain the only instance in history of the voluntary abdication of dictatorship." [46] It may be for that reason that it was preceded by an editorial which was without doubt one of the most painful pieces of rationalization ever published in the history of liberal journalism. It sought to explain the newest wave of trials for alleged treason and sabotage in Russia, involving a group of the most famous figures in Bolshevik history. Despite the quibbling and apologetics, the *Nation* was reluctant to accept the charges against Zinoviev, Kamenev, Trotsky and others, yet at the same time eager to believe that there was some case against them; "We do not mean to deride the charges," it hastily covered after some ruminations, adding a rueful comment which reflected on their haste to accept the new constitution as evidence that the Soviet Union was about to legislate ineffable political purity: "It was to be expected that under the velvet glove of the new Soviet constitution there would still be the firm outlines of the iron hand." [47] But the *Nation* had not expected it.

Neither had the large majority of other liberals. The *New Republic*'s saddened editorial comment was characteristically titled "Another Blow At the Dream." Like the *Nation*'s, the agitation of this group of editors was intense, the news "received with a sinking feeling," and "especially disquieting to those who do not credit such charges, but accept the government's account at face value." [48] The scurrying which filled the liberal camp was akin to the commotion likely to occur with the loosing of a cat in a dove cote.

By October, *Nation* views had stiffened a bit; great disappointment was expressed that these trials, like the earlier ones, were "conducted in a manner foreign to democratic ideals of justice," while issuing the judgment that "the pre-trial conduct of the government-controlled press was particularly shocking," with its "overwhelming presumption of guilt." "It is at least a question whether the proceedings could be in any true sense a trial," was the modest conclusion, but of course since the case of the accused was not being considered, this was sheer understatement. Trotsky, interned in Norway by the Minister of Justice, Trygvie Lie, shortly after the trials began, was one defendant whose views should have been reaching the outside, not being in Russia at all, but there was little more than notice taken of this by American liberals. Nevertheless, for its mild criticisms of the Moscow trials, the *Nation* did get a full-page denunciation in the December 22 *New Masses*. "It [the *Nation*] has encouraged the serious libel that the Moscow trial was not genuine," the pro-trial *New Masses* loudly complained.[49] Bad blood between the erstwhile sympathetic publications now multiplied rapidly.

The trouble was actually only beginning. The last week of January, 1937 saw a larger and even more spectacular list of accused hauled before Red courts on even more sensational charges, accused of collusion with Hitler Germany, plots with Trotsky to assassinate Stalin and to let loose a campaign of incredible havoc within Russia. From this point on, a great watershed in liberal thinking, writing and expression was crossed. The civil war among the defenders and repudiators of these trial charges was about to begin. Among the editorial camps there began a program of defensive back-tracking which sought to exonerate the Stalinists by asserting that the world was now divided into "Fascist" and "democratic" camps, which in their view provided a mantle of protection to the Communists for whatever went on internally in Russia, since their acts were so obviously intended to extend the life of "democracy" in the world. But the blithe years of extravagant pro-Red praise and excuses were about to yield a crop of bitter critiques from many readers and some writers, who insisted that this was not the issue at all, and preferred to see no reason for taking the part of the Russian dictator, now that their rationale had pitched them so implacably against those of Germany and Italy. Coupled with the growing chorus of anti-Communist Left denunciation of Stalinist conduct in Spain, the two sallies became part of one actual internal revolt within liberal ranks.

The earliest reports on this new wave of trials found both liberal weeklies seeking comfort in the dispatches of Walter Duranty to the New York *Times,* whose first accounts indicated "a clear belief in the validity of the confessions" of the accused, as the *Nation* put it. "The horror of the new Moscow trials is inescapable," it nevertheless concluded. The most bothersome part of them all seemed to be that the logic of the situation put the Soviet government in a bad light regardless of the outcome; if the accused were innocent, then it would be impossible to excuse the government for the methods they had used to conduct the trials, while if the men were guilty, then Russia was "so riddled with conspiracies" that it could not "lay claim to the trust that liberals have thus far accorded it," and the editorial of January 30 seemed to think that this latter eventuality would be worse to stand up under.[50] The *New Republic* was no less disoriented, but clung to its belief that Duranty's judgment was correct, and felt that the foreign consequences were by far the most serious in the long run view: [51]

> It gives aid and encouragement to the Fascist forces in Italy, Germany and Japan at a time when it really does begin to seem true that the world is divided into two camps, Fascist and democratic, and that democracy is fighting for its life . . . the tragedy involved in them [the trials] is more than merely Russian; it is a tragedy for the whole world.

One could hardly accuse the editors of not trying to salvage something of comfort to the Soviet regime. In answer to a letter-writing critic who protested their sympathy with the Communists, and rebelled at identification of the Soviet Union with the democracies, the editorial rebuttal blandly commented, "There are two broad aspects of democracy, political and economic. Soviet Russia has the second, but not the first. It nevertheless is a part, and an important part, of the anti-Fascist front." [52]

The *Nation's* most labored editorial effort at portraying the trials in a favorable light up to this stage was published on February 6, despite a paragraph of mild chiding. It also contained the advance statement of a new suggested policy twist for liberals: indefinitely suspended judgment on the Russian actions. Despite the promptness with which the "inside" was smoked out into the open in the affairs of the nations whose governments it despised, the *Nation* pleaded dense ignorance in the final analysis on the Soviet; "It is possible that it will be another hundred years before all the actual facts about the recent Soviet trials are known," it ventured, and quietly recommended that "Meanwhile it is the task of progressives all over the world to appraise without any political or emotional commitments the meaning and implications of what has happened in Russia." [53] Similar detachment with respect to German, Italian, Spanish and Japanese affairs might have rendered them utterly invulnerable to spiritual mobilization in another war.

But all of the *Nation's* readers and writers were not ready to collaborate on such a program of breath-holding on tip-toe. The same issue containing this appeal published an angry piece by Paul Ward, defending fellow-journalists Vladimir Romm and Karl Radek as the most unlikely Russians to be involved in "the fantastic plot Vishinsky laid bare," [54] while Trotsky's defenders were growing more vocal by the day. The touchiness of this head-on collision even impelled the *Nation* a few weeks later to print two reviews of the just-published *The Revolution Betrayed,* by Trotsky, a warm and friendly one by Benjamin Stolberg and an utterly hostile one by Fischer, whose resentment of Trotsky's attack on Stalin smoldered throughout the review—the same Fischer who protested in his dispatch of June 17, 1936 that he "violently disliked the raucous paeans of praise for Stalin which are repeated in this country [Russia] with benumbing frequency and monotony." But apparently he was as repelled at this moment by demolishing criticism from ideological antagonists of the formidability of Trotsky.[55]

The *New Republic* had much the same experience, and likewise soon showed serious evidence of the strain produced by the split within its ranks. Its February 17 editorial, "Russian Politics in America," admonished the readership "not to be naïve enough to suppose that in a controversy of this kind Trotsky is any more a protagonist of liberal democracy than Stalin," and supported the new doctrine of suspended judgment: [56]

It is the responsibility of believers in civil liberty to hold their minds open for any further evidence that may be presented. But it does not seem to us that it is their responsibility, on the basis of arguments such as these, to assert positively that the confessed traitors were not guilty and did not have a fair trial, or on the other hand to assert positively that they were guilty.

But the decay of the liberal ranks went on, and side-taking grew more brisk. In the *New Republic,* Lion Feuchtwanger, the passionate scourge of Hitler, was prominent among the "anti-Nazis" who accepted the Moscow trials completely on their face value,[57] in support of the now wary editorial friendliness toward the official Soviet explanations. But more critical voices began to rise, mainly in the letters to the editor, including Martha Gruening and Norman Thomas in these early weeks of 1937.[58]

The incident which touched off a major fulmination of this enlarging volcano was an eight-column review by Cowley of the *The Case of the Anti-Soviet Trotskyite Center* in April,[59] about the longest review ever published in the *New Republic.* He revealed that he was completely convinced that the trial of the new group of defendants was fair, adding "It seems to me that the confessions were undoubtedly sincere." He scoffed at critics' insinuations of pressure, intimidation, threats to relatives, deprivations, loss of sleep, drugs, and what might be known later as "Darkness-at-Noon" and "brain-washing" circumstances; "the behavior of the prisoners on the witness stand," declared this editor of a journal beseeching its readers to suspend their judgment, "was certainly that of guilty men lacking popular support and ashamed of the deeds that had brought them there."

Yet Cowley was badly torn and shaken by this event, and could not conceal his anxiety over Stalin, one of the earliest occasions in which the Soviet dictator was subjected to deprecation in this publication by anyone, yet softened in terms of total impact:

I am not a "Stalinist" except in so far as I deeply sympathize with the aims of the Soviet Union, and in so far as I believe that Stalin and his Political Bureau have in general followed wiser policies than those advocated by his enemies. I do not believe he is infallible as a statesman or a guide. . . . The public adoration of this one leader is to me a disheartening feature of Soviet life.

Furthermore, Cowley was split between defending the Soviet and cautioning American "progressives" against total commitment to it as a guide for future American action. It was his conviction now that the record made it necessary "to revise and revalue our whole attitude toward the Soviet Union," and that it was unfortunate that liberals and radicals were adopting the position everywhere that the Soviet Union was "the answer to their personal problems." The U.S.S.R. was still "in construction," Cowley explained, and

To this new society we owe our loyalty, but not our blind loyalty. With its strength and weaknesses, its present shortcomings and its promise for the future, it is still the most progressive force in the world. For the Soviet Union to be attacked and destroyed by Fascist powers would be a catastrophe from which I very much doubt that our present civilization could recover.

Again, a prominent liberal editor had interpreted the underlying basis of the support for domestic Communist action and policy; the field of foreign politics was the dominant consideration.

The marathon Cowley review drew enthusiastic letters of praise from Upton Sinclair, Jerome Davis, Mark Starr and L. B. Boudin, and a sour-sweet one from John Chamberlain, who rejoiced at Cowley's courage finally to attack the Stalin "father-image," long propagated by Anna Louise Strong, which Chamberlain said had been "sticking in his crop" for a long time. But a thunderous wave of dissent rolled in from other sources. One of the most fiery came from Dwight MacDonald, and one a few days later just as fiery from Sidney Hook. MacDonald pounded Cowley for siding with Stalinist views.

Hook wanted to know how Cowley concluded that because Trotsky hated the Stalin regime this made him guilty of the specific crimes for which he was tried *in absentia* at Moscow. Hook now doubted all the Soviet trials since 1931.[60]

The critic who drew the most attention was Waldo Frank. When he expressed his doubt over the validity of the trials in the May 12 *New Republic*, the Communist press fell upon him like no other liberal, mainly because of his intimate part in the campaigning of the Browder-Ford Communist Party presidential team in the fall of 1936, and his major parts in a number of powerful pro-Communist activities in the latter months of 1936 and into 1937.[61] His criticism was almost treated as a defection, and the after-effects were most revealing. When he was bitterly attacked by Browder, Frank promptly wrote a letter to the *New Masses* protesting his persistence as "a faithful friend of the Soviet Union" and calling upon his "many friends in the U.S.S.R." to exonerate him from the charges of devotion to Trotskyism which were resounding in the *New Masses*.[62] Reinhold Niebuhr's spirited defense of Frank from Browder's "venomous reply" to the latter's doubts as to the Moscow trial picture sounded the same note: "No one has been a more consistent supporter of Russia and the cause of the Soviets than Mr. Frank," Niebuhr flared. His anger at Browder for what he considered an ill-tempered attack upon an important "revolutionary writer" aroused him to great heights, of which the following statement was the pinnacle: [63]

These observations are made by one who believes that the present policy of the Communist Party is immeasurably superior to that of the Trotskyites. It is a responsible policy and theirs is an irresponsible one. Trotskyite fanaticism is a peril to the revolutionary cause today. But that does not prove that Trotsky conspired with Japan or Germany or that the Moscow trials are wholly honest. It is just barely possible that the rulers of Russia, forced by the world situation to opportunistic statesmanship, foolishly thought it necessary to tar the more intransigent Marxist foes with the taint of Fascism in order to neutralize the charges of these foes against them.

Again the world political situation was being trundled out to buttress the Stalinist action, although Niebuhr's defense was somewhat specious compared with the more forthright defenses based sheerly on the mortal threat posed by Russia's rivals. If the policies of the Communist Party were as "immeasurably superior" as Niebuhr claimed they were, then their malfunctioning should have been blamed for the "opportunistic statesmanship" to which their executors were being driven, and not the nebulous entity called "the world situation," which was as much a *product* of Communist policy as it was an agent acting *upon* Communist policy. But the world situation of 1937 in the fellow-traveler's eye was a strictly one-dimensional one.

Fred Rodell tried to keep the cause of liberal agnosticism toward the Stalin-Trotsky controversy going in a *New Republic* plea to all liberals to refuse to take part "in a violent quarrel based on insufficient evidence," [64] but the passage of time was actually making the difference of opinion more profound, and the parties to it more implacable. When the American Writers' Congress in the first week of June, 1937 turned over their platform to Browder, who launched into a ferocious attack on Trotsky and his "liberal stooges," more fireworks exploded. MacDonald was stirred into writing what was probably the longest letter to the editor that the *Nation* ever consented to publish, denouncing the AWC as a Communist Party "maneuver," accusing it of denying invitations to Wilson, Hacker, Lewis Corey, Hook, Stolberg and James T. Farrell, thus, along with permitting Browder's speech, "slandering" or "excluding" "a considerable group of eminent anti-Fascist writers" merely because of their known insistence on criticizing the regime in Russia.[65] Henry Hart of the AWC the following week (June 26, 1937) wrote almost as long a letter in angry defense against MacDonald's charges, most of the letter being devoted to attacking MacDonald for calling the organization a "Communist maneuver." [66] It was regrettable for MacDonald that the United States Attorney-General did not support him in his charge until 1944.

In the meantime the open season on Old Bolsheviks had been extended in Russia. The arrest, trial, and execution of eight prominent Red Army generals in the second week of June, including the "almost legendary hero" Marshal Tukhachevsky, youthful military genius of the Revolution, brought about new prostrations among American liberals persisting in their vision of the "Dream." A sad and grieving *Nation* editorial paragraph on June 19 regretted that the executions had "provided a field day for the enemies of Moscow at a time when Soviet policy in Europe needed all the friends it can find." [67] Four days later the *New Republic,* still protesting editorially that there was "no reason to question the probity or the ability of Soviet prosecutors and courts, civil or military," and still lambasting the Trotsky defenders, felt that this new series of executions, involving persons so high in military echelons, was evidence of "weak morale within the Soviet Union," and went on to plot out the implications, again in terms of foreign politics: [68]

Friends of the Soviet Union have been hoping, and even from time to time observing, that this sort of thing would be outgrown with time. It was to be expected soon after the revolution. But if now, after 20 years, plots and counter plots still dominate the scene, a chilling influence is bound to be exerted on all those who expected something better. The blow that all these incidents have delivered to the prestige of the Soviet Union throughout the world is at present beyond measure.

Although a mild chiding was again directed at Russian leadership for what was taking place, no change of heart was evident. One of those least-influenced by the trials wrangle was Schuman. In his review of William Henry Chamberlin's *Collectivism* in the *New Republic* on June 23, he admitted that "it is not to be denied that the Bolshevik Party, as a disciplined brotherhood employing terror, propaganda and pageantry in a new technique of oligarchy, was the pattern upon which Mussolini and Hitler fashioned their own weapons of power." But he was eager to accept the Communists' own word as to their ideals and goals, and concluded that they were attainable if they said they were so. He was ready to grant Chamberlin's skepticism that the Soviet Union was moving in the direction of liberty, democracy and well-being but he was inclined to be far more charitable. Despite being shaken by the purge trials in progress, Schuman was still of the belief that the charges against the defendants were correct. And he felt confident in the asserted Communist goal of material prosperity eventuating; "If efficiency in production is achieved, prosperity is possible, because an economy resting upon public monopoly (unlike the Fascist economies resting upon private monopoly) is capable of expanding mass consumption almost indefinitely." Schuman felt that the issue of the trials could be effectively blotted out under a mountain-range heap of consumer goods.[69]

Three weeks later the junior liberal weekly published a special article by Walter Duranty which was an unqualified testament in favor of the Stalin regime's interpretation of the trials ever since that of Kirov's alleged killers in 1934. His accent was also in terms of foreign politics, praising the United States for recognizing the Soviet in 1933 and thus providing them with a barrier against much greater pressure from the Japanese in Asia, and permitting an atmosphere and environment in which "the Red Army and the Soviet war industry gained prodigiously in efficiency and strength," while currently emerging as "a positive adversary instead of a potential obstacle" in the Spanish war. Duranty accepted without a tremor the story of a Fascist-inspired plot with disaffected Red leaders, and expressed grim satisfaction that now "the 'Trojan horse' of the Kremlin's enemies is broken and its occupants destroyed."[70]

This was an article which would not have been rejected by a Communist publication anywhere on earth, and it contributed high-octane fuel to the flaming criticism of the *New Republic-Nation* editorial policy of pro-Soviet teetering on the opinion high-wire. A week earlier Max Eastman's rude blast at both editorial staffs had been published in the *New Republic*, and Duranty's article appearing on its heels made a number of observers wonder what kind of policy upheaval was racking the journal. Eastman described the Russian situation as a "counter-revolution," featured by the killing of more "trusted Bolsheviks" in the past eight months than Jacobins who had been guillotined after the collapse of Robespierre. Eastman went on to say that these circumstances were understood better "by almost every low-brow rag in this country than they are by the *Nation* and the *New Republic*." And the reason? [71]

> It seems to me it is because the editors of these papers, although at heart democratic liberals, have been deceived by their hope of Russia and despair of America into imagining they were Bolsheviks or something near it. They have mistaken Russia's return to bourgeois standards for their own approach to proletarian revolutionism. They have mistaken their emotional dislike of "Trotskyism" for a loyalty to Communism.

The new wave of executions, involving the reputed military commanders, even stimulated Villard to make a separate attack on Stalin in the *Nation* for July 10; "Eight Benedict Arnolds at once" was a story which even he could not swallow. His bitter review of the effects of "Stalin's continuation of his legal murders" and wholesale assault on liberals still defending Stalin and the purges stressed the fact that the latter people were now growing even louder in demanding that the United States fight again "to save democracy," and Villard was having none of that. His chief reward for this contribution was a stern rebuke from Carl Marzani, writing from Oxford, England, whose long *Nation* letter six weeks later fumed that Villard should question the guilt of the executed generals. As for the war issue, he advised Villard, "The only policy, if any, that can prevent war is not to preach Lansbury pacifism but to rally the democracies around the Franco-Soviet pact." [72] The blood bath in Russia was to be ignored; the firming of Communist foreign policy was the order of the day to Russia's liberal friends.

Fischer, still in Moscow, did not illumine the *Nation*'s readers on what he knew about this new purge outburst. Not until February 10, 1940, when engaged in writing a massive attack on the Stalinist system, did he reveal that it was his conclusion that it was strictly motivated by the discovery of strong anti-Stalin sentiment in the Red Army and in the secret police, and not that they were German spies. On this latter date he announced that "It is significant that on May 11, 1937, the very day on which Marshal Tukhachevsky was demoted and a month before he and his generals were executed, political commissars were introduced in the Red Army. These commissars, *Pravda* said, are 'the eyes and ears of the Communist Party in the ranks of the Army.' " [73]

All summer and fall of 1937 the conflict among the liberals bloomed and ripened. By the time the execution list reached the 600-mark it produced a revulsion in its first *New Republic* editor, Brailsford, who expressed his horror in a separate article titled "What Has Happened In Russia?" Condemning the killings as "an act of barbarism," his disillusion was complete: [74]

English socialists who have worked for a United Front at home and a common inter-policy on that basis between London, Paris and Moscow, look out after these executions on ruins. No path runs clear through the debris. With some reservations, we had thought Stalin more nearly right over policy than Trotsky. But after this bloodbath one has to realize that in a land where loyal opposition is impossible there can be neither stability nor health.

Another explosion rocked the same journal before the end of the year, a charge by Felix Morrow that the editors of the *New Republic* were "working for Stalinism under the guise of being a liberal organ." Morrow's pointed barb at the editors produced an odd repudiation: [75]

Mr. Morrow seems to be affected by a violent rush-to-the-brain of Russian politics. He also seems to think that a liberal magazine should give equal space to all sides of every question. For the last eight years the *New Republic* has ceased to call itself a liberal magazine in order to avoid misconceptions of this sort, which seem to be inherent in the word "liberal." While trying to preserve the best qualities of liberalism, it prefers to be known as progressive.

But editorial policy on Russia did not change, and the *New Republic* continued to have Russian politics "on the brain" fully as much as Felix Morrow, with grasping for any kind of straws to help illustrate its support of the Russian trials as evidence that the criticism and splitting among liberals had shaken them far more than yet admitted. As support for the Soviet assertion that a massive spy ring was being broken up by trials and executions, the *New Republic* pointed out just after Christmas 1937 the case of Juliette Poyntz, long known as a Communist Party labor activity figure, who had been disclosed as a long-time secret agent for the Immigration Bureau of the Department of Labor and active in the deporting of radical aliens. "When things like this can happen in the United States, it becomes more credible that the Soviet government has to protect itself against a horde of spies and traitors," [76] the editorial rumbled, although the implication of the story was that the American Communist Party was the aggrieved entity in this incident.

On its part, *Common Sense* was as agitated by the Moscow trials as its weekly elder cousins, but gradually leaned toward a critical and withdrawal policy. After conceding that some economic achievements had been made in Russia since the Communists had taken over, its six-column editorial for October, 1937 concluded that the political manifestations of Communism in Russia had been essentially reactionary, and that there had been far too much intrigue, plotting and violence; even Hitler's list of purgees of June, 1934 was no longer very substantial compared to what the Soviet regime had annihilated only since August, 1936. As for recommended procedure, its independent position commanded first place: [77]

We American progressives should watch Europe, including the Soviet Union, from a safe distance, learn what can be learned, but apply our intelligence to finding our own way forward. We want neither Europe's wars, nor Europe's revolutions, nor Europe's absolutisms.

For a time in early 1938 the liberal editorial position clung to the line that Russia was so far away that it rendered any precise knowledge of what was going on there quite impossible. Lengthy reports in great detail on Germany and Japan, replete with meticulous addenda had long featured liberal foreign news reporting, and a goodly volume of such information, albeit far more charmingly presented, about Russia was also on record. But with the coming of the trials, a façade of bewilderment went up almost at once. On January 5, the *New Republic* stubbornly reiterated its old position, "We see no reason at present for modifying the opinion we have expressed on several previous occasions, that it is impossible for persons at this distance from Russia to say with authority what is going on there." At the same time some comfort was attempted to be extracted from a *Saturday Evening Post* story by John D. Littlepage and Demaree Bess which supported the view that the executed persons in the Soviet Union had really been guilty, and their trials not frameups.

This attitude continued even into the fourth big roundup of famous Bolshevik figures in the first few days of March, including notables such as Bukharin and Rykov. On March 9 the *New Republic* issued a bland recognition that another purge was under way, again wearily acknowledged it was still another of the "world's great tragedies," but warned anyone against thinking this was evidence of Communist weakness. The likelihood of war between Russia and the Japanese-German East-West coalition was being considered imminent, and the report concluded brightly that "The USSR is in many ways the strongest nation on earth—as Japan and Germany may find out to their cost." [78]

The *Nation* expressed horror over this latest series first, its March 12 editorial showing painful reluctance to believe the charges, referring to the Soviet legal system as "a travesty of justice," but finally conceding that the story that Russia was badly wormeaten by "disaffection" must be true, and that "the whole government apparatus" must be in a total state of demoralization. But the desire to say something compensatory led to the reaching out to blame Hitler Germany for it all, German policy being responsible for creating in the Soviet Union "a psychological state of war," from whence came the impulse to rapid industrialization, a "vast arms program," and the "universal atmosphere of suspicion and overcharged patriotism," thus opening up avenues for the expression of pre-existing "profound political differences." There was no statement as to what had been responsible for the immense Red military buildup in the years prior to Hitler's coming. Another omission in this long editorial was any mention of Trotsky, that he was really the chief defendant even if not in Russia, that he had not confessed to anything, and contradicted the entire proceedings.[79] The *Nation* printed only two letters by Franz Höllering and James Rorty critical of their evasiveness on the trials this time around.

Villard far exceeded his previous harsh words on Russia in this issue. He described the news as "simply appalling," insisted it deprived the Communists "of the sympathy of those liberals the world over who, without being in the least committed to Communism, have still felt that no more remarkable experiment in human government has ever been undertaken in modern times," that Stalin and the Kremlin were "undermining every good the revolution sought to accomplish," and that the Soviet was "digging its own grave by exhibiting a blood lust without parallel," which he now placed ahead of both Hitler and the Czar in severity.[80]

Four days later the *New Republic* made its first really serious facing-up to the consequences of the purges on foreign affairs in an unmistakable expression of disillusion over the Soviet Union: "It can scarcely be true that so many prominent and trusted persons were out-and-out conspirators for Fascism or the return of capitalism or the handing out of territory to foreign enemies," the editorial protested; "It is a strain on credulity to assert that they planned so many murders, poisonings and massacres."

Again the main damage was assessed as happening to Russia's relations with the rest of the world; [81]

Whatever the truth concerning the defendants may be, it is an obvious fact that hardly anything more disastrous to Soviet prestige in the rest of the world can be imagined. The effect of the repeated trials and executions is incalculably great. They came just as large areas of public opinion in Europe, America and Asia were becoming more warmly sympathetic with the aims and achievements of Russian socialism.

The damage done to the Popular Front everywhere was no less great, it went on, and had "sent a chill over every suggestion of faith in, or cooperation with, the Stalin regime," especially in the United States, which was deeply lamented. Timed with Hitler's easy absorption of Austria it represented a dark moment for liberals who had especially incubated anti-Fascist dreams. But it is to be noted that again the entire procedure was weighed far more in relation to foreign political prestige than as internal news. The major liberal concern was still with the outside consequences of the trials, not their intrinsic qualities or their essential truth or falseness.

An indication of the state of anxiety which the event had engendered in Bliven was reflected in his amazing four-column signed "Letter to Stalin" on March 30. The senior editor of the *New Republic,* writing in the manner of a fond well-wisher toward the Soviet Union, recommended a series of idealistic politico-legal-judicial reforms in the Soviet procedure of handling alleged oppositionists, all in the hope of recapturing the good will of the "democratic" world, now badly shocked by the latest dozen and a half Red notables hurried off to death by firing squads. Bliven was especially distressed by the pretrial confessions, but felt in extenuation that "Soviet court procedure in most types of trials is admirable." He called on Stalin to abolish the death penalty in order to avoid any comparison with Italy and Germany; "For you to abolish the death penalty would do more than any other single thing you could do to prove that the dictatorship of the proletariat is not on all fours with the dictatorships of the Fascists." Bliven's closing plea was even more incredible, an exhortation to Stalin to step aside as Communist dictator for eighteen months to deflate the entire charge of dictatorship: "I am profoundly convinced that nothing you could do for the USSR by remaining in office for that length of time could be as great a service as the demonstration that among 190,000,000 comrades no one is indispensable, that those foreign critics who lump together 'Hitler, Stalin and Mussolini' have been and are altogether wrong." The ingenuous and innocent flavor of this long open dispatch stands out as an expression of persistent liberal faith in a Soviet dream steadily growing more sour by the minute.[82]

Bliven and the *Nation* were both promptly flayed by the *New Masses* for this new outburst of Russian criticism, despite frequent evidences of softness. The editorials in the issues of March 22 and subsequently accused the two liberal weeklies of having undermined the

Soviet Union for twenty years, and now contributing mightily to the growing vitality of Russia's German and Japanese enemies in Central Europe, China and Spain by convincing everyone that the Reds were in a deep funk of panic, confusion and disintegration, instead of doing what they should have been doing, building "faith in the Soviet Union and in its peoples' front movement in all countries." Bliven was so disturbed by the personal attack that he wrote to the *New Masses* and complained of being misrepresented, that he was not really a hostile critic at all; "There are many matters as to which the *New Republic* and the *New Masses* are in agreement and the forces of reaction are so strong at the present time that those who are fighting for a progressive view ought to emphasize their agreements and not their disagreements." But this peace offering which was published on April 12 was not sufficient to bring about his forgiveness for his attitude and stands on the trials and collective security.[83]

The *New Republic*'s principal pro-Soviet voices in the succeeding months were Cowley and Heywood Broun, while Stewart essayed in this capacity on the *Nation*. Cowley and Stewart were the only two persons associated with the liberal editorial staffs among the 137 signers of a statement exonerating the Stalin regime of any malfeasance in conducting the 1938 trials, which was published on May 3 in the *New Masses*.[84] Two weeks later Cowley reviewed the 800-page official *The Case of the Anti-Soviet Bloc of Rights and Trotskyites* in the *New Republic,* and after four long columns of comment emerged completely convinced that the entire parade of confessions outlined in the volume showed nothing whatever which might incline him not to believe that the Stalin regime's case was essentially sound, correct and true.[85] There was a serious crisis for the journal, its readers and editors to come to grips with here.[86] In logical pursuit of their anti-Fascist commitment, unless evidence could be uncovered that the accused were innocent, then the Stalinist case had to be supported, for if the accused were just trying to weaken the Soviet Union, then it followed that the *New Republic* liberals had to approve whatever fate was visited upon the accused by the regime.

Stewart, back with the *Nation* in September after another visit to Russia, brought back an interpretation of the trials quite in contradiction to the generally accepted version which was causing such agonies of indecision among liberals. His "Progress and Purges in Soviet Russia" asserted that they were the result and not the cause of popular discontent "from below," and that the leadership really was vested in the younger generation, which was bitterly unhappy over purely internal circumstances. They had finally exploded after a decade of inward seething "at the evidences of inefficiency and injustice which they saw around them," and the victims of their wrath were the purgees of the whole series of trials.[87] This was obviously not corroborative of the conventional case which interpreted the trials as defenses against internal subversion on behalf of Russia's foreign enemies.

But the damage had just about been completed to liberal unity on Russia. Even such implacable haters of Trotsky as Niebuhr approved of the final report of the Dewey Commission of Inquiry, led by the famous liberal educator, which had gone into the charges against Trotsky made in the various Moscow trials, and found him innocent, a report which became generally known in July, 1938. Niebuhr's own pontifical summary of the significance of the trials in the *Nation* two months before the Dewey report stressed the damage the trials had done to Marx's theories of the State and human behavior, while testifying to his deep faith in Marxism as "an essentially correct theory and analysis of the economic realities of modern society." Nor could he resist a parting comment in which he still preferred to be found on the side of Stalin "relativism" if the struggle had consisted only of the ideological issue of Stalinism versus "the unstatesmanlike absolutism of Trotsky." [88]

The bloom and nobility were disappearing fast from the Soviet corona in the eyes of more and more liberals as more details of the trials unfolded. The suspicion that the Russian story was another sordid struggle for power was growing, with the result that a fully developed area for disillusion was in existence by the time the Communists put aside collective security and embarked on their "Russia First" venture in August, 1939. For a goodly contingent of liberals this was the most frightful spiritual shock of the century, but for the dissidents who made the prodigious disturbance over the trials of 1936–1938, it was much less so; their return to reality had been in progress.

The logic of the disillusioned over the savagery of the Russian execution programs was to lead to the conclusion that the Hitler and Stalin systems had much in common, albeit devoted to the propagation of the interests of two major rival states. When Max Eastman prepared his essay "Stalinism Becomes Fascism" for publication in the magazine *Liberty,* the *Nation* sold advertising space to that journal to announce its appearance, an act which drew a thunderous condemnation of all concerned in the *New Masses* late in December, 1938.[89] But the sentiment was now at large, soon to be given wider circulation by Ignazio Silone's *School for Dictators,* a book which also aroused defenders of the Stalin regime to fury.[90] But for many liberals now much sickened by it all, it was possible to quietly let the subject of the trials go by the board and to concentrate on foreign affairs, in which department the defense of Russia against the German and Japanese powers of darkness still gave promise of experiencing strong feelings of righteousness.

SOME NOTES ON RUSSIAN FOREIGN POLICY
BETWEEN THE FRENCH AND GERMAN PACTS

As has been seen, the emergence of a dynamic regime in Germany produced among other things the somersault in Soviet Russian foreign policy which found it eagerly seeking friends among the nations it once professed such contempt for, the products of which included recognition by the United States, entry into the League of Nations, and the beginning of the series of "non-aggression pacts" with neighbors of Germany. American liberals, hoping for greater cordiality between the United States and the Soviet after recognition, enjoyed a rather short season of expectancy. The running-aground on the Red glacier on the subject of pre-1917 Russian debts accomplished the feat of halting any closer official get-together, on which theme the prior discussion of the subject of Russo-American relations and their interpretation by American liberals ended. But for the Russians it was the threshold leading to a more expansive foreign venture, not the end of the wall. The high-flying Popular-Front, Collective-Security, Non-Aggression-Pact days lay just around the corner.

The *Nation* expressed much indignation with the State Department when it terminated the discussions with the Communists in February, 1935, and issued a bitter rebuke for the summary abruptness with which the conversations were concluded.[91] It was matched by a dispatch from Fischer published on April 3, whose irritation with the State Department and its curtness underlined the deference which the Soviet was beginning to get from European countries, now that Germany was showing definite restlessness with the status quo other states dearly wanted to preserve. Other countries were currying Russian favor, complained Fischer, but "The provincial United States State Department" was dealing with the Soviet Union "as though it were Panama or Albania." [92] There was an almost personal sense of indignation in his grievance.

The sun broke through in May, with the signing of the Russo-French and Russo-Czech agreements, both carefully fitted into interstices in the League of Nations to give them respectability. The *Nation* advanced the opinion that "advocates of collective security" would be able to find little that they could quarrel with in these arrangements,[93] and hoped they would have the effect of making the Germans back down from their expansionist goals, in harmony with its the-enemy-is-basically-a-coward theory, so deeply internalized among collective security exponents. That they just stimulated the Germans to go on to more energetic promotion of counter-actions on their own behalf was ignored temporarily, and credited to basic German evil later on, as the consequences of the iron-ring policy bore somewhat unexpected and appalling fruit. The immediate situation called forth a notice of Stalin's expression of sympathy to Laval and his concern with French security, and the notation of the first political consequence of the pact in France; the Russian leader's policy "cut the ground from under the resistance of French radicals to French militarism." [94] So the liberals had a bitter aftertaste to their joy over the strengthening of Russia. The French could not be promising military support to the Communists without building up their own forces and simultaneously smothering their domestic Communists and others agitating against arms. In a new way, liberal devotion to Russia and peace was resulting in an inextricable clash of conflicting interests.

The *Nation* found its way out of this rather easily. Its editorial of May 29, 1935 made it clear that the welfare of Russia was first on the agenda. This statement admitted that these pacts were "weakening the ties of international Communism" and that "Capitalist governments, if they get into a war in which Russia is their ally, will be reasonably insured against the danger of a general strike by radical labor," a bland admission that the Russian State had a prior call on the loyalty of Communists of other lands, whose actions might with sureness be expected to hinge on orders from Moscow, since the comment frankly admitted that the Communist parties elsewhere in the world were following Russian foreign policy. What of the peace movement, now that Communists would have to align with Russian military buildups? As far as France was concerned, the *Nation* quietly concluded, "The defense of pacifism would seem to be left to nonresisters." Another long spike had been silently driven into the center of liberal pacifist and peace pretensions; the ill-fitting relationship of pacifism and collective security politics needed nothing else to portray its obviousness.

Fischer underlined this with his comment on the Stalin-Laval formula from Moscow in June; "Moscow long ago realized that the interests of the world revolutionary movement must be sacrificed to the interests of the Soviet Union as a power," he frankly stated, adding that it was "easy to understand Germany's objection to a step which unites the two strongest Continental powers." But he warned Laval and the French not to think he had come back to Paris with "the scalp of the French Communist Party;" [95]

The Bolsheviks say "The U.S.S.R. is a workers' state. The Franco-Russian alliance gives it peace and the possibility of establishing socialism. We appear to be playing capitalism's game by throwing the Communist International to the wolves. Actually the capitalists are playing our game by protecting us against the armed attacks of an aggressive Fascism. If the foreign Communist parties must suffer from this relationship, they should understand that in the end the cause of revolution will be served best by serving the Soviet Union first."

The words might just as well have been Fischer's own, or the *Nation*'s editorial policy, for there were no words of objection from any liberal to where collective security was leading. There should not have been any confusion or acrimony among liberals a little over four years later when the Soviet abandoned this gambit. The *New Masses,* with which the liberal press had a first-cousin relationship as a consequence of the substantial cross-migration of editors and staff, had spelled it out quite adequately at its launching. It was Russian, and not French or Czech, security which was understood in the term "collective security," and there was no effort to conceal this. But not only that; the boasting of Communist military strength in 1935 made the clear impression that future war involvement would not mean merely the keeping intact of Russia's frontiers as of the moment. With allies, its expansion was a guaranteeable consequence of victory. There was a dual aspect to the insistent pro-Communist propaganda that Russia was in persistent danger of attack by "reactionary capitalist" states; its corollary was the repeated allegation that these potential attackers were corrupt and weak, thus their easy defeat by Communism implied their absorption by the Communists. It could hardly be expected that the vanquished would be left to incubate more corrupt and weak capitalism.

A glance at a few contemporary expressions of such views is in order. On April 2, 1935 the *New Masses* published a substantial editorial titled "The March Toward Moscow," which brushed off Hitler as the head of a state with an economic system on the verge of utter collapse, and which was desperately in need of war with Russia to keep afloat, having adopted conscription and massive rearmament to solve German unemployment. German conscription was, however, just a few weeks old at that moment. The editorial then came to grips with the other side of the picture by declaring that "The Soviets in recent years have been forced to curtail the socialization program in order to build up the largest and most powerful fighting machine in all Europe," and spelled out some of its growth: [96]

Nevertheless, though the danger of war upon the Soviets is great, we must not forget that for the past two years they have been watching the distant armies of their enemies approach and can readily place two million men in the field. Though they have not made the actual figures of their mechanical potentials public, they have published the increase in the production of war materials. In the last two years [1933–1935] the Soviet air forces have been increased by 300 per cent, the number of light tanks by 760 per cent, heavy artillery by 210 per cent, machine guns by 215 per cent.

Earl Browder's comment on the Franco-Soviet pact in the June 4 issue bluntly announced that "This pact is a concrete example of the Leninist policy of utilizing the antagonisms among the imperialist powers in order to promote the interests of the working class, of the world proletarian revolution." But a long editorial on August 13 made the issue of the "beyond-security" aspect of these pacts more obvious: [97]

From a long-run point of view it is plain that the anti-Nazi coalition with which the U.S.S.R. now cooperates can only postpone war, not prevent it. . . . The object again is postponement, not prevention, since prevention of war is impossible save through a world victory of Communism. But within a few more years the Soviet Union will be so powerful that neither Germany nor Japan will dare to attack. The Second Imperialist War, if deferred until this time, will be the suicide of the imperialist powers themselves, not an attack on the U.S.S.R. Meanwhile, any European power which attacks the Soviet Union will be faced by war with France and Czechoslovakia. Moscow postpones war by preparedness, both military and diplomatic. When war comes, Moscow will be ready. And in war's bloody aftermath of social and economic collapse, the Comintern, which has necessarily been quiescent in the now vanishing epoch of capitalistic stability, will face new opportunities and new tasks.

The Soviet Union's memorable plunge into collective security Popular-United Front international politics took place accompanied by the expression of such realistic sentiments as these in the frankly pro-Communist press, but American liberals reflected little of the substance or implications of them. The alliance between Communism and other forces was endorsed as a genuine pooling of forces for the mutual protection of everybody. The breach among liberals on this issue came only when the campaign to enlist the United States into the gathering got under way. Then a substantial group demurred, remembering the League of Nations. But no significant group came to the conclusion that collective security as it was unfolding was not a beneficial matter for Russia's European neighbors. In fact, the editorial position developed in both the major liberal weeklies was that it was the Communists who adopted the liberal suggestion of such action in the first place and not the other way around, and when the Soviet abandoned the program, they were subjected to vociferous abuse, especially from the *Nation,* for having stepped out of a relationship into which they had been invited. But by 1939 the *Nation* had developed a fixed view on the desirability of the destruction of

Hitler as a sole war goal, and bitterly suffered from the loss of any potential participant in this endeavor.

The latter half of 1935 was a mainly unbroken period of tribute to Russia from the liberal press for its sudden and profound change in practical foreign politics. The only event which produced harsh and discordant notes was the calling of the first meeting of the Communist International in six years during the summer in Moscow, an event which was explained by liberal organs in America as a supplementary step to the Popular Front program in the collective security tandem. From the Communist point of view, this Comintern meeting was the official christening of the Popular Front, and at first the liberals did not object to looking upon the Popular Front as its product, as in the case of the *New Republic*'s editorial of August 7.[98] The following month, the editorial position of this weekly like that of the *Nation* had become more enthusiastic about it than the Communists, and considered the latter to be *converts* to the idea.[99] This view grew out of the assumption that the Communists had recognized their mistake in Germany of quarreling with the liberals, socialists and other "anti-Fascist" elements, and were now willing to join hands with these elements and forget their previous unpleasantries.

The *Nation,* in its major editorial on the emergence of this new political strategy on August 7, "Moscow Offers An Olive Branch," did not at first indulge in this view that the liberal tail was finally wagging the Communist elephant. It was content to relate it to the rapid emergence of the Soviet as a world power and the consequent changed behavior on the diplomatic and tactical front. This long-delayed Comintern meeting the editors hailed as "strategically a brilliant maneuver," and felt that if the policy were to prove successful, "the U.S.S.R. will have done more to strengthen its defenses than could be accomplished by a dozen mutual security pacts." There was no illusion here that Russia had joined some gigantic mutual insurance company for the ultimate comfort and well-being of all concerned. The *Nation* further explained that the "revolutionary elements" in the political democracies were going to have to keep these states intact and suppress the "manifestations of fascism therein," as "Ironically enough, the revolutionary opponents of democracy are inevitably driven to its defense in order to keep intact any of the liberties which permit them to pursue their revolutionary ends."[100] This was a roundabout way of saying that the Communists abroad, in terms of long-range goals, would first have to join with non-Communist elements to crush their big threat, Fascism, and this achieved, they could then proceed to "pursue their revolutionary ends" with a minimum of disturbance and discomfort.

Contrary to the weeklies, *Common Sense* greeted the announcement of the Popular Front with a bark of disapproval. Its September,

1935 editorial took an exceedingly bleak outlook on it, especially in America, and considered its "cooperation" with liberal and democratic forces here and elsewhere in reality a "flank attack" on them just as much as a protective device against Fascism, as well as betrayal of any anti-war position they might have once affirmed; [101]

> The Communists have now gone over to the reckless position that some wars may be good wars. In a war against Germany, for instance, Communists will be ordered to fight with the capitalistic powers allied with the Soviet Union. The Russian Party which controlled the [Comintern] Congress dictated this final about-face for its own national political ends.

And in the December issue, John Chamberlain, in his acerbic "Would Socrates Be a Marxist?," vigorously attacked the relationship of the Popular Front to Soviet foreign policy and charged that the Communist Party in Russia would be "ready to sell out the United Front at any psychologically propitious moment," in the advancement of Russian national goals.[102] This was rank heresy at such an early date among liberals, although the two statements were remarkable suspicions and unspecific anticipations of the *Pakt* by nearly four years.

Majority liberal thinking overcame these doubts and reservations, however, and the following three years were the most fruitful for the growth of the Popular Front form of collective security. "Peace" and rearmament of the Soviet Union found ready apologists here, and the word "Communist" tended to disappear and blend into the generic term "anti-Fascist." "The existing peace is a bad sort of peace, but this bad peace is in any event better than war," observed George Dimitroff in the *New Masses* on May 26, 1936,[103] and this summarized the Communist view of the purpose of the Popular Front in these unstable years of waxing German-Japanese strength and uncertainty as to Soviet power. In the meantime, the liberal press did not let up an iota in its publicity on the warlike intentions of Russia's antagonists, East and West. There was a spiritual affinity between such reportage in these circles and the commentators on foreign news most frequently published in the first two years of the Popular Front in the *New Masses*, John Strachey and Joseph Freeman.

For some liberals the Popular Front drive carried embarrassing consequences. The enlistment in the military defense of Russia did great harm to the simultaneous campaigns within the United States against the munitions industry and military education, as well as the general anti-war and pacifist movement. The abrupt change of Communist direction not only deprived liberals of support in these programs, but found them facing a back-fire. The Communists developed a positive-good theory of rearmament for Russia, and it made curious reading alongside the earlier and still-persisting liberal crusades against this policy for America. Louis Fischer displayed his particular form of infection in a *Nation* piece early in April, 1936 titled "The Soviets Face the Threat of War": "The Soviet Union is the only country in Europe where intensive armament activity coincided with a sharp rise in the living standards of the nation," he announced with an undertone of pride, and added: "The Soviet Union, thanks to its new industries, has become a military giant." [104] The Popular Front was indeed incubating a wondrous split personality among American liberals. But of course this attitude was not a mere local phenomenon. The Comintern was producing this approach quite generally. "The Left Prepares For War," Ludwig Lore's report on a European trip was titled in the *Nation* early in December, 1937. He related with some gusto in a long article that, following his contacts with the Communist and Socialist Parties and the Social Democrats in all European countries, he could say that they had all abandoned pacifism, and were all backing every arms and army buildup in every country, as part of a quiet and firm preparation for a final showdown war with "Fascism" and the loosing of a social revolution of far-reaching consequences upon all of Europe at its conclusion.[105] But, of course, Communist Parties had been voting for pro-military budgets everywhere since late 1936. The reason for the loss of interest and support for the Nye investigation in America at the same time hardly needed to be interpreted by the oracle at Delphi.

The contradiction in all this for America continued to puzzle and irritate some commentators in the liberal press throughout the era of greatest vitality of the Popular Front. When Browder's *What Is Communism?* was reviewed by Louis Hacker in the April 22, 1936, *Nation,* he was not convinced by Browder's contempt for the neutrality legislation of the Roosevelt Administration, his vociferous support for the League of Nations and his earnest recommendation of United States "cooperation" for peace with the Soviet Union. Browder, in faithful Leninist manner, had outlined the customary Popular Front's "militant peace program" that would not be in any way pacifist, and which upon the outbreak of a war, would convert an international "imperialist" struggle into a proletarian-led civil war everywhere. But Hacker pointed out that this would be impossible to achieve in the United States if it became an ally of the Soviet Union in a future war, as Browder was indirectly suggesting.[106] Niebuhr pointed this out again early in 1938 reviewing Browder's *The People's Front* in the same liberal weekly. Despite his admitted sympathy with Browder's "Stalinist revisionism," he still thought the foreign policy picture developed by Browder was exceedingly cloudy when posed alongside the ideal Leninist formula: [107]

. . . while the Party wants peace it also wants powerful allies on the side of Russia in an eventual conflict. In other words, the fortuitous alliance between Russia and the satisfied imperial powers makes impossible a completely realistic analysis of the present international situation from the official Communist perspective.

The gist of these mild objections was that despite its talk of a world policy as the outcome of the Popular Front, Russian willingness to team up with powerful states not allied to it in ideology simply meant that Russia was acting as a powerful state with selfish interests of its own, and not as the front-line leader of a world proletarian program aiming to upset the entire national state system and initiate international stateless egalitarian socialism. But the will to believe the outward paraphernalia of the Popular Front was too strong; believers needed more dramatic forms of betrayal by Russia than this in order to lose their faith in the purity of purpose among the Communists.

The view of Frederick Schuman on the importance of the Popular Front to the United States, which was included in his review of William H. Chamberlin's *Collectivism: A False Utopia* in the *New Republic* for June 23, 1937, was not only a rebuke to "liberals" such as Chamberlin, who saw unpalatable elements in both German and Russian organizational forms but a classical statement of the case for adhering to the Russian-oriented collective security scheme: [108]

. . . the menace to liberalism comes obviously not from the Left but from the Right. And obviously, if freedom is to survive, it will be because the Western democracies stand united with Moscow against the Fascist threat. This union is an imperative political necessity in the present world crisis. The liberals who seek to tar enemies and allies with the same brush give comfort to the foe and do liberalism a disservice. Before 1933, orthodox Communists were unable to distinguish between liberals and Fascists. They have since recognized their error. Liberals who cannot distinguish between Communists and Fascists fall into similar error. Here, paradoxically, the Fascists are more nearly right. There is a hard kernel of truth in the Fascist contention that liberalism and Communism are akin. In ultimate ideals and in immediate interests, democracy and Sovietism are not enemies but brothers. In closer union and in gradual assimilation between these faiths, freedom may yet find salvation.

Schuman entertained no doubts about the ultimate product of the Popular Front and bothered not at all with its likely clash with pure Leninist doctrine. By far the majority of liberals reflected this view during the 1935–1938 period.

And indeed there was a minimum of evidence stressed during this period to warrant otherwise, in view of the repeated reaffirmations of growing Soviet strength and devotion to peace, and the spreading influence of pro-Russian sympathy on all levels, a product of a steadily favorable press toward the Communists and an across-the-board denigration of Hitler Germany. The *New Republic* rejoiced editorially on September 2, 1936 that a *Review of Reviews* poll of its readers indicated that in case of a Russo-German war, they would support Russia by a 2–1 margin. A Gallup poll twenty-six months later, after Munich, raised the proportion to over 4 to 1, a fact which gave the *New Masses* great comfort at that time.[109]

Frank Hanighen, no longer exclusively involved in chronicling the sins of munitions makers, was now in tune with new developments. His "Armies Over Europe" in the September 5, 1936 *Nation* stated quite flatly that "In morale Russia ranks easily above the other powers," and that "In case of a war it is certain that the Russian army will display the extraordinary spirit of the French revolutionary army of 1793." Its German opponents might promote a formidable opposition through clever propaganda, he conceded, "But experience in the last war demonstrated that as far as morale is concerned, democracies have a better chance to stand adversity than autocracies." [110] Russia's status as a "democracy" was not at issue.

But the majority of the commentaries of the period stressed Russian peace policies, even if it involved mention of their armed might. The *New Republic* hailed Soviet foreign policy as "realistic, direct and coherent" in the Spanish war though Russia was really interested in a comprehensive neutrality on the part of all nations there, even while its military personnel and material were arriving.[111] Bliven's signed editorial on November 18 of this year, "Russia and Peace, 1936" dismissed any need for concern over the towering military buildup in the Soviet, since it was being assembled to promote peace; [112]

Soviet Russia is giving the world an important object lesson in the possibilities of peace. Although the presence of implacable and aggressive enemies on her borders, east and west, compels her still to maintain a large military establishment, all competent, impartial experts are agreed that of herself she constitutes no threat to peace—the only great power of which this is true. She will not commit aggression because, among other reasons, no living soul within her borders would benefit from aggression.

Through 1937 it was much the same story. Even *Common Sense* dropped its guard after the promulgation of the new Russian constitution to sound a note on the peace horn; "Only in the Soviet Union, where the new constitution at least expresses a *will* toward wider liberties and human fulfillment, is there any desire for peace," and in February, 1937 it announced without comment that the Red Army budget for the coming year was up 35.6% over that for 1936–1937.[113]

After the Sino-Japanese war once more broke into large-scale operations in the summer of 1937, peace continued to be the key word. Yakhontoff's *New Republic* article "The USSR In the Oriental Crisis" on September 29 gave forth a comforting reassurance of the innocence of Soviet intentions in Asia as against the blackheartedness of the Japanese, and with no hesitance announced that "there is no risk in asserting that the U.S.S.R., in spite of her great military strength, is definitely devoted to the cause of peace." [114] For liberals there were no Russian participations in the Spanish and Chinese wars that might be construed under any heading but peaceable fighting. For, as the *New Republic* asserted in its editorial "Siberian Dynamite" on August 10, 1938, "Soviet Russia is on the whole the most pacific of the great powers." [115]

Nor were Russian actions and agitations considered to have any part in stimulating the Italo-German-Japanese Anti-Comintern Pact of November, 1937. The significance of this to the *Nation* was expressed in a horrified editorial on November 13: "It is a simple truth that the civilization of the world is threatened by extinction . . . The anti-Communist pact, uniting Italy with Germany and Japan, presents this major threat in concrete and detailed terms; the Fascist international is organized and prepared for united action." [116]

THE IDEOLOGICAL CLIMATE
PRIOR TO THE HITLER-STALIN PACT

The majority of American liberals took the position that the anti-Communist program of Germany, Italy and Japan in its separate national phases was invalid; when they joined in formal association in pursuit of such a goal, the liberals were even more hostile. In fact, this stimulated dissident factions toward a positive reaction of their own, in which the Soviet Union was advanced as the only real barrier to these three states, or Fascism, and pleaded more strongly that if only the Western democracies would cooperate, then Fascism's defeat was a certainty. It was the opposite side of the coin presented by the anti-Communist Pact, and the hope of this materializing was the dynamic behind liberal opinionizing from the end of 1937 until August 1939. With very rare exceptions no breath escaped which concerned itself in any way with the order most likely to prevail thereafter. The puzzled agony of the "liberators" in Germany between 1945 and 1948 stands as testimony that the failure to have thought very much about it was widely shared. Only then did the bankruptcy of unqualified and thoughtless military victory sink in, and its cost since then and into the future threatens to reach figures which only astronomers may be able to handle. But the scene in Europe in 1945 was only the materialization of liberal dreams and exhortations between 1937 and 1939, albeit a two year period of dark and dismal discouragement set in before the anti-Fascist "pact" was clothed in military flesh.

Basic to the liberal urging of a Western democracies-*cum*-Soviet combine was a grim rejection of the creeping doubt among the less-devoted that Russia and its German adversary were not as far apart as the vociferous Communist press and its liberal affiliates-in-spirit insisted. Those who persisted in tying Communism and Fascism in a single bundle before the Pact of 1939 were bitterly resented and fought, although they were to enjoy immense satisfaction when the two regimes came to an understanding on that occasion. The pro-Soviet position was that for the democracies to fight both simultaneously was unrealistic, and that the only real enemy of democracy was Fascist Germany and Japan, on the basis of what they were doing as well as saying. It involved silence on the militarism of Russia and Red China or explaining such activities as purely defensive gestures, an idea many of the more innocent accepted for years. In fact, even the hardier souls who sharply questioned Soviet military growth never got around to a similar position on China. No Communist uprising ever enjoyed the overall ideological camouflage which American liberals threw over Red China until its victory was complete. But before 1939 the major task was to head off those who suspected that Russian devotion to democratic liberalism was more affectation than conviction. Thus the picture of a benevolent Russia with nothing but careful and limited policies of self defense and integrity of frontiers was kept upright, and at some cost. It became a greater burden after the bold talk of an imminent overthrow of Hitler and the establishment of a Communist Germany of 1931–1935 was abandoned.

Because Russia's ambitions differed from those of Germany and Japan, many American liberals concluded she had no national ambitions at all, other than scrupulous protection of the boundaries she had acquired after the season of border wars of 1918–1921. One would have gathered from their defenses that Russia had no interest in frontier rectification as did the Germans, and that their seeming acceptance of these earlier settlements had been made for all time, which thus qualified them for consideration as superior morally to the Germans. Furthermore, in most of the books written by liberal authors on the world and especially the Central European scene between 1935 and 1939 the struggle for control here was nearly always posited as a German versus a Franco-British showdown, with either side dominating in the manner of Versailles. The 1918–1929 thinking covered the entire situation, as there was but the faintest consideration of the Soviet Union as an interested participant beyond the spectator level. The Popular Front dynamics required the maintenance of the image of the innocent defender and the possibility that "defense" might bring the Soviet Union deep into Europe was rarely given the slightest contemplation. The persistent image of the Soviet as the most pacific big state on earth effectively barred such thinking. A decade and a half of constant salesmanship of Russia as a peaceful land of socialism chased out of mind the idea that it was a potential actor in the manner of the imperialist countries, and this view was never stronger than just before Russia showed an interest in Polish and Baltic real estate.

But there was more to the Popular Front than merely an association which helped the Russians feel secure. On countless occasions emphasis was laid on this as a comprehensive program aimed at shoring up the material and psychological resources of all states likely to consider themselves under threat as a result of the expansion of Germany, Italy and Japan. Hence, when the Russians began early in 1938, probably as a consequence of the blending of the Anti-Comintern Pact, the trouble at home, and the bad war news from both the Spanish and Chinese sectors, to show far more sensitivity toward their own defense than that of others, liberal agitation, apprehension and concern in America began to gather and spread. The swift German success in effecting the union with Austria in March undoubtedly hastened the defensive action, but it stimulated unrest among liberal protagonists of the Popular Front here.

A speech by Maxim Litvinov in June, 1938 touched off an anxious editorial in the *Nation* on "the growing tendency of Soviet Russia to withdraw from active leadership in the struggle for European security," and noted in particular that although he reassured all the Communists would honor their bi-lateral "mutual assistance" pacts, still they intended, as the editorial put it, to place "far more trust" in "the efficacy of the Red Army than in these instruments for the defense of the Soviet frontiers." It went on to explain in the following words, "This will be disappointing to those who have looked to the Soviet Union for leadership in the struggle for peace. But it was inevitable that the collapse of collective action would eventually isolate even its strongest proponent." [117] This reasoning did not necessarily follow, as it could as easily be advanced that the Russians were using collective security to shore up Soviet frontiers from the beginning, which the Communist and fellow-traveler press here freely admitted, and were backing away from it when it no longer seemed to have any future for serving their purposes.

But other liberal press voices were not as despairing as this. Stewart, back from his Russian visit, was calmly confident that the Soviet could be depended upon to maintain their "traditional anti-fascist policy," and that a rapprochement with the Germans was utterly out of the question. Despite the inactivity during the Austrian affair, he felt sure they would back the Czechs in their current dispute with Germany, and that on the wider level, there was no change in the Comintern policy, and that the Communist Party was cooperating in Spain, China and France; "I have it on the best of authority that the Soviet Union has not abandoned its hope of collective action," he reassured everyone; "It recognizes as clearly as ever that peace is indivisible, that war in any section of the world is a threat to all." Litvinov's words were still echoing. But Stewart had eyewitness reports to make to underscore the reasons for his confidence: [118]

. . . the Soviets have exhibited few of the degenerative weaknesses of the older powers. Their army and airforce are second to none in Europe. This year's harvest will be the largest in Russian history. Soviet leadership has repeatedly shown itself capable of decisive action in an emergency. Because of this fact, the Czechs are probably justified in their matchless optimism.

The Czech crisis will be discussed in the context of German affairs subsequently, but the continued passive Russian role, at first disquieting, soon found apologists. As the world moved into the even more distressing year of 1939 the anxieties about the ultimate fate of the Soviet pacts ballooned in size. But Fischer reported that the Soviet and Stalin would be forced to bolster them and the French and British empires as well, "lest Fascism become too strong to cope with." [119] While the newly-added foreign reporter, Geneviève Tabouis, commenting specifically on the Soviet pact with France in the *Nation* on January 28, 1939 praised Soviet diplomacy during the Czech crisis for its correctness, expressing deep faith in the pact with Russia as a positive insurance against trouble for France with Germany, as well as trust in the permanency of post-Munich implacability of the Communists toward Hitler.[120]

Excuses were even found to wash away the significance of Russian actions outside the collective security lines, even those giving aid and comfort to its nominal antagonists. News that the Soviet intended to ship quantities of petroleum products to both Italy and Germany started to make the rounds late in February. The *Nation*, which had always maintained that such trade was unthinkable, was quite convinced that such dispatches were a grievous exaggeration.[121] The *New Republic* bristled at criticism of the Communist action, instead, and defended it briskly. Its February 22 editorial "Russia and the Old School Tie" scoffed at moral indignation expressed in some Western circles and suggested that such sentiments were now out of order, after Franco-British knuckling down before Hitler's demands in

Czechoslovakia. This editorial stressed a point long made in the Communist and sympathizer papers, namely, that the later maneuver had been an attempt on the part of British and French leaders to divert Hitler eastward, the basis of the Communist "appeasement" case. The Reds were now retaliating and indicating that Hitler and the Fascists might find somewhat less resistance if he struck westward; "they are practical idealists who don't propose to sacrifice their own country." [122] This was a novelty in the liberal weeklies; the Soviet Union was being mentioned in the context of Russian national patriotism, after twenty years of portraying it as the center of international stateless pacifist socialism.

As if to add emphasis to this position, Stalin's famous March, 1939 speech before the All-Russian Communist Congress gave official support to the view that the Munich settlement had been a deliberate attempt to isolate the Soviet, the British prime minister, Chamberlain, being charged with hoping that Germany and Russia would destroy each other. This thesis had been ricocheting off the pages of American liberal papers for six months, the result being that Stalin's mention brought but very quiet statements, that in the *New Republic* on March 22 being especially restrained and sober.[123] In a chop-licking comment on April 1 the *Nation* corroborated Stalin's charge on the nature of Munich, and beamed at the re-entry of Russia into European politics on its own terms after a long period of neglect, especially into the plans of Central Europe. Now that Poland, "long an implacable enemy of the Soviets," had discovered the comfort of having Russia as a potential supporter in the face of "Nazi pressure," it was only to be expected that Chamberlain would be bringing England in behind, after Germany had completed its absorption of all of Czechoslovakia, and it was about time that the British leader discovered "the existence of the one great power which has been consistently anti-Fascist in its foreign policy." It found grounds for an even more exciting possibility: [124]

The sudden shift in the British attitude toward the Soviet Union is bound to have its effects in the United States. If Britain's long-range interests coincide at this moment with those of Moscow, the same can be said even more emphatically of those of this country. For in addition to serving as a bulwark against Nazi aggression in Europe, the Soviet Union stands as a potential check against Japanese aggrandizement in the Far East, where American interests are even more directly threatened. These two great countries, controlling between them the greater part of the world's resources, might still avert war if they worked closely together.

This was essentially the plaintive call of Robert Dell as well as editorial policy, for as the critical moment for Russia drew near, it became even clearer that the Soviet could not have too many friends. Dell also subscribed to the Communist interpretation of the meaning of "appeasement," where the endangering of Russia far more than the dissolution of Czechoslovakia bothered the liberals above all.[125] And in the temporary wrath against England and France, the falling back on one of the great hopes of the decade made a comfortable cushion in the immediate period of liberal anguish over the situation. The most elaborate statement of this "conspiracy of appeasement" theory was undoubtedly that of Schuman in his soon-published book *Europe on the Eve*. In the meantime, it did not appear as if the Communists were going to wait long for the evolvement of liberal hopes for their well-being; the *New Republic* mentioned quietly on March 29 that Klementi Voroshilov had announced the doubling of the Red Army, which it estimated at two and a half to three million men of the moment.[126] No comments were considered necessary on the effect of this on the economy which presumably had found the formula for supplying both guns and butter.

The resignation of Maxim Litvinov as Soviet Foreign Commissar was the trigger event signalling the final turn of the diplomatic wheel and an outburst of foreboding liberal comment. In a prolonged editorial comment on May 17, the *New Republic* divined a possible change in the dropping of the persistent proponent of collective security, which policy, amazingly enough, it now admitted had been a matter of "national selfishness" as followed by the Russians, who had used it since "it was necessary to stop Hitler before he became powerful enough to challenge the USSR." Now it was admittedly a failure on this count, and the suspicion was voiced that Russia was now possibly going to subscribe to Hitler's bi-lateral non-aggression treaty offer, which the German leader had put on the counter for all nations for some time. But this seemed incredible: "One can scarcely believe that the Soviet government has at this late date fallen for the Nazi argument against which it has for so long been warning others." [127] The *New Republic* showed its vexation also at Hitler's charge that so far as his objectives were concerned they had all been gained without war, and that the real warmakers and disturbers of the peace were those who were urging resistance to his moves. The troublesome part of this was that his actions, in revision of Versailles, had not taken him from the frontiers of 1914 Germany, and now that he was seeking a revision of Danzig and the Polish Corridor, it hardly implied that he had designs on Patagonia, now that hostile propaganda was whipping up old charges of Teutonic world conquest aims again.

Another sober rationalization of Soviet diplomatic behavior in terms of Russian national interest featured the *New Republic*'s editorial page the 24th of May as well. The outlining of the goals which they might become involved in fighting for was most significant, in

view of the fact that collective security had not yet been entirely abandoned as a desirable state of international affairs; [128]

> If the Soviet Union fights, she will do so in her own interest and that of
> socialism, and not for some vague general principles of democracy under
> capitalism which she can share with England and France. . . . When
> nations fight for self-interest, you know where to find them, and they stay
> put. When they are animated by higher and abstract ideals, you can never
> be sure that tomorrow the ideal will not be gone and the ally with it.

This was a new pinnacle in realism for this journal, and a statement
which could have been used to illustrate justifiably the behavior of
every state on the planet as well as Russia.

The malicious glee in the discomfiture of the Daladier and Chamberlain governments over the coyness of the Soviet Union in the bargaining of the spring and early summer of 1939 reached a peak in the
writings of Schuman, which matched his anxiety over the possibility
of a Hitler-Japanese assault on Red Russia and the logic of a Stalin-
Hitler rapprochement to head this off. His "Toward a New Munich"
in the *New Republic* on May 31 contained all the basic ingredients of
what was likely to occur, although a "stop-Hitler alliance" was far
more preferred by both Schuman and the editors. The insuperable
hurdles of the moment were the personalities of Chamberlain and
Daladier, their bargaining with Stalin being subjected to torrents of
abuse and repeated accusations once more that they were really trying
to set up a situation which would pit Russia against Germany, leaving
them as sideline spectators. This advice was for England and France
to dump these leaders and their foreign ministers, and to get on with
the "encirclement" of Germany.[129] Who might lead the British into
such a program was not mentioned, but the *New Masses* had elevated
Churchill into a hero's niche since Munich, and his alacrity to admit
the Red Army into Central Europe at that time had led to his being
quoted with glee in this publication and the American official Communist press as well during these days.

The *New Masses* of course recoiled like a bee-bitten horse from all
talk of a possible Hitler-Stalin understanding. It poured vitriol on
General Krivitsky in the issue of July 4 for making allegations in
the *Saturday Evening Post* that such an action was quite likely,[130] but
several other sources suggested it as well. Subsequent research by I. F.
Stone and others, printed in the lip-chewing days after it had become
a fact, indicated that in view of the numerous rumors of this type cir-
culating fully six months before, the synthetic surprise and shock
evinced by its consummation was especially artificial dissimulation.
But the liberals played on the collective-security organ to the very last
minute, whatever the liberals may have been thinking or substituting

for thought. When the Communists published Litvinov's speeches between April 4, 1934 and September 21, 1938 under the title *Against Aggression,* Stewart took time out from his *Nation* editorial duties to review it for the *New Masses,* describing it as "an unsurpassable handbook" for anyone who wanted to know about Soviet foreign policy and Communist devotion to collective security.[131] It was ironic that it was reviewed so graciously just two weeks before the *Pakt.*

A week earlier still another testimonial to liberal disbelief in any such eventuality had been published by the *New Republic,* an analytical piece by Edmund Stevens, the *Manchester Guardian*'s Moscow correspondent. He made very clear the ideological fixation on Russia prevailing among liberals: [132]

. . . the likelihood that Russia will continue to "sit on the fence" does not mean that she is going to fall into the lap of Germany. Fundamental differences of aims and interests between the Soviet and Nazi systems render this highly improbable. When Western observers, accustomed by the empiricism of democratic politics and impressed by superficial resemblances, predict a Russo-German rapprochement, they overlook the deep-rooted social antagonism and the important role of doctrinaire ideology in shaping and controlling the mass mind in Eastern Europe. Hitler could no more make friends with Soviet Russia than he could with the Jews.

Probably even more unfortunate from the point of view of liberal unity as well as ideological integrity was the dovetailing at this same period of the consequences of the years of internal dispute over Russian internal affairs and the direction of Communist policies in general. In the four months prior to the *Pakt,* with liberals solemnly reassuring one another that a Hitler-Stalin agreement was unthinkable solely on ideological grounds, the resentment toward Russian Communism that had raced through the Trotsky adherents and several other splinters of liberal-left forces reached full flower. The contribution of this collection of dissidents to the discomfiture of the orthodox pro-Russian liberal press and majority was immense, reaching its peak at the very moment of the Russo-German understanding.

The principal instigators of the final act of this uprising against the twenty-year vision of Communist Russia were two groups, the Committee for Cultural Freedom, of which John Dewey was chairman, and the League for Cultural Freedom and Socialism, the chairman of which was Dwight MacDonald, the latter a splinter group of the former, but fully as articulate. And the reputation of those who banded together in these groups was so formidable that they could not be ignored.

The policy statement of the CCF, signed by 95 liberal notables, was published in both the liberal weeklies in their last issues of May,

1939. It drew long and hostile editorials in both, that in the *Nation* being signed by Freda Kirchwey. They were alarmed and appalled at the unequivocal condemnation of totalitarianism everywhere including Russia, and they charged the CCF with splitting tactics in trying to herd all the Communists to one side in the liberal left faction. The Kirchwey critique especially resented the addition of Russia to the list of condemned governments. She spiritedly defended Communists for having constructed and run "a string of organizations—known as 'fronts' by their opponents—which clearly serve the cause not of 'totalitarian doctrine' but of a more workable democracy." She refused to answer to the CCF's call to fight the Communists here or elsewhere, and pleaded instead for the emergence of "an era of good-will and decency" on the liberal-left. "There is virtue in merely refusing to shoot," she ended her repudiation of the CCF.[133]

The *New Republic*'s even longer review was more transparently defensive, and revealed the double standard of judging one regime by its acts and another by its professed abstract ideals once more: [134]

In lumping together the Fascist powers with the U.S.S.R., the Committee shows, we feel, a regrettable lack of historical perspective. It clearly implies that Fascism and Communism are both completely incompatible with freedom for the individual. But while this charge is true of Fascism, it is clearly not true of the theory of a socialist commonwealth.

The rejection of the CCF's case went on to lay the responsibility for all the objectionable features of Soviet Russia upon Russian traditions and the emergencies caused by the revolutionary era and its aftermath, although the CCF had made it abundantly clear that their case was not against "the theory of a socialist commonwealth" but the existing Soviet political and socio-economic system.

These editorial responses touched off severe attacks in response, by Sidney Hook upon the *Nation,* and by George W. Hartmann and especially Ferdinand Lundberg upon the *New Republic,* which both journals published and kept running for weeks. Hook's offense at the Kirchwey preference for the Third International rather than equal condemnation with the Third Reich was one of the sharpest of all rebuffs by a many-times-published colleague. Hook charged her with giving the Reds "protective coloration," and insisted that [135]

The entire question of the role of the Communist Party in this and other countries is too large to discuss here. Suffice it to say that proofs abound that whether on American soil or in Spain, France, or any country you please, its primary loyalty is to the Kremlin, and not to peace, democracy, or intellectual freedom.

This was probably the first time that anything like this about the Communists had ever been said in the *Nation,* but the outlook of this journal and its editors on foreign affairs was entirely a product of having refused to take such a position in the previous decade.

Kirchwey clung stubbornly to her position in rebuttal, urging that the mutual recriminations on the Left be abandoned, and basing the largest part of her plea for the lifting of the condemnation of the Communists solely on their performance in Spain, ignoring Hook's assertion that the Communist Party in Spain had been fighting for a Kremlin goal. She was firmly defended in this position of calling for Left unity again in a letter by Charles A. Madison.[136]

The *New Republic* just as vigorously protested the charges of Lundberg that it was "Stalinist," and went on to say that "many things that have been done inside the Soviet Union are good; its foreign policy has been a steady influence for peace." It dodged Lundberg's charge that five to ten million peasants had been killed in the forced collectivization of agriculture and the assassination of several ex-Communists in four Western European countries in the previous five years, but could not suppress the impulse once more to reject the attack on the conduct of the purge trials; "We have seen no evidence conclusive to us that the political trials were 'frameups,' at least as a whole." [137]

Increasing sensitivity and the issuing of manifestoes occupied the liberal publications during the rest of the spring and early summer of 1939, as the left-liberal split yawned wider by the week. MacDonald's "revolutionary league of artists and writers" in the LCFS especially leaped upon the Writers' Congress, long a liberal impeccable, and deposited upon the *Nation* in mid-July another extended declaration, uniformly condemning Germany, Italy and Russia, while reserving special unfriendly mention for the "progressive cultural circles" which castigated the Fascist "deification" of Hitler and Mussolini while engaged simultaneously in a similar glorification of Stalin and "unqualified support of Roosevelt." Most of it was devoted to a scathing attack on the Communists and the whole "democratic front" movement, with its now unconcealed advocacy of "a new war for 'democracy.'" These groups and individuals it dismissed as nothing but "apologists for the Kremlin, utterly intolerant of all dissenting opinion from the Left"; "to the war drive of the Fascist powers they reply with a war drive of their own." [138]

The final step in this drama, now that these two groups of liberals had called for a comprehensive rejection of Stalinism and a condemnation of Communism, was reaction in the form of a mighty open letter signed by over 400 prominent persons, including two editors from each of the two liberal weeklies, titled "To All Active Supporters of Democracy and Peace". The statement identified the supporters of the CCF and LCFS as "individuals who have for years had as their chief political objective the maligning of the Soviet people and their government," and went on to list "ten basic points" in which they insisted Russia and the Fascist powers were in diametrical opposition and in eternal hostility, which turned out to be an admirable condensation of what had been the intellectual fare of the pro-Communist press for two decades, and a classic restatement of the Popular Front catechism at the very moment the Soviet Union was about to blow it sky-high. The signatories included T. A. Bisson, Henry P. Fairchild, Waldo Frank, Leo Huberman, Matthew Josephson, George Kaufman, Rockwell Kent, John A. Kingsbury, Max Lerner, Klaus Mann, Harvey O'Connor, Clifford Odets, Frederick L. Schuman, George Seldes, I. F. Stone, William Carlos Williams, Dashiell Hammett, Richard Wright, Vincent Sheean, Granville Hicks, Corliss Lamont, Emil Lengyel, Robert Morss Lovett, Maxwell D. Stewart, Harry F. Ward, Donald Ogden Stewart, Louis Untermyer and scores of other famous liberals in the literary, theatrical and artistic world, undoubtedly the most impressive group of persons ever assembled on a statement published in the liberal papers between the world wars.[139]

It was also the most unfortunately-timed manifesto ever published in the entire decade prior to the outbreak of the Second World War. Dated August 10, 1939 it appeared in the *New Republic* in its issue of August 23, the day the *Nichtsangriffspakt* was signed by the Communist and German foreign ministers. But the timing was even more grisly in the case of the *Nation;* their issue of this week did not appear until August 26.[140] The lameness of this passionate act of faith on the part of so many prominent Americans in the never-ending implacability of Russia and Germany stands as one of the most staggering acts of bad judgment in the history of American intellectual life.

THE GREAT BETRAYAL
BEGETS THE GREAT REJECTION

A large part of American liberalism never recovered from the Litvinov "peace is indivisible" slogan despite the Soviet action in August, 1939. They were horrified to learn that Stalin considered both Litvinov and his slogan to be expendable, but they continued to be guided by the slogan as if this had not happened. When Communists switched to the "war of rival imperialisms" interpretation of the new war which exploded a few days after the *Pakt,* which liberals in a towering stack of literature had approved as a correct diagnosis of World War One. The liberals stubbornly refused to be budged from their "war against Fascism" position, a position the Communists had unceasingly worked into shape since 1935. For 22 months it was an unpleasant and bitter position, made whole again by the Soviet entry into the war via German invasion in June, 1941. Still more evidence piled up a few months later when the Communists continued a Russia-First policy of maintaining a strict neutrality toward Japan after the United States went to war with this nation, but excuses were invented to explain once more this discrepancy in the alleged seamless gown of peace, which the Reds had created but refused to wear.[141]

By the time of the *Pakt*, the liberals who had been most ardent in flirting with the Soviet Union had gone on too long to make an impartial withdrawal possible. A thinly-concealed favorable predisposition toward the Soviet Union prevailed regardless, and even in some cases survived the Russo-Finnish war a few months later. Liberal choice of the Russian over the German form of totalitarianism still was the deciding psychic influence, and the conviction of the ultimate beatification of the Soviet Union and the similar sureness of the utter and completely unqualified depravity of Germany lay behind the choice. Despite some defections, a portion of the previous Popular Front groups continued to express great warmth toward Russia even after the *Pakt*. Even those upon whom black disillusion descended in August, 1939 continued to be much more obsessed with the "horrible consequences of tyranny" in Germany than with its evidences in Russia. The apparent defection of Russia into the German camp did not dislodge them from their determination to see Germany crushed. The Communist-Popular Front propagandists had builded better than they knew, even though there were many occasions in the next two and a half years when they wished their edifice had not been so durably constructed.

Even among those liberals who reflected hostility toward Stalin and Russian Communism after the *Pakt* there was a forced, almost false tone to their criticism, which was discernible even after the Finnish war got under way, an event which loosened some of the most devoted liberal affections for Russia. It probably could not have been otherwise. In one sense, liberals were not given sufficient time to incubate a full-fledged indignant attitude. After 20 unbroken years of having Russia posed as the Coming Society and the polar opposite to capitalist and (especially in the 30s, Hitlerian) socio-economic systems, during which time only faint breezes of criticism had ever been permitted to rustle the pages of liberal literature, it was probably asking too much for a summary reversal. By tending to adhere to attitudes acquired during the period of Communist comradeship and tutelage, their ultimate mobilization for war against the enemies of Russia was virtually assured at the end of the *Pakt* period. Other agents were able to keep the flame of belligerence burning, and for somewhat different objectives. And though the official liberal attitude after June 1941 was that of a gruff parent accepting a returned prodigal, it was more a picture of a reconciliation of a family resulting from the return of a once-deserting father.

But the *Pakt* period was an interesting one, intellectually, sprinkled with anguished announcements of deep disappointment in Communist Russia by fellow-traveling liberals, and even more sensational recantations by Communists who sought refuge among the liberals. It is largely these episodes that comprise the Great Rejection of Communist leadership, along with the civilized expressions of outrage from the editorial staffs of the main liberal publications. The *Nation* was stunned by the *Pakt*. Its cross but subdued editorial of August 26, "Red Star and Swastika," covered all sorts of issues in an effort to understand what had happened and was mainly devoted to speculation on the likely consequences. It now admitted the Russians had been playing a double game with both England and Germany since April, conceded with some ill grace that the Reds had a case for independent action on the basis of the opaque Chamberlain negotiations, and referred to Chamberlain as "a double-crosser who has been double-crossed." But the major pique with the Soviet was over its abdication from the "leadership of the anti-Fascist front the world over." An ally in a war against Germany had been lost. "The disillusion which will follow among the Left forces here and abroad will be bitter," it predicted,[142] as the loss of faith where none should have ever been planted in the first place swelled across the country. The following week there was much exultation over the trouble the *Pakt* had caused to both the American Communist Party and the various pro-Hitler "shirt organizations," although there were no comments upon those elements in the country which had not been inclined to separate them very far originally. With the war now under way, figures such as Villard began to realize the relationship of this emotional tie to pressures toward participating in the combat and he concluded with great heat that the lesson to be derived from the Russo-German understanding was that Americans should at all costs stay out of "this conscienceless power-politics game," and not let bitterness over the consequences feed "the delusion that we have got to back England and France in order to save democracy for the world."[143]

The *New Republic* commented in shocked, somber tones on August 30 that "Not for a long time has such a paralyzing piece of news struck the world as the announcement of the Russo-German treaty of non-aggression," and confessed to utter innocence that it was "imminent." It also found Hitler's decision more astounding, in view of its contradiction of "his long anti-Comintern crusade," although Stalin's contradiction of his long anti-Fascist collective security "crusade" was fully as astounding. The impulse to think well of the Soviet could not repress the hope that the *Pakt* might yet be still another front behind which Stalin was continuing his search for military support.[144] By the end of the following month this was obviously not the case, and another editorial followed the *Nation*'s lead in describing the shattering effect of this act upon the Popular Front concept: [145]

The strength of the Soviet Union throughout the world has hitherto rested . . . on a widespread faith among humble folk—and some not so humble—that she constituted a bulwark of honesty and humanity in a treacherous world. Her proudest boast was the clear and simple line of her foreign policy. The more the Soviet Union was attacked by her natural enemies, the stronger the faith grew. But, except among devout Communists, it has now been lost; henceforth the power of the Russian state abroad must rest on fear rather than trust.

The season of sensitivity over fellow-travelerism promptly set in on the last echoes of the *Pakt*. The stock of the Communist Party was tending toward the bottom, and "fellow travelers are dropping like ripe plums in a hurricane," the *New Republic* mournfully narrated on September 6, especially concerned over the abuse being felt by front group leaders because of prior Red support.[146] In the *Nation* three weeks later James Wechsler's extended "Stalin and Union Square" went into the dark days which had befallen the Party, with its fierce internal fights and resignations. Wechsler had a difficult time separating his own genuine alarm over what the *Pakt* had done to the "anti-Fascist collective security" front of 1935–1939 from his own critique of the plight of the Communists and those who refused to renounce them. On the whole Wechsler felt at this point that the bulk of American Communists had too much of an "emotional investment" in their "faith," the major article of which was "the incorruptibility of the U.S.S.R." In this immediate period of wheeling and milling, he discerned only the Social Democratic Federation and their organ the *New Leader* sticking implacably to the Popular Front position that Hitlerism had to be "smashed," that the war was an "anti-Fascist" one, and that American military intervention should be forthcoming if it was thought necessary to achieve this goal.[147] The Communist goal of having Central Europe converted into a political vacuum for investment by themselves was being supported vigorously by the very elements that appeared to be most affronted by Communist behavior.

The *Nation* was fully in accord with this as well, but in the first few confused weeks after the *Pakt* it was essential to become separated from the fixations of the previous period, an important element of which was a new stance as distinct from the Communists as possible. It was not to be achieved in an entirely painless way, even though the employment of former running partners of the Communist press such as Wechsler to dissect Communism was part of the separation process. Editorially it was still a substantial struggle, with the memories of the months just prior to the *Pakt* still hot and strong. The tenderness on the issue of prior identification with Russian policy was the worst aspect, especially since it was a wounded area always being opened up by liberals who still remembered the fury of the contest over the Soviet purge trials and the *Nation*'s stand during their tenure. Five weeks after the Russo-German agreement, the *Nation* was still defending itself from charges of previous pro-Stalinism in a wide number of areas, on this latter occasion as a result of a sulphurous letter from James T. Farrell. The reply to Farrell was substantially what was used in rebuttal to all such charges now, that it had been Stalin who agreed with the *Nation,* not the reverse, and that "When he shifted sides, we stayed put." [148] It was a line that impressed none of Trotsky's friends, nor the other liberal-left which had made a major issue out of Communist behavior in Spain, and their treatment by the Stalinist forces in general. It took many months of steadily-growing implacability toward the Communists to rub off from the *Nation* the reputation it had acquired in the eyes of liberal dissidents, although the struggle over the merits of Soviet Russia was promptly replaced by another which was fought over the role the United States should play in the new European war.

The discomfiture of the Communists and defections from their ranks figured prominently in the next eight months or more, embellished by abrasive blows from long-time well-wishers who no longer wanted to be identified with their past. The retreat of the fellow-travelers was far more impressive than Party resignations at this time, and of the latter, very few took up the battle again within the liberal breastworks. Of these the most important was Granville Hicks. In the campaign of embarrassing Communists, the liberal press confined itself to those who remained identified with the Party. Earl Browder was a favorite target, and Quincy Howe took extended impish pleasure in badgering him in a review of Browder's *Fighting for Peace,* since its fervent Popular Front line was already outdated when it was published—in actuality, as Howe pointed out, a breath from 1938. Browder's July 5, 1939 speech at Charlottesville, Virginia, where he told an audience that an understanding between Hitler and Stalin was as unlikely as the United States Chamber of Commerce electing him as its president, was held up for special comment and ridicule. Howe, a partisan of Charles A. Beard and one of the most articulate liberal critics of collective security, wound up his September 6 *New Republic* demolition of Browder's book with the comment, "Our liberal internationalists have long since forfeited all claims to serious attention. The Communists have not yet acquired such a disastrous record for misinterpretation, but this book of Mr. Browder's is an ominous beginning." [149] Two weeks later, the *New Republic* for once did not denounce the Dies Committee when it reported Ben Gitlow's testimony, and Browder's naming of liberal groups used as "transmission belts" for Communist ideas, as well as his admission of having gone abroad on a false passport.

It took additional blows to liberal equilibrium after the war was under way, including the Russian part in the partition of Poland and the absorption of the Baltic States in the first two weeks of October 1939, to steel the *New Republic* toward the Soviet Union. Its fierce editorial attack on October 11 was its most realistic talk on Russia to date: [150]

A good many of the people who are morally outraged at the behavior of Soviet Russia are so because they have been naïve enough to take Communist propaganda at its face value. Because of the constant iteration from official party sources, the unwary assumed that the leaders in the Kremlin really believed in democracy, that they regarded Hitler and Nazism as the greatest menace to the world, and that in order to scotch that menace they were ready to support even imperialist capitalist democracies like Britain and France.

Those who believed this, it went on to illustrate, had been most indiscreet;

It should have been remembered all the time that if Communists joined democratic and popular fronts, it was not because they cherished democratic ideals. . . . Likewise it was clear to the discerning that the worldwide Communist drive against Nazism and Fascism coupled with the support for collective security was not really the ideological crusade that it appeared to be, but rather a means of winning allies for the Soviet Union, in case she should be attacked by the Third Reich, coupled with a means of discouraging that attack.

This Olympian view was just what the *New Republic* had denounced as cynical reaction a few short months before, and anyone who had the temerity to take such a detached stand then ran the risk of seeming guilty of befriending "the enemies of democracy." But at this point the editors were pleading that it was not the above that shocked them but the new Soviet territorial landgrabs, mainly on the grounds once more that these were not in line with "socialist" views on power politics, and the general reprehensibility of acquisition of the territory of one's neighbors. Again it was a falling-back on a literal translation of socialist scriptures and accepting Soviet statements as of 1920 as final for all time, which was at the base of their discomfort.[151] By mid-November, 1939 the Communist position was being referred to as a "line," with the added illuminating comment, "People all over the world have awakened to the fact that any policy of the several national Communist Parties is dictated by the necessities of the Soviet government." [152] The *Pakt* and its aftermath had indeed wrought vast political education.

But the account was not entirely without its tortuous twists and turns hereafter. On both an editorial and personal basis the lapses and hedgings continued, testifying to the painful nature of the divestment of all the previous fixations on Russian Communism. Granville Hicks began the parade of prominent figures to qualify their faith in the Soviet Union and the Communist Party in a long and memorable letter addressed to the *New Republic* which appeared on October 4, 1939, shortly after he had resigned from the staff of the *New Masses*. It was a hot indictment of the Communist Party leadership and the Soviet for their reversal on the Popular Front, yet it was modified by a refusal to denounce the Soviet Union and a promise to defend the Communist Party. For the former he offered in extenuation, "After all, the Soviet Union is a socialist commonwealth, and, even if it makes mistakes, its fate is of the utmost concern to every believer in socialism." As for the American Communist Party, he asserted, "I know that no progressive movement is safe if the Party is suppressed."

The florid religious quality of this testimonial prompted a scathing letter from Max Eastman which appeared on October 25, describing Hicks's resignation as "the best example so far of the Split Libido common to the Fellow Travelers of Stalin," and insisting that what Hicks and others should have been saying at the time was "I was wrong—you cannot serve democracy and totalitarianism," but noting with regret that "It seems too bad that nobody in the *Nation* and the *New Republic* has the clarity of heart and mind to say it." [153]

An even more pointed rejection followed from Vincent Sheean, the author of one of the most impressive defenses of the Russians for their part in the *Pakt,* which appeared in the *New Masses* on September 19.[154] Seven weeks later the *New Republic* began publication of the first of two articles by him, "Brumaire: The Soviet Union as a Fascist State," the strongest condemnation of the Soviet Union thus far printed in this weekly. Sheean proved to be a thoroughly angered and disillusioned Soviet well-wisher; in a preliminary statement he admitted, "these two articles will constitute the first criticism I have ever made of the Soviet Union, and the first time I have ever been willing to discuss Stalin or even, in fact, to mention him in print." [155] Such reverence toward the Russian leader while he and his journalist colleagues had been savagely attacking Hitler on an almost daily basis for seven years gives some idea why the liberal readers got a lopsided view in the hall of political monsters; the mirrors had been arranged to show only those regimes hostile or unsympathetic to Communist Russia.

In the case of Sheean the *New Republic* felt called upon to accompany his fierce pieces with a long editorial, recalling that "there are few writers on international affairs whose views will command more respect among those of progressive leanings," and also making it plain that editorial opinion was not as harsh as his, which was that of one "most deeply committed to the Soviet Union's previous foreign policy." The editors now claimed that their long-standing refusal to commit themselves to collective security warranted their assertion of having held balanced views on Russia for a long time on this subject, a claim not substantiated by all that had appeared in defense of the Communists regardless of opposition on this issue, since the journal had simply opposed American participation in such schemes. But it used this as a point from which to leap off in describing the use of the League of Nations and collective security as a brilliant, "hard-headed piece of *Realpolitik*," splitting the other nations and gaining the allies it needed for the proper circumstances. It also claimed that Soviet anti-Fascism was a pose; "The ideological mumbo-jumbo in which it was clothed was an instance of the thoroughness with which the Soviet Union forces follow through any line adopted." It now defended the Russian acquisition of Polish and Baltic territory as justified, and necessary for their own defense, and even at this late date, again the obverse of its German position, found grounds on which to exculpate the Communists for the employment of terrorism, espionage, and purges to wipe out Old Bolsheviks and other alleged enemies, "whole ranks of people who had developed ability to do things," "together with many innocent persons." But, after a long recital of a catalog of treachery and blood, the *New Republic* did not think that the Soviet deserved Sheean's bitter condemnation.[156] Its views on Communism in the United States were much harsher, however, and in other countries outside of Russia as well. Communism, they now advised, did not and had not "for a long time sincerely represent any genuine international movement," and was not "a secure repository of the trust of workers or intellectuals in other nations."

Expressions of shock, disillusionment and distress ran through the *Nation* as well during these late fall days. One of the most profoundly shaken by the *Pakt* was Max Lerner, whose "Revolution in Ideas" on October 21 was the rumination of a spectator evaluating the ruins of a catastrophic earthquake. His lame and diaphanous value judgment by which it still might be possible to separate the political sheep and goats was the product of a person with nothing to say at the moment but under a fierce agony of trying to have a constructive comment to contribute in a time of disaster.[157]

Villard's column on November 4 was an announcement that he had lost all hope of seeing anything good now coming out of the Soviet "experiment"; the *Pakt* was also the *coup de grâce* to his faith, which had been under siege since the shooting of Kirov. He confessed that the liberal writers should have been more diligent in 1935–1936 in calling attention to Russian oil sales to Mussolini at the very time the Communists were leading in the outcry against Italian actions in Ethiopia. He also admitted his growing doubts about the Russian protestations of peace-loving while watching their deep commitment in the undeclared war in Mongolia, "but I was assured that the guilt was solely Japan's, and moreover, that the diversion was helping China and so helping democracy." Crestfallen by their sudden peace with Japan and their Polish, Baltic and Rumanian territorial snatches, Villard shouted, "the Russian government has revealed itself as a common despoiler and robber. . . . It is not only just as bloody as the others, but just as crooked, treacherous, and criminal." [158] The *Pakt* had indeed made possible a glorious moment of impartiality toward dictatorships. One may only speculate as to what liberal foreign policy might have been after 1929 if its innocence toward the Soviet Union had never existed.

The liberal scene was not without its unreconstructed holdouts. The answer to such contrite and abusive figures as Sheean was Schuman's "Machiavelli in Moscow" in the *New Republic* for November 29. It was a shout of enthusiastic admiration for Stalin and his adroit maneuvering of both Hitler and the Western nations out of position. He snorted at liberal complaints, hesitation, condemnations and reservations, and voted unconditionally for Stalin as a master politician. The military security of the U.S.S.R. came first, said Schuman, in plumbing Red decisions. If the socialist dream-world should now become impossible to conceive of evolving in Russia any more, then that was the price to be paid for the present situation; "The U.S.S.R. is a great power," Schuman trumpeted in pride. The twenty-five years of blood spilled since 1914 seemed to have been for the purpose of permitting Russia to re-emerge in the image of 1914, but under different management. He firmly supported the Stalin purges as efforts to wipe out German agents in Russia, and he blamed the joining of hands with Hitler upon the Anglo-French refusal to permit the Soviet to extend "military protection" to Finland, Poland, Rumania and the three Baltic states; Stalin's strategy was "ethically indistinguishable" from that of Hitler, Chamberlain, Mussolini or Daladier, Schuman insisted, "It is merely more successful." [159]

Schuman obviously went far beyond the point of defense which the editors had reached when trying to modify Sheean's attack; they now issued a stiff editorial criticism of Schuman, declaring that the somersault taken by the Communists was far too great for the ordinary person to perform, and gave their reason: [160]

The fact is that for years the Comintern had bent all its energies to convincing the plain people of the world that Hitler was their worst enemy, and that they would join with anybody else—even with imperialistic Britain and France—to defeat him. It had advocated support of the New Deal and of democratic forces in all other countries to stem the attack of domestic reactionaries. And the fact is that without warning it made friends with Hitler, turned its hostility against Hitler's enemies and ditched the democratic movements. People with simplicity of mind resent the discovery that their burning convictions of yesterday were nothing but a necessity of Moscow's foreign policy. . . . The overnight reversal is proof to them that Moscow was acting as a nationalist state rather than as leader of a world movement. Moscow's betrayal did not begin with its shift; it began with the insincere propaganda for collective security and the Popular Front. Such people will have difficulty in enthusiastically supporting Moscow's line in the future.

The *New Republic* was wrong in its last statement, as events after June 22, 1941 bore out. But its stand was a common denominator of the half-abashed, half-truculent declarations of Hicks, Sheean and others, a self-consciousness which projected on to the Comintern, Stalin and the Soviet Union their own feelings of rage and sense of betrayal. The message was "you have made a mistake in alienating us," not "we were simple-minded for having accepted your propaganda verbatim as a true statement of the world situation." Having spared no heights of invective in building Hitler into a demon surpassing anything known since the Old Testament, they now had the exquisite pain of having to try to accept him as at least a neutral figure, and the effort to rub off seven years of self-induced hostility was an achievement they found impossible to realize, however easily the Stalinists could. And in insisting in going on with the Popular Front war against Hitler on the old basis it is little wonder that they began to feel alone on a bleak plateau once teeming with partisans. The lost security of purpose which the halcyon Popular Front days had supplied was the real issue.

This central idea pervaded the next series of defections, which was touched off by Russia's invasion of Finland in December, 1939. The first of these in the *New Republic* was Ralph Bates, the faithful chronicler of the Spanish Civil War from the Communist point of view, who had found it possible to survive the *Pakt,* but could not rationalize this latter event. And as had most of the others, he was convinced his support of the Popular Front policy of the Comintern was a defense of himself and his politics: [161]

We never dreamed that the whole policy would be ditched at a moment's notice and a complete face-about accomplished by the very country that had in reality originated that policy. . . . It was the collective-security and the Popular Front policies that actually created vast bodies of liberalism and anti-Fascism. . . . In effect, the Communists pointed at Hitler and said, "there is your enemy; fight him." Now they declare, "This is an imperialist war, turn against your own governments." That is why I, and many others, resent the change and cannot believe the honesty of it.

Bates thus testified to the success of the Communists in implanting the anti-Hitler hate and their failure to uproot it, although its continuation did them no harm, since the destruction of Hitler hardly meant a situation less favorable to the spread of more Communism. Those who despised the Communists for abandoning the fight had the unenviable lot of waging a war-program which was bound to help no one but the Communists in the final analysis.

Niebuhr also gave vent in the *Nation* to disillusion and disappointment with Soviet Russia early in the Finnish war period—an elephantine grappling with the obvious. He no longer expressed sympathy with the "millions outside the boundaries of Russia" who clung to their image of the Soviet as the leader of a proletarian world order, when "all the evidence points to the fact that the defensive, and possibly the imperialistic, requirements of the Russian state, rather than the strategic considerations of the workers' cause, determine Russian policy." He was willing now to express the same kind of realism which had been seizing other figures famous in the pages of the liberal press; "The pretensions of Russia must be judged as those of any other nation," he now advised; "Its transcendent disinterestedness in the field of world politics is an illusion." [162] For over ten years, Marxist liberals had been excoriating those who had been saying this, Left and Right alike. The latter-day awakening was slightly anticlimactic. But the pre-dispositions of the era still remained. With the scales removed from liberal eyes on the Russian situation, and with hostility rising, there still was none of the surefooted venomous determination to annihilate expressed toward Stalinist Russia that had saturated their attitudes toward Germany. The Popular Front was dead, yet never more alive.

The *Nation* showed its pique toward Russia and its grim thoughtlessness toward its friends abroad through its grinding war directed against Finland by publishing on December 16, 1939 the first real critique of the Soviet as a militarist state in Alan Mather's "Militarism vs. Socialism in Russia," reminiscent of scores of similar pieces which had been written about National Socialist Germany in the previous seven years. It described much the same things as had been alleged in its Teutonic neighbor—a quarter of the budget devoted to national defense arms spending (at that time considered a frightfully large percentage), a declining standard of living, wages plummeting, a steady diversion of labor toward armaments, work speed-up and many other evidences of the movement of the Soviet economy toward the practices of its much-scorned adversaries. Even worse, said the author, "having embarked upon armament competition, the home of socialism has had to resort, first, to a new creation of classes, and then to that same forceful maintenance of class relationships which underlies the military economies of other lands." [163] It was strange to see this in a journal which not long before could cite with casual aplomb and almost approval the Soviet Union having the world's largest army and air force.

The Finnish war proved to be the solvent which melted even such adamant partisans as Ludwig Lore and Malcolm Cowley, who used their respective reviews of Walter G. Krivitsky's *In Stalin's Secret Service* in January, 1940 to write scathing words of the post-*Pakt* Soviet. Cowley described it as the last in "a series of writings and events that have caused me to change my judgment of Soviet Russia." [164] The Moscow Express was losing passengers at a rapid rate by now, even though Cowley's review was largely a seven-column attack on Krivitsky's veracity. It was not until September of the same year that the *New Republic* finally joined those elements on the Left which had been growing increasingly vocal on the far-reaching arms of the Russian espionage and assassination system, when it commented on the killing of Trotsky in Mexico. Its editorial "The Old Man" thought that there was a "fair likelihood that the Russian secret service had a hand in this plot, as in several others." The *Nation* in February, 1941 also came around to suspecting the GPU as responsible for the murder of Krivitsky in Washington, D. C. His alleged "suicide" was considered highly suspect.[165]

The most important defection which the Finnish war detonated in the *Nation* was that of its long-time Moscow correspondent Fischer, who had written more lines in praise of the Communists in the past seventeen years and influenced more people on their attitudes toward the Soviet Union than probably all other liberal journalist specialists on Russia combined. His "Russia—Twenty Years After" in the same issue for February 10, 1940 was the most destructive attack on Stalin this journal had yet published. The war against Finland and the emergence of nationalism he considered to be the final blows in the undermining of "faith in its internationalism." The capitalist order he now admitted had emerged from the depression in much improved condition, while the difficulties of the Communist economy had "dashed the hopes of many who had seen the millennium in terms of socialist industry and trade." More important, "the attempt to democratize Soviet dictatorship was a failure," he stated without qualification; "As a result, pro-Soviet sympathies in the capitalist world are now certainly at their lowest ebb since 1917." [166] Fischer's relapse was one of the most startling and sensational of the period.

New Republic editorial policy sought to discriminate among the outspoken attackers of Stalin and Russia, and published resentful critiques of some of the more aggravating, especially Benjamin Stolberg and Eugene Lyons. This sparked spirited letters in their defense by John Chamberlain and Edmund Wilson late in January, 1940, which included gratuitous attacks on their own part on the personalities whom this publication preferred as guides in the new pastime of genteel Communist-baiting of a respectable sort.[167] But the editors thought that the critics it did not appreciate had made a point quite clear, one which was now editorially acceptable; "Many persons, including the editors of the *New Republic,* have been slow and reluctant to accept the thesis that the socialist experiment in Russia is a failure, that the rest of the world should follow a much different path, that this is a blocked road to Utopia." [168] They would not accept it as an "indictment" of Russia, nevertheless. But five weeks later (February 26, 1940) the *New Republic*'s editorial "Sixteen Propositions," a striking suggestion for sweeping revamping of liberal thinking on Russia, came to negative conclusions on some aspect of the Soviet Union and Soviet life in fourteen proposals,[169] fully as harsh a verdict on Russia as that of the critics who had previously been chided for their extravagant abuse. Not all the readers enjoyed this, and the sociologist Robert S. Lynd eventually contributed a serious complaint to the editors about their "essentially negative slant" on Russian Communism.[170]

Running simultaneously in the *Nation* was another major critique by Lewis Corey, a three-part post-mortem titled "Marxism Reconsidered," which now came to such pallid conclusions as "There is a totalitarian potential in the socialist economic system," and "The Socialist system of collective ownership is compatible with totalitarianism." [171] The endless debating over the alleged abyss which separated Communism and Fascism which had featured the earliest years of the Russo-German conflict-in-the-making seemed like prehistory at this point, but it had taken a series of the most stunning events of the modern era to shock Left-liberalism out of its idealist fixations on the nature of the socio-politico-economic system of Communist Russia.

The defections continued, although many of them trailed in the dust after the war broke out in the vast campaigns of the spring and summer of 1940. The liberal press was mainly in a state of near-hysteria at this point as Hitler's forces rolled over the Franco-British forces at will, and spared little time or attention for an issue which now seemed settled forever. The *Nation* did take a moment to congratulate another famous defector, John Strachey, when the latter severed relations with the London *Daily Worker* and took up the cudgels as a patriotic Englishman in May, charging British Communists with favoring a German victory.[172] For all practical purposes, this intensely emotional period of shedding of deep ties with Communism was brought to an end by the man who had started it off, Granville Hicks. His *Nation* piece, "The Blind Alley of Marxism" on September 28, 1940 was much more disillusionist than his original secession a year earlier, appalled by what he had supported the several years past, especially "the Marxist concept of power and the Marxist concept of history." [173] The effect of the *Pakt* and its impact on American liberals, as well as the interpretation of Russian affairs from that point to the entry of the United States into the war, will be examined again subsequently in the context of the war.

THE PARALLEL BATTLEFIELD:
REVIEWING THE BOOKS ON SOVIET RUSSIA

An important ingredient to the flavor of Popular Front times down to Russian involvement in the Second World War was the estimation and evaluation of the literature dealing with Russian and Communist affairs. In many ways the publishing business itself was attuned to the intellectual climate in America, as the pulse of book releases often fitted in appropriately with the crises on ideological and political issues. But the reviews and reviewers performed a separate function as a thermometer registering the maximum and minimum temperatures of affection for the Popular Front and Soviet Russia in liberal circles. A secondary source for divining this spirit can be obtained from a scanning of the reviews of the numerous "proletarian" novels which streamed from the publishing houses throughout the 1930's in parallel columns with the accounts of history and public affairs and also with the persistent "Visit the Soviet Union" advertisements of the travel agents and groups sponsoring Russian tours for the more enthusiastic. The 1934–1937 period was the peak of brightest promise among enamored liberals; no group wished harder to see something that was not there. And only on rare occasions did the liberal press see anything incongruous or humorous in the party-line wandering and the use of the rubber yardsticks of Communist literary criticism into which they had become enmeshed themselves,[174] especially in 1935 and 1936, when liberal contributions to the Communist or Communist-line press were commonplace.

As the Popular Front swung into action, the accent on books favorable to Soviet Russia took up the stride. The trickle of critical volumes persisted for awhile, accompanied by severe reception, and then faded out, gaining life once more when the controversy over Trotsky and the trials exploded in 1937. A laboratory example was Ella Winter's simultaneous review of Louis Fischer's *Soviet Journey* and Eugene Lyons' *Moscow Carrousel* in the *New Republic* in May, 1935, the former hailed for its idyllic picture of the Soviet, the latter darkly suspect because of his accent on the somber aspects of the Communist scene.[175] A similar fate to Lyons' was met by William Henry Chamberlin's *The Russian Revolution* the following month in the same journal at the hands of Cowley, who hardly agreed with a line in the entire book because he was so affronted by its anti-Bolshevik tone.[176] No less condemnatory was Fischer in the *Nation* four months later. He was of the conviction that Chamberlin did not understand the nature of the Communist Revolution at all; "Its primary purpose was the transfer of power from the exploiting to the exploited classes," he added as a corrective to Chamberlin's account. But his principal objection to the book was Chamberlin's failure to contribute to an understanding of what had happened since 1921.[177] An official Soviet publication could hardly have expected a more faithful product. Far preferable in these times were the praises of journalists, not their critiques. Villard in the *Nation* in November, 1935 could scarcely restrain himself in greeting Walter Duranty's *I Write As I Please,* while Robert Morss Lovett also attained heights of rhapsody over Anna Louise Strong's *This Soviet World* a year later, at a time when the peak point of Soviet influence was being reached. At the same time the *New Masses* editor Joseph Freeman's *An American Testament* was reviewed by Cowley, perhaps the classic account in the entire decade of a conversion to Communism.[178]

The major literary contribution of this early Popular Front period to the enhancement of Communist Russia was the stupendous work by Sidney and Beatrice Webb, *Soviet Communism: A New Civilization?* George Soule's paean of praise in the March 18, 1936 *New Republic* resolutely concluded, "Within its 1174 pages every important question about the Soviet Union receives an answer. The job has been done once and for all; any future book must take this as a basing point." Abram Harris in the *Nation* the same week came to somewhat similar conclusions, describing it as "without question, the definitive account of the political and economic system of the U.S.S.R." But apparently his review was far from ardent enough, for Fischer chided him in a separate letter from Moscow in June, condemning his review as "most inadequate"; he was especially indignant that Harris, a professor of economics at Howard University, had not noticed that the Webbs had accepted Communist theory; "No mention is ever made of the very significant fact that here we see the Webbs, the parents of

Fabianism, the originators of the theory of the "inevitability of grad-
ualness," converted to revolution and accepting the doctrine of the
end justifying the means." [179]

In such an intellectual climate, the fate of books denunciatory of
contemporary Soviet internal policies could be predicted. A readership had been developed for books describing the experiences of persons who had lived for a time under totalitarian political orders, especially that of Hitler Germany, in the period just prior to the Popular
Front, although there had existed a literature of similar sort dealing
with Russia ever since the books by Emma Goldman and Alexander
Berkman in 1923–1925. The latter-day variety was to get an even
more ferocious reception by American liberals in general, and in the
liberal press in particular. Cowley, reviewing George Kitchin's *Prisoner of the OGPU* in September, 1935, actually rejoiced at the
author's predicament, and referred to his account of his treatment by
the Bolshevik police as "the truth about spraying apple orchards as
written from the point of view of the woolly aphis and the codling
moth." Joseph Barnes reviewed Kitchin in the same week for the
Nation, and was torn between the desire to destroy Kitchin personally
and to disparage his account by imputation of serious character
defects, and to admit that his experiences were quite plausible. He
particularly resented Kitchin's ignoring of the things which he
thought should have been advertised about internal Russian affairs,
especially the Five Year Plan, and in summary concluded that Kitchin
had "simply produced some more glib tales for those who still refuse
to believe that revolutions are expensive." The same reception
greeted Andrew Smith's *I Was A Soviet Worker,* brought out by Dut-
ton in the spring of 1936. Eleanor Gray in *Common Sense* mercilessly
shook this book, describing it ultimately as "bought, body and soul,
by Hearst." In connection with Kitchin and the *Nation,* however, it
was interesting to note in the issue following the reception given by
Ludwig Lore to Wolfgang Langhof's *Rubber Truncheon* and Stefan
Lorant's *I Was Hitler's Prisoner,* precisely the same kind of book
but devoted to the excesses of the German instead of the Russian
police. Lore treated them as a form of scripture.[180]

The apology for Russian violence and brutality while simultaneously devoting heated indictments of precisely the same sort of thing
when done in Germany was quite common at this time, and overtones
of this favoritism persisted, an obvious factor in opinion-formation,
even in books which gained wide general readership. John Gunther's
Inside Europe, a very successful book which furnished tens of thousands of people with their clichés about Europe which lasted through
the end of the war, in fact, was an example of this. In George Seldes'
review, he especially commended Gunther for his portraits of Hitler in the grip of hysterical weeping fits and Mussolini engaging

in sinister sadism, but even more approved of his mild, warm chapter on the Bolshevik Revolution and the Soviet Union, which had been prefaced by the remark, "No revolution can be made with silk gloves." William P. Vogel, Jr. reached the pinnacle of acclaim for Gunther in *Common Sense* for April, 1936 when he enthused,[181]

Perhaps the best lesson of the book is the essential normality of Stalin, the deep strain of humanity beneath his ruthless political severity. One feels that the terror caused by him and his elimination of Trotsky as well as his other enemies can, on purely pragmatic grounds, be excused. He had an idea and he made it work, to the greater glory of a large population and their greater happiness.

In general the other major figures in the "socialist commonwealth," Marx and Lenin, shared the same kind of veneration in the pre-purge years of the Popular Front. The reviews of Henri Barbusse's *Stalin* and the re-issue of Franz Mehring's *Karl Marx* in separate issues of the *Nation* in December, 1935 were symptomatic of the deep respect felt among the liberal Marxian fellow travelers. Lore was actually embarrassed by the total absence of criticism of the Soviet leader by Barbusse, but revealed his towering esteem of Marx in hailing the book by Mehring, "the renowned historian of German Social Democracy," as "truly remarkable." Lore's review of *The Letters of Lenin* in April, 1937 began with the declaration, "Truly, there can be no more fitting monument to the great Lenin than that which he himself created in these simple, unstudied self-portraits." [182] Schuman's review in the *New Republic* two months later went somewhat beyond this in a burst of unrestrained praise: [183]

The writer of them emerges as a peculiarly singleminded genius, possessed of enormous learning and analytical insight. But one feels, inescapably, that the secret of his leadership, and of his all-but-miraculous achievement, lay less in his remarkable intellectual gifts than in his character as a man, a friend and a comrade. In these roles he here stands self-revealed in simple dignity, perhaps the greatest figure of our times.

The source of Schuman's ferocity toward Hitler and his anti-Communist program, and some inkling as to why he was one of the first liberals in America to call for a declaration of war on Germany, is partially uncovered here. But by June, 1937, with the controversy over the purges beginning to reach glowing heat, extra emotion expended on behalf of Lenin was due partly to his role as a diversionary figure and a unity-symbol, especially among the pro-Stalinist liberals such as Lore and Schuman, with panic steadily increasing. By

September, 1938 Lore displayed the effect of this racking controversy by his gentle review of utterly contradictory biographies of Lenin by P. Kerzhentsev and Christopher Hollis, offering the following mild suggestion; "Somewhere between the two the truth will lie. Where, each reader will have to judge for himself or leave it to posterity to answer." [184]

Marx went through a similar distillation during the Popular Front-purge period. As late as September, 1936, Lewis Mumford could find even such a generalized book as Jan Huizinga's *In The Shadow of Tomorrow* greatly objectionable for failing "to show a special appreciation for the work of Marx," [185] but a year later, with the purge trial controversial flames glaring brightly, Edmund Wilson could review all three of the mighty books on Marx written or edited by Sidney Hook in a single sitting and indicate little evidence of being impressed, influenced or pleased by the subject.[186]

The purge trials upheaval had stimulated a burst of books on Russia and Communism, and now a healthy portion were distinctly critical and unfavorable, although the majority of these were products of disillusioned ex-Communists or the emotionally-attached, or partisans of the Trotsky brand of Communism as opposed to that of the reigning Stalinists. One of the most influential was Trotsky's own volume, *The Revolution Betrayed,* which touched off one of the oddest transferrals of allegiance during the period. It was reviewed with exceptional disfavor in the *New Republic* by Bertram D. Wolfe on June 16, 1937, even though he thought Trotsky had proved that Russia was not "marching toward socialism," and that the Stalinists might not "conceivably build a society superior to capitalist economy in productivity, culture and well-being." Five months later Wolfe reviewed *The Case of Leon Trotsky* by John Dewey and other members of the Preliminary Committee of Inquiry, in Mexico, and now was emerging as a defender of Trotsky against the charges made in Moscow at the trials, but he still thought that Trotsky was wrong in insisting that the Stalin regime was so degenerate that it could not permit an opposition in the Communist Party in Russia. It was Wolfe's view that Trotsky had been made the chief defendant *in absentia* in order to make a case against this opposition.[187]

Among the new books which bore down heavily on the Stalinist regime was that by Fred Beal, *Proletarian Journey,* the odyssey of an American Communist who was able to hold up under two periods of residence in Russia, and who now repeated what ex-radicals had been saying since the time of the Kronstadt rebellion. James Rorty received it with a whoop of applause in the *Nation* in October, 1937.[188] But by far the most advanced of the new literary demolition experts in the *Nation* was Edmund Wilson, who reviewed twelve books on Russia in November and December of this same year. He dismissed Lion Feuchtwanger's *Moscow, 1937* as a product of the Soviet "publicity service," intended only to repair the damage among Communists all over the world by the views of André Gide in his *Retouches à Mon Retour de l'URSS.* But he had unconcealed praise for Pierre Hubart's *En URSS,* Eugene Lyons' *Assignment in Utopia* and *Russia Twenty Years After* by Victor Serge, all either ex-Reds or sympathizers at one time. Wilson identified Lyons now as a man "who had spent some of the best years of his life whooping it up for the Soviets," forgetting his own days at this pastime especially between 1931 and 1936.[189]

Matthew Josephson reviewed the Lyons, Gide and Serge books, along with Max Eastman's booklet *The End of Socialism in Russia* in a long group-review in the *New Republic,* and his regret at the severity of the criticism was the most obvious feature of his six columns of small-print comment. He was particularly repelled by the new tendency to assert that Bolshevism had become a replica of Fascism, insisting that the situation was otherwise; Fascism had borrowed the worst aspects of Bolshevism but had rejected "nearly all its promising and redeeming features." Lyons' sensitivity to Josephson's skepticism and reservations resulted in a long angry letter, which the *New Republic* published on December 29, 1937, striking back at the reviewer as "typical of the know-nothing attitude of an entire class of American intellectuals in relation to Russia." [190]

The general anti-Stalin tone of the book reviews in the *Nation* stimulated Granville Hicks into a major article in the *New Masses* in the first week of December, "A '*Nation*' Divided," charging that there was a serious split on this liberal weekly, with its editorial page consistently pro-Stalin and its book review section now captured by a group sympathetic to Trotsky. He maintained that pro-Stalin books were not being reviewed at all, as well as being reviewed in a hostile manner, while anti-Stalin books were receiving cordial reception. In his unhappiness he conceded that the *Nation* was on the whole "friendly to the Soviet Union and would not willingly aid its enemies," but he was sorry that its liberal audience was being exposed to "a little clique of anti-Communists." This long and bitter hammering was similar to the lecture Hicks had read in 1934 to the New York *Times*'s "Red-baiting book review section." Perhaps he should have waited a week, for four days later Wilson reviewed in the *Nation* five publications dealing with the Stalin charges against Trotsky, and expressed the point-blank view that Trotsky was innocent as charged on all counts. It underlined Hicks's allegation, however; there was a serious disagreement between the editorial and book-review sections on the staff of the *Nation* when it came to the subject of the Stalin-Trotsky controversy.[191]

The Russo-German agreement of August, 1939 seemed to be a signal for publishers to open the flood-gates on books critical of Russia, Stalin and Communism, although the event meant nothing with respect to Germany since books even non-committal toward Hitler Germany since 1933 could have been counted on the fingers of one person's hands with fingers left over, and the *Pakt* simply insured the continuance of the previous implacability. For liberal well-wishers toward Stalin it was a literary tragedy, however. The release of Boris Souvarine's forcefully-critical *Stalin* was expertly timed, but its reviews in both liberal weeklies, by Schuman in the *New Republic* and by Hans Kohn in the *Nation,* were by men reluctant to part with their pleasant visions of the Russian dictator. Schuman's caustic essay revealed that he did not find a line in its 704 pages meeting with his approval, and he insisted on filing a brief in defense of the book's subject despite his own unhappiness over the scuttling of the Popular Front, the *Pakt,* and the Polish invasion: [192]

Stalin has read Machiavelli and has become the most astute diplomat of the century. His sole political interests are defense of the USSR and propagation of world revolt. The war between the bourgeois powers which he helped to precipitate will enhance the security of the Soviet Union and in its inevitable aftermath, promote social revolution. . . . Among contemporary leaders, the man in the Kremlin bids fair to be the only survivor.

Kohn did not take this bold tack, but sought to undermine Souvarine's reliability by telling the readers that the book was not well-documented. This aroused a curt reproof from Max Nomad, who suggested to Kohn in a letter to the editors of the *Nation* three weeks later that the reviewer see the readily-available original French edition, with its "26 large pages of sources in compact small type," [193] presumably enough to satisfy the most demanding academic critic.

As the period of the *Pakt* stretched into that of war, books unfriendly to the Soviet seemed to parallel the disastrous fortunes of the Anglo-French "Allies" against the Germans. Max Eastman's *Stalin's Russia and the Crisis in Socialism* and his *Marxism: Is It Science?* were features of the indictment of Russian collectivism in 1940, greeted with enthusiasm and approval by Abram Harris and Louis Hacker. Undoubtedly the behavior of the Communists in the past ten months had a considerable part to play in their major drop of prestige in the liberal press. The estimate of Harris, "What Eastman's book seems to show is that planning, socialist or otherwise, contains the seeds of totalitarianism," [194] would hardly have qualified for publication a year before, while Hacker's description of *Marxism* as "a brilliant analysis of the windy Teutonic metaphysics whose prisoner and victim Marx always was" not only signalled a stupendous turn-about by a man who had been hailed by liberals as the outstanding Marxist historian in America, but testified to the degree to which things German had sagged when the Germanic influences on Communism's key figure could be separated for specific disparagement.

Late in the summer of 1940 came Freda Utley's *The Dream We Lost,* the lead item in another series of disillusionist volumes by ex-Communists, written in a far darker vein than those which characterized the 1931–1937 period. Hers was an especially hard book for liberals to take, after having been brought up on two decades of an almost unbroken shout of approval of things Communist, especially her conviction that the Hitlerian system was milder than the Stalinist, and an easier one under which to live. Richard H. Rovere, newly-relapsed from the *New Masses* editorial staff and a reviewer of books on occasion for the *New Republic,* was quite repelled by this view, more so than Margaret Marshall in the *Nation.*[195] There was even an opportune moment to hark back to the flavor of the mid-20's and mention briefly the anarchist critique of G. P. Maximov, *The Guillotine at Work: Twenty Years of Terror in Russia,* which made all previous accounts of Soviet terrorism and blood-letting seem very tame by comparison.[196]

The scene was not entirely focussed on anti-Communism. Despite the increasingly war-committed sympathies of liberalism, and the consequently rising indignation at the Russian absence from the anti-Hitler coalition, a few books managed to appear which continued in the spirit of the pre-*Pakt* days or ignored that anything like it had ever occurred. Serge Chakotin's *The Rape of the Masses,* with its entire devotion to Hitler and Mussolini as creators of dictatorial systems, was a breath from 1935, while Hewlett Johnson's *The Soviet Power* was so massive a piece of praiseworthy apology that it could not be ignored. Freda Utley's January 6, 1941 *New Republic* review, "Dean in Cloud-Cuckoo Land," was about the most hostile review of a pro-Soviet book to be published in a liberal journal. It provoked a stream of angry letters from well-known friends of the Soviet who had not yet defected despite the events since August, 1939, and who had not been influenced by the liberal affection-transfer to Britain in its struggle for survival with Hitler Germany. When Isidor Schneider, Ella Winter and John A. Kingsbury wrote letters challenging the repeated Utley assertion that the National Socialist system was not as ruthless as the Communist, she shot back, "if Hitler had not been somewhat less ruthless than Stalin the world might be as ignorant of conditions in Germany as it is of the state of Russia; Stalin never let *his* victims out of the country to tell the tale whereas Hitler has allowed thousands of Jews, socialists and liberals *to* leave Germany." [197]

Jan Valtin's *Out of the Night* struck the right chord among the liberals in the post-*Pakt* era of 1939–1941, and prior to the involvement of Russia in the war. Its dark portrait of both Communist and National Socialist parties in Germany and their various intrigues suited the mood of hostility toward both, and favorable reviews in the *Nation* and *New Republic* in January 1941 by Wolfe and Franz Höllering excited an angry American Communist and fellow traveler assault. The *Nation* especially critized the *Daily Worker* for giving Valtin the "Schmelka Ginsberg treatment," a reference to Krivitsky, by alleging that the author was a fictitious person. They were able to poke fun at this charge because the Communist daily had once printed Valtin's picture. The *Nation* conducted a vigorous campaign to prevent Valtin from being deported back to Germany, but many liberals lived to take up the Communist charge that he was a liar, after June 22, 1941, when the Great Reconciliation set in.[198]

Several extremely unfriendly books just managed to be published and reviewed before the German invasion of Russia reversed the presses and started a strong flow of pro-Soviet books once more. Arthur Koestler's *Darkness at Noon,* memorializing the Moscow trials, obtained friendly reception in both liberal weeklies, although Cowley still could not bring himself to believe the citation of figures, even in a work disguised as fiction, of the Red slave labor camps and the mass deaths by starvation. Liberals in the main continued to reject these accounts, although they proved capable of believing similar charges against the Germans without the faintest reservation or doubt.

But the end was not yet in sight. Manya Gordon's *Workers Before and After Lenin* and Louis Fischer's autobiographical chronicle of miscalculation, *Men and Politics,* contributed especially damaging body-blows to the illusions about Communist Russia; they were the culmination of the sledge-hammer blows struck at rosy liberal views of Russia between 1919 and 1939. The Gordon account was one of the strongest, assaulting the Communist theory that Russia prior to 1917 was a hell, that no industry existed, and that the Stalinist era was tending to Utopia. Her thesis that the Russian worker had suffered a net loss over the years, plus the extirpation of his unions, once described by a *New Republic* editorial as the very essence of Fascism, and the conversion of them by the Russian State into speed-up agencies, was very disillusioning. Freda Utley's remarks in review, "There is no unemployment pay or poor relief in the Soviet Union," and "Unemployment is liquidated by the simple device of liquidating the unemployed," were harsh footnotes for a remarkable book, almost unbelievable for it to be reviewed in a liberal magazine.[199] A year later or two years earlier it would undoubtedly have been fortunate to escape being deposited in a trash-can.

Lewis Gannett and Cowley reviewed Fischer's *Men and Politics* in the second week of May, 1941. Their deep sympathy for the author's personal turmoil was unconcealed, Cowley's excuse being couched in especially articulate terms: [200]

> It is the story of the author as an individual, but it is also the collective tragedy of a whole order or type in Western civilization, composed of the men whose profession was handling ideas and whose aim as a group was to mold the future through good will and intelligence. In Russia, many of them were purged and the others became cynics. In the West, their moral position was weakened by the Russo-German pact, while their social position in the whole continent of Europe was destroyed by the German invasion. Wherever they are living today, even in their own homes they are exiles. The country for which they actually fought and from which they were driven was the future.

No finer tribute to the tenacity of the love for Communism and the stubborn refusal to admit the obvious was committed to print during this period of estrangement.

The June 23, 1941 issue of the *New Republic* contained the ultimate in the period of literary estrangement from the Communists, a harshly critical review of books written by John Strachey and Earl Browder by Louis Fischer. The titles, *A Faith to Live For,* and *The Way Out,* seemed to characterize the situation. The faith in Russia had been saved by the "way out," the German attack on the Soviet the day before. Again a matter of timing was the issue. Liberal abuse of Communist Russia came to an abrupt halt, and the exigencies of the war and the unpredictabilities of world politics ignited another period of almost limitless tribute.

MARXIST RESIDUES AND
THE FLUCTUATING FORTUNES
OF DOMESTIC COMMUNISM: A SUMMARY

As time goes by it grows more impressive that the greatest feat of propaganda in centuries has been the success of the Russian Communist movement in inducing large numbers of people in scores of nations to reject and spurn their own country and to devote themselves to the advancement of the security and comfort of the citizens of Russia. Nothing quite compares to the intense appeal of this campaign in bringing about such an amazing and fundamental alteration in what otherwise is assumed to be the expectable behavior in this age of national state groupings. Never had so many ostensible citizens of numerous states so bitterly attacked their own and so consistently defended every twist and turn of the policies of a national rival. It will puzzle people for a long time.

The success of the "anti-Fascist" program of the 1930s must start here, with an understanding that basic to it all was the establishment of the thesis that anything proclaiming itself "anti-Fascist" was ipso facto "democratic" and beyond the faintest question. Hence evolved the practice of never identifying Communists as anything but "anti-Fascists" unless forced to do so. The corollary to this was the parallel thesis posed to the non-Communists to accept, that Communism and Fascism represented the really fundamental choices which had to be made ultimately, drawn up as the images of Light and Dark. Once these two approaches had become internalized, everything that followed was self-explanatory. "Anti-Fascism" without its complement of full devotion to Communism would have meant little to liberal and radical opinion-makers, and they would hardly have risen to their heights of vituperative condemnation of Fascism with just sympathy and support for Franco-British continental and colonial aims as motivation. There simply was not enough steam left in this feeble business, especially after all that had been done to deflate them after the First World War.

As the Popular Front ballooned, beginning in 1935, the "anti-Fascist" and "anti-Nazi" programs reflected the same sort of growth health. At its height even the liberal weeklies, as we have seen, preferred to place little emphasis on "liberal" to the advantage of "progressive" as a correct label for their new stance. For the tendencies in the country which still persisted in criticizing Communism and pointing out Communists, there developed as a counterthrust one of the most effective political blackmail terms of the century, "Red-baiting." There was no opposite to this term in the Popular Front period, and in essence there never has been one. Liberals adopted it generally, even though a few began to suffer from twinges of pain over it after 1937 and began to think that maybe there was something for which Communists might be "baited," though these individuals were a minority. Frederick Schuman's comprehensive attack on the Hearst press in an April, 1935 article in the *New Republic* for its pursuit of him for his consistent pro-Soviet public positions was one of the most eloquent statements incorporating both the "anti-Nazi" and "Red-baiting" slogans, the first designating his approach and the latter that of the Hearst organization.[201] The same month the same journal devoted an entire page to a Cowley review of a Communist pamphlet costing two cents, which consisted of the posing of Communist as against liberal views in the context of an interview between Stalin and H. G. Wells. It was intended not only to help give circulation to views prevailing in "the socialist state that exists in a sixth of the world," but to give substance to the journal's own change of heart in this era and its reluctance to stand as a liberal interpreter.[202]

Some idea of the confusion this produced could be seen from parallel stories dealing with Granville Hicks in the June 12, 1935 *New Republic* on the occasion of his dismissal from his position at Rensselaer Polytechnic Institute; one column identified him as "an editor of the *New Masses* and an avowed Communist," while in the adjoining one he was "a Communist sympathizer who has never yet been accused of propagandizing in his classes." [203] This lapse was not common; the word "Communist" was not used by either liberal weekly in the Popular Front period if "democratic" or "revolutionary" or "anti-Fascist" could possibly be substituted. One of the outstanding examples was that of the Brazilian Communist Party leader Luis Carlos Prestes, identified by such terms or as "the great leader of the movement for liberation" throughout the pre-Pearl Harbor decade.[204] Even at the very height of the furious contest over the Moscow trials and Trotsky, hesitance to identify non-Russian Communists as such was evident among editors and contributors alike. The *Pakt* had a limited effect on this disposition.

As has been seen, it was late in the prewar decade before the liberals could bear to compare Hitlerism and Stalinism in any sense except as polar opposites, and then only in a modified and hesitant manner. As rival self-elected elites, American liberals had not the inclination or basic orientation to conceive of them; the Communist and Fascist personalities were different in kind, which was a corollary of the definitions of Fascism and Communism which circulated among liberals in the era of maximum affection toward the latter. Peter Odegard, reviewing the symposium *Dictatorship in the Modern World* edited by Guy Stanton Ford, in the *Nation* on March 18, 1936 gave an extended exposition of the distinction again, as supplied by Hans Kohn in his portion of the symposium, "Communist and Fascist Dictatorships: A Comparative Study"; [205]

The similarity in method of Fascist and Communist dictatorships has tended to obscure the fundamental contrasts in origin and purpose which they embody. Both, it is true, are for the moment anti-democratic. But the Communist's opposition is based on the identification of contemporary democracy with monopoly capitalism, whereas the Fascist assault is based on the assumption that democracy is but the advance agent of equalitarian socialism. Communism is secular, scientific and pragmatic; and in theory, at least, represents the logical culmination of the democratic principles of liberty and equality. The recent liberalization of election methods in Russia and the relaxation of repressive measures are cited as evidence of the essentially democratic purpose of the Communist regime. Moreover, Communism is internationalist in outlook. Fascist dictatorship is charismatic, nationalistic and permanent. It represents a philosophy of regimentation and inequality as the enduring principle of social organization.

Kohn's was about the last major definition in the classic form which evolved in the depression years, and came unfortunately just before the eruption of the 1936 series of Moscow trials. Reservations and hedging grew with liberal unhappiness over Russian affairs. When Norman Thomas reviewed Earl Browder's *What Is Communism?* in the *New Republic* just about at the conclusion of the Ethiopian war, he was quite blunt in sizing Browder up as a nationalist because he was loyal to the national goals of Russia.[206] But hostile definitions of Communism as such made no headway for some time, nor were they accepted among liberals in general. In the *New Republic* the views of persons unfriendly to Communism were frequently treated as humor in a column headed "The Bandwagon." The assumption seemed to be that only those friendly to Communism deserved respect when defining it, whereas Fascism and other systems were best defined by their firmest enemies. The *New Republic* also took a split-personality approach to the subject of Fascist, National Socialist and Communist activities in the United States. It admitted in a major editorial in September, 1937, "Italy and Germany in America," that there were no more than 20,000 members in Fascist groups and "bunds" in the entire country, but denounced the idea that they were insignificant for the reason of fewness. On the other hand, the Communist Party, though very much larger, was considered no threat because of its small size, and the editors insisted that it was entirely supported by funds of American origin, while the German and Italian sympathizers were supposedly all financed from overseas.[207] This was a significant aspect of the ideological stacking which made one variant of the totalitarian world appear to be an appealing order but its apparent rivals the most unspeakable form of human society ever devised. But beginning in 1938, some of the wind currents in American liberalism began to shift slightly. Calvin B. Hoover's *Dictators and Democracies,* one of the very first volumes to deal with the similarities rather than the differences of the Italian, German and Russian systems, received a favorable *Nation* review at the hands of Abram Harris.[208] Stray liberal heretics began to advance the view that the Fascist regimes were actually middle-class anticapitalist dictatorships, and no longer the product of reactionary billionairies trying to stave off the collapse of their world. Later in the year, when liberal book reviewers, far more enchanted by Trotsky than by the ruling regime in Russia, began to refer to the latter's American partisans as "Stalinoids," the emergence of a realistic view of domestic Communism took place simultaneously.

The persistent signs of growing liberal coolness toward the American Communists by mid-1938 were not only a product of the grinding controversy over the relative qualities of Stalinism and Trotskyism and the second thoughts on the purges, but also due in part to the persistent attacks on the two liberal weeklies in the *New Masses* and *Daily Worker,* as well as the *New Republic's* private skirmish with Browder over the merits of collective security. The 1938 Communist Party convention ignited a wave of anti-Communist bitterness for a few months. *Common Sense* commented satirically, "Wrapped in the American flag so tightly the hammer and sickle were practically invisible, the Communist Party staged one of its most impressive national conventions, to the tune of *Yankee Doodle.*" [209] The *New Republic's* response to this event was an editorial "The New Communist Line," which expressed the same kind of puzzlement at the absence of avowals to produce socialism, the patriotic talk and the testimonials to the memory of Jefferson, Paine, Jackson, Lincoln, the Declaration of Independence and the Constitution.[210] Suspicion that something was afoot could not be suppressed, although there was no willingness to accept Max Eastman's torrid attack on the Party as a secret society taking its orders on all vital questions from a foreign dictator and differing little from the Hitler and Mussolini regimes, with their "same vaguely intended proletarian and socialistic ideals the Communists use." The *New Republic,* even yet revolted at the idea of speaking of them in the same breath, was still convinced the Communist Party was "on the side of democracy," and cited its fighting for civil liberties, union principles and social legislation, although it did not discuss the Party's attitude toward such subjects in Soviet Russia. The junior liberal weekly persisted in thinking it could take the Communists or leave them, depending on their day-to-day behavior, despite this new wave of temporary objectivity toward them. Both weeklies were caught in a crossfire of Communist criticism in the summer of 1938, growing out of this suspicion toward the Party's new line and a review of Browder's latest book, *The People's Front.* The *Nation's* editorial response was especially spirited in rejecting Communist charges that they were "aiding the enemy and disunity" by their criticism; it was the liberal conviction that "anti-Fascists" of non-Communist discipline had every right to criticize the Communist Party without abuse from Party leaders or rank and file. In the meantime, the Communists continued their praises of American traditional objects of veneration, while seeking to find some common ground to unite the United States and the Soviet Union, to the discomfiture of many liberals.

On the opposite side of the critical line, the liberals championed the Communists and defended them in particular against the charges of the Dies Committee. In its vehement denunciation of this investigatory body, the *New Republic* on August 31, 1938, utterly rejected the idea that the Communists were of the slightest danger to the country, insisting that "the Communists today are not acting as a revolutionary group; they are so committed to the policy of cooperation with all democratic forces that one can hardly tell them from the New Deal Democrats." [211] To this degree the new Communist affection for patriotic symbolic gestures had paid substantial public relations dividends. It seemed exceedingly difficult to detect where this new position dove-tailed with the current interests of the Soviet Union, thus it was thought best to act as if there was no relation between them at this moment. At the same time, liberal journalism had no difficulty in taking on the Communist press characteristic of imputing the most sinister sort of motives to political opponents, especially rightists, universally referred to as "fifth column" groups, when the term became popularized after emerging from the context of Spanish Civil War politics.[212]

From 1937 on there was a distinct liberal "revisionist" attempt to tailor Marxism to the liberal views of the day, in an effort to rub off the more unpalatable features, which were considered of great damage as a consequence of widespread publicity to Russian operational realities. Some reference has been made to the ultimate fate of this attempt in connection with the disillusionment with Russia. Max Lerner was the first and perhaps the most articulate of this liberal adaptationist element, but his efforts were not especially welcomed by Communists or the pro-Communist press. A substantial piece of his in the *Nation* late in 1938 titled "Six Errors of Marxism," was replied to in the *New Masses* by A. B. Magil on December 6 in a retort titled "Six Errors of Max Lerner." It was an airy dismissal of Lerner as a confused but well-wishing friend of Marxism despite his "superficial generalizations"; "Marxists would certainly welcome greater intellectual vigor and circumspection in their critics," Magil sniffed. When Lerner's *It Is Later Than You Think* appeared shortly thereafter, Magil pursued this as well, categorizing it as "an attempt to fuse Marxism with the ideology of middle-class liberalism," and was still piqued at what he interpreted as Lerner's "inverted type of Red-baiting," while taking comfort in his call for "an uncompromising struggle versus Fascism." Paul Sweezy followed the path of Magil in his review of Lerner's *Ideas Are Weapons* later in the year, after the war had begun. Although a collection of more than 60 smaller pieces Lerner had written since 1930, Sweezy detected a "unity to the whole" which was a product of the author's "method and point of view," "in its fundamental outlines, clearly Marxian." But Sweezy hastened to point out that Lerner was not a "faithful follower" or even a close student of Marx; it was "a kind of generalized Marxism," blended with liberalism, and thought that its "typically liberal wishful thinking" undermined its otherwise serious contribution.[213]

The effort of Lerner and others to bridge over the widening split among the orthodox Marxists of Communist persuasion and the liberals was not successful. The camps took up their defenses within liberal ranks, and either supported such statements as Harold Laski's "Why I am a Marxist," in the January 14, 1939 *Nation* [214] or tended to veer over to such views as *Common Sense* advanced in a six-column editorial in the autumn of 1938, "Marx Over Europe." This scathing attack began with the statement, "It is our belief that a major reason for the sorry pass in which Europe and the world now find themselves is due to the continuing intellectual prestige of the myths preached by Marx," and fastened that down with the delineating observation that "The advance guard of human thought is everywhere weighed down with useless Marxist baggage." *Common Sense* took special care to point out that [215]

> To a greater extent than perhaps realized, the best liberal and progressive minds, even in America, base their thinking on assumptions derived from the 90-year-old Marxist doctrines. For example, the only intelligent weeklies of opinion in America, the *Nation* and the *New Republic*, are unable to escape from the assumption that the working class is by nature the only true progressive class.

This memorable defection from the liberal front on Marxism assaulted it as unable to explain the business cycle, called its two-class orientation mere nonsense, and its economics and its claim to "science" no more than philosophical mumbo jumbo; "Its strength, like that of Fascism or any other myth, is emotional." But it was not brushed off as inconsequential; *Common Sense* admitted it occupied a most dangerous vantage point in international affairs, where Marxians were posing "the false issue and unreal slogan of 'Fascism versus democracy'":

> The vested interests of France and England will fight for their empires while the liberals, under the Marxist influence, will back them up, against the overwhelming instinct of the mass of the people. How can democracy be an issue, when it is the Soviet dictatorship that opposes the Fascist dictatorship, and capitalist imperialism in the democratic states that opposes Fascist imperialism? But the liberals have been persuaded that the Soviet dictatorship is a dictatorship of the working class (which has a "historic" mission) while the Fascist dictatorships are of the capitalist class and therefore represent the forces of sin or evil (or "night" as Strachey puts it in his *What Are We To Do?*, a wholly religious book.)

The concluding salute was as uncomfortable a verdict as any handed down by a liberal periodical in the pre-war period; "The Hitler myths of blood and soil are obvious monstrosities but the delusions of Marx may perhaps be no less a peril to the happiness of mankind."

The rejection of Marxism gained ground after the *Pakt* and the outbreak of war, but the issue of domestic Communism stayed in a front-running position. Communists continued to be "anti-Fascists" in the 1939–1941 period, for although an understanding existed between Hitler and Stalin, there was no evidence from any Communist or fellow-traveler publication that American Communists favored a Hitler victory. Furthermore, some Communists kept fighting even though most of those in Europe were not doing so. Russia might have pacts with Germany and Japan, but Chinese Communists were still at war, and presumably were receiving Russian supplies during this period. Thus the American liberals were seriously torn on the Communist issue, attacking and defending the Communists on the basis of their checkered war behavior.

On the home front the situation was not less racking. The *New Republic* became especially disturbed when the prominent Socialist lawyer and American Labor Party figure, Louis Waldman, refused to take part in an American Civil Liberties Union conference on civil liberties because some of the cooperating organizations were in his estimate "Communist fronts." The journal editorially tried to salve the situation, urged attendance anyway, and pleaded for faith in the "democratic process" while urging voting down those "whose hearts are in Moscow, not in the United States." But in the following five months neither of the liberal weeklies wanted any part of the Dies Committee investigation. The *New Republic* early in November, 1939 grew especially angry at the Committee's naming of the American League for Peace and Democracy (*né* American League Against War and Fascism) as a Communist front, and especially the listing of all its members.[216] This was in a way a fitting climax to the pacifist movement of 1931–1939 and its gradual blending of all good and bad wars as a result of the contact with the determining Red line. Editorials and comments describing this as a "witch hunt" and a "Red hunt" continued for weeks, and one particularly naïve inversion of the situation by the *New Republic* political columnist "T.R.B." was memorable: [217]

The popular front movement of the last four years produced a great and largely hopeful change in the political temper of the country. It carried liberalism to social and geographical groups that never before had been touched by it. Because most popular front organizations admitted Communists to membership, we must now consider whether this movement is to be swept away.

This was an interpretation of an "innocent club" which must have produced broad smiles on the face of every Communist leader in the western hemisphere.

The *Nation* was no less vigorous and energetic in condemning all suggestions of investigating Communist activities, despite its eager support of all similar proposals of inquiries of the nature of various "shirt" and "bund" groups alleged to be more than friendly with the German or Italian regimes. On February 24, 1940, a *Nation* editorial lauded Attorney General Robert H. Jackson for dismissing an indictment against sixteen persons charged with recruiting soldiers for service with the Communists in the late-lamented Spanish war, which had followed a raid on the New York City headquarters of the Abraham Lincoln Brigade.[218] It was rather late in the season for denying Communist involvement in this venture, what with all the admissions by the disenchanted, whatever may have been the innocence of the individual soldiers fighting in the Spanish front lines in believing that their fighting participation was in a crusade of cosmic purity against the unspeakable horrors of Fascism. But there was a slightly hypocritical touch to the Roosevelt Justice Department attacking the Communists in 1940 for having recruited Americans for foreign service, when sympathizers with England were encouraging American pilots to enlist for service in the British and Canadian air forces at the same time. Frowns for "recruiting for a foreign army" did not apply here.

But what Eastman had once labeled as liberalism's "split-libido" on American Communism continued. Closely related but now relapsed associates such as Wechsler and Rovere essayed in the liberal weeklies as experts on the subject, wrote mild but querulous pieces expressing mystification at the persistence of the movement in membership strength, but indicated they had acquired little wisdom through their years of contacts. When Wechsler expressed wonderment in the *Nation* at how a Communist-sponsored rally was able to draw 20,000 attendants to Madison Square Garden in New York City shortly after the Second World War had begun, Norman Thomas essayed at illuminating the scene for him in a letter to the editors a short while later: [219]

Under the line which made them a kind of left wing of the New Deal, Communists have been far more successful than the general public realizes in placing their people in jobs in various organizations—in white collar projects of the WPA and even in the Civil Service. By ways I cannot stop to describe they have managed to maintain a high degree of job control. Part but not all the explanation of the 20,000 people at Madison Square Garden is to be found in this job control.

Charity continued to be the major liberal virtue toward the Communists despite occasional sallies of this sort, which of course did not have official editorial espousal despite their publication. It was complicated by a generous measure of confusion. The mixed reception accorded Ben Gitlow's *I Confess: The Truth About American Communism* underlined this. Rovere hailed it in the January 29, 1940 *New Republic* as "one of the few intelligent critical essays on American Communism," but Robert Bendiner in the *Nation* two months later could not resist comprehensive unkindness toward Gitlow as much as toward the Communists.[220]

The *Nation*'s rage at Dies for his persistence in working away at the thesis of Communists in federal government employment did not slack. Even when so notable a leftist as Thomas boldly charged the same, and openly credited the effectiveness of the Communist bosses over the federal jobholders in their patronage ring with being responsible for the discipline still persisting in spite of opposition to the Roosevelt Administration's foreign policy, it did not impress them very much.[221] In November, 1940 it ran a vitriolic review of Dies's *The Trojan Horse in America* by Wechsler, now a labor reporter for the new leftist daily newspaper PM in New York City. Wechsler favored an investigation of the Dies Committee. The *New Republic* was no less repelled by the Dies Committee investigation of Communists. An editorial on December 9, 1940, expressed the fervent hope that Congress would abandon it soon.[222] Two weeks before a *Nation* editorial hoped that the wife of Earl Browder would be permitted to depart voluntarily from the country, upon the charge that she had entered the country illegally. On this occasion it remarked that the Attorney-General was unable to suspend the deportation of aliens belonging to organizations "advocating overthrow of the government by force," but the *Nation* quietly interposed, "Whether the Communist Party is such an organization has not yet been decided upon by the Supreme Court." [223] With the war going the way it was, and in view of the Communist Party position on it, a verdict more kindly than this could hardly have been expected. Nor were the liberal weeklies so estranged from domestic Communism as to deny it the advantages of their circulation for advertising purposes. The November 18, 1940, *New Republic* carried a halfpage ad soliciting subscriptions to the *Daily Worker,* and the entire back cover of its issue of February 17, 1941, announced the coming 30th anniversary issue of the *New Masses.*

By this time the war in Europe had overshadowed all other considerations by a wide margin, and liberal attitudes toward Communism in the United States hinged more directly on this fact than all other previous and sustaining issues combined. When the hysteria attending the easy Hitler triumph in June, 1940,[224] swept American liberals along as well as all other elements in the country not credited with as much intellectual stamina, the Communists had been subjected to intense and exaggerated castigation. Their cries of "warmonger" at the British and French, their opposition to American help to either, their bitter antagonism toward the Roosevelt "defense" program and their refusal to consider the Hitlerian victory as any kind of physical threat to the United States drew heated liberal reproach.[225] Their continuation along this course into the early months of 1941, with the National Committee of the CPUSA issuing probably the strongest denunciation of the Lend-Lease proposal in its January 23, 1941, broadside in the *Communist*, "Defeat Roosevelt's War-Powers Bill! Get Out and Stay Out Of War!" and the *New Masses'* corrosive full-page boxed editorial "This Criminal War" in their thirtieth anniversary number on February 19, did not elevate their esteem among the liberal weeklies, now both solidly committed to seeing the United States involved.[226] But the gravitational pull of the past ten years was far too strong to allow a comprehensive rejection of the Communists.

This was vividly illustrated in their reviews and comments on the publication of the scorching volume by Eugene Lyons, *The Red Decade*. Niebuhr reviewed it in the *Nation* in September, while the book was considered so important by the *New Republic* that it was reviewed as an editorial by Bliven, one of the few times a book had been so treated in the previous two decades. Niebuhr, now disenchanted with the Communists, largely approved of Lyons' severe indictment but he bridled in hostility at Lyons' charge that the liberal weeklies had clung to an intimate Soviet orientation until the *Pakt;* "I have the evidence in my files," he shouted back, "that the *Nation* was publishing reams of criticism of Stalinism in a period in which Lyons accuses it of being completely compliant." Having joined the editorial staff that week, Niebuhr apparently felt that the challenge was sufficiently grave to call forth hyperbole of this sort.[227]

Bliven, in an agitated five-column review, though he did not feel impelled to essay a defenseless tack such as Niebuhr's, in his turn tried to defend his journal against charges of pro-Communism as well. But he did make a point that Lyons had not dealt sufficiently with the *New Republic* in its cooling-off period in the past eighteen months. It was worth noting that he did not fall back on a much-repeated point of the past, his distinguishing the *New Republic* and the Communists on the issue of collective security, since from the previous fall the *New Republic* had gone over to it while the Communists had rejected it. And he overstressed the domestic policies on which the Communists and the *New Republic* had been in accord.[228] But what both reviewers shied away from was the towering pile of material in both weeklies which in the past ten years had been written in consistent praise of and in sympathy for Soviet Russia as a foreign state. In terms of gross weight it surely would have outweighed Niebuhr's "reams" of criticism. What tended to detract from the full impact of such a book as Lyons' *Red Decade* was that, with the German invasion of Russia already a three-month-old fact, a new help-Russia crusade was already under way, and the ideological and intellectual carpenters were already on the scene beginning the foundations of a new "Red Decade," which was to make the one just ended seem like little more than a weak prologue. The previous decade of harmony with the Comintern made the return of American liberals to support of the cause of Communist Russia mostly effortless: the transition was as easy and painless as participation had been in the pre-*Pakt* years.

One may speculate on what might have transpired had not the Comintern built such an incandescent hate of Hitler in the hearts and minds of its brilliant literary sympathizers in America. It is obvious that without this psychological baggage they might have adopted a more detached view toward European totalitarian systems, one which might have been far more beneficial to the advancement of United States interests, in the long run. The emotional declarations of war on the part of the liberal intellectuals years before the actual shooting began must be associated with the resumption of the road to war by the United States. The opposite side of this foreign affairs coin is the liberal position on Germany, which the examination of the liberal stand on Russia and Communism now makes essential to an understanding of the whole in its proper ideological and political context.

NOTES

1 *Nation,* July 3, 1935, p. 2.
2 *Nation,* July 10, 1935, p. 35.
3 *New Republic,* August 7, 1935, pp. 354–355.
4 *Nation,* October 9, 1935, p. 394; Kunitz in *New Masses,* November 26, 1935, pp. 12–14.
5 *Nation,* October 9, 1935, p. 394.
6 Soule, "Europe: Four Expectations," *New Republic,* November 13, 1935, pp. 7–9. The first of Soule's articles in the "Does Socialism Work?" series was sub-titled "How People Live In the Soviet Union," *New Republic,* February 5, 1936, pp. 356–359. Soule's collected articles sold as a pamphlet for 25¢, and the editors advised the readers that it contained "forthright and sound information."
7 *Common Sense,* December, 1935, p. 5.
8 *New Republic,* November 27, 1935, p. 78.
9 *Nation,* May 1, 1935, pp. 506–508.
10 *New Republic,* May 29, 1935, p. 110.
11 The Soviet Travel Division's advertisement in the *New Republic* for May 13, 1936, p. 26, read "Visit Soviet Russia with Joshua Kunitz." The price was announced as $469. The separate Soviet tours described by Rothschild in *Nation,* April 29, 1936, pp. 562–563.
12 The *Nation* carried advertisements between April 22 and June 10, 1936 to the effect that a tour of Russia for five weeks under Fischer's direction would leave New

York on July 7. But Fischer remained in Russia until "early September," and on October 8, 1936, wrote to the *Nation*, his piece datelined Madrid.

13   See for example advertisement in *New Republic*, May 19, 1937, p. 56.

14   The tourist class price of this trip was listed as $614.

15   See advertisement in *Nation*, July 1, 1939, p. 28.

16   Intourist advertisement in *Nation*, February 26, 1936, p. 251.

17   Rodman review in *Common Sense*, July, 1935, pp. 27–28; Lovett review in *New Republic*, August 14, 1935, p. 24. Joseph Freeman, reviewing the book in the *Communist*, August, 1935, pp. 777–784, declared, "A combination of Marxist intellectual discipline with a lyric gift has imparted to Joshua Kunitz's study of Soviet Asia unique literary qualities." Only *Common Sense* identified Kunitz as an editor of the *New Masses*.

18   Kisch's book was actually published first in Germany in 1932. Strong review in *New Republic*, May 8, 1935, pp. 374–375; Stewart review in *Nation*, April 10, 1935, pp. 424–425.

19   *New Republic*, February 9, 1938, p. 27.

20   Advertisement in *New Republic*, December 11, 1935, p. 145; Seaver review of Gorky in *New Republic*, June 24, 1936, p. 214.

21   Adamic review in *Nation*, December 5, 1934, p. 655; Simpson review in *New Republic*, January 15, 1936, p. 291; *Nation* editorial January 16, 1935, p. 59.

22   See for example Kunitz, "Jews In the Soviet Union," *New Masses*, August 28, 1934, pp. 19–21; editorial "On the Communist Approach To Zionism," *Communist*, July, 1936, pp. 666–670.

23   *Nation*, August 28, 1935, p. 231.

24   *Nation*, October 9, 1935, p. 409.

25   *Nation*, February 5, 1936, p. 143.

26   See especially James Waterman Wise, "Are All Jews Communists?," *New Masses*, October 29, 1935, p. 10, a bitter attack on the American Jewish Committee, B'nai Br'ith and the Jewish Labor Committee for a statement denying Jewish affiliation with Communism and charging Communism with being also the foe of Judaism and the Jews in general. The *New Masses* sometimes referred to the New York *Post* as "the English edition of the *Jewish Daily Forward*," because its staff included several Jewish Social Democrats who wrote hostile stories about the Communists.

27   Porter Niles, "Pogrom In September," *New Masses*, September, 1936, pp. 8–10; MacDonald, "Spivak vs. Superspivak," *Common Sense*, April, 1936, p. 24; Schuman review in *Nation*, June 27, 1936, pp. 849–850.

28   "Soviet Democracy," *Nation*, June 17, 1936, pp. 761–762.

29   Fischer, "The New Soviet Constitution," *Nation*, June 17, 1936, pp. 772–774.

30   *Nation*, August 1, 1936, pp. 139–140.

31   *New Republic*, June 24, 1936, p. 187.

32   *New Republic*, December 9, 1936, pp. 160–161.

33   *Nation*, November 21, 1936, pp. 596–598.

34   "Russia and the World," *Nation*, November 13, 1937, p. 521.

35   Stewart, "Twenty Years Of Progress," *Nation*, November 13, 1937, pp. 523–527. There were occasional criticisms of internal social affairs to be seen in the *Nation*. Alice Withrow Field's "Prostitution In the Soviet Union," in the issue for March 25, 1936, began naïvely, "It comes as something of a shock to many persons to learn that the Soviet Union has not yet succeeded in eliminating one of the grossest forms of human exploitation—the prostitution of women's bodies" (pp. 373–374), while Fischer in his "The New Soviet Abortion Law," on July 18, 1936, pp. 65–67, slashed out, "The new Soviet law of June 27, 1936 on abortions, divorces, alimony, and so on, is a blot on Moscow's inspiring record for advanced social legislation." The editorial for August 1, 1936, p. 114, referred to this law reluctantly as "class legislation," and commented that the prohibitive cost had reduced the number of divorces 90% in 20 days.

36   See his "U.S.S.R. In 1936," *Nation*, October 10, 1936, pp. 412–414, datelined "Kiev, early September."

37   *New Republic*, January 25, 1939, pp. 326–327.

38   *New Republic*, February 8, 1939, p. 3.

39   *Nation*, February 11, 1939, p. 163.

40 "Young Man Showing His Muscles," *New Republic*, May 31, 1939, p. 87.

41 *Nation*, December 21, 1940, pp. 631–633.

42 *Nation*, July 11, 1936, p. 31.

43 Milton Howard, reviewing Wilson's *Travel In Two Democracies* in the *New Masses*, September 1, 1936, pp. 23–25, quoted Wilson as saying of Russia, "Here you are at the moral top of the world, where the light never goes out."

44 Published in *Nation*, February 20, 1937, pp. 210–211.

45 *New Republic*, January 20, 1937, pp. 348–350. But Cowley admitted he was in agreement with Wilson in his principal conclusions.

46 Fischer, "Soviet Democracy: Second View," *Nation*, August 22, 1936, pp. 205–207.

47 " 'Old Bolsheviks' On Trial," *Nation*, August 22, 1936, p. 201.

48 *New Republic*, August 26, 1936, p. 58.

49 "The Moscow Trials," *Nation*, October 10, 1936, p. 409; *New Masses*, December 22, 1936, p. 20.

50 *Nation*, January 30, 1937, p. 114.

51 "Another Russian Trial," *New Republic*, February 3, 1937, pp. 399–400. "It seems to us that the weight of the evidence supports Mr. Duranty's view—that the confessions are true."

52 *New Republic*, February 17, 1937, p. 51.

53 "Behind the Soviet Trials," *Nation*, February 6, 1937, p. 143.

54 *Nation*, February 6, 1937, p. 147.

55 Reviews in *Nation*, April 10, 1937, pp. 401–406.

56 *New Republic*, February 17, 1937, pp. 33–34.

57 *New Republic*, March 31, 1937, p. 242.

58 Thomas, in a letter to the *New Republic*, February 24, 1937, p. 75, had regarded the Soviet Union as "a mighty bulwark against Fascist aggression." See also list of liberal sympathizers with Trotsky in *New Republic*, March 17, 1937, p. 169.

59 *New Republic*, April 7, 1937, pp. 267–270, for citations in two paragraphs below.

60 MacDonald in *New Republic*, May 19, 1937, pp. 49–50; Hook in *New Republic*, June 2, 1937, p. 104.

61 Frank was deeply involved in Communist politics in the fall of 1936–1937. He was listed by the *Nation* as chairman of a Henri Barbusse Memorial Committee meeting sponsoring an anti-Hitler address by Ernst Toller at Mecca Temple the last week of October, and a speaker, along with Joseph Freeman and Elizabeth Gurley Flynn at a Professional Groups for Browder and Ford meeting at Edison Hotel, at which Rockwell Kent was chairman, the same week. Early in January, 1937 he was chairman of the "American Society for Technical Aid to Spanish Democracy," an organization of which John Howard Lawson was secretary and Earl Browder treasurer, and professedly engaged in enlisting skilled workmen to work behind the Loyalist lines. *Nation*, October 14, 1936, 501; January 16, 1937, p. 81.

62 Frank's letter in *New Masses*, May 25, 1937.

63 Niebuhr's letter in *New Republic*, June 9, 1937, p. 132. Browder's letter attacking Frank was in the issue for May 26.

64 *New Republic*, May 19, 1937, pp. 33–34.

65 *Nation*, June 19, 1937, p. 714.

66 *Nation*, June 26, 1937, p. 741.

67 *Nation*, June 19, 1937, p. 691.

68 *New Republic*, June 23, 1937, p. 174.

69 *New Republic*, June 23, 1937, p. 201.

70 Duranty, "The Riddle Of Russia," *New Republic*, July 14, 1937, pp. 270–271.

71 *New Republic*, July 7, 1937, p. 253.

72 Villard's column in *Nation*, July 10, 1937, p. 46; Marzani's letter published in *Nation*, August 21, 1937, pp. 206–207.

73 Fischer, "Russia—Twenty-two Years After," *Nation*, February 10, 1940, pp. 182–186.

74 *New Republic*, July 28, 1937, pp. 323–325.

75 The exchange between Morrow and the editors was published in the issue for November 10, 1937.

76 *New Republic*, December 29, 1937, p. 210.

77 "USSR and USA," *Common Sense*, October, 1937, pp. 3–5.

78 *New Republic,* March 9, 1938, p. 117.
79 "Russian Tragedy, Act III," *Nation,* March 12, 1938, pp. 287–288.
80 *Nation,* March 12, 1938, p. 302.
81 "Moscow Loses Caste," *New Republic,* March 16, 1938, pp. 151–152.
82 *New Republic,* March 30, 1938, p. 216–217.
83 The *New Masses* attack was titled "The Editorial Jitters," published in the issue of March 22, 1938, p. 10; Bliven's letter in *New Masses,* April 12, 1938, p. 19.
84 *New Masses,* May 3, 1938, p. 19.
85 *New Republic,* May 18, 1938, pp. 50–51. Strangely enough, Cowley confessed to being much frightened by the reports of the condemned, and declared that "one lesson of these trials" was "a new respect and affection for the political virtues of the old-fashioned liberals." See also "Moscow Trial: II," *New Republic,* May 25, 1938, p. 81.
86 Pro-Stalin readers of the *New Republic* roasted Bliven for some time after his famous open letter, and some of their letters were published; see especially the aggravated ones in the issues for April 13, 1938, pp. 306–307 and April 27, 1938, pp. 361–362.
87 Stewart, "Progress and Purges In Soviet Russia," *Nation,* September 17, 1938, pp. 265–267.
88 Niebuhr, "Russia and Karl Marx," *Nation,* May 7, 1938, pp. 530–531; *Nation,* July 30, 1938, pp. 112–113. In his May 7 article, Niebuhr said, "in the opinion of the present writer Marxism is an essentially correct theory and analysis of the economic realities of modern society. It is correct in its analysis of the unavoidable conflict between owners and workers in an industrial society, correct in regarding private ownership of the means of production as the basic cause of periodic crises and technological unemployment, and correct in its insistence that the communal ownership of the productive process is a basic condition of social health in a technical age."
89 *New Masses,* December 27, 1938, p. 12.
90 *New Masses,* January 17, 1939, p. 26. The attack on Silone was headed "Deserter's Plea."
91 "Slamming the Door On Russia," *Nation,* February 13, 1935, p. 173.
92 Fischer, "The Soviet-American Break," *Nation,* April 3, 1935, p. 385.
93 *Nation,* May 15, 1935, p. 559.
94 *Nation,* May 29, 1935, p. 615.
95 Fischer, "The Franco-Soviet Alliance," *Nation,* June 19, 1935, pp. 704–705.
96 *New Masses,* April 2, 1935, p. 9.
97 "The Peace Policies Of Moscow," *New Masses,* August 13, 1935, pp. 6–7. Browder's comment on the Franco-Soviet pact in *New Masses,* June 4, 1935, p. 20.
98 *New Republic,* August 7, 1935, p. 345.
99 "USA vs USSR," *New Republic,* September 11, 1935, pp. 116–117.
100 *Nation,* August 7, 1935, p. 145.
101 *Common Sense,* September, 1935, p. 6.
102 *Common Sense,* December, 1935, pp. 6–8.
103 Compare especially with Peffer's statement in *Harper's,* June, 1936, pp. 31–32; see Chapter 18, note 73. Dimitroff's statement in article "What Is the People's Front?," *New Masses,* May 26, 1936, pp. 9–11.
104 *Nation,* April 8, 1936, pp. 442–444.
105 *Nation,* December 11, 1937, pp. 643–645.
106 Hacker review in *Nation,* April 22, 1936, pp. 527–528.
107 Niebuhr review in *Nation,* February 26, 1938, pp. 247–249. See also letter from Theodore Brameld to *Nation,* March 12, 1938, pp. 311–312, attacking Niebuhr for charging that Browder and the new Communist Party line deviated from Marx, Lenin and Popular Front tactics.
108 *New Republic,* June 23, 1937, p. 201.
109 *New Republic,* September 2, 1936, p. 87; *New Masses,* December 20, 1938, p. 9.
110 *Nation,* September 5, 1936, pp. 268–270.
111 *New Republic,* October 21, 1936, pp. 295–296.
112 *New Republic,* November 18, 1936, p. 68.
113 *Common Sense,* February, 1937, p. 5.
114 *New Republic,* September 29, 1937, pp. 204–206.
115 *New Republic,* August 10, 1938, p. 4.

116 "Russia and the World," *Nation*, November 13, 1937, p. 521.
117 *Nation*, July 2, 1938, p. 2.
118 Stewart, "Russia's Role in the European Crisis," *Nation*, August 27, 1938, pp. 199–201.
119 Fischer, "America and Europe," *Nation*, July 22, 1939, pp. 97–101.
120 Tabouis, "That Franco-Soviet Pact," *Nation*, January 28, 1939, pp. 115–117.
121 *Nation*, February 25, 1939, p. 219.
122 *New Republic*, February 22, 1939, p. 59.
123 "Will America Save Europe?," *New Republic*, March 22, 1939, pp. 180–181.
124 "Rediscovery Of Russia," *Nation*, April 1, 1939, pp. 364–365.
125 Dell, "Americans Or England," *Nation*, February 25, 1939, pp. 227–229. In this essay Dell went on to say, "My opinion is that the future of the world is in the hands of the United States and Russia, and that sooner or later you in America will recognize this and act accordingly. There is no real difficulty in the way of an accommodation between the United States and Russia, for the Russian government is now the most realistic and, in the true sense of the term, the most opportunistic in the world." Dell also expressed his indignation at charges in the United States, France and Britain that the Munich capitulation was partly due to "the ambiguous attitude of Russia" in his article "Phil La Follette Is Right," *Nation*, April 29, 1939, pp. 487–488.
126 *New Republic*, March 29, 1939, p. 207.
127 *New Republic*, May 17, 1939, pp. 32–33.
128 "Russia and Mr. Chamberlain," *New Republic*, May 24, 1939, pp. 60–61.
129 Schuman, "Toward the New Munich," *New Republic*, May 21, 1939, pp. 91–93.
130 Much of this was discussed in a nine-column editorial, "General Krivitsky Exposes Himself," *New Masses*, July 4, 1939, pp. 7–10.
131 *New Masses*, August 8, 1939, pp. 24–25.
132 *New Republic*, August 2, 1939, pp. 357–358.
133 Kirchwey, "Red Totalitarianism," *Nation*, May 27, 1939, pp. 605–606.
134 "Liberty and Common Sense," *New Republic*, May 31, 1939, pp. 89–90.
135 Hook-Kirchwey exchange in *Nation*, June 17, 1939, pp. 710–711.
136 Madison letter in *Nation*, June 17, 1939, p. 712.
137 Editorial exchange with Lundberg in *New Republic*, June 28, 1939, pp. 217–218.
138 *Nation*, July 15, 1939, pp. 83–84.
139 *New Republic*, August 23, 1939, p. 63.
140 "To All Active Supporters of Democracy and Peace," *Nation*, August 26, 1939, p. 228.
141 One of the most generous apologies for the Soviet abandonment of its "historic role" as "leader in the fight for collective security against Fascist aggression" was that of Harold Laski in his "British Labor's War Aims," *Nation*, September 30, 1939, pp. 340–342. Another impressive pro-Soviet apologetic was that of Albert Guérard, published in *Nation*, September 23, 1939, p. 331.
142 *Nation*, August 26, 1939, pp. 211–212.
143 *Nation*, September 2, 1939, pp. 230–231; Villard's column on page 247 of same issue.
144 *New Republic*, August 30, 1939, p. 85.
145 "What Stalin Has Lost," *New Republic*, September 27, 1939, p. 197.
146 *New Republic*, September 6, 1939, p. 114.
147 Wechsler, "Stalin and Union Square," *Nation*, September 30, 1939, pp. 342–344. Wechsler noted the resignation of Granville Hicks and Richard H. Rovere's withdrawal from the editorial board of the *New Masses*.
148 *Nation* exchange with Farrell in issue of September 30, 1939, p. 359.
149 *New Republic*, September 6, 1939, p. 138.
150 *New Republic*, October 11, 1939, p. 257, for this and subsequent citation.
151 Brailsford claimed to have been at Minsk in 1920, and charged now that Lenin had encouraged the Poles to take "too much" in their post-war territorial settlement.
152 "The New Communist Line," *New Republic*, November 15, 1939, p. 97. On the first anniversary of the *Pakt* the editors compared it to the Sacco-Vanzetti executions as one of "the heaviest blows that liberals have suffered in modern times." *New Republic*, September 2, 1940, p. 293.

153 Hicks's letter in *New Republic,* October 4, 1939, pp. 244–245; Eastman's commentary in *New Republic,* October 25, 1939, p. 344. See also *New Masses,* October 3, 1939, p. 21, "G.H. Resigns".

154 *New Masses,* September 19, 1939, p. 9.

155 *New Republic,* November 8, 1939, pp. 7–9. The second article appeared the following week, pp. 104–106. On the Communist reaction see Joseph North, "Vincent Sheean, Summer Soldier," *New Masses,* December 19, 1939, pp. 21–24. His articles and a *Saturday Evening Post* eulogy of Winston Churchill infuriated the pro-Soviet camp.

156 "Common Sense About Russia," *New Republic,* November 15, 1939, pp. 98–100.

157 Lerner, "Revolution In Ideas," *Nation,* October 21, 1939, pp. 435–437.

158 *Nation,* November 4, 1939, p. 499. The wave of realism also touched the *Nation's* editorial chief Freda Kirchwey. In her signed editorial "Dictator's Dilemma," November 18, 1939, pp. 540–541, she confessed that she believed Russia for some time had been "moving away from its revolutionary internationalism toward a strongly nationalist state capitalism."

159 Citations in above paragraph from Schuman, "Machiavelli In Moscow," *New Republic,* November 29, 1939, pp. 158–160.

160 "Power Politics and People," *New Republic,* November 29, 1939, p. 155.

161 Bates, "Disaster In Finland," *New Republic,* December 13, 1939, pp. 221–225. Bates's closing statement read, "It is hard to lose the affection and respect of so many friends whose bravery and devotion I admire. Nevertheless, I am getting off the train. It will have to be a flying jump, and no doubt the passengers in the compartments behind will shoot at me as they clatter by. I had thought the train was bound for a fertile place in the sun; but I have found out that it is rushing toward the Arctic north, where it will be buried beneath vast drifts of snow and be forever more silent." See also Steve Nelson, "Answering Ralph Bates," *New Masses,* January 9, 1940, p. 24, especially his comments on a Bates speech to the International Brigade in Spain on the Jarama front in May, 1937, "How To Win the War—Eight-Point Program Of the Communist Party In Spain."

162 Niebuhr, "Ideology and Pretense," *Nation,* December 9, 1939, pp. 645–646.

163 *Nation,* December 16, 1939, pp. 671–673.

164 Lore review of Krivitsky in *Nation,* January 6, 1940, p. 24; Cowley review of Krivitsky in *New Republic,* January 22, 1940, pp. 120–123.

165 "The Old Man," *New Republic,* September 2, 1940, p. 292; *Nation,* February 22, 1941, pp. 199–200.

166 *Nation,* February 10, 1940, pp. 182–186.

167 *New Republic,* January 22, 1940, pp. 118–119.

168 "Americans and Russia," *New Republic,* January 15, 1940, pp. 70–72.

169 *New Republic,* February 26, 1940, pp. 264–265.

170 Said Lynd, "I regard the effort of the Soviet Union to knit the whole life of the person on collective farm or in the city into an inter-functioning whole through social and cultural as well as economic activism as the most important sociological development going on in the world today. . . . If the USSR succeeds in making man "belong" in an endless web of spontaneous human functions with his fellows, it will have done something no contemporary capitalist nation has done. . . ." Letter to *New Republic,* April 1, 1940, p. 443.

171 Corey series in *Nation,* February 17, 1940, pp. 245–248; February 24, 1940, pp. 272–275; March 2, 1940, pp. 305–307. Citations in text from first article. See also responses to articles on p. 329 and after in March 2, 1940 issue.

172 *Nation,* June 1, 1940, pp. 66–67.

173 *Nation,* September 28, 1940, pp. 264–267.

174 One of these rare occasions took place late in 1935 in the fourth of a series in the *Nation* on American literary critics written by Margaret Marshall, an editor, and Mary McCarthy, titled "Our Critics, Right Or Wrong." Number Four, "The Proletarians," exposed the Communists to a witty puncturing of the party line and the sidling up to the once-hated "bourgeois" now that the Popular Front had been adopted. It provoked a sharp letter from Isidor Schneider, now a *New Masses* editor and one time *Nation* contributor, who said in part, "the courting of middle-ground writers is not done . . . as a piece of social climbing; and it is eager, not because we want to make

high-toned friends, but to unite writers against Fascism." "The Proletarians," *Nation,* December 4, 1935, pp. 653–655; Schneider's letter in *Nation,* December 18, 1935, p. 711.

175   *New Republic,* May 29, 1935, pp. 80–81.

176   *New Republic,* June 12, 1935, p. 142.

177   *Nation,* October 2, 1935, pp. 387–388.

178   Villard review of Duranty in *Nation,* November 27, 1935, pp. 626–627; Lovett review of Strong in *New Republic,* October 21, 1936, p. 333; Cowley review of Freeman in *New Republic,* October 28, 1936, p. 356.

179   Soule review of Webbs in *New Republic,* March 18, 1936, pp. 171–172; Harris review of Webbs in *Nation,* April 22, 1936, pp. 518–520; Fischer's letter from Moscow, May 20, 1936, published in *Nation,* June 10, 1936, p. 756.

180   Cowley review of Kitchin in *New Republic,* September 11, 1935, p. 134; Barnes review of Kitchin in *Nation,* September 11, 1935, pp. 305–306 (Barnes was identified by the editors as "formerly Russian expert on the American Council of the Institute of Pacific Relations," on p. 301 of this same issue); Gray review of Smith in *Common Sense,* April, 1936, p. 29; Lore reviews of Langhof and Lorant in *Nation,* September 18, 1935, pp. 335–336. See also Michael Gold, "Satevepost and Revolution: New Escapees from the Soviets," *New Masses,* April 28, 1936, p. 15, ridiculing stories of flight from Communist concentration camps.

181   Vogel review of Gunther in *Common Sense,* April, 1936, p. 29.

182   Lore review of Barbusse in *Nation,* December 4, 1935, pp. 656–657, his review of Mehring in *Nation,* December 18, 1935, pp. 719–720, his review of Lenin's letters in *Nation,* April 24, 1937, pp. 480–481. In this latter review Lore declared, "This reviewer is not a Trotskyite. He believes that Trotsky's present policies are wrong and harmful to the interests of the international working class."

183   *New Republic,* June 9, 1937, p. 139.

184   *Nation,* September 17, 1938, pp. 273–274.

185   *New Republic,* September 30, 1936, pp. 230–231.

186   Wilson reviewed *Towards An Understanding of Karl Marx, The Meaning Of Marx* and *From Hegel To Marx* in six columns of small print in *New Republic,* August 4, 1937, pp. 366–368.

187   Wolfe's review of Trotsky in *New Republic,* June 16, 1937, pp. 164–165; of the Dewey report in *New Republic,* November 24, 1937, p. 79.

188   *Nation,* October 9, 1937, pp. 384–385.

189   Wilson reviews titled "Russia: Escape From Propaganda," *Nation,* November 13, 1937, pp. 530–535. Reader reaction to Wilson's sharp criticisms of the Soviet Union was very hostile, if the letters published in the issue of December 4, 1937, p. 627, were any indication of general sentiment.

190   *New Republic,* December 29, 1937, pp. 229–230.

191   Wilson's review titled "Stalin, Trotsky and Willi Schlamm," *Nation,* December 11, 1937, pp. 648–653. The *Nation's* editors reacted very hotly to Hicks's charges in the *New Masses,* and maintained that it was their policy to select reviewers from "the writers who still remain outside the intellectual trade barriers that surround the various totalitarian camps." December 11, 1937, pp. 631–632. According to Hicks's partial box-score (*New Masses,* December 7, 1937, pp. 8–11), 9 books hostile to the Communists were reviewed favorably in the *Nation,* and only 7 books friendly to the Communists were so treated. On the other hand, he claimed that 22 books friendly to the Communists had been reviewed in a hostile manner, and four pro-Communist books had not been reviewed at all. He blamed Joseph Wood Krutch and Margaret Marshall for "having made the book section of the *Nation* an organ of the Trotskyites." See also Hicks, "White Guards On Parade: Reviewing the New York Times' Red-Baiting Book Review Section," *New Masses,* October 2, 1934, pp. 17–22.

192   Schuman, "Stalin As Satan," *New Republic,* October 4, 1939, pp. 249–250.

193   Kohn's review in *Nation* for October 7, 1939; Nomad's letter in issue for October 28.

194   *Nation,* June 8, 1940, pp. 711–714. See also Edmund Wilson, "Max Eastman in 1941," *New Republic,* February 10, 1941, pp. 173–176, a revindication of Eastman for his stand during the long period of liberal-Communist "understanding" prior to August, 1939.

195   Marshall review of Utley in *Nation*, September 7, 1940, p. 196; Rovere review of Utley in *New Republic*, September 23, 1940, p. 424.

196   *Nation*, January 4, 1941, p. 28.

197   Utley review on p. 26; see also *New Republic*, February 3, 1941, p. 151 for her exchange with Schneider, Winter and Kingsbury.

198   Höllering review of Valtin in *Nation*, January 18, 1941, pp. 77–78; Wolfe review of Valtin in *New Republic*, January 27, 1941, p. 123. See also *Nation*, May 10, 1941, pp. 543–544, on Valtin deportation efforts, and also "The Krivitsky Affair," *Nation*, July 8, 1939, pp. 32–33 for origins of the unhappiness over the "Schmelka Ginsberg" charges.

199   *Nation*, March 29, 1941, pp. 384–386.

200   Cowley in *New Republic*, May 12, 1941, pp. 669–670. Gannett's review in *Nation*, May 10, 1941, pp. 559–560.

201   *New Republic*, April 17, 1935, pp. 287–288. Schuman's denunciation of the "Fascist bludgeoning" of scholars and professors, with the implication that such events were about to begin in America, omitted a discussion of the fate of "capitalist" or "Fascist" professors in the universities of the Soviet Union.

202   *New Republic*, April 24, 1935, p. 317.

203   See articles in *New Republic*, June 12, 1935, pp. 114–115.

204   See *New Republic*, November 25, 1940; the entire back page (736) was devoted to an appeal by the Council for Pan-American Democracy to President Getulio Vargas of Brazil to release Prestes, identified only as "Honorary Chairman of the National Liberation Alliance."

205   *Nation*, March 18, 1936, pp. 353–354. See also Carl T. Schmidt's review of *Fascism For Whom?* by Max Ascoli and Arthur Feiler, *New Republic*, August 2, 1939, pp. 370–371.

206   *New Republic*, May 6, 1936, pp. 373–374.

207   *New Republic*, September 22, 1937, pp. 173–174.

208   *Nation*, February 12, 1938, pp. 188–190.

209   *Common Sense*, July, 1938, p. 7. See also Alexander Trachtenberg, "The Soviet Union and the American People," *The Communist*, September, 1939, pp. 867–886.

210   *New Republic*, June 15, 1938, p. 144. Anna Louise Strong wrote a strong condemnatory letter to the *New Republic* for its aloof approach, partially printed in the issue of June 29, 1938, p. 219.

211   "The Dies Committee Mess," *New Republic*, August 31, 1938, p. 90.

212   See especially Theodore Draper, "The New Treason: 'Fifth Column' Within the Democracies," *New Masses*, July 5, 1938, pp. 15–16. Of interest in this context was the reception given to the book by Alfred McClung Lee and Elizabeth Lee, *The Fine Art of Propaganda* (Harcourt, 1939), which got its loudest acclaim in the Communist press, since its subject, which it denigrated, was the Rev. Charles E. Coughlin, an implacable anti-Communist adversary on the radio. The book's stereotyped propaganda "tricks of the trade," repeated wearily in thousands of college classrooms in the next two decades, actually rendered the political vocabulary of the world useless if one were to be guided by it, and if it were universally applied. The Communists assumed that the book was written for their use against their opponents; "a valuable contribution to the democratic struggle against Coughlinism," Samuel Sillen exulted in the *New Masses*, August 29, 1939, pp. 23–24.

213   *New Masses*, December 6, 1938, pp. 5–8; *New Masses*, February 21, 1939, pp. 24–27. Sweezy's evaluation in *Nation*, December 2, 1939, pp. 616–617. Lerner's "Six Errors Of Marxism" in *New Republic*, November 16, 1938, pp. 37–38, in which he declared that "for all its shortcomings," it was still "the most useful and illuminating body of social thought in our world."

214   Said Laski, "The time has come for a central attack on the structure of capitalism. Nothing less than wholesale socialization can remedy the position." *Nation*, January 14, 1939, pp. 59–61.

215   *Common Sense*, September, 1938, pp. 3–5, for this and subsequent citation.

216   "Washington Witch-Hunt," *New Republic*, November 8, 1939, pp. 5–6.

217   "Case History Of A Red Hunt," *New Republic*, December 6, 1939, p. 189.

218   *Nation*, February 24, 1940, p. 267.

219   *Nation*, October 14, 1939, p. 423. See also Rovere, "Factions On the Far Left,"

New Republic, April 18, 1940, pp. 468–470. Rovere was convinced that the non-Communist Left would not work with the Communist Party on anything from now on, and that it was "certain" that the former, especially the Socialists, would resist United States intervention in the war.

220 Rovere, "Apostate," *New Republic,* January 29, 1940, pp. 154–155. Bendiner review of Gitlow in *Nation,* March 23, 1940, pp. 397–398. Part of the hostility to Gitlow may have been due to his emphasis on Ludwig Lore, long associated with the *Nation.* Gitlow referred to him as "one of the most decent of the Communist leaders in America," and in Gitlow's opinion, few men in America had done as much as Lore to establish Communism here. Gitlow, *I Confess,* pp. 235–238.

221 See also Irwin Ross, "Why Communists Stay That Way," *New Republic,* March 25, 1940, pp. 403–405.

222 *New Republic,* December 9, 1940, p. 773. Wechsler review of Dies in *Nation,* November 23, 1940, p. 507. Both liberal weeklies gave publicity to George Seldes' newest book, *Witch Hunt,* during this time, and also carried advertising of Hewlett Johnson's *The Soviet Power,* both published by Modern Age Books.

223 *Nation,* November 9, 1940, p. 434.

224 During the campaigns the *Nation,* after citing the London newsletter *The Week* as a detached and reliable source on foreign news on several past occasions, finally revealed that its editor, Claude Cockburn, was "associated under another name with the London *Daily Worker* and is known to have an inside track to the Russian embassy in London." *Nation,* May 18, 1940, pp. 609–610.

225 See in particular "The Communist Party Line," *New Republic,* June 3, 1940, p. 745.

226 *The Communist,* February, 1941, pp. 115–119; *New Masses,* February 19, 1941, p. 57.

227 *Nation,* September 20, 1941, pp. 256–257.

228 Bliven, "The Scotch Plaid Decade," *New Republic,* October 6, 1941, pp. 432–434.